FIFTY STATE CONSTRUCTION LIEN AND BOND LAW

Second Edition

VOLUME 1

FIFTY STATE CONSTRUCTION LIEN AND BOND LAW
Second Edition

VOLUME 1

ROBERT F. CUSHMAN
STEPHEN D. BUTLER
Editors

ASPEN LAW & BUSINESS
A Division of Aspen Publishers, Inc.
Gaithersburg New York

This publication is designed to provide accurate and authoritative information in regard to the subject matter covered. It is sold with the understanding that the publisher is not engaged in rendering legal, accounting, or other professional services. If legal advice or other professional assistance is required, the services of a competent professional person should be sought.

— From a *Declaration of Principles* jointly adopted by
a Committee of the American Bar Association and
a Committee of Publishers and Associations

A Division of Aspen Publishers, Inc.
A Wolters Kluwer Company
www.aspenpublishers.com

Printed in the United States of America

1 2 3 4 5 6 7 8 9 0

Library of Congress Cataloging-in-Publication Data

Fifty state construction lien and bond law / Robert F. Cushman, Stephen D. Butler, editors.—2nd ed.
p. cm.
ISBN 0-7355-1371-6 (Volume 1)
0-7355-1372-4 (Volume 2)
0-7355-1063-6 (Set)
1. Mechanics' liens—United States—States. 2. Insurance, Surety and fidelity—United States—States. I. Title: 50 state construction lien and bond law. II. Cushman, Robert Frank, 1931–. III. Butler, Stephen D.

KF900.Z95 F53 1999
346.7304'4—dc21

99-055748

About Aspen Law & Business

Aspen Law & Business—comprising the former Prentice Hall Law & Business, Little, Brown and Company's Professional Division, and Wiley Law Publications—is a leading publisher of authoritative treatises, practice manuals, services, and journals for attorneys, financial and tax advisors, corporate and bank directors, and other business professionals. Our mission is to provide practical solution-based how-to information keyed to the latest legislative, judicial, and regulatory developments.

We offer publications in the areas of banking and finance; bankruptcy; business and commercial law; construction law; corporate law; pensions, benefits, and labor; insurance law; securities; taxation; intellectual property; government and administrative law; real estate law; matrimonial and family law; environmental and health law; international law; legal practice and litigation; and criminal law.

Other Aspen Law & Business products treating construction law issues include:

Alternative Clauses to Standard Construction Contracts (Second Edition)
Architect and Engineer Liability: Claims Against Design Professionals (Second Edition)
Calculating Construction Damages
Calculating Lost Labor Productivity in Construction Claims
California Construction Law (Sixteenth Edition)
Construction Bidding Law
Construction Change Order Claims
Construction Claims Deskbook: Management, Documentation, and Presentation of Claims
Construction Defect Claims and Litigation
Construction Delay Claims (Third Edition)
Construction Dispute Resolution Formbook
Construction Documentation (Third Edition)
Construction Industry Forms (Second Edition)
Construction Industry Insurance Handbook
Construction Joint Ventures: Forms and Practice Guide
Construction Law Handbook
Construction Law Library on CD-ROM
Construction Litigation: Practice Guide with Forms
Construction Litigation: Representing the Contractor (Second Edition)
Construction Litigation: Representing the Owner (Second Edition)
Construction Management: Law Practice
Construction Scheduling: Preparation, Liability, and Claims
Construction Subcontracting: A Legal Guide for Industry Professionals
The Construction Subcontracting Manual: Practice Guide with Forms
Design-Build Contracting Claims
Design-Build Contracting Formbook
Design-Build Contracting Handbook
Differing Site Condition Claims

Handling Construction Defect Claims: Western States (Third Edition)
Legal Guide to AIA Documents (Fourth Edition)
1999 Wiley Construction Law Update
Practical Guide to Construction Contract Surety Claims
Proving and Pricing Construction Claims (Second Edition)
State-by-State Guide to Architect, Engineer, and Contractor Licensing
Sweet on Construction Industry Contracts: Major AIA Documents (Fourth Edition)

ASPEN LAW & BUSINESS
A Division of Aspen Publishers, Inc.
A Wolters Kluwer Company
www.aspenpublishers.com

SUBSCRIPTION NOTICE

This Aspen Law & Business product is updated on a periodic basis with supplements to reflect important changes in the subject matter. If you purchased this product directly from Aspen Law & Business, we have already recorded your subscription for the update service.

If, however, you purchased this product from a bookstore and wish to receive future updates and revised or related volumes billed separately with a 30-day examination review, please contact our Customer Service Department at 1-800-234-1660, or send your name, company name (if applicable), address, and the title of the product to:

ASPEN LAW & BUSINESS
A Division of Aspen Publishers, Inc.
7201 McKinney Circle
Frederick, MD 21704

ABOUT THE EDITORS

Robert F. Cushman is a partner in the international law firm of Pepper Hamilton LLP and serves as legal counsel to numerous construction owners, developers, contractors, suppliers, and bonding companies. He concentrates on construction, surety, and fidelity claim litigation and construction and development business matters. Mr. Cushman is a member of the bar of the Commonwealth of Pennsylvania and is admitted to practice before the Supreme Court of the United States and the U.S. Claims Court. He has served as Executive Vice President and General Counsel of the Construction Industry Foundation and as Regional Chairman of the Public Contract Law Section of the American Bar Association. He is a member of the International Association of Insurance Counsel. Mr. Cushman is an experienced arbitrator for the International Chamber of Commerce and the American Arbitration Association. He is a member of the CPR Institute for Dispute Resolution national construction panel and is one of twelve mediators/arbitrators from the United States who serve on the panel of the Commercial Arbitration and Mediation Center for the Americas (CAMCA). This joint venture of Canadian, Mexican, and U.S. arbitral institutions is aimed at serving the needs of the business and legal communities when disputes arise between NAFTA-based partners. Mr. Cushman is a founding fellow of the American College of Construction Lawyers. He is a nationally recognized lecturer on all phases of construction and surety law and is the editor and coauthor of numerous business, construction, real estate, and insurance books. Mr. Cushman is the permanent Chairman of the Andrews Conference Group *Construction Superconference* and is the Organizing Chairman of the Forbes Magazine conferences on *Project Financing and Construction, Rebuilding America's Infrastructure, The Latin American Market,* and *Federal Facility Cleanup.*

Stephen D. Butler is Manager of litigation for the Bechtel group of companies in San Francisco. He is the Bechtel representative to the Center for Public Resources, a non-profit ADR organization in New York, and he served on the CPR Construction Industry Task Force. He is a member of the ABA's Forum on the Construction Industry, the Forum's ADR Subcommittee. He is an experienced arbitrator and is a member of the AAA's Large Complex Case and Construction Panels. He is a frequent lecturer on all phases of construction law, and he has authored and coauthored a number of construction-related texts, including several in the Aspen series.

SUMMARY OF CONTENTS

VOLUME 1

CONTENTS

VOLUME 1

VOLUME 2

ABOUT THE CONTRIBUTORS

Michael F. Albers is a shareholder in the Dallas, Texas office of Jenkens & Gilchrist and concentrates his practice in the areas of construction law and commercial real estate development. He has represented owners, developers, contractors, and lenders in construction documentation, dispute resolution, project acquisition, financing, and development activities. Mr. Albers is the practice group leader of the firm's national Construction and Government Contracts Section and specializes in manufacturing and industrial construction projects. He is a member of the Texas and the American Bar Associations and has served on the Texas and Dallas Bar Associations' Construction Law Sections. Mr. Albers has written for and participated in the presentation of various programs concerning construction law, including the Practicing Law Institute's Construction Contracts Seminars, the Texas Bar Advanced Real Estate Program, and the ABA/Joint Program on Bankruptcy in the Construction Industry. He is a contributing author to a number of books published by John Wiley & Sons and Aspen Law & Business, including *Construction Failures* (1989), *Proving and Pricing Construction Claims* (1990), *Fifty State Construction Lien and Bond Law* (1992), and *State-by-State Guide to Architect, Engineer, and Contractor Licensing* (1999).

Bernard L. Balkin is a senior partner in the law firm of Sandler, Balkin, Hellman, Weinstein & Witten, P.C. in Kansas City, Missouri. He is a graduate of the University of California at Berkeley and Harvard Law School and has engaged in surety, construction, public contract, and real estate practice for the last 40 years. He is admitted to practice before the Supreme Court of Missouri, the Supreme Court of the United States, and the Courts of Appeal of the Fourth, Fifth, Sixth, Eighth, Ninth, and Tenth Circuits, as well as numerous federal and state administrative boards and agencies. He has authored and presented several papers related to surety, construction, contract, and franchising law. Mr. Balkin is a founder and past President of the Surety Claims Institute and a former Vice Chair of the Fidelity and Surety Law Committee of the Tort and Insurance Practice Section of the American Bar Association.

Lisa A. Banick is a partner in the law firm of Garrity, Avignone, Banick & Whetstone in Bozeman, Montana, where she concentrates on business law, real estate, litigation, and construction law. Ms. Banick received a B.S. in Civil Engineering from the University of Virginia, and a J.D., magna cum laude, from New York Law School. A member of the New York, New Jersey, and Montana bars, she is also an associate member of the American Society of Civil Engineers. Ms. Banick has written about a variety of construction law topics.

Dennis J. Bartlett is a member of the firm of Kerr Friedrich Brosseau Bartlett, LLC in Denver, Colorado. He received his B.A. from the University of Notre Dame in 1980 and his J.D. from Notre Dame Law School in 1985. He is a member of the Denver, Colorado and American Bar Associations. He is also a member of the ABA Forum on the Construction Industry and the Section of Tort Insurance Practice and is Vice Chair of its Fidelity and Surety Law Committee. Mr. Bartlett specializes in construction, surety, fidelity, engineer professional liability, and commercial litigation.

Harry R. Blackburn is a partner in the Philadelphia, Pennsylvania law firm of Harry R. Blackburn & Associates, P.C. Mr. Blackburn is a graduate of American International College and Western New England College of Law. Mr. Blackburn has concentrated his practice in the areas of surety and fidelity litigation, construction, and commercial litigation and represents surety and fidelity companies, general contractors, subcontractors, architects, and engineers. He has lectured extensively and authored numerous articles. He is presently the Chairman of the Pan-American Congress and Trade Show and is an advisor to the Director of International Commerce for the State of New Jersey. In addition, he is a member of the Philadelphia Hispanic Chamber of Commerce, the ABA International Law Subcommittee of Fidelity and Surety Law Division, and a member of the Board of Directors of the Engineers Club of Philadelphia. Harry R. Blackburn & Associates, P.C. has offices located in Philadelphia, Pennsylvania; Cherry Hill, New Jersey; and San Juan, Puerto Rico.

Axel Bolvig, III is a partner with the Birmingham, Alabama office of Bradley Arant Rose & White LLP. His primary areas of practice are litigation and construction contracts. He graduated magna cum laude with a B.S.E. degree in civil engineering from Duke University and also received his J.D. from Duke. He is licensed to practice before the Alabama Supreme Court, and he is admitted in the United States District Courts for the Northern and Southern Districts of Alabama, as well as the United States Courts of Appeals for the Fifth and Eleventh Circuits. Mr. Bolvig has represented owners, general contractors, sureties, designers, suppliers, and specialty contractors in connection with contract negotiations, construction disputes, and other matters.

Terrence L. Brookie is a partner in the Indiana law firm of Locke Reynolds LLP. He practices in the areas of construction law, fidelity and surety law, and commercial litigation. He is a member of the Hamilton County, Indiana and the American Bar Associations. He is a member of the ABA's Forum on the Construction Industry (Division 7, Steering Committee), the Construction Litigation Committee, and the Section of Tort and Insurance Practice, Fidelity and Surety Law Section. He holds a B.A. degree from Denison University (1978) and a J.D. from Indiana University School of Law, Indianapolis (1981).

Debra L. Brown is a senior associate with the law firm of Pierce Atwood in Portland, Maine. She received a B.S. degree in General Engineering from the

U.S. Naval Academy. She worked for five years as an officer and project manager in the Navy Civil Engineer Corps and is a registered Professional Engineer in Maine. Ms. Brown received her J.D. from Boston University School of Law and her practice focuses on construction-related matters.

Alan W. Bryson is the Managing Clerk/Paralegal in the law firm of Postner & Rubin, New York, New York. He is a graduate of Columbia University and has been a managing clerk for more than 33 years. His specialization is in legal procedures and training attorneys to follow proper legal procedures.

Federico Calaf-LeGrand is of counsel to the Philadelphia law firm of Harry R. Blackburn & Associates, P.C. He is a partner in the law firm of Reichard & Calaf in San Juan, Puerto Rico. Mr. Calaf-LeGrand is a graduate of Catholic University of Puerto Rico and the University of Puerto Rico Law School. Mr. Calaf practices in the areas of banking, commercial litigation, and patent law. He was appointed by the Supreme Court of the Commonwealth of Puerto Rico to the Board of Examiners and is a member of the Board of Directors of the Notary's Association of Puerto Rico and the Board of Directors and Audit Committee of Santander National Bank.

Edward M. Callahan, Jr. is a partner in the Roseland, New Jersey law firm of Clancy, Callahan & Smith. He has been a member of the New Jersey Bar since 1965 and is admitted to practice in the United State District Court, the United States Tax Court, and the Third Circuit Court of Appeals. He has been counsel to the Northern New Jersey Chapter, Inc. of the National Electrical Contractors Association for over 20 years, and his private law practice principally involves construction claims, labor law, and construction industry matters. He is presently a consultant to the coalition formed by the construction industry in New Jersey for reform of the New Jersey Mechanics' Lien Law.

David W. M. Conard is a partner in the Burlington, Vermont law firm of Little, Cicchetti & Conard, P.C. He received his A.B. degree from Dartmouth College in 1982 and his J.D. from the University of Colorado School of Law in 1986. He is a member of the Chittenden County, Vermont and American Bar Associations and is a member of bar committees relating to real estate and construction law, including the ABA Forum on the Construction Industry. Mr. Conard's practice emphasizes construction, real estate, and real estate-based commercial lending.

Richard Conner is a partner in the Greensboro, North Carolina office of Conner Gwyn Schenck PLLC. Since 1972, his principal area of practice has been construction law. Mr. Conner received his undergraduate degree from Guilford College, and his J.D. from the University of North Carolina. A coauthor of *Construction and Design Law,* Mr. Conner is a fellow in the American College of Construction Lawyers and serves as general counsel to the Construction Management Association of America.

Victor E. Covalt, III is a partner with Ballew, Schneider & Covalt in Lincoln, Nebraska, a firm serving individual, commercial, and business clients. His practice emphasizes banking, business, bankruptcy, and commercial litigation.

Mr. Covalt is graduate of the University of Nebraska, receiving a B.A. with distinction in 1976 and a J.D. with high distinction in 1981. He is a former editor-in-chief of the *Nebraska Law Review.* He is also a coauthor of Smith & Covalt, "Should the Surety Stand on Its Equitable Subrogation Rights or File Its Indemnity Agreement Under the Commercial Code?" (Nebraska Law Review 1990).

James L. Csontos is a partner with the Phoenix, Arizona law firm of Jennings, Haug & Cunningham, LLP, where he practices in the firm's Surety and Construction Litigation Section. Mr. Csontos is a graduate of Arizona State University, where he earned his B.S. degree, magna cum laude, in general business administration in 1982 and his J.D., cum laude, in 1986. He is admitted to practice before the state and federal courts of Arizona and serves on the Executive Counsel of the Construction Section of the Arizona Bar Association.

Paul E. Davis is associated with Conner Gwyn Schenck PLLC in its Raleigh, North Carolina office. His principal area of practice is construction litigation. Mr. Davis received his undergraduate degree and his J.D. from the University of North Carolina. He is a member of the Council of the Construction Law Section of the North Carolina Bar Association. A coauthor of *Construction and Design Law,* Mr. Davis has written extensively in the construction law field.

Mary C. Dirkes is an associate attorney at Clark Hill P.L.C. in Detroit, Michigan. She received her B.S. in Civil Engineering from the University of Michigan and her J.D. from Wayne State University, cum laude. She has been involved in a wide variety of litigation matters, including construction, commercial, and products liability litigation.

William Alexander Fead is a member of the Burlington, Vermont law firm of Paul, Frank & Collins, Inc., where his practice is focused on drafting and negotiating construction and design contracts, as well as representing clients in claims and dispute resolution proceedings. He is active in numerous professional and trade associations, including the Design-Build Institute of America (DBIA), where he serves as an Advisory Board member. He is a regular speaker and author on design-build and other construction law topics.

Andrew J. Friedrich is a member of the firm of Kerr Friedrich Brosseau Bartlett, LLC in Denver, Colorado. He received his B.A. from the University of Colorado in 1965 and his J.D. from the Univeristy of Colorado in 1968. He is a member of the Denver, Colorado and American Bar Associations, the ABA Forum on the Construction Industry, its Fidelity and Surety Law Committee, Section of Tort and Insurance practice, and the Defense Counsel Research Institute. Mr. Friedrich practices primarily in the areas of construction, professional liability, fidelity and surety, insurance, and commercial litigation.

Donald G. Gavin is a founding principal in the law firm of Wickwire Gavin, P.C. in Vienna, Virginia; Madison, Wisconsin; and Los Angeles, California. He earned a degree in Economics from the Wharton School, a J.D. from the University of Pennsylvania School of Law, and a Master of Law Degree in government procurement law from George Washington University. His practice emphasizes public contract law, environmental law, and construction and surety matters, and he lectures frequently throughout the country on subjects dealing with construction, government contracts, and hazardous waste and treatment facilities for professional associations, as well as universities and governmental agencies. Mr. Gavin has authored and coauthored numerous books, articles, and other publications and is on the advisory committee to BNA's Federal Contracts Reports. Mr. Gavin has been elected a fellow of the American Bar Foundation and the Public Contract Law Section, and he is also currently Vice Chairman of the Fidelity and Surety Committee of the Tort and Insurance Practice Section of the American Bar Association. He is also Chair of its Federal Regulations and Environmental and Toxic Tort Law Subcommittees, and he is a member of the Construction Law Section of the Virginia Bar Association.

Douglas Gigler is a member of the firm of Nilles, Hansen & Davies, Ltd. in Fargo, North Dakota. He practices in the areas of commercial litigation and insurance defense. He received his J.D. from the University of North Dakota in 1992.

Jeffrey G. Gilmore is a shareholder in the law firm of Wickwire Gavin, P.C. in Vienna, Virginia; Madison, Wisconsin; and Los Angeles, California. His practice emphasizes construction law involving a broad range of private and public projects. He earned a B.A. degree in Economics from Miami University and received his J.D. from the College of William and Mary, Marshall-Wythe School of Law. Prior to joining the firm, he served as a law clerk with the Supreme Court of Virginia. He frequently lectures on various aspects of construction, lien, and surety law. He received an appointment by the Fairfax County Circuit Court as a commissioner in chancery of the court with responsibility for conducting evidentiary hearings on mechanics' lien disputes and other chancery matters. Mr. Gilmore's clients include various participants in the industry, such as design professionals, contractors, developers, sureties, and government owners.

Kimbell D. Gourley is a shareholder in the Boise, Idaho law firm of Eberle, Berlin, Kading, Turnbow & McKlveen, Chartered, where he practices primarily in the areas of commercial litigation, commercial transactions, and bankruptcy law. A graduate of the University of Portland, Mr. Gourley received his J.D. degree from the University of Idaho, where he was executive editor of the *Idaho Law Review.* Mr. Gourley is a member of the Idaho State Bar, the American Bar Association, and the Idaho State Bankruptcy Law Section. Mr. Gourley has lectured previously at seminars on the topics of bankruptcy and creditor collections and has been an instructor for the American Institute of Bankers on the Uniform Commercial Code.

Maura A. Greene is a partner in the Professional Practices Group at Burns & Levinson LLP in Boston, Massachusetts. She represents architects, engineers, surveyors, lawyers, accountants, and real estate brokers, providing advice on contract-related issues and handling the defense of claims. She represents clients in trials in the state and federal courts in Massachusetts and in alternative dispute resolution settings. She received a J.D. degree from Suffolk University Law School and an A.B. from Smith College.

David J. Hatem is a partner in the Boston, Massachusetts law firm of Burns & Levinson LLP. He is the chairman of the firm's Professional Practice Group. Mr. Hatem concentrates his practice on the liabilities of professionals, particularly architects, engineers, construction management professionals, and environmental professionals, as well as lawyers and accountants. He is a frequent speaker and author of numerous published articles on issues of professional liability. Mr. Hatem received his J.D. degree and his B.A. degree, magna cum laude, from Boston University.

William F. Haug is a partner in the law firm of Jennings, Haug & Cunningham, LLP in Phoenix, Arizona and is a member and past President of the State Bar of Arizona. He is a member of the State Bar's Construction Law Section and a past Chair of the Fidelity and Surety Law Committee of the Torts and Insurance Practice Section of the American Bar Association. He is a member of the Forum Committee on the Construction Industry and former Editor of the Hard Hat Case Notes Section of its publication, *The Construction Lawyer.* He also drafted Arizona's Little Miller Act and its mechanics' lien bond statutes and is the author of numerous articles relating to the construction industry and contract bonds.

David M. Hayes is a senior member of Clark Hill P.L.C. in Detroit, Michigan. He received his B.A. from Western Michigan University and his J.D. from Wayne State University, where he was an Editor of the *Wayne Law Review.* Mr. Hayes has been involved in a wide variety of sophisticated and complex litigation matters throughout the country, as well as in Canada. He specializes in construction litigation, corporate and commercial litigation, products liability, and antitrust law. He has lectured nationally on construction litigation and is the author of articles concerning both construction law and civil procedure.

Dan A. Haynes is a partner in the Connecticut law firm of Pepe & Hazard, where he focuses his practice on domestic and international construction and federal government contracting. He earned a B.S. from American University and a J.D. from Georgetown University Law Center. An experienced lecturer and author on construction law, Mr. Haynes is a member of the Connecticut, District of Columbia, and Virginia bars.

Eugene J. Heady is an attorney with the law firm of Smith, Currie & Hancock, LLP in Atlanta, Georgia. Mr. Heady practices in the areas of construction law, government contracting, and litigation. Mr. Heady earned a B.S. degree in Engineering from the University of Hartford in 1981, where he was inducted into the Kappa Mu Honorary Engineering Society, and he earned his law degree, cum laude, from Texas Tech University School of Law in 1996. He served as the Editor-in-Chief of the *Texas Tech Law Review* and as an Editor of the *Texas Tech Legal Research Board.* Mr. Heady's published work includes "Stuck Inside These Four Walls: Recognition of Sick Building Syndrome Has Laid the Foundation to Raise Toxic Tort Litigation to New Heights," 26 Tex. Tech. L. Rev. 1041 (1995) (republished in *Legal Handbook for Architects, Engineers and Contractors* (Clark Boardman Callaghan 1996)); "Contractors' Amending AIA A401–1997: Standard Form of Agreement Between Contractor and Subcontractor," in *Alternative Clauses to Standard Construction Contracts* (Aspen Law & Business 1998); and "Subcontractors' Amending AIA A401–1997: Standard Form of Agreement Between Contractor and Subcontractor," in *Alternative Clauses to Standard Construction Contracts* (Aspen Law & Business 1998). Mr. Heady lectures frequently on construction law and on Georgia construction lien and public contract bond law. Mr. Heady is a member of the State Bars of Georgia, Texas, Colorado, and Florida. Mr. Heady is also a member of the ABA Forum on the Construction Industry and Scribes: The American Society of Writers on Legal Subjects.

Richard Henderson is a member of the firm of Nilles, Hansen & Davies, Ltd. in Fargo, North Dakota. He practices in the areas of commercial litigation, concentrating in disputes relating to the construction industry. He received his J.D. degree from the University of Chicago in 1983.

Buckner Hinkle, Jr. is a partner in the Lexington, Kentucky law office of Stites & Harbison, which has offices in Lexington, Louisville, Frankfort, and Hyden, Kentucky; Jeffersonville, Indiana; Atlanta, Georgia; and Washington, D.C. His practice focuses on the construction industry, with emphasis on contract negotiation and drafting and resolution of disputes through litigation, arbitration, or alternative means. Mr. Hinkle is also a corporate officer and general counsel for Hinkle Contracting Corporation, a Kentucky highway contractor and aggregate producer. Mr. Hinkle is a graduate of the University of the South and the University of Kentucky College of Law. He is a member of the American College of Construction Lawyers and the Governing Committee of the ABA Forum on the Construction Industry, former Chair of the Forum's Contract Documents Section, and former Chair of the Construction and Public Contract Law Section of the Kentucky Bar Association. He is also a member of the American Arbitration Association panel of arbitrators and mediators and is a frequent contributor to construction seminars and publications.

Weldon R. Johnson is a partner in the Columbia, South Carolina firm of Barnes, Alford, Stork & Johnson, L.L.P. He is a graduate of Wofford College and the University of South Carolina School of Law. He is a member of the Fidelity and Surety Law Committees of the International Association of Defense Counsel and the American Bar Association. Mr. Johnson is the author of the South Carolina section of the *Payment Bond Manual* published by the American Bar Association.

Patrick J. Keating is a retired partner of the Detroit, Michigan law firm of Clark Hill P.L.C. and is a past President of the Michigan bar. From 1980 through 1982, he served as an advisor to the Michigan House of Representatives committee, which drafted Michigan's construction lien law. Throughout his career, Mr. Keating specialized in construction law matters and served as chairman of the Michigan State Bar Real Property Law Section. He has lectured nationally on construction litigation and is the author of several articles on construction liens and litigation.

Courtney R. Kepler is a partner in the law firm of Brown & Drew in Casper, Wyoming. He is a graduate of the University of Wyoming College of Law. He has extensive experience in construction litigation and in contract and bond law as it is applied in Wyoming. He has represented owners, contractors, and subcontractors.

Jocelyn L. Knoll is a senior associate in the Minneapolis, Minnesota law firm of Fabyanske, Westra & Hart, P.A., where she concentrates her practice in the areas of construction law and insurance law. Ms. Knoll received her B.S. from the University of New Hampshire and her J.D. from the William Mitchell College of Law, magna cum laude. She is currently on the Governing Board of the Minnesota State Bar Association Section of Construction Law.

Harvey C. Koch is the senior partner of the New Orleans, Louisiana law firm of Koch & Rouse. He is a graduate of Tulane University and its School of Law and is admitted to practice before the Louisiana Bar. He has devoted a major portion of his practice to complex commercial law and litigation, encompassing all aspects of the construction process, including complex construction and intellectual property litigation and arbitration. The Governor of Louisiana appointed Mr. Koch to the Louisiana Architects Selection Board, which he chaired in 1981, the Louisiana Engineers Selection Board, which he chaired in 1982, and the Louisiana Design Professionals Selection Appellate Board, which he chaired in 1983. Mr. Koch also served as the 1990–1991 Chair of the Fidelity & Surety Law Committee of the Tort and Insurance Practice Section of the American Bar Association. He founded the Section of Fidelity, Surety and Construction Law Section of the Louisiana State Bar Association and served as its first Chairman. He is a member of the American Arbitration Association's Panel for Complex Construction Contracts and International Arbitrators and has served as a member, as well as Chairman, of arbitration panels dealing with complex construction projects and innovative construction procedures and techniques of all kinds and description. Mr. Koch is a former Vice Chairman of the Fidelity & Surety Law Committee of the International Association of Insurance Counsel and currently serves as a member of the Committee on International Construction Projects of the International Bar Association, the ABA Forum on the Construction Industry, and the Public Contracts, Tort and Insurance Practice, and International Law Sections of the American Bar Association. In addition, Mr. Koch was a member of the Consultative Group, *Restatement of the Law Third, Suretyship* of the American Law Institute. He is a member of the National Bond Claims Association and a member of the Board of Directors of the Surety Claims Institute and currently serves on the Board of the Governors of the American College of Construction Lawyers. Mr. Koch has authored, coauthored, and edited numerous articles and publications and has lectured extensively regarding construction law and the relationship between contractors, subcontractors, sureties, banks, engineers, and architects.

Kenneth R. Kupchak is a director of the Honolulu, Hawaii law firm of Damon Key Leong Kupchak Hastert. For over 20 years, his practice has centered on all aspects of construction law, from international joint ventures to complex multiparty litigation and the acquisition of three of the Pacific Basin's leading contractors. He serves on the Steering Committee for the Dispute Avoidance and Resolution Division of the ABA's Forum on the Construction Industry and is a Fellow of the American College of Construction Lawyers.

Christopher J. Lamb is a partner in the Wilmington, Delaware office of Pepper Hamilton LLP. He specializes in debtor-creditor law and has extensive experience representing financial institutions and businesses in construction lending, workouts, and bankruptcies. As part of his practice, he deals frequently with mechanics' liens and the claims of sureties on bonds.

C. Russell Lewis is an associate with the Anchorage, Alaska office of Oles Morrison Rinker & Baker LLP. Mr. Lewis concentrates his practice on construction litigation and employment and labor law. In addition to practicing law, Mr. Lewis served as project manager for several multimillion dollar projects in the Southcentral Region of Alaska and served a term as a member of Alaska's Workers' Compensation Board. Mr. Lewis graduated from Gonzaga University School of Law in 1998 and holds a B.S. degree in Mechanical Engineering from LeTourneau University. Mr. Lewis is a member of the Alaska Bar Association and American Bar Association, and he practices exclusively in Alaska in both state and federal forums.

Kent W. Lindsay is a partner in the Construction and Government Contracts Department in the San Francisco, California office of Thelen Reid & Priest LLP. Mr. Lindsay has represented owners, developers, contractors, subcontractors, and material suppliers, among others, in a wide variety of construction and commercial matters. He is a graduate of the University of California, Hastings College of the Law.

John A. Lucas is a resident litigation partner at Hunton & Williams in Knoxville, Tennessee. He received his B.S. in Engineering from the U.S. Military Academy at West Point and his J.D. from the University of Texas School of Law.

R. Lee Mann, III is an associate with the Atlanta, Georgia law firm of Kilpatrick Stockton LLP, where he practices construction and government contracting law. Mr. Mann has litigated and arbitrated a wide variety of construction and government contract disputes for subcontractors, suppliers, contractors, and owners on public and private projects throughout the United States. He frequently prosecutes and defends mechanics' lien actions. Mr. Mann earned a Bachelor of Industrial Engineering degree with highest honors from the Georgia Institute of Technology in 1985 and was inducted into the Phi Kappa Phi, Tau Beta Pi, and Alpha Pi Mu Honor Societies. He earned his law degree, magma cum laude, from the University of Georgia School of Law in 1995, where he was a Woodruff Scholar, Managing Editor of the *Georgia Law Review,* and a member of the Order of the Coif. Mr. Mann is a member of the State Bars of Georgia and Florida and is admitted to practice before the United States Court of Federal Claims.

Ronald A. May is a partner in the firm of Wright, Lindsey & Jennings in Little Rock, Arkansas. He graduated from the University of Iowa and Vanderbilt

University Law School. He is a member of the International Association of Defense Counsel and a former Chairman of its Fidelity and Surety Committee. Mr. May has been a frequent contributor to the annual fidelity and surety law survey of the *Defense Counsel Journal.* In addition to his professional activities, he is Chairman of the board of the Arkansas Cancer Research Center and a member of the Arkansas Ethics Commission.

Robert L. Meyers, III has been a construction transaction and dispute resolution practitioner for over 30 years. Mr. Meyers maintains an active practice in Dallas, Texas, representing virtually all participants in the construction industry, including owners, general contractors, subcontractors, design professionals, and sureties. He has served as Chairman of the ABA Litigation Section Construction Litigation Committee, Chairman of the Dallas Bar Association Construction Law Section, Chairman of the State Bar of Texas Construction Law Section, and on the Board of Governors. He is currently Secretary of the American College of Construction Lawyers. Mr. Meyers has spoken and written extensively on construction law topics as a faculty member for the PLI National Construction Seminar for 14 years, the State Bar of Texas Construction Law Conference for 10 years, the Construction Litigation Superconference for 10 years, and various programs of the American College of Construction Lawyers. He has coauthored the *SMU Law Review Texas Construction Law Update* for the past several years and chapters in various construction law treatises, including the Aspen Law & Business (formerly Wiley) Construction Law Series.

Brian W. Mullins is a member of the Madison, Wisconsin and Vienna, Virginia law firm of Wickwire Gavin, P.C., where his practice concentrates on construction contracts and claims. He has represented all parties to the construction, design, and development process including owners, contractors, design professionals, sureties, and suppliers. Mr. Mullins is a District Vice-Chair for the Public Contracts Section of the American Bar Association and is an officer and director of the Construction and Public Contract Law Section of the State Bar of Wisconsin. He has contributed to and presented numerous construction law publications. He is a member of the Panel of Construction Arbitrators for the American Arbitration Association, the Construction Financial Management Association, the National Society of Professional Engineers, and the Legal Advisory Committee for AGC of Wisconsin.

Anna H. Oshiro is a director of the law firm of Damon Key Leong Kupchak Hastert in Honolulu, Hawaii, where she practices construction law on behalf of design professionals, general contractors, subcontractors, developers, and material suppliers. She has contributed to numerous construction industry publications and has lectured on Hawaii's new procurement code. She is a member of the ABA Litigation Section, the ABA's Forum on the Construction Industry, and Hawaii's Building Industries Association.

John F. Panzarella is an associate in the law firm of Trenam, Kemker, Scharf, Barkin, Frye, O'Neill & Mullis, P.A., where he concentrates his practice in the areas of commercial, general civil, and construction litigation. He received his B.S.B.A. degree and J.D. degree, with honors, from the University of Florida and his M.B.A. degree from the University of South Florida. Mr. Panzarella is a member of the Hillsborough County Bar Association and the Litigation and Business Law Sections of the American Bar Association.

Paige Alan Parker is a partner in the Boise, Idaho firm of Moore, Baskin & Parker. He received his Ph.D. in 1981 in Political Science from the University of Florida and his J.D., summa cum laude, from the University of Idaho Law School in 1986. The bulk of Mr. Parker's practice is in the areas of lien, bond, and insurance law.

Louis R. Pepe is a partner in the Connecticut law firm of Pepe & Hazard, LLP, where he concentrates on construction law, representing contractors, owners, and sureties. He received his undergraduate and master's degrees from Rensselaer Polytechnic Institute in Troy, New York and his J.D. with distinction from Cornell Law School. He has presented seminars in construction contract litigation throughout the Northeast and has authored numerous articles on the subject.

R. Timothy Phoenix is a director of Hoefle, Phoenix & Gormley, P.A. in Portsmouth, New Hampshire. He received his B.S. from the University of New Hampshire and his J.D. from the Franklin Pierce Law Center in Concord, New Hampshire. Mr. Phoenix is a founder of a small general practice firm, where he concentrates on the areas of small business representation, including construction, development, real estate, bankruptcy, and general litigation.

Jotham D. Pierce, Jr. is a member of the Portland, Maine law firm of Pierce Atwood. He is a graduate of Bowdoin College and Harvard Law School. His practice has concentrated on the representation of owners, contractors, and suppliers in construction-related matters for approximately 19 years and includes litigation in state and federal courts and various alternative dispute resolution matters, including mediation and arbitration. Mr. Pierce was Chairman of the Practicing Law Institute Construction Contracts program from 1974 to 1986 and a panel member from 1987 to 1999. He is a fellow of the American College of Construction Lawyers and has been Chairman of the ABA Litigation Section, Construction Litigation Committee.

David M. Powell is a partner in the firm of Wright, Lindsey & Jennings in Little Rock, Arkansas. He graduated from Davidson College and Duke University Law School and specializes in construction litigation, commercial transactions, and professional liability.

William K. Renno is an associate with the Anchorage, Alaska, office of Oles Morrison Rinker & Baker LLP. Mr. Renno concentrates his practice on construction litigation, environmental issues, products liability law, and complex general civil litigation. In addition to practicing law, Mr. Renno served as a project coordinator and worked as a journeyman carpenter on several multimillion dollar projects throughout Alaska. Mr. Renno graduated cum laude from University of Puget Sound School of Law in 1988 and holds a B.S. degree in Construction

Management/Industrial Technology from Northern Michigan University. Mr. Renno is a member of the Alaska Bar Association and American Bar Association, and he practices exclusively in Alaska in both state and federal forums.

Carl G. Roberts is a partner in the Litigation Department of Ballard Spahr Andrews and Ingersoll, LLP in Philadelphia, Pennsylvania and is a member of the firm's Construction Law Group, Information Technology Law Group, Project Finance Group, and Workouts and Failed Transactions Group. Some particular areas in which Mr. Roberts concentrates his practice include construction litigation and workout matters related to project finance and other lending transactions. Mr. Roberts also has considerable experience in noncompetition and trade secrets litigation, particularly involving technology concerns and in computer software contracting litigation. Mr. Roberts has been a member of the section council for the American Bar Association's Law Practice Management Section. He is presently a member of the section's Magazine Editorial Board and Columns Editor for the magazine. He has written articles on applications of computer technology to the practice of law, has been a speaker and writer on technology, ethics, and computer use in litigation, and has given several seminars on law practice management for CEELI in Warsaw, Poland. His article, "Ethical Considerations in Providing Legal Information Over the Internet," was published in the *1997 Symposium Issue* of *The Professional Lawyer.* He is on the board and is a past President of the Philadelphia Chamber Ensemble and is a member of the Penn Hillel Committee of Hillel of Greater Philadelphia. Mr. Roberts is a graduate of Harvard College (B.A. in Economics, cum laude, 1970) and the University of Pennsylvania (J.D. 1974).

Chris L. Rhodes, III is a senior partner in the Tulsa, Oklahoma law firm of Rhodes, Hieronymus, Jones, Tucker & Gable, where he practices in the areas of corporate, suretyship, and insurance defense.

E. Mabry Rogers is a partner with the Birmingham, Alabama office of Bradley Arant Rose & White LLP, where his primary areas of practice are litigation and construction contracts. A cum laude graduate of Yale University, he received his law degree, cum laude, from Harvard Law School in 1974. He is licensed to practice in all Alabama courts and various other courts around the country, including the United States Supreme Court. Mr. Rogers has represented owners, contractors, subcontractors, suppliers, designers, and sureties. In addition to lecturing at various construction seminars, he is the author of several books and chapters of books and has had several construction-related articles published. He has served as an arbitrator for the American Arbitration Association and as a special master for the courts. Mr. Rogers is a member of the American College of Construction Lawyers.

Robert A. Rubin is a partner in the New York, New York law firm of Postner & Rubin. He received a B.C.E. from Cornell University and a J.D. from Columbia University. His practice is limited to construction matters, principally the resolution of complex construction disputes. Mr. Rubin has authored and coauthored many texts and articles on construction law. He is a fellow of the American Society of Civil Engineers, fellow (President—1999) of the American College of Construction Lawyers, and a member of The Moles. Mr. Rubin is also a licensed professional engineer and a member of the New York City, State, and American Bar Associations.

Ethan W. Schmidt, of the law firm of Schmidt, Schroyer & Moreno, P.C., practices construction law and civil litigation in Rapid City, South Dakota. His construction clients include contractors, subcontractors, suppliers, and insurance companies, dealing with all facets of contract consulting. Mr. Schmidt represents clients by drafting and interpreting contract documents, preparing mechanics' liens, and negotiating and litigating other matters relating to the construction industry. He received his B.S. degree in banking and finance from the University of Nebraska and his J.D. degree from the University of North Dakota School of Law. He is a member of both the South Dakota and Nebraska Bar Associations and presents educational construction seminars.

Laurence Schor is a partner in the Washington, D.C. law firm of McManus, Schor, Asmar & Darden, LLP, where he concentrates his practice on all phases of construction and government contract law. He is the former managing partner of the Washington, D.C. office of Smith, Somerville & Case, LLC and has served as the Assistant General Counsel, U.S. Army Corps of Engineers, and as attorney at the Marshall Space Flight Center for NASA. He has authored articles and course manuals on government contract and construction topics and lectures regularly for professional groups on issues arising in these areas. Mr. Schor is a member of the American Bar Association, Public Contracts Section, where he was Chairman of the Construction Committee and served as Budget and Financial Officer, and is a member of and lecturer for the Forum Committee on the Construction Industry. He is also a member of the Federal Bar Association. He holds a Bachelor's degree in Business Administration from Southern Methodist University, a law degree from the University of Texas, Austin, School of Law, and a Master of Laws degree from George Washington University, with an emphasis in government procurement. He is a founding member, served on the Board of Governors, and is currently Treasurer, of the American College of Construction Lawyers.

Walter J. Sears, III is a partner with the Birmingham, Alabama office of Bradley Arant Rose & White LLP, where his primary areas of practice are litigation and construction contracts. He graduated cum laude from Princeton University and received his J.D. from the University of Virginia Law School. Mr. Sears is licensed to practice in all Alabama courts, as well as various other courts around the country, including the United States Supreme Court. He has substantial experience representing contractors, owners, subcontractors, suppliers, designers, and sureties. He has authored and edited several books and chapters of books on construction-related matters and has lectured at various construction seminars.

Gary F. Sheldon is a construction attorney with the Connecticut law firm of Pepe & Hazard, LLP, where he focuses his practice on the representation of owners, sureties, general contractors, and subcontractors in a wide variety of construction-related disputes. He received his B.S. degree in Mechanical Engineering from Clarkson University and his J.D. degree from the University of Connecticut School of Law. He is a member of the Connecticut and New York bars.

Stanley P. Sklar is Chair of the Construction Practice Group of Bell, Boyd & Lloyd, Chicago, Illinois. He graduated from Northwestern University School of Law, is an elected member of the American College of Real Estate Lawyers, and is a founding fellow and past President of the American College of Construction Lawyers. Mr. Sklar is a former Chair of the Chicago Bar Association Subommittee on Mechanics' Liens and former Chair of its Real Property Committee. He is also Co-Chair of a special committee of the Circuit Court of Cook County, Illinois regarding mandatory arbitration of mechanics' lien foreclosure actions. He is a certified Mediator and Arbitrator for the American Arbitration Association and a member of its National Training Faculty for Commercial Arbitrators.

David W. Slaughter is a partner in the law firm of Snow, Christensen & Martineau in Salt Lake City, Utah. He received a B.A., magna cum laude, from Brigham Young University in 1975. After serving three years' active duty as a commissioned officer in the United States Army, he returned to Brigham Young University, earning his J.D., magna cum laude, in 1981 from the J. Reuben Clark Law School, where he was a member of the *Brigham Young University Law Review* and its Lead Articles Editor. Mr. Slaughter joined his present firm in 1982, following a judicial clerkship with Judge Malcolm R. Wilkey on the United States Court of Appeals for the District of Columbia Circuit. His practice focuses on complex corporate and commercial litigation and dispute resolution, including construction and surety matters. Mr. Slaughter is also an arbitration panelist for the American Arbitration Association and serves as a regional panelist for complex construction cases.

Michael F. Smith is a senior associate who serves as the director of legal research and writing with the Tulsa, Oklahoma law firm of Rhodes, Hieronymus, Jones, Tucker & Gable, where he practices in the areas of insurance defense, environmental, manufacturers' product liability, and appellate practices.

Robert J. Smith is a member of the Madison, Wisconsin and Vienna, Virginia law firm of Wickwire Gavin, P.C. A former professor of extension and civil and environmental engineering at the University of Wisconsin in Madison, Mr. Smith is a registered professional engineer. He received civil engineering and law degrees from the University of Wisconsin. His professional practice is devoted to the representation of owners, contractors, and design professionals. He is a fellow in the American College of Construction Lawyers and is the past Chairman of the American Society of Civil Engineers Committee on Contract Administration and the Engineers Joint Contract Documents Committee.

James R. Snyder is a Member in the Charleston, West Virginia office of the law firm of Jackson & Kelly PLLC. He received a B.A. degree in Economics from the University of Notre Dame in 1973 and a J.D. from West Virginia

University in 1977. He is a member of the West Virginia and Michigan bars. He practices in the areas of environmental litigation and construction litigation.

Jeffrey D. Stone is a shareholder of Pingel & Templer, P.C. in Des Moines, Iowa. He received his B.S. in Construction Engineering in 1976 from Iowa State University and his J.D. from Drake University in 1992, graduating as a member of the Order of the Coif. He is a member of the American, Iowa, and Polk County Bar Associations.

David B. Stratton is a partner in the Wilmington, Delaware office of Pepper Hamilton LLP. He specializes in debtor-creditor law and has extensive experience representing financial institutions and businesses in construction lending, workouts, and bankruptcies. As part of his practice, he deals frequently with mechanics' liens and the claims of sureties on bonds.

Robert T. Strickland is a partner in the Columbia, South Carolina firm of Barnes, Alford, Stork & Johnson, L.L.P. He is a graduate of Clemson University and the University of South Carolina School of Law.

Neal J. Sweeney is a partner in the Atlanta, Georgia law firm of Kilpatrick Stockton LLP. He practices exclusively in the area of construction law and litigation, with further concentration in federal, state, and local contracting. Mr. Sweeney received his undergraduate degree from Rutgers University and his law degree, with honors, from George Washington University. He has handled claims, litigation, and arbitration throughout the United States, involving hospitals, office buildings, military bases, and major civil works. His written works on construction law topics have been published in several books and periodicals, including "Winning Strategies for Proving and Pricing Claims" in *Proving and Pricing Construction Claims,* Second Edition (Aspen Law & Business 1996). He has also been the editor of the annual *Wiley Construction Law Update* since 1992.

Bradley G. Taylor practices law in the Bellevue, Washington office of Marston & Heffernan, P.L.L.C., where he concentrates on construction, real property, and business matters. He holds B.S. degrees in Civil Engineering and Construction Management from Washington State University and a J.D. degree from Seattle University School of Law (formerly University of Puget Sound School of Law). He has worked in the construction industry in numerous capacities, including construction claims analyst, estimator/engineer, and field office engineer.

Dean B. Thomson is a shareholder in the Minneapolis, Minnesota law firm of Fabyanske, Westra & Hart, P.A., where he practices in the area of construction, surety, and insurance law representing owners, contractors, subcontractors, sureties, developers, and design professionals. He received his B.A. from Carleton College and his J.D. from the University of Minnesota, cum laude. While serving as past Chairperson of the Minnesota State Bar Association Section of Construction Law, Mr. Thomson was actively involved in amending the mechanic's lien and bond statutes that are the subject of Chapter 24. He is also a member of the National Construction Dispute Resolution Council of the American Arbitration Association and a Steering Committee Member for Division 1 of the ABA Forum on the Construction Industry. Mr. Thomson is a frequent author on construction law, and he regularly lectures at various state and national societies of architects, sureties, and general contractors on all aspects of construction disputes.

Richard M. Trachok, II is a partner in the law firm of Bible, Hoy & Trachok in Reno, Nevada and specializes in construction litigation. He received his undergraduate degree from the University of Nevada, graduated summa cum laude from California Western School of Law, and received his LL.M. from Cambridge College in the United Kingdom. He is a member of the American Bar Association's Forum Committee on the Construction Industry and is an arbitrator with the American Arbitration Association. Mr. Trachok lectures frequently before construction industry groups and is an adjunct professor in the Engineering department of the University of Nevada, Reno, teaching construction law.

John S. Vento is a shareholder in the Tampa, Florida office of Trenam, Kemker, Scharf, Barkin, Frye, O'Neill & Mullis, P.A., where he practices primarily in the areas of construction law, federal acquisition law, and business litigation. He received his J.D., with honors, from Duquesne University School of Law (1974) and an LL.M. from the University of Michigan Law School (1979). He was also a National Endowment for the Humanities Fellow at Yale Law School (1980). He is the past Co-Chair of the American Bar Association's Committee on Construction Litigation and a charter member of the ABA's Forum Committee on the Construction Industry. He frequently presents programs in construction contract litigation for the American Bar Association and other trade groups, such as the Associated General Contractors (AGC). Mr. Vento is a certified commercial and construction arbitrator for the American Arbitration Association and has represented the Association in arbitration litigation. He also serves as a mediator in construction and commercial disputes for the American Arbitration Association as well as in private disputes.

Stephen G. Walker is senior counsel of Bechtel Corporation in San Francisco, California and a member of its legal department's claims group. He is also a registered civil engineer, a member of several bar and engineering groups, and an arbitrator on the Large Complex Case Panel of the American Arbitration Association.

Christopher C. Whitney is a partner in the Providence, Rhode Island and Boston, Massachusetts based law firm of Little, Bulman & Whitney. A trial lawyer who devotes much of his practice to construction matters, he is a member of the Governing Committee of the American Bar Association's Forum on the Construction Industry. He received his B.A. from Dartmouth College, with honors, and his J.D. from Georgetown University, with honors.

Keith Witten is a member of the Board of Directors of Sandler, Balkin, Hellman, Weinstein & Witten, P.C., in Kansas City, Missouri. He has engaged in the practice of fidelity and surety law for over 25 years. He received a B.A. degree from Auburn University in 1968 and his J.D. degree from the University of Kansas School of Law in 1971, where he was an editor of the *Kansas Law Review.* He has been admitted to practice before the United States Supreme Court, the United

States Courts of Appeals for the Sixth, Eighth, Ninth, and Tenth Circuits, and the United States District Courts for the District of Kansas, the Western District of Missouri, and the District of Arizona, as well as the courts of Kansas and Missouri. He is a Vice Chair of the Fidelity and Surety Law and Litigation Committees of the Torts and Insurance Practice Section of the American Bar Association and secretary of the Surety Claims Institute.

Robert M. Wright is a partner in the Baltimore, Maryland and Washington, D.C. law firm of Whiteford, Taylor & Preston. His practice is concentrated on construction law and surety law, where he represents owners, contractors, sureties, and design professionals. Mr. Wright acts as counsel to the National Constructors Association, whose members consist of some of the largest engineering and construction firms in the United States. He is a member of the American Arbitration Association Panel of Construction Industry Arbitrators and Mediators, the Fidelity and Surety Law Committee, and the Forum Committee on the Construction Industry of the American Bar Association. He has served as Co-Chairman of the Steering Committee for Construction Cases of the Maryland State Bar Association. Mr. Wright is an author of publications by the Maryland Institute for the Continuing Professional Education of Lawyers on Surety Bonds and the Maryland Mechanics' Lien Law.

Ron A. Yarbrough is a partner in the Jackson, Mississippi law firm of Ott & Purdy, P.A. He received his B.A. from Millsaps College and his J.D. from University of Memphis. He practices primarily in the areas of construction litigation, construction surety and fidelity law, and commercial contract litigation. Mr. Yarbrough has written a number of articles on construction and surety law, including articles published in *The Mississippi Law Journal* and *Handling Fidelity, Surety, and Financial Risk Claims,* Second Edition (John Wiley & Sons 1990), and is a frequent seminar speaker on those topics. He is member of the American Arbitration Association's National Panel of Construction Arbitrators and the American Bar Association Forum on the Construction Industry.

Michael A. Yoshida is a director of the firm of Damon Key Leong Kupchak Hastert in Honolulu, Hawaii. Following work in the construction industry and graduation from the University of Hawaii School of Law in 1979, he served as a law clerk to the Honorable Jon J. Chinen, United States Bankruptcy Judge for the District of Hawaii. Since joining the firm in 1980, he continues to utilize his expertise in bankruptcy law and creditor's rights, the main emphasis of his practice. Mr. Yoshida also practices in the areas of commercial litigation, mortgage and lien foreclosures, real property law, and real property transactions.

Saphronia R. Young is an associate with the Anchorage, Alaska office of Oles Morrison Rinker & Baker LLP. Ms. Young concentrates her practice on construction litigation, labor, surety, and procurement law. In addition to practicing law, Ms. Young is involved in a variety of community service projects and is a member of the National Association of Women in Construction. Ms. Young graduated from the University of Missouri School of Law at Kansas City in 1992 and holds a B.A. degree in Geology from the University of Kansas. Ms. Young is a member of the Alaska Bar Association, Missouri Bar Association, Kansas Bar Association, and American Bar Association and is licensed to practice in Alaska, Missouri, and Kansas in both state and federal forums.

James A. Zehren is a partner at Stoel Rives LLP, a multistate firm headquartered in Portland, Oregon. His practice is concentrated in construction and design law, including business transactions, preventative law, and dispute resolution. His practice emphasizes preparation of contract documents, licensing and registration issues, and lien and bond claims. Mr. Zehren is currently a member of the Construction Section of the Oregon State Bar as well as the Forum on the Construction Industry of the American Bar Association. He has authored various articles on construction and design law topics and has spoken on lien and bond law and related subjects.

Timothy F. Zitzman practices with Hunton & Williams in Knoxville, Tennessee. He graduated from the University of Tennessee in 1990 and the Washington & Lee School of Law in 1996.

PREFACE

There are three ways in which contractors, subcontractors, and material suppliers to construction projects can assure that they will be paid.

The first is by having a good contract with a solvent and honest party. The Aspen Law & Business series of construction litigation books addresses alternatives, ramifications, problems, and solutions in this regard. The second way is by perfecting lien rights, and the third is by perfecting bond rights. This handbook is designed to provide the information essential to determining and perfecting lien and bond rights.

A lien is a charge upon the real estate. Its origin dates back to early England, when "mechanics," those who worked with their hands, were given a "charge" against the property on which they worked. It was felt that one who put value into property should be recompensed. Today, every state has a lien law.

One cannot lien a public project, as opposed to a private project. Therefore, the federal government and all of our states have bond statutes to protect unpaid suppliers of labor and materials. These bond laws vary from state to state, just as lien laws do.

Contractors, subcontractors, material suppliers, lawyers, and credit managers must be as familiar with the lien and bond laws of the applicable jurisdiction as they are with the contracts they or their clients sign.

We chose a preeminent construction law firm in each state to address the information essential for filing a lien or perfecting a bond claim. The mechanics' lien portion for each state covers who may claim, how to file the claim, where to file, when the claim must be filed, duration of the lien, contents of the notice, extent of the lien, priority of the lien, and leading decisions. The payment bond portion for each state covers the amount of the bond, the labor and materials covered, the notice requirement, time limitations, contracts that are excluded from bonding, procedures to follow, place for suit, special provisions, and key decisions.

The construction industry now has at its fingertips a handbook that delivers practical working knowledge of each state's bond and lien laws (with citations to appropriate statutes) and a knowledgeable firm and attorney within each state (the chapter authors) to contact for detailed discussion.

Philadelphia, Pennsylvania
San Francisco, California
December 1999

ROBERT F. CUSHMAN
STEPHEN D. BUTLER

FIFTY STATE CONSTRUCTION LIEN AND BOND LAW
Second Edition
VOLUME 1

CHAPTER 1

FEDERAL PAYMENT BOND LAW

Laurence Schor[1]

---

[1] This chapter was updated with the assistance of Tamra Miller from the corresponding chapter in the First Edition, written by Robert F. Cushman and Mason Avrigian, Jr.

§ 1.01 MILLER ACT PAYMENT BONDS

The Miller Act[2] was enacted by Congress in 1935 and is the federal legislation that requires surety bonds on federal public works projects. The Miller Act applies to any contract in excess of $100,000[3] that is for the "construction, alteration, or repair of any public building or public work of the United States."[4] If a project fits within those requirements, a contract cannot be awarded unless the prime contractor[5] provides two surety bonds, with a surety or sureties satisfactory to the United States, as follows:

1. A performance bond for the protection of the United States in an amount deemed adequate by the contracting officer;[6] and
2. A payment bond for the protection of persons supplying labor or materials in the prosecution of the work under the contract, in an amount prescribed in the statute.[7]

The contracting officer is authorized to waive the performance and payment bond requirements for so much of the work as is performed in a foreign country if it is impractical for the contractor to furnish the bonds.[8] Likewise, the bonding requirement in § 270a(a) is not exclusive. Congress expressly authorized the contracting officer to require "a performance bond or other security" in addition to or in cases other than those specified in § 270a(a).[9]

The federal government requires the payment bonds for a particular and definite purpose. On private construction projects, subcontractors (and possibly others) providing labor and materials can secure payment through mechanics' and materialmen's liens allowed by state law. These state law lien rights are discussed

---

[2] Act of Aug. 24, 1935, c. 642, 49 Stat. 793 (codified at 40 U.S.C. § 270a et seq. (1988)). The Miller Act repealed its predecessor, the Heard Act (Act of Aug. 13, 1894, c. 280, Stat. 278, *as amended by* Act of Feb. 24, 1905, c. 778, 33 Stat. 811), but essentially reinstated the basic provisions of the earlier Heard Act. *See* Clifford E. MacEvoy Co. v. United States *ex rel.* Calvin Tomkins Co., 322 U.S. 102, 105 (1944).

[3] The original contract amount in the 1935 legislation was $2,000. The amount was changed to $25,000 by an amendment in 1978. Act of Nov. 2, 1978, Pub. L. No. 95–585, 92 Stat. 2484. In 1994, the contract floor was raised to $100,000. Federal Acquisition Streamlining Act of 1994, Pub. L. No. 103–355 § 4104, 108 Stat. 3243 (1994).

[4] 40 U.S.C. § 270a(a) (1986). The types of construction projects subject to the Miller Act are discussed in **§ 1.03.**

[5] Throughout this chapter, the term *prime contractor* refers to the entity that enters into a contract with the United States to perform a public works contract.

[6] 40 U.S.C. § 270a(a)(1) (1986).

[7] *Id.* § 270a(a)(2). Section 270a(a)(2) provides that payment bonds shall be in the following amounts: (1) for contracts under $1 million, the bond penal sum must be 50% of the contract amount; (2) for contracts in excess of $1 million but less than $5 million, 40% of the contract amount; and (3) for contracts in excess of $5 million, the payment bond must be in the amount of $2.5 million.

[8] *Id.* § 270a(b).

[9] *Id.* § 270a(c).

throughout the successive chapters of this book. On federal government projects, however, subcontractors and others supplying labor and materials do not have lien rights because the doctrine of sovereign immunity precludes liens against government property.[10] Thus, unpaid suppliers of labor and materials have no recourse against the improvements and are left with only common law contract actions to obtain payment. The Miller Act payment bond is intended to bridge that gap and to substitute the surety bond for the mechanics' lien. The payment bond, therefore, serves a number of purposes. It provides payment security to subcontractors and others providing labor and materials on federal construction projects and therefore encourages broader participation in those projects, and it enables the government to meet its equitable obligation to see that those whose work has gone into the construction of a public project are paid.[11]

This chapter examines the substantive and procedural requirements for prosecuting payment bond claims under the Miller Act. Although the focus here is federal statutory requirements and case law, it is important to note that state bond statutes are often patterned after the Miller Act, so-called "Little Miller Acts." In the absence of controlling state court decisions, courts interpreting state bond statutes often look to federal court decisions under the Miller Act for guidance.[12]

§ 1.02 BOND FORM

The Federal Acquisition Regulation (FAR) specifies the form of payment bond to be used under the Miller Act.[13] The bond form is mandatory and may not be altered without written approval of the administrator of general services. Unlike payment bonds issued on most private projects, the bond form required by the FAR does not contain certain limitations on the surety's liability that are specified in the statute. For example, the bond form does not contain the notice and suit limitation provisions specified in the statute.[14] These conditions, however, are read into the bond and are binding on the surety and any claimants. This is because a statutory bond is to be reviewed in light of the statute creating the duty to give the security, and the provisions of the statute are, therefore, read into the bond itself.[15] One court has held that if the bond specifies less than the minimum

---

[10] F.D. Rich Co. v. United States *ex rel.* Indus. Lumber Co., 417 U.S. 116, 121–22 (1974); Arvanis v. Noslo Eng'g Consultants, Inc., 739 F.2d 1287, 1289 (7th Cir. 1984); Chicago Rigging Co. v. Uniroyal Chemical Co., 718 F. Supp. 696, 698 (N.D. Ill. 1989).

[11] Pearlman v. Reliance Ins. Co., 371 U.S. 132, 141 (1962); Henningsen v. United States Fidelity & Guar. Co., 208 U.S. 404, 410 (1908); United States Fidelity & Guar. Co. v. United States, 475 F.2d 1377, 1381 (Ct. Cl. 1973).

[12] *See* Lite-Air Prods., Inc. v. Fidelity & Deposit Co., 437 F. Supp. 801 (E.D. Pa. 1977); Solite Masonry Units Corp. v. Piland Constr. Co., 232 S.E.2d 759 (Va. 1977); Montgomery County Bd. of Educ. v. Glassman Constr. Co., 225 A.2d 448 (Md. 1967).

[13] 48 C.F.R. § 53.301–25-A (1991).

[14] 40 U.S.C. § 270b (1986).

[15] American Cas. Co. v. Irvin, 426 F.2d 647 (5th Cir. 1970) (citing Maryland Cas. Co. v. United

coverage required by the statute, the statute is read into the bond and the surety is held to have provided the minimum coverage so specified in the statute.[16]

On the other hand, statutory requirements do not generally restrict coverage of the bond. Risks that are required to be covered by the terms of the statute will be deemed covered by a bond given pursuant to the statute if the bond so provides and if enforcement is not contrary to public policy.[17]

§ 1.03 PUBLIC WORK OF THE UNITED STATES

The Miller Act does not define what constitutes a "public work of the United States" subject to the payment and performance bond requirements. The question sometimes arises either before a contract is awarded to determine if Miller Act bonds are required or during or after completion of a particular project, when a subcontractor or supplier has not been paid by the prime contractor and no bond was posted at the beginning.

Public work as used in the Miller Act is construed broadly. In *United States v. Irwin,*[18] the Supreme Court adopted a broad interpretation, holding that *public work* encompasses any projects historically constructed or carried on either directly or by public authority or with public aid to serve the interests of the general public.[19] The Court expressly rejected an argument that *public work* was limited to projects in which title to the improvements, buildings, or land was vested in the United States.[20] In *Peterson v. United States ex rel. Marsh Lumber Co.,*[21] the Sixth Circuit held that the term *public work* does not have a technical meaning but is to be understood in its plain, obvious, and rational sense. The court held that *public work* includes any work in which the United States is interested, which is done for the public, and for which the United States is authorized to expend funds.[22]

A broad array of projects has been held to constitute public works projects subject to the Miller Act bond requirements.[23] These include interstate highway projects,[24] construction of a jet propulsion laboratory to be operated by a private

States, 251 U.S. 342 (1919)); *see also* Mayor of Baltimore v. Fidelity & Deposit Co., 386 A.2d 749 (Md. Ct. Spec. App. 1978).

[16] *See* Mayor of Baltimore v. Fidelity & Deposit Co., 386 A.2d 749 (Md. Ct. Spec. App. 1978).

[17] American Cas. Co. v. Irvin, 426 F.2d 647 (5th Cir. 1970).

[18] 316 U.S. 23 (1941).

[19] *Id.* at 29.

[20] *Id.* (citing Peterson v. United States *ex rel.* Marsh Lumber Co., 119 F.2d 145, 147–48 (6th Cir. 1941)).

[21] 119 F.2d 145 (6th Cir. 1941).

[22] *Id.* at 147.

[23] *See generally* Annotation, *What Constitutes Public Work Within Statute Relating to Contractor's Bond,* 48 A.L.R.4th 1170 (1984).

[24] United States *ex rel.* Motta Constr. v. Able Bituminous Contractors, Inc., 640 F. Supp. 69 (D. Mass. 1986).

institute,[25] railroad construction projects,[26] and construction of a post library at a military post.[27]

Alternatively, certain projects using federal funds have been held not to be public works projects under the Miller Act. In *Chicago Rigging Co. v. Uniroyal Chemical Co.,*[28] the district court considered whether a contract to demolish government buildings was a contract to which the Miller Act bonding requirements applied. The particular contract at issue involved handling and removing asbestos fibers and, thereafter, demolishing and disposing three army ammunition plant buildings.[29] The court held that the contract did *not* fall within the Miller Act because it involved solely demolition and not any further construction.[30] The court distinguished another case holding that a contract for the removal of asbestos material followed by installation of concrete slabs fell within the ambit of the Miller Act.[31]

§ 1.04 CLAIMANTS UNDER THE MILLER ACT

The Miller Act requires a payment bond "for the protection of all persons supplying labor and material" in a public works project by the United States.[32] The payment bond does not, however, cover "all" persons supplying such labor or material. Coverage is limited by § 270b(a) of the Act to those who had a contractual relationship with the prime contractor or with a subcontractor.[33] The parties covered by a Miller Act payment bond are limited to the following:

1. Material suppliers and laborers under contract with the prime contractor;
2. Subcontractors to the prime contractor; and
3. Sub-subcontractors, material suppliers, and laborers under contract with the subcontractor.

Figure 1-1 illustrates who is and who is not covered by a Miller Act payment bond.

Determining the status of the proposed claimant is critical to any Miller Act claim analysis, both substantively and procedurally. The proposed claimant's

---

[25] Fidelity & Deposit Co. v. Harris, 360 F.2d 402 (9th Cir. 1966).

[26] Peterson v. United States *ex rel.* Marsh Lumber Co., 119 F.2d 145, 147–48 (6th Cir. 1941).

[27] United States *ex rel.* Gamerston & Green Lumber Co. v. Phoenix Assurance Co., 163 F.2d 713 (9th Cir. 1958).

[28] 718 F. Supp. 696 (N.D. Ill. 1989).

[29] *Id.* at 698.

[30] *Id.* at 700 (citing United States v. Kimrey, 489 F.2d 339, 340–42 (8th Cir. 1974)).

[31] *See* United States *ex rel.* Universal Eng'g, Inc. v. Scientific Coating Co., No. C-86–3683, slip op. at 1, 1988 WL 4786 (N.D. Cal. Jan. 4, 1988), *cited in* Chicago Rigging Co. v. Uniroyal Rigging Co., 718 F. Supp. 696, 701 n.7 (N.D. Ill. 1989).

[32] 40 U.S.C. § 270a(a) (1986).

[33] *Id.* § 270b(a); *see* F.D. Rich Co. v. United States *ex rel.* Indus. Lumber Co., 417 U.S. 116, 122 (1974); Clifford E. MacEvoy Co. v. United States *ex rel.* Calvin Tomkins Co., 322 U.S. 102 (1944).

FIGURE 1-1. PARTIES COVERED BY MILLER ACT PAYMENT BOND.

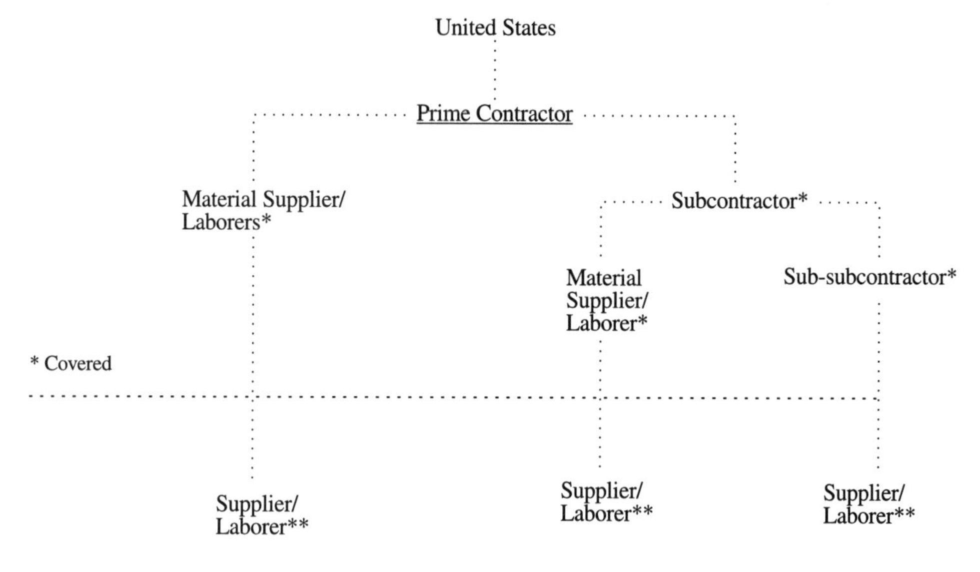

position in **Figure 1-1** will determine (1) if it can make a claim on the bond and (2) how to prosecute that claim.

[A] Contracts with Prime Contractor

The law is clear that parties under direct contract with the prime contractor are entitled to make a claim on the payment bond for work performed and materials supplied.[34] Thus, material suppliers, laborers, and subcontractors that have express or implied contractual relationships with the prime contractor on a project are protected by the bond. Moreover, those parties that deal directly with the prime contractor, whether under express or implied contracts, are not required to give the statutory 90-day notice before making a claim on a Miller Act bond.[35]

The language in § 270b(a) of the Miller Act expressly provides that the contract with the prime can be "express or implied."[36] The concept of implied contracts with the prime contractor has generated a significant amount of litigation

[34] Clifford E. MacEvoy Co. v. United States *ex rel.* Calvin Tomkins Co., 322 U.S. 102, 105 (1944).

[35] United States *ex rel.* Billows Elec. Supply Co. v. E.J.T. Constr. Co., 517 F. Supp. 1178, 1183 (E.D. Pa. 1981), *cert. denied,* 459 U.S. 856 (1982); United States *ex rel.* Greenwald-Supon, Inc. v. Gramercy Contractors, Inc., 433 F. Supp. 156, 160 (S.D.N.Y. 1977).

[36] 40 U.S.C. § 270b(a) (1986).

and is important for both procedural and substantive reasons. First, because claimants under contract with the prime contractor are exempt from the 90-day notice required of other parties, claimants often attempt to establish an implied relationship with the prime contractor either to avoid the notice requirement or to validate a claim if the 90-day notice was not given or was improper in form or substance. Second, and possibly more important, parties often attempt to establish implied contracts with the prime contractor in order to have standing to maintain a Miller Act claim. If a party does not have a direct contract with the prime, it can make a claim only if it was a supplier, laborer, or sub-subcontractor to a subcontractor. The term *subcontractor* as used in the Miller Act has a technical meaning, and all parties under contract with the prime contractor are not subcontractors for purposes of the Miller Act.[37] Accordingly, if a company supplies labor or materials to a material supplier to the prime contractor, that company has no standing to make a claim on the bond.[38] This strict rule can be avoided if the company can establish (1) that the middle party—the material supplier under contract with the prime contractor—was in fact a subcontractor to the prime (thereby making the company a supplier to a subcontractor and covered by the bond)[39] or (2) that it had an implied contract with the prime contractor.

The term *implied contract* as used in the Miller Act is interpreted as a contract implied in fact, not implied in law.[40] If an implied contract is alleged, the courts will analyze the facts to determine if an actual contract can be inferred from the circumstances, conduct, acts, or relations of the parties showing some form of tacit understanding.[41] The rule is that the general contractor or the subcontractor must actually assume an obligation to pay for the labor or materials. In *United States ex rel. Greenwald-Supon v. Gramercy Contractors,*[42] the district court considered a claim against the prime contractor and its surety by a sub-subcontractor of an air conditioning subcontractor on a housing project at the United States Military Academy at West Point. The plaintiff sought to recover amounts not paid by the subcontractor for labor and materials supplied on the project. The facts showed that during the construction period, the prime contractor knew of the plaintiff's work and knew specific details of the plaintiff's problems in recovering payments for work performed.[43] More important, in consideration for the plaintiff's promise to remain on the project and complete its work, the prime

[37] The meaning of *subcontractor* as used in the Miller Act is discussed in detail in § **1.04[B]**.

[38] Clifford E. MacEvoy Co. v. United States *ex rel.* Calvin Tomkins Co., 322 U.S. 102, 105 (1944).

[39] The factors used by the courts to determine if middle parties are subcontractors are discussed in § **1.04[B]**.

[40] Fidelity & Deposit Co. v. Harris, 360 F.2d 402, 409 (9th Cir. 1966).

[41] *See* United States *ex rel.* Greenwald-Supon, Inc. v. Gramercy Contractors, 433 F. Supp. 156, 161 (citing United States *ex rel.* Hargis v. Maryland Cas. Co., 64 F. Supp. 522 (S.D. Cal. 1946)).

[42] 433 F. Supp. 156 (S.D.N.Y. 1977).

[43] *Id.* at 160.

contractor agreed not to make final payment to the subcontractor until it received a release from the plaintiff.[44]

The sub-subcontractor argued that it had an implied contract with the prime contractor, and therefore the 90-day notice requirement did not apply. The prime contractor argued that it did not have any direct contract with the plaintiff and that it only agreed to delay payment to its subcontractor pending receipt of notice that the subcontractor satisfied its payment obligations.[45] The court rejected the prime contractor's defense. The court found an implied contract based on the facts that (1) the prime contractor was aware that plaintiff was performing work on the project under contract with the subcontractor and was aware of the nature of the work, (2) in its letter to the plaintiff, the prime contractor "explicitly agreed" not to make final payment to the subcontractor unless the plaintiff was paid, (3) the plaintiff continued work based on the prime contractor's assurances, and (4) the defendant knew the precise nature and extent of the outstanding obligations owed to the plaintiff.[46] The court held that because an implied contract existed, the plaintiff was not bound by the notice provisions of § 270b(a).[47]

Implied contracts have also been found in other circumstances. When a general contractor agreed with a material supplier to a subcontractor that the general contractor would make payments directly to the supplier to satisfy an unpaid balance and to pay for all future deliveries, the court found an implied contract.[48] When a prime contractor has agreed with its subcontractor to pay for materials and equipment provided to the subcontractor directly and to deduct any amounts so paid from amounts due the subcontractor, a direct obligation to a materialman to the subcontractor has been found.[49] Finally, an implied contract has been found when a prime contractor guarantees amounts owed by a subcontractor to its material suppliers.[50]

Alternatively, certain things have been held not to create implied contracts. The courts consistently hold that joint check arrangements, in which the prime contractor agrees to pay its subcontractor and material supplier or laborer by joint check to ensure payment to the latter, do not create direct contractual relationships between the prime and the lower-tier claimant for purposes of the Miller Act.[51]

---

[44] *Id.* at 160–61.

[45] *Id.* at 161.

[46] *Id.* at 161–62.

[47] *Id.* at 162.

[48] *See* United States *ex rel.* Billows Elec. Supply Co. v. E.J.T. Constr. Co., 517 F. Supp. 1178 (E.D. Pa. 1981), *aff'd,* 688 F.2d 827 (3d Cir.), *cert. denied,* 459 U.S. 856 (1982).

[49] United States *ex rel.* Hargis v. Maryland Cas. Co., 64 F. Supp. 522 (S.D. Cal. 1946).

[50] United States *ex rel.* W.F. Foley & Bros. v. United States Fidelity & Guar. Co., 113 F.2d 888 (2d Cir. 1940).

[51] *See* United States *ex rel.* Youngstown Welding & Eng'g Co. v. Travelers Indem. Co., 802 F.2d 1164 (9th Cir. 1986); United States v. Hesselden Constr. Co., 404 F.2d 774 (10th Cir. 1968); United States *ex rel.* Metal Mfg., Inc. v. Federal Ins. Co., 656 F. Supp. 1194 (D. Ariz. 1987); United States *ex rel.* Fordham v. Parker, Inc., 504 F. Supp. 1066, 1072 (D. Md. 1980).

An assignment of the proceeds due under a subcontract to a material supplier so that the supplier will continue to perform, which the prime contractor approves, has also been held not to create a direct obligation between the prime contractor and the materialman.[52]

[B] Subcontractors

A subcontractor to a prime contractor is given special status under the Miller Act. A subcontractor does not have to give the 90-day notice required of other claimants on the bond. This is because the subcontractor deals directly with the prime contractor, and because of that relationship, the prime contractor should be fully aware of the work performed by the subcontractor and amounts paid or not paid for work performed. More important, if a party is a subcontractor, the statute creates rights against the bond in those parties under contract with the subcontractor. Thus, it is often very important for second-tier claimants to determine that the middle party is a subcontractor to the prime, rather than an ordinary supplier of materials or labor.

The term *subcontractor* is not defined in the Miller Act. The term has a technical rather than ordinary meaning, and the cases have established guidelines to make the determination. A direct contract with the prime contractor is a clear prerequisite to subcontractor status.[53]

The substance of the relationship with the prime contractor is, however, the controlling factor in making the determination. Courts analyze the function being carried out by the purported subcontractor. In the *MacEvoy* case,[54] the Supreme Court held that a subcontractor under the Miller Act is "one who performs for and takes from the prime contractor a specific part of the labor or material requirements of the original contract."[55] This standard has been interpreted as requiring analysis of the "substantiality" of the relationship between the subcontractor and the prime contractor and the importance of that relationship in terms of the overall project.[56]

The Supreme Court addressed the above standards in *F.D. Rich Co. v. United States ex rel. Industrial Lumber Co.*[57] In *Rich,* the Court considered whether a material supplier, Industrial Lumber, had standing to make a claim on the Miller Act bond. This turned on whether the middle party, Cerpac Company, was a subcontractor. In this case, the prime contractor, Rich, entered into two contracts with Cerpac for a federal housing project. One contract required Cerpac to install

---

[52] United States v. Van de Riet, 316 F.2d 912, 915 (4th Cir. 1963).

[53] J.W. Bateson Co. v. United States, 434 U.S. 586, 590 (1978).

[54] Clifford E. MacEvoy Co. v. United States *ex rel.* Calvin Tomkins Co., 322 U.S. 102 (1944).

[55] *Id.* at 108–09.

[56] *See* United States *ex rel.* Parker-Hannifin Corp. v. Lane Constr. Co., 477 F. Supp. 400, 410 (M.D. Pa. 1979) (citing F.D. Rich Co. v. United States *ex rel.* Indus. Lumber Co., 417 U.S. 116 (1974)); *see also* Aetna Cas. & Sur. Co. v. United States, 382 F.2d 615, 617 (5th Cir. 1967).

[57] 417 U.S. 116 (1974).

custom millwork; the other required Cerpac simply to supply all standard exterior plywood. Cerpac entered into a purchase order with Industrial Lumber to supply all of the lumber. The Court held Cerpac to be a subcontractor because it not only supplied certain standard items to be incorporated into the project (plywood) but also performed custom milling work and took over part of the contract requirements from the prime contractor.[58] In so holding, the Court also noted a close and long-standing relationship between Cerpac and the prime contractor and also, significantly, the fact that the prime was in a position to require a bond from Cerpac and thereby secure itself against any loss resulting from Cerpac's default.[59]

The subcontractor determination is based on the facts of each case. Courts analyze a variety of factors including:

1. The dollar value of the subcontracts as a percentage of the prime contract;
2. Whether the purported subcontractor performed on-site installation work or any other on-site work;
3. Whether the purported subcontractor's work involved identifiable parts of the prime contract;
4. Whether the items to be provided by the purported subcontractor were stock items or materials or had to be specially manufactured to meet project specifications;
5. Whether the subcontractor was required to provide shop drawings;
6. Whether the purported subcontractor could be "backcharged" for correcting unacceptable work;
7. Whether the purported subcontractor was required to give a bond;
8. Whether the subcontractor received progress payments or received payment upon invoicing for the items of work performed; or
9. Whether the purported subcontractor included sales tax in its invoice.[60]

Material suppliers often argue that the middle party is a subcontractor rather than an ordinary supplier because the purported subcontractor agreed to provide "customized materials" for the construction project. This argument allows the suppliers to avoid the rule that suppliers to material suppliers do not have standing to make a claim on the bond.[61]

Although an agreement to provide custom materials is not *per se* sufficient to establish the relationship of responsibility and importance necessary to render

---

[58] *Id.* at 124.

[59] *Id.*

[60] *See* Aetna Cas. & Sur. Co. v. United States, 382 F.2d 615 (5th Cir. 1967); United States *ex rel.* Clark v. Moon, Inc., 698 F. Supp. 665 (S.D. Miss. 1988); United States *ex rel.* Parker-Hannifin Corp. v. Lane Constr. Co., 477 F. Supp. 400 (M.D. Pa. 1979).

[61] *See* Clifford E. MacEvoy Co. v. United States *ex rel.* Calvin Tomkins Co., 322 U.S. 102, 111 (1944); *see also* Brown & Root, Inc. v. Gifford Hill & Co., 319 F.2d 65 (5th Cir. 1963); Fidelity & Deposit Co. v. Van Harris, 360 F.2d 402 (9th Cir. 1966); United States *ex rel.* Potomac Rigging Co. v. Wright Contracting Co., 194 F. Supp. 444 (D. Md. 1961).

the provider a subcontractor,[62] it is given substantial qualitative weight in support of finding subcontractor status.[63] The determination requires analysis of all relevant facts, and it is difficult to lay down a general rule to resolve all cases. The district set forth the following guidelines in *United States ex rel. Parker-Hannifin Corp. v. Lane Construction Corp.*[64]:

(1) a party who supplies fungible goods which are part of his general inventory, such as sand and gravel, and the production of which does not require a specialized or customized manufacturing process in order to meet specifications of the prime contract is generally held to be a material supplier rather than a subcontractor regardless of the cost of the materials;

(2) if an item is to be custom manufactured by the purported subcontractor according to the specifications found in the prime contract and the purported subcontractor bears a portion of the responsibility for the design and fabrication of the goods including the responsibility to prepare shop drawings in accordance with prime contract specifications . . . it is likely that the [party providing the items is a subcontractor under the Miller Act].

In *Parker-Hannifin* the court held that a company that agreed with the prime contractor to custom manufacture flow gates for a dam project in accordance with the government's specifications and to prepare shop drawings for the flow gates was a subcontractor even though it had no installation responsibility. The plaintiff, Parker-Hannifin, as the supplier of hydraulic cylinders for the flow gates, was therefore entitled to claim on Lane's bond.

Consistent with *Parker-Hannifin,* a number of courts have held that an agreement to provide customized materials to meet the specifications in the prime contract qualifies the providing party as a subcontractor under the Miller Act, thereby allowing lower-tier suppliers to make claims on Miller Act payment bonds.[65] Alternatively, certain courts have rejected claims that providing materials

---

[62] *See* United States *ex rel.* Parker-Hannifin Corp. v. Lane Constr. Co., 477 F. Supp. 400, 411 (M.D. Pa. 1979); Aetna Casualty & Sur. Co. v. United States, 382 F.2d 615, 617 (5th Cir. 1967).

[63] United States *ex rel.* Consolidated Pipe & Supply Co. v. Morrison-Knudsen Co., 687 F.2d 129, 134–35 (6th Cir. 1982).

[64] 477 F. Supp. 400, 411 (M.D. Pa. 1979).

[65] *See* United States *ex rel.* Consolidated Pipe & Supply Co. v. Morrison-Knudsen Co., 687 F.2d 129 (6th Cir. 1982) (customized fabricated pipe); United States *ex rel.* Wellman Eng'g Co. v. MSI Corp., 350 F.2d 285 (2d Cir. 1965) (hydraulic system for opening and closing doors), *rev'd on other grounds,* 336 F.2d 636 (4th Cir. 1964); United States v. Monaco & Son, 222 F. Supp. 175 (D. Md. 1963) (all material for heat distribution system); Miller Equip. Co. v. Colonial Steel & Iron, 383 F.2d 669 (4th Cir. 1967), *cert. denied,* 390 U.S. 955 (1968) (custom-fabricated steel girders); Cooper Constr. Co. v. Public Hous. Admin., 390 F.2d 175 (10th Cir. 1968) (kitchen cabinets); United States v. John A. Johnson & Son, 137 F. Supp. 562 (W.D. Pa. 1955) (millwork supplier); Basich Bros.

to meet project specifications is sufficient to make the middle party a subcontractor.[66]

In *United States ex rel. CTI Ltd., Inc. v. Mellon Stuart Co.,*[67] the court held that a performing guarantor who exercised its option to assume its defaulting subcontractor's duties and obligations on the project qualified as a subcontractor entitled to sue under the payment bond. Because the guarantor entered into a separate and distinct contract with the principal to supply labor and materials and did in fact assume the completion of the project, the claimant ceased being "merely a guarantor."[68] The court distinguished the facts of this case from *United States ex rel. Gold Bond Building Products v. Blake Construction Co.,*[69] in which the Fifth Circuit held that a guarantee agreement did not establish the requisite relationship between a supplier and subcontractor to entitle the former to Miller Act protection.

[C] Straw Parties and Sham Transactions

Parties that do not have express or implied contracts with the prime contractor or with a subcontractor on a federal project are generally precluded from making a claim on a Miller Act payment bond. The particular facts of the case may, however, give that party an alternative. If the purported claimant can establish that higher-tier parties, who effectively bar the claim, are not legitimate or are installed only as straw parties to limit claims on the bond, a court has grounds to disregard the formal relationships and allow the lower-tier party to make a claim on the bond.

The circuit court allowed a claim on this basis in *Glen Falls Insurance Co. v. Newton Lumber & Manufacturing Co.*[70] That case involved claims by suppliers to a purported sub-subcontractor. The prime contractor, DMH Enterprises, had negotiated a subcontract with Whitestone Construction Company for carpentry and millwork on a defense housing project. The prime contractor, however, structured the transaction so that Whitestone was a sub-subcontractor. An individual who was a close friend and relative of the president of DMH was installed as the purported subcontractor. Suppliers to Whitestone brought suit to enforce

---

Constr. Co. v. United States *ex rel.* Turner, 159 F.2d 182 (9th Cir. 1946) (supplier of gravel in accordance with project specifications).

[66] *See* Aetna Cas. & Sur. Co. v. United States *ex rel.* Gibson Steel Co., 382 F.2d 615 (5th Cir. 1967) (miscellaneous steel products in accordance with project specifications); United States *ex rel.* Pioneer Steel Co. v. Ellis Constr. Co., 398 F. Supp. 719 (E.D. Tenn. 1975); United States *ex rel.* Potomac Rigging Co. v. Wright Contracting Co., 194 F. Supp. 444 (D. Md. 1961) (precast concrete cribbing); United States v. Lembke Constr. Co., 370 F.2d 293 (10th Cir. 1966) (concrete); Brown & Root, Inc. v. Gifford-Hill & Co., 319 F.2d 65 (5th Cir. 1963).

[67] 860 F. Supp. 556 (N.D. Ill. 1994).

[68] *Id.* at 562.

[69] 820 F.2d 139 (5th Cir. 1987).

[70] 388 F.2d 66 (10th Cir. 1967), *cert. denied,* 390 U.S. 905 (1968).

claims on the bond, and the court ruled that the contract between DMH and the individual was a sham and that Whitestone was the true subcontractor. The court focused on the facts that the individual installed as the subcontractor did not provide any labor or materials on the project and that the prime contractor had no intention of imposing any real contractual obligations on the purported subcontractor. The court held that the true purpose of the arrangement was to insulate the prime contractor from liability under the Miller Act.[71]

An alter-ego theory has also been used to disregard parties in a contracting framework so that parties not otherwise covered by the bond can make claims. In *United States ex rel. M.A. Bruder & Sons, Inc. v. Aetna Casualty & Surety Co.*,[72] the district court recognized that an alter-ego theory can be used to gain standing to make a claim against the bond if the facts permit.

Even if a party in the contracting framework is not installed for illegitimate purposes, a court still might disregard a party that serves no function in the construction project. For example, in *United States ex rel. Hillsdale Rock Co. v. Cortelyou & Cole, Inc.*,[73] the circuit court considered whether Stanford University was, in fact, a contractor for purposes of the Miller Act. The facts showed that Stanford entered into a contract with the Atomic Energy Commission (AEC) for development of a linear accelerator center at the university. In that contract, Stanford was required to develop procedures for subcontractors for the actual construction work. Stanford "subcontracted" with defendant Cortelyou and Cole (C&C). C&C, in turn, contracted with Bottari Co., and Bottari purchased materials from the use-plaintiff, Hillsdale Rock Company. Bottari did not pay for the materials purchased from Hillsdale. Stanford required the purported subcontractor, C&C, to provide a Miller Act payment bond in favor of Stanford and the United States. Hillsdale filed a claim for payment for the materials on C&C's bond.

The court allowed Hillsdale's claim on the ground that Stanford was not really the prime contractor but in reality an agent of the owner of the project, the United States. The court specifically noted that Stanford performed none of the construction work and merely acted in the AEC's place to contract for the construction work. Because Stanford was not viewed as the prime contractor and C&C was, Hillsdale became a supplier to a subcontractor to C&C (Bottari), and therefore was covered by the Miller Act bond.[74]

§ 1.05 CLAIMS COVERED BY MILLER ACT PAYMENT BOND

A Miller Act payment bond is conditioned on payment to all persons "supplying labor and materials in the prosecution of the work" provided for in

---

[71] *Id.* at 69.

[72] 480 F. Supp. 659 (D.D.C. 1979) (the court disregarded an entity in the contracting framework that was an alter ego of a subcontractor and held that a material supplier to that straw party was entitled to make a claim on the bond as a party under contract with a subcontractor).

[73] 581 F.2d 239 (9th Cir. 1978).

[74] *Id.* at 241–42.

the prior contract.[75] Although the provision is relatively clear, a number of disputes arise as to whether certain charges incurred in connection with supplying labor and materials are covered by the bond.

[A] Labor Charges

Labor charges incurred in connection with work under the prime contract are clearly covered by the statute and generally do not pose a problem. Actual wages to laborers performing work are surely covered by the bond. If the minimum wage rate is statutorily proscribed, the bond is interpreted to cover those wage rates. Thus, amounts due for wages under the Fair Labor Standards Act are recoverable against the bond.[76] It is important to note, however, that a labor union generally does not have rights under the Miller Act to sue on the bond on behalf of union members, unless individual employees (assuming they have standing as claimants) assign their claims to the union.[77]

Disputes about labor charges usually do not, however, concern wages and wage rates, but rather other charges relating to the labor. In *United States ex rel. Sherman v. Carter*,[78] the Supreme Court considered whether contributions to a union health and welfare fund that the contractor was obligated to pay, in addition to basic wages, on a "per hour" basis under the terms of a collective bargaining agreement were covered by a Miller Act bond. The contractor paid all laborers the direct wages but did not pay the contributions in full. The trustees of the health and welfare fund brought suit on the payment bond, and the surety argued that the contribution claims were not "wages" due to the contractor's employees and that, because the laborers received all wages, they were paid in full.[79] The Supreme Court disagreed. Because the contractor agreed to pay the contributions under the collective bargaining agreements, the Court held that the contributions were part of the compensation for the work done by the laborers and that the labor charges would not be "paid in full" until all contributions were paid.[80] Thus, the court recognized that amounts that an employer agrees to contribute to union trust funds can be recovered by the individual employees or their representatives under a Miller Act bond.[81]

Amounts owed to the government for withholding taxes was an area of

---

[75] 40 U.S.C. § 270a(a) (1988). *See* Annotation, *What Constitutes Supplying Labor and Material "In the Prosecution of the Work" Provided for in the Primary Contract under Miller Act,* 79 A.L.R.2d 843 (1978).

[76] Hines Lumber Co. v. Kalady Constr. Co., 227 F. Supp. 1017 (N.D. Ill. 1964). *But see* United States *ex rel.* Ken's Carpet Unlimited, Inc. v. Interstate Landscaping Co., No. 92–6571 (6th Cir. Sept. 6, 1994) (holding that subcontractor had no obligation to pay Davis-Bacon Act wages due to prime contractor's failure to insert DBA wage scale into subcontract).

[77] United Bhd. of Carpenters v. Woerful Corp., 545 F.2d 1148 (8th Cir. 1976).

[78] 353 U.S. 210 (1957).

[79] *Id.* at 217.

[80] *Id.* at 217–18.

[81] J.W. Bateson Co. v. United States, 434 U.S. 586, 588 n.1 (1978).

dispute between the Internal Revenue Service (IRS) and sureties before the Miller Act was amended in 1966. The question was whether the IRS could make a claim on the bond if the contractor withheld taxes based on employee wages (thereby allowing the employees a credit on tax returns) and did not pay the amounts over to the government. The preamendment cases held that the IRS did not have a claim on the bond.[82] In 1966 Congress amended the Miller Act to make sureties on Miller Act performance bonds liable for withheld payroll taxes if the government provides time limits.[83] The written notice is a precondition to the government's right to make a claim on the bond. On non-Miller Act projects, however, the surety is generally not liable for payment of withheld taxes unless the applicable statute or the bond itself provides coverage.[84]

[B] Materials

In addition to labor, the Miller Act allows recovery for one who supplies "material" to a federal construction project. It does not protect the supplier of capital equipment. If a person intends to make a claim on the bond for unpaid materials, the first step must be to determine if the items are "materials" under the Miller Act.

The cases have established the *substantial consumption test* to determine if a thing is a material covered by the bond or unprotected capital equipment. In *United States ex rel. Sunbelt Pipe Corp. v. United States Fidelity & Guaranty Co.,*[85] Judge Haynsworth explained the distinction as follows:

> A thing which may reasonably be expected to be removed by the contractor and used in subsequent jobs is a part of the contractor's capital equipment, but something which is reasonably expected to have no utility or economic value to the contractor after the completion of the work may be classified as material.[86]

In making the "material" or "capital equipment" determination, courts approach the problem from the perspective of the reasonable expectation of the

---

[82] United States Fidelity & Guar. Co. v. United States, 201 F.2d 118 (10th Cir. 1952); Westover v. Wilma Simpson Constr. Co., 209 F.2d 908 (9th Cir. 1954).

[83] 40 U.S.C. § 270a(d) (1986). Section 270a(d) provides that the United States must give the surety written notice within 90 days after the contractor files a return for any particular period and that no notice can be given more than 180 days after the date a return was required to be filed under Title 26 of the United States Code.

[84] *See* United States v. Pennsylvania Dep't of Highways, 349 F. Supp. 1370 (E.D. Pa. 1972); United States v. Maryland Casualty Co., 323 F.2d 473 (5th Cir. 1963); United States v. Crossland Constr. Co., 217 F.2d 275 (4th Cir. 1954).

[85] 785 F.2d 468 (4th Cir. 1986).

[86] *Id.* at 470; *see also* United States *ex rel.* J.P. Byrne & Co. v. Fire Ass'n, 260 F.2d 541 (2d Cir. 1958).

supplier.[87] For example, when a supplier of tires for heavy earth-moving equipment "reasonably expected them to have been substantially used up in the work under the contract," the court held the tires to be materials even though the tires were not consumed because of a work stoppage.[88] Likewise, claimants that supplied fuel,[89] groceries,[90] coal and water,[91] transportation,[92] and lumber for concrete forms[93] have all been held to have supplied materials for payment bond claims on the substantial consumption theory.

Alternatively, certain items have been held not to be materials even though used in performance of the work. Sureties have been held not liable for reusable pipe that was welded but not destroyed,[94] or wheelbarrows used but not consumed in the work.[95]

There is no requirement that the materials furnished to the bonded project actually be incorporated into the work.[96] One court has stated that "[i]t is immaterial to [a materialman's] right to recovery that the materialman deliver the materials to the jobsite or that such materials actually be used in the prosecution of the work."[97] The test focuses on the supplier's knowledge and intent. Recovery is generally allowed if (1) the materials were supplied in the prosecution of the work provided for in the contract, (2) the claimant was not paid, (3) the claimant had a good-faith belief that the materials were intended for the specified work, and (4) the Act's jurisdictional requirements have been satisfied.[98] Thus, when the supplier's invoices and delivery tickets identified the bonded project, and its credit

---

[87] United States *ex rel.* Brothers Builders Supply Co. v. Old World Artisans, Inc., 702 F. Supp. 1561, 1566 (N.D. Ga. 1988).

[88] United States *ex rel.* J.P. Byrne & Co. v. Fire Ass'n, 260 F.2d 541, 544 (2d Cir. 1958).

[89] Glassell-Taylor Co. v. Magnolia Petroleum Co., 153 F.2d 527 (5th Cir. 1946).

[90] Brogan v. National Sur. Co., 246 U.S. 257 (1918); Equitable Casualty & Sur. Co. v. Helena Wholesale Grocery Co., 60 F.2d 380 (8th Cir. 1932).

[91] United States *ex rel.* Sadler & Co. v. French Dredging Co., 52 F.2d 235 (D. Del. 1931).

[92] Standard Accident Ins. Co. v. United States *ex rel.* Powell, 302 U.S. 442 (1938).

[93] United States *ex rel.* Trover v. Tompkins, 72 F.2d 383 (D.C. Cir. 1934); *compare* United States *ex rel.* Cruiliher & Huguely, Inc. v. Baird & Co., 73 F.2d 652 (D.C. Cir. 1934) (wooden planks used as decking over steel beams are not materials and not covered by bond).

[94] United States *ex rel.* Sunbelt Pipe Corp. v. United States Fidelity & Guar. Co., 785 F.2d 468 (4th Cir. 1986).

[95] Ibex Indus., Inc. v. Coast Line Waterproofing, 563 F. Supp. 1142 (D.D.C. 1983).

[96] United States *ex rel.* Lanahan Lumber Co. v. Spearin, 496 F. Supp. 816 (M.D. Fla. 1980) (delivery to jobsite or actual use in prosecution of work is immaterial to right of recovery under § 2706(a)); United States *ex rel.* Tom P. McDermott, Inc. v. Woods Constr. Co., 224 F. Supp. 406 (N.D. Okla. 1963); United States *ex rel.* Westinghouse Elec. Supply Co. v. Endebrok-White Co., 275 F.2d 57 (4th Cir. 1960).

[97] United States *ex rel.* Carlson v. Continental Cas. Co., 414 F.2d 431, 433 (5th Cir. 1969) (citations omitted).

[98] United States *ex rel.* Balzer Pac. Equip. Co. v. Fidelity & Deposit Co., 895 F.2d 546, 550 (9th Cir. 1990); United States *ex rel.* Krupp Steel Prods., Inc. v. Aetna Ins. Co., 831 F.2d 978, 980 (11th Cir. 1987).

manager testified that the materials were intended for the particular project, there was a presumption that the materials were used for the bonded project, and the defendant bore the burden to overcome that presumption.[99]

A related question concerns materials that are intended for the bonded project but are diverted to another project. The good-faith test applies here too. The materialman must in good faith believe, or have reason to believe, that the material was intended for the specified project work.[100] A diversion of the material by another party to a different project will not defeat an otherwise valid Miller Act claim if the materialman acts in good faith.[101] Therefore, the surety's liability for materials supplied in the prosecution of work generally extends to materials that the contractor diverts from a bonded project to another project when the supplier has no constructive knowledge of the contractor's intended diversion of the materials at the time they are furnished.[102]

[C] Equipment

Charges for equipment purchased and used to perform the contract work are generally not covered by a Miller Act payment bond. This is based on the rule discussed in **§ 1.05[B]** that the Miller Act does not cover items that can be characterized as "capital investments" unless they are expected to be "substantially consumed" during the construction project.[103] Because equipment can typically be used on other projects, courts generally deny recovery for the cost of purchased equipment.[104]

[D] Equipment Rental

Equipment rental, however, is different from equipment purchases. If a contractor or subcontractor rents equipment for use on a particular job, the payment bond will cover unpaid obligations under the rental contract. This is based on the theory that the "use" of the machinery was consumed in the work, and not the machinery itself.[105] Recovery is allowed for the rental cost while the

---

[99] United States *ex rel.* Krupp Steel Prods., Inc. v. Aetna Ins. Co., 831 F.2d 978, 980 (11th Cir. 1987).

[100] *Id.*

[101] Glassell-Taylor Co. v. Mangolis Petroleum, 153 F.2d 527 (5th Cir. 1946).

[102] United States *ex rel.* J.P. Byrne & Co. v. Fire Ass'n, 260 F.2d 541 (2d Cir. 1958); *see also* United States *ex rel.* Westinghouse Elec. Supply Co. v. Endebrok-White Co., 275 F.2d 57 (4th Cir. 1960); United States *ex rel.* Carlson v. Continental Cas. Co., 414 F.2d 431, 433 (5th Cir. 1969).

[103] *See* United States *ex rel.* Sunbelt Pipe Corp. v. USF&G, 785 F.2d 468 (4th Cir. 1980); Ibex Indus. v. Coastline Waterproofing, 563 F. Supp. 1142 (D.D.C. 1983).

[104] *See* United States *ex rel.* Eddies Sales & Leasing v. Federal Ins. Co., 634 F.2d 1050 (10th Cir. 1980).

[105] United States *ex rel.* Carter-Schneider-Nelson, Inc. v. Campbell, 293 F.2d 816 (9th Cir. 1961), *cert. denied,* 368 U.S. 987 (1962).

equipment is being used on the project, as well as the cost of maintaining or repairing the equipment, if the rental contract puts those obligations on the renter.[106]

[E] Insurance Premiums

Insurance premiums are not labor or material and are generally not recoverable under the Miller Act. The Eighth Circuit recently confirmed this role when it held that a prime contractor and its surety were not liable for a subcontractor's unpaid premiums for workers' compensation insurance and general liability insurance because they do not constitute labor or materials.[107]

[F] Consequential Damages

Payment bonds typically allow recovery for amounts "justly due" to those who supply labor and materials. Claimants argue that this includes consequential damages, including delay damages, lost profits, attorneys' fees, and prejudgment interest, so that they are put in the same position as if there had been no default. The surety argues, however, that it is liable only for the actual cost of labor and materials used on the job, and not for any consequential costs.

There is a split of authority over whether delay damages are recoverable under the Miller Act. Some courts deny delay damages on the ground that the claimant's recovery is limited to the price in the contract. Because the damages claimed are for "delay" rather than for "labor and material," these courts reject claims for delay damages under Miller Act bonds.[108]

Other courts reject delay damage claims based on state law. For example, in *United States ex rel. Seminole Sheet Metal v. SCI, Inc.*,[109] the Eleventh Circuit considered a subcontractor's claim for damages resulting from delay by the architect in approving material submissions. The court rejected the delay damage claim on the basis that state law governed whether the contractor breached the contract and was, therefore, liable for delay damages. The subcontract contained a no-damages-for-delay clause, and the court held that because none of the

---

[106] *See* United States *ex rel.* Carlisle Constr. Co. v. Coastal Structures, Inc., 689 F. Supp. 1092 (M.D. Fla. 1988); United States *ex rel.* Mississippi Rd. Supply Co. v. H.R. Morgan, Inc., 542 F.2d 262 (5th Cir. 1976), *cert. denied,* 434 U.S. 828 (1977).

[107] United States *ex rel.* Cobb-Strecker-Dunphy & Zimmerman, Inc. v. M.A. Mortenson Co., 894 F.2d 311 (8th Cir. 1990); *see also* United States *ex rel.* West v. Peter Kiewit & Sons Co., 235 F. Supp. 500 (D. Alaska 1964).

[108] McDaniel v. Ashton-Mardian Co., 357 F.2d 511 (9th Cir. 1960); United States *ex rel.* E&R Constr. Co. v. James Constr. Co., 390 F. Supp. 1193 (M.D. Tenn. 1972), *aff'd,* 489 F.2d 756 (6th Cir. 1974); United States *ex rel.* Pittsburgh-Des Moines Steel Co. v. MacDonald Constr. Co., 281 F. Supp. 1010 (E.D. Mo. 1968).

[109] 828 F.2d 671 (11th Cir. 1987).

exceptions to the clause under Florida law applied, the subcontractor had no claim on the bond for delay damages.[110]

The cases, however, appear to be moving toward allowing delay damages under the Miller Act as part of the amounts "justly due." In *United States ex rel. Mariana v. Piracei Construction Co.,*[111] the district court considered whether a Miller Act surety was liable to a subcontractor for the increased costs of performing the subcontract, which resulted solely from delay in commencement of the project and were not attributable to the subcontractor. The court held the surety liable for delay damages on the grounds that the claims were within the literal language of the statute because the subcontractor sought out-of-pocket expenses for labor and materials and that recovery would promote the remedial purpose of the Miller Act and the public interest in the smooth completion of construction projects.[112] Other courts have likewise allowed recovery of delay damages under the Miller Act.[113]

A subcontractor's right to recover profits has been the subject of a number of cases with inconsistent results. For instance, the court ruled in *MAI Steel Service, Inc. v. Blake Construction Co.* that "a claim for profits does not involve actual outlay and thus falls outside both the letter and spirit of the Miller Act."[114] Similarly, in *Consolidated Electrical & Mechanicals, Inc. v. Biggs General Contracting, Inc.,* the court ruled that lost profits could not be recovered, stating that "the Miller Act was not meant to replace subcontractors' state contract remedies, which allow for recovery of lost profit."[115] However, some courts have allowed profits in Miller Act claims. These courts have emphasized that it is generally recognized that a reasonable profit is part of the amount justly due for labor and materials provided on a government project.[116]

Miller Act claimants routinely attempt to recover attorneys' fees as part of their damages. Recovering attorneys' fees is, however, very limited. State statutes authorizing award of attorneys' fees do not provide grounds to recover fees in

---

[110] *Id.* at 675–76. The *Seminole* case implies that if a state law exception to a no-damages-for-delay clause applies to the particular facts of a case, delay damages might be recoverable against the bond.

[111] 405 F. Supp. 904 (D.D.C. 1975).

[112] *Id.* at 906–07.

[113] *See* United States *ex rel.* Heller Elec. Co. v. Klingensmith, Inc., 670 F.2d 1227 (D.C. Cir. 1982) (holding that Miller Act surety is liable for the value of materials and services provided and therefore liable for delay damages).

[114] 981 F.2d 414 (9th Cir. 1992).

[115] 167 F. 3d 432 (8th Cir. 1999).

[116] *See* United States for Use of D&P Corp. v. Transamerica Ins. Co., 881 F. Supp. 1505 (D. Kan. 1995) (holding that plaintiff was entitled to recover for overhead and profit); United States *ex rel.* Woodington Elec. Co. v. United Pac. Ins. Co., 545 F.2d 1381 (4th Cir. 1976); United States *ex rel.* Reichenberg v. Montgomery, 155 F. Supp. 384 (E.D. Pa. 1957), *aff'd,* 253 F.2d 427 (3d Cir. 1958).

Miller Act claims. The Supreme Court rejected the use of state law to recover attorneys' fees on the ground that the Miller Act is a federal cause of action, and the substantive rights and remedies available are matters of federal law.[117] However, in a recent case the U.S. Court of Appeals for the Fifth Circuit affirmed a District Court decision that awarded attorneys' fees to a subcontractor who had filed a claim against the contractor's Miller Act bond as well as claims under Texas state law for extra work and delay damages. In reaching its decision, the Fifth Circuit relied on state law claims that allowed recovery for attorneys' fees.[118]

In cases that were pursued only under the Miller Act, there have been a few circumstances where attorneys' fees have been awarded. If the contract under which the claimant performed specifically provides for recovery of attorneys' fees, the fees have been held to be recoverable.[119] Attorneys' fees have also been held to be recoverable when the opposing party in a Miller Act claim acts in bad faith.[120]

Prejudgment interest is recoverable on Miller Act claims on one of two theories. First, if the claimant's contract provides for payment of interest, the contract provides the basis for an award of interest.[121] Second, if the contract does not provide for interest, it may be recoverable under state law. Although a Miller Act claim is a federal action based on federal law, the Act does not provide any standards for awarding prejudgment interest, and courts look to state law to award interest on claims.[122] Although the courts agree that state law can provide the basis for interest, the circuits differ on the time from which it begins to accrue.[123]

---

[117] F.D. Rich Co. v. United States, 417 U.S. 116 (1974); *see also* United States *ex rel.* Leno v. Summit Constr. Co., 892 F.2d 788 (9th Cir. 1989); Howell Crane Serv. v. USF&G, 861 F.2d 110 (5th Cir. 1988); United States *ex rel.* Pensacola Constr. Co. v. St. Paul Fire & Marine Ins. Co., 710 F. Supp. 638 (W.D. La. 1989). *See generally* Annotation, *Recovery of Attorney's Fees in Miller Act (40 USC §§ 270(a)-270(e)) Litigation,* 4 A.L.R. Fed. 685 (1967).

[118] *See* U.S. fubo Varco Pruden Buildings v. Reid & Gary Strickland Co., 161 F.3d 915 (5th Cir. 1998).

[119] United States *ex rel.* C.J.C., Inc. v. Western States Mechanical Contractors, Inc., 834 F.2d 1533 (10th Cir. 1987). *But see* United States *ex rel.* Krupp Steel Prods. v. Aetna Ins. Co., 831 F.2d 978 (11th Cir. 1987) (supplier could not recover attorney's fees even though fees were allowed under supplier subcontractor contract and subcontract).

[120] *See* United States *ex rel.* Mid Seven Transp. v. Blinderman Constr. Co., 735 F. Supp. 272 (N.D. Ill. 1990); United States *ex rel.* Gen. Elec. Supply Co. v. Minority Elec. Co., 537 F. Supp. 1018 (S.D. Ga. 1982); KW Indus. v. National Sur. Co., 855 F.2d 640 (9th Cir. 1988).

[121] United States *ex rel.* Billows Elec. Supply Co., 517 F. Supp. 1178 (E.D. Pa. 1981), *aff'd,* 688 F.2d 827 (3d Cir.), *cert. denied,* 459 U.S. 856, 103 S. Ct. 126 (1982).

[122] United States *ex rel.* Seminole Sheet Metal, Inc. v. SCI, Inc., 828 F.2d 671, 678 (11th Cir. 1987).

[123] *Compare id.* (interest runs from date liquidated debt is due) *with* Golden W. Constr. Co. v. United States, 304 F.2d 753 (10th Cir. 1962) (surety not liable for interest until demand is made under bond) *and* United States *ex rel.* Sherman v. Carter, 301 F.2d 467 (9th Cir. 1962).

[G] Breach-of-Contract Damages

In a Miller Act claim, the claimant can recover either the contract price for the labor and materials provided or the "reasonable value" of those items. If the labor and materials were provided under a contract with specified prices and the amounts due were simply not paid even though the claimant fully performed, the claimant's action is on the contract for the contract price. If, however, one of the parties breaches the contract and causes the other to cease work, the courts have held that the claimant has an action on the Miller Act bond to recover the value of labor and materials provided on a quantum meruit theory. It is well established that an action in quantum meruit is available to a subcontractor from a breaching contractor under the Miller Act.[124] Quantum meruit damages have been allowed in at least two situations. First, when there is a substantial breach of a contract, the subcontractor can forgo a suit on the contract and sue for the reasonable value of its performance.[125] Damages are measured based on "the amount for which such services could have been purchased from one in plaintiff's position at the time and place the services were rendered."[126] The impact of this rule is that recovery is not limited by the contract and the claimant can recover the value of services provided irrespective of limitations in the contract.[127]

To determine the proper "value of performance" under a quantum meruit theory, courts will deduct the cost of any corrective action necessitated by the claimant's work.[128]

The second ground for quantum meruit recovery is when the subcontractor has performed work outside the terms of the contract that benefits the prime contractor. If these "extras" are performed, the subcontractor is entitled to recover their "reasonable value."[129]

See also Annotation, *Award of Prejudgment Interest under the Miller Act,* 66 A.L.R. Fed. 904 (1981).

[124] *See* United States *ex rel.* C.J.C., Inc. v. Western States Mechanical Contractors, Inc., 834 F.2d 1533, 1539 (10th Cir. 1987) (citations omitted). *See also* Annotation, *Quantum Meruit Recovery by Subcontractor under Miller Act (40 USCS §§ 270a et seq.),* 26 A.L.R. Fed. 746 (1973).

[125] United States *ex rel.* C.J.C., Inc. v. Western States Mechanical Contractors, Inc., 834 F.2d 1533, 1550 (10th Cir. 1987) (citations omitted).

[126] United States *ex rel.* Coastal Steel Erectors, Inc. v. Algernon Blair, Inc., 479 F.2d 638, 641 (4th Cir. 1973).

[127] *Id.*

[128] United States *ex rel.* C.J.C., Inc. v. Western States Mechanical Contractors, Inc., 834 F.2d 1533, 1540 (10th Cir. 1987); *see also* Leo Spear Constr. Co. v. Fidelity & Casualty Co., 446 F.2d 439, 443–44 (2d Cir. 1971).

[129] United States *ex rel.* C.J.C., Inc. v. Western States Mechanical Contractors, Inc., 834 F.2d 1533 (10th Cir. 1987); *see also* Continental Cas. Co. v. Allsap Lumber Co., 336 F.2d 445, 455–56 (8th Cir. 1964), *cert. denied,* 379 U.S. 968 (1965) (breach of contract by prime contractor and work performed outside the contract by subcontractor allowed trial court to disregard "express" contract and award damages in quantum meruit).

§ 1.06 NOTICE REQUIREMENTS

The Miller Act requires that any person under contract with a subcontractor, who has no direct contract with the prime contractor, must give written notice of a claim to the prime contractor "within ninety days from the date on which such person did or performed the last of the labor or furnished or supplied the last of the material for which [the] claim is made."[130] The statute provides that the notice must state with substantial accuracy "the amount claimed and the name of the party to whom the material was furnished or supplied or for whom the labor was done or performed."[131] Satisfying this notice requirement is a condition precedent to maintaining an action on a Miller Act payment bond by any party that does not have a direct contract with the prime contractor.[132]

[A] Who Must Give Notice

The Miller Act is clear that any party who has standing to make a claim on the bond and who does not have a direct contract with the prime contractor must give the 90-day notice. Thus, parties under contract with subcontractors must provide notice; subcontractors, material suppliers, and laborers under direct contract with the prime contractor do not have to give the 90-day notice as a condition to making a claim on the bond. The Act creates this distinction because there is no reason to require notice from subcontractors and others under direct contract with the prime contractor because the prime already knows that such a subcontractor or materialman is, or claims to be, unpaid. Notice is required of claimants not under contract with the prime contractor so that the prime contractor can protect itself by withholding payments otherwise due to a subcontractor until the subcontractor satisfies the outstanding debts.[133]

The Miller Act is clear that the notice must be given directly to the prime contractor.[134] The purpose of the notice requirement is only satisfied if notice is so given. Accordingly, an unpaid supplier to a subcontractor cannot rely on a letter

---

[130] 40 U.S.C. § 270b(a) (1986). The federal courts are in disagreement about whether the 90-day notice provision requires that notice be received by the contractor on or before the 90th day. *See* **§ 1.06[C].**

[131] *Id.*

[132] United States *ex rel.* John D. Ahern Co. v. I.F. White Contracting Co., 649 F.2d 29 (1st Cir. 1981).

[133] *See* United States *ex rel.* Honeywell v. A&L Mechanical Contractors, Inc., 677 F.2d 383 (4th Cir. 1982); United States *ex rel.* Kinlan Sheet Metal Works, Inc. v. Great Am. Ins. Co., 537 F.2d 222 (5th Cir. 1976).

[134] 40 U.S.C. § 270b(a) (1988). United States *ex rel.* Keener Gravel Co. v. Thacker Constr. Co., 478 F. Supp. 299 (E.D. Mo. 1979). If the prime contractor no longer exists at the time of notice, the notice must be given to the prime's successor. *See* Bush v. Maryland Casualty Co., 320 F.2d 939 (5th Cir. 1963).

demanding payment to the subcontractor with a copy to the general contractor.[135] Likewise, the notice to the prime contractor must be presented by or on authority of the claimant.[136] Thus, that same unpaid supplier cannot rely on a letter to the prime contractor from the subcontractor of which the supplier had no knowledge.[137]

If a claimant has an otherwise valid claim on a bond, but is or may be barred by the 90-day notice requirement, it can do one of two things if the facts permit. First, the claimant can attempt to establish a direct contractual relationship with the prime contractor so that it becomes a subcontractor and does not have to give notice. The claimant can succeed here if it can establish (1) that it had an implied contract with the prime contractor[138] or (2) that a party in the contracting framework is a "straw party" or a sham.[139]

Alternatively, the claimant can argue that the prime contractor waived the notice requirement or is estopped from asserting it as a defense. The focus here is on the prime contractor's actions or representations and the impact on the claimant. Anything the prime contractor does that would reasonably lead the unpaid claimant to believe that it would be paid without having to provide the 90-day notice gives a court grounds to find that the notice requirement has been waived or that the prime contractor is estopped from asserting it.[140]

[B] Form, Content, and Manner of Delivery

The Miller Act requires the 90-day notice to be in writing, and the courts consistently hold that oral notice, by telephone or otherwise, does not satisfy the statutory requirement.[141]

The content of the notice is most important. The written notice must inform the prime contractor, expressly or by implication, that the claimant is looking to

---

[135] United States *ex rel.* San Joaquin Blocklite v. Lloyd E. Tull, Inc., 770 F.2d 862 (9th Cir. 1985).

[136] *Id.; see also* United States *ex rel.* J.A. Edwards & Co. v. Thompson Constr. Corp., 172 F. Supp. 161 (S.D.N.Y. 1959), *aff'd sub nom.* United States *ex rel.* J.A. Edwards & Co. v. Peter Reiss Constr. Co., 273 F.2d 873 (2d Cir.), *cert. denied,* 362 U.S. 951 (1960).

[137] *See* United States *ex rel.* San Joaquin Blocklite v. Lloyd E. Tull, Inc., 770 F.2d 862, 865 (9th Cir. 1985).

[138] Implied contracts with the prime contractor and the recognized grounds therefor are discussed in § **1.04[A].**

[139] Straw parties and sham transactions are discussed in § **1.04[C].**

[140] United States *ex rel.* Franklin Paint Co. v. Kagan, 129 F. Supp. 331 (D. Mass. 1955).

[141] *See* United States *ex rel.* Brothers Builders Supply Co. v. Old World Artisans, Inc., 702 F. Supp. 1561 (N.D. Ga. 1988) (telephone call is not proper form of notice); United States *ex rel.* Fordham v. Parker, Inc., 504 F. Supp. 1066 (D. Md. 1980) (same); *see also* United States *ex rel.* Acme Transfer & Trucking v. Kaiser, 270 F. Supp. 215 (E.D. Wis. 1967); United States *ex rel.* Excavation Constr., Inc. v. Glen-Stewart-Pickney Builders & Developers, Inc., 388 F. Supp. 289 (D. Del. 1975).

the prime contractor for payment of the subcontractor's unpaid bill.[142] The notice must also inform the prime contractor of the approximate amount claimed[143] and the subcontractor for whom the work was performed.[144]

Finally, the Act provides that the 90-day notice must be served on the contractor by registered mail or in any manner in which a United States marshal is authorized to serve summons.[145] The courts, however, give liberal construction to this requirement. The statutory provision is generally held to be a means of proving receipt and not a mandatory requirement.[146] Courts generally hold that if written notice is provided, by regular mail or otherwise, the contractor has actual notice, and the notice will not fail because it was not sent in the prescribed manner.[147]

[C] Time Period for Giving Notice

The Miller Act provides that the claimant must give written notice to the prime contractor within 90 days of the last date upon which the claimant furnished labor or material for which the claim is made. Determining that "last date" is critical to the claim. The determination is complex, and it is important for both determining when the 90-day notice must be given and when the one-year time period for bringing suit begins to run. The timing of the 90-day notice has raised a number of issues and has generated a significant body of case law addressing those issues.[148]

The 90-day time period is computed in accordance with Rule 6(a) of the

---

[142] United States *ex rel.* Blue Circle W., Inc. v. Tucson Mechanical Contracting, Inc., 921 F.2d 911, 914 (9th Cir. 1990); United States *ex rel.* Jinks Lumber Co. v. Federal Ins. Co., 452 F.2d 485 (5th Cir. 1971); United States *ex rel.* Charles R. Joyce & Son, Inc. v. Baehner, Inc., 326 F.2d 556 (2d Cir. 1964). *See generally* Annotation, *Sufficiency of Notice to Public Works Contractor on United States Project under Miller Act (40 USCS § 270b(a)),* 98 A.L.R. Fed. 778 (1987).

[143] United States *ex rel.* Honeywell, Inc. v. A&L Mechanical Contractors, Inc., 677 F.2d 383 (4th Cir. 1982); United States *ex rel.* Pool Constr. Co. v. Smith Rd. Constr. Co., 227 F. Supp. 315 (D. Okla. 1964).

[144] Apache Powder Co. v. Ashton Co., 264 F.2d 417 (9th Cir. 1959).

[145] 40 U.S.C. § 270b(a) (1988).

[146] United States *ex rel.* Moody v. American Ins. Co., 835 F.2d 745 (10th Cir. 1987).

[147] Fleisher Eng'g & Constr. Co. v. United States, 311 U.S. 15 (1940); United States *ex rel.* Moody v. American Ins. Co., 835 F.2d 745 (10th Cir. 1987); United States *ex rel.* Hillsdale Rock Co. v. Cortelyou & Cole, Inc., 581 F.2d 239 (9th Cir. 1978) (regular United States mail); United States *ex rel.* Kelly-Mohrhusen Co. v. Patnode Co., 457 F.2d 116 (7th Cir. 1972). *But see* United States *ex rel.* Denie's Sons Co. v. Bass, 111 F.2d 965 (6th Cir. 1940) (failure to give written notice by registered mail was fatal to right to sue); United States *ex rel.* Betts v. Continental Cas. Co., 230 F. Supp. 557 (W.D. Pa. 1964) (same).

[148] *See generally* Annotation, *Timeliness of Notice to Public Works Contractor on Federal Project of Indebtedness for Labor and Material Furnished,* 69 A.L.R. Fed. 600 (1985).

Federal Rules of Civil Procedure.[149] The 90 days begins to run the day after the last day labor or materials were supplied. The notice must be given on or before 90 days thereafter. Although the Miller Act does not address the issue of whether the 90-day notice is based on the date of mailing by the claimant or the date of receipt by the defendant, the majority of courts have determined that the notice must be *received* within 90 days.[150] In *United States ex rel. Lincoln Electric Products Co. v. Greene Electrical Service,*[151] the court considered defendant's argument that a supplier's notice was invalid because it was not *received* by the contractor on the 90th day. The court rejected that argument and held that the notice was effective when it was *registered and mailed* on the 90th day.[152]

In *United States ex rel. Pepper Burns Insulation, Inc. v. Artco Corp.*,[153] the Fourth Circuit disagreed with Lincoln Electric and interpreted the 90-day notice requirement as meaning that notice must be *received* within 90 days of the date on which labor was last performed or materials were last furnished.

The standard used to determine the date that the 90-day period begins to run is whether the work was performed or the material supplied as part of the original contract or for the purpose of correcting defects or making repairs following inspection of the project.[154] When materials required under a contract were not supplied with the claimant's final material delivery to the project, but were delivered for the first time thereafter, the 90-day period ran from the later date—the actual date the items were first supplied to the project.[155] The 90-day period will not, however, run from the date materials are provided to replace previously supplied but defective items.[156]

Determining the last date upon which materials were supplied to a project pursuant to a contract involving multiple deliveries is frequently disputed. The

---

[149] *See* United States *ex rel.* Lincoln Elec. Prods. Co. v. Green Elec. Serv., 252 F. Supp. 324, 327 (E.D.N.Y. 1966).

[150] *See* Pepper Burns Insulation, Inc. v. Artco Corp., 970 F.2d 1340 (4th Circuit 1992); U.S. fubo Greenwald-Supon, Inc. v. Gramercy Contractors, 433 F. Supp. 156 (S.D.N.Y. 1977).

[151] 252 F. Supp. 324 (E.D.N.Y. 1966).

[152] *Id.*

[153] 970 F.2d 1340 (4th Cir. 1992), *cert. denied,* 506 U.S. 1053 (1993).

[154] United States *ex rel.* Greenwald-Supon, Inc. v. Gramercy Contractors, Inc., 433 F. Supp. 156, 162 (S.D.N.Y. 1977).

[155] United States *ex rel.* Raymond Bergen, Inc. v. DeMatteo Constr. Co., 467 F. Supp. 22, 24–25 (D. Conn. 1979). The 90-day notice period for a supplier has been held to commence on the date the supplier last delivered material to the subcontractor, not the date it delivered the last material to the job site, because delivery to the job site was not required under the Miller Act. United States *ex rel.* Brothers Builders Supply v. Old World Artisans, Inc., 702 F. Supp. 1561 (N.D. Ga. 1988).

[156] United States v. Hesseldon Constr. Co., 404 F.2d 774 (10th Cir. 1968); United States *ex rel.* G.E. Co. v. H.I. Lewis Constr. Co., 375 F.2d 194 (2d Cir. 1967). *But see* United States *ex rel.* G.E. Co. v. G.I. Johnson & Son, Inc., 310 F.2d 899 (8th Cir. 1962) (timely notice given within 90 days from date two defective items were redelivered to site after they were replaced at no additional cost).

issue is whether notice must be given within 90 days of each delivery or within 90 days of the last delivery. In *United States ex rel. A&M Petroleum, Inc. v. Santa Fe Engineers, Inc.,*[157] the Fifth Circuit considered a claim based upon a series of diesel fuel deliveries to a construction project. The claimant made 15 deliveries of diesel fuel and related supplies to the project from November 15, 1984 to June 5, 1985 pursuant to purchase orders issued by a subcontractor. The subcontractor failed to make full payment, and the supplier gave notice to the contractor on August 8, 1985 within 90 days after the last delivery. The contractor refused to pay the claim and argued that the supplier's notice was ineffective for the early deliveries. The district court agreed and held that the notice was untimely except as to the last delivery on June 5, 1985.[158] The circuit court reversed that order and directed judgment in favor of the supplier. Citing a long line of precedent decisions, the court held that the supplier need only give notice within 90 days after the last delivery.[159]

A different result has been reached when the delivery to which the 90-day notice applies is outside the ambit of a series of deliveries. For example, in *United States ex rel. J.A. Edwards & Co. v. Peter Reiss Construction Co.,*[160] the Second Circuit held that when a gap of more than 90 days occurred between a series of material deliveries, a notice given for the later deliveries was ineffective as to the earlier deliveries. The court focused on the fact that 90 days elapsed after the first series of deliveries, and the contractor was, therefore, free to make payments to the subcontractor and free from liability to the supplier.[161]

On the other hand, it has been held that when a claimant has a single contract with a subcontractor to supply material or a job, a 90-day gap in deliveries will not prevent the later delivery from being the last date of material deliveries for purposes of the notice requirement, and the additional delivery triggers a new 90-day period for giving notice for the entire claim.[162]

The sale of additional materials on a bonded project which are not part of the claim will not resurrect a claim to recover payment for materials that is barred because timely notice was not given. Thus, when a supplier sold materials to a subcontractor and did not provide timely notice to the prime contractor to make a claim on the bond, the suppliers' subsequent sale of additional materials directly

---

[157] 822 F.2d 547 (5th Cir. 1987).

[158] *Id.* at 548.

[159] *Id.* (citations omitted). *But see* United States *ex rel.* Burak, Inc. v. Sovereign Constr. Co., 338 F. Supp. 657 (S.D.N.Y. 1972) (notice requirement in § 270b(a) bars claims on individual purchase orders for material delivered more than 90 days before date of notice).

[160] 273 F.2d 880 (2d Cir. 1959), *cert. denied,* 362 U.S. 951 (1960).

[161] 273 F.2d at 881–82; *see also* United States *ex rel.* Burak Inc. v. Sovereign Constr. Co., 338 F. Supp. 657, 661 (S.D.N.Y. 1972) (citing same rule).

[162] National Sur. Corp. v. United States *ex rel.* Way Panama, S.A., 378 F.2d 294 (5th Cir.), *cert. denied,* 389 U.S. 1004 (1967); *see also* United States *ex rel.* Edwards v. Peter Reiss Constr. Co., 273 F.2d 880, 883 (2d Cir. 1959).

to the prime contractor did not create a new 90-day time period within which to give the statutory notice.[163]

Although the notice must be given within 90 days after the last day labor or materials were supplied to the project, the question that sometimes arises is whether notice given *before* that last date is timely for purposes of the Miller Act. The federal circuits are split on the issue. Some courts hold that such premature notice is not timely because of the plain meaning of the statute ("within ninety days from the date").[164] Other courts hold such early notice to be timely for any labor or materials provided before the date of the notice.[165]

§ 1.07 COMMENCING SUIT WITHIN ONE YEAR

The Miller Act requires claimants to commence suit on the payment bond within one year after the last day on which the claimant performed labor or supplied materials on the project.[166] Most state payment bond statutes and private payment bonds likewise contain a one-year limitation.[167] Like the 90-day notice requirement, the one-year suit limitation raises a variety of issues and has generated substantial case law.[168]

The courts hold that the one-year limitation is a jurisdictional prerequisite and is a limitation on the substantive rights conferred by the statute.[169] The one-year limitation is not merely a statute of limitations that can be waived if not properly plead but, as a jurisdictional prerequisite, can be raised at any time, even on appeal for the first time.[170] This is particularly important in Miller Act cases

---

[163] United States *ex rel.* Olmstead Elec., Inc. v. Neosho Constr. Co., 599 F.2d 930 (10th Cir. 1979); *see also* United States *ex rel.* Harris Paint Corp. v. Seaboard Sur. Co., 437 F.2d 37 (5th Cir. 1971).

[164] *See* Drave Corp. v. Robert B. Kerris, Inc., 655 F.2d 503 (3d Cir. 1981); United States *ex rel.* Kinlan Sheet Metal Works, Inc. v. Great Am. Ins. Co., 537 F.2d 222 (5th Cir. 1976); United States *ex rel.* San Joaquin Blocklite v. Lloyd E. Tull, Inc., 770 F.2d 862 (9th Cir. 1985).

[165] *See* United States *ex rel.* Honeywell, Inc. v. A&L Mechanical Contractors, Inc., 677 F.2d 383 (4th Cir. 1982); United States *ex rel.* Laborer's Pension Trust Fund v. Safeco Ins. Co., 707 F. Supp. 286 (E.D. Mich. 1988); United States *ex rel.* Moody v. American Ins. Co., 835 F.2d 745 (10th Cir. 1987).

[166] 40 U.S.C. § 270b(b) (1986).

[167] *See, e.g.,* AIA A311–1970 (one-year period runs from date upon which principal ceased work on bonded project (unless limitation is prohibited by law)) and AIA A312–1970 (one-year period commences on earlier of dates on which claimant gave contractor written notice of claim or last date upon which anyone furnished labor or material under construction contract).

[168] *See* Annotation, *Construction and Application of Miller Act Provision (40 USCS § 270b(b)) Limiting Time for Suits on Payment Bonds,* 10 A.L.R. Fed. 553 (1969).

[169] *See* United States *ex rel.* Celanese Coatings Co. v. Gullard, 504 F.2d 466 (9th Cir. 1974); United States *ex rel.* Lank Woodwork Co. v. CSH Contractors, Inc., 452 F. Supp. 922 (D.D.C. 1978). *See also* United States *ex rel.* Brothers Builders Co. v. Old World Artisans, Inc., 702 F. Supp. 1561 (N.D. Ga. 1988) (satisfying one-year limitation is condition precedent to claim).

[170] *See* Chicago Rigging Co. v. Uniroyal Chem. Co., 718 F. Supp. 696 (N.D. Ill. 1989); United

in the federal courts, where the defendants can argue that the court lacks subject matter jurisdiction if the one-year suit limitation is not satisfied.

As with the 90-day notice, federal courts apply the principles of Rule 6(a) of the Federal Rules of Civil Procedure to calculate the one-year limitation period for Miller Act claims.[171] The one-year period commences running on the day *after* the last day on which labor or materials were supplied and ends in the next calendar year, on the date one day before the starting date.[172] Thus, when materials were last supplied on May 20, 1959, a suit commenced on May 20, 1960 was held to be timely.[173] Moreover, the district court in *Bailey v. Faux*[174] held that the tolling provisions of Rule 6(a) also apply to Miller Act claims.

The suit on the payment bond cannot be commenced until after the expiration of 90 days after the one-year period begins to run.[175] Within the first 90 days, the surety cannot be sued. If the suit is commenced before the 90-day period expires, it is premature and may be dismissed. If the dismissal occurs after the one-year period expires, the claimant will have lost the claim against the bond.

A claimant who is barred from pursuing a claim under a payment bond for failure to satisfy the jurisdictional prerequisite of commencing suit within the one-year limitation period may be able to obtain an equitable lien on retainage funds. In *United States Fidelity & Guaranty Co. v. Ernest Construction Co.,*[176] the court held that although the surety had no obligation to the subcontractor under the payment bond once the subcontractor failed to file a timely claim, the subcontractor's right to the retainage held by the surety had priority over both the surety and the government's claims to the retained funds.

Determining the "last day" that materials were supplied or labor performed is a more difficult question. The one-year period runs from the last date labor was

States *ex rel.* Celanese Coatings Co. v. Gullard, 504 F.2d 466 (9th Cir. 1974); *see also* United States *ex rel.* Soda v. Montgomery, 253 F.2d 509 (3d Cir. 1958); United States *ex rel.* Statham Instruments, Inc. v. Western Cas. & Sur. Co., 359 F.2d 521 (6th Cir. 1966).

[171] Bailey v. Faux, 704 F. Supp. 1051, 1054 (D. Utah 1989); *see also* United States *ex rel.* Altman v. Young Lumber Co., 376 F. Supp. 1290 (D.S.C. 1974); United States *ex rel.* Pre-Fab Erectors, Inc. v. A.B.C. Roofing & Siding, Inc., 193 F. Supp. 465 (S.D. Cal. 1961). *But see* United States *ex rel.* Magna Masonry v. R.T. Woodfield, 709 F.2d 249 (4th Cir. 1983) (holding Rule 6(a) does not apply to Miller Act limitations period without identifying method to calculate one-year period).

[172] Bailey v. Faux, 704 F. Supp. 1051 (D. Utah 1989).

[173] United States *ex rel.* Pre-Fab Erectors, Inc. v. A.B.C. Roofing & Siding, Inc., 193 F. Supp. 465 (S.D. Cal. 1961).

[174] 704 F. Supp. 1051 (D. Utah 1989) (when the end date fell on a date the court was closed, suit was held to be timely under Rule 6(a) when filed on next open date).

[175] 40 U.S.C. § 270b(a) (1986) ("Every person who has furnished labor or material in the prosecution of the work . . . who has not been paid in full therefor before the expiration of a period of ninety days after [the last day labor or materials were supplied] . . . [has] the right to sue on [the] payment bond. . . . ")

[176] 854 F. Supp. 1545 (M.D. Fla. 1994).

performed or materials supplied in furtherance of the original contract and not from a date when repair or corrective work was performed.[177] Materials supplied to replace defective items previously supplied,[178] or work done solely to make repairs or corrections to work previously performed[179] does not qualify as work done under the original contract and, therefore, cannot commence the one-year period. Likewise, work performed or material supplied solely to gain coverage under the bond will not be considered in measuring the one-year period.[180] However, if an item of work was never supplied to the project, it will be considered original contract work when it is finally supplied.[181] In all cases, the burden of proof is on the claimant to prove that the labor or materials were provided in furtherance of the original contract.[182]

The one-year period begins to run from the last day materials or labor were supplied, even if those items supplied on the last day are not part of the claim. Thus, a suit brought by a subcontractor within one year of its last furnishing of labor and materials for the project, but which was not filed within one year of the materials and labor at issue in the suit, was held to be timely.[183] Subcontractors making claims can rely on work performed by sub-subcontractors to compute the one-year period and do not have to establish that the "last day" of work was with their own forces.[184]

The one-year limitation period provides the surety with a very strong defense

---

[177] United States *ex rel.* Billows Elec. Supply Co. v. E.J.T. Constr. Co., 517 F. Supp. 1178, 1181 (E.D. Pa. 1981), *aff'd,* 688 F.2d 827 (3d. Cir.), *cert. denied,* 459 U.S. 856 (1982).

[178] *Id.* (materials delivered to correct malfunctioning public address system held not materials furnished under original contract).

[179] United States*ex rel.* Magna Masonry, Inc. v. R.T. Woodfield, Inc., 709 F.2d 249 (4th Cir. 1983); United States *ex rel.* H.T. Sweeney & Son, Inc. v. E.J.T. Constr. Co., 415 F. Supp. 1328 (D. Del. 1976).

[180] United States *ex rel.* First Nat'l Bank of Jackson v. USF&G, 240 F. Supp. 316 (N.D. Okla. 1965).

[181] United States *ex rel.* Lank Woodwork Co. v. CSH Contractors, Inc., 452 F. Supp. 922 (D.D.C. 1978).

[182] United States *ex rel.* Billows Elec. Supply Co. v. E.J.T. Constr. Co., 517 F. Supp. 1178, 1181 (E.D. Pa. 1981).

[183] United States *ex rel.* Drywall Contractors, Inc. v. Aetna Casualty & Sur. Co., 725 F.2d 650 (11th Cir. 1984); United States *ex rel.* Altman v. Young Lumber Co., 376 F. Supp. 1290 (D.S.C. 1974). *But see* United States *ex rel.* McGrath v. Travelers Indem. Co., 253 F. Supp. 330 (D. Ariz. 1966) (one-year period begins on day after end of labor for which claim is being made and *not* from last day any labor was performed under contract); United States *ex rel.* Brothers Builders Supply v. Old World Artisans, Inc., 702 F. Supp. 1561 (N.D. Ga. 1988) (holding that a subcontractor's cross-claim against the surety was timely under the one-year limitation because the subcontractor sought indemnity or contribution for sums it might owe a supplier; therefore, the court ruled, the cross-claim dated back to the date the original claim was filed).

[184] United States *ex rel.* Joseph T. Richardson, Inc. v. E.J.T. Constr. Co., 453 F. Supp. 435 (D. Del. 1978); United States *ex rel.* H.T. Sweeney & Son, Inc. v. E.J.T. Constr. Co., 415 F. Supp. 1328 (D. Del. 1976).

to an untimely claim. The surety may, however, be equitably estopped from raising the timeliness defense by its acts or representations.[185] To establish equitable estoppel, it is not necessary to show actual fraud. It is only necessary to show that the person estopped misled by statements or conduct another person to the latter's prejudice.[186] Thus, when the surety acknowledged a claim, made payments thereon, corresponded with the parties, and presented the appearance of taking an active part in trying to secure payment, the surety was equitably estopped from raising the limitations defense.[187]

Most cases finding the surety equitably estopped involve some representations by the surety acknowledging the claim and making promises to pay it.[188] Settlement discussions, however, without more have been held insufficient to constitute estoppel.[189]

In *United States ex rel. B&B Welding v. Reliance Insurance Co.,*[190] the district court considered a subcontractor's claim that the surety was estopped from raising the limitations defense. The facts indicated that the suit was commenced almost 19 months after the last day of work. The court rejected the estoppel argument and held that even if the surety's actions created an estoppel for part of the 19 months, the claimant could not wait to commence suit approximately 6 months after the time "it should reasonably have become apparent that [the surety] was neither representing nor promising that it would acknowledge and pay the claim." Thus, the claim was barred.[191]

§ 1.08 JURISDICTION AND VENUE REQUIREMENTS

The Miller Act requires suits to be brought in the federal district court "for any district in which the contract was to be performed and executed and not elsewhere."[192] Exclusive jurisdiction is given to the federal courts irrespective of

---

[185] *See generally* Annotation, *Defendant in Miller Act Suit As Estopped from Defending on Ground that Suit Was Not Commenced Within Time Specified in 40 USCS § 270b(b),* 11 A.L.R. Fed. 922 (1971).

[186] *See* United States *ex rel.* Bagnal Builders v. United States Fidelity & Guar. Co., 411 F. Supp. 1333, 1337 (D.S.C. 1976); *see also* United States *ex rel.* Humble Oil & Ref. Co. v. Fidelity & Cas. Co., 402 F.2d 893 (4th Cir. 1968); McWalters & Bartlett v. United States *ex rel.* Wilson, 272 F.2d 291 (10th Cir. 1959) (estoppel requires deception relied upon by other party to that party's detriment).

[187] United States *ex rel.* Bagnal Builders v. United States Fidelity & Guar. Co., 411 F. Supp. 1333, 1338 (D.S.C. 1976).

[188] United States *ex rel.* Nelson v. Reliance Ins. Co., 436 F.2d 1366 (10th Cir. 1971); United States *ex rel.* Humble Oil & Ref. Co. v. Fidelity & Cas. Co., 402 F.2d 893 (4th Cir. 1968); United States *ex rel.* E.E. Black, Ltd. v. Price-McNemar Constr. Co., 320 F.2d 663 (9th Cir. 1963).

[189] Sam Finley, Inc. v. Pilcher, Livingston & Wallace, Inc., 314 F. Supp. 654 (S.D. Ga. 1970).

[190] 743 F. Supp. 129 (E.D.N.Y. 1990).

[191] *Id.* at 133.

[192] 40 U.S.C. § 270b(b) (1986).

the amount in controversy or citizenship of the parties. The claims cannot be brought in a state court even if agreed upon by the parties, and a claim made in the state court will not toll the one-year limitation period.[193]

Proper venue is the district in which the contract is being performed. The defendants can waive improper venue by failing to make timely objection, or, if an objection is made, the suit may be transferred to the proper district.[194]

§ 1.09 WHEN CONTRACTOR DOES NOT PROVIDE BOND

A question that often arises is what, if any, remedy is available to a subcontractor or other Miller Act claimant if either the bond was never provided or the claimant cannot recover on the bond. The case law provides direction on these issues.

The cases provide that a claimant has no cause of action against the United States or the prime contractor *under the Miller Act* if the payment bond was never posted.[195] The federal courts follow Justice Cardozo's analysis in *Strong v. American Fence Construction Co.*[196] (decided under the Heard Act): "The statutory liability, which in turn is inseparably linked to the statutory remedy, assumes the existence of a bond as an indispensable condition. Till then, there is neither federal jurisdiction nor any right of action that can rest upon the statute."[197]

If the claimant is a subcontractor and a bond was not provided, the subcontractor has a direct contract action against the prime. This remedy may, of course, be of little use if the prime is unable to pay. If the claimant is more remote than a subcontractor (that is, a sub-subcontractor or supplier to a subcontractor), the remedies against the prime contractor are very limited. One recognized theory is a "breach of promise" action against the prime for failing to provide a bond.[198] This is based on the theory that the second-tier claimant is a third-party beneficiary of the promise to provide the bond. Establishing the promise is the difficult element of the claim. This theory could be applied when the prime contractor signed and submitted a bid for the claimant. Bid documents on public projects typically contain an undertaking to comply with all applicable laws and regulations and to supply the required performance and payment bonds.

An unpaid subcontractor's recourse against the United States is equally

---

[193] United States *ex rel.* Harvey Gulf Int'l Marine, Inc. v. Maryland Cas. Co., 573 F.2d 245 (5th Cir. 1978).

[194] 28 U.S.C. §1406(a) (1986); *see* United States *ex rel.* Caswell Equip. Co. v. Fidelity & Deposit Co., 494 F. Supp. 354 (D. Minn. 1980).

[195] *See* Universities Research Ass'n, Inc. v. Coutu, 450 U.S. 754, 777 n.28 (1981); *see also* Harry F. Ortlip Co. v. Alvey Ferguson Co., 223 F. Supp. 893, 894–95 (E.D. Pa. 1963); Strong v. American Fence Constr. Co., 245 N.Y. 48, 156 N.E. 92 (1927) (Heard Act) (Cardozo, C.J.).

[196] 245 N.Y. 48, 156 N.E. 92 (1927).

[197] *Id.* at 52, 156 N.E. at 93.

[198] *See* Strong v. American Fence Constr. Co., 245 N.Y. 48, 53, 156 N.E. 92, 93 (1927); *see also* Gallagher & Speck, Inc. v. Ford Motor Co., 226 F.2d 728 (7th Cir. 1955).

limited when the prime contractor does not provide a payment bond. In *Arvanis v. Noslo Engineering Consultants, Inc.*,[199] the court addressed the following question: "who is left holding the bag when a prime contractor on a federal construction project fails to obtain a Miller Act payment bond and then defaults without paying his subcontractors?"[200] In that case, Noslo was the prime contractor on a United States Army construction project. Noslo failed to obtain a payment bond as required by the Miller Act. Noslo defaulted on the contract, failed to pay two subcontractors for materials and services provided on the project, and filed for bankruptcy. The two subcontractors sued the United States after they determined that the prime contractor did not provide the payment bond. They alleged that the United States was negligent in failing to require Noslo to provide the Miller Act bond and in failing to retain sufficient funds to protect unpaid subcontractors. The court first addressed whether the United States owed any duty to require Miller Act bonds. The court held that it did not as follows:

> Appellants argue that the Miller Act requires the government to insist that its contractors furnish Miller Act payment bonds. This is incorrect. The statute requires only that contractors obtain performance and payment bonds. The statute places no affirmative obligation on the government, and says absolutely nothing about what happens when the contractor fails to furnish the bond. The Act grants a very narrow and specific right to those in [subcontractors'] position: the right to sue on the bond (if there happens to be one).[201]

The court next addressed the claim concerning negligent failure to retain adequate funds to protect unpaid subcontractors. The court held that the "retainage" claim was barred by the government's sovereign immunity.[202]

A related but somewhat different question is whether a subcontractor has any direct rights for payment against the United States when the prime contractor and the surety (if applicable) fail to pay the subcontractor. Unpaid subcontractors often attempt to obtain payment through funds held by the United States under the prime contract in the form of retainage. Although a subcontractor may have equitable rights to the retained funds, it does not have standing to sue the United States to enforce those rights.

The Court of Claims addressed this question in *United Electric Corp. v. United States*.[203] In that case, the plaintiff, United Electric, was a subcontractor to a prime contractor, Standard Conveyor Company, on a materials-handling system project for the United States Air Force. The subcontractor performed, but

---

[199] 739 F.2d 1287 (7th Cir. 1984).

[200] *Id.* at 1288. *See also* Automatic Sprinkler Corp. v. Darla Envtl. Specialists, Inc., 53 F.3d 181 (7th Cir. 1995).

[201] *Id.* at 1290.

[202] *Id.* at 1292.

[203] 647 F.2d 1082 (Ct. Cl. 1981).

the prime contractor defaulted and subsequently filed bankruptcy. The payment bond surety refused to pay the subcontractor on the ground that the bond did not cover the materials provided by the subcontractor.[204] The United States held a percentage of sums due under the prime contract as retainage. The retainage exceeded the amount claimed by the subcontractor, and the subcontractor sued the United States to recover from the retainage.

The Court of Claims granted the government's motion to dismiss on the ground that the subcontractor had no standing to sue the United States.[205] The court held that subcontractor claims against the United States are barred by the doctrine of sovereign immunity, based on the controlling axiom that "the United States may be sued only to the extent that it allows its sovereign immunity to be waived."[206] Because none of the waiver provisions applied, the subcontractor had no grounds to sue.

Although the court in *United Electric* squarely held that a subcontractor has no standing to sue the United States, the court confirmed, in accordance with prior cases, that an unpaid subcontractor has an equitable lien on the funds retained by the government.[207] This equitable lien gives the United States the right to pay laborers and materialmen,[208] but subcontractors and other claimants have no right to enforce the equitable lien and compel the United States to make payment.[209]

In *Kennedy Electric Co. v. United Postal Service,*[210] the Tenth Circuit reached a different result, although on distinguishable facts. The *Kennedy* case also involved a suit by a subcontractor to recover amounts due for labor and materials out of funds retained by the United States Postal Service. The prime contractor

---

[204] *Id.* at 1082–83.

[205] *Id.* at 1083–84.

[206] *Id.* at 1084 (citing 28 U.S.C. § 1491 (1986)).

[207] *See* United Elec. Corp. v. United States, 647 F.2d 1082 (Ct. Cl. 1981); Continental Cas. Co. v. United States, 164 Ct. Cl. 160 (1964).

[208] Continental Cas. Co. v. United States, 164 Ct. Cl. 160, 162–63 (1964).

[209] United Elec. Corp. v. United States, 647 F.2d 1082, 1086 (Ct. Cl. 1981). The court in *United Electric* provided a lengthy discussion of a subcontractor's equitable rights in the retainage held by the United States. In accordance with its prior decision on the issue in United States Fidelity & Guar. Co. v. United States, 201 Ct. Cl. 1, 475 F.2d 1377 (1973), which reconciled the Supreme Court's decisions in United States v. Munsey Trust Co., 332 U.S. 234 (1947), and Pearlman v. Reliance Insurance Co., 371 U.S. 132 (1962), the court concluded that although a subcontractor has equitable rights to the retainage, it has no standing to sue the United States to enforce those rights. 647 F.2d at 1086. It is important to note, however, that if a payment bond surety pays a subcontractor (or other bond claimant), the surety gains rights to proceed against the retainage. By making the payment, the surety gains equitable rights from its subrogation to the subcontractors' claims, and its standing to sue the United States (its ability to enforce its equitable rights) comes from the fact that it is also subrogated to and stands in the shoes of the prime contractor, which has privity of contract with the United States. *Id.; see* Pearlman v. Reliance Ins. Co., 371 U.S. 132 (1962). If the government pays the retainage funds to the wrong party, it may be liable to the surety for its mistake. Transamerica Premier Ins. Co. v. United States, 32 Fed. Cl. 308 (1994).

[210] 508 F.2d 954 (10th Cir. 1974).

did not provide payment and performance bonds in violation of the Miller Act.[211] The Postal Service argued that sovereign immunity barred the subcontractor's suit. The court rejected that defense and affirmed the district court's judgment in favor of the subcontractor. The court held that as an independent establishment with the general capacity (given by Congress) to "sue and be sued," the postal service was amenable to suit by a subcontractor.[212] The Court of Claims in *United Electric* distinguished *Kennedy* on this point and held that the postal service, as an independent agency, is different from subordinate units of the federal government, like the Air Force, that fall within the government's sovereign immunity.[213]

---

[211] *Id.* at 955.

[212] *Id.* at 959.

[213] United Elec. Corp. v. United States, 647 F.2d 1082, 1084 (Ct. Cl. 1981).

CHAPTER 2

ALABAMA

Axel Bolvig, III
E. Mabry Rogers
Walter J. Sears, III

§ 2.01 INTRODUCTION

On private projects, Alabama does not require prime contractors to furnish the owner with bid, performance, or payment bonds, and Alabama law provides contractors, subcontractors, and suppliers with certain mechanics' lien rights.

On public projects, Alabama does not provide contractors with any mechanics' lien rights. Bid bonds are required on public projects in Alabama. On public projects of $50,000 or more, Alabama requires prime contractors to furnish a performance bond in the full amount of the prime contract and a payment bond of at least 50 percent of the amount of the prime contract. Although statutory and case law in Alabama establish that first- and second-tier contractors, their subcontractors, and material suppliers are protected by a payment bond on a public project, it is not clear whether material suppliers to material suppliers are protected.

In Alabama, there are three principal statutes governing bonds and mechanics' liens. The principal Alabama statute governing performance and payment bonds may be found at Alabama Code §§ 39-1-1 *et seq.* (1975).[1] The Alabama statute governing bid bonds may be found at §§ 39-2-1 *et seq.* The Alabama mechanics' lien statute may be found at §§ 35-11-210 *et seq.*

§ 2.02 BOND LAW

[A] General Concepts

As in other jurisdictions, Alabama treats the construction surety bond relationship as a tripartite relationship and treats bonds as tripartite contracts.

Construction surety bonds usually have one obligee, which is typically an owner or general contractor, and joint and several obligors, which are typically the general contractor or subcontractor and its surety.

The Alabama Statute of Frauds requires that surety contracts, which include construction bonds, be in writing.[2] In addition, traditional principles of contract interpretation apply to construction surety bonds in Alabama. For example, the surety bond and the underlying contract will be construed together and treated as though embodied in one instrument.[3] The court, in interpreting the provisions of the contract and bond, will look to the intentions of the parties concerned.[4] Moreover, when called upon to interpret a construction bond, Alabama courts "will consider its nature, facts and circumstances leading up to and attending its

---

[1] All statutory citations, unless otherwise noted, are to ALA. CODE (1975).

[2] ALA. CODE § 8-9-2; *See* American Cas. Co. v. Devine, 275 Ala. 628, 157 So. 2d 661 (1963).

[3] Pacific Ins. Co. v. Wilbanks, 283 Ala. 1, 214 So. 2d 279 (1968).

[4] *Id. See also* Acstar Ins. Co. v. American Mechanical Contractors, Inc., 621 So. 2d 1227 (Ala. 1993).

execution, relation and condition of parties, nature and situation of subject matter, and apparent purpose of making the contract."[5]

With regard to choice of law, Alabama follows the traditional view that a contract is governed by the law of the place where it was made, unless the parties intend the law of some other place to govern or unless it is to be wholly performed in some other place.[6] Alabama recognizes the right of the contracting parties to choose the law of a particular state to govern the contract, so long as the consequences of the choice-of-law provision are not likely to be contrary to Alabama law or public policy.[7]

As in other jurisdictions, the liability of the surety on the bond is coextensive with that of its principal on the underlying obligation. Thus, in Alabama, the contractor's liability on the contract is the limit of the liability of the surety on the bond (up to the penal amount), and the liability of the contractor is a necessary element of the case against the surety.[8] Accordingly, the surety may raise any defense available to the principal in an action on the bond other than defenses personal to the principal.[9] For example, the surety may invoke a pay-when-paid provision in a subcontract to defeat payment bond claims of subcontractors.[10] Alabama also recognizes the surety defense of discharge when the parties to the underlying contract, without notice to or consent of the surety, materially alter the obligations of the underlying contract such that injury or prejudice to the surety results.[11]

[B] Bid Bonds

Section 39-2-4 requires bidders on public works projects to file with their bids either a cashier's check drawn on an Alabama bank or a bid bond payable to the awarding authority for an amount not less than five percent of the awarding authority's estimated costs or of the contractor's bid, but in no event more than $10,000. The bidder to whom the award is made must enter into a written contract and furnish the required performance and payment bonds and evidence of any insurance required by the bid documents within the period specified in the invitation for bids, or if no period is specified, within 15 days after the prescribed forms have been presented for signature. The awarding authority may grant an

---

[5] Pacific Ins. Co. v. Wilbanks, 283 Ala. 1, 214 So. 2d 279 (1968).

[6] *Ex parte* Owen, 437 So. 2d 476 (Ala. 1983); *see* First Nat'l Life Ins. Co. v. Fidelity & Deposit Co. of Md., 525 F.2d 966 (5th Cir. 1976).

[7] Craig v. Bemis Co., 517 F.2d 677 (5th Cir. 1975).

[8] American Cas. Co. v. Devine, 275 Ala. 628, 157 So. 2d 661 (1963).

[9] Commercial Standard Ins. Co. v. Alabama Surface Mining Reclamation Comm'n, 443 So. 2d 1245 (Ala. Civ. App. 1983) (statute of limitations); *but see* Government St. Lumber Co. v. AmSouth Bank N.A., 553 So. 2d 68 (Ala. 1989) (guarantor waived right to assert defenses of principal in contract of guaranty).

[10] *See* James E. Watts & Sons Contractors, Inc. v. Nabors, 484 So. 2d 373 (Ala. 1985).

[11] United Bonding Ins. Co. v. W.S. Newell, Inc., 285 Ala. 317, 232 So. 2d 616 (1970).

extension of time to execute the required documentation not exceeding five days in the event of extenuating circumstances.[12]

Should the successful bidder fail to execute a contract and furnish the required bonds and insurance within the applicable time period, the awarding authority will retain from the proposal guaranty the difference between the amount of the low bid and the amount of the proposal of the next lowest bidder. If no other bids are received, the full amount of the proposal guaranty will be retained.[13] Once the low bidder has signed the contract, if the awarding authority fails to execute the contract and issue a notice to proceed within applicable time limits (unless both parties agree to an extension of time), the contractor may withdraw its bid without forfeiture of the proposal guaranty.[14]

In Alabama, the contractor and surety historically have been able to avoid liability on the bid bond or proposal guaranty in the event of a bid mistake. Alabama courts have held that a contractor may withdraw its bid, without liability for the proposal guaranty, if it can show that the proposed price is greatly out of proportion to the value of the work and that the awarding authority knows or should have known a mistake has been made.[15] However, lower Alabama courts have issued at least two opinions that may limit the contractor's ability to obtain relief.[16]

In these cases, the courts have strictly construed § 39-2-7, which provides that in case of error in the extension of prices in bids, unit prices will govern, and in case of discrepancy between prices shown in figures and in words, the words will govern. In one case, the figures indicated a bid item as $80,600, but the price was written in words as $8,600. In another case, the figures showed a bid item as $368,000, but the words indicated only $368. The contractor and surety were denied relief in both cases.[17]

In 1997, the Legislature amended § 39-2-11 to allow (except for contracts let by the Department of Transportation) withdrawal of bids without forfeiture under certain circumstances. The statute allows withdrawal if (1) the mistake renders a bid substantially out of proportion to that of other bidders, (2) the mistaken bidder sends written notification to the awarding authority within three working days after bid opening, and (3) the mistaken bidder presents clear and convincing documentary evidence no later than three working days after bid opening that it made such a mistake due to calculation or clerical error, an

[12] ALA. CODE § 39-2-8.

[13] *Id.* § 39-2-11.

[14] *Id.*

[15] *Ex parte* Perusini Constr. Co., 242 Ala. 632, 7 So. 2d 576 (1942).

[16] Clark Constr. Co. v. Alabama Highway Dep't, 451 So. 2d 298 (Ala. Civ. App. 1984); Montgomery Bridge & Eng'g v. Alabama Highway Dep't, 440 So. 2d 1114 (Ala. Civ. App. 1983).

[17] Clark Constr. Co. v. Alabama Highway Dep't, 451 So. 2d 298 (Ala. Civ. App. 1984); Montgomery Bridge & Eng'g v. Alabama Highway Dep't, 440 So. 2d 1114 (Ala. Civ. App. 1983).

inadvertent omission, or a typographical error. In no event shall a mistake of law, judgment, or opinion constitute a valid ground for withdrawal.[18]

When it enacted these statutory grounds for withdrawal in the event of a bid mistake, the Legislature did not repeal or revise § 39-2-7, described above. In the event of a conflict between the two, the later enactment will presumably govern.

[C] Performance Bonds

Although Alabama does not require contractors to provide performance bonds on private projects, Alabama statutes require the prime contractor to furnish a performance bond in the full amount of the contract price on projects with awarding authorities for public works of $50,000 or more.[19] An awarding authority is any governmental board, commission, agency, body, authority, instrumentality, department, or subdivision of the state, its counties and municipalities.[20] Industrial development boards do not fall within this definition, although they are public corporations established by the state, county, or city. Thus, industrial board projects are not subject to bonding requirements; however, industrial development board property may be made subject to mechanics' liens.[21]

As stated in **§ 2.02[A],** Alabama recognizes that a surety may be discharged from its obligation under a performance bond when the parties to the underlying obligation, without notice to or consent of the surety, materially alter the underlying obligation to the injury or prejudice of the surety.[22] With results depending on the particular facts of each case, Alabama courts have addressed the discharge defense in the contexts of alterations in retainage and frequency of progress payments,[23] changes in drawings and specifications,[24] and changes in the makeup of an arbitration panel established to hear disputes arising out of the underlying contract.[25] The surety's knowledge of and consent to changes in the underlying obligation can, under appropriate circumstances, operate as a waiver of the surety's right to discharge.[26]

In Alabama, if the contractor breaches the underlying contract and is found

---

[18] Ala. Code § 39-2-11.

[19] *Id.* § 39-1-1.

[20] *Id.* § 39-2-1. The definition excludes the State Docks Department and any entity exempted by statute from the competitive bid laws.

[21] George A. Fuller Co. v. Vulcan Materials Co., 293 Ala. 199, 301 So. 2d 74 (1974); Abell-Howe Co. in Industrial Dev. Bd., 392 So. 2d 221 (Ala. Civ. App. 1980).

[22] United Bonding Ins. Co. v. W.S. Newell, Inc., 285 Ala. 317, 232 So. 2d 616 (1970).

[23] *Id.;* Continental Casualty Co. in Public Bldg. Auth., 381 F.2d 10 (5th Cir. 1967); Maryland Cas. Co. in Cunningham, 234 Ala. 80, 173 So. 506 (1937); First Nat'l Bank in Fidelity & Deposit Co., 145 Ala. 331, 40 So. 415 (1906); Fidelity & Deposit Co. of Md. in Robertson, 136 Ala. 379, 34 So. 933 (1903).

[24] United Bonding Ins. Co. v. W.S. Newell, Inc., 285 Ala. 317, 232 So. 2d 616 (1970); Maryland Cas. Co. v. First Nat'l Bank of Eufaula, 276 Ala. 575, 165 So. 2d 359 (1964).

[25] MacKay & McDonald v. Dodge & McKay, 5 Ala. 388 (1843).

[26] *See* First Nat'l Bank of Birmingham v. Hendrix, 241 Ala. 675, 4 So. 2d 407 (1941); Culwell v. Edmondson, 221 Ala. 424, 129 So. 2d 276 (1930).

to have been properly declared in default, the performance bond surety will be held responsible for the damages resulting from the contractor's breach. When the performance bond surety elects to complete the defaulted contract, however, the surety is subrogated to any remaining balance of contract payments yet to be paid under the contract.[27] In the case of the surety that elects not to complete, the measure of damages is usually the cost to complete the work from the date of default less the amount remaining to be paid under the contract.[28] Whether or not the surety elects to complete the work or elects to hire a contractor to complete the work, the surety still may be responsible for such items as actual delay damages,[29] liquidated delay damages,[30] other consequential damages,[31] interest,[32] and attorneys' fees, if there is a statute or express provision in the contract or performance bond providing for attorneys' fees.[33]

Finally, on private jobs, the performance bond surety's subrogation rights to unpaid contract balances enjoy priority over the "unpaid balance" lien claims of subcontractors and materialmen. Unpaid balance lien claimants are entitled to share pro rata all sums remaining unspent, if any, upon completion of construction of the project.[34]

[D] Payment Bonds

On private projects, Alabama law does not require contractors to furnish payment bonds.

On public projects of $50,000 or more, Alabama law requires prime contractors to furnish a payment bond in an amount not less than 50 percent of the contract price.[35] The obligation of the bond includes reasonable attorneys' fees incurred by successful claimants in civil actions on the bond.[36] The Alabama statute requiring payment bonds on public projects was patterned after the Miller Act[37] and was enacted for the same purposes.[38] Accordingly, courts will interpret

---

[27] *See* United States Fidelity & Guar. Co. v. Bass, 619 F. 2d 1057 (5th Cir. 1980); Pacific Ins. Co. v. Wilbanks, 283 Ala. 1, 214 So. 2d 279 (1968); United States Fidelity & Guar. Co. v. First Nat'l Bank of Lincoln, 224 Ala. 375, 140 So. 755 (1932).

[28] *See* Fox v. Webb, 268 Ala. 111, 105 So. 2d 75 (1958).

[29] United Bonding Ins. Co. v. W.S. Newell, Inc., 285 Ala. 317, 232 So. 2d 616 (1970); Huntsville Elks' Club v. Garrity-Hahn Bldg. Co., 176 Ala. 128, 57 So. 750 (1912).

[30] Cotton States Mut. Ins. Co. v. Conner, 387 So. 2d 125 (Ala. 1980); *see also* City of Albertville v. United States Fidelity & Guar. Co., 272 F. 2d 594 (5th Cir. 1960).

[31] Maryland Cas. Co. v. Cunningham, 234 Ala. 80, 173 So. 506 (1937) (rent for temporary living quarters).

[32] Union Indem. Co. v. State, 221 Ala. 1, 127 So. 204 (1930).

[33] Mason v. City of Albertville, 276 Ala. 68, 158 So. 2d 924 (1963).

[34] Pacific Ins. Co. v. Wilbanks, 283 Ala. 1, 214 So. 2d 279 (1968).

[35] ALA. CODE § 39-1-1.

[36] *Id.*

[37] 40 U.S.C.A. § 270a–270d (1986).

[38] Headley v. Housing Auth., 347 So. 2d 532 (Ala. Civ. App. 1977).

the Alabama statute and the Miller Act in the same manner.[39] In Alabama, the state and some political subdivisions thereof are protected by sovereign immunity and are not liable for failure to require a payment bond from the prime contractor in accordance with the statute.[40] For other political subdivisions and agencies, however, statutes and interpretive decisions permit a suit against the governmental entity, and a suit for failure to require bonding in violation of the statute may be maintained.[41]

Although the statutory and case law in Alabama establish that first- and second-tier subcontractors[42] and suppliers of materials to the prime contractor and its subcontractors[43] are protected by a payment bond on a public project, it is not clear whether material suppliers to material suppliers are protected.[44] Because suppliers to suppliers do not have mechanics' lien rights in Alabama[45] and because the protections afforded by the public bond statutes are a substitution for lien rights, it could be argued that such suppliers were not intended to be protected by a payment bond on a public project. On the other hand, because the statutes are to be liberally construed, it could be argued that such suppliers are protected.

Alabama cases have broadly construed the statutory phrase "labor, material or supplies" furnished for or in the prosecution of the work. For example, gasoline, oil, and lubricating outfit;[46] saws, a truck, maintenance of the truck, maintenance of the saws, and electric cable;[47] general supervision;[48] profit;[49] prepaid freight charges;[50] and even materials furnished for the project in good faith but diverted to another job[51] have been held to be "labor, materials or supplies" for which the surety is liable under the payment bond.

Even when a payment bond is not literally in statutory form, if it was given for the purposes named in the statute and accepted and acted upon as such, the payment bond statute will be read into the bond.[52]

---

[39] Price v. H.L. Coble Constr. Co, 317 F.2d 312 (5th Cir. 1963); Waterworks, Gas & Sewer Bd. v. Buchanan Contracting Co., 294 Ala. 402, 318 So. 2d 267 (1975).

[40] *See* Warrior Hinkle, Inc. v. Andalusia City Sch. Bd., 469 So. 2d 1285 (Ala. 1985). *See In re* Monarch Tile, Inc., 219 B.R. 622 (Bankr. N.D. Ala. 1998) (Highway Department not liable for failing to require payment bond).

[41] *See* Housing Auth. v. Headley, 360 So. 2d 1025 (Ala. Civ. App. 1978).

[42] Price v. H.L. Coble Constr. Co., 317 F. 2d 312 (5th Cir. 1963).

[43] Sparks Constr., Inc. v. Newman Bros., 51 Ala. App. 690, 288 So. 2d 749 (1974).

[44] *Id.*

[45] *See* Pinecrest Apartments, Ltd. v. R.P. McDavid Co., 535 So. 2d 126 (Ala. 1988).

[46] State *ex rel.* Wadsworth v. Southern Sur. Co., 221 Ala. 113, 127 So. 805 (1930).

[47] Price v. H.L. Coble Constr. Co., 317 F.2d 312 (5th Cir. 1963).

[48] *Id.*

[49] *Id.*

[50] Columbus Rock Co. v. Alabama Gen. Ins. Co., 153 F. Supp. 827 (M.D. Ala. 1957).

[51] Riley-Stabler Constr. Co. v. Westinghouse Elec. Corp., 396 F.2d 274 (5th Cir. 1968); Columbus Rock Co. v. Alabama Gen. Ins. Co., 153 F. Supp. 827 (M.D. Ala. 1957); S.T. Bunn Constr. Co. v. Cataphote Inc., 621 So. 2d 1325 (Ala. Civ. App. 1993).

[52] Waterworks, Gas & Sewer Bd. v. Buchanan Contracting Co., 294 Ala. 402, 318 So. 2d 267 (1975); American Cas. Co. v. Devine, 275 Ala. 628, 157 So. 2d 661 (1963).

In Alabama, as elsewhere, the time limits and notice requirements of the bond statute must be followed strictly. Under the statute, claimants on the payment bond must give written notice to the surety of the amount and nature of the claim at least 45 days in advance of bringing suit to enforce their rights under the statute and bond.[53] This notice is a condition precedent to thc bringing of an action.[54] The giving of notice by registered or certified mail, postage prepaid, addressed to the surety at any of its places of business or offices is deemed sufficient under the statute.[55]

An action on a payment bond must be instituted within one year from the date of final settlement of the contract. Before final settlement, however, on public contracts of $50,000 or more in amount, the contractor must give notice of final completion of the contract by advertisement in a newspaper of general circulation published within the city or county wherein the work was performed for a period of four successive weeks.[56] Final settlement shall not occur until 30 days after such notice.[57]

A civil action on the payment bond may be brought on the bond against the contractor and the surety, or either of them, in the county in which the work is to be or has been performed or in any other county where venue is otherwise allowed by law.[58]

If the contractor or surety fails to pay the claim in full within 45 days of the date the claimant mailed notice of the claim, the claimant is entitled to recover a reasonable attorneys' fee based on the result, plus interest on the claim from the date of the notice.[59] Either party may make an offer of judgment more than 15 days before trial. If the judgment obtained by the offeree is less favorable than the offer, he is liable for the attorneys' fees and costs incurred by the offeror after making the offer.[60]

[E] Additional Bond Issues

In Alabama, there is no statutory provision or common law precedent that allows a cause of action for bad faith against a surety.[61] In addition, in two

---

[53] ALA. CODE § 39-1-1.

[54] Lloyd Wood Constr. Co. v. Conn-Serve, Inc., 285 Ala. 409, 232 So. 2d 649 (1970).

[55] ALA. CODE § 39-1-1.

[56] *Id.*

[57] *Id.* For contracts less than $50,000, one week's notice is required; final settlement may be one week after such notice.

[58] *Id.*

[59] *Id.* The condition that the fee be "based on the result" was added to the statute in 1997. There is, as yet, no case law construing its meaning.

[60] ALA. CODE § 39-1-1.

[61] *But see* Hightower & Co. v. United States Fidelity & Guar. Co., 527 So. 2d 698 (Ala. 1988) (allegations of surety bad faith involved in procedural question over whether motion to dismiss was properly converted to motion for summary judgment).

unpublished decisions, Alabama courts have expressly refused to recognize the tort of bad faith in the surety context.[62]

§ 2.03 LIEN LAW

[A] General Concepts

The general provisions of the Alabama statute providing for liens may be found at §§ 35-11-1 *et seq.,* and the provisions specifically addressing mechanics' and materialmen's liens may be found at § 35-11-210 et seq. The purpose of mechanics' liens is to provide contractors, subcontractors, and suppliers with a security mechanism on private construction projects in Alabama, including the projects of industrial development boards. A mechanics' lien right is a significant security device because it places a lien against the owner's property for the debt of the owner or the contractor and operates as an encumbrance on the owner's interest in its property. Because mechanics' lien rights are created by statute in derogation of the common law, the statutory requirements are strictly enforced—particularly the procedural and notice requirements.[63]

Mechanics' liens do not attach to publicly owned property in Alabama. If title to the land is held by the state or a political subdivision thereof, no mechanics' lien right is afforded contractors and materialmen working on the project.[64] Projects performed by industrial development boards, however, are not subject to this protection, and a lien will attach to properties held by industrial development boards.[65] The Alabama statute provides for two types of mechanics' liens, known as the *full price lien* and the *unpaid balance lien.*

[B] Basic Provisions: Full Price and Unpaid Balance Liens

The Alabama mechanics' lien statute distinguishes between those persons having a direct contractual relationship with the owner of the property or land upon which the buildings or improvements are to be constructed (the original contractor) and other persons, such as subcontractors and suppliers, who deal directly with the original contractors.[66] An original contractor has a lien right in the full amount of its contract with the owner (a full price lien).[67] Persons or

---

[62] *See* United States *ex rel.* Sprinkler Contractors, Inc. v. McPheters, No. 81-AR-1909-S (N.D. Ala. Feb. 22, 1983); TSP Corp. v. Smith & Sons, Inc., No. 84-504-927-WAT (Cir. Ct. Jefferson Co., Apr. 10, 1985).

[63] Hartford Accident & Indem. Co. v. American Country Clubs, Inc., 353 So. 2d 1147 (Ala. 1977); First Colored Cumberland Presbyterian Church v. W.D. Wood Lumber Co., 205 Ala. 442, 88 So. 433 (1921).

[64] *See* Rayborn v. Housing Auth., 276 Ala. 498, 164 So. 2d 494 (1964); Scruggs v. Mayor, 155 Ala. 616, 46 So. 989 (1908).

[65] Abell-Howe Co. v. Industrial Dev. Bd., 392 So. 2d 221 (Ala. Civ. App. 1980).

[66] Ala. Code § 35-11-210.

[67] *Id.*

entities not in privity with the owner have unpaid balance lien rights. Some material suppliers not in privity with the owner may be able to obtain full price lien rights by giving written notice to the owner, before furnishing material to the project, that material will be furnished to the contractor or subcontractor and that a lien is claimed for the full price thereof.[68] If the owner fails to object in writing to the lien claim "before the material is used,"[69] the owner's silence creates an implied contract to pay the materialman and forms the contractual basis to support a full price lien.[70] This notice also must be given to the owner's construction lender, if its identity can be reasonably determined.[71] Finally, the statute appears to make the advance notice full price lien available only to a materialman not in privity with the owner and not to those supplying labor and services.[72]

All other persons or entities not having contracts with the owner (and which are not materialmen that have provided advance notice of a full price lien) are entitled to an unpaid balance lien. Such persons are entitled to a lien on the unpaid balance of contract funds due from the owner to the original contractor at the time a written notice is given to the owner and to a lien on the building and land to the extent of the unpaid balance.[73] This notice, given under § 35-11-218, is different from the advance notice required for a materialman to obtain a full price lien, which is given under § 35-11-210. The § 35-11-218 notice, when given, establishes the amount of the unpaid balance in the hands of the owner to which the claimant's lien attaches. The notice must be in writing, must state that a lien is claimed, and must set forth the amount of the lien, the work performed, and the person from whom the money is owed.[74] Finally, the § 35-11-218 notice should be given to the construction lender as well as the owner, if its identity can be reasonably determined.[75]

Mechanics' liens are not perfected until the lien claimant obtains a money judgment against the debtor.[76] The Alabama Court of Civil Appeals has held that an owner who received a § 35-11-218 notice for an unpaid balance lien from a supplier defeated the lien when he paid out the unpaid balance to the general contractor before the supplier could perfect its lien by obtaining a judgment against the contractor.[77] Because it is unlikely that a lien claimant will be able to obtain a judgment against its debtor before the time limits within which it must notify the owner (see **§ 2.03[D]**), this result would seem to frustrate the purpose of the lien statutes by allowing an owner to pay out the unpaid contract balance

---

[68] *Id.* The statute provides a form for such notice.

[69] *Id.*

[70] Buettner Bros. v. Good Hope Missionary Baptist Church, 245 Ala. 553, 18 So. 2d 75 (1944).

[71] *See* Bailey Mortgage Co. v. Gobble-Fite Lumber Co., 565 So. 2d 138 (Ala. 1990).

[72] *See* Crane Co. v. Sheraton Apartments, Inc., 257 Ala. 332, 58 So. 2d 614 (1952).

[73] *Id.; see also* ALA. CODE §§ 35-11-210, -218.

[74] ALA. CODE § 35-11-218.

[75] *See* Bailey Mortgage Co. v. Gobble-Fite Lumber Co., 565 So. 2d 138 (Ala. 1990).

[76] *Ex parte* Grubb, 571 So. 2d 1119 (Ala. 1990).

[77] Burch v. First Coastal Bldg. Supply, 606 So. 2d 146 (Ala. Civ. App. 1992), *cert. denied,* 1992 Ala. LEXIS 1312 (Ala. Oct. 23, 1992).

free of a lien even though he has received notice of a lien. The court apparently did not consider the argument that, although perfection of a lien by judgment is necessary for enforcement, the perfected lien could be said to attach retroactively as of the date of the notice.

[C] Other Basic Aspects of Liens

In Alabama, only original contractors, subcontractors, and their subcontractors and suppliers possess mechanics' lien rights. The mechanics' lien statute does not extend lien rights to a supplier of materials to another supplier.[78] In addition, a mechanics' lien claim must arise out of a contract for performing work or furnishing materials for the construction or repair of a building or improvement upon land.[79]

The requirement that a mechanics' lien claim be supported by a contract may be satisfied by establishing the existence of either a written or oral contract between the original contractor and the owner. In Alabama, the lack of a contract defeats a claimant's lien rights.[80]

In Alabama, the type of services rendered or materials furnished can affect the claimant's entitlement to a lien right. For example, clearing, grading and excavation work,[81] drilling a well,[82] and constructing a coal mine[83] have all been determined to be an improvement to property sufficient to support a lien. The architect or engineer who prepares drawings, plans, and specifications for a building and superintends its erection is entitled to a lien.[84] However, a surveyor who stakes out a subdivision and draws maps does not "perform work" for a "building or improvement" within the meaning of the statute such that lien rights would obtain.[85] Generally, the labor or materials must be expended on something that has attached to or become part of the land and adds substantial value to the property.[86] What is a "building or improvement" is determined by the courts on a case-by-case basis.[87] Liens do not cover finance charges or attorneys' fees.[88]

The extent of the property made subject to a lien depends upon whether the property or land is situated within the corporate limits of a city or a town. When

---

[78] Pinecrest Apartments, Ltd. v. R.P. McDavid Co., 535 So. 2d 126 (Ala. 1988).

[79] ALA. CODE § 35-11-210.

[80] *See* First Colored Cumberland Presbyterian Church v. W.D. Wood Lumber Co., 205 Ala. 442, 88 So. 433 (1921).

[81] Mazel v. Bain, 275 Ala. 531, 133 So. 2d 44 (1961).

[82] Wilkinson v. Rowe, 266 Ala. 675, 98 So. 2d 435 (1957).

[83] Central Trust Co. v. Sheffield & B. Coal, Iron & Ry., 42 F. 106 (C.C. Ala. 1890).

[84] *See* Hughes v. Torgerson, 96 Ala. 346, 11 So. 209 (1892).

[85] Wilkinson v. Rowe, 266 Ala. 675, 98 So. 2d 435 (1957).

[86] Wade v. Glencoe Lumber, 267 Ala. 530, 103 So. 2d 730 (1958).

[87] Mazel v. Bain, 275 Ala. 531, 133 So. 2d 44 (1961).

[88] Sherman v. Greater Mt. Olive Baptist Church, 678 So. 2d 156 (Ala. Civ. App. 1996).

the property is located within a city or town, the lien extends to the owner's interest in the land "to the extent in area of the entire lot or parcel."[89] If the property is not in a city or town, the lien extends to the owner's interest in the improvement and "one acre in addition to the land upon which the building or improvement is situated."[90] The mechanics' lien statute does not extend the lien to cover improvements off the land upon which the building or improvements are made, even if part of one project on the land.[91]

Finally, the lien only extends to the owner's interest in the land. Therefore, if the original contractor performs tenant improvements for a lessee, and the lease allows construction of tenant improvements, the lien extends to the tenant's leasehold interest and not to the owner's interest in the land.[92]

[D] Procedural and Notice Requirements

In order to obtain (or perfect) a lien, all potential lienors must take certain actions within the time limits prescribed by the statute. Failure to adhere strictly to the requirements of the statute will result in a loss of lien rights because Alabama courts will not recognize an equitable lien when the statutory procedures are available.[93] For material suppliers without contracts with the owner who seek full price liens, the first step is service of written notice of intent to claim a lien on the owner and construction lender, in accordance with § 35-11-210, before the supplied material is used in connection with the project. The first step for unpaid balance claims (which usually occur when the original contractor or subcontractor fails to pay) is for the claimant to serve the owner and construction lender with written notice of intent to file a lien, under § 35-11-218, before filing a verified statement of lien.

The second step for persons not having contracts with the owner (and the first step for original contractors, who are not required to give notice to the owner) is filing a verified statement of lien in the probate court of the county or counties where the property is situated. Original contractors must file a verified statement of lien within six months after the last item of work has been performed or the last item of material has been furnished.[94] Laborers must file within 30 days after the last item of work has been furnished.[95] Every other claimant must file within

---

[89] ALA. CODE § 35-11-210.

[90] *Id.; see also* O'Grady v. Bird, 411 So. 2d 97 (Ala. 1981).

[91] *See* Slow Contracting Co. v. RUN, 285 Ala. 301, 231 So. 2d 743 (1970); Eufaula Water Co. v. Addyson Pipe & Steel Co., 89 Ala. 552, 8 So. 25 (1890).

[92] ALA. CODE § 35-11-212. *But see* Kirkpatrick Concrete Co. v. Birmingham Realty Co., 598 So. 2d 796 (Ala. 1992) (lessor may be estopped to deny mechanics' lien on freehold if it has knowledge of and benefits from permanent improvements).

[93] Covington County Bank v. R.J. Allen & Assocs., 462 F. Supp. 413 (M.D. Ala. 1977); McClesky v. Finney, 272 Ala. 194, 130 So. 2d 183 (1961).

[94] ALA. CODE § 35-11-215.

[95] *Id.*

four months after the last item of work or material has been furnished.[96] The form and contents of the verified statement of lien are set forth in the statute at § 35-11-213. These requirements must be carefully followed, for deficiencies such as inaccurate designation of the owners of the property[97] or inadequate description of the property[98] may result in loss of lien rights.

The third step for perfection of lien rights in Alabama (and the second step for original contractors) is filing suit to enforce the lien. Suit must be commenced within six months after maturity of the entire indebtedness.[99] Ordinarily, this maturity date will be when the last labor was performed or the last materials were furnished.[100] However, the maturity date may also depend upon the lien claimant's billing practices or expectations.[101]

Finally, the lien claimant must establish liability for the debt for which the lien is claimed and must obtain a money judgment against the debtor.[102] If, for example, a subcontractor cannot obtain a money judgment against the original contractor (such as due to a stay in bankruptcy), the lien cannot be perfected and enforced. A lien filed pursuant to the mechanics' lien statute remains inchoate and loses all force and vitality unless an action is brought and prosecuted to final judgment.[103]

A lien claimant may, at his option, join all parties having an interest in the subject property to the suit to enforce the lien. However, any parties not so joined by the claimant are not bound by the judgment or proceedings therein.[104] Before filing suit to enforce a lien, the lien claimant should review the probate court records to determine whether any party has acquired an interest in the property after the filing of the verified statement of lien. If so, that party should be joined in the suit to enforce the lien if the lien is to have any binding effect on that party's interest in the property.[105]

---

[96] *Id.*

[97] Architechnology, Inc. v. Federal Deposit Ins. Corp., 769 F. Supp. 1208 (S.D. Ala. 1991).

[98] *In re* Jones, 131 B.R. 743 (Bankr. N.D. Ala. 1991).

[99] ALA. CODE § 35-11-221.

[100] *See, e.g.,* Yeager v. Coastal Mill Work, Inc., 510 So. 2d 188 (Ala. 1987).

[101] *See* Starek v. TKW, Inc., 410 So. 2d 35 (Ala. 1982).

[102] *Ex parte* Grubbs, 571 So. 2d 1119 (Ala. 1990). *See also* Burch v. First Coastal Bldg. Supply, 606 So. 2d 146 (Ala. Civ. App. 1992) (owner may pay off any unpaid balance due to contractor prior to lien claimant's judgment against debtor, to prevent unpaid balance lien from attaching). *See* discussion of this case in text at n.77.

[103] Lily Flagg Bldg. Supply Co. v. J.M. Medlin & Co., 285 Ala. 402, 232 So. 2d 643 (1970); United States v. Costas, 273 Ala. 445, 142 So. 2d 699 (1962).

[104] ALA. CODE § 35-11-223.

[105] Birmingham Lumber and Building Materials, Inc. v. Lovejoy, 705 So. 2d 440 (Ala. Civ. App. 1997) (party who purchased property and properly recorded the deed after a materialman's lien was filed, but prior to commencement of the lien perfection action, was not bound by a judgment entered against the prior owner of the property based on the lien where the subsequent purchaser was not joined as a party to the suit to enforce the lien).

[E] Waiver of Lien Rights

The lien created by the Alabama statute may be subordinated, waived, or released by contract.[106] However, the presumption is that the right to the lien exists if the claimant has brought itself within the protection of the statute by complying with all of the prescribed formalities. The defendant must show that the claimant has knowingly surrendered or waived its lien.[107]

The Alabama statute contains a provision that requires an original contractor, upon request by the owner, to furnish a list of all materialmen, laborers, and employees who have furnished any material, who have done any labor, or who may be under contract to do so.[108] If the original contractor fails to provide the owner with such a list, or if the contractor fails to pay any materialman, subcontractor, or laborer, the original contractor forfeits its mechanics' lien rights under the statute.[109]

[F] Lien Priorities

In Alabama, competing mechanics' lien claimants stand on equal footing, except for original contractors, whose liens are subordinated to those of lien claimants not in privity of contract with the owner.[110] If the original contractor defaults and does not complete the work, however, any unpaid balance remaining to be paid under the contract may be used first by the owner to pay a third party to complete the work.[111] Among lien claimants other than the original contractor, there is no priority on the basis of the date of filing of the verified statement of lien,[112] or upon the date that notice is given to the owner of the claim,[113] or upon which claimant began supplying materials first;[114] so, such claimants will share pro rata to the extent funds are available for distribution.

The original contractor holds the last priority among lien claimants and will be paid any remaining balance after the liens of all of its subcontractors and materialmen have been paid.[115]

With respect to mortgages and other encumbrances, mechanics' liens enjoy priority when the competing encumbrance was created subsequent to "the com-

---

[106] Vulcan Painters v. MCI Constructors, 41 F.3d 1457 (11th Cir. 1995); Wayne J. Griffin Electric v. Dunn Constr., 622 So. 2d 314 (Ala. 1993).

[107] *See* Noland Co. v. Southern Dev. Co., 445 So. 2d 266 (Ala. 1984); Floyd v. Rambo, 250 Ala. 101, 33 So. 2d 360 (1948).

[108] Ala. Code § 35-11-219.

[109] *Id.*

[110] *Id.* § 35-11-228.

[111] *See* Knox v. Jones, 268 Ala. 389, 108 So. 2d 369 (1959).

[112] LeGrand v. Hubbard, 216 Ala. 164, 112 So. 826 (1927).

[113] *Id.; see also* Rayborn v. Housing Auth., 276 Ala. 498, 164 So. 2d 494 (1964).

[114] *See* O'Grady v. Bird, 411 So. 2d 97 (Ala. 1981).

[115] *See* Baker Sand & Gravel Co. v. Rogers Plumbing Co., 228 Ala. 612, 154 So. 591 (1934).

mencement of work on the building or improvement."[116] In addition, if the building or improvement upon which the mechanics' lien is claimed is separable from the land, without impairing the value of the security of any prior mortgage or encumbrance, the mechanics' lien will enjoy priority over prior encumbrances with respect to the separable improvement.[117] The term "commencement of work" means the time that the material for which a lien is sought is incorporated into the building or improvements or at least furnished therefor at the construction site.[118] When a lender obtains a security interest in the land after construction has begun, but fails to obtain a subordination agreement from potential lienors, those lienors who have commenced work will enjoy priority over the subsequent mortgage.[119]

[116] ALA. CODE § 35-11-211. *See* Builder's Supply Co., Inc. v. Compass Bank, 724 So. 2d 525 (Ala. Civ. App. 1998) (the taking of a permanent mortgage, which was recorded after the lien claimant began furnishing materials, did not extinguish the security interest created initially by the construction mortgage and provisions in the permanent mortgage indicated that the parties' intent was to protect the bank's secured interest in the same real estate described in both mortgages; consequently, the bank's mortgages had priority over the materialman's lien).

[117] ALA. CODE § 35-11-211.

[118] Gamble's Inc. v. Kansas City Title Ins. Co., 217 So. 2d 923 (Ala. 1969).

[119] O'Grady v. Bird, 411 So. 2d 97 (Ala. 1981).

CHAPTER 3

ALASKA

William K. Renno
C. Russell Lewis
Saphronia R. Young

§ 3.01 LIENS

[A] Lien Definitions and General Information

Alaska's lien statutes attempt to mirror the effect of other lien statutes, namely to "give unpaid contractors, workers, and materials suppliers a security interest in the real estate which they have improved. . . ."[1] The statutory scheme used in Alaska generally accomplishes this goal, although there are limitations applicable as to who may file a lien, what property may be made subject to a lien, and timeliness requirements in lien actions.

[1] Applicable Statutes

Alaska's statutory lien provisions are found in Alaska Stat. §§ 34.35.005 *et seq.* The statutes provide comprehensive guidance for the foreclosure of liens.[2] The statutes also codify the rights and remedies available to workers and materialmen in the Mechanics and Materialmen section.[3]

[2] Types of Liens or Other Encumbrances to Secure Payment

Alaska employs two devices to assure parties who have supplied goods or services for a project that they will be paid. The first method is the Mechanics'/Materialmen's lien.[4] This method encumbers the property in the amount of unpaid labor or goods invoices.[5] The second device is the stop-notice given to lenders.[6] The stop-notice is only applicable if invoices for payment for goods, services, or equipment have become past due.[7] Taken together, the two methods provide an effective "before and after" means of making sure that the money on a project is distributed to persons with claims for goods, services, and labor.

[B] Persons/Entities Entitled to Lien Rights

The party seeking to claim on a lien must meet certain eligibility standards.[8] Only those parties that have provided materials or services to the building at the direction of the owner or the owner's agent in accordance with an existing contract can assert a Mechanics' or Materialmen's lien.[9] In the case of a general contractor,

---

[1] Grant S. Nelson and Dale A. Whitman, REAL ESTATE FINANCE LAW, § 12.4 (3d ed. 1994).

[2] ALASKA STAT. §§ 34.35.005–34.35.045.

[3] *Id.* §§ 34.35.050–34.35.120.

[4] *Id.*

[5] *Id.* § 34.35.050.

[6] *Id.* § 34.35.062.

[7] *Id.*

[8] *Id.* § 34.35.050.

[9] *Id.*

the supervision of others who perform the services or provide the labor is sufficient to vest the right to lien in the general contractor.[10]

Another threshold requirement is the claimant's burden to show that the materials provided were incorporated in the project.[11] The burden to show the incorporation of the materials rests upon the claimant. However, the burden does not require personal knowledge and can apparently be satisfied if the party that provides the materials makes "conscientious effort" to determine where the materials will be used.[12]

[C] Land or Property Subject to Liens

If a person or entity falls within the class that can assert lien rights, the remaining question involves the property sought to be liened. Is it the type of property subject to lien? This question involves two types of property—land and other property.

To be subject to a lien, land must pass a two-part test. First the land must be situated under, or in reasonable proximity to, a building or other structure that was benefited by the materialmen's or mechanics' labor and goods.[13] A mine site that was benefited by labor or materials is likewise subject to lien.[14] The second test is in the form of a limitation. Only the interest that is owned by the person who causes the work to be done is lienable.[15]

[D] Steps for Asserting Lien Rights Under Mechanics' and Materialmen's Lien Laws

A person or entity who fits in the class of persons who can file a lien, and who has identified a property subject to lien, must still take certain steps in the appropriate order to place a valid lien.

[1] Notice of Right to Lien

A person about to furnish material or services to a property should provide a notice of right to lien. This notice places the burden of proof on the property owner to dispute that the labor and services benefited the property.[16] This notice must contain certain provisions regarding information about the project.[17]

---

[10] *Id.; id.* § 34.35.050(6).

[11] *Id.* §34.35.050(3).

[12] Dannemiller v. Amfac Distribution Corp., 566 P.2d 645, 649 (Alaska 1977).

[13] Alaska Stat. § 34.35.055(a).

[14] *Id.*

[15] *Id.* § 34.35.055(b).

[16] *Id.* § 34.35.064(a).

[17] *Id.* The required contents of the Notice of Right to Lien are (1) a legal description sufficient for identification of the real property; (2) the name of the owner; (3) the name and address of the claimant; (4) the name and address of the person with whom the claimant contracted; (5) a general

The Notice of Right to Lien must also contain a statement specified by statute.[18]

[2] Recordation of Notice of Right to Lien

The Notice of Right to Lien can be filed in the recorder's office at any time after the potential lien claimant either enters a contract for or first furnishes labor, material, or services.[19]

[3] Owner's Notice of Completion

Alaska statutes provide that the owner of real property which "may be subject to lien" may announce the date of the completion of work on the property.[20] This Notice of Completion must contain certain information regarding the project, as required by statute.[21] The filing or lack thereof by the owner triggers different subsequent time deadlines.[22]

[4] When a Notice of Completion is Filed

When a Notice of Completion is filed, a potential lien claimant who receives advance notice of the filing of the Notice of Completion has 15 days to file a claim of lien.[23] Likewise, a lien claimant who *has not* given notice of a right to lien must file a claim within 15 days of the recording of the Notice of Completion.[24] A claimant who records a Notice of Right to Lien has 90 days after either the actual completion of the construction contract or the last date of furnishing goods or services for the improvement of the property.[25] A claimant who has

---

description of the labor, materials, services, or equipment provided or to be provided; and (6) a statement that the claimant may be entitled to record a claim of lien.

[18] The statement must be in the same type face as the previous requirements of the notice and must read: "WARNING: Unless provision is made for payment of sums that may be due to the undersigned, your above property may be subject to foreclosure to satisfy those sums even though you may pay a prime contractor or other person for the labor, material, service, or equipment furnished by the undersigned."

[19] ALASKA STAT. § 34.35.067.

[20] *Id.* § 34.35.071.

[21] *Id.* The Notice of Completion must be in writing and signed by the owner and it must include: (1) the date of completion of the building or other improvement; (2) the name and address of the owner; (3) the nature of the interest or estate of the owner; (4) the legal description of the property sufficient for identification; and (5) the name of the general contractor.

[22] *See* ALASKA STAT. § 34.35.068.

[23] *Id.* § 34.35.068(b)(1)(A).

[24] *Id.* § 34.35.068(b)(1)(B).

[25] *Id.* § 34.35.068(b)(2)(A).

recorded a right to lien but otherwise receives no advance notice of the recording of the Notice of Completion has 90 days in which to file a claim of lien.[26]

[5] When a Notice of Completion is Not Filed

If the owner does not file a Notice of Completion, a lien claimant must file a lien claim no later than 90 days after either (1) the completion of the construction contract; or (2) the last day the claimant furnishes goods, services, or labor for the project.[27]

[6] The Claim of Lien

Assuming the timeliness requirements are met, there are distinct requirements for the actual claim of lien. The claim of lien is required to state: (1) the real property subject to the lien, with a legal description sufficient for identification; (2) the name of the owner; (3) the name and address of the claimant; (4) the name and address of the person with whom the claimant contracted; (5) a general description of the labor, materials, services, or equipment furnished for the construction, alteration, or repair, and the contract price of the labor, materials, services, or equipment; (6) the amount due to the claimant for the labor, materials, services, or equipment; and (7) the date the last labor, materials, services, or equipment were furnished.[28] All of the recitals in the claim of lien must be verified by an oath of the claimant or of "another person having knowledge of the facts."[29]

[E] Foreclosure: The Means of Benefiting from a Lien

Once a party has filed a lien, to realize any tangible benefit from that lien, the lien must be foreclosed. Alaska law provides that foreclosure suits may be brought in the district court if there is adequate monetary jurisdiction in the district court.[30] Otherwise, the foreclosure action must be brought in superior court.[31]

The foreclosure statutes and the case law addressing foreclosures provide several items worthy of note. First, in a successful foreclosure action, all money expended on drawing and filing a lien claim is recoverable, as are reasonable attorneys' fees in the foreclosure action.[32] Second, a lien foreclosure action is

---

[26] *Id.* § 34.35.068(b)(2)(B).
[27] *Id.* § 34.35.068(a)(2).
[28] *Id.* §§ 34.35.70(c)(1)–(7).
[29] *Id.* § 34.35.70(c).
[30] *Id.* § 34.35.005(a).
[31] *Id.*
[32] *Id.* § 34.35.005(b).

given priority on the civil calendar.[33] Finally, a mechanic's or materialmen's lien is paramount to a homestead exemption on a residence.[34]

[F] Defenses to a Lien Claim

There are several defenses that a property owner can assert against the lien claim or the foreclosure of a lien. Some of these are general defenses and some are available only in specific fact patterns.

[1] Threshold Requirements

The first step to defend against a lien claim is to ascertain if the claimant is a person who is entitled to claim a lien. Did the claimant furnish goods, services, labor, or materials that were incorporated in the project? If not, then there is no basis for a lien claim.

[2] Contractor Registration

Alaska law provides two procedural defenses to a lien claim. First, in order to bring an action in a court of Alaska, a contractor must be properly registered.[35] Second, if the contractor is a corporation, it must submit proof of payment of its biennial taxes before it can bring an action in the courts of Alaska.[36] The filing of the corporation's biennial report is also a prerequisite to bringing suit.[37]

[3] "Bonding Around" a Lien

Alaska law provides that a property owner may post bond to free the property from the effects of a claimed lien or a threatened lien.[38] "Bonding around" a lien is not actually a defense to a lien, but rather a means of freeing the property while the validity of the claim of lien is determined.

In order to bond around a lien, the property owner (or a prime contractor or subcontractor) must post a bond in the amount of one and one-half times the claimed lien.[39] This bond must be dedicated to pay the alleged claimed lien and the cost of any suit to enforce the claimed lien.[40] If a properly executed bond is

---

[33] *Id.* § 34.35.005(c).

[34] *Id.* § 09.38.065(2)(B). *See also* Munn v. Thornton, 956 P.2d 1213, 1221 (Alaska 1998).

[35] ALASKA STAT. § 08.18.151.

[36] *Id.* § 10.06.848(a).

[37] *Id.*

[38] *Id.* § 34.35.072.

[39] *Id.*

[40] *Id.*

posted, the lien and any action to foreclose the lien will no longer have any effect on the property.[41]

[4] Warranty Work

The lien statutes specifically provide that any "[l]abor, materials, services, or equipment furnished . . . to satisfy warranty obligations or to remedy defective or unsatisfactory construction" does not create any lien liability.[42] Accordingly, any lien claimed on the basis of work required under a contractual warranty is invalid.

[5] Strict Timeline Construction

The Alaska courts have recognized that lien statutes are remedial in nature and should be liberally construed.[43] However, when the existence of a lien depends on fulfilling statutory requirements, the mandate of liberal construction is set aside.[44] Alaska statutes provide that a lien is only valid if filed within the appropriate time periods.[45] These elements are combined to require strict compliance with the filing deadlines. The Alaska Supreme Court has held that the requirement to comply with the applicable timeline must be enforced in order to reinforce the "significance of filing . . . a lien."[46]

[6] Breach of Contract

Property owners may be able to assert a defense of breach of contract against a contractor's foreclosure of a lien. When a contractor fails to complete a "considerable portion" of the contract work, that contractor cannot foreclose any lien arising under the contract.[47]

[7] Prime Contractor's Duty to Defend

A property owner may be able to look to a prime contractor for both defense and indemnity related to a lien claim.[48] If a lien claim is filed based on the

---

[41] *Id.*

[42] *Id.* § 34.35.071(e).

[43] H.A.M.S. Co. v. Electrical Contractors of Alaska, Inc., 563 P.2d 258, 263 (Alaska 1977) (citations omitted).

[44] *Id.*

[45] Alaska Stat. § 34.35.068(c).

[46] Brooks v. R&M Consultants, Inc., 613 P.2d 268, 270 (Alaska 1980) (citations omitted).

[47] Gillis v. Gillette, 184 F.2d 872, 876, 13 Alaska 55, 63 (9th Cir. 1950). Although the cited authority is somewhat aged, the concept of breach of contract as defense to lien foreclosure is still supported in Oregon. *See, e.g.,* Bend Tarp & Liner, Inc. v. Bundy, et al., 961 P.2d 857, 861, 154 Or. App. 372, 379 (Or. App. 1998) (breach of contract bars foreclosure of a lien). Oregon law is the basis for Alaska's lien law. *See Gillis, supra,* and cases cited therein.

[48] Alaska Stat. §§ 34.35.100(a) and (b).

provision of materials or labor to a prime contractor, the property owner can withhold money in an amount equal to the claimed lien from the contractor during the pendency of any lien action.[49] Should the lien action result in a judgment against the property owner (or the property of the owner), the owner can reduce the money owed to the contractor.[50] Alternatively, the owner can demand money back from the prime contractor if the claimed lien amount exceeds the amount remaining to be paid to the contractor.[51] Importantly, the property owner is authorized to demand repayment from the contractor for any settlements that the owner reaches directly with the party claiming a right to lien.[52]

[8] Waiver

Alaska law specifically allows for liens to be waived.[53] However, there are two important restrictions on the availability of a waiver. These restrictions focus on the parties that may waive a lien and on the time in which the waiver has effect.

First, individuals may not waive lien rights.[54] Individuals, as contemplated by the statute, are the craft workers who actually perform work on the site, rather than contractors.[55] Therefore, contractors may waive lien rights, but individual workers cannot.[56]

The second restriction applies to the time of the waiver. To be effective, waivers can only be retrospective. Any waiver that purports to waive future claims or benefits will not be given effect.[57]

[G] Lien Priorities

Alaska generally follows the rule of "first in time, first in right" regarding priority of encumbrances on land. Specifically, Alaska statutes provide that a prior encumbrance will be superior to a lien that arises after the encumbrance is recorded.[58]

Alaska statutes grant a priority to "individual[s] actually performing labor upon a building," even if the lien from that labor is subsequent in time to a prior encumbrance.[59] The protection and priority granted those individuals also extends

---

[49] *Id.* § 34.35.100(a).

[50] *Id.* § 34.35.100(b).

[51] *Id.* § 34.35.100(c).

[52] *Id.*

[53] *Id.* § 34.35.117(a).

[54] *Id.* § 34.35.117(b).

[55] *See* Nystorm v. Buckhorn Homes, Inc., 778 P.2d 1115, 1122–24 (Alaska 1989).

[56] *Id.* at 1124. Although individual workers may, in fact, execute lien waivers, those waivers will not be given any effect. *Id.*

[57] Alaska Stat. § 34.35.117(a).

[58] *Id.* § 34.35.060(a).

[59] *Id.* § 34.35.060(c).

to any employee benefit trusts acting on behalf of individuals who supplied labor for the improvement on the property.[60]

[H] Stop Lending Notices

Alaska provides the stop-lending notice as another means of protecting those claimants who furnish "labor, material, service, or equipment" for a project.[61] This remedy is available only if the claimant has furnished an invoice and that invoice is past due.[62]

The stop-lending notice is created by the claimant and must contain several items of information.[63] Once a stop-lending notice is received by a lender, it remains in effect for 90 days, or until revoked by the claimant.[64] The lender must then cease disbursement or face varying degrees of liability to the claimant.[65]

Project owners (and general contractors) are under a significant burden relating to construction financing. Owners must submit a certificate attesting to the proposed use of any construction financing proceeds prior to receiving those proceeds.[66] These certificates must include the amount of funds going to each prime contractor.[67] Should the owner then fail to disburse the funds according to the certificate, criminal penalties will apply.[68] Any claimant who files a stop-lending notice is entitled to see all the certificates filed for the project, as well as any funds the lender has allocated for the project that remain undistributed.[69]

[I] Conclusion

Alaska's lien law statutes provide a comprehensive scheme for the protection of those who perform services on construction projects. Although the burden on the lien claimant to pay attention to timelines and other procedural matters is significant, the protection available through the lien and foreclosure process ensures that legitimate construction debts will be paid.

---

[60] *Id.*

[61] *Id.* § 34.35.062(a).

[62] *Id.*

[63] *Id.* §§ 34.35.062(a)(1)–(6). These instructions essentially require the claimant to identify the project, the real property which is improved, the person to whom the labor or material is furnished, the claimant, and the unpaid amount due to the claimant. The notice must also contain instructions from the claimant to the lender to stop any future disbursements to the project.

[64] *Id.* § 34.35.062(b).

[65] *Id.* § 34.35.062(c).

[66] *Id.* § 34.35.062(f).

[67] *Id.*

[68] *Id.* § 34.35.062(h).

[69] *Id.* §§ 34.35.062(i)(1)-(2).

§ 3.02 BONDS

[A] General Information

At first glance, one might be tempted to believe Alaska lacks a full compendium of surety cases to guide the practitioner through the complex maze of the rights and obligations of the claimant, the principal, the surety, and the obligee. However, as this section demonstrates, there is sufficient authority available to determine that Alaska recognizes the traditional principles of suretyship but places those principles within the framework of modern analysis found in other jurisdictions, as well.

[1] Reliance Upon Federal Case Law

In Alaska, most bond claims are brought against public construction bonds. In these claims, Alaska borrows heavily from the federal scheme. One court stated, "The Little Miller Act is the stepchild of the federal Miller Act, 40 U.S.C. § 270a-270d, and is substantially similar in all respects."[70] The Alaska Act, like the federal Act, is clearly remedial in nature. There is no question that a remedial statute is to be liberally construed to effectuate its purposes.[71]

[2] Basic Types of Construction Bonds

In Alaska, there are four types of bonds, generally, that cover construction obligations. The first is the contractors' license bond. Alaska imposes a requirement that all construction contractors register with the Commissioner of the Department of Commerce and Economic Development prior to engaging in construction.[72] The second is the public construction bid bond;[73] the third is the public works bond required under Alaska's "Little Miller Act."[74] The fourth is the federal Miller Act bond.[75] Finally, parties may require bonds as part of their private contracting negotiations.

[B] License Bonds Generally

Alaska imposes the license bond requirement as part of the State's contractor registration scheme to ensure scrupulous and competent contracting.[76] It is unlaw-

---

[70] Hyundai Constr. Co. v. Kalmbach, Inc., 502 P.2d 856 (Alaska 1972).

[71] State *ex rel.* Smith v. Tyonek Timber, Inc., 680 P.2d 1148, 1157 (Alaska 1984).

[72] ALASKA STAT. §§ 08.18.071 *et seq.*

[73] *Id.* § 36.30.120.

[74] *Id.* § 36.25.010(a).

[75] 40 U.S.C.A. § 270(a).

[76] State *ex rel.* Smith v. Tyonek Timber, Inc., 680 P.2d 1148, 1157 (Alaska 1984).

ful for an entity to even submit a bid in Alaska prior to obtaining the certificate of registration by the Department of Commerce and Economic Development.[77] Registration requires a surety bond, liability and property damage insurance, and a registration fee.[78] The statute exempts minor or inconsequential work,[79] but any work repairing, altering, or constructing buildings in excess of $10,000 requires registration, licensing, and bonding.[80] Not all typical construction services fall within the scope of the statutes, however. Quarrying, for example, does not involve structures and is exempted from the registration requirements.[81]

[1] Enforcement of Registration Requirements

The state gives teeth to the statute by prohibiting unlicensed contractors from bringing actions to collect compensation for performance of the work, or for breach of a contract for which registration is required.[82] While the court may find that a contractor has substantially complied,[83] one court found the contractor did not substantially comply because it failed to register or obtain bonding, and was not insured.[84] Courts have permitted the unregistered contractor to assert counterclaims as a set-off, however.[85]

If a contractor has been registered, bonded, and insured, the department is to notify the contractor of any lapse and provide twenty days for it to reinstate coverage prior to prohibiting the contractor from undertaking new construction work.[86] This may occur when a judgment has reduced the bonding available below the statutorily required amounts,[87] although the surety will not be liable for aggregate claims in excess of the state penal sum of the bond.[88]

[2] Coverage of the License Bond and Nonaggregation of the Penal Sum

There are fewer cases in Alaska discussing when a claimant may recover against a contractor's license bond, and the dearth of cases may be explained by the relatively low penal sums available.[89] The statutes contemplate coverage for

---

[77] Lost Valley Timber v. Power City Constr., Inc., 809 F.2d 590, 592 (9th Cir. 1987).

[78] Gross v. Bayshore Land Co., 710 P.2d 1007, 1012 (Alaska 1985).

[79] ALASKA STAT. § 08.18.161(9).

[80] *Id.* § 08.18.011(a).

[81] Olsen & Sons Logging, Ltd. v. Owens, 607 P.2d 949 (Alaska 1998).

[82] ALASKA STAT. § 08.18.151.

[83] Hale v. Vitale, 751 P.2d 488 (Alaska 1988).

[84] Gross v. Bayshore Land Co., 710 P.2d 1007 (Alaska 1986).

[85] Sumner Dev. Corp. v. Shivers, 517 P.2d 757 (Alaska 1974).

[86] 12 A.A.C. 21.160.

[87] *Id.; see also* Attorney General Opinion No. J-66-485-78, 1979 WL 22966 (1979).

[88] ALASKA STAT. § 08.18.071.

[89] $10,000 for general contractors; $5,000 for specialty contractors pursuant to ALASKA STAT. § 08.18.071.

taxes, labor, equipment, material, claims for breach of contract, and claims for negligent construction.[90] However, the bond does not cover claims for labor, equipment, or material supplied to the contractor but not incorporated into construction.[91]

[C] Bid Bonds

Bid bonds are required for all competitive sealed bidding on public contracts in excess of $100,000, or for other contracts when the agency deems it advisable.[92] The purpose of the bid bond is to ensure the contractor executes the contract as bid. Forfeiture of the bid bond acts to prevent contractors from withdrawing bids after opening when doing so would permit a competitive advantage.[93] Thus, if the agency permits a contractor to withdraw the bid based upon a legitimate clerical mistake, the agency cannot then maintain an action against the bidder or his bond.[94] Furthermore, one case refused summary judgment against the surety when failure to execute the contract rested upon discovery by the bidder that performance would be impossible or impracticable.[95]

[D] Purpose and Scope of "Little Miller Act" Bonds

For public construction bonds, Alaska's "Little Miller Act"[96] is substantially founded upon the federal Miller Act,[97] and state courts interpret the Act accordingly.[98] Payment and performance bonds are required for contracts in excess of $100,000 for the construction, alterations, or repair of a public building or of public work.[99] The primary purpose of the payment bond is to secure payment of persons who furnish labor and materials to the public project,[100] in lieu of lien rights against public property.[101] Public supply contracts are not within the scope of coverage.[102]

---

[90] ALASKA STAT. §§ 08.18.071(1)(2)(3) and 08.18.081.

[91] Balboa Ins. Co. v. Senco Alaska, Inc., 567 P.2d 295 (Alaska 1977).

[92] ALASKA STAT. § 36.30.120; 2 A.A.C. 12.810.

[93] Alaska Intern. Constr., Inc. v. Earth Movers of Fairbanks, Inc., 697 P.2d 626 (Alaska 1985).

[94] ALASKA STAT. § 36.30.160; 2 A.A.C. 12.170.

[95] Merl F. Thomas Sons, Inc. v. State, 396 P.2d 76 (Alaska 1964).

[96] ALASKA STAT. §§ 36.25.010–36.25.025.

[97] 40 U.S.C.A. § 270(a).

[98] State *ex rel.* Palmer Supply Co. v. Walsh & Co., 575 P.2d 1213 (Alaska 1978).

[99] ALASKA STAT. § 36.25.010(a).

[100] State *ex rel.* White v. Neal & Sons, 489 P.2d 1016 (Alaska 1971).

[101] Anchorage Sand & Gravel v. Alaska Dock & Bridge Builders, Inc., 14 Alaska 642 (D.C. Alaska 1954).

[102] Municipality of Anchorage v. Tatco, Inc., 774 P.2d 207 (Alaska 1989).

[1] Time Limitations

The primary distinction between the federal and state statutory schemes is the definition of what triggers the time period during which actions must be brought. Alaska's statutory scheme provides that "no suit may be started after the expiration of one year after the date of final settlement of the contract."[103] Alaska requires a specific administrative act by the public owner for the bar period to commence.[104] Thus, the one-year period does not begin to run until approval of the final pay estimate and release of retainage.[105] Moreover, any time period within the language of the bond itself will not be enforced absent a showing of prejudice by the surety related to the late filing of suit.[106]

[2] Notice Requirements

Alaska requires persons not having a direct contract with the bonded contractor to provide notice within 90 days of the date on which they last provided labor or material to the project.[107] The notice must be sent by registered mail and provide the amount claimed, and the name of the person to whom the material or labor was provided.[108]

[3] Substantiating the Claim

Once suit has been filed, the bond claimant faces the same hurdles in Alaska as it does under federal cases and traditional surety law. For example, Alaska recognizes the "source of funds" rule. That is, when the creditor knows or reasonably should know that payments are being made from funds earned on the bonded project, the claimant must show that the account for that particular project was properly credited,[109] such that the claim against the bond is accordingly reduced.

Alaska cases also interpret the coverage to extend only to items furnished for the bonded project.[110] Thus, only equipment "substantially consumed" on the project is a bonded obligation, and a claim for crane rental costs was therefore limited to the time period the equipment was used on the bonded project.[111] Moreover, only obligations within the bonded contract come within the scope of coverage. Thus, when the bonded prime contract was for labor only, and the bond itself covered items required "in the performance of the contract," a subcontractor

---

[103] Alaska Stat. § 36.25.020(c).

[104] Safeco Ins. Co. of Am. v. Honeywell, 639 P.2d 996 (Alaska 1981).

[105] *Id.*

[106] Alaska Energy Auth. v. Fairmont Ins. Co., 845 P.2d 420 (Alaska 1993).

[107] Alaska Stat. § 36.25.020(b).

[108] *Id.*

[109] State *ex rel.* Palmer Supply Co. v. Walsh & Co., Inc., 575 P.2d 1213 (Alaska 1978).

[110] McGee Steel Co. v. State *ex rel.* McDonald Indus. Alaska, Inc., 723 P.2d 611 (Alaska 1986).

[111] *Id.*

could not sue on the payment bond for materials furnished to the project by a sub-subcontractor.[112] Additionally, persons who fail to register as contractors under Alaska's statutory licensing scheme, § **3.02[B]**, *supra,* may not maintain a payment bond action against a surety.[113]

[E] Other Bonds and General Surety Principles

Miller Act claims brought in federal courts in Alaska do not differ from those brought in other jurisdictions. Therefore, both federal and private bonds are discussed simultaneously in this section. As elsewhere, the surety is entitled to raise most of the defenses the bonded principal could assert, such as waiver, estoppel, and official immunity.[114] Moreover, if the contract requires arbitration with the bonded principal, the surety may rely upon that provision to stay the obligee's suit against it. Of course, both the surety and the claimant would be bound by the result of the arbitration.[115]

[1] The Surety's Options When a Claim is Filed

The surety in Alaska has the traditional option of investigating the claim and "doing nothing" in the belief that its principal has valid defenses. The surety must make a good faith investigation, however.[116] If investigation reveals the principal is in default of the bonded contract, the surety may either buy back its bond or finance the project to completion.[117]

[2] The Surety's Right to Indemnity

Alaska also recognizes the surety's right to indemnity from the principal for amounts paid under the bond, and the principal may seek to recover those amounts as damages against third parties.[118] This is true even when the principal and surety entered into a settlement agreement compromising the amount the principal would pay the surety from the third-party litigation.[119]

[3] The Surety's Right of Subrogation

Alaska courts will enforce the surety's right of subrogation, and do not require the surety to conform with the U.C.C. in securing those rights.[120] Impair-

---

[112] SKW/Eskimos, Inc. v. Sentry Automatic Sprinkler Co., 723 P.2d 1293 (Alaska 1986).

[113] State *ex rel.* Smith v. Tyonek Timber, Inc., 680 P.2d 1148 (Alaska 1984).

[114] Integrated Resources Equity Corp. v. Fairbanks North Star Borough, et al., 799 P.2d 195 (Alaska 1990).

[115] Loyal Order of Moose, Lodge 1392 v. Int'l Fidelity Ins. Co., 797 P.2d 622 (Alaska 1990).

[116] *Id.*

[117] Alaska Nat'l Bank of the North v. Gwitchyaa Zhee Corp., 639 P.2d 984 (Alaska 1981).

[118] Geolar, Inc. v. Gilbert/Commonwealth Inc. of Michigan, 874 P.2d 937 (Alaska 1994).

[119] *Id.*

[120] Alaska State Bank v. General Ins. Co. of Am., 579 P.2d 1362 (Alaska 1978).

ment of subrogation rights will only discharge the surety to the extent of its prejudice, however.[121] Thus, when the state entered into a settlement agreement with the bonded principal that impaired the surety's subrogation interest, the court did not discharge the surety outright. Rather, the state was precluded from immediate suit against the surety and would be forced to await a further default of the principal under the settlement agreement.[122]

[4] Limiting the Surety's Claim of Discharge

Similarly, the surety in Alaska is not discharged by nonmaterial alterations in the nature of the indebtedness or the time of payment.[123] As noted above, Alaska courts will not enforce restrictive readings of the bond without a showing of prejudice to the surety should the provision not be upheld.[124] The federal cases from the Ninth Circuit appear to require a showing of prejudice, as well.[125]

Even the private surety may be estopped by its conduct to raise the traditional defenses sureties would otherwise enjoy. In one instance, the court found that the individual sureties' conduct precluded them from raising the argument that a claimant had destroyed their subrogation interest in collateral.[126]

[F] Conclusion

The legislature has defined surety "insurance,"[127] and sureties are subject to the obligations of good faith and fair dealing.[128] The surety and insurance contexts are the only areas in Alaska law where breach of the covenant gives rise to actions sounding in tort.[129] Nonetheless, a review of Alaska case law indicates courts balance that burden by recognizing the obligations of claimants to substantiate bond claims according to the applicable statutes, contracts, and bonds.

---

[121] State v. McKinnon, 667 P.2d 1239 (Alaska 1983).

[122] *Id.*

[123] Bradford v. First Nat'l Bank of Anchorage, 932 P.2d 256 (Alaska 1997).

[124] Alaska Energy Auth. v. Fairmont Ins. Co., 845 P.2d 420 (Alaska 1993); Weaver Bros., Inc. v. Chappel, 684 P.2d 123, 125–26 (Alaska 1984).

[125] *See, e.g.,* Transamerica Ins. Co. v. City of Kennewick, 785 F.2d 660 (9th Cir. 1986).

[126] Hull v. Alaska Fed. Sav. & Loan Ass'n of Juneau, 658 P.2d 122 (Alaska 1983).

[127] Alaska Stat. § 21.12.080.

[128] Loyal Order of Moose, Lodge 1392 v. International Fidelity Ins. Co., 797 P.2d 622 (Alaska 1990).

[129] Municipality of Anchorage v. Gentile, 922 P.2d 248 (Alaska 1996).

CHAPTER 4
ARIZONA

William F. Haug
James L. Csontos

§ 4.01 INTRODUCTION AND QUICK SUMMARY OF ARIZONA BOND AND LIEN LAW

In Arizona, the principal statutes governing construction bonds are known as Arizona's "Little Miller Act," Ariz. Rev. Stat. §§ 34–222 *et seq.*, and Arizona's "Procurement Code," §§ 41-2501 *et seq.* Arizona's mechanics' lien law is found at Ariz. Rev. Stat. §§ 33-981 *et seq.* In addition to the statutes identified above, potential bond or lien claimants should also be aware of coverage offered under Ariz. Rev. Stat. §§ 32-1101 *et seq.* (contractors' license bond statutes and prompt pay provisions), § 33-1003 (bond in lieu of mechanics' lien rights) and § 33-1004 (mechanics' lien discharge bond).

[A] Private Project Lien and Bond Rights

On private projects, Arizona does not require prime contractors to furnish any kind of bond, with the exception of a license bond that is required of all contractors licensed to do business in Arizona.[1] On residential, but not commercial, construction projects, unpaid subcontractors, material suppliers and laborers will have certain rights to assert certain claims against the contractor's license bond.[2]

Although there exists no statutory requirement that contractors provide a bond on private projects, Arizona law does provide that an owner may require the prime contractor to provide a bond that meets certain statutory requirements, thereby prohibiting the recording of a lien against the property. Such bonds are known as *bonds in lieu of lien rights.*[3] Owners of private projects are also free to require common law payment bonds.

On private projects, Arizona law does provide parties who perform labor or furnish professional services, materials, machinery, fixtures or tools with certain mechanics' lien rights. Such rights may be waived, but only if the waiver is in a form substantially the same as the waiver and release forms specified by statute.[4]

[B] Public Project Lien and Bond Rights

On all public projects in excess of $25,000, and some projects below $25,000, Arizona requires that prime contractors furnish bid bonds in the amount of ten percent of the bid and performance and payment bonds, each in the full amount of the prime contract. The payment bond provides coverage to anyone who furnishes labor or material to the project and has a direct contractual

[1] ARIZ. REV. STAT. § 32-1052(E).

[2] Hatch Cos. Contracting v. Arizona Bank, 170 Ariz. 553, 826 P.2d 1179 (App. 1991).

[3] ARIZ. REV. STAT. § 33-1003 (Supp. 1998).

[4] *Id.* § 33-1008 (Supp. 1998).

relationship with the prime contractor or one of the prime contractor's subcontractors.

On public projects, Arizona does not provide contractors with mechanics' lien rights. Unpaid contractors, subcontractors and suppliers may have an equitable lien against unpaid contract proceeds, but the priority of such lien may be behind that of a surety that has paid claims.[5]

§ 4.02 BOND LAW

[A] General Concepts

The interpretation of the surety's obligations under a construction bond depends upon if the bond is statutory or contractual. If the bond is provided to fulfill a statutory requirement, the bond is a statutory bond and the terms of the statute control. "Whatever is included in the bond, and not required by the law, must be read out of it, and whatever is not expressed and ought to have been incorporated, must be read as if inserted in to it. . . ."[6]

If the construction bond is not a statutory bond, the normal rules of contract construction apply.[7] If the terms of the bond or controlling statute are ambiguous and susceptible of more than one reasonable meaning, the terms of the bond may be construed against the surety.[8]

[B] Bid Bonds

Arizona does not require prime contractors to furnish bid bonds on private projects. However, prime contractors are required under both of Arizona's public contracting statutory schemes to furnish a bid bond to guarantee that the bidder will enter into a contract if the contract is awarded. The bid bond must be in the amount of ten percent of the bid.[9] Statutory bid bonds are "spread bonds," and are liable for the spread between the bonded bid and the next highest bid.[10]

Under Arizona law, if the prime contractor is able to establish that its bid contains a material mistake, made as a result of a computational error and not a

---

[5] General Acrylics v. United States Fidelity & Guar. Co., 128 Ariz. 50, 623 P.2d 839 (App. 1980).

[6] Porter v. Eyer, 80 Ariz. 169, 294 P.2d 661 (1956) (quoting from 11 C.J.S., Bonds, § 40 (1938)); *see also* United States Fidelity & Guar. Co. v. St. Mary's Hosp. of Tucson, 10 Ariz. App. 346, 458 P.2d 966 (1969); Paul Schoonover, Inc. v. Ram Const., Inc., 129 Ariz. 204, 630 P.2d 27 (1981); Maricopa Turf, Inc. v. Sunmaster, Inc., 173 Ariz. 357, 842 P.2d 1370 (App. 1992).

[7] Western Sur. Co. v. Horrall, 111 Ariz. 486, 533 P.2d 543 (1975); Cushman v. National Sur. Corp. of New York, 4 Ariz. App. 24, 417 P.2d 537 (1966).

[8] Cushman v. National Sur. Corp. of New York, 4 Ariz. App. 24, 417 P.2d 537 (1966); Employment Sec. Comm'n v. Fish, 92 Ariz. 140, 375 P.2d 20 (1962).

[9] Arizona's Little Miller Act, ARIZ. REV. STAT. § 34-201(A) (Supp. 1998); Arizona's Procurement Code, *id.* § 41-2573(A) (1999).

[10] *Id.* §§ 41-2542 and 41-2573 (1999).

judgmental error, the prime contractor may be allowed to withdraw its bid and the bid bond surety will thereby avoid any liability under its bond.[11] For projects governed by the Arizona Procurement Code, the provisions describing how and when a bid may be withdrawn or corrected are specified by statute.[12] If withdrawal is permitted, then no action may be brought against the bidder or the bid bond surety.[13]

[C] Performance Bonds

In Arizona, there are two statutory provisions requiring payment and performance bonds on public projects. Arizona's original "Little Miller Act" is found under Title 34 of Public Buildings and Improvements and is applicable to all state, county, city and local public agencies not covered under Arizona's version of the Procurement Code.[14]

Arizona's Procurement Code, Ariz. Rev. Stat. §§ 41-2501 *et seq.*, is applicable to all state agencies, except the Arizona Department of Transportation, the Board of Regents (the governing body controlling the state's three universities) and certain other specified state agencies.[15] All of the exempted state agencies, and any other public entities not specifically included, can elect to come under Arizona's Procurement Code.[16] The Arizona Department of Transportation has its own statutory bond provisions, which merely incorporate by reference the Little Miller Act bond requirements.[17] Many of the exempted state agencies have adopted regulations in substantial compliance with the bond requirements of the Procurement Code and Little Miller Act.[18]

The various statutes providing for performance and payment bonds on public projects contain differences without much distinction. In 1992, the Arizona Legislature "unified" the bond requirements by incorporating by reference into the Title 28 and Title 41 bond statutes the applicable provisions of the Little Miller Act found at Title 34.[19]

On public projects performed under Arizona's Little Miller Act, the prime contractor is required to provide a payment and performance bond in the full amount of the contract regardless of the size of the contract.[20] If the project is

---

[11] Marana Unified Sch. v. Aetna Cas. & Sur. Co., 144 Ariz. 159, 696 P.2d 711 (App. 1984).

[12] ARIZ. REV. STAT. § 41-2533(F) (1999).

[13] *Id.* § 41-2573(C) (1999).

[14] For information on Arizona's Little Miller Act, *see generally* Haug, William F., *Little Miller Act,* 5 Ariz. Bar. J No. 2, at 13 (1969).

[15] ARIZ. REV. STAT. § 41-2501 (1999).

[16] *Id.* § 41-2501(C) (1999).

[17] *Id.* § 28-6713(C) (1998).

[18] *See, e.g.,* Maricopa Turf, Inc. v. Sunmaster, Inc., 173 Ariz. 357, 842 P.2d 1370 (App. 1992).

[19] *See* Chapter 27 of Laws 1992, Arizona Legislative Service (West 1992).

[20] ARIZ. REV. STAT. § 34-222(A)(1) (Supp. 1998).

controlled under Arizona's Procurement Code, and less than $25,000, the public agency has some discretion in following the bidding and bonding requirements.[21]

Under either of the two statutory frameworks, the law requires that the performance bond be solely for the protection of the contracting party that awarded the contract. This requirement eliminates the prime contractor's subcontractors, suppliers and laborers from the list of potential performance bond claimants.[22]

Arizona's Little Miller Act and Procurement Code do not provide a limitation period in which suit against a performance bond must be brought. Under Arizona law, the general statute of limitations on contracts is six years.[23] However, the general statute of limitations may not be applicable against the state or public agency.[24] Contracts of insurance and suretyship may shorten this period of limitation to a period no less than two years.[25]

[D] Payment Bonds

[1] Private Projects

Arizona law does not require prime contractors to provide payment bonds on private projects. Any owner may, in accordance with its contract, require a prime contractor—and any prime contractor may require its subcontractors—to provide payment bonds conditioned on what ever notice, limitations and other conditions that may be found in the bond itself. On projects with such bonds, potential bond claimants must obtain a copy of the bond to discover the conditions and limits of coverage that may exist.

If the owner or prime contractor on a private project desires to keep the project free of mechanics' liens, the prime contractor may provide a payment bond in lieu of lien rights. Such bonds are then conditioned in accordance with Arizona's Little Miller Act.[26] A bond in lieu of lien rights must be in the full amount of the prime contract and solely for the protection of those performing labor or professional services or furnishing materials, machinery, fixtures or tools to the prime contractor or its subcontractors. The payment bond must be recorded in the county where the project is to be built and must include a copy of the prime contract and a legal description of the property on which the project is to be built.[27] If properly recorded, the project becomes a "public project" for the purposes of all potential lien claimants except the prime contractor, who retains its lien rights.

[21] *Id.* § 41-2574(A) (1999).

[22] Haug, *Little Miller Act,* 5 Ariz. Bar J. No. 2, at 13 (1969).

[23] Ariz. Rev. Stat. § 12-548 (1992).

[24] *Id.* § 12-510(1992).

[25] *Id.* § 20-1115 (1990); W. J. Kroeger Co. v. Travelers Indem. Co., 112 Ariz. 285, 541 P.2d 385 (1975); Zuckerman v. Transamerica Ins. Co., 133 Ariz. 139, 650 P.2d 441 (1982).

[26] Ariz. Rev. Stat. § 33-1003 (Supp. 1998).

[27] *Id.* § 33-1003(B) (Supp. 1998).

The payment bond in lieu of lien rights has the same conditions as a Little Miller Act payment bond.[28] All notice and limitations provisions of the Little Miller Act payment bond are applicable to the payment bond in lieu of lien rights. If not properly recorded, the payment bond may be a "common law" bond, and will be conditioned in accordance with whatever provisions are found in the bond form.[29]

If no payment bond in lieu of mechanics' lien is recorded for a private project, and a lien is recorded against the property, the lien may be removed by the owner or prime contractor providing a mechanics' lien discharge payment bond. The party desiring to have the mechanics' lien discharged must execute the payment bond as principal, and the payment bond must be in an amount equal to one and one half times the amount of the lien and conditioned for the payment of the judgment which would have been rendered against the property.[30]

Upon recordation of the payment bond, the mechanics' lien is discharged from the property. After recordation, the bond must be served upon the lien claimant within a "reasonable time" who must, if suit is pending, institute proceedings within 90 days to add the principal and surety as parties to the foreclosure suit.[31] The lien claimant must also release any lis pendens that was recorded against the property.[32]

[2] Public Projects

On all public projects governed by Arizona's Little Miller Act, and on all projects over $25,000.00 governed by Arizona's Procurement Code, the prime contractor is required to provide a payment bond in the full amount of the prime contract solely for the protection of claimants supplying labor or materials to the prime contractor or any of its subcontractors in the prosecution of the work provided for in the prime contract.[33]

On public projects, claimants who have a direct contractual relationship with a subcontractor, but no direct contractual relationship with the prime contractor, must serve the prime contractor with a preliminary 20-day notice and a 90-day post-completion demand for payment to enforce their payment bond claim.[34]

---

[28] *Id.* § 33-1003(B) (Supp. 1998).

[29] Hartford Accident & Indem. Co. v. Federal Ins. Co., 172 Ariz. 104, 834 P.2d 827 (App. 1992).

[30] ARIZ. REV. STAT. § 33-1004(B) (Supp. 1998).

[31] Arizona Rules of Civil Procedure require that the principal on a bond be joined in any suit against the surety unless the principal is insolvent, bankrupt or unavailable for service. Rule 17(f), ARIZ. R. CIV. P.; SCA Constr. Supply v. Aetna Cas. & Sur. Co., 157 Ariz. 64, 754 P.2d 1339 (1987).

[32] Hatch Cos. Contracting v. Arizona Bank, 170 Ariz. 553, 826 P.2d 1179 (App. 1991).

[33] Arizona's Little Miller Act, ARIZ. REV. STAT. § 34-223 (Supp. 1998); Arizona's Procurement Code, *id.* § 41-2574 (1999).

[34] Arizona's Little Miller Act, *id.* § 34-223(A) (Supp. 1998); Arizona's Procurement Code, *id.* § 41-2574(D) (1999). Under both the Little Miller Act and the Procurement Code, the preliminary 20-day notice requirements are found at *id.* § 33-992.01, subsection C, paragraphs 1, 2, 3 and 4 and subsections D, E, and I.

The preliminary notice must be served by mail no later than 20 days after the claimant first furnished labor or provided materials to the job site and must include a general description of the labor or materials furnished, an estimate of the total price, the name and address of the claimant, the name of the person who contracted for the labor or materials and the legal description, subdivision plat, street address or other sufficient description of the location of the job site. The proper form to use is spelled out in Ariz. Rev. Stat. § 33-998.01 and the failure to use the proper form can result in a subsequent bond claim being declared invalid.[35]

If preliminary notice is not given within 20 days after the claimant first provided labor or materials to the job site, the claimant may still provide the prime contractor with preliminary 20-day notice, but only the labor or materials provided within 20 days prior to the service of the preliminary notice, and at any time thereafter, may be included in the payment bond claim.[36]

In addition to the preliminary notice, claimants having a direct contractual relationship with a subcontractor, but no direct contractual relationship with the prime contractor, must also provide the prime contractor with a post-completion demand for payment. The demand for payment must state with substantial accuracy the amount of the claim and the name of the party to whom the materials were furnished or for whom the labor was performed.[37] The demand must be served within 90 days from the date on which the claimant performed the last of the labor or furnished the last of the material for which the claim is made. At least one court has held that the demand must be received by the prime contractor within 90 days.[38]

Under Arizona's Little Miller Act and Procurement Code, service of the preliminary notice and the post-completion demand must be made by registered or certified mail sent to any address where the prime contractor maintains an office, conducts business or resides.[39] Failure to send the notice by registered or certified mail may not be fatal if the prime contractor actually received the notice.[40] Failure to provide the prime contractor with preliminary notice and a post-completion demand may cause the claim against the payment bond to be invalid.[41]

On school district projects covered by the Arizona Procurement Code, if the

---

[35] MLM Constr. Co. v. Pace Corp., 172 Ariz. 226, 836 P.2d 439 (App. 1992).

[36] Ariz. Rev. Stat. § 33-992.01(E) (Supp. 1998).

[37] Arizona's Little Miller Act, *id.* § 34-223(A) (Supp. 1998); Arizona's Procurement Code, *id.* § 41-2574 (1999).

[38] Maricopa Turf, Inc. Sunmaster, Inc., 173 Ariz. 357, 842 P.2d 1370 (App. 1992).

[39] Arizona's Little Miller Act, Ariz. Rev. Stat. § 34-223(A); Arizona's Procurement Code, *id.* § 41-2574(D).

[40] Western Asbestos Co. v. TGK Constr. Co., 121 Ariz. 388, 590 P.2d 927 (1979); Maricopa Turf, Inc. Sunmaster, Inc., 173 Ariz. 357, 842 P.2d 1370 (App. 1992).

[41] Stratton v. Inspiration Consol. Copper Co., 140 Ariz. 528, 683 P.2d 327 (App. 1984); Greaig v. Park West Constr. Co., 130 Ariz. 576, 637 P.2d 1079 (App. 1981).

prime contract provides that the general contractor shall require payment bonds from some or all of its subcontractors, then those payment bonds are also conditioned in accordance with the applicable statute. A bond claimant under such bond must satisfy all notice requirements as a condition to making a bond claim.[42]

Because coverage under both statutory payment bonds extends only to claimants who have a direct contractual relationship with the prime contractor or one of its subcontractors, the definition of the term "subcontractor" is important in determining if a particular claimant may pursue a claim against the bond. If the party with whom the claimant had a direct contractual relationship is a supplier to the prime contractor, and not the prime contractor's subcontractor, then the claimant's claim is barred.[43]

Because the distinction between a supplier and a subcontractor may be the difference between a valid and invalid payment bond claim, the distinction has been the subject of litigation. Although the difference between a supplier and a subcontractor is usually easy to understand, when the "supplier" manufactures specially ordered goods, such as prefabricated buildings or specially designed light fixtures, the distinction is not quite as clear.[44] Other examples of this problem are found in cases involving sand and gravel suppliers and suppliers of certain types of specially manufactured goods.[45]

The Arizona Court of Appeals in *Tiffany Construction Co. v. Hancock & Kelley Construction Co.*[46] recognized that the distinction between a supplier and a subcontractor may not be clear and offered the following factors to be considered in making such a determination:

(a) Does the custom in the trade consider the supplier a subcontractor or a materialman?
(b) Are the items supplied generally available in the open market or are they "customized?"
(c) In determining whether the material is "customized," do the plans and specifications call for a unique product, or are these specifications merely descriptive of what is to be furnished?
(d) Does the supplier's performance constitute a substantial and definite delegation of a portion of the performance of the prime contract?

---

[42] Norquip Rental Corp. v. Sky Steel Erectors, Inc., 175 Ariz. 199, 854 P.2d 1185 (App. 1993).

[43] Advance Leasing & Crane Co. v. Del E. Webb Corp., 117 Ariz. 451, 573 P.2d 525 (App. 1977).

[44] *See, e.g.,* Clifford F. MacEvoy Co. v. United States *ex rel.* Calvin Tomkins Co., 322 U.S. 102 (1944); F. D. Rich Co. v. United States *ex rel.* Indus. Lumber Co., 417 U.S. 116 (1974).

[45] Tiffany Constr. Co. v. Hancock & Kelley Constr. Co., 24 Ariz. App. 504, 539 P.2d 978 (1975) (supplier of rock chips not a subcontractor); United States *ex rel.* Wellman Eng'g Co. v. MSI Corp., 350 F.2d 285 (2d Cir. 1965) (off-site manufacturer of hydraulic systems held to be a subcontractor); *see also* Jacobsen Constr. Co. v. Industrial Indem. Co., 657 P.2d 1325 (Utah 1983).

[46] 24 Ariz. App. 504, 539 P.2d 978 (1975).

Even if the claimant did not give the required notice, or is not a proper claimant under the bond, the claimant may be entitled to seek payment directly from the prime contractor or owner under a theory of unjust enrichment.[47] To be successful under such a theory, the claimant must establish that the owner or prime contractor has not fully paid the amounts due under the contract, thus making the acceptance of the labor or materials furnished by the claimant "unjust."

If the claimant did provide all required notices and wishes to bring suit under the payment bond, such suit must be brought no sooner than 90 days nor later than one year after the claimant last furnished labor or materials to the project.[48] The suit must be brought in the name of the claimant and must include as defendants the principal and surety.[49] Work done for the purpose of correcting defects or making repairs may not toll the running of the one year limitation.[50]

§ 4.03 LIEN LAW

[A] General Concepts

The Arizona statutes providing for mechanics' liens are found under Article Six of Title 33, Arizona Revised Statutes. The primary purpose of Arizona's mechanics' lien statutes is to protect the right of contractors and material suppliers who enhance the value of the property of another. An incidental purpose of Arizona's mechanics' lien statutes is to protect the rights of the owner whose property is subject to such a lien.[51] Like other remedial statutes, Arizona courts have liberally construed the mechanics' lien statutes to accomplish the goal of protecting those who furnish labor and material, and have accepted substantial compliance with some of the statutes' requirements as sufficient to enforce otherwise valid lien rights.[52] Although substantial compliance is sometimes the rule, strict compliance with the deadlines imposed by the statutes is still required.[53]

Although the general purpose is very broad, there are significant exclusions to the right to record a mechanics' lien. One such exclusion is the exception of public projects from the operation of the mechanics' lien statutes.[54] Unlicensed

[47] Flooring Systems, Inc. v. Radisson Group, Inc., 160 Ariz. 224, 772 P.2d 578 (1989); Commercial Cornice & Millwork, Inc. v. Camel Constr. Services Corp., 154 Ariz. 34, 739 P.2d 1351 (App. 1987); Murdock-Bryant Constr., Inc. v. Pearson, 146 Ariz. 48, 703 P.2d 1197 (1985).

[48] Ariz. Rev. Stat. § 34-223(B) (Supp. 1998).

[49] *Id.* § 34-223(B) (Supp. 1998); SCA Constr. Supply v. Aetna Cas. & Sur. Co., 157 Ariz. 64, 754 P.2d 1339 (1987).

[50] Honeywell, Inc. v. Arnold Constr. Co., 134 Ariz. 153, 654 P.2d 301 (App. 1982).

[51] Arizona Gunite Builders, Inc. v. Continental Cas. Co., 105 Ariz. 99, 459 P.2d 724 (1969).

[52] Gene McVety, Inc. v. Don Grady Homes, Inc., 119 Ariz. 482, 581 P.2d 1132 (1978); Advanced Living Ctr. v. T. J. Bettes Co., 11 Ariz. App. 336, 464 P.2d 656 (1970).

[53] James Weller, Inc. v. Hansen, 21 Ariz. App. 217, 517 P.2d 1110 (1973).

[54] Wells-Stewart Constr. Co. v. Martin Marietta Corp., 103 Ariz. 375, 442 P.2d 119 (1968) (prime contractors on public projects are required to provide payment bonds for the protection of those who are in direct contract with the prime contractor or any of its subcontractors).

contractors and persons who furnish professional services but do not hold a valid certificate of registration are also excluded from the right to record a mechanics' lien.[55] Other exclusions and limitations are discussed in the following sections.

[B] Basic Provisions

Arizona's lien law provides that a lien may be recorded by "every person who labors or furnishes professional services, materials, machinery, fixtures or tools in the construction, alteration or repair of any building, or other structure or improvement. . . ."[56] This protection extends only to those who provide such labor, services or materials at the instance of the owner or the "owner's agent."

For the purposes of Arizona's mechanics' lien statutes, the *owner's agent* is defined as "[e]very contractor, subcontractor, architect, builder or other person having charge or control of the construction, alteration or repair, either wholly or in part, of any building, structure or improvement[.]"[57] This definition of agent generally limits lien rights to those who have a direct contractual relationship with the owner, prime contractor or any of the prime contractor's subcontractors.[58] A supplier to a supplier, or a supplier to a second tier subcontractor may not have lien rights under Arizona law.[59]

An important exception to the general rule regarding who may claim a lien occurs when the improvement involves owner occupied one-family or two-family residences.[60] On such projects, only a party having a written contract executed by the owner-occupant is permitted to record a mechanics' lien against the property.[61] Mechanics' liens are also not permitted on private projects on which a payment bond in lieu of mechanics' lien rights has been recorded.[62]

Every mechanics' lien, if properly recorded and perfected, relates back to and attaches on the first day labor was commenced or materials were furnished to the project.[63] Thus, all lien claimants on a project are on equal footing without

---

[55] ARIZ. REV. STAT. § 33-981(C) and (E) (Supp. 1998); *see also id.* §§ 32-1101 *et seq.* (Supp. 1998) regarding contractors license requirements and *id.* §§ 32-101 *et seq.* (Supp. 1998) regarding certificate of registration requirements for architects, engineers, land surveyors, etc.; Aesthetic Property Maintenance, Inc. v. Capitol Indem. Corp., 183 Ariz. 74, 900 P.2d 1210 (1995) (holding the substantial compliance with licensing regulations may be sufficient).

[56] *Id.* § 33-981(A) (Supp. 1998).

[57] *Id.* § 33-981(B) (Supp. 1998).

[58] If a lease provides that the tenant is to construct improvements, the lessee is an "agent" of the owner for mechanics' lien purposes, and the lessee's contractor can enforce a lien right against the leased premises. Bobo v. John W. Lattimore Contractor, 12 Ariz. App. 137, 468 P.2d 404 (1970); *compare with* Hayward Lumber & Inv. Co. v. Graham, 104 Ariz. 103, 449 P.2d 31 (1968) in which the lease did not require the construction of improvements and the lien was not allowed.

[59] B.J. Cecil Trucking, Inc. v. Tiffany Constr. Co., 123 Ariz. 27, 597 P.2d 184 (App. 1979).

[60] ARIZ. REV. STAT. § 33-1002 (1990).

[61] *Id.* § 33-1002(B) (1990); Guarriello v. Sunstate Equip. Corp., 187 Ariz. 596, 931 P.2d 1106 (App. 1996)

[62] ARIZ. REV. STAT. § 33-1003 (Supp. 1998).

[63] *Id.* § 33-992 (Supp. 1998).

reference to the date of recording or to the time of performing the work or furnishing the professional services or materials.[64] If the property is foreclosed, and there are not sufficient proceeds of sale to discharge all liens, the proceeds are shared on a prorated basis among all lien claimants.[65] The Arizona courts have held that no deficiency judgment is ordinarily permitted against the property's owner unless the owner has a direct contractual relationship with the lien claimant or is otherwise liable to the claimant for payment of the debt.[66]

In calculating the amount of the lien claim, the general rule is that the amount is limited to the reasonable value that the labor, services or materials actually provided or incorporated in the project has to the owner.[67] Although prime contractors and others in direct contract with the owner may be entitled to lien for the contract price, a subcontractor's lien is limited to the reasonable value of the labor and materials furnished.[68] The "reasonable value" of the work done and materials supplied is not limited to the actual cost, but may include profit and overhead.[69] Although a subcontractor is limited to the reasonable value of the labor and materials furnished, the subcontractor may use the contract amount as *prima facie* evidence of the reasonable value of the work performed.[70]

In any event, the contract amount is the upper limit as to reasonable value and any discounts for prompt payment and the like must be given to the owner.[71] If the lien claimant is not in direct privity with the property owner, the lien claimant is not entitled to its contractual rate of interest, and is instead limited to the statutory rate of interest.[72]

[C] The 1998 Amendments

In 1998, the Arizona legislature passed substantial amendments to Arizona's lien laws. The amendments included changes to the definition of "completion"

---

[64] *Id.* § 33-1000(A) (Supp. 1998). Under the 1998 amendments to § 33-992(A) (Supp. 1998), construction lenders who record a deed of trust or mortgage within ten days after commencement of the work will still have priority over mechanic lien claims.

[65] *Id.* § 33-1000(B) (Supp. 1998).

[66] James Weller, Inc. v. Hansen, 21 Ariz. App. 217, 517 P.2d 1110 (1973); Costanzo v. Stewart, 9 Ariz. App. 430, 453 P.2d 526 (1969).

[67] ARIZ. REV. STAT. § 33-981(B) (Supp. 1998); Parker v. Holmes, 79 Ariz. 82, 284 P.2d 455 (1955).

[68] Lenslite Co. v. Zocher, 95 Ariz. 208, 388 P.2d 421 (1964); Wahl v. Southwest Sav. & Loan Ass., 106 Ariz. 381, 476 P.2d 836 (1970).

[69] Parker v. Holmes, 79 Ariz. 82, 284 P.2d 455 (1955).

[70] Lanier v. Lovett, 25 Ariz. 54, 213 P. 391 (1923).

[71] Cashway Concrete & Materials v. Sanner Contracting Co., 158 Ariz. 81, 761 P.2d 155 (App. 1988) (holding that amount of lien was limited to the contract amount, less the discount offered for prompt payment, even though the time for prompt payment has long since passed).

[72] Environmental Liners, Inc. v. Ryley, Carlock & Applewhite, 187 Ariz. 379, 930 P.2d 456 (App. 1996).

and changes to the deadlines for recording liens. The 1998 amendments also added Stop Notices to the weapons available to unpaid contractors and suppliers.

The amendments, reported at Chapter 277, Laws 1998, took effect as follows:

> This act is applicable to the construction, alternation or repair of any building or other structure or improvement of any nature if labor was commenced or materials were commenced to be furnished on or after the effective date of this act.

The effective date of the act was August 21, 1998.

Projects in which labor was commenced or materials were commenced to be furnished prior to the effective date of the new amendments, but completed perhaps years later, will be governed by the pre-amendment definition of "completion" and the pre-amendment deadlines. The result is that there will be an overlap of which law applies, depending upon when labor was commenced or materials were commenced to be furnished to the project. Because of the overlap of the old statutory requirements, a lien claimant must know when the project was commenced in order to know what lien rights are available.

[D] Lien Law Notice Requirements

Except for persons performing actual labor for wages, every party who performs labor or furnishes professional services, materials, machinery, fixtures or tools must serve the owner or reputed owner, the prime contractor or reputed prime contractor and the construction lender, if any, or reputed construction lender with written preliminary 20-day notice. As strange as it may seem, this provision requires the prime contractor serve itself with preliminary notice, although there are no reported decisions holding a lien invalid because the contractor failed to serve itself.[73]

Service may be made by mailing, with a certificate of mailing, the notice to the residence or place of business of the party to be served or by registered or certified mail sent to the party's residence or business address. If service is by mail, service is deemed complete upon the time of deposit of such mail.[74] Actual receipt of the preliminary notice is not required.[75]

A claimant need give only one preliminary notice with respect to all labor, professional services, materials, equipment, fixtures and tools supplied unless the actual total price exceeds by 20 percent the estimated total price, in which case an additional preliminary 20 day notice must be given; or unless such labor, professional services, materials, equipment, fixtures and tools supplied are sup-

---

[73] Ariz. Rev. Stat. § 33-992.01 (Supp. 1998).

[74] *Id.* § 33-992.01(G) (Supp. 1998).

[75] Columbia Group, Inc. v. Jackson, 151 Ariz. 76, 725 P.2d 1110 (1986).

plied to more than one subcontractor, in which case separate preliminary 20-day notices must be provided.[76]

The notice must include a general description of the labor, professional services, materials, equipment, fixtures or tools furnished or to be furnished, the name and address of the claimant and the person with whom the claimant contracted, a description of the location of the job site and a statement that basically tells the owner that nothing is necessarily wrong but that the owner may want to take certain precautions to protect the property from liens.[77] One such precaution an owner can take is to require the prime contractor to provide a payment bond in lieu of mechanics' lien rights.[78] Another precaution available to the owner is the use of joint checks, payable to all who have given preliminary 20-day notices.[79]

The statute provides a form to use for serving preliminary 20 day notice, although any form in substantial compliance with the statutorily provided form is acceptable.[80] However, any material deviation from the statutory form could result in an invalid lien claim.[81]

Because the preliminary 20-day notice must include information that may not be known to the claimant, the claimant may request the information from the owner. Within ten days after receipt of such a request, or within ten days of receipt of a preliminary 20-day notice, the owner is required to provide the claimant with the name of the owner, prime contractor, construction lender and description of the location of the project.[82] If the claimant relies on the information provided by the owner, and such information proves to be false, the owner is prevented from raising as a defense any inaccuracy of the information supplied by the owner and included in the notice.[83] The owner's failure to respond to a request for information does not excuse the claimant from timely serving a preliminary notice. However,

---

[76] ARIZ. REV. STAT. § 33-992.01 (G) and (H) (Supp. 1998).

[77] *Id.* § 33-992.01(C)(5) (Supp. 1998). The required statement is as follows:

"In accordance with Arizona Revised Statutes § 33-992.01, this is not a lien and this is not a reflection of the integrity of any contractor or subcontractor.

Notice to Property Owner: If bills are not paid in full for the labor, professional services, materials, machinery, fixtures or tools furnished or to be furnished, a mechanic's lien leading to the loss, through court foreclosure proceedings, of all or part of your property being improved may be placed against the property. You may wish to protect yourself against this consequence by either: (1) Requiring your contractor to furnish a release signed by the person or firm giving you this notice before you make payment to your contractor. (2) Using any other method or device which is appropriate under the circumstances."

[78] *Id.* § 33-1003 (Supp. 1998).

[79] Brown Wholesale Elec. Co. v. Beztak of Scottsdale, Inc., 163 Ariz. 340, 788 P.2d 73 (1990) (endorsement of joint check deemed receipt of all moneys owed up to the amount of the joint check.).

[80] ARIZ. REV. STAT. § 33-992.01(D) (Supp. 1998).

[81] MLM Constr. Co. v. Pace Corp., 172 Ariz. 226, 836 P.2d 439 (App. 1992).

[82] ARIZ. REV. STAT. § 33-992.01(I) (Supp. 1998).

[83] *Id.* § 33-992.01(J) (Supp. 1998).

if the owner's information comes after the claimant serves its preliminary notice, the claimant has an additional 30 days after receipt of the owner's information to serve an amended preliminary notice.[84]

[E] Waiver and Release of Lien Rights

Arizona's lien statutes includes four statutory waiver and release forms.[85] These forms are Conditional and Unconditional Waivers and Releases on Progress Payment and Conditional and Unconditional Waivers and Releases on Final Payment. Unless in substantial compliance with the statutory forms, no other waiver and release forms are effective for releasing lien claims.

The progress payment forms are effective for all labor and materials delivered to the project through the effective date stated in the release. Retention, pending change orders and work done after the effective date of the release are reserved.

The final waiver and release forms are full and final waivers and releases. The form includes a space for the claimant to insert any disputed amount that the claimant believes remains.

The distinction between conditional and unconditional waivers and releases is conditional waivers and releases are only valid if the payment referred to in the waiver and release actually was made. Before any party may rely upon a conditional waiver and release, payment must be verified. On the other hand, unconditional waivers and releases are valid even if payment is never made. For that reason, unconditional waivers and releases must include the following "Surgeon General" style of warning:

> Notice: This document waives rights unconditionally and states that you have been paid for giving up those rights. This document is enforceable against you if you sign it, even if you have not been paid. If you have not been paid, use a conditional release form

The statutory forms are substantially similar to the waiver and release forms previously used in California and, if not carefully used, could result in the waiver and release of a valid claim.[86]

[F] Perfection of Lien Rights

To perfect a mechanics' lien, the claimant must record a notice and claim of lien with the county recorder of the county in which the property or some part of the property is located and, within a reasonable time thereafter, serve a copy

---

[84] *Id.* § 33-992.01(J) (Supp. 1998).

[85] *Id.* § 33-1008 (Supp. 1998).

[86] Halbert's Lumber, Inc. v. Lucky Stores, Inc., 8 Cal. Rptr. 2d 298, 6 Cal. App. 4th 1233 (1992).

upon the owner. Service may be made by first class registered or certified mail or by any manner that a summons and complaint may be served.[87]

If the construction project is a multibuilding project, the lien claimant may be required to apportion its lien against the multiple buildings or lots. The Arizona courts will allow a blanket lien, without apportionment, if apportionment is impractical.[88]

The time by which the notice and claim for lien must be recorded may vary depending on when the first of the labor or materials were provided to the project (by anyone), whether the claimant is a prime contractor or not and whether the owner recorded a notice of completion.

Regardless of which version of Arizona's lien law applies, strict compliance with the statutory time elements in recording notices and claims for liens is required.[89] Substantial compliance with other requirements may be sufficient to perfect a mechanics' lien.[90]

[1] Pre-1998 Amendment Deadlines and Definition of Completion

For projects that commenced prior to August 21, 1998, prime contractors are required to record their notice and claim for lien within the earlier of 90 days after *completion* or, if a notice of completion has been recorded and served, within 45 days after such recordation.[91]

If the claimant is not a prime contractor, then the notice and claim of lien must be recorded within the earlier of 60 days after *completion* or, if a notice of completion has been recorded and served, within 35 days after such recordation.[92]

For the purposes of timely recording a notice and claim for lien, completion of the project is defined as the earliest of the following events:

- Actual completion of the work.
- Written acceptance by the owner or agent of the work.

---

[87] Old Adobe Office Properties, Ltd. v. Gin, 151 Ariz. 248, 727 P.2d 26 (App. 1986). If service is made by registered or certified mail, service will be complete upon the sender obtaining a certificate of mailing, receipt of registration or receipt of certification.

[88] CS&W Contractors, Inc. v. Southwest Sav. & Loan Association, 180 Ariz. 167, 883 P.2d 404 (1994); S.K. Drywall, Inc. v. Dev. Financial Group, Inc., 165 Ariz. 588, 799 P.2d 1362 (App. 1990), *vacated in part,* 169 Ariz. 345, 819 P.2d 931 (1991).

[89] James Weller, Inc. v. Hansen, 21 Ariz. App. 217, 517 P.2d 1110 (1973).

[90] *Id.; but compare* Commercial Cornice & Millwork v. Camel Constr. Servs. Corp., 154 Ariz. 34, 739 P.2d 1351 (App. 1987) (holding that the failure to state the date the material was first furnished caused the lien to be invalid).

[91] ARIZ. REV. STAT. § 33-993(A) (Supp. 1997). The notice of completion is defined in *id.* § 33-993(C) (Supp. 1997) as a written notice which the owner or its agent may record at any time after completion for the "purpose of shortening the lien period." If a notice of completion is recorded, the owner is required under *id.* § 33–993(F) to mail by certified or registered mail a copy of the notice to the prime contractor and all parties who supplied preliminary 20-day notice.

[92] *Id.* § 33-993(A) (Supp. 1997).

- Final inspection and written acceptance by the governmental body which issued the building permit.
- Cessation of labor for a period of 60 consecutive days, except such cessation due to strikes, shortage of materials or acts of God.[93]

If the project is residential, then occupation or use of the building, structure or improvement, or any part thereof, constitutes completion.[94]

[2] Post-1998 Amendment Deadlines and Definition of Completion

For projects that commenced on or after August 21, 1998, prime contractors, subcontractors, materialmen and professionals all are required to record their notice and claim for lien within the earlier of 120 days after *completion* or, if a notice of completion has been recorded and served, within 60 days after such recordation.[95]

For purposes of establishing a lien, *completion* means the *earliest* of:

- Thirty days after final inspection and written final acceptance by the governmental body issuing the building permit
- Cessation of labor for a period of 60 consecutive days, except when such cessation is due to a strike, shortage of materials or act of God.[96]

If no building permit is issued or if the governmental body that issued the building permit does not issue final inspections and written final acceptances, then *completion* means the last date on which any labor, materials, fixtures or tools were furnished to the property.[97]

If the improvement consists of the construction for residential occupancy of more than one *separate building,* each building is a separate work and the time within which to record a lien begins to run upon the completion of each building.[98] A *separate building* means one structure and any garages or other appurtenant buildings in a multibuilding residential project or subdivision.[99]

---

[93] *Id.* § 33-993(B) (Supp. 1997).

[94] *Id.* § 33-993(B)(2) (Supp. 1992); Union Rock & Materials Corp. v. Scottsdale Conf. Center, 139 Ariz. 268, 678 P.2d 453 (App. 1983).

[95] ARIZ. REV. STAT. § 33-993(A) (Supp. 1998). The notice of completion is defined in *id.* § 33-993(C) (Supp. 1998) as a written notice which the owner or its agent may record at any time after completion for the "purpose of shortening the lien period." If a notice of completion is recorded, the owner is required under *id.* § 33-993(F) (Supp. 1998) to mail by certified or registered mail a copy of the notice to the prime contractor and all parties who supplied preliminary 20-day notice.

[96] *Id.* § 33-993(C) (Supp. 1998).

[97] *Id.* § 33-993(D) (Supp. 1998).

[98] *Id.* § 33-993(B) (Supp. 1998).

[99] *Id.* § 33-993(B) (Supp. 1998).

If the work performed is an *improvement at the site* that is not included in a contract for the construction of a building, the improvement is a separate work and the commencement of the improvement is not the commencement of the construction of the building.[100] Likewise, the completion of *improvement at the site* work is a separate date of *completion* for the purposes of calculating the deadline for recording a lien. *Improvement at the site* is defined as (1) the demolition or removal of improvements, trees or other vegetation, (2) the drilling of test holes, (3) the grading or filling at the property, (4) the construction of sewers or other public utilities, and (5) the construction of streets, highways or sidewalks.[101]

[3] Pre-1998 Amendment Contents of Notice and Claim of Lien

The notice and claim of lien must be made under oath by someone with knowledge of the facts and must contain the following seven items of information:

1. The legal description of the land and improvements charged with the lien.
2. The name of the owner or reputed owner and the name of the party by whom the claimant was employed.
3. A statement of the terms of the contract if oral or a copy of the contract if written.
4. A statement of the claimant's demand, deducting all just credits and offsets.
5. A statement of the date of completion, using the definition of completion discussed above.
6. A statement of the date that the labor, materials, machinery, fixtures or tools were first furnished to the jobsite.
7. A statement of the date the preliminary 20 day notice was served and a copy of such notice and proof of service.[102]

[4] Post-1998 Amendment Contents of Notice and Claim of Lien

The contents of the Notice and Claim of Lien for projects commenced on or after August 21, 1998 are the same as for pre-1998 amendment projects with the exception that the statement of the date the claimant first provided labor or materials to the project (paragraph 6, above) is no longer required.[103] There is no penalty for continuing to include this information in a Notice and Claim of Lien,

[100] *Id.* § 33-992(E) (Supp. 1998).
[101] *Id.* § 33-992(E) (Supp. 1998).
[102] *Id.* § 33-993(A)(1) through (7) (Supp. 1997).
[103] *Id.* § 33-993(A)(1) through (6) (Supp. 1998).

and it may be beneficial to know this information to confirm that the preliminary 20-day notice was timely served.

[G] Foreclosing the Lien

A mechanics' lien properly recorded will expire on its own six months after recording unless an action to foreclose the mechanics' lien is brought within such time.[104] A foreclosure action that is included in an amended complaint will not relate back to the date of the original filing.[105] To maintain the priority enjoyed by the mechanics' lien, a lis pendens or notice of pendency of action must be filed and recorded to give notice that the lien has not expired and that there is litigation affecting title to the property pending.[106] If the owner or prime contractor provides a mechanics' lien discharge bond, the claimant must amend its complaint to include the principal and surety on the lien discharge bond within 90 days after receipt of the bond, and record a release of the lis pendens.[107]

[H] Stop Notices

The 1998 amendments to the mechanics' lien statutes included the addition of a new statutory remedy to protect a contractor's or supplier's right to receive payment. This new remedy is the *Stop Notice,* which is provided for at Ariz. Rev. Stat. §§ 33-1051 *et seq.* (Supp. 1998). Prior to the effective date of the 1998 amendments, Stop Notices did not exist in Arizona, although they have been used in California for many years. Arizona's new statutory provisions are similar and sometimes identical to California's Stop Notice statutes for private projects. Based upon the similarity, the Arizona courts will no doubt look to California law for guidance.[108]

A Stop Notice is a notice served upon the project owner or construction lender in which a claimant describes the work performed and the unpaid balance and demands that the owner or construction lender withhold that amount from the next payments to the prime contractor or, if served upon the construction lender, from the payments due to the owner or prime contractor.

A Stop Notice may be bonded. A Bonded Stop Notice is a Stop Notice

---

[104] *Id.* § 33-998 (Supp. 1998).

[105] United Pac. Ins. Co. v. Cottonwood Properties, Inc., 156 Ariz. 149, 750 P.2d 907 (App. 1987).

[106] ARIZ. REV. STAT. §§ 12-1191 (Supp. 1998) and 33-998 (Supp. 1998); Scottsdale Memorial Health Sys., Inc. v. Clark, 157 Ariz. 461, 759 P.2d 607 (1988).

[107] ARIZ. REV. STAT. § 33-1004 (Supp. 1998); Hatch Cos. Contracting v. Arizona Bank, 170 Ariz. 553, 826 P.2d 1179 (App. 1991).

[108] Paul C. Helmick Corp. v. Lucky Chance Mining, Co., 127 Ariz. 82, 618 P.2d 252 (App. 1980) ("Since the language of our lien statute is substantially similar to the California statute, the construction placed thereon by the California courts should be very persuasive, if not controlling.").

supported by a bond in the amount of 125 percent of the claim set forth in the Stop Notice.[109]

[1] Who May Serve a Stop Notice

Any person entitled to record a lien and who has provided a preliminary twenty-day notice, other than the prime contractor, may serve a Stop Notice upon the owner. This limits the application of Stop Notices to private projects that are not owner-occupied residential construction. Any person entitled to record a lien, including the prime contractor, may serve a Stop Notice or Bonded Stop Notice upon the construction lender.[110]

[2] Stop Notice Forms

A Stop Notice is a written notice that is signed and verified by the claimant or its agent and that states in general terms all of the following:

- The name and address of the claimant.
- A description of the labor, professional services, materials, machinery, fixtures or tools furnished or agreed to be furnished by the claimant.
- The name of the person to or for whom the labor, professional services, materials, machinery, fixtures or tools were furnished or agreed to be furnished.
- The total amount in value of the labor, professional services, materials, machinery, fixtures or tools agreed to be furnished.
- The amount in value of the labor, professional services, materials, machinery, fixtures or tools already furnished.
- The amount of any of payment received by the claimant.[111]

The Stop Notice of not invalid by reason of any defect in form if it is sufficient to substantially inform the owner of the information required above.[112]

[3] Serving a Stop Notice

A Stop Notice may be served upon an owner by delivery to the owner, personally, or by leaving the Stop Notice at the owner's residence with a person of suitable age and discretion or at the owner's place of business. A construction lender must be served by delivery to the branch manager or other responsible officer or person at the office or branch that administers or holds the construction

---

[109] Ariz. Rev. Stat. § 33-1051 (Supp. 1998).
[110] *Id.* §§ 33-1053 through 33-1056 (Supp. 1998).
[111] *Id.* § 33-1051 (Supp. 1998).
[112] *Id.* § 33-1052 (Supp. 1998).

monies. A Stop Notice or Bonded Stop Notice may be served by certified mail with the same effect as by personal service.[113]

A Stop Notice may be served any time prior to the expiration of the time within which that person's lien shall be recorded.[114] This time may be shorted upon written demand by the owner or construction lender.[115] Under the 1998 amendments, effective from August 21, 1998 through August 6, 1999, the owner or construction lender may make a written demand that a Stop Notice be served, then any Stop Notice or Bonded Stop Notice must be served within thirty days after written demand. Failure to do so resulted in a forfeiture of all lien rights.[116] In 1999, these sections were amended to provide that a claimant merely forfeits its Stop Notice rights, but retains its lien rights, if it fails to respond to a demand for Stop Notices.[117]

[4] Effect of Service Upon Owner and Lender

A Stop Notice served upon the owner requires the owner to withhold from the prime contractor or anyone acting under the prime contractor's authority sufficient monies due or that become due to answer the Stop Notice claim. If a payment bond conditioned in accordance with Ariz. Rev. Stat. § 33-1003 (bond in lieu of lien rights) was recorded, the owner may, but is not required, to withhold sufficient monies. If a bond in lieu of lien rights is recorded, and the owner elects not to withhold, the owner is required to supply the claimant with a copy of the bond within 30 days after receipt of the Stop Notice.[118]

When served with a Stop Notice, a construction lender may, and when served with a Bonded Stop Notice, must withhold from any amounts due or that become due to the owner, the prime contractor or anyone acting under the prime contractor's authority, sufficient monies to answer the Stop Notice claim. If a payment bond conditioned in accordance with Ariz. Rev. Stat. §33-1003 (bond in lieu of lien rights) was recorded, a construction lender served with a Bonded Stop Notice may, but is not required, to withhold sufficient monies.[119]

If a bond in lieu of lien rights is recorded, and the Stop Notice claimant makes a written request for notice of the construction lender's election to withhold and provides the construction lender with a self-addressed, stamped envelope, the construction lender must furnish a copy of the payment bond in lieu of lien rights if it elects not to withhold the monies. The copy of the bond must be furnished within 30 days after the making of the election. If the construction lender fails to

---

[113] *Id.* § 33-1056 (Supp. 1998).

[114] *Id.* § 33-1056 (Supp. 1998).

[115] *Id.* §§ 33-1054 and 33-1055 (Supp. 1998).

[116] *Id.* §§ 33-1054 through 33-1056 (Supp. 1998).

[117] *Id.* §§ 33-1054 and 33-1055 (Supp. 1999). These amendments are effective on August 6, 1999.

[118] *Id.* § 33-1057 (Supp. 1998).

[119] *Id.* § 33-1058 (Supp. 1998).

furnish a copy of the payment bond, and certain conditions are satisfied, the construction lender can avoid liability for not withholding monies pursuant to a Bonded Stop Notice if it furnishes a copy of the bond.[120]

If the monies withheld or required to be withheld pursuant to a Stop Notice are insufficient to pay in full all valid claims, the monies shall be distributed among the claimants in the same ratio that their claims bear to the aggregate of all such valid claims, regardless of the order in which the Stop Notice claims were made or actions filed.[121]

[5] Foreclosing a Stop Notice

An action against an owner or construction lender to enforce payment of claims stated in a Stop Notice or Bonded Stop Notice may be commenced after ten days from the date of service of the Stop Notice but not later than three months after the expiration of the period within which claims of liens must be recorded, unless all parties required to be parties to the claim stipulate in writing to an extension of time to bring the action for not more than three additional months.[122]

An action to enforce a Stop Notice should include all interested parties. This may include all parties above the Stop Notice claimant in the chain of contract, and may also include all subcontractors and suppliers of the Stop Notice claimant who have served their own Stop Notices. Any claimant filing an action to enforce a Stop Notice shall, within five days of commencing the action, serve a Notice of Commencement of Action upon the same persons and in the same manner as provided for service of a Stop Notice or Bonded Stop Notice.[123]

Any person who has served a Stop Notice or Bonded Stop Notice may join in an action to enforce a Stop Notice, and when there are separate actions pending, on motion by the owner or construction lender, the actions shall be joined, and all claimants shall be required to adjudicate their claims in that action.[124]

In an action against an owner or construction lender to enforce a Bonded Stop Notice, the prevailing party shall be awarded reasonable attorney fees from the party held liable by the court for payment of the claim and any amount awarded on the claim shall include interest at the legal rate (10 percent) computed from the date the Bonded Stop Notice was served on the owner or construction lender.[125]

[6] Release of a Stop Notice

An owner or construction lender may release monies withheld pursuant to a Stop Notice or Bonded Stop Notice upon receipt of a release of Stop Notice

---

[120] *Id.* § 33-1058(B) (Supp. 1998).
[121] *Id.* § 33-1060 (Supp. 1998).
[122] *Id.* § 33-1063 (Supp. 1998).
[123] *Id.* §§ 33-1055 and 33-1063 (Supp. 1998).
[124] *Id.* § 33-1065 (Supp. 1998).
[125] *Id.* §§ 33-1066 and 33-1067 (Supp. 1998).

given by the Stop Notice claimant or upon service by an owner, construction lender, prime contractor or subcontractor who disputes a Stop Notice or Bonded Stop Notice claim of a Stop Notice Release Bond in the amount of 125 percent of the Stop Notice claim, or upon the entry of an order of dismissal or settlement of an action to enforce a Stop Notice claim.[126] If no action is commenced within the time permitted or extended, the Stop Notice ceases to be effective and the monies shall be released to the contractor or other person to whom they are due.[127]

[7] Penalties for a False Stop Notice

Any person who wilfully gives a false Stop Notice or Bonded Stop Notice or willfully includes in the notice any labor, professional services, materials or equipment not furnished for the property described in the notice forfeits all right to participate in the pro rata distribution of monies, forfeits all right to record a Notice and Claim of Lien, and is subject to the penalties described under Ariz. Rev. Stat. § 33-420, which includes a penalty of $5,000 or treble actual damages, plus costs and attorney fees, against anyone who records a false or invalid lien.[128]

---

[126] *Id.* § 33-1062 (Supp. 1998).
[127] *Id.* § 33-1063(B) (Supp. 1998).
[128] *Id.* § 33-1061 (Supp. 1998).

CHAPTER 5

ARKANSAS

Ronald A. May

§ 5.01 INTRODUCTION

The Arkansas bond and lien laws were enacted in a piecemeal fashion, are frequently redundant, and have been amended from time to time under parochial influences careless of the public good. Notwithstanding this, the laws are effective and have usually been interpreted appropriately by the courts. The current lien law was originally enacted in 1895,[1] although it seems to have been based on earlier legislation going back to at least 1873. Consequently, it has some quaintly archaic phraseology. It protects the claims of workers and material suppliers for buildings, boats, and vessels. Strangely, in a populist frontier state, the law has always been strictly construed.

The hodgepodge of laws governing surety bonds for construction projects is, of course, of more recent vintage in Arkansas jurisprudence. One chapter of the Arkansas annotated statutes provides that the bond shall cover claims for labor and materials, including but not being limited to "fuel oil, gasoline, camp equipment, food for workers, feed for animals, premiums for bonds and liability and workers' compensation insurance, rentals on machinery, equipment and draft animals, and taxes."[2]

Another chapter contains the more organic provisions making bonds mandatory on public projects exceeding $20,000 and on church or charitable projects involving $1,000 or more and optional on private projects.[3] The Arkansas statutory contract bond law has no resemblance at all to the so-called Little Miller Acts.

§ 5.02 BOND LAW

[A] General Concepts

The purpose of the bond laws was to substitute the bond's obligation on public projects for the security of the statutory lien available on private projects.[4] Contracts for more than $20,000 by the state, its subdivisions, counties, municipalities, school districts, or other taxing units are simply forbidden unless accompanied by bond in the amount of the contract.[5] As noted in **§ 5.01,** the amount of the contract is much lower on church construction, but failure to require a bond on church construction can lead to the imposition of a lien,[6] which would not occur on a public contract.

Unlike the lien law, the bond law is liberally construed.[7] There are no

---

[1] 1895 Ark. Acts 146. Currently ARK. CODE ANN. §§ 18-44-101 *et seq.* (Michie 1987).

[2] 1929 Ark. Acts 368. Currently ARK. CODE ANN. §§ 22-9-401 *et seq.* (Michie 1987), based on earlier legislation from 1911.

[3] 1953 Ark. Acts 351. Currently ARK. CODE ANN. §§ 18-44-501 *et seq.* (Michie 1987).

[4] *See discussion in* Oliver Constr. Co. v. Williams, 152 Ark. 414, 238 S.W. 615 (1922).

[5] ARK. CODE ANN. § 18-44-503 (Michie Supp. 1991).

[6] Milord v. Arkmo Lumber & Supply Co., 272 Ark. 462, 615 S.W. 2d 349 (1981).

[7] Detroit Fidelity & Sur. Co. v. Yaffe Iron & Metal Co., 184 Ark. 1095, 44 S.W. 2d 1085 (1932).

distinctions between first-, second-, or third-tier suppliers to subcontractors.[8] If the materials are actually used in the construction, the supplier to a subcontractor is deemed to be in privity with the construction contract.[9] However, a remote supplier to another materialman is not entitled to the bond's protection.[10] The bond is supposed to be filed with the circuit clerk,[11] but this requirement is rarely observed, with no apparent prejudice to bond claimants.

[B] Enforcing Liability

Both bond laws provide that an action on a bond must be brought within six months from the date final payment is made on the contract.[12] However, the Arkansas legislature has seen fit to extend that time to 12 months for contracts with the State Building Services.[13] A large number of court decisions have grafted exceptions on this limitation, so great care must be exercised in electing to rely on limitations as a defense.[14] It has long been clear that a claimant need not join the contractor in a suit on a bond.[15] Venue is in any county where the beneficiary of the bond resides or the loss occurred.[16]

A particularly difficult problem for sureties is presented by the Arkansas penalty and attorneys' fees statute.[17] This law makes it mandatory that the trial court award a penalty of 12 percent and a reasonable attorneys' fee to a party that is successful in recovering under an insurance policy or a bond. The award is not discretionary and does not depend on bad faith or similar concepts. Because the attorneys' fee is frequently 25 to 40 percent of the recovery, the total penalty can be quite severe. It is necessary that the successful claimant show that the claim was denied by the surety before suit was filed. It was formerly necessary that the claimant recover the exact amount of its claim before the penalty and fees could be awarded. In practice, this meant that sureties did not often have to pay the extra amounts because it was rather rare that a claimant on a construction bond recovered exactly the amount for which it sued. In 1991, the Arkansas legislature amended the statute to allow recovery if the amount recovered was within 20 percent of the amount demanded.[18] This will undoubtedly add significantly to the exposure of sureties in Arkansas.

---

[8] *Cf.* 40 U.S.C. §§ 270a-270f (1988) (making distinctions between tiers).

[9] *See, e.g.,* River Valley, Inc. v. American States Ins. Co., 287 Ark. 386, 699 S.W. 2d 745 (1985).

[10] Sweetser Constr. Co. v. Newman Bros., 236 Ark. 939, 371 S.W. 2d 515 (1963).

[11] Ark. Code Ann. § 18-44-507 (Michie 1987).

[12] *Id.* §§ 18-44-508 and 22-9-403.

[13] *Id.* §§ 18-44-503(b) and 22-9-403.

[14] *See, e.g.,* Berry Asphalt Co. v. Western Sur. Co., 223 Ark. 344, 266 S.W. 2d 835 (1954), in which the court read a common law obligation into the bond, giving rise to a five-year limitation of action. *See also* United States Fidelity & Guar. Co. v. Little Rock Quarry Co., 309 Ark. 269, 830 S.W. 2d 362 (1992).

[15] Holcomb v. American Sur. Co., 184 Ark. 449, 42 S.W. 2d 765 (1931).

[16] Ark. Code Ann. § 23-79-204 (Michie 1987).

[17] Ark. Code Ann. § 23-79-208 (Michie Supp. 1991).

[18] *Id.* § 23-79-208(d). *But cf.* R.J. "Bob" Jones Excavating Contractor v. Firemens Fund Ins.

[C] Other Provisions

A 1993 enactment requires bonds for subcontractors under certain circumstances, and provides specific penalties for failure to provide a bond.[19]

[D] Exceptions

The Arkansas legislature has tampered unintelligently with the coverage of the bond laws. The fundamental bonding law of 1953 is also written to exempt contracts with the Arkansas State Highway and Transportation Department.[20]

§ 5.03 LIEN LAW

[A] General Concepts

The 1895 legislature obviously tried to do everything it could to enumerate the persons protected by the Arkansas lien laws as well as the types of contracts involved. In language finally modernized in 1995, the law now provides:

> Every contractor, subcontractor, or material supplier as defined in § 18-44-107, who supplies labor, services, material, fixtures, engines, boilers or machinery in the construction or repair of an improvement to real estate, or any boat or vessel of any kind, by virtue of a contract with the owner, provider, contractor, or subcontractor, or agent thereof, upon complying with the provisions of this subchapter, shall have, to secure payment, a lien upon the improvement and on up to one (1) acre of land upon which the improvement is situated, or to the extent of any number of acres of land upon which work has been done or improvements erected or repaired.[21]

As already noted, the law has been strictly construed because it was an extraordinary remedy not available to every merchant or worker.[22] Unlike the liberality extended to suppliers claiming under surety bonds, the lien statute requires that there be actual privity of contract between the supplier and the subcontractor or contractor.[23] Likewise, the burden is on the materialman to show that the materials for which a lien is claimed were used in the improvements on which the lien is sought.[24] On the other hand, the apparent requirement that there be a contract with an owner is tempered considerably by the fact that the courts

Co., 324 Ark. 282, 920 S.W.2d 483 (1996), which affords some relief to a surety that makes a good faith defense of claim against its principal.

[19] *Id.* § 18-44-502. Presumably such contract bonds are covered under ARK. CODE ANN. § 27-67-206(f) (Michie 1987).

[20] ARK. CODE ANN. § 22-9-404.

[21] *Id.* § 18-44-101 (Michie 1987).

[22] Christy v. Nabholz Supply Co., 261 Ark. 127, 546 S.W. 2d 425 (1977).

[23] Valley Metal Works v. A.0. Smith-Inland, 264 Ark. 341, 572 S.W. 2d 138 (1978).

[24] Ragsdell v. Gazaway Lumber Co., 11 Ark. App. 188, 668 S.W. 2d 60 (1984).

have always regarded the owner's prime contractor as the owner's representative in order to establish the necessary privity.[25] A contractor claiming under the lien laws is limited to materials furnished or labor actually performed and is not entitled to a lien for profits.[26] However, a supplier of materials is entitled to a lien for its profit.[27]

[B] Procedure for Establishing Lien

In the somewhat archaic procedure established under this old law, the laborer or supplier wishing to obtain a lien is required, within 120 days after the labor is performed or the materials furnished, to file with the clerk of the circuit court in the county where the improvement is located what is called "a just and true account of the demand due or owing to him" along with a correct description of the property to be charged with the lien.[28]

However, it is not all that simple. Before the laborer or supplier files with the circuit clerk, the claimant must give the owner, or the owner's agent, or both of them 10 days' notice. Elaborate provisions are set forth as to the manner in which the notice is to be served, which include notice by mail "addressed to the person to be served with a return receipt requested and delivery restricted to the addressee or the agent of the addressee."[29] However, neither of these cumbersome procedures is necessary if the claimant simply files suit to impress a lien and does so within 120 days of the work performed or materials supplied.[30]

Unhappily, these procedures were given an additional spin when the Arkansas legislature enacted a new notice provision in 1979 but modified substantially in 1995.[31] The new notice provision is thoroughly incoherent but boils down to a requirement that the principal contractor furnish the owner a particularly formalized notice before the furnishing of the materials or the labor. The notice is in the form of an acknowledgment by the owner that labor and materials will be utilized in the construction and that the owner may become liable for payment therefor. Because it would be difficult or even impossible to get the owner's acknowledgment in most cases, the provision allows the principal contractor to give the notice by certified mail before labor and materials are furnished. The notice can now be incorporated in the contract itself. The terms of the notice should be strictly complied with. However, the initial notice is *not* a prerequisite to the assertion of a lien on commercial projects or residential projects containing more than four units.

---

[25] *See, e.g.,* Gillison Discount Bldg. Materials v. Talbot, 253 Ark. 696, 488 S.W. 2d 317 (1972).

[26] Withrow v. Wright, 215 Ark. 654, 222 S.W. 2d 809 (1949).

[27] John E. Bryant & Sons Lumber Co. v. Moore, 264 Ark. 666, 573 S.W. 2d 632 (1978).

[28] Ark. Code Ann. § 18-44-117(a) (Michie 1987).

[29] *Id.* § 18-44-114(b)(1) (Michie Supp. 1991).

[30] Burks v. Sims, 230 Ark. 170, 321 S.W. 2d 767 (1959).

[31] Ark. Code Ann. § 18-44-115 (Michie 1987).

If a supplier to a commercial construction project has not received payment, the claimant must send a written notice of non-payment both to the general contractor and the property owner within 75 days of the date on which the supplies were provided.[32] This notice must state that the supplier is entitled to payment but has not yet been paid and must further provide: (1) a general description of the material, (2) the amount due and unpaid, (3) the name and address of supplier, (4) the name of the person who contracted with the supplier, (5) the job site location, and (6) a bold-faced statement as set forth in the statute.[33] The 75-Day Notice of Nonpayment is *not* a prerequisite to the assertion of lien for material supplied for use in a residential construction project.

When the claimant has run the gauntlet of notices and filed suit, such action must be commenced within 15 months after filing the lien[34] (unless, of course, the claimant chooses to file within the 120-day period and avoid filing the lien itself). The action must be filed, according to the statute,[35] in the circuit court of the county where the property is located. However, a number of Arkansas Supreme Court decisions have allowed the action to proceed in chancery court, which has become the customary forum for such cases. The contractor can be compelled to defend the action for the owner.[36] A claimant may, in addition, be awarded an attorneys' fee.[37]

[C] Effect of Lien

In ordinary circumstances, the labor and materials supplier's lien has a priority. However, when a construction lender has obligated itself to furnish construction funds, it may obtain a priority.[38]

This is a highly technical area of the law, and extreme care must be taken by a construction lender if it wishes to establish its priority.

From the beginning, however, it has been well established that the lien has a priority over later encumbrances;[39] the law now provides detailed priorities and should be studied closely.

[D] Other Provisions

In the event that a lien is properly established, the owner, contractor, construction money lender, or any other person affected by the lien may file with the

---

[32] *Id.* § 18-44-115(e)(2).

[33] *Id.* § 18-44-115(e)(2).

[34] *Id.* § 18-44-119.

[35] *Id.* § 16-13-304.

[36] *Id.* § 18-44-124.

[37] *Id.* § 18-44-128.

[38] United States v. Westmoreland Manganese Corp., 134 F. Supp. 898 (E.D. Ark. 1955). *Cf* Lyman Lamb Co. v. Union Bank, 237 Ark. 629, 374 S.W. 2d 820 (1964).

[39] ARK. CODE ANN. § 18-44-110 (Michie 1987).

circuit court clerk where the lien is filed a bond in double the amount of the lien conditioned upon the payment of the lien if it is found that the property was subject to the lien. Upon the filing of the bond, the circuit court clerk is obliged to give the lien claimant three days' notice, within which time the lien claimant may question the sufficiency of the bond. At the expiration of the three days, the lien shall be discharged by the entry of a marginal notation by the clerk.

On private projects for which a bond has been furnished a lien claimant, for the purpose of pressuring the owner, may file a lien even though it has a better claim under the bond. The filing of such a lien, of course, can interfere with construction or permanent financing. By following the cross-bond procedure set forth above, this harassing technique can be nullified.[40] Likewise, a lien claimant who has been paid is subject to criminal penalties if the claimant fails to discharge its lien.[41] As one might expect, there has been remarkably little effort to prosecute under this section, and such prosecution has been relatively ineffective.[42]

---

[40] *Id.* § 18-44-118.

[41] *Id.* § 18-44-132.

[42] *See, e.g.*, Reno v. State, 241 Ark. 127, 406 S.W. 2d 372 (1966), reversed for failure to admit evidence of defendants insolvency and "inexperience."

CHAPTER 6

CALIFORNIA

Kent W. Lindsay
Stephen G. Walker

§ 6.01 INTRODUCTION

There are three distinct forms of remedy available to contractors and material suppliers on construction projects in California to assist in the collection of debts: the mechanics' lien, the stop notice, and the payment bond.[1]

The availability of any of these remedies in a particular case depends on whether the project on which work is performed is a public work of improvement or a private project, and whether the claimant is an original contractor (also known as a *general* or *prime contractor*) on the one hand, or a subcontractor or materialman on the other hand.

A *public work* is defined in California as any work of improvement contracted for by a public entity.[2] A *public entity* means the state, the Regents of the University of California, a county, city, district, public authority, public agency, or any other political subdivision or public corporation in the state.[3]

An *original contractor* is any contractor who has a direct contractual relationship with the owner.[4] A *subcontractor* is a contractor who has no direct contractual relationship with the owner.[5] A *materialman* is any person furnishing materials or supplies to be used or consumed in any work of improvement.[6]

Original contractors, subcontractors, and materialmen who otherwise qualify are all entitled to mechanics' liens in California, but only on private works of improvement. Mechanics' liens are prohibited on public works by the doctrine of sovereign immunity.[7] Stop notices may be filed on both private and public projects, although on public projects, stop notices are permitted only by subcontractors and materialmen and not by original contractors.[8] Payment bonds are also permitted on both public and private works and are required on public projects with a value of more than $25,000.[9]

The rules regarding mechanics' liens, stop notices, and payment bonds are generally found in "The Mechanics' Lien Law" contained in the California Civil Code, Division 3, Part 4, Title 15, §§ 3082 to 3267. The basic right to a mechanics' lien is found in the California Constitution at Article XIV, § 3.

§ 6.02 MECHANICS' LIENS

The California Constitution guarantees to "mechanics, persons furnishing materials, artisans, and laborers of every class" a lien upon the property upon

---

1 *See* §§ **6.02–6.04.**

2 Cal. Civ. Code § 3100 (Deering 1986 & Supp. 1999).

3 *Id.* § 3099.

4 *Id.* § 3095.

5 *Id.* § 3104.

6 *Id.* § 3090.

7 Miles v. Ryan, 172 Cal. 205, 157 P. 5 (1916).

8 Cal. Civ. Code § 3181 (Deering 1986 & Supp. 1999).

9 *Id.* § 3247.

which they bestow labor or furnish materials for the value of the labor done or material furnished.[10] The categories of claimants mentioned in the California Constitution are not intended to be exclusive and have been broadly interpreted by the legislature to include:

> mechanics, materialmen, contractors, subcontractors, lessors of equipment, artisans, architects, registered engineers, licensed land surveyors, machinists, builders, teamsters, and draymen, and all persons and laborers of every class performing labor upon or bestowing skill or other necessary services on, or furnishing materials or leasing equipment to be used or consumed in or furnishing appliances, teams, or power contributing to a work of improvement.[11]

In order to qualify to claim a lien, a claimant must have made a direct contribution to a work of improvement.[12] A materialman to a materialman does not contribute directly to a project, and thus is not entitled to claim a lien.[13]

The statute defines "work of improvement" very broadly to include the "construction, alteration, addition to, or repair, in whole or in part, of any building, wharf, bridge, ditch, flume, aqueduct, well, tunnel, fence, machinery, railroad or road, the seeding, sodding, or planting of any lot or tract of land for landscaping purposes, the filling, leveling, or grading of any lot or tract of land, the demolition of buildings, and the removal of buildings."[14]

Lien rights do not accrue in California before a project has commenced.[15] A project is considered to have begun when there has been physical work performed on the project that is clearly discernible by anyone.[16]

The only exception to this rule is that an owner may choose to have the preparatory "site work," essentially the demolition, grading, site preparation, and utilities work, performed under separate contract from the main construction project. Under this circumstance, "the site improvement shall be considered a separate work of improvement and the commencement thereof shall not constitute a commencement of the [main] work of improvement."[17]

A materials supplier is entitled to a mechanics' lien only for material "used or consumed" on the project.[18] The early rule was quite strict, requiring that the

---

[10] Cal. Const. Art. XIV, §3.

[11] CAL. CIV. CODE § 3110 (Deering 1986 & Supp. 1999).

[12] M. Marsh, CALIFORNIA MECHANICS' LIEN LAW AND CONSTRUCTION INDUSTRY PRACTICE § 4.6 (6th ed. 1996).

[13] *Id.*

[14] CAL. CIV. CODE § 3106 (Deering 1986 & Supp. 1999).

[15] M. Marsh, CALIFORNIA MECHANICS' LIEN LAW AND CONSTRUCTION INDUSTRY PRACTICE § 4.12 (6th ed. 1996) (citing MacDonald v. Filice, 252 Cal. App. 2d 613, 60 Cal. Rptr. 832 (1967)).

[16] *Id.* § 4.156.

[17] CAL. CIV. CODE § 3135 (Deering 1986 & Supp. 1999).

[18] *Id.* § 3110.

material be incorporated into and actually form a part of the finished structure.[19] It is now settled, however, that when material is used upon and is instrumental in producing the project, the material has been "used or consumed" and the claimant is entitled to a lien therefor.[20] Thus, for example, it has been held that a claimant is entitled to a lien for form lumber that cannot be said to have been incorporated into the finished structure, but which nevertheless is "consumed" during the project.[21]

[A] Notice Requirements

Every lien claimant, except one under direct contract with the owner (that is, an original contractor) or one performing actual labor for wages or an express trust fund, is required to serve a "Preliminary 20-day Notice" on the project owner, the original contractor, and the construction lender, if any, to be entitled to enforce a lien.[22] The preliminary notice must be served not later than 20 days after the claimant has first furnished labor, service, equipment, or materials to the jobsite, although a claimant serving a preliminary notice more than 20 days after first performing work still may claim for the labor, services, equipment, or labor provided in the 20 days preceding the service and thereafter.[23]

The purpose of the preliminary 20-day notice is to give the owner and the construction lender advance notice of all potential lien claimants so they can protect the property from liens. With preliminary notice, for example, an owner can issue joint checks to the general contractor and its subcontractors or require the original contractor to obtain lien releases from all those who have served preliminary notices before the owner releases progress payments.

An owner cannot waive the right to have the preliminary notice served.[24] An owner may be estopped, however, to assert a claimant's failure to comply with the preliminary notice requirements when the owner has *actual* knowledge of the work of improvement and of the contribution of the claimant.[25] This narrow exception developed by the case law has been applied only in a few cases, and ought not be viewed as neutralizing the otherwise strict preliminary notice requirements.

The preliminary 20-day notice must be served on the owner or reputed owner of the project, the original contractor or reputed contractor, and the construction lender or reputed construction lender, if any.[26] A claimant who contracts with a

---

[19] Stimson Mill Co. v. Los Angeles Traction Co., 141 Cal. 30, 74 P. 357 (1903).

[20] Olson-Mahoney Lumber Co. v. Dunne, 30 Cal. App. 332, 159 P. 178 (1916).

[21] *Id.*

[22] CAL. CIV. CODE § 3097(a) (Deering 1986 & Supp. 1999).

[23] *Id.* § 3097(c), (d).

[24] *Id.* § 3097(e).

[25] *See, e.g.,* Truestone, Inc. v. Simi W. Indus. Park II, 163 Cal. App. 3d 715, 209 Cal. Rptr. 757 (1984).

[26] CAL. CIV. CODE § 3097(a) (Deering 1986 & Supp. 1999).

subcontractor is not required to serve a preliminary 20-day notice on that subcontractor, and failure to provide notice to subcontractors does not affect the validity of the notice.[27] The identity of the construction lender may be difficult to ascertain by a supplier who is somewhat removed in the project hierarchy. Building permits, deeds of trust, and other documents filed with the county recorder, however, should include the name of the lender and should be reviewed. A contractor who fails to review such records may be charged with constructive notice of the documents' content, and the failure to serve a preliminary notice on a construction lender may be a fatal defect when the lender's identity could have been gleaned from such a review.[28]

[1] Contents of Preliminary 20-day Notice

The required contents of a preliminary 20-day notice are set out exactly in the California Civil Code.[29] The notice must include:

1. A general description of the labor, service, equipment, or materials furnished or to be furnished, and an estimate of the price thereof;
2. The name and address of the person furnishing the labor, service, equipment, or materials;
3. The name of the person who contracted for purchase of the labor, service, equipment, or materials;
4. A description of the jobsite sufficient for identification;
5. A "Notice to Property Owner" in boldface type, notifying the owner that unpaid bills could result in lien proceedings and foreclosure.

The statute provides the exact warning language to be included in the notice. In two recent cases, courts have rejected preliminary notices that varied only slightly from (and in one case even added to) the language required by the legislature.[30]

All of the requirements of the statute are satisfied by the use of the printed four-part snap-out form available from building exchanges and large stationery suppliers in California. It is strongly recommended that claimants use this printed form.

[2] Service of Preliminary 20-day Notice

The completed notice must be served by personal delivery or by first class registered or certified mail.[31] At least one court has held that the requirement for

---

[27] *Id.* § 3097(e).

[28] M. Marsh, California Mechanics' Lien Law and Construction Industry Practice § 4.25 (6th ed. 1996) (citing Romak Iron Works v. Prudential Ins. Co. of Am., 104 Cal. App. 3d 767, 163 Cal. Rptr. 869 (1980)).

[29] Cal. Civ. Code § 3097(c) (Deering 1986 & Supp. 1999).

[30] Harold James, Inc. v. Five Points Ranch, Inc., 158 Cal. App. 3d 1, 204 Cal. Rptr. 494 (1984); Fuller v. American Forest Prods. Co., 204 Cal. App. 3d 482, 252 Cal. Rptr. 30 (1988).

[31] Cal. Civ. Code § 3097(f) (Deering 1986 & Supp. 1999).

registered or certified mail when serving by mail is not subject to interpretation and must be strictly complied with.[32] The statute requires a "proof of service affidavit" showing the time, place, and manner of service, the name and address of the party upon whom the notice was served, and if the notice was served by mail, the return receipt of certified or registered mail.[33] The preliminary notice should also be filed with the county recorder in the county where the jobsite is located. County recorders are obligated to notify parties who have filed 20-day preliminary notices whenever a notice of completion or cessation is recorded on the project.

Contractors who perform residential construction work are subject to additional notice requirements in California. Such contractors are required to provide a "Notice to Owner" explaining the statutory lien procedures before entering into a home improvement or swimming pool contract.[34]

[B] Recording the Claim of Lien

A general contractor must record its "claim of lien" after it completes its contract and within 60 days after a notice of completion or notice of cessation is recorded, or if no notice of completion or cessation is recorded, within 90 days after the work of improvement is completed.[35]

A subcontractor or material supplier must record its claim of lien within 30 days after a notice of completion or notice of cessation is recorded, or if no notice of completion or cessation is recorded, within 90 days after the completion of the work of improvement.[36]

These time limits run from the date the entire project is complete, not the time that a particular claimant finished its work. A framing contractor, for example, may finish its work very early on a project, but the time within which its lien must be filed is measured from the date that the last work is performed by the last contractor on the project.

A notice of completion, in order to validly shorten the period within which liens must be filed, must be signed and verified by the owner or its agent, state the name and address of the owner and general contractor, describe the site sufficient for identification, and be recorded within 10 days following actual completion of the project.[37] A notice of cessation must contain the same substantive information and is effective only if there has been a continuous cessation of labor for at least 30 days before the date it is recorded.[38]

---

[32] IGA Aluminum Projects, Inc. v. Manufacturers Bank, 130 Cal. App. 3d 699, 181 Cal. Rptr. 859 (1982).

[33] CAL. CIV. CODE § 3097.1 (Deering 1986 & Supp. 1999).

[34] CAL. BUS. & PROF. CODE §§ 7018.5, 7159 (West 1975 and Supp. 1994).

[35] CAL. CIV. CODE § 3115 (Deering 1986 & Supp. 1999).

[36] *Id.* § 3116.

[37] *Id.* § 3093.

[38] *Id.* § 3092.

When no notice of completion is recorded, a project is deemed complete, and the 90-day limitation for recording liens begins to run when:

1. The owner or its agent begins to occupy or use the work of improvement, accompanied by a cessation of labor thereon; or
2. The work is accepted by the owner or its agent; or
3. There is a cessation of labor for a continuous period of 60 days, or a cessation of labor thereon for a continuous period of 30 days or more if the owner files for record a notice of cessation.[39]

For purposes of this section, the owner's "occupation" of the work must be open and entire.[40] "Acceptance" must also be open, and must be sufficient to provide notice to claimants that the work has been accepted and that the period within which liens are required to be filed has begun to run.[41]

[1] Contents of the Claim of Lien

The claim of lien must be a written statement, signed and verified by the claimant or the claimant's agent, containing:

1. A statement of the claimant's demand after deducting all just credits and offsets;
2. The name of the owner or reputed owner, if known;
3. A general statement of the kind of labor, services, equipment, or materials furnished by the claimant;
4. The name of the person to whom the claimant was employed or to whom the claimant furnished the labor, services, equipment, or materials;
5. A description of the site sufficient for identification.[42]

A mistake or error in a claim of lien will not generally cause the lien to fail. The statute provides that no mistake or error in the statement of the demand, or the amount of credits and offsets allowed, or the balance asserted to be due the claimant, or in the description of the property against which the lien is recorded will invalidate the lien unless a court finds that the mistake or error was made with the intent to defraud or that an innocent third party without direct or constructive notice of the lien purchases the property, and the defect or error makes the claim so deficient that it does not put the innocent party on further inquiry in any manner.[43]

---

[39] *Id.* § 3086.

[40] M. Marsh, California Mechanics' Lien Law and Construction Industry Practice § 4.36 (6th ed. 1996).

[41] *Id.*

[42] Cal. Civ. Code § 3084 (Deering 1986 & Supp. 1999).

[43] *Id.* § 3261.

[C] Foreclosure Proceedings

A claimant must file suit to foreclose its mechanics' lien within 90 days of the date that its claim of lien is recorded. No lien

> binds any property for a longer period of time than 90 days after the recording of the claim of lien, unless within that time an action to foreclose the lien is commenced in a proper court. . . . If the claimant fails to commence an action to foreclose the lien within the time limitation provided in this section, the lien automatically shall be null and void and of no further force and effect.[44]

The only way that the 90-day limitation period can be extended is by the recording of a "Notice of Credit" in the office of the county recorder, signed by the lien claimant and the owner expressly extending the time within which a foreclosure action may be commenced.[45] The credit allows the lien to continue in force until 90 days after the expiration of the credit, but in no case longer than one year from the time of completion of the work of improvement.[46]

The "proper court" in which to commence the foreclosure action is the county where the real property, or some part thereof, is situated.[47] The lien claimant must name as defendants in the action, all junior encumbrances. Because a claimant may not know the identity of all such junior lienholders at the time the foreclosure action is commenced, California law permits the designation of fictitious defendants (commonly denominated as "Doe" defendants).[48] Plaintiff is then permitted to amend its complaint to state the true identity of the Doe defendants at the time the identities are ascertained.

[1] Lis Pendens

Upon the commencement of the foreclosure action, the lien claimant should immediately record a "Notice of Pendency of Action" (lis pendens) with the county recorder. The lis pendens takes the place of the lien as a claim on the property, and provides constructive notice to subsequent purchasers or encumbrancers of the property of the recordation of the lien and the existence of the foreclosure action.[49] The lis pendens provides important protection to lien claimants, but it also clouds title to the property. Therefore, when an owner believes a lis pendens has been recorded improperly, he or she may file a motion to have the lis pendens expunged, and the burden of proof is on the lis pendens claimant to show by a preponderance of the evidence the probable validity of its

---

[44] *Id.* § 3144.
[45] *Id.*
[46] *Id.*
[47] CAL. CIV. PROC. CODE § 392 (Deering 1986 & Supp. 1999).
[48] *Id.* § 392.
[49] CAL. CIV. CODE § 3146 (Deering 1986 & Supp. 1999).

claim.[50] If the claimant cannot meet its burden, the court must order the lis pendens removed.[51] The court may condition an order expunging the lis pendens on the property owner's giving an undertaking in an amount that will indemnify the claimant if it prevails on its lien claim.[52] The prevailing party on a motion to expunge a lis pendens is entitled to its reasonable attorneys' fees, unless the court finds that the other party acted with substantial justification or that imposing such fees and costs would be unjust under the circumstances.[53]

Lis pendens claimants should be aware that, at any time after a lis pendens has been recorded, and upon the motion of any person with an interest in the property, a court may require the claimant to give the moving party an undertaking as a condition of maintaining the lis pendens.[54]

[2] Attorneys' Fees

In general, there is no right to attorneys' fees in an action to foreclose a mechanics' lien, as such fees are not included in the value of the labor done or material furnished by the lien claimant. This is so even when an underlying contract provides for attorneys' fees.[55] Of course, if the suit to foreclose a lien includes other causes of action (such as a breach of contract claim in an action by a general contractor), attorneys' fees may be recoverable under one of the other causes of action.

At least one court has held that "delay/interest" damages also are not part of the value of labor, services, equipment or materials furnished and may not be included in a claim of lien. "The function of the mechanics lien is to secure reimbursement for work actually contributed to the job, not to facilitate recovery of consequential damages or to provide leverage for imposing claimant's view as to who caused the breakdown in the contract."[56]

[D] Priority of Liens

Properly recorded mechanics' liens relate back to the date of the commencement of the project and are entitled to priority over all encumbrances attaching after the commencement of the project.[57] On nearly every project, however, the construction lender will record a deed of trust before the commencement of the work, and thus the deed of trust is nearly always of a higher priority than all mechanics' liens. There is no relative priority between lien claimants; all liens,

---

[50] Cal. Civ. Proc. Code § 405.32 (West 1973 & Supp. 1994).

[51] *Id.* § 405.32.

[52] *Id.* § 405.33.

[53] *Id.* § 405.38.

[54] *Id.* § 405.34.

[55] *See* Abbett Elec. Corp. v. Citicorp Real Estate, Inc., 230 Cal. App. 3d 355, 281 Cal. Rptr. 362 (1991).

[56] Lambert v. Superior Court, 228 Cal. App. 3d 383, 279 Cal. Rptr. 32 (1991).

[57] Cal. Civ. Code § 3134 (Deering 1986 & Supp. 1999).

regardless of when recorded, are deemed to date from the commencement of the work.[58]

[E] Waivers and Releases

Neither the owner nor the original contractor may waive, affect, or impair the claims and liens of other persons without that person's written consent.[59] Furthermore, mechanic's lien rights may only be waived if the claimant provides a written waiver and release that follows substantially the forms contained in Civil Code § 3262, subdivision (d).[60] That section provides the precise language for four different lien waivers: (1) a conditional waiver and release upon progress payment; (2) an unconditional waiver and release upon progress payment; (3) a conditional waiver and release upon final payment; and (4) an unconditional waiver and release upon final payment. The forms define the extent of the release provided, and specifically exclude release of contract retention not yet received, and extras provided after the date of the release. The waiver and release forms also provide that execution of a lien release does not affect the contract rights of the parties, including rights based upon rescission, abandonment, or breach of contract.

[F] Bond to Release Lien

Civil Code § 3143 provides that an owner, contractor or subcontractor who disputes the correctness or validity of a lien may record a bond from a corporate surety in a penal sum equal to one and one-half times the amount of the lien and thereby remove the lien as an encumbrance on the property.[61] The bond is substituted as security for the underlying claim, guaranteeing payment of amounts to which the claimant eventually establishes entitlement. A release bond allows an owner to sell or or refinance its the property without compromising a disputed claim.

Any person who records a lien release bond is required to provide notice of that fact to the lienholder by certified or registered mail.[62] The lien claimant thereafter may be required to withdraw its lis pendens and to amend its complaint to substitute a cause of action on the bond for the lien foreclosure claim.

§ 6.03 STOP NOTICES

The *stop notice* is a notice to the party paying for a work of improvement, that is, the owner, the construction lender, or the disbursing officer of a public entity, that money is due the stop notice claimant. A properly served stop notice

---

[58] *Id.*

[59] *Id.* § 3262(a).

[60] *Id.* § 3262(d).

[61] *Id.* § 3143.

[62] *Id.* § 3144.5.

can obligate the party paying for the work to withhold from the debtor sufficient sums to pay the stop notice claim.[63]

A valid stop notice thus is a claim on the undisbursed construction funds. This is an important remedy on public projects for which mechanics' liens are not permitted. It is also important, however, on private projects because a mechanics' lien is a claim against the property and is only as valuable as the owner's equity in the property. On a private project built with a construction loan, the deed of trust is typically recorded before construction begins and thus has priority over all mechanics' liens (which date from the time that construction begins). When the deed of trust and other encumbrances exceed the market value of a property, a mechanics' lien is of no value. A stop notice claim, on the other hand, is a claim against the construction fund and ensures that any undisbursed funds will be used to pay the claim regardless of the market value of the property. The rules regarding stop notices on private projects and public projects differ slightly.

[A] Stop Notices on Private Projects

On a private project, any person entitled to a mechanics' lien, except a general contractor, may serve a stop notice on the project owner, and the owner must withhold the amount claimed in the stop notice from the general contractor unless the general contractor has recorded a payment bond for the project.[64] Failure of an owner to withhold the required funds may give the stop notice claimant the right to a personal judgment against the owner.[65]

[1] Bonded Stop Notices

Any claimant on a private project, including a general contractor, may also serve a bonded stop notice on the construction lender.[66] A *bonded stop notice* is a stop notice given to a construction lender, accompanied by a bond in a penal sum equal to 125 percent of the amount of the claim and conditioned that if the defendant prevails in an action on the stop notice, the claimant will pay all costs and damages arising out of the claim up to the penal amount of the bond.[67] The prevailing party in an action to enforce payment of a claim pursuant to a bonded stop notice is entitled to recover, as part of its award, attorneys' fees and interest at the legal rate from the date of service of the bond stop notice.[68]

The lender is obligated to withhold the sums claimed in any bonded stop notice served by a general contractor, whether a payment bond has been recorded or not. The lender must also withhold the sums claimed in a bonded stop notice

---

[63] *Id.* § 3103.

[64] *Id.* § 3161.

[65] M. Marsh, California Mechanics' Lien Law and Construction Industry Practice § 5.4 (6th ed. 1996).

[66] Cal. Civ. Code § 3159 (Deering 1986 & Supp. 1999).

[67] *Id.* § 3083.

[68] *Id.* §§ 3176, 3176.5.

served by any other person unless a payment bond has been recorded on the project.[69] If a payment bond has been previously recorded, the lender may elect not to withhold funds pursuant to the stop notice, but if the stop notice claimant serves a written request for notice of the lender's election to withhold, accompanied by a self-addressed, stamped envelope at the time the bonded stop notice is served, the lender must furnish the claimant a copy of the payment bond within 30 days of the election not to withhold.[70] The construction lender is only required to withhold the net amount of all claims of the original contractor, subcontractors, and material suppliers.[71]

[B] Stop Notices on Public Projects

The stop notice remedy on a public project is in lieu of the mechanics' lien rights available on private projects and constitutes a lien on the contractor's fee held by the public agency.[72] Any person entitled to a mechanics' lien other than a general contractor may serve a stop notice upon the public entity responsible for the public work.[73]

Thereafter, the public entity is required to withhold from the general contractor sums "sufficient to answer the claim stated in the stop notice and to provide for the public entity's reasonable cost of any litigation thereunder."[74] If the general contractor disputes the validity or correctness of the stop notice, the public entity may, in its discretion, permit the contractor to file a release bond in an amount equal to 125 percent of the stop notice claim. The public entity is then required to release the withheld money.[75]

[1] General Contractor's Right to Challenge Stop Notice

The general contractor may also seek release of the stop notice by summary proceedings if it believes that the claim is improper, excessive, or is not warranted under the law.[76] The general contractor must file with the public entity an affidavit setting forth the legal and factual grounds upon which it bases its claim for release of the stop notice.[77] The public entity must then serve upon the stop notice claimant, either personally or by registered or certified mail, a copy of the affidavit and a notice setting forth a time between 10 and 20 days after service of the

[69] *Id.* § 3162.

[70] *Id.*

[71] *Id.* § 3162.

[72] M. Marsh, California Mechanics' Lien Law and Construction Industry Practice § 6.3 (6th ed. 1996) (citing United States Fidelity & Guar. Co. v. Oak Grove Union Sch. Dist., 205 Cal. App. 2d 226, 22 Cal. Rptr. 907 (1962)).

[73] *Id.* § 3181.

[74] *Id.* § 3186.

[75] *Id.* § 3196.

[76] *Id.* § 3197.

[77] *Id.* § 3198.

affidavit for the stop notice claimant to file a counteraffidavit.[78] If the claimant files no counteraffidavit, the public entity is obligated to release the withheld funds.[79]

If the claimant does file a counteraffidavit, either party may file an action in the appropriate superior court for a declaration of the respective rights of the parties. The superior court is required to schedule a hearing on the matter within 15 days of the filing of the action.[80] The affidavit and the counteraffidavit constitute the pleadings in the matter, and the contractor bears the burden of proof at the hearing.[81]

[2] Release of Retentions

For all public works contracts entered into on or after January 1, 1993, the owner must release all retentions within 60 days after completion of the project. *Completion* occurs upon one of the following events:

1. Occupation, beneficial use, the enjoyment of the work of improvement, accompanied by a cessation of work; or
2. Acceptance of the work of improvement; or
3. Cessation of labor on the work of improvement for a continuous 100-day period; or
4. Cessation of labor for 30 continuous days if the public agency records a notice of cessation or a notice of completion.[82]

If there is a dispute between the public entity and the original contractor, the public entity may withhold from the final payment an amount not to exceed 150 percent of any disputed payment.[83] If the public entity retains an amount equal to or less than 125 percent of the estimated value of the work yet to be completed, it must distribute undisputed retentions within 90 days.[84] If the public entity retains an amount greater than 125 percent of the estimated value, it must distribute undisputed retentions within 60 days after the work is completed.[85]

[C] Notice Requirements

As with mechanics' liens, stop notice claimants (except a general contractor serving a bonded stop notice on the construction lender on a private project) must serve a preliminary 20-day notice to be entitled to enforce their stop notices.[86] On

---

[78] *Id.* § 3199.
[79] *Id.* § 3200.
[80] *Id.* § 3201.
[81] *Id.* § 3202.
[82] CAL PUB. CONT. CODE § 7107 (WEST 1985 & SUPP. 1999).
[83] *Id.* § 7107(c).
[84] *Id.* § 7107(g).
[85] *Id.*
[86] CAL. CIV. CODE §§ 3160, 3183 (Deering 1986 & Supp. 1999).

a private project, the preliminary 20-day notice is the same as the preliminary notice required of a mechanics' lien claimant.[87]

On a public project, the preliminary 20-day notice is required by a separate statute, and the requirement is mandatory.[88] A preliminary 20-day notice should be served within 20 days after the claimant first furnishes services or materials to the jobsite.[89] However, if the claimant files a preliminary notice sometime thereafter, its claim will be limited to services and material supplied within 20 days prior to the notice, and at any time thereafter. When the price to be paid a subcontractor on a project exceeds $400, the failure of the subcontractor to give the preliminary 20-day notice constitutes grounds for disciplinary action by the registrar of contractors.[90] The preliminary notice must be served either personally or by registered or certified mail to the general contractor and to the public agency concerned, and the transmittal and notice requirements are strictly construed.[91] The preliminary notice to the public agency should be sent to the office of the disbursing officer of the department constructing the work.

[D] Service of Stop Notice

A stop notice must be served within either 30 days after the recordation of a notice of completion or cessation (60 days for an original contractor) or 90 days after the completion of the work of improvement if no notice of completion or cessation has been recorded.[92] As a matter of practice, subcontractors or material suppliers should, in the absence of a recorded notice of completion or cessation, serve their stop notices within 90 days after they last furnish services or materials to the project. The court of appeal has held that, for public works, a complete work stoppage for 30 days constitutes a cessation of labor and completion of the work of improvement for purposes of the statute, requiring that the claimant serve a stop notice within 90 days after completion of the work of improvement.[93] When a claimant serves a stop notice on a public project, the claimant should include with the stop notice served on the public entity a check for two dollars. The public entity is thereafter required to give the claimant notice of completion, cessation of labor, or acceptance of the project, the dates from which the time to commence an action to enforce a stop notice are calculated.[94]

---

[87] *Id.* § 3160.

[88] *Id.* §§ 3098, 3183.

[89] *Id.* § 3098.

[90] *Id.* § 3098(b).

[91] *Id.* § 3098(a); San Joaquin Blocklite, Inc. v. Willden, 184 Cal. App. 3d 361, 228 Cal. Rptr. 842 (1986).

[92] CAL. CIV. CODE §§ 3160 (private project), 3184 (public project) (Deering 1986 & Supp. 1999).

[93] W.F. Hayward Co. v. Transamerica Ins. Co., 16 Cal. App. 4th 1101, 1103, 20 Cal. Rptr. 2d 468, 469 (1993).

[94] CAL. CIV. CODE § 3185.

[E] Contents of Stop Notice

A stop notice must be in writing, signed and verified by the claimant or its agent, and state in general terms:

1. The kind of labor, services, equipment, or materials furnished or agreed to be furnished by the claimant;
2. The name of the person to whom the claimant furnished labor, services, equipment, materials;
3. The value of that which was furnished by the claimant; and
4. The name and address of the claimant.[95]

In the case of a private project, the stop notice must be served either personally or by registered mail on the owner or its agent. If a stop notice is served on the construction lender, it must be served on "the manager or other responsible officer" at the office or branch of the lender administering or holding the construction funds.[96] On a public project, the stop notice is served on the disbursing officer of the entity constructing the project or on the director of the department which let the contract in the case of a public work for the state.[97]

[F] Action to Enforce Stop Notice

An action against the owner or construction lender to enforce a stop notice may be brought no earlier than 10 days after the date of service of the stop notice and no later than 120 days after recordation of a notice of completion or cessation, or 180 days after completion of the work of improvement if no notice of completion or cessation has been recorded (that is, "not later than 90 days following the expiration of the period within which claims of lien must be recorded" [or within which stop notices must be filed]).[98] Within five days of filing the action, a stop notice claimant must give notice of the commencement of the action to all the parties upon whom a stop notice was served.[99] If a claimant fails to commence an action to enforce the claim within the time required, the stop notice ceases to be effective, and the party holding the money is obligated to pay it over to the persons to whom it is due.[100]

[G] Priority of Stop Notices

On a private job, no assignment by a project owner or contractor of construction loan funds is entitled to priority over the claims of stop notice claimants,

[95] *Id.* § 3103.
[96] *Id.*
[97] *Id.*
[98] *Id.* §§ 3172 (private project), 3210 (public project) (Deering 1986 & Supp. 1999).
[99] *Id.* §§ 3172 (private project), 3211 (public project).
[100] *Id.* §§ 3172 (private project), 3210 (public project).

whether the assignment occurs before or after service of stop notices.[101] On both public and private projects, when the total undisbursed construction funds are insufficient to satisfy fully the claims of all stop notice claimants, the funds are required to be distributed among all claimants in the same ratio that the respective claims bear to the aggregate of all valid claims.[102] This pro rata distribution is required to be made without regard to the order of time in which stop notices are served or actions thereon are commenced.[103]

§ 6.04 PAYMENT BONDS

A payment bond is a bond with "good and sufficient sureties" conditioned for the payment of the claims and giving claimants a direct right of action against the sureties on claims "brought to foreclose the liens provided for in this title or in a separate suit brought on the bond."[104]

[A] Public Projects

As noted, a payment bond is mandatory on public projects involving an expenditure in excess of $25,000. The bond is required to be approved by the public entity, and must be in a sum equal to one hundred percent of the amount of a contract under $5 million, and fifty percent of the amount of a contract between $5 million and $10 million, and twenty-five percent of a contract that exceeds $10 million.[105]

A payment bond on a public project must, by its terms, be for the benefit of all persons authorized to serve a stop notice, that is, all persons other than the general contractor.[106] The filing of a stop notice, however, is not a condition precedent to the maintenance of an action against the surety on the payment bond. A payment bond action may be commenced separately against the surety and without the filing of any action against the public entity.[107]

[1] Notice Requirements

A preliminary 20-day notice now is required to make a claim on a public works payment bond.[108] The legislature, however, created a "second chance" notice to cover the situation where a payment bond claimant has not served a preliminary 20-day notice. In that event, a claimant may serve a written notice to surety within 15 days *after* a notice of completion has been recorded, or, if no

[101] *Id.* § 3166 (Deering 1986 & Supp. 1999).
[102] *Id.* §§ 3167 (private project), 3190 (public project).
[103] *Id.*
[104] *Id.* § 3096.
[105] *Id.* §§ 3247, 3248.
[106] *Id.* § 3096.
[107] *Id.* § 3250.
[108] *Id.* § 3098.

notice of completion has been recorded, within 75 days *after* completion of the work as a whole.[109] The written notice to surety must describe the kind of labor, services, equipment, or materials furnished or agreed to be furnished by the claimant; the name of the person or company to or for whom the labor, services, equipment, or materials were furnished; and the amount in value, as near as may be determined, of any labor, services, equipment, or materials already furnished or to be furnished. The written notice must be served by personal delivery or by registered or certified mail, return receipt requested, to the surety and the bond principal.[110]

[2] Action on Payment Bond

An action may be brought against a surety on a payment bond at any time after the claimant has furnished its last labor or materials, but the suit must be commenced within six months after the period in which stop notices may be filed, that is, within 6 months and 30 days after the recording of a notice of completion or cessation, or within 6 months and 90 days after project completion when no notice of completion or cessation is recorded.[111]

[3] Mandatory Award of Attorneys' Fees to Prevailing Party

The Civil Code provides for an award of reasonable attorneys' fees to the prevailing party in an action against the surety on a payment bond.[112] The California Court of Appeal held that, in an action against a surety on a public works payment bond, the court must award attorneys' fees pursuant to Civil Code § 3250 to the prevailing party, regardless of whether the principal would have been liable for attorneys' fees pursuant to contract or any other statute.[113]

[B] Private Projects

On a private project, no lien claimant may maintain an action on the bond unless the claimant has given a 20-day private work preliminary notice to the surety, or given written notice of its claim to the surety within 15 days of recordation of a notice of completion or cessation, or 75 days from the date of completion or cessation if no notice is recorded.[114] Service of the written notice to the surety may be made personally or by registered or certified mail.[115]

---

[109] *Id.* §§ 3252 (public works) and 3242 (private works)
[110] *Id.* §3227.
[111] *Id.* § 3249.
[112] *Id.* § 3250.
[113] Liton Gen. Eng'g v. United Pac. Ins., 16 Cal. App. 4th 577, 584, 20 Cal. Rptr. 2d 200 (1993).
[114] CAL. CIV. CODE § 3242 (Deering 1986 & Supp. 1999).
[115] *Id.* § 3227.

If a payment bond has been recorded in the county recorder's office in the county where the work of improvement is located, any suit brought against the surety on the bond must be filed within six months after completion of the work of improvement.[116] If the payment bond has not been recorded, the claimant has four years within which to bring an action against the surety.

[116] *Id.* § 3240.

CHAPTER 7

COLORADO

Dennis J. Bartlett
Andrew J. Friedrich

§ 7.01 INTRODUCTION

On private projects Colorado law does not require that any performance or payment bonds be furnished. Mandatory protection to labor, equipment and material providers is afforded by the statutorily available mechanics' lien.[1] Performance and payment bonds on private projects are generally applied according to their own written terms and in accord with common law principles.

For state and local public works projects, no mechanics' lien is available. By statute, every general contractor on a public works project in excess of $50,000 must post a surety bond.[2] The bonds are intended to provide remedies similar to the mechanics' lien protections that are not applicable to public works.[3] Another remedy available to the labor or material claimant on a public work is to tie up payments due the general contractor by timely filing of a verified statement of claim.[4]

§ 7.02 BOND LAW

[A] General Concepts

As with all contract based legal work, the first essential of handling a bond matter is to obtain and read the operative documents. In the construction contract surety context, those operative documents are the bonds, the contract being bonded, and, in the case of public work, any statutes or regulations under which the bonds are given.

The law of suretyship has its own key terms. The surety is, of course, the person or entity who has agreed to be financially responsible for the contractor's performance of its contract. The contractor is the principal. The party with whom the contractor has contracted is the obligee—most typically the project owner. If a subcontractor has bonded the performance of its contract to the general contractor, in that relationship the general contractor is the obligee. Each bond gives rise to a tripartite relationship involving the principal, the surety, and the obligee. Each of the parties has obligations to each of the other parties.

It is a fundamental of surety law that if the principal is not liable the surety is not liable.[5] The existence and extent of the surety's liability is dependent upon the principal's liability.

Construction projects most typically involve performance and payment bonds. In basic terms, the performance bond is to guarantee to the obligee that

---

[1] COLO. REV. STAT. §§ 38-22-101 *et seq.* (1998).

[2] *Id.* §§ 38-26-101 *et seq.* (1998).

[3] Continental Cas. Co. v. Rio Grande Fuel Co., 119 P.2d 618 (Colo. 1942).

[4] COLO. REV. STAT. § 38-26-107 (1998).

[5] Bushman Constr. Co. v. Air Force Academy Hous., Inc., 327 F.2d 481 (10th Cir. 1964).

the principal's contract will be performed.[6] The payment bond is to provide for the payment of those supplying labor and material to the project. The performance and payment obligations are sometimes combined into a single bond. These may be preceded by a bid bond to assure that a successful bidder will undertake and perform the contract.

A surety's obligations are contractual in nature and are defined by the terms of the bond.[7] A surety's obligations cannot be expanded without its consent.[8] Matters that materially increase a surety's risk without its knowledge or consent may operate to the discharge of the surety to the extent that it has been prejudiced.[9] A surety cannot be bound to a contract different from that for which it executed the bond.[10]

A surety contract is to be construed according to the plain meaning of its terms.[11] A surety bond is to be interpreted as other contracts, giving effect to the intent of the parties. "To ascertain that intent, a court should look to the bond and other instruments to which the bond refers."[12] When a bond is given pursuant to statute, it is the terms and requirements of the statute that control.[13]

To have a binding surety obligation, the bond must be in writing, must be signed by the surety, and must be delivered by the surety out of its possession and control with the intention that it go into force and effect. Further, the obligee must accept the surety bond, but such acceptance may be inferred.[14]

The failure to make claim or bring suit within time limits expressed in the bond or any applicable statutes or regulations may result in defeat of any claim on the bond.[15]

---

[6] General Ins. Co. v. City of Colorado Springs, 638 P.2d 752 (Colo. 1981).

[7] People v. National Sur. Co., 176 P. 948 (Colo. 1918).

[8] Haberl v. Bigelow, 855 P.2d 1368 (Colo. 1993); People v. Smith, 645 P.2d 864 (Colo. Ct. App. 1982).

[9] National Union Fire Ins. Co. v. Denver Brick & Pipe Co., 427 P.2d 861 (Colo. 1967). A common example is the surety defense of prepayment. If the owner has paid the contractor more than it should have under the construction contract, the surety may be discharged to the extent it can show prejudice from the prepayment. However, Colorado has now ruled that the surety cannot avail itself of a prepayment defense when the bonded contract provides that payments do not constitute acceptance of defective work or relieve the contractor from its obligations. Brighton Sch. Dist. 27J v. Transamerica Premier Ins. Co., 923 P.2d 328 (Colo. Ct. App. 1996), *aff'd on other grounds,* 940 P.2d 348 (Colo. 1997).

[10] Empson v. Aetna Cas. & Sur. Co., 206 P. 378 (Colo. 1922).

[11] Fuqua Homes, Inc. v. Western Sur. Co., 616 P.2d 163 (Colo. Ct. App. 1980).

[12] Western Sur. Co. v. Smith, 914 P.2d 451, 453 (Colo. Ct. App. 1995), *cert. denied,* (Colo. 1996); Edmonds v. Western Sur. Co., 962 P.2d 323 (Colo. Ct. App. 1998).

[13] CPS Distribs., Inc. v. Federal Ins. Co., 685 P.2d 783 (Colo. Ct. App. 1984). The rule of construction of ambiguities against the drafter is, of course, often invoked against insurers and sureties. It should not, however, be applied where the form of bond is one prescribed by government requirements, the contract documents, is an A.I.A. form, or otherwise is not the product of the surety's own draftsmanship.

[14] Tanco, Inc. v. Houston Gen. Ins. Co., 555 P.2d 1164 (Colo. 1976).

[15] *E.g.,* Fountain Sand & Gravel Co. v. Chilton Constr. Co., 578 P.2d 664 (Colo. Ct. App. 1978).

[B] Bid Bonds

A bid bond is intended to assure that the successful bidder will in fact enter into the contract and provide the required performance and payment bonds. Depending upon the form used, the bid bond may provide for the forfeiture of a given amount or may call for payment to the owner of the difference between the bidder's price and the contract price the owner ends up having to pay for a replacement contractor.

Colorado law requires that contractors bidding on state public works projects with an estimated price to exceed $50,000 deliver bid security to the state.[16] The bid security may be a surety bond, the equivalent in cash, or some other form of security satisfactory to the state. The bid security provided is to be at least five percent of the bid. After the bids are opened, the bid security remains irrevocable for the period specified in the instructions to bidders. However, an inadvertently erroneous bid may be withdrawn if the bidder submits proof that clearly and convincingly demonstrates that a bidding error was made.[17]

[C] Performance Bonds

On Colorado public works projects, every contractor who is awarded a contract exceeding $50,000 must file a performance bond with the appropriate governmental agency conditioned upon the faithful performance of the contract and providing that if the contractor or its subcontractors fail to pay for any labor, materials, team hire, sustenance, provisions, provender, supplies, rental machinery, tools, or equipment, that the surety will pay for the same together with interest at the rate of eight percent per annum.[18] The performance bond, or other security satisfactory to the owner, must be in an amount equal to 50 percent of the contract price.[19]

The statute does not provide for a time limitation on performance bond claims by the obligee. However, at least as to payment bond obligations contained within the performance bond, actions must be commenced within six months of completion of the work or within 90 days after the date fixed for final settlement, whichever is longer.[20] However, if the bond provides for a longer period of time to sue, the bond provision will control.[21]

On private projects, a time limitation provided for in the bond will control so long as it is reasonable.[22] The applicable period if no limitation is stated in the

---

[16] Colo. Rev. Stat. § 24-105-201 (1998).
[17] *Id.* § 24-103-202(6).
[18] *Id.* § 38-26-106.
[19] *Id.* § 38-26-106(1); *id.* § 24-105-202(1)(a) (state contracts, with exceptions).
[20] Rocky Mountain Ass'n of Credit Management v. Marshall, 615 P.2d 68 (Colo. 1980).
[21] Montezuma Plumbing & Heating, Inc. v. Housing Auth., 651 P.2d 426 (Colo. Ct. App. 1982).
[22] Hepp v. United Airlines, 540 P.2d 1141 (Colo. Ct. App. 1975).

bond has not been judicially determined, and arguments can be made for times ranging from two to six years.[23]

[D] Payment Bonds

On public works projects, every contractor awarded a contract exceeding $50,000 must provide a bond conditioned upon the prompt payment of all persons supplying labor, materials, rental machinery, tools, or equipment used in the work.[24] However, the public body is not liable for failure to require a contractor to supply such a bond.[25]

Actions on these bonds must be commenced within six months of completion of the contract, although if a bond provides for a longer time, the bond language will control.[26] Completion means eventual completion of the work, not, for example, when the original contractor may have defaulted on or abandoned the work.[27] However, an action may also be maintained against the bond if such an action is commenced within 90 days after the date of final settlement.[28] That limitation is in the alternative to the six month period provided for, and the claimant may choose the longer of the two.[29] The minimal level of protection required is two tiered—that is, suppliers, laborers, and materialmen of a contractor or its subcontractors may pursue a claim against the bond.[30] "Subcontractor" is expansively defined to include sub-subcontractors who assume a substantial specified portion of the work.[31] However, a supplier to a materialman would have no claim under the bond.[32]

It has been held that items such as fringe benefits due under a collective bargaining agreement are proper items for which claim can be made,[33] although the purchase of equipment has been held not to be recoverable.[34]

---

[23] Colo. Rev. Stat. §§ 13-80-101, -103.5, -104 (1998).

[24] *Id.* § 38-26-105. Payment bonds on state projects, with exceptions, are to be for fifty percent of the contract price. *Id.* § 24-105-202(1)(b).

[25] School Dist. No. 28 v. Denver Pressed Brick Co., 14 P.2d 487 (Colo. 1932).

[26] Montezuma Plumbing & Heating, Inc. v. Housing Auth., *supra* note 21.

[27] Allen v. Wells, 227 P. 833 (Colo. 1924); Colo. Rev. Stat. § 38-26-105 (1998).

[28] Colo. Rev. Stat. § 38-26-107 (1998).

[29] Rocky Mountain Ass'n. of Credit Management v. Marshall, *supra* note 20.

[30] Colo. Rev. Stat. §§ 38-26-105 to -107 (1998).

[31] South Way Constr. Co. v. Adams City Serv., 458 P.2d 250 (Colo. 1969); Koybayashi v. Meehleis Steel Co., 472 P.2d 724 (Colo. Ct. App. 1970).

[32] Lovell Clay Prods. v. Statewide Supply Co., 580 P.2d 1278 (Colo. Ct. App. 1978). In Western Metal Lath v. Acoustical & Constr. Supply, Inc., 851 P.2d 875, 881 (Colo. 1993), a supplier to a material supplier argued that the statutory scheme, by not providing him any remedy at the same time it provided a supplier to a subcontractor a remedy, violated the equal protection clause. That argument was rejected; the Colorado Supreme court held that the Act was constitutional and did not violate the equal protection guarantees of the Colorado Constitution.

[33] Trustees of Colo. Carpenters & Millwrights Health & Benefit Trust Fund v. Pinkard Constr. Co., 604 P.2d 683 (Colo. 1979).

[34] CPS Distribs. Co. v. Federal Ins. Co., 685 P.2d 783 (Colo. 1984).

Attorneys' fees are generally not recoverable against the bond, but they may be recoverable if that obligation is expressly assumed under the bond.[35] The statutory scheme for state public works nowhere provides that attorneys' fees are recoverable.[36] Prejudgment interest is recoverable from a surety only from the time that a claimant gives notice and delivers the demand for payment to the surety.[37]

[E] Labor and Material Claims On Performance Bonds

The performance and payment bonds may sometimes be combined into a single bond or the performance bond may itself expressly state a payment obligation. In those instances, it is generally clear that the labor and material claimant may claim on the performance bond. More typically, however, there are separate performance and payment bonds, and it has sometimes happened that there is a performance bond only.[38] In those cases the issue may arise whether the labor and material claimant may recover against the performance bond. Under Colorado law whether a third party may assert any rights against a performance bond depends upon the language of the bond interpreted with reference to the underlying contract for which it was issued.[39]

[F] Good Faith and Fair Dealing

While there is a Colorado case holding that in a contract action a surety could be held liable for punitive damages,[40] that ruling probably is no longer valid.[41] It is now, however, settled that under Colorado law a performance bond surety may be subjected to bad faith liability to the owner.[42] The standard for liability is whether the surety's conduct is unreasonable and the surety knows its conduct is unreasonable or recklessly disregards the fact that its conduct is unreasonable.[43] The Colorado appellate courts have not yet ruled upon whether labor and material claimants may also maintain bad faith claims against sureties.

---

[35] Cement Asbestos Prods. Co. v. Hartford Accident & Indem. Co., 592 F.2d 1144 (10th Cir. 1979).

[36] COLO. REV. STAT. §§ 38-26-101 *et seq.* (1998).

[37] Autocon Indus., Inc. v. Western States Constr. Co., 728 P.2d 374 (Colo. Ct. App. 1986).

[38] There is, however, no good reason ever to have a performance bond alone without a payment bond. Bond premium typically is based on the contract price and there is no extra charge to have a payment bond along with the performance bond.

[39] *See* Montezuma Plumbing & Heating, Inc. v. Housing Auth., *supra* note 21; National Union Fire Ins. Co. v. Denver Brick & Pipe Co., *supra* note 9.

[40] Riva Ridge Apartments v. Robert G. Fisher Co., 745 P.2d 1034 (Colo. Ct. App. 1987).

[41] In Mortgage Fin., Inc. v. Podleski, 742 P.2d 900 (Colo. 1987), it was held that punitive damages are not available in breach of contract actions. (Despite the order in which the two cases appear in the Pacific Reporter, *Mortgage Finance* was decided after *Riva Ridge.*)

[42] Transamerica Premier Ins. Co. v. Brighton Sch. Dist. 27J, 940 P.2d 348 (Colo. 1997).

[43] *See* COLO. REV. STAT. § 10-3-1113 (1998).

However, the ruling giving performance bond obligees such a right relied upon payment bond cases from other jurisdictions in so doing.

Colorado's unfair claim settlement practices statute does apply to sureties. Although that act has been held not to give rise to a private civil action, in a bad faith case willful conduct of the kind set forth therein may be considered in determining whether delay or denial of payment of a claim was unreasonable if the delay or denial and the claimed damage was caused or contributed to by prohibited conduct.[44]

Absent a contractual provision, attorneys' fees may not be awarded either for bad faith itself or for establishing liability on the bond in the presence of bad faith conduct.[45]

[G] Indemnification of Surety

While a surety paying the debt of its principal has common law rights of indemnification from the principal, far more significant as a practical matter are the surety's rights under the written indemnity agreement, without which a surety bond generally will never get written in the first place.[46] The surety may also require the posting of collateral in order to obtain issuance of a bond. Once a claim has been made against the surety, indemnity agreements typically allow the surety to call for collateral, give it rights with respect to contract funds, and otherwise secure its position.

§ 7.03 LIEN ON FUNDS: PUBLIC PROJECTS

In addition to the other remedies provided on public projects, a claimant may assert a lien on contract funds. A subcontractor, supplier, or materialman may, before the date of advertised final settlement, file with the owner a verified statement of claim asserting a claim against any contract funds held by the owner.[47] The owner must advertise the date of final settlement, at least twice, ten days prior thereto by publication of a notice in a newspaper of general circulation in the counties where the work was contracted for and where it was performed.[48] If such a claim is filed, the owner must hold funds sufficient to cover the claim for a period of 90 days after final settlement. The claimant must, within that 90-day period, commence an action against the contractor and file a notice of lis pendens. If an action is commenced and the requisite notice of lis pendens is filed, the government body must hold the funds as a stakeholder pending the outcome of

[44] *Id.* §§ 10-3-1113 and 1104(1)(h)(I) to (XIV).

[45] Bernhard v. Farmers Ins. Exchange, 915 P.2d 1285 (Colo. 1996).

[46] *See* Wilson & Co., Eng's and Architects v. Walsenburg Sand & Gravel Co., 779 P.2d 1386 (Colo. Ct. App. 1989).

[47] Colo. Rev. Stat. § 38-26-107 (1998).

[48] *Id.* § 38-26-107(1).

that litigation. The surety need not be a party to that action.[49] The governmental body holding the funds is not required to pay interest to either the contractor or the subcontractor for the period of time it holds the funds, even though it appreciates a benefit therefrom.[50]

§ 7.04 LIEN LAW

[A] General Concepts

The right to a mechanics' lien and the procedures to establish and enforce the lien exist in Colorado solely by way of statute.[51] The lien process is broadly available to those who supply labor, equipment, services, or materials to any sort of private construction or improvement on land.[52] In order ultimately to look to the property as a secured source of payment, the statutory requirements must be complied with. Although loss of lien rights precludes recourse to the property for payment of the debt on a secured basis, it does not mean that other possible avenues of recovery are foreclosed.[53]

[B] Basic Provisions

Lien rights are available to virtually all who supply labor, materials, equipment, design, or superintendence to any construction, improvement, alteration, or

---

[49] South-Way Constr. Co. v. Adams City Serv., 169 Colo. 513, 458 P.2d 250 (1969).

[50] *See* Elliott Elec. Supply Co. v. Adolfson & Peterson, Inc., 765 P.2d 1079 (Colo. Ct. App. 1988).

[51] The General Mechanics' Lien Act is found at COLO. REV. STAT. §§ 38-22-101 *et seq.* (1998). Although not a subject of this chapter, it should be noted that a different and separate article, *id.* §§ 38-24-101 *et seq.*, applies for those who furnish labor or materials to oil or gas or other wells, pipelines, pumping stations, refineries, and the like. Mining properties, however, are within the general statute, albeit with some differences in application. *Id.* § 38-22-104. Water wells have now been held to be within the separate provisions of §§ 38-24-101 *et seq.* rather than the general statute. Aspen Drilling Co. v. Hayes, 876 P.2d 86, 87-89 (Colo. Ct. App. 1994), *cert. denied* (1994).

[52] Public property cannot be subjected to mechanics' liens. Western Lumber & Pole Co. v. City of Golden, 130 P. 1027, 1028 (Colo. Ct. App. 1913). This is true even when the property became public by dedication and the work for which a lien is claimed "relates back" to a period preceding the dedication to the public. City of Westminster v. Brannen Sand & Gravel Co., 940 P.2d 393 (Colo. 1997).

[53] COLO. REV. STAT. § 38-22-124 (1998). The preservation of other remedies under this section extends to claims of unjust enrichment that may lie against the property owner, Frank M. Hall & Co. v. Southwest Properties Venture, 747 P.2d 688, 690-91 (Colo. Ct. App. 1987), *cert. denied* (1988), as well as to claims for the debt itself, breach of contract to pay, and the like. *See, e.g.*, Hayutin v. Gibbons, 139 Colo. 262, 266-67, 338 P.2d 1032, 1035 (1959). However, the right to pursue a claim of unjust enrichment has been curtailed. In DCB Constr. Co., Inc. v. The Central City Dev. Co., 965 P.2d 115, 122 (Colo. 1998), the court held that to impose liability under an unjust enrichment claim on the landlord owner the contractor had to establish "improper, deceitful or misleading conduct" by the landlord.

repair of any structure or improvement upon land, as more particularly and exhaustively described in the statute.[54] Although the statute is worded and construed broadly for the protection of those who supply labor and materials, the scope of the statute is not without limitation. Those who have been found outside the protection of the statute include a supplier of materials only to a materialman[55] and one who supplied a contractor with labor for the benefit of the contractor only.[56] Liens may not extend to late charges.[57] Notable inclusions by specific statutory language are tools; curb, gutter, and sidewalk work adjacent to the property; and architects and engineers, including design and specifications as well as superintendence.

Although the work must be at the instance of the property owner or the owner's agent, those who are held to be agents are broadly described.[58] Moreover,

---

[54] COLO. REV. STAT. § 38-22-101(1) (1998). This key section reads as follows:

> Every person who supplies machinery, tools, or equipment in the prosecution of the work, and mechanics, materialmen, contractors, subcontractors, builders, and all persons of every class performing labor upon or furnishing directly to the owner or persons furnishing labor materials to be used in construction, alteration, improvement, addition to, or repair, either in whole or in part, of any building, mill, bridge, ditch, flume, aqueduct, reservoir, tunnel, fence, railroad, wagon road, tramway, or any other structure or improvement upon land, including adjacent curb, gutter, and sidewalk, and also architects, engineers, draftsmen, and artisans who have furnished designs, plans, plats, maps, specifications, drawings, estimates of cost, surveys, or superintendence, or who have rendered other professional or skilled service, or bestowed labor in whole or in part, describing or illustrating, or superintending such structure, or work done or to be done, or any part connected therewith, shall have a lien upon the property upon which they have supplied machinery, tools, or equipment or rendered service or bestowed labor or for which they have furnished materials or mining or milling machinery or other fixtures, for the value of such machinery, tools, or equipment supplied, or services rendered or labor done or material furnished, whether at the instance of the owner, or of any other person acting by his authority or under him, as agent, contractor, or otherwise for the machinery, tools, or equipment supplied, or work or labor done or services rendered or materials furnished by each, respectively, whether supplied or done or furnished or rendered at the instance of the owner of the building or other improvement, or his agent; and every contractor, architect, engineer, subcontractor, builder, agent, or other person having charge of the construction, alteration, addition to, or repair, either in whole or in part, of said building or other improvement shall be held to be the agent of the owner for the purposes of this article.

[55] Schneider v. J.W. Metz Lumber Co., 715 P.2d 329, 331-32 (Colo. 1986).

[56] Kern v. Guiry Bros. Wall Paper Co., 60 Colo. 286, 153 P. 87 (1915). This case does not explain how claimant's work was of benefit solely to the contractor. Whether the ruling currently amounts to a meaningful restriction on lien rights is questionable.

[57] Independent Trust Corp. v. Stan Miller, Inc., 796 P.2d 483, 493-94 (Colo. 1990). Similarly, unearned bonuses at the time of the owner's breach are not lienable. *See* LSV, Inc. v. Pinnacle Creek, LLC, 1999 Colo. Ct. App. LEXIS 161 (Colo. Ct. App. June 10, 1999). The lien does, however, extend to interest at the rate provided in the contract or, if none, 12 percent. COLO. REV. STAT. § 38-22-101(5) (1998).

[58] COLO. REV. STAT. § 38-22-101(1) (1998).

work is, in any event, deemed to be at the instance of an owner unless the owner within five days after learning of the work gives certain prescribed notification.[59]

The lien attaches to "so much of the lands wherein such building, structure, or improvement is made as may be necessary for the convenient use and occupation of such building, structure, or improvement, and the same shall be subject to such liens,"[60] and to the entire building, erection, or improvement.[61] When a claimant supplies labor or materials for two or more improvements being constructed by the same person and under the same contract, the claimant can apportion between the improvements, but if apportionment cannot readily and definitely be made, one lien claim can be made against all the improvements and related land.[62]

As more fully outlined in **§ 7.04[C],** the lien must be established and perfected by notice and recording procedures. Although the statutes are to be liberally construed in favor of lien claimants, strict construction is the rule in determining whether the right to a lien exists; compliance with statutory requirements must be established.[63]

Upon payment of a lien and costs after filing, the lien claimant following request is obligated to record acknowledgement of satisfaction.[64]

If the claim is not paid and the claimant is determined to pursue action to foreclose the lien, action must be commenced within six months after completion of the improvement or furnishing of the last labor or material, and within that same time a notice stating that the action has been commenced, commonly called a notice of *lis pendens,* must be recorded with the clerk and recorder for the county where the property is located.[65] Abandonment by discontinuance of all labor, work, services, and furnishing of materials for a three-month period is deemed equivalent to completion.[66] A lien cannot hold the property for more than a year from the date of filing unless claimant files an affidavit within 30 days after each annual anniversary of filing that the improvement has not been completed.[67]

When there are multiple mechanics' liens filed against a project, it is not necessary for each lien claimant to file a separate suit and record a notice of lis pendens,[68] but every claimant who wishes to preserve lien rights must be sure to

---

[59] *Id.* § 38-22-105. The notification procedure is as described in **§ 7.04[F].**

[60] COLO. REV. STAT. § 38-22-103(1) (1998).

[61] *Id.* § 38-22-103(2).

[62] *Id.* § 38-22-103(4). Application of the blanket lien provision is discussed in Independent Trust Corp. v. Stan Miller, Inc., 796 P.2d 483 (Colo. 1990).

[63] *See, e.g.,* Richter Plumbing & Heating, Inc. v. Rademacher, 729 P.2d 1009, 1012 (Colo. Ct. App. 1986), *cert. denied* (1986).

[64] COLO. REV. STAT. § 38-22-118 (1998).

[65] *Id.* § 38-22-110.

[66] *Id.* § 38-22-109(7).

[67] *Id.* § 38-22-109(8).

[68] *Id.* § 38-22-111; Bulow v. Ward Terry & Co., 396 P.2d 232, 235-36 (Colo. 1964).

have either started its own action and filed notice of lis pendens or to have been named or joined in an action for which notice of lis pendens has been properly given, before expiration of the time stated. All persons who have filed lien statements are to be made parties in any action,[69] as are the owner and all other parties having any interest in the property whose title or interests are to be charged with or affected by the lien.[70]

The statute contains provisions on service of process, personal as well as lien judgments,[71] sale of the property, and disposition of proceeds.[72] Redemption rights exist as in cases of sale of real estate on execution.[73]

In addition to lien rights and procedures, the statute also provides for a bonding procedure to preclude liens and provide alternative protection to claimants[74] and procedures for withholding of contract funds to secure payment of those working on or supplying the project.[75]

[C] Notice Requirements

Any person seeking a mechanics' lien must record a lien statement. However, the lien claimant must first serve a notice of intent to file lien statement.[76] At least 10 days before filing the lien statement, a notice of intent must be served by personal service or by registered or certified mail, return receipt requested, on both the owner or reputed owner and the principal or prime contractor. An affidavit that such service or mailing has been accomplished must be filed for record along with the lien statement. Failure to timely serve and record the notice of intent is fatal to any lien.[77]

Lien statements must be filed for record in the office of the clerk and recorder for the county where the property, or the principal part thereof, to be affected by the lien is situated.[78] Generally, the filing must be done before the expiration of

---

[69] COLO. REV. STAT. § 38-22-111(2) (1998).

[70] *Id.* § 38-22-111(3). Section 38-22-115 states that "[p]rincipal contractors and all other persons personally liable for the debt for which the lien is claimed" are to be made parties to lien enforcement actions. However, Bulow v. Ward Terry & Co., 396 P.2d 232, 234 (Colo. 1964), found the principal contractor to be a proper party but not a necessary party when the contract was for more than $500 and was not recorded.

[71] COLO. REV. STAT. § 38-22-113 (1998).

[72] *Id.* § 38-22-114.

[73] *Id.* § 38-22-114(1).

[74] Discussed in **§ 7.04[F].**

[75] Separate procedures exist under COLO. REV. STAT. §§ 38-22-102(4)-(7) AND 38-22-126 (1998).

[76] COLO. REV. STAT. § 38-22-109(3) (1998).

[77] Everitt Lumber Co. v. Prudential Ins. Co., 660 P.2d 925 (Colo. Ct. App. 1983); Daniel v. M.J. Dev., Inc., 603 P.2d 947 (Colo. Ct. App. 1979).

[78] COLO. REV. STAT. § 38-22-109(1) (1998). The recording fee is five dollars per page. *Id.* § 30-1-103(1).

four months after the day on which the lien claimant last performed labor or last furnished material,[79] except that statements "for labor and work by the day or piece, but without furnishing material therefor" must be filed after performance of the labor and before two months after completion of the building or other improvements.[80] Lien statements may be amended to cure mistakes or more fully complying with the lien act, but only within the time for filing.[81]

Special time requirements may be applicable if a lien claimant is to attain priority over the bona fide purchaser for value of a single or double family dwelling. In such instances, provided that the lien claimant is other than a laborer or mechanic working by the day or piece without furnishing material, and provided further that the purchaser does not have actual notice at the time of conveyance of the unpaid amounts due and the lien statement was not recorded before the conveyance, and, further, a notice to extend was not filed before conveyance or within one month after completion, the lien statement must be recorded within two months after completion of the building to encumber the interest of the bona fide purchaser for value.[82]

Required contents of the lien statement are: the name of the owner or reputed owner of the property, or if that information is not known to the claimant, a statement to that effect; the name of the person claiming the lien, the name of the person who furnished the material or performed the labor for which the lien is claimed, and when the lien is claimed by a subcontractor, the name of the contractor or, if the contractor's name is not known to the lien claimant, a statement to that effect; a description of the property to be charged with the lien; and a statement of the amount due claimant.[83] Signature is to be by the party claiming the lien or some other person on behalf of the claimant, and verification is required.[84]

Care must be taken in stating the amount due. To knowingly file a lien for an amount greater than is due and without a reasonable possibility that the amount claimed is due results in forfeiture of all rights to the lien and liability for attorneys' fees and costs incurred in defending against the lien.[85] Further, the lien statement can only be for the amount due at the time of filing. Recording of a lien for the full amount before all work has been completed is ineffective as to

---

[79] *Id.* § 38-22-109(5).

[80] *Id.* § 38-22-109(4).

[81] *Id.* § 38-22-109(6).

[82] *Id.* § 38-22-125.

[83] *Id.* § 38-22-109(1). This requirement does not mean that a general contractor must separately name in its statement of lien each subcontractor that remains unpaid or the amount due each such subcontractor. FCC Constr., Inc. v. Casino Creek Holdings, Ltd., 916 P.2d 1196, 1199 (Colo. Ct. App. 1996).

[84] Colo. Rev. Stat. § 38-22-109(2).

[85] *Id.* § 38-22-128. *See also id.* § 38-35-109(3) (1998) and LSV, Inc. v. Pinnacle Creek, LLC, 1999 Colo. Ct. App. LEXIS 161 (Colo. Ct. App. June 10, 1999).

work performed subsequent to filing.[86] The lien can only be for the amount due for labor actually performed or material actually supplied, not for the full contract price when it has not been fully performed.[87]

The specified times for lien statement recording can be extended by filing a notice to extend with the appropriate clerk and recorder within the original time.[88] This extends the time for filing a lien statement to four months after completion of the improvement or six months from the date of filing the notice, whichever occurs first. Although such a notice automatically terminates six months after the date of filing, if the improvement still is not then completed, before the termination date a claimant may file a new or amended notice to remain in effect an additional six months from date of filing or four months from completion, whichever occurs first.

The notice of intent and lien statement are commonly combined into a single document that includes the affidavits of service or mailing on owner and contractor. This procedure has been found to comply with the statute, so long as the service or mailing is made at least 10 days before the lien is actually filed.[89] In calendaring due dates for perfecting liens, it is essential to include not just the due date for filing of the lien statement, but also a date 10 or more days in advance of that for complying with the notice requirements.

[D] Waiver

The right to claim a mechanics' lien may be waived before, during, or after the work, but the waiver must be for consideration, must be express, and any doubts or ambiguities are to be resolved against waiver.[90] Only the person who would otherwise be entitled to a lien can waive the right to a lien; one cannot waive the lien rights of another.[91]

[E] Lien Priority

A mechanics' lien relates back to the time of the commencement of work under the contract between the owner and the first contractor, or if that contract

---

[86] Sperry & Mock, Inc. v. Security Sav. & Loan Ass'n, 37 Colo. Ct. App. 357, 549 P.2d 412, *cert. denied* (1976).

[87] Heating & Plumbing Eng'rs, Inc. v. H.J. Wilson Co., 698 P.2d 1364 (Colo. Ct. App. 1984), *cert. denied* (1985) (lien forfeited and attorneys' fees and costs assessed for improper contract price lien filing). *See also LSV, Inc., supra* note 85.

[88] COLO. REV. STAT. § 38-22-109(10) (1998).

[89] Manguso v. American Sav. & Loan Ass'n, 782 P.2d 866, 868 (Colo. Ct. App. 1989).

[90] Western Fed. Sav. & Loan Ass'n v. National Homes Corp., 167 Colo. 93, 445 P.2d 892 (1968); Bishop v. Moore, 137 Colo. 263, 265, 323 P.2d 897, 898 (1958); Ragsdale Bros. Roofing, Inc. v. United Bank of Denver, 744 P.2d 750 (Colo. Ct. App.), *cert. denied* (1987); Mountain Stone Co. v. H.W. Hammond Co., 39 Colo. Ct. App. 58, 564 P.2d 958, *cert. denied* (1977).

[91] COLO. REV. STAT. § 38-22-119 (1998); Aste v. Wilson, 14 Colo. Ct. App. 323, 59 P. 846 (1900).

is not in writing, to the time of commencement of work on the structure or improvement.[92] This, however, does not mean that a lien cannot attach until actual commencement of physical work on the project itself. For example, the first delivery of materials to the site can provide the attachment date even though construction work has not then begun,[93] and the architect's or engineer's commencement of design work provides an attachment date though before actual construction.[94]

The mechanics' lien then has priority over any lien or encumbrance created subsequent to the attachment date for the mechanics' lien, even if earlier created but not recorded until after that attachment date, provided that the mechanics' lien claimant did not have actual notice.[95] All mechanics' liens on a project have the benefit of the attachment date of the first attaching lien.[96] As between mechanics' liens, priority is first given to laborers or mechanics working by the day or piece, but who do not furnish material; second to subcontractors and materialmen; and third to principal contractors.[97]

[F] Remedies of Owner

Recording the contract may serve to limit the owner's lien exposure to the amount of the contract price. To gain this limitation, the contract must be in writing and signed by the parties and be for more than $500. The contract or a memorandum thereof must contain certain specified information and further must be recorded with the clerk and recorder of the county where the property, or its principal portion, is situated, and the contract must comply with certain statutory requirements. Recording must take place before the commencement of any work under the contract.[98]

An owner may also seek to protect the property from liens by use of performance and payment bonds posted before commencement of work. To secure

[92] Colo. Rev. Stat. § 38-22-106(1) (1998).

[93] *See, e.g.,* Sontag v. Abbott, 344 P.2d 961, 964-65 (Colo. 1959).

[94] *See, e.g.,* Bankers Trust Co. v. El Paso Pre-Cast Co., 192 Colo. 468, 472–73, 560 P.2d 457, 460-61 (1977). However, architectural services provided to the contractor before the contractor has a contract with the owner cannot be the basis for the first attaching lien for priority purposes. Printz Serv. Corp. v. Main Elec., Ltd., 949 P.2d 77 (Colo. Ct. App. 1997), *rev'd in part on different issue,* Main Elec. Ltd. v. Printz Serv. Corp., 1999 Colo. LEXIS 235 (Colo. Mar. 15, 1999).

[95] Colo. Rev. Stat. § 38-22-106(1) (1998). A lien claimant's actual notice prior to starting work of a prior but then unrecorded security interest in the property prevents that claimant from having priority over the preexisting interest. *Actual notice* is defined as "such notice as is positively proved to have been given to a party directly and personally, or such as the party is presumed to have received personally because the evidence within the party's knowledge was sufficient to put the party upon inquiry." Powder Mountain Painting v. Peregrine Joint Venture, 899 P.2d 279 (Colo. Ct. App. 1994), *cert. denied* (Colo. 1995).

[96] Colo. Rev. Stat. § 38-22-106(1).

[97] *Id.* § 38-22-108.

[98] *Id.* §§ 38-22-101(2) and (3) and 38-22-102.

this protective effect, there must be both a performance bond and a labor and material payment bond, each for 150 percent of the contract price, executed by the principal contractor and a qualified corporate surety.[99] Further, notice of the bond must be filed with the clerk and recorder of the county where the property is located before the commencement of work, and the principal contractor must on the property post notice that notice of bond has been filed with the clerk and recorder and make copies of the bond available to all serving the project.[100] Should the surety become bankrupt or insolvent, lien rights exist the same as if no bond had been filed.[101] When a lien is filed on a project bonded pursuant to the statute, the lien is deemed released upon recording of a notice signed by principal and surety acknowledging the existence of the bond and that the lien claimant is entitled to claim the benefits of the bond; if the principal and surety fail to execute and record the acknowledgment within 30 days after written demand, all lien claimants can enforce their lien claims the same as if no bond had been filed.[102] Action on a bond must be brought within six months after completion of the last work on the project.[103] Those having claims of less than $2,000 can use a special procedure requiring the surety to make payment if the claim is not controverted after specified notice.[104]

An owner who leases property can protect the property from liens in consequence of improvements or other construction at the instance of the tenant. To do so, the owner-lessor must, within five days after obtaining notice of the construction, give notice by service or posting that the owner's interest will not be subject to any lien by personally serving written notice to that effect on all persons working on or supplying the project or within that same time posting and keeping posted such a notice in a conspicuous place on the property.[105]

Special protection is afforded the owners of single-family residences against the risk of having to pay twice for the same work. It is an affirmative defense to a lien claim that the owner has paid an amount sufficient to satisfy the owner's contractual and legal obligations to the principal contractor or any subcontractor for the purpose of payment to the subcontractor or supplier of materials or services to the job if the property is an existing single-family dwelling unit; is a residence constructed by the owner or under contract by the owner before occupancy as

---

[99] *Id.* § 38-22-129(1).

[100] *Id.* § 38-22-129(3).

[101] *Id.* § 38-22-129(5).

[102] *Id.* § 38-22-129(4).

[103] *Id.* § 38-22-129(2).

[104] Under Colo. Rev. Stat. § 38-22-130 (1998), one having a claim for less than $2,000 is to serve the principal contractor and surety with an affidavit, including reasonably available documentary evidence. If the affidavit is not controverted within 45 days, the surety is to forthwith pay the claim.

[105] *Id.* § 38-22-105(2). A notice of nonliability is effective even if given before the owner has notice of construction or intended construction. Frank M. Hall & Co. v. Southwest Properties Venture, 747 P.2d 688, 690 (Colo. Ct. App. 1987), *cert. denied* (1988).

owner's principal residence; or is a single-family owner-occupied dwelling unit.[106] By its terms, the defense does not exist in favor of the builder or developer of multiple residences, except as to their own occupied primary residence.

Once a mechanics' lien has been filed, the property owner can free the property from the lien by substitution of bond.[107] The bond is to be for one and one-half times the amount of the lien plus costs allowed to date, shall be conditioned as specified in the statute, is filed with the clerk of the district court for the county where the property is located, and must be approved by a judge of that court. Upon filing of such bond, the lien is released and discharged. The bond is substituted for the lien, and any action on the bond is subject to the same time limitation as an action on the lien.

---

[106] COLO. REV. STAT. §§ 38-22-102(3.5) and -113(4) (1998). Koch Plumbing & Heating, Inc. v. Brown, 835 P.2d 610 (Colo. Ct. App. 1992).

[107] COLO. REV. STAT. §§ 38-22-131 through 133.

CHAPTER 8

CONNECTICUT

Louis R. Pepe
Dan A. Haynes
Gary F. Sheldon

§ 8.01 INTRODUCTION

On private projects, Connecticut law does not require prime contractors to furnish any kind of bonds. However, Connecticut law does provide certain mechanic's lien rights on private projects. Connecticut law generally does not provide any mechanic's lien rights on public projects.

On public projects in excess of $25,000, Connecticut requires the awarding authority to include a provision in each general contract for the contractor to furnish a payment bond in the full amount of the prime contract on or before the date the contract is awarded.[1] Payment bonds on public projects in Connecticut are posted "for the protection of persons supplying labor or materials in the prosecution of the work provided for in the contract for the use of each such person."[2] Connecticut law does not require that a performance bond be posted on public projects, but one is nonetheless generally required by the awarding authority.

In Connecticut there are two principal sets of statutes governing bonds and mechanic's liens. The Connecticut statutes governing payment bonds can be found at Connecticut General Statutes §§ 49-41 *et seq.* (Little Miller Act). These statutes are generally referred to as the Little Miller Act because they are modeled in part on the Federal bond statute, the Miller Act.[3] The Connecticut mechanic's lien law can be found at Connecticut General Statutes §§ 49-33 *et seq.*

§ 8.02 BOND LAW

[A] General Concepts

In Connecticut, each construction surety bond has three parties: (1) an obligee, the beneficiary of the bond, typically the owner or general contractor; (2) a principal, typically the general contractor or subcontractor; and (3) the surety. In an action on the bond, the liability of the surety is no greater than that of its principal[4] and generally cannot exceed the penal sum. As in other jurisdictions, Connecticut surety contracts must be in writing and signed by the surety against whom the claim is made.[5] Although the liability of the surety is generally

---

[1] CONN. GEN. STAT. § 49-41(a).

[2] *Id.* Whether a project is a public work for purposes of CONN. GEN. STAT. § 49-41 has been held to turn on the degree of governmental connection with the particular work. L. Suzio Constr. Co. v. New Haven Tobacco, Inc., 28 Conn. App. 622, 611 A.2d 921 (1992) (holding that a publicly assisted, private commercial development project is not a public work); Gerrity Co. v. Pace Constr., Inc., 18 Conn. L. Rptr. No. 4, 141 (J.D. Bridgeport 1996)(holding that a municipal housing authority project is a "public work").

[3] Dysart Corp. v. Seaboard Sur. Co., 240 Conn. 10, 16, 688 A.2d 306 (1997). *See* 40 U.S.C. §§ 270a–270d.

[4] Star Contracting Corp. v. Manway Constr. Co., 32 Conn. Supp. 64, 66, 337 A.2d 669 (1973).

[5] CONN. GEN. STAT. § 52-550(a)(2).

measured by the express terms of the bond, when the bond conflicts with the terms of a statute under which it is furnished, the statutory language will establish the minimum protection of the bond.[6] However, the bond can provide greater protection than required by statute.[7] Except for statutory payment bonds discussed later in this chapter,[8] a surety bond may not limit the time for filing an action on a performance or payment bond to less than three years.[9]

In 1999, the Connecticut legislature passed a new law, *An Act Concerning Fairness in Financing in the Construction Industry,* Connecticut Public Act No. 99-153 (the "Fairness Act"), to provide additional protection to persons who provide services, labor or material on contruction projects in Connecticut.[10] This protection includes the award of interest, costs, attorney's fees and penalties for violations of the "prompt pay" provisions.[11] The Fairness Act further provides that the surety is not liable for these damages, unless the applicable bond "expressly reference[s]" the Fairness Act and states that the surety is obligated for these damages.[12]

[B] Bid Bonds

In Connecticut, a bid bond guarantees the owner that the lowest responsible bidder will enter into the contract for which the bid was submitted. Typically, the bond will provide a penal sum in a set amount in the event the contractor refuses to enter into the contract after an award is made or refuses to deliver required bonds after an award is made.[13] Bid bonds are frequently required by the terms of the bid documents for public and private projects. It is generally within the discretion of the awarding authority to require that a bid bond be posted. However, bid bonds, or some other form of security, are statutorily required on state public works projects of $50,000 or more.[14] The bond must represent at least ten percent

---

[6] MacDonald v. Standard Accident Ins. Co., 19 Conn. Supp. 257, 111 A.2d 347 (1955).

[7] Herbert S. Newman & Partners, P.C. v. CFC Constr. Ltd. Partnership, 236 Conn. 750, 674 A.2d 1313 (1996).

[8] By statute, the applicable limitations period for actions on a public works payment bond is one year. CONN. GEN. STAT. § 49-42(b)

[9] CONN. GEN. STAT. § 38a-290.

[10] The Fairness Act applies to all private commercial and industrial construction contracts entered after October 1, 1999 and establishes a fifteen day "prompt pay" requirement as a default for contracts between owners, contractors, subcontractors and suppliers within the scope of the Fairness Act. Conn. Public Act No. 99-153. The Fairness Act also modifies the law applicable to mechanic's liens; these provisions are addressed in other sections of this chapter.

[11] Conn. Public Act No. 99-153.

[12] *Id.* § 9.

[13] *See* L.F. Pace & Sons, Inc. v. Travelers Indem. Co., 9 Conn. App. 30, 514 A.2d 766 (1986), for a discussion of bid bonds.

[14] CONN. GEN. STAT. § 4b-92.

of the bid.[15] On state highway projects, a bid bond is required in an amount equal to at least one-third of the amount of the bid.[16]

[C] Performance Bonds

Although contractors are not statutorily required to provide performance bonds on either public or private contracts in Connecticut, such bonds are nonetheless common in the state. Public authorities in Connecticut have discretionary authority to require performance bonds.[17] Performance bonds are not permitted, however, on state projects on which the total estimated cost for labor and material is less than $25,000.[18] Similarly, subcontractors may not be required by the awarding authority to provide performance bonds on state projects on which the total estimated cost of subcontract work is less than $50,000.[19] Notwithstanding these limitations, nothing prevents a general contractor from requiring nonstatutory performance bonds from its subcontractors by contract.

Generally, the amount of the performance bond is either the contract price or some percentage thereof. The performance bond is a three-party instrument requiring performance by the surety when the principal defaults on its obligations in the underlying construction contract with the obligee. The performance bond obligee may be the project owner or may be a general contractor that required the performance bond from a subcontractor.[20] To trigger the surety's performance bond obligations, the bond obligee must have fully satisfied its own contractual obligations as well as any notice requirements to the surety. If so, and if the bond principal has failed to perform its obligations, the obligee may make demand upon the surety for performance.

The concept underlying the performance bond is that the contractor is expected to perform the construction contract, but if the contractor fails to perform, the surety's obligations may arise.[21] The surety's performance obligations are enumerated in the bond instrument.[22] The bond usually binds a principal and

---

[15] *Id.*

[16] *See* State of Connecticut Department of Transportation, Standard Specifications, for Roads, Bridges and Incidental Construction, Form 815 (1995).

[17] CONN. GEN. STAT. § 49-41(a).

[18] *Id.* § 49-41(b)

[19] *Id.*

[20] Through the use of a dual obligee rider, a lender may become an obligee along with the owner.

[21] City of New Haven v. Eastern Paving Brick Co., 78 Conn. 689, 698, 63 A. 517 (1906).

[22] Pittsburgh Plate Glass Co. v. Dahm, 159 Conn. 563, 567, 271 A.2d 55 (1970); Nor'easter Group, Inc. v. Colossale Concrete, Inc., 207 Conn. 468, 476 n.7, 542 A.2d 692 (1988). On state projects in Connecticut, the terms of the performance bond are usually not negotiable. For example, the Connecticut Department of Transportation form requires indemnification of the obligee for all loss due to the principal's noncompliance with the contract. Moreover, the surety, by executing the bond, waives notice of any changes up to a twenty-five percent change in the contract price. The terms of the Department of Transportation bond also require the surety to waive notice of time

surety to performance of the underlying contract. The bond terms may specifically require performance to an obligee's satisfaction. In the event of default and termination of the contractor by the owner, the surety typically may: (1) complete performance of the contract itself; (2) arrange for completion of the contract; or (3) pay the owner its reasonable costs to complete the project up to the penal sum of the bond.

The bond obligee, generally the owner, is the intended beneficiary of the performance bond. In the event of the principal's failure to perform the underlying contract, the obligee should carefully review the terms of the performance bond to make its claims on the bond in compliance with the terms of the bond and the underlying contract. The obligee must comply with any contractual requirements for declarations of default and termination as well as any conditions imposed in the bond for notice to the parties.[23] The obligee may make demand on the surety for completion, and for payment of certain related costs such as temporary safety and security measures, liquidated damages if any, as well as incidental and consequential damages, all subject to the terms of the bond and underlying contract. In short, the obligee may make claims against the surety for the damages that the bond principal would have been liable for pursuant to the terms of the underlying contract, provided such claim is consistent with the terms of the performance bond and within the penal sum of the bond.[24]

Although payment of subcontractors is generally a contractual performance obligation of the general contractor, a subcontractor is not the intended beneficiary on a performance bond, and may not seek recourse for nonpayment against a performance bond.[25]

Not only does the surety step into the shoes of the principal and assume the obligations of performing the contract work, but the surety is also subrogated to the bonded contractor's rights to payment. Pursuant to its subrogation rights, a surety has the right to file and enforce a mechanic's lien for work performed by the principal and any replacement contractor hired by the surety to complete the work.[26]

[D] Payment Bonds

On private projects, Connecticut law does not require contractors to furnish payment bonds.

---

extension by the parties. Under these terms, the surety relies entirely on the contract administration skills of its principal.

[23] Gillman v. Pedersen, 182 Conn. 582, 584, 438 A.2d 780 (1981).

[24] City of New Haven v. Eastern Paving Brick Co., 78 Conn. 689, 698, 63 A. 517 (1906).

[25] C&M Warehouse, Inc. v. Eastern Trucking, 12 Conn. L. Rptr. No. 15, 490 (J.D. Hartford/New Britain at Hartford 1994).

[26] Saint Francis Hosp. and Med. Ctr v. B&T Contractors, Inc., PJRCV960564910S (J.D. Hartford-New Britain at Hartford 1997).

On public projects in excess of $50,000, prime contractors must furnish a payment bond in the full amount of the contract price.[27] Similarly, the state may require subcontractors to provide a payment bond for subcontracts in which the total estimated costs of labor and materials is $50,000 or greater.[28] Notwithstanding the limitation, the general contractor is not prevented from requiring nonstatutory payment bonds from its subcontractors by contract.

It is the contractor's contractual obligation to provide a payment bond on public projects.[29] The Connecticut Supreme Court held that the awarding authority cannot be held liable for failure to ensure that a contractor provides a payment bond.[30] However, if no payment bond is in place, a subcontractor may claim an equitable lien against any undispersed funds.[31]

The bond statute was originally enacted in response to a Connecticut Supreme Court decision,[32] which precluded the enforcement of a mechanic's lien on public property. The payment bond is "for the protection of persons supplying labor or materials in the prosecution of the work provided for in the contract for the use of each such person."[33]

Subcontractors, as parties having a direct contractual relationship with the general contractor, are covered by the statutory bond. The bonds themselves usually include subcontractors as claimants in the body of the document. Sub-subcontractors, or second-tier subcontractors, are also covered by the bond, according to the express language of the statute, because they have a "direct contractual relationship with the subcontractor."[34] Suppliers who provided materials to the contractor or its subcontractor would also be included in the coverage of a bond. The coverage afforded by the statutory payment bond appears to be limited to second-tier subcontractors and suppliers.[35] Ultimately, the determination

[27] CONN. GEN. STAT. § 49-41(a). Consultants are explicitly excluded from the requirement of supplying payment bonds.

[28] *Id.*

[29] *Id.*

[30] O&G Indus., Inc. v. Town of New Milford, 229 Conn. 303, 640 A.2d 110 (1994).

[31] Ten Hoeve Bros., Inc. v. City of Hartford, No. 930704020 (J.D. Hartford-New Britain at Hartford 1996).

[32] National Fireproofing Co. v. Town of Huntington, 81 Conn. 632, 71 A. 911 (1909).

[33] CONN. GEN. STAT. § 49-41(a).

[34] *Id.* § 49-42(a).

[35] American Masons' Supply Co. v. F.W. Brown Co., 174 Conn. 219, 226-28, 384 A.2d 378 (1978). *See also* Dysart Corp. v. Seaboard Sur. Co., 240 Conn. 10, 688 A.2d 306 (1997) (bar that cashed payroll checks of subcontractor's employees not entitled to claim against the bond when checks were returned for lack of funds); Summit Crane Co. v. Continental Metalcraft, Inc., No. 93035564 (J.D. New Haven at New Haven 1996) (third-tier supplier not entitled to claim against the bond). *But see* Semco Mfg. Inc. v. B-G Mechanical Contractors, Inc., No. CV93-0522990S (J.D. Hartford/New Britain at Hartford 1994); Palumbo v. Aetna Cas. & Sur. Co., No. CV95-0368671 (J.D. New Haven at New Haven 1995) (third-tier supplier's claim upheld based on relationship with second-tier subcontractor).

of who is covered depends upon the contractual relationship of the potential claimant to the bond principal.

Potential claimants under a Little Miller Act bond may secure a copy of the bond from the awarding authority.[36] By statute, application for a copy of the bond must be made after labor and/or materials are supplied and remain unpaid.

Connecticut's Little Miller Act will be interpreted liberally to effectuate the purposes and intent of the Act.[37] However, timing requirements are deemed jurisdictional and are subject to a strict interpretation.[38] For purposes of the Little Miller Act, *material* includes rental value of equipment.[39] Under a liberal interpretation, most items of labor and materials incorporated into the project, or supplied with a reasonable expectation that they will be incorporated into the project, will be covered by the bond. However, there is no firm rule, "for the facts and circumstances of each case are the sole determination of the definition."[40] In Connecticut, the language of the bond statute will be read into the bond, and, to the extent conflicts occur between the bond and the statute, the statutory language will control.[41] The language of the bond, however, can be broader than the statutory language; to include coverage for services and materials beyond those covered by § 49-42.[42]

Some items are certain to be covered under the bond. Labor is explicitly included within the bond coverage.[43] Recoverable labor costs include union pension and health benefits, the recoverability of which is not preempted by the Employee Retirement Income Security Act (ERISA), 29 U.S.C. §§ 1001 *et seq.*[44] Materials are similarly covered. If allowed to be stored off site pursuant to the contract, materials supplied and stored off site may be covered by the bond. That portion of equipment that is "consumed in the process of the work is also covered under the statutory payment bond."[45] Payment for architectural services may be recoverable under the bond if the services are incoporated into the improvements.[46]

---

[36] CONN. GEN. STAT. § 49-43.

[37] Okee Indus., Inc. v. National Grange Mut. Ins. Co., 225 Conn. 367, 623 A.2d 483 (1993).

[38] *Id.*

[39] CONN. GEN. STAT. § 49-42(c).

[40] International Harvester Co. v. L.G. DeFelice & Son, Inc., 151 Conn. 325, 330, 197 A.2d 638 (1964).

[41] *Id.*

[42] Herbert S. Newman & Partners, P.C. v. CFC Constr. Ltd. Partnership, 236 Conn. 750, 674 A.2d 1313 (1996).

[43] CONN. GEN. STAT. § 49-41(a).

[44] Eacott v. Ins. Co. of N. Am., 40 Conn. App. 777, 673 A.2d 587 (1996); Bleiler v. Cristwood Constr., Inc., 72 F.3d 13 (2d Cir. 1995).

[45] International Harvester Co. v. L.G. DeFelice & Son, Inc., 151 Conn. 325, 337, 197 A.2d 638 (1964).

[46] Herbert S. Newman & Partners, P.C. v. CFC Constr. Ltd. Partnership, 13 Conn. L. Rptr. No. 5, 154 (J.D. New Haven at New Haven 1994), *aff'd,* 236 Conn. 750, 674 A.2d 1313 (1996).

Lost profits are recoverable under the bond, but only with respect to work actually performed.[47] A claimant may also recover "out of pocket" delay costs, including the rental value of idle equipment, standby labor costs, and costs incurred but not billed.[48] Connecticut's payment bond statute explicitly provides for the award of interest on moneys found to be due under the payment bond.[49] This interest does not accrue against the bond until the date of service of the claim, or the date the interest is due, whichever is later.

For all payment bonds issued after October 1, 1994, an unpaid subcontractor is entitled to seek payment under the bond 60 days after the applicable "payment due date" established by the prompt pay statute, Connecticut General Statutes § 49-41a.[50] If a first-tier subcontractor's labor or material was included in a requisition submitted by the bonded contractor, and paid by the awarding authority, the payment due date is 30 days from the date the general contractor receives payment from the awarding authority.[51] The payment due date for a second tier subcontractor is 30 days after the first-tier subcontractor receives payment from the general contractor which encompasses labor or material furnished by the second-tier-subcontractor.[52] If the work claimed was not included on a requisition, the payment due date is the date the subcontractor last performed the labor or provided the services for which the claim is made.

The claimant must also provide the bond principal with a copy of the notice.[53] The notice must contain the following information: (1) the amount of the claim, with substantial accuracy; (2) the parties to whom or for whom the labor or materials were supplied; and (3) a detailed description of the project on which the labor and/or materials were supplied. Compliance with the statutory notice requirements is a precondition to recovery on the bond and is also a jurisdictional prerequisite to bringing suit on the bond.[54] An insubstantial deviation from the content requirements of the notice will not invalidate the notice, however, as the

---

[47] Blakeslee Arpaia Chapman, Inc. v. EI Constructors, Inc., 239 Conn. 708, 721, 687 A.2d 506 (1997).

[48] *Id.*

[49] CONN. GEN. STAT. § 49-42.

[50] *Id.* In 1994, the statutory timing requirements for filing bond claims on public projects changed. The former provisions continue to apply to all bonds issued before October 1, 1994. Conn. Public Act No. 94-188. Prior to the effective date of this change, the determining factor was when the last of the material, services or equipment was furnished.

[51] CONN. GEN. STAT. § 49-42. It is unclear whether the subcontractor's work must be included in the contractor's requisition to the owner or whether work requisitioned by the subcontractor to the contractor or directly to the owner will bring the work within this provision. *See* J.J. Landerman Roofing Co., Inc. v. Orlando Annulli & Sons, Inc., CV9764108S (J.D. Tolland at Rockville 1998).

[52] *Id.*

[53] CONN. GEN. STAT. § 49-42(a). Although the statute requires that the principal receive a "copy" of the notice, a separate notice may satisfy this requirement as well. KMK Insulation, Inc. v. A. Prete and Son Constr. Co., Inc., 49 Conn. App. 522, 715 A.2d 799 (1998).

[54] Suzio Asphalt Co. v. Connecticut Indem. Co., No. 713 18 (J.D. Middlesex at Middletown 1994).

statute contains elements requiring liberal construction of form and content and strict construction of timing requirements.[55]

Any suit on the bond must be brought in the superior court in the judicial district where the contract was performed. Such suits are privileged with respect to assignment for trial.[56] A suit on the bond must be commenced within one year after the "payment due date," previously discussed, pursuant to the prompt payment statute.[57] If the contracting authority has not paid the applicable requisition, then the action is limited only by the statute of limitation for contracts.[58] In the case of a person whose labor or materials were not included in a requisition or estimate, then suit must be brought within one year from the date the materials and labor were last supplied to the project.[59] Connecticut courts lack jurisdiction to entertain a bond claim that has been filed beyond the one-year limitations period.[60]

The surety has a period of 90 days after service of the notice of the claim to make payment under the bond or deny liability. If a claim is denied, or the surety otherwise fails to respond within 90 days, the claimant may bring an action against the bond, but must do so within the one-year limitations period.[61] The failure of a surety to respond within 90 days does not extend or excuse the one-year statute of limitations period for filing a claim on the bond.[62] A surety's failure to respond to a claim as required by statute may, however, subject the surety to claims of unfair trade practices.[63] However, notwithstanding a claimed violation of Connecticut General Statutes § 49-42, an unfair trade practices claim may not lie against a surety absent a violation of the Connecticut Unfair Insurance Practices Act,[64] Connecticut General Statutes §§ 38a-815 *et seq.*

---

[55] Okee Indus., Inc. v. National Grange Mut. Ins. Co., 225 Conn. 367, 623 A.2d 483 (1993). *See also* KMK Insulation, Inc. v. A. Prete and Son Constr. Co., Inc, 49 Conn. App. 522, 715 A.2d 799 (1998).

[56] CONN. GEN. STAT. § 49-42(a).

[57] *Id.* § 49-42(b).

[58] J.J. Landerman Roofing Co., Inc. v. Orlando Annulli & Sons, Inc., CV976108S (J.D. Tolland at Rockville 1998).

[59] *Id.*

[60] American Masons Supply Co. v. F.W. Brown Co., 174 Conn. 219, 384 A.2d 378 (1978); Pittsburgh Plate Glass Co. v. Dahm, 159 Conn. 563, 271 A.2d 55 (1970).

[61] CONN. GEN. STAT. § 49-42(a).

[62] Major Machinery Corp. v. Woodland Brokers Ltd., 7 Conn. L. Rptr. 223 (J.D. Hartford/New Britain at Hartford 1992); Fisher Skylights, Inc. v. CFC Constr. Ltd. Partnership, 79 F.3d 9 (2d Cir. 1996).

[63] *See* Blakeslee Arpaia Chapman v. United States Fidelity & Guar. Co., 11 Conn. L. Rptr. 169 (J.D. New London at New London 1994); Premier Roofing Co. v. Insurance Co. of N. Am., 13 Conn. L. Rptr. No. 17, 544 (J.D. Danbury 1995); Production Equip. Co. v. Blakeslee Arpaia Chapman, Inc., 15 Conn. L. Rptr. No. 17,558 (J.D. New Haven at Meriden 1996); *but see* United States Fidelity & Guar. Co. v. Resolution Trust Corp., 20 Conn. L. Trib. No. 12, 5 (D. Conn. 1994); City of Waterbury v. Aetna Ins. Co., 13 Conn. L. Trib. No. 20, 489 (J.D. Litchfield 1987).

[64] Mountain Laurel Constr., L.L.C. v. Brennan Constr. Co., No. 960557319 (J.D. Hartford-New

Costs will be awarded to the prevailing party, with interest allowed at the rate specified in the underlying contract, or, if the contract is silent, at the interest rate provided by statute.[65] Additionally, attorneys' fees may be awarded to either party if it appears that the claims of the claimant or the defenses of the surety are without substantial basis in fact or law.[66]

In defending a bond claim, the surety may avail itself of any defense available to the general contractor.[67] However, good faith payment by the general contractor to a first-tier subcontractor is not a defense to a bond claim by a second-tier contractor.[68]

A bond claimant may also obtain a prejudgment attachment against a surety to secure its bond claim by showing probable cause to sustain the validity of the claim and by showing that the bond is insufficient to secure the claim, that is, that the claim is beyond the penal sum of the bond or that the surety is in a precarious financial condition.[69]

A bond claimant must pay attention to both the content and the timing requirements for the notice of claim. In *Okee Industries, Inc. v. National Grange Mutual Insurance Co.,*[70] the Connecticut Supreme Court discussed the level of compliance necessary to effectuate proper notice in terms of both content and timing. The Court held that the timing provisions of the payment bond statute must be strictly observed, but the provisions dealing with service and content are subject to a standard of substantial performance.[71] Under this standard, the Court held that a subcontractor had complied with the statutory notice requirements when the notice was timely although the subcontractor had failed to serve a copy of the official notice of claim on the general contractor. The Court found that the subcontractor had adequately placed the contractor on notice of its claim through previous correspondence.[72]

Britain at Hartford 1996). *But see* Premier Roofing Co., Inc. v. Ins. Co. of N. Am., 1995 WL107186 (Conn. Super. 1995); Blakeslee Arpaia Chapman v. United States Fidelity & Guar. Co., 11 Conn. L. Rptr. 169 (1994).

[65] CONN. GEN. STAT. § 37-3a.

[66] *Id.* § 49-42(a). A claimant may also be entitled to recover costs, interest, penalties and attorney's fees from the principal under the Fairness Act, Conn. Public Act No. 99-153. The surety's liability is controlled by the terms of the bond.

[67] Blakeslee Arpaia Chapman v. El Constructors, Inc., No. 040938 (J.D. Litchfield at Litchfield 1995), *aff'd,* 239 Conn. 708, 687 A.2d 506 (1997).

[68] KMK Insulation, Inc. v. A. Prete & Son Constr. Co., 14 Conn. L. Rptr. No. 10,329 (J.D. Bridgeport at Bridgeport 1995), *remanded on other grounds,* 49 Conn. App. 522, 715 A.2d 799 (1998).

[69] Blakeslee Arpaia Chapman, Inc. v. El Constructors, Inc., 32 Conn. App. 118, 628 A.2d 601 (1993).

[70] 225 Conn. 367, 623 A.2d 483 (1993).

[71] *Id.* at 374–76.

[72] *Id.* at 376. *See also* Summit Crane Co. v. Continental Metalcraft, Inc., No. 93035564 (J.D. New Haven at New Haven 1996).

After October 1, 1999, prepayment bond claim waivers are not enforceable on private commercial or industrial projects.[73]

§ 8.03 LIEN LAW

[A] General Concepts

The Connecticut mechanic's lien statutes can be found at Connecticut General Statutes §§ 49–33 *et seq.* ("lien law"). The purpose of the lien law is to provide contractors and subcontractors on private contracts with security for payment.[74] A mechanic's lien is a significant security device because it places a lien against the owner's property as the debt of the owner and operates as an encumbrance on the owner's interest in its property.

It is common for construction lenders to obtain a mortgage interest in the project and to require the owner, as a term of the construction loan, to ensure that the property will not be encumbered by mechanics' liens. A failure to do so may operate as a default on the loan and prevent the release of further financing for the project until such liens are released. The owner often passes this obligation on to the contractor by expressly requiring the contractor to satisfy or discharge all mechanics' liens on the project. Under the circumstances, a mechanics' lien is often a powerful incentive for the owner or the contractor to settle the payment claim in order to prevent the withholding of essential funding for the project.

The Connecticut mechanics' lien statutes have withstood constitutional scrutiny.[75] Although the lien law is a statutory right in derogation of the common law, its provisions are interpreted liberally to effect the remedial purpose of furnishing security for payment to those who provide services or materials.[76] However, the courts have required strict compliance with the timing requirements in the statute as a jurisdictional issue.[77]

---

[73] "Any provision in a construction contract or any periodic lien waiver issued pursuant to a construction contract that purports to waive or release the right of a contractor, subcontractor or supplier engaged to perform services, perform labor or furnish materials under the construction contract to (1) claim mechanic's lien, or (2) make a claim against a bond, for services labor or materials which have not yet been performed and paid for shall make a claim against a bond, for services, labor or materials which have not yet been performed and paid for shall be void and of no effect." Conn. Public Act No. 99-153, § 4(a). The Fairness Act also provides for interest, fees and penalties for nonpayments under construction contracts. A surety is only liable for these costs to the extent that the bond expressly references the public act and includes coverage of these costs.

[74] F.B. Mattson Co., Inc. v. Tarte, 247 Conn. 234, 237-38, 719 A.2d 1158 (1998).

[75] PDS Eng. & Constr., Inc. v. Double RS, 42 Conn. Supp. 460, 627 A.2d 959 (1992).

[76] *F.B. Mattson,* 247 Conn. at 238.

[77] Swift & Upson Lumber Co. v. W.L. Hatch Co., 115 Conn. 494, 162 A.19 (1932).

[B] Basic Provisions

In Connecticut, the right to file a mechanics' lien is statutory.[78] In Connecticut, any person with a claim of more than $10 for "materials furnished or services rendered in the construction, raising, removal or repairs of any building or any of its appurtenances or in the improvement of any lot or in the site development or subdivision of any plot of land" may file a mechanic's lien.[79]

The claim must arise out of an agreement with, or the consent of, the owner, or of some person having authority to act on behalf of the owner. In the case of a materialman that files a lien, the requisite agreement or consent of the owner does not necessitate privity in the form of a contract assented to by the owner between the original contractor and the supplier. The owner's authorization to the original contractor for procurement of the materials is sufficient owner consent.[80] When an owner hired a management company to operate a landfill, a contractor's supply of fill material to the landfill at the direction of the management company and without knowledge or consent of the owner of the property was insufficient to support a lien.[81] The determination of consent requires a finding that the owner intended to subject its interest in the property to a lien as if the owner had directly requested the work.

Generally, mechanic's lien rights only extend to persons who provide labor or material that enhances the property in some physical manner, lays the groundwork for the physical enhancement of the property, or plays an essential part in the scheme of physical improvement.[82] The services must be directly associated with the physical construction or improvement of the land.[83] Services provided in the improvement of a lot, which are not "incorporated or utilized in any building or appurtenance" are only lienable if they involve "site development" or "subdivision" of the lot.[84] In *Ceci Brothers,* the Court found that the landscaping and maintenance services provided were not lienable under this test.[85]

The general contractor, by virtue of its direct dealings with the property owner, possesses lien rights.[86] Subcontractors and entities who have contracted

---

[78] CONN. GEN. STAT. § 49-33.

[79] *Id.*

[80] Robles v. Lyon & Billard Co., CV970259867S (J.D. New Haven at Meriden 1997).

[81] Quinnipiac Real Estate and Dev. Corp. v. Cherry Hill Constr. Co., Inc., CV970398294 (J.D. New Haven at New Haven 1997).

[82] New England Sav. Bank v. Meadow Lakes Realty Co., 243 Conn. 601, 615, 706 A.2d 465 (1998); Schadtle v. TLC Homes, Inc., CV98-0578705s (Super. Ct. 1998).

[83] Thompson & Peck, Inc. v. Division Drywall, 241 Conn. 370, 380, 696 A.2d 326 (1997).

[84] Ceci Brothers, Inc. v. Five Twenty-One Corp., 51 Conn. App. 773, 724 A.2d 541 (1999).

[85] *Id.* at 778.

[86] Pursuant to their subrogation rights, performance bond sureties may also have standing to file mechanics' liens for work performed by the bonded contractor or by a takeover contractor hired by

with subcontractors, also possess lien rights.[87] It is uncertain whether a claimant beyond the second tier possesses lien rights under Connecticut law. Architects and engineers also possess lien rights provided that their plans are used in the construction of the building or improvement.[88] No Connecticut cases squarely address the rights of other entities such as a supplier of dumpster services or fuel. However, if a direct relationship can be shown to a first-tier subcontractor and the material or service can be shown to have benefited the property, the right to lien will most likely be upheld.

An estimating company providing estimating services to a general contractor has no right to file a lien, as the estimate does not attach any increment of value to the land.[89] Design, surveying, and engineering services, however, are lienable services, even if no physical improvements are made to the property.[90] A firm that performed surveying and engineering work in the site development and subdivision of a plot of land possessed lien rights.[91] Snow removal services are not lienable.[92] Charges for insurance premiums are not lienable.[93] A mechanics' lien was not permitted to secure payment for 30 kitchen cabinets when only four were actually installed.[94]

A home improvement contractor who fails to comply with the Connecticut Home Improvement Act, Connecticut General Statutes § 20-429, may not lien for work performed while in noncompliance.[95] However, a subcontractor's lien will not be invalidated because the general contractor failed to comply with the Home Improvement Act.[96]

---

the surety. Saint Francis Hosp. and Med. Ctr. v. B&T Contractors, Inc., PJRCV960564910S (J.D. Hartford-New Britain at Hartford 1997).

[87] Seaman v. Climate Control Corp., 181 Conn. 592, 595-96, 436 A.2d 271 (1980). The mechanics' lien rights of such subcontractors are based on the doctrine of subrogation. As such, the subcontractor may recover only to the extent the general contractor could recover from the property owner. W.G. Glenney Co. v. Bianco, 27 Conn. App. 199, 604 A.2d 1345 (1992).

[88] Marchetti v. Sleeper, 100 Conn. 339, 123 A. 845 (1924).

[89] Estimating Servs. Assocs., Inc. v. Forge Square Assocs. Ltd. Partnership, No. 56744 (J.D. Middlesex July 11, 1991).

[90] Design Professionals, Inc. v. Sammartino, 11 Conn. L. Rptr. 99 (J.D. Tolland 1994).

[91] New England Sav. Bank v. Meadow Lakes Realty Co., 243 Conn. 601, 614–15, 706 A.2d 465 (1998).

[92] Greenfield Village v. Gilbert Landscaping, No. 960562319S (J.D. Hartford-New Britain at Hartford 1996); Landscape Management Servs., Inc. v. Farmington Plaza Assocs., No. 940539633 (J.D. Hartford-New Britain at Hartford 1996).

[93] Thompson & Peck, Inc. v. Division Drywall, Inc., 241 Conn. 370, 696 A. 2d 326 (1997).

[94] Duran v. Kitchen/Bath Showcase, 21 Conn. L. Rptr. No. 5, 185 (J.D. New Haven at Meriden 1998).

[95] Meadows v. Higgins, 49 Conn. App. 286, 714 A.2d 51 (1998), *rev'd on other grounds,* 249 Conn. 155, ___ A.2d ___ (1999); Town & Country v. Schiller, 9 CSCR 598 (J.D. Stamford/ Norwalk at Stamford 1994).

[96] O'Donnell v. Rindfleisch, 13 Conn. App. 194, 204, 535 A.2d 824 (1988); Fink v. Olson, 18 Conn. L. Rptr. No. 7, 259 (J.D. Bridgeport at Bridgeport 1997); Baxter v. Quoka, I Conn. L. Rptr. 817 (J.D. 1990). *But see* Feola v. Capitol Contractors, Inc., 6 CSCR 819 (J.D. Waterbury 1991).

The lien statute grants lien rights to those persons rendering site development services. Thus, a site contractor may file a blanket lien upon an entire subdivision including residences that have been sold provided proper notice has been given.[97] A lienor may not, however, file a lien against a single lot in a subdivision for materials and services provided to the entire subdivision. A mechanic's lienor has the option to file a blanket lien against the entire plot of land that has been subdivided, or to file individual liens on the individual lots. However, if a lienor chooses the latter approach, each lien must be limited to the value of labor and materials provided to each respective lot.[98] A lien against an entire condominium complex was upheld, even though the materials and labor were not incorporated into every condominium unit. The court reasoned that the labor and materials were incorporated into common areas that benefited the entire condominium complex.[99] A lien was held invalid because the contractor filed the lien against only one of three parcels on which he worked, and made no attempt to allocate the work among the three parcels.[100]

Work done in connection with fixtures will also give rise to lien rights against the real property if the fixture becomes part of the realty.[101] A mechanic's lien may not be filed against a right of access, however, because such a property interest may not be assigned, transferred, mortgaged, or sold under execution as a separate and distinct entity.[102]

The general rule is that public property is not subject to lien.[103] However, if the property is not being used to fulfill a governmental function but is being used in a proprietary capacity, the immunity from lien may be lost and a lien maintained.[104] It has also been held that housing authority property is subject to a lien.[105]

Private real estate is clearly subject to mechanics' lien. However, the lien claimant must satisfy the requirements of Connecticut law that the lien arises out of "an agreement with" or "consent of" the owner. Because of the "agreement" or "consent" requirement, the contractor working for a tenant has a dilemma. A tenant, such as a shop owner in a mall, does not own the underlying land, therefore, the contract with the tenant shop owner does not support a lien right against the underlying fee. The mall owner must consent for the fee interest to be subject to a lien. Consent has been narrowly construed by Connecticut's courts.

[97] Pomarico v. Gary Constr., Inc., 5 Conn. App. 106, 497 A.2d 70 (1985).

[98] Butch v. Thangamutha, 37 Conn. App. 547, 657 A.2d 684 (1995).

[99] First National Bank v. Hemingway Ctr. Ltd. Partnership, 846 F. Supp. 186 (D. Conn. 1994).

[100] New England Sav. Bank v. Meadow Lakes Realty Co., 44 Conn. App. 240 (1997), *aff'd on other grounds,* 243 Conn. 601 (1998).

[101] Stone v. Rosenfield, 141 Conn. 188, 104 A.2d 545 (1954).

[102] Harkins v. Girouard Estates, Inc., 31 Conn. App. 485, 625 A.2d 1388 (1993).

[103] National Fireproofing Co. v. Town of Huntington, 81 Conn. 632, 71 A. 911 (1909).

[104] Jon Constr. Co. v. City Place Venture, 12:11 Conn. L. Trib. 18 (1986).

[105] Joseph L. McHugh Corp. v. Hartford Hous. Auth., 12:11 Conn. L. Trib. 18 (1986).

The consent must be shown to give rise to an "implied contract" to pay.[106] The mere granting of permission or acknowledgment of work being performed is not enough.

The claimant may also consider filing a lien against the lessee's leasehold interest. The right to lien a leasehold interest was supported in an early superior court decision, but has been consistently rejected since.[107] However, in 1999, the Connecticut legislature passed a new law, *An Act Concerning Fairness in Financing in the Construction Industry* (the "Fairness Act"), Connecticut Public Act No. 99–153, to provide additional protection to persons who provide services, labor or material on contruction projects in Connecticut.[108] As part of the Fairness Act, the Connecticut Mechanic's Lien statutes are amended to expressly permit a lien on the leasehold interest.[109]

At the time of commencement of work, the contracting property owner must hold title to or have an equitable interest in the land.[110] Even when the work continues after the owner takes title, a lien reflecting a commencement date prior to the transfer of title is not valid absent the agreement or consent of the previous owner.[111] A lien on after-acquired property is invalid.[112] The lien is valid only if the owner/seller of the property, at the time of the construction contract, had a sufficient equitable interest in the work being performed.[113] Such an equitable interest will probably be found only if the real estate sales contract requires the work to be done or reflects that the work will benefit the seller of the property.[114]

---

[106] St. Catherine's Church Corp. v. Technical Planning Assocs., Inc., 9 Conn. App. 682, 684–85, 520 A.2d 1298 (1987). *See* RJB Contracting, Inc. v. Hi-G Co., 15 Conn. L. Rptr. No. 4,128 (J.D. Hartford/New Britain at New Britain 1995) (landlord's involvement in planning of construction was insufficient to show that landlord impliedly or expressly consented to be liable for work requested by lessee). *But see* Basser v. B&G Piping Co., 1 Conn. Ops. 800 (J.D. Ansonia-Milford at Milford 1995) (when lease expressly contemplated and consented to certain tenant improvements to property, and when lease provided that any improvements would become property of owner upon termination of lease, court found the requisite owner consent to sustain lien).

[107] Battistelli v. Jacobson, 13 Conn. Supp. 196 (1944). *But see* Stamford Wrecking Co. v. Bank of Boston Connecticut, No. CV98-016 3266S (J.D. at Stamford, 1998); Calabrese Constr. v. Costco Wholesale, No. 012344 (J.D. Waterbury at Waterbury 1996); Stodolink v. Arney, Inc., 3 Conn. L. Rptr. 422 (J.D. Fairfield at Bridgeport 1991); Ebenstein & Ebenstein v. Smith Thibault Corp., No. 34552 (J.D. Hartford-New Britain at Hartford 1988).

[108] The Fairness Act applies to all private commercial and industrial construction contracts between owners, contractors, subcontractors and suppliers entered after October 1, 1999. Conn. Public Act No. 99-153. The Fairness Act also modifies the law applicable to bonds; these provisions being addressed in other sections of this chapter.

[109] Conn. Public Act No. 99-153.

[110] New England Sav. Bank v. Meadow Lakes Realty Co., 243 Conn. 601, 622, 688 A.2d 345 (1998) (commencement date prior to owner taking title to the land invalidates the lien).

[111] *Id.*

[112] *Id.* at 618-20.

[113] Centerbrook, Architects & Planners v. Laurel Nursing Servs., Inc., 224 Conn. 580, 620 A.2d 127 (1993).

[114] DiCesare-Bentley Eng'g, Inc. v. Queensgate Ltd. Partnership, 9 Conn. L. Rptr. 39 (J.D. New London at New London 1993).

Under certain circumstances, a subsequent purchaser may also be liable, as owner, for work performed at the direction of the prior owner. Typically, a purchaser will only take title to the property after addressing the disposition of any mechanics' liens, by requiring that the liens be discharged or released prior to sale, by considering the value of the liens in the purchase price, or by escrowing an appropriate sum of money pending disposition of the liens. However, when a lien for work performed for the prior owner is filed against the property after title has been transferred to the purchaser, these protections may not be available. In cases in which the purchaser was aware that the prior owner was making improvements to the property at or about the time of the closing, the purchaser has been charged with notice of potential liens for the work and held liable for the value of that work under the lien.[115]

There is scant case law in Connecticut addressing the issue of what costs may be included in the amount of a lien. Labor, materials, and services clearly come within the scope of the statute.[116] The claim must be for "materials furnished" and "services rendered." A narrow view of these provisions has been taken by Connecticut courts, which hold that the materials or services must actually be used in the project.[117] Any attempt to include a particular cost in a lien should be supported by an argument that the item claimed somehow became used or incorporated into the project. After applying this rule, consider including the cost of the following items in any lien: rental equipment, temporary work, overhead, and delay-related damages. Both contractual and statutory interest are secured by the lien.[118]

[C] Notice and Recording Requirements

Connecticut's lien law contains various notice and recording requirements that are strictly enforced.

Generally, all those claimants not in privity of contract with the owner must provide a notice of intent to file a lien. The notice must be served upon the owner of the building or property and the general contractor, if the general contractor has filed the required affidavit.[119] A notice of intent to lien need not be given prior to recording a lien, and service of the lien certificate itself meets the statutory notice of lien requirements.[120] The Connecticut Supreme Court held that a mort-

---

[115] Waterbury Lumber & Coal Co. v. Asterchinsky, 87 Conn. 316, 87 A. 739 (1913); Sullivan v. Buckland Meadow Assoc., Docket No. 9251236 (J.D. Tolland at Rockville 1996).

[116] CONN. GEN. STAT. § 49-33.

[117] Lewin & Sons, Inc. v. Herman, 143 Conn. 146, 120 A.2d 423 (1956).

[118] CONN. GEN. STAT. § 52-249; S.J. Smith Constr., Inc. v. Home Depot U.S.A., 21 Conn. L. Rptr. No. 3, 80 (J.D. Stamford 1998).

[119] CONN. GEN. STAT. § 49-35 provides that a general contractor is entitled to the same notice of lien as an owner only if the general contractor files on the land records of the town where the project is located an affidavit: (1) stating the number under which the general contractor conducts business; (2) stating the general contractor's business address; and (3) describing the project. This affidavit must be filed by the general contractor no later than 15 days after commencing work.

[120] H&S Torrington Assoc. v. Lutz Eng'g Co., 185 Conn. 549, 555, 441 A.2d 171 (1981).

gagee bank is not an owner for purposes of the mechanic's lien statute, and thus is not entitled to receive notice of the lien.[121]

In order for a lien to attach to individual units of a condominium development, each individual owner must be served.[122] Failure of such service will result in the lien not attaching to the property of the individual owners. Property owned in the name of a partnership also creates an interesting problem. In the case of a general partnership in which all the partners can be identified and served, it would be prudent to serve all of the partners. However, in the case of a limited partnership or a general partnership with numerous or unidentified partners, service on a general partner or agent registered with the secretary of state in the manner prescribed in the lien law will suffice.[123]

The notice of intent to lien must be served after work has commenced but no later than 90 days after work has ceased. As discussed below, the certificate of mechanics' lien must also be recorded within 90 days of the last work. The 90 days is counted by excluding the last day worked but including the 90th day.[124] When the 90th day falls on a holiday or weekend, it is advisable to record the lien and provide notice beforehand. The general rule is that the last day of work will control unless the contractor unreasonably delayed the completion of trivial or inconsequential work after substantial completion.[125] However, work after substantial completion, if requested by the owner, will be sufficient to extend the lien period.[126] Although the issuance of a certificate of occupancy may be a factor among many for determining the last day of lienable work, the mere issuance of a certificate is not dispositive of the issue.[127]

In *F. B. Mattson Co. v. Tarte,*[128] the Connecticut Supreme Court clarified that work requested by the owner is lienable even if the work was trivial and unreasonably delayed by the contractor.[129] The date of substantial completion will only control as the "last worked" date when all work furnished after that date was: (1) unreasonably delayed by the contractor; and (2) at the contractor's initiative, not the owner's request.[130] Further, the *Mattson* court held that the removal of equipment is lienable work if it requires "repair to the building."[131]

---

[121] Red Rooster Constr. Co. v. River Assocs., Inc., 224 Conn. 563, 620 A.2d 118 (1993).

[122] Papa v. Greenwich Green, Inc., 177 Conn. 295, 416 A.2d 1196 (1979).

[123] Fischbach-Natkin Co. v. Hartford Parkview Assocs. Ltd. Partnership, 9:16 Conn. L. Trib. 17 (1983).

[124] R&R Pool & Spa, Inc. v. Robert Disney, 15:11 Conn. L. Trib. 22 (1989).

[125] Martin Tire & Rubber Co. v. Kelly Tire & Rubber Co., 99 Conn. 396, 122 A. 102 (1923).

[126] F.B. Mattson Co., Inc. v. Tarte, 247 Conn. 234, 237–38, 719 A.2d 1158 (1998).

[127] *Id. See also* Jackson v. Fortunato, CV880096695 (J.D. Stamford-Norwalk at Stamford 1997) (fifteen "punchlist" items performed subsequent to the issuance of a certificate of occupancy did not constitute "trivial" work, and thus constituted lienable work).

[128] 247 Conn. 234, 719 A.2d 1158 (1998).

[129] 247 Conn. at 240.

[130] *Id.*

[131] *Id.* at 241–42.

The removal of roof brackets in *Mattson* required the replacement of shingles and other work totalling sixteen hours. The Court determined that this work was lienable and that the lien was valid.[132]

The only thing required to be stated in the notice of intent to lien is that the claimant has furnished or has commenced to furnish materials or services and intends to claim a lien therefor.[133]

Care must be taken to follow the service requirements. All owners and general contractors, when applicable, must be properly served. Failure to properly serve all property owners will invalidate the lien.[134] Service on a condominium association is insufficient to protect the statutory and constitutional rights of the individual condominium unit owners.[135] When a lienor provides an overly inclusive property description, failure to provide notice to all owners, including the owners of the overly inclusive portions of the description, may render the lien invalid.[136] The failure to serve all joint property owners may render the lien invalid, even when the lien is to be enforced only against one of them.[137] The owner or general contractor must receive in-hand or abode service if they reside in the same town as the project.[138] If the owner or general contractor does not live in the same town as the project, but a known agent resides in the town, a notice may be served upon the agent. Otherwise, service by certified mail may be directed to the place where the owner or general contractor resides.[139] In cases where it is not clear whether the entity "resides" in the town, service at the "in town" address and certified mail to any other likely address(es) is prudent. It is imperative that these rules be carefully followed. Failure to strictly adhere to the statutory service requirements will deprive the court of jurisdiction and require discharge of the lien.[140]

The lien must be recorded in the land records of the town where the project is located within 90 days of the last day worked.[141] Within the same 90-day period, but no later than 30 days after the lien is recorded, a copy of the lien must be served on all property owners.[142] When work on one project proceeds under different contracts and the work overlaps, a single lien may be filed for both contracts within the time that work ceased on the entire project.[143] However,

---

[132] *Id.*

[133] CONN. GEN. STAT. § 49-35.

[134] Round-house Constr. Corp. v. Telesco Masons Supplies Co., 168 Conn. 371, 362 A.2d 778 (1975); Kababik v. Hydraulic Repair Co., Inc., 7 Conn. L. Rptr. No. 10, 280 (J.D. Ansonia/Milford at Milford 1992).

[135] Papa v. Greenwich Green, Inc., 177 Conn. 295, 416 A.2d 1196 (1979).

[136] Milone & MacBroom, Inc. v. Bysiewicz Corp., 9 Conn. L. Rptr. 404 (J. D. Middlesex 1993).

[137] Diversified Floors, Inc. v. Shaw, 8 Conn. L. Rptr. 611 (J.D. Hartford/New Britain at Hartford 1993).

[138] *Id.*

[139] Optima Invs. v. Scinto, 12:10 Conn. L. Trib. 14 (1986).

[140] Nadeau v. Bagley, No. 54613 (J.D. Tolland at Rockville 1994).

[141] CONN. GEN. STAT. § 49-34.

[142] *Id.*

[143] Waterbury Constr. Co. v. Northeast Drywall, Inc., 12:44 Conn. L. Trib. 9 (1986).

contract work for another party on the same project may not be sufficient to extend the last day of work performed under a separate contract.[144]

Connecticut statutes set forth what must be stated in the lien.[145] First, the basis for the claim must be stated. It must identify whether the lien derives from an agreement with the property owner or consent of the property owner.[146] The property liened must be described, the amount of the lien must be stated, the persons against whom the lien is claimed must be named, and the first and last days of work must be stated.[147] The last day of work, while not an enumerated requirement found in the statute, should nonetheless be stated, as this date is required to determine the lien's validity. In the alternative, the lien should state the lien is recorded within 90 days of the last work performed. The lien statement must also contain a statement "that the amount claimed is justly due, as nearly as the same can be ascertained."[148] Even absent the magic words "the amount claimed is justly due," a lien properly sworn to, which states the amount of the lien, substantially complies with the "justly due" requirement. The entire lien statement must then be subscribed and sworn to by the claimant. This requirement must be strictly followed.[149] The lien must be signed by the lienor, not its attorney.[150] Finally, dishonest or fraudulent statements can be grounds for the invalidation of the lien.[151]

The failure to include a commencement date may render the lien invalid.[152] An incorrect commencement date may also invalidate the lien.[153] Incorrectly naming the owner of the property may invalidate the lien.[154]

The party filing the lien must be the same entity that performed the work on the property. When a company contracted to perform under an unregistered

---

[144] Connecticut Resources Recovery v. Archer, 17 Conn. L. Trib. 27 (J.D. Ansonia-Milford at Milford 1991).

[145] CONN. GEN. STAT. §§ 49-33 *et seq.*

[146] *Id.* § 49-33.

[147] *Id.* § 49-34.

[148] *Id.;* Technico-Op v. Alvin Constr. Co., No. 0321181 (J.D. Fairfield at Fairfield 1996).

[149] J.C. Penney Properties, Inc. v. Peter M. Santella Co., 210 Conn. 511, 555 A.2d 990 (1989); Red Rooster Constr. Co. v. River Assocs., Inc., 224 Conn. 563, 620 A.2d 118 (1993).

[150] Brochu v. Northwest Lumber & Hardware, Inc., 11 Conn. L. Rptr. 160 (J.D. Litchfield at Litchfield 1994).

[151] Morici v. Jarvie, 137 Conn. 97, 75 A.2d 47 (1950). Even when there is no evidence that an oral oath or other oath-taking ceremony was administered, the presence of a signed statement swearing to the truth of the facts stated in the certificate of lien has been held sufficient. Technico-Op v. Alvin Constr. Co., No. 0321181 (J.D. Fairfield at Fairfield 1996).

[152] Brochu v. Northwest Lumber & Hardware, Inc., 11 Conn. L. Rptr. 160 (J.D. Litchfield at Litchfield 1994).

[153] Systematics, Inc. v. Forge Square Assocs. Ltd. Partnership, 13 Conn. L. Rptr. No. 15, 497 (J.D. Middlesex at Middletown 1995).

[154] Fisher Skylights, Inc. v. Mashantucket Pequot Indian Tribe, 9 CSCR 843 (J.D. New London at Norwich 1994). *But see* Big Y Trust v. Wesco Distribution, Inc., 15 Conn. L. Rptr. No. 15, 501 (J.D. Windham at Putnam 1995) (incorrectly naming owner did not invalidate lien when actual owner received notice of lien and there was no evidence that it was misled by incorrect reference).

trade name, and later filed a lien under its official corporate name, the lien was declared invalid because the entity that filed the lien was not the same entity with an enforceable contract on which to base its claim.[155]

When insubstantial deviations exist, aside from the omission of statutorily required content, courts will not invalidate the lien if the mistakes were made in good faith and do not prejudice the property owner. For example, the failure to state an intention to lien will not invalidate the lien.[156] Depending on the degree of error, an overly inclusive or defective property description may not render the lien invalid.[157] The extent to which an interested party would be mislead is relevant to this determination. An incorrect statement of the amount due will not invalidate the lien.[158] A lienor may also introduce evidence substantiating a completion date other than the date stated in the lien.[159] In fact, a mechanics' lien may secure payment for additional work performed after the filing of the lien.[160] When a lien inadvertently misdesignated a former corporation as the lienor instead of the surviving successor corporation, the lien was nonetheless valid.[161]

The lien certificate is served in the same manner as the notice of intent. Although Connecticut law does not explicitly state that the lien must be served on the general contractor, it is advisable that a subcontractor do so.

[D] Foreclosure

Once the lien has been perfected by proper service, notice, and recording, the lienor has one year to commence an action to foreclose the lien.[162] Mechanic's liens are foreclosed in the same manner as a mortgage.[163] In addition, the lienor must file a lis pendens on the land records within the one-year period, evidencing the foreclosure action.[164] Failure to commence an action or file a lis pendens within the one-year period renders the mechanic's lien invalid and automatically dis-

[155] Schwartz v. Best Constr. & Dev. Co., No. CV95-0142999 (J.D. Stamford/Norwalk at Stamford 1995).

[156] H&S Torrington Assocs. v. Lutz Eng'g Co., 185 Conn. 549, 555–56, 441 A.2d 171 (1981).

[157] Burque v. Naugatuck Lumber Co., 113 Conn. 350, 353, 155 A. 414 (1932); Milone & MacBroom, Inc. v. Bysiewicz Corp., 9 Conn. L. Rptr. 404 (J.D. Middlesex 1993).

[158] Morici v. Jarvie, 137 Conn. 97, 102, 75 A.2d 47 (1950).

[159] Westland v. Goodman, 47 Conn. 83, 86 (1879).

[160] Anthony Julian R.R. Constr. Co. v. Mary Ellen Drive Assocs., 39 Conn. App. 544, 664 A.2d 1177 (1995), *cert. denied,* 235 Conn. 930, 667 A.2d 800 (1995).

[161] Tilcon Connecticut, Inc. v. J.E Barrett & Sons, Inc., CV97574226 (J.D. Hartford-New Britain at Hartford 1998).

[162] In the event of bankruptcy by the property owner, the one-year period to foreclose a lien is extended by 11 U.S.C. § 108(c) until 30 days after receipt of notice of termination of the bankruptcy stay. Incorporated Constr. Ltd. v. New England Sav. Bank, 13 Conn. L. Rptr. No. 10, 332 (J.D. Hartford/New Britain at Hartford 1995). CONN. GEN. STAT. § 49-39.

[163] CONN. GEN. STAT. § 49-33(h). *See also id.* § 49-47a.

[164] *Id.* § 49-39.

charges the lien as a matter of law.[165] The lis pendens must also be served on the property owner by a sheriff or indifferent person, by abode service or certified mail in the same manner as the lien.[166]

When foreclosing on a mechanic's lien, the foreclosure complaint must set forth (1) all prior and subsequent encumbrances of record upon the subject property;[167] (2) the amount of each encumbrance; (3) the date of each encumbrance; (4) the date each encumbrance was recorded; and (5) the date of commencement for the mechanic's lien.[168] A party need not, however, plead the existence of a lienable fund from which the lien may be satisfied.[169]

The plaintiff in a successful mechanic's lien foreclosure action is also entitled to recover reasonable attorney's fees and costs pursuant to Connecticut General Statutes § 52-249.[170] The recovery of attorney's fees incurred on appeal is also allowed.[171] Although not recoverable under existing caselaw, after October 1, 1999 attorneys' fees will also be recoverable on a bond substituted for a mechanic's lien.[172]

[E] Waiver

Prior to October 1, 1999, advance lien waivers in construction contracts were enforceable on all projects in Connecticut. However, on that date, the Fairness Act, Public Act No. 99-153, becomes effective and forbids all pre-payment lien waivers for all private commercial and industrial construction projects within the State of Connecticut, including lien waivers found in prime contracts and subcontracts.[173] It is expected that this prohibition will be applied only to waivers related

---

[165] *Id.* § 49-40a; H.G. Bass Assocs., Inc. v. Ethan Allen, Inc., 26 Conn. App. 426, 601 A.2d 1040 (1992). If a lien has expired, the continued existence of the unreleased lien will not affect title or marketability of property.

[166] CONN. GEN. STAT. § 52-325(c).

[167] Although other mechanics' liens must be identified in the complaint, the other lien holders are not necessary parties and need not be joined as defendants to the foreclosure action. D&G Plumbing & Heating Co. v. Malon, 13 Conn. L. Rptr. No. 11 (J.D. Tolland at Rockville 1995).

[168] CONN. PRACTICE BOOK § 10-69.

[169] Pagnelli Constr. v. United Natural Foods, Inc., No. 970569803 (J.D. Hartford-New Britain at New Britain 1998).

[170] A. Secondino & Sons, Inc. v. Loricco, 19 Conn. App. 8, 561 A.2d 142 (1988).

[171] Stergue v. Serpico, 17 Conn. L. Rptr. 360 (J.D. Danbury 1996).

[172] Conn. Public Act No. 99-153.

[173] "Any provision in a contruction contract or any periodic lien waiver issued pursuant to a construction contract that purports to waive or release the right of a contractor, subcontractor or supplier engaged to perform services, perform labor or furnish materials under the contruction contract to (1) claim a mechanic's lien, or (2) make a claim against a bond, for services, labor or materials which have not yet been performed and paid for shall be void and of no effect." Conn. Public Act No. 99-153, § 4(a).

The scope of the Fairness Act is limited to commercial or industrial buildings requiring a certificate of occupancy and expressly excludes public construction. *See* Conn. Public Act No.

to commercial and industrial construction contracts entered after the effective date of the Fairness Act and not to waivers on existing contracts.

The use of lien waivers is often mandated by the owner whose construction financing is contingent upon unencumbered property. After the effective date of the Fairness Act, parties to contracts within the scope of the Fairness Act will retain the ability to agree to subordinate lien rights to mortgage or security interests for this purpose. The Fairness Act also has no effect on the validity of lien waivers given in exchange for payment.

Beyond the scope of the Fairness Act, lien waivers may be supportable without payment.[174] The "consideration" being that a contractor is motivated to release the lien by "the expectation that his employer will put in funds out of which he hopes to be paid in whole or part."[175] A lien waiver is invalid, however, when it fails to describe the property to which it applies.[176] When the language is clear and unambiguous, the waiver is upheld as a matter of law.[177]

Partial lien waivers are also common in Connecticut. They generally come in two varieties. One type waives the right to claim a lien up to the amount paid. The other type waives the right to claim a lien for all work up to a certain date. Execution of the second type, if the language is unambiguous, will most likely lead to a waiver of the right to lien for claimed extra work accomplished within the period covered by the waiver. As such, contractors should be extremely cautious before signing partial lien waivers of this type.

Although advance lien waivers are generally enforceable,[178] enforcement may be inappropriate when an advance waiver appears inconsistent with the parties' intentions reflected in other provisions of the agreement. One superior court refused to enforce a subcontractor's full advance lien waiver because the subcontractor subsequently executed two partial lien waivers, each of which were restricted to work performed between specific dates.[179] However, the Connecticut Appellate Court has upheld an advance lien waiver provision in a subcontract,

---

99-153, § 1(2). This limited scope may not apply to the revisions to existing statutes: permitting liens on leaseholds; and providing for attorney's fees on mechanic's lien bonds, which do not reference the limiting definitions of the Fairness Act. Conn. Public Act No. 99-153, §§ 7 and 8. *See* CONN. GEN. STAT. §§ 49-33(h) and 52-249 (1999).

[174] *See supra* note 171 for the scope of the Fairness Act.

[175] Bialowans v. Minor, 209 Conn. 212, 550 A.2d 637 (1988). Lien waivers are not executory promises but fully executed promises, thus rendering the doctrine of consideration inapplicable. A&J Painting, Inc. v. Percy, No. CV-93-52434-S (J.D. Tolland 1993).

[176] J. Iapaluccio, Inc. v. Anderson, No. 322734 (J.D. Danbury at Danbury 1996) (lien waiver referred to an attached property description, which was missing).

[177] Cadoux Corp. v. Rollinson, 13:34 Conn. L. Trib. 16 (1987); Townsend v. Barlow, 101 Conn. 86, 124 A. 832 (1924); Yang v. Stevenson Millwork, No. CV 95-0144885 (J.D. Stamford/ Norwalk at Stamford 1995).

[178] *But see* Conn. Public Act No. 99-153.

[179] Nutmeg Housing v. Acequia Constr., No. CV 125182 (J.D. Waterbury 1995).

notwithstanding language in the subcontract that also required the execution of ongoing partial lien waivers.[180]

A contractor cannot bargain away the lien rights of its subcontractors.[181] However, the contractor may be contractually obliged to discharge all liens. An owner may enforce a subcontractor's lien waiver, especially when lien waivers are necessary for the owner to obtain construction financing for the project.[182] Furthermore, a subcontractor's waiver survives the contractor's breach of contract.[183]

[F] Lien Priority

In Connecticut, the precedence and amount of a lien is determined by statute.[184] First, precedence is governed by the first day worked, not the day of filing. Thus, the lien statute is not a race statute. In the case of a mortgage, the mortgagee's precedence is established by the date of recording. If the lienor commenced work before the recording of the mortgage, the lienor will have precedence.[185] Second, Connecticut follows the so-called New York rule, limiting the amount of all liens to the amount due from the owner to the original general contractor,[186] including contractual interest[187] and presumably contractual attorney's fees and penalties. Thus, an owner need only pay once for the project.[188]

The fact that mechanics' lien priorities relate back to the contractor's first day of work can cause problems for mortgagees when an owner finalizes financing arrangements *after* a project has begun, thereby placing the mortgagees' priority behind the lien of any contractor who began work before the mortgage was recorded on the land records. To avoid this problem, and to induce financing for a project, it is common for a mortgagee to require subordination agreements[189]

---

[180] Snydergeneral Corp. v. Lee Parcel 6 Assocs. Ltd. Partnership, 43 Conn. App. 32, 681 A.2d 1008 (1996).

[181] Pero Building Co. v. Smith, 6 Conn. App. 180, 504 A.2d 524 (1986).

[182] Fourth New London NSB Quarters, Inc. v. Wyoming Valley Contractors, Inc., 22 Conn. Supp. 293, 170 A.2d 737 (1961); Townsend v. Barlow, 101 Conn. 86, 124 A. 832 (1924).

[183] 22 Conn. Supp. at 296.

[184] CONN. GEN. STAT. §§ 49-33 and 49-36.

[185] Gruss v. Miskinis, 130 Conn. 367, 34 A.2d 600 (1943).

[186] When the general contractor on a new home was not to be paid by the property owner, but by a future third-party purchaser of the home, there existed no lienable fund to support a subcontractor's mechanic's lien. Fox Cliff Blocks v. Balf Co., No. CV 95-57060 (J.D. Tolland at Rockville 1995).

[187] S.J. Smith Constr., Inc. v. Home Depot U.S.A., 21 Conn. L. Rptr. No. 3, 80 (J.D. Stamford 1998).

[188] Seaman v. Climate Control Corp., 181 Conn. 592, 605-07, 436 A.2d 271 (1980).

[189] The relative priority of lienors and other encumbrances can be modified by the execution of a subordination agreement. Generally, a subordination agreement only affects the relative priorities of the parties to the agreement by reversing their respective priorities in relation to one another, but such an agreement does not affect the priorities of persons who are not parties to the agreement.

from contractors who have begun work on the project prior to the recording of the mortgage on the land records. Under such an agreement, the contractor agrees to subordinate its lien fights to the priority of the mortgage. These agreements remain enforceable after Connecticut Public Act No. 99-153 comes into effect.

With respect to competing mechanics' lienors, the general rule is one of apportionment, but there are exceptions. For instance, one exception arises if an encumbrance other than a lien is recorded during construction. In this event, three classes of priority are established in the following order: (1) all liens originating before the encumbrance; (2) the encumbrance; and (3) all liens originating after the encumbrance.[190] No lienor in its respective class has priority over other lienors in the class.

If the lienable fund is insufficient to pay all liens, all subcontractors will get paid in full first and the general contractor will be paid whatever is left.[191] If the fund is insufficient to pay all subcontractors, they will be paid on a pro rata basis, and the general contractor will be paid nothing.

In addition to following the New York rule limiting the amount of all liens to the amount due from the owner to the original general contractor, Connecticut also allows the owner to deduct from the potential lienable fund any good faith payments made to the original contractor, and in the case of a default of the original general contractor, to deduct reasonable completion costs and any damages resulting from the default.[192] Payments are made in "good faith" if they are paid after they are due and before the owner receives notice of the subcontractor's lien.[193] Under the statutory definition of a "good faith" payment, a naive and well-intentioned owner is not protected when it makes final payment to the general contractor after receiving notice of a subcontractor's lien.[194]

The owner may not safely make advance payments to the general contractor without giving at least five days' advance written notice to all persons "known to have furnished materials or rendered services" on the project.[195] The five-day notice requirement, however, applies only to subcontractors working on the project at the time of the advance payment, not to subcontractors who may commence work on the project after the advance is made. Therefore, when a subcontractor first came on the project several weeks after the owner made an advance payment to the general contractor, the subcontractor could not claim that the earlier advance was made in bad faith due to the owner's failure to provide notice to those sub-

---

See Duraflex Sales & Serv. Corp. v. W.H.E. Mechanical Contractors, 110 F.3d 927 (2d Cir. 1997); RJB Constr. Inc. v. Hi-G Co., 2 Conn. Ops. 107 (J.D. Hartford-New Britain at New Britain 1995).

[190] *See* CONN. GEN. STAT. § 39-33(d).

[191] *Id.* § 49-35(b).

[192] *Id.* § 49-33(f). Rene Dry Wall Co. v. Strawberry Hill Assocs., 182 Conn. 568, 572-75, 438 A.2d 774 (1980).

[193] CONN. GEN. STAT. § 49-33(f).

[194] J.J. Mottes Co. v. Plourde, CV 93-52770 (J.D. Tolland at Rockville 1995).

[195] *Id.* Notice of advance payment must be given five days prior to the payment. CONN. GEN. STAT. § 49-36(c).

contractors working on the project at the time of the advance.[196] An initial "deposit" given to the contractor by the owner prior to construction, although it was not a construction progress payment, was still a payment made in good faith to which the owner was entitled a setoff against a subcontractor's mechanics' lien.[197]

[G] Lien Discharge or Reduction

Under Connecticut General Statutes § 49-35a, an owner may apply to the Superior Court for a hearing to determine whether the lien should be discharged or reduced.[198] The burden is initially on the lienor to establish "probable cause" to sustain the validity of the lien.[199] Probable cause is established by showing a bona fide belief in the existence of facts essential under the law to support the action which would warrant a person of ordinary caution, prudence, and judgment, under the circumstances, to entertain the action.[200] If probable cause is established, then the owner must prove the invalidity or excessiveness of the lien by "clear and convincing" evidence.[201]

Under this procedure, the court may: (1) deny the owner's application; (2) declare the lien invalid; (3) reduce the lien amount; or (4) discharge or reduce the lien upon the posting of a bond to indemnify the lienor for any damages as a result of the discharge or reduction.[202] A judicial decision rendered pursuant to this statute is deemed a final judgment[203] and is appealable within seven days from issuance of the court order.[204] The order is stayed pending the expiration of the appeal period.[205] The discharge (reduction) order takes effect upon the recording of a certified copy on the land records.[206] The court clerk may not provide a certified copy during the appeal period.[207] This stay applies only to the order to "discharge" a lien and not the dismissal of liens upon the posting of a bond, discussed in **§ 8.03[H]**.

An application to discharge or reduce a mechanics' lien invokes a special

---

[196] Waterbury Landfill Assocs. v. Eastern Co., No. 0122318 (J.D. Waterbury at Waterbury 1996).

[197] Mancini v. Landmark Excavating, 14 Conn. L. Rptr. No. 12,371 (J.D. Waterbury 1995).

[198] An application to discharge or reduce the lien must be filed in the Judicial District where the lien may be foreclosed. CONN. GEN. STAT. § 49-35a(a).

[199] *Id.* § 49-35b(a).

[200] Pero Bldg. Co. v. Smith, 6 Conn. App. 180, 504 A.2d 524 (1986).

[201] CONN. GEN. STAT. § 49-35b(a).

[202] *Id.* § 49-35b(b). If the owner's application is denied, the lienor still must commence a timely foreclosure action to enforce the lien.

[203] *Id.* § 49-35c(A).

[204] *Id.* § 49-35c(b). If the lien is discharged by the court during trial, as opposed to by the special application procedures of § 49-35a, a party is entitled to the normal 20-day period for appealing final judgments. New England Sav. Bank v. Meadow Lakes Realty Co., 235 Conn. 663, 668 A.2d 712 (1996).

[205] CONN. GEN. STAT. § 49-35c(b).

[206] *Id.* § 49-35c(d).

[207] *Id.*

statutory proceeding that is not the equivalent of an ordinary civil action. Therefore, the filing of counterclaims is not permitted.[208]

If there is an arbitration agreement between the parties, the validity of the lien may be a question for the arbitrator, requiring that the lien discharge proceedings be stayed pending arbitration.[209]

[H] Substitution of Lien Bond

When the validity of a lien is questionable, the Connecticut statutes provide an opportunity for "the owner of that real estate, or any person interested in it," to make application to the Superior Court that the lien be dissolved upon the substitution of a "bond, with sufficient surety."[210] This procedure may be preferred when the owner wants to avoid the time and expense of a full hearing to discharge the lien or when the contractor has a contractual obligation to remove the lien from the land records.

A cash bond held in escrow will also satisfy the bond requirement.[211] The "interested person" language of § 49-37 has been interpreted to provide a contractor with standing to bring such an application.[212] Although the statute requires that the court be satisfied that "the applicant in good faith intends to contest the lien," such applications are liberally granted by the courts.[213] This statute is designed to facilitate a transfer of property by dissolution of the lien and at the same time ensure the continued existence of assets from which the lienor may satisfy its claim if it should later prevail and obtain judgment on the merits of the lien.[214]

After the court orders the bond substitution and returns the order to the court clerk, the applicant has 10 days within which to file a certified copy of the court's order on the land records, which automatically discharges the mechanic's lien as a matter of law.[215] The 10-day period, however, is not mandatory and may be deviated from without prejudice to the lienor's rights.[216]

Parties may also agree to substitute a mechanics' lien bond voluntarily in

---

[208] Baxter v. Quoka, 3 Conn. L. Rptr. 425 (J.D. Ansonia-Milford at Milford 1991); Griswold Rubber Co. v. Connecticut Concrete Co., No. CV960053966S (J.D. Windham at Putnam 1997).

[209] Grisanti v. Round Hill Properties, Ltd., No. CV 970160887S (J.D. Stamford-Norwalk at Stamford 1998).

[210] CONN. GEN. STAT. § 49-37(a). An application to substitute a bond for mechanic's lien may be filed in any Judicial District. However, the court's substitution order must be returned to the court clerk of the judicial district where the lien is recorded. *Id.* Any surety authorized to do business in the state is "sufficient." *Id.* § 52-189.

[211] Snelser v. Newick, No. CV980408679 (J.D. New Haven at New Haven 1998).

[212] Henry E. Raab Connecticut, Inc. v. J.W. Fisher Co., 183 Conn. 108, 438 A.2d 834 (1981).

[213] CONN. GEN. STAT. § 49-37(a).

[214] Henry F. Raab Connecticut, Inc. v. J.W. Fisher Co., 183 Conn. 108, 438 A.2d 834 (1981).

[215] CONN. GEN. STAT. § 49-37(a).

[216] H.C. Tedford Assoc. v. Federal Deposit Ins. Corp., 9 Conn. L. Rptr. 503 (J.D. Ansonia-Milford at Milford 1993).

exchange for release of a mechanics' lien. Such a voluntary substitution of a lien bond will be treated as a substitution under that statute and will not deprive the court of jurisdiction to discharge or modify the bond pursuant to § 49–37, and does not alter the one-year limitations period for bringing suit on the bond.[217] When a bond is substituted by agreement the court will incorporate the terms of the mechanics' lien bond statute to effectuate its remedial purpose.

Once a bond is substituted, the principal or surety on the bond may seek discharge of the bond by a procedure similar to the discharge of a mechanics' lien.[218] Once a bond is substituted, however, some mechanics' lien defenses become impractical and are no longer available. Specifically, insufficient equity in the property may not be used to defeat or reduce the lien bond.[219]

The lienor still has one year from the date of perfecting the original lien within which to bring suit on the bond.[220] Suit on the bond is a much easier process than foreclosing on the mechanics' lien, because prior and subsequent encumbrancers are no longer involved in the action. The only proper parties are the surety, the bond principal (usually the owner or contractor), and the lienor. Although a bond may be substituted during a pending lien foreclosure action, a bond may not be substituted after judgment has entered and while an appeal is pending.[221] If a foreclosure action was commenced on the lien prior to substitution of the bond, all other previously cited parties must be dropped from the suit.[222]

Prior to October 1999, attorneys' fees were not generally recoverable on a bond substituted for a mechanics' lien.[223] One case suggested that the lien must expressly claim or include an additional value for attorneys' fees in order to secure such fees by the lien.[224] Effective October 1, 1999, the Fairness Act amends Connecticut General Statutes § 52–249 to expressly provide for attorney's fees in the enforcement of a bond substituted for a mechanic's lien.[225]

[I] Invalid Liens

As discussed in **§ 8.03[G]**, only an owner may seek immediate discharge or reduction of a mechanic's lien under Connecticut General Statutes § 49-35a. Typically, a contractor seeking to discharge or reduce a lien must first substitute

---

[217] New Haven Windstrial Co. v. Six Carpenters, Inc., 12 Conn. L. Trib. No. 21, 37 (J.D. New Haven at New Haven 1986).

[218] CONN. GEN. STAT. § 49-37(b).

[219] First Fed. Sav. & Loan Ass'n v. Barrett, 11 Conn. L. Rptr. No. 20, 634 (J.D. Waterbury 1994).

[220] CONN. GEN. STAT. § 49-37(a).

[221] Anthony Julian R.R. Constr. Co. v. Mary Ellen Drive Assocs., 12 Conn. L. Rptr. No. 9, 298 (J.D. Ansonia-Milford at Milford 1994), 39 Conn. App. 544, 664 A.2d 1177 (1995), *cert. denied,* 235 Conn. 930, 667 A.2d 800 (1995).

[222] H.C. Tedford Assoc. v. Federal Deposit Ins. Corp., 9 Conn. L. Rptr. 503 (J.D. Ansonia-Milford at Milford 1993).

[223] Conn. Public Act No. 99-153.

[224] Snelser v. Newick, CV980408679 (J.D. New Haven at New Haven 1998).

[225] Conn. Public Act No. 99-153.

a bond and then attempt to discharge the bond under the procedures set forth in Connecticut General Statutes § 49-37. Connecticut, however, has an additional statute, Connecticut General Statutes § 49-51, that permits "any person having an interest in any real or personal property described in any certificate of the lien, which lien is invalid but not discharged of record" to give written notice to the lienor by certified mail to discharge the lien.[226] The "interested person" language is given the same interpretation as similar language in the bond substitution provisions of Connecticut General Statutes § 49-37, which has been construed to include a contractor as an "interested person."[227] Notice must be sent directly to the lienor, not the lienor's attorney.[228]

If the lienor fails to release the lien within 30 days of the notice, the interested person may apply to the Superior Court for a discharge of the lien.[229] An application to discharge the lien filed prior to the expiration of 30 days from the notice date will not be entertained.[230]

If the court determines that the lien was filed without "just cause," it may allow, in its discretion, damages at the rate of $100 per week after the expiration of the 30-day notice period, not to exceed $5,000 or a sum not to exceed the actual loss sustained by the aggrieved person, including attorneys' fees, whichever is greater. Accordingly, § 49-51 provides a contractor or owner an expedient mechanism to discharge liens and an opportunity to recover the damages and expenses incurred to discharge the lien, especially when the lien was clearly invalid, or filed in bad faith.[231] The award of damages under the statute is discretionary with the court and will probably be assessed only if the lienor is shown to have acted in a frivolous or incompetent manner.[232]

If a lienor has just cause to believe that the mechanics' lien was valid, even if it is later proven invalid, damages are not warranted under the statute, especially where the plaintiff has not proven actual damages caused by the invalid lien.[233] A finding of bad faith, however, is not required in order to justify the award of damages and attorneys' fees under the statute.[234]

If a lien has expired for the lienor's failure to foreclose within the one-year

---

[226] CONN. GEN. STAT. § 49-51(a).

[227] PDS Eng'g & Constr., Inc. v. Double RS, 42 Conn. Supp. 460, 627 A.2d 959 (J.D. Hartford/New Britain at Hartford 1992); Henry F. Raab Connecticut, Inc. v. J. W. Fisher Co., 183 Conn. 108, 438 A.2d 834 (1981).

[228] Guilford Yacht Club Ass'n, Inc. v. Northeast Dredging, Inc., 192 Conn. 10, 468 A.2d 1235 (1984).

[229] CONN. GEN. STAT. § 49-51(a).

[230] Quail Run Village v. Benedetto, 6 Conn. L. Rptr. 163 (J.D. Middlesex 1992).

[231] *See* Juros v. York, No. CV92-50970 (J.D. Tolland at Rockville 1995) (awarding damages under § 49-51 for the knowing filing of a baseless lien and with improper motive).

[232] Quail Run Village v. Benedetto, 6 Conn. L. Rptr. 163 (J.D. Middlesex 1992); Huckabee Plumbing v. Falco, 4 Conn. L. Rptr. 5 (J.D. Fairfield 1991).

[233] Richard Riggio & Sons, Inc. v. Galiette, 46 Conn. App. 63, 66-67, 698 A.2d 336 (1997).

[234] *Id.* at 66.

limitation, the lien is automatically discharged as a matter of law. Under such circumstances, the court will not assess damages under § 49-51 for the plaintiff's failure to release the lien after it expired, as it is of no legal effect.[235]

If a party has either received satisfaction of its lien claim or received a court judgment denying its claim, the party must, upon written notice from any interested party to the property, file a release of the lien on the land records within 10 days of the notice. Failure to release the lien within the prescribed period may subject the lienor to monetary penalties in an amount to be determined by the court, but not to exceed one-half of the amount of the lien.[236]

[235] Oxford Paint & Hardware v. Baxter, No. CV-91-036876-S (J.D. Ansonia/Milford at Milford 1992).

[236] Conn. Gen. Stat. § 49-59.

CHAPTER 9

DELAWARE

David B. Stratton
Christopher J. Lamb

§ 9.01 INTRODUCTION

Delaware law requires "non resident contractors"[1] to obtain a license[2] and to file a special surety bond with the Delaware Department of Finance.[3] These non-resident contractor requirements are applicable to both private and public projects.

With respect to private projects, Delaware requires performance bonds only in connection with the construction of certain roads and streets outside the corporate limits of cities and towns. In these circumstances, the developer is required to post a performance bond with the Delaware Department of Transportation.[4] Although this bond is generally limited to 10 percent of the estimated cost of construction, under certain circumstances the Department of Transportation may require a 100-percent bond.[5]

Pursuant to the Delaware State Procurement Act,[6] statutory procurement procedures, including bonding requirements, have been materially revised. Under the state's revised procurement procedures, a bid bond or bid security must be posted only if required by the agency involved.[7] Such bond or security must be either (1) a "good and sufficient bond to the State for the benefit of the agency involved"; or (2) a "security of the bidder assigned to the agency for a sum equal to at least 10% of the bid."[8]

Certain mechanics' lien remedies are available to contractors, subcontractors, and suppliers in Delaware in connection with private projects and, when the state has waived its right to sovereign immunity, in connection with public construction projects as well. The principal Delaware statute governing mechanics' liens is known generally as the mechanics' lien statute, Delaware Code Annotated title 25, §§ 2701 *et seq.* (1985 & Supp. 1990).[9]

---

[1] DEL. CODE ANN. tit. 30, § 2501 (1997).

[2] *Id.* § 2502 (1997 & Supp. 1998). In addition to the licensing requirement, Delaware also requires contractors to register as a tax withholding agent, file statements of contracts awarded by general contractors, subcontractors, and construction managers to nonresident contractors, file monthly or quarterly statements of amounts paid to subcontractors, file an unemployment compensation liability form, and certify that workers' compensation insurance coverage is in effect. Instructions and the required forms are contained in a packet that is available from the State of Delaware, Department of Finance, Division of Revenue, Carvel State Building, 820 North French St., Wilmington, DE 19801.

[3] DEL. CODE ANN. tit. 30, § 375 (1997).

[4] *Id.* at tit. 17, § 508(b) (1995 & Supp. 1998).

[5] *Id.*

[6] *Id.* at tit. 29, §§ 6901 *et seq.* (1997).

[7] *Id.* § 6927(a).

[8] *Id.*

[9] Effective December 1999, the mechanics' lien statute was substantially revised to provide liens for construction management services, to change the time limitations for filing liens (i.e., within 180 days for contractors and within 120 days for others), and to amend certain pleading requirements. Del. Sen. Bill No. 130, as amended by House Amend. No. 1 (to be codified at DEL. CODE ANN. tit. 25, §§ 2701 *et seq.*). A complete analysis of the new law will be included in the next Supplement.

§ 9.02 BOND LAW

[A] General Concepts

It should be noted at the outset that the Delaware case law dealing with construction bonds and sureties is not extensive. Nonetheless, in addition to the statutory material pertaining to non-resident contractors and public works projects, there are enough cases to provide meaningful guidance on how to approach construction bonds in the state of Delaware.

The concept of a construction bond or surety in Delaware is the same as in other jurisdictions. That is, a bond is a contract whereby one party (the surety) agrees to perform the obligations of another party (the obligor) if the obligor fails to perform its obligations to the obligee.[10] As in other jurisdictions, Delaware requires that a surety contract be reduced to writing and signed by the party against whom the surety contract will be charged.[11] There is an exception to the writing requirement when a contractor has given an oral guarantee to the materialmen of a subcontractor, but this exception appears to be limited to the facts of a single Delaware case from 1956.[12]

In the event that the surety is called upon to perform the obligations of the obligor, the surety may subsequently recover from the obligor what it has paid out on behalf of the obligor. Furthermore, the surety takes the benefit of all remedies that the obligee may have had against the obligor.[13]

An often-litigated issue is the question of who may recover against the surety in the event of a default by the obligor.[14] In the construction context, these cases typically involve an action by a subcontractor to recover against the general

---

[10] W.T. Rawleigh Co. v. Warrington, 199 A. 666, 667 (Del. Super. 1938) ("According to the ordinary meaning of that term, a surety is a person 'who binds himself for the payment of a sum of money, or for the performance of something else for another, who is already bound for the same.'").

[11] No action shall be brought to charge any person upon any agreement . . . to charge any person to answer for the debt, default, or miscarriage, of another, in any sum of the value of $25 and upwards, unless the contract is reduced to writing, or some memorandum, or notes thereof, are signed by the party to be charged therewith, or some other person thereunto by him lawfully authorized in writing.

DEL. CODE ANN. tit. 6, § 2714 (1993).

[12] S&S Builders, Inc. v. DiMondi, 126 A.2d 826 (Del. 1956) (subcontractor's materialman could recover against contractor after subcontractor's failure to pay for concrete blocks when contractor had given materialman oral assurances of payment).

[13] Hartford Accident & Indem. Co. v. Long, 245 A.2d 800 (Del. Ch. 1968); Royal Indem. Co. v. Alexander Indus., Inc., 211 A.2d 919 (Del. 1965).

[14] *See, e.g.,* State v. American Ins. Co., 559 A.2d 1247 (Del. 1989) (action against bond provided pursuant to DEL. CODE ANN. tit. 29, § 6909 (1985 & Supp. 1990)); Certain-Teed Prods. Corp. v. United Pac. Ins. Co., 389 A.2d 777 (Del. Super. 1978) (action against bond provided pursuant to DEL. CODE ANN. tit. 29, § 6909 (1997)).

contractor's surety for failure to pay for materials, labor, and wages.[15] The real significance of these cases is their highlighting of the importance of careful drafting when preparing the surety agreement.

For example, bonds executed pursuant to Delaware's public works projects statute[16] will always be construed by the courts to provide for the minimum coverage required by the statute.[17] However, because a surety arrangement is simply a form of contract,[18] the parties may provide for broader coverage.[19] In interpreting surety agreements, as with all contracts, the courts will look to the intent of the parties.[20] That is, at the time the surety agreement was entered into, did the surety and the obligor intend that the protection of the bond would be available to parties beyond the obligor's subcontractors?[21]

Finally, it should be noted that when the bond or surety is required by statute, the "obligation of the surety must be determined in light of the purposes to be served by the law requiring such bond."[22]

Obviously, the drafting element is important for all parties involved. For the obligor/contractor and the surety/bonding company, the terms of the agreement are critical to understanding the limits of each party's exposure in the event of a default or other indemnifiable event. For the potential obligee/subcontractor, the terms of the agreement will govern if, how, and how much the subcontractor will recover if the obligor fails to pay the subcontractor.[23] Although this may seem to

---

[15] *See, e.g.,* State v. American Ins. Co., 559 A.2d 1247 (Del. 1989) (action against bond provided pursuant to DEL. CODE ANN. tit. 29, § 6909 (1975 & Supp. 1990)); Certain-Teed Prods. Corp. v. United Pac. Ins. Co., 389 A.2d 777 (Del. Super. 1978) (action against bond provided pursuant to DEL. CODE ANN. tit. 29, § 6909 (1997)).

[16] DEL. CODE ANN. tit. 29, § 6927 (1997).

[17] *See* Certain-Teed Prods. Corp. v. United Pac. Ins. Co., 389 A.2d 777, 779 (Del. Super. 1978).

[18] "The general rules of construction of contracts are applicable to suretyship or bail undertakings." State v. Mitchell, 212 A.2d 873, 886 (Del. Super. 1965) (discussing bail bond arrangement).

[19] *See, e.g.,* Bar Steel Corp. v. Read, 277 A.2d 678 (Del. 1971) (modifications to surety agreements, when not contrary to public policy, are permissible).

[20] Delmar New, Inc. v. Jacobs Oil, 584 A.2d 531 (Del. Super. 1990).

[21] *See e.g.,* Royal Indem. Co. v. Alexander Indus., Inc., 211 A.2d 919 (Del. 1965). *See also* State v. Interstate Amiesite Corp., 297 A.2d 41, 44 (Del. 1972) (parties may provide that contractor bear all liability claims against subcontractor, but such contract provisions must be "crystal clear and unequivocal"). *See also* Quality Elec. Co. v. Eastern States Constr. Serv., Inc., 663 A.2d 488 (Del. 1995) (when surety agreement contains limitation language found in DEL. CODE ANN. tit. 29, § 6909(d), supplier to subcontractor cannot maintain an action against general contractor and its surety; absent such an express limitation, however, supplier can bring such an action).

[22] State v. Fidelity & Deposit Co. of Md., 194 A.2d 858, 861 (Del. 1963) (notice provision placed in bond issued pursuant to Delaware Public Works Project statute held to be surplusage).

[23] *See, e.g.,* Rumsey Elec. Co. v. University of Del., 358 A.2d 712, 714 (Del. 1976) (when a party seeks to recover "under a contract as to which he is a third-party beneficiary, he must take that contract as he finds it"); Rumsey Elec. Co. v. University of Del., 334 A.2d 226, 230 (Del. Super. 1975) (third party's "right to sue must be measured by the terms of the agreement between the principals"), *aff'd,* 358 A.2d 712 (Del. 1976). *See also* Pierce Assocs., Inc. v. Nemours Found.,

be stating the obvious, it is critical that each party connected with the surety agreement understand who will be potentially liable to whom under the bond.

[B] Bid Bonds

Delaware law does not require bid bonds on private projects. A *public works contract* is defined as "construction, reconstruction, demolition, alteration and repair work and maintenance work paid for, in whole or in part, with public funds."[24] Under the state's revised procurement procedures, the bright-line requirement of a bid bond for any project with a cost in excess of $10,000 has been eliminated, with the result that a bid bond or bid security now must be posted only if required by the agency involved.[25] Such bond or security must be either (1) a "good and sufficient bond to the State for the benefit of the agency involved"; or (2) a "security of the bidder assigned to the agency for a sum equal to at least 10 percent of the bid."[26]

Although not mandated by statute, the state agency controlling the project may place additional requirements on the submission of bids. For example, in some circumstances the agency may require a consent of surety. A *consent of surety* is a "written acknowledgment by an insurance or bonding company that it will issue a performance bond on behalf of the bidding company in the event that the contract be awarded to it."[27] As a result, the bidder is well advised to carefully read the bidding information provided by the agency.

[C] Performance and Payment Bonds

With respect to private projects, Delaware requires the filing of a bond only in connection with the construction of "any new road or street outside the corporate limits of any city or town and intended to be dedicated by the owner thereof to the public use."[28] It seems clear that this statute is primarily aimed at new developments. The stated purpose of this bond is to ensure the "faithful performance and satisfactory completion of the obligations imposed by [the statute]."[29] The bond must be filed with the Department of Transportation before the commencement of any construction of such streets or roads.[30]

Generally, the Department of Transportation may not require a bond in

865 F.2d 530, 536 (3d Cir.1988) ("a contractor and subcontractor may agree to confer upon an owner rights which are enforceable directly against the subcontractor; however, an intent to do so must be found in the contract documents"), *cert. denied,* 492 U.S. 907 (1989).

[24] DEL. CODE ANN. tit. 29, § 6901(15) (1997).

[25] *Id.* § 6927(a).

[26] *Id.*

[27] McDaniel v. Department of Corrections, Civ. Action No. 6142, 1980 WL 6371 (Del. Ch. Apr. 15, 1980) (discussing agency's waiver of consent of surety requirement) (Brown V.C.).

[28] DEL. CODE ANN. tit. 17, § 508 (1995 & Supp. 1998).

[29] *Id.* § 508(b).

[30] *Id.*

excess of 10 percent of the estimated cost of the construction. If, however, the developer "has been adjudged by the Department to be in violation of [the statute] and/or has not maintained a satisfactory record of compliance on repair and construction completion," the Department of Transportation may require a bond, certified check, or other security up to 100 percent of the cost of construction.[31]

With the exception of the developer's street and road construction bond, Delaware does not require performance or payment bonds in connection with private projects.

For each public works contract, the successful bidder must execute a performance and payment bond in a sum equal to 100 percent of the contract price.[32] This bond must be executed simultaneously with the formal contract. In addition to the bond, the successful bidder must:

> purchase adequate insurance for the performance of the contract, and, by submission of a bid, [is deemed to have agreed] to indemnify and save harmless and to defend all legal or equitable actions brought against the State, any agency, officer and/or employee of the State, for and from all claims of liability which is or may be the result of the successful bidder's actions, during the performance of the contract.[33]

The statute provides a broad range of parties who may maintain an action against the public works bond. These parties include "every person furnishing materials or performing labor under the contract."[34] The breadth of this provision does not, however, mean that the right of action is unlimited.[35] Absent express language in the surety agreement to the contrary, recent Delaware decisions indicate that the notion of "privity of contract" will control recoveries against the statutory performance bond.[36] In other words, unless the surety agreement specifically includes parties such as the suppliers or employees of subcontractors, or

---

[31] *Id.*

[32] *Id.* at tit. 29, § 6927(d) (1997). The statute does not differentiate between payment and performance, but rather combines the two concepts into one bond. The state may, at its discretion, waive the bond and other form of security, with such waiver to be stated in the bid specifications. *Id.* § 6927(h).

[33] *Id.* § 6929.

[34] DEL. CODE ANN. tit. 29, § 6927(f) (1997).

[35] *See, e.g.,* State v. American Ins. Co., 559 A.2d 1247 (Del. 1989) (statute did not confer on employees of subcontractor an unqualified right of action against prime contractor or its surety in the absence of a contractual relationship between the prime contractor and the employees). *Cf.* State *ex rel.* Christopher v. Planet Ins. Co., 321 A.2d 128 (Del. Super. 1974) ("There is no basis under the subsection for confining its application to those who dealt directly with the general contractor"). It should be noted that the *American Insurance* decision, while giving some deference to *Planet Insurance,* does seem to limit its reach.

[36] State v. American Ins. Co., 559 A.2d 1247, 1249 (Del. 1989); Certain-Teed Prods. Corp. v. United Pac. Ins. Co., 389 A.2d 777 (Del. Super. 1978) (under the express terms of the bond, materialman had cause of action against surety despite lack of privity of contract with general contractor).

the contractor has a separate contractual relationship with such parties, these parties will not be able to maintain an action against the surety. This result reinforces the importance of carefully drafting the surety agreement.

Finally, if a party is entitled to bring an action against the public works bond, it must do so within three years of the date the last work was done on the contract.[37] The statute does not define "the date the last work was done on the contract," and the Delaware courts have not rendered a reported decision on this issue. This is, of course, a factual issue that the courts will have to resolve on a case-by-case basis.[38]

The statute permits the parties to contractually reduce the statute of limitations to "1 year following the date on which the successful bidder ceased work on the contract."[39] This reduction must be set forth explicitly in the surety agreement.

[D] Non-Resident Contractor Bonds

The state of Delaware is somewhat unique in its requirement that non-resident contractors file a surety bond with the State Department of Finance. The purpose of this bond is to "guarantee the payment of state income taxes, state occupational or business licenses, unemployment compensation contributions and income taxes withheld from wages of employees, together with any penalties and interest thereon."[40] The non-resident contractor bond must be filed before any work commences on the applicable contract.[41]

Generally speaking, a *non resident contractor* is defined as any "general contractor, prime contractor, construction manager, subcontractor or other type of construction contractor" who does not regularly maintain a place of business in the state of Delaware.[42] If the contractor is a partnership or joint venture composed of more than one entity and one of these constituent entities maintains a regular place of business in the state of Delaware, then the contractor will be considered a "resident contractor." [43]

The amount of the non-resident contractor's bond is as follows:

1. On contracts of $20,000 or more, the bond must equal 6 percent of the contract or subcontract price.[44]

---

[37] DEL. CODE ANN. tit. 29, § 6927(f) (1997).

[38] Rumsey Elec. Co. v. University of Delaware touched upon the issue, but in that case, the parties had stipulated to the completion date. 334 A.2d 226, 229 (Del. Super. 1975).

[39] DEL. CODE ANN. tit. 29, § 6927(f) (1997).

[40] *Id.* at tit. 30, § 375 (1997).

[41] Division of Revenue, Technical Information Mem. 86–10 (Dec. 29, 1986).

[42] DEL. CODE ANN. tit. 30, § 2501 (1997).

[43] *Id.* § 2501(3).

[44] *Id.* § 375.

2. On cost-plus contracts of $20,000 or more, the bond must equal 6 percent of the contractor's or subcontractor's estimated cost and profit.[45]
3. When the aggregate of two or more contracts in one calendar year is $20,000 or more, the bond must equal 6 percent of the aggregate amount of such contracts.[46]
4. When the contract is less than $20,000, no non-resident contractor bond is required.

In lieu of the bond just described, the Department of Revenue will accept cash bonds, irrespective of the size of the contract or contracts covered by the bond.[47] Additionally, the Department of Revenue may accept bank letters of credit in the amounts described.[48] Requests for authorization to accept bank letters of credit must be made by letter to the Delaware director of revenue.

§ 9.03 LIEN LAW

[A] General Concepts

Delaware law provides for a general mechanics' lien in a statute known generally as the Delaware mechanics' lien statute.[49] The lien statute provides contractors, subcontractors, and suppliers with a mechanism for obtaining security for the payment of goods and services provided on private and certain public construction projects in Delaware. The mechanics' lien afforded to such entities by the lien statute constitutes a lien on the owner's interest in the property, which relates back to the date on which services were first rendered or goods were first delivered by the contractor,[50] and thus represents a significant security device. As with the mechanics' liens of other states, the lien rights afforded contractors, subcontractors, and suppliers in Delaware do not derive from common law[51] but are statutorily created. As such, the procedural requirements set forth in the lien statute will be strictly enforced by the courts and must be scrupulously observed by those seeking to perfect their lien rights.

It is important to keep in mind that mechanics' liens may not be filed against the state of Delaware or its agencies, and a mechanics' lien will not attach to state-owned property unless the state or an agency of the state has waived its

---

[45] *Id.*

[46] *Id.*

[47] *Id.* § 375(a)(1). *See also* Division of Revenue, Technical Information Mem. 90-10-A (Mar. 1, 1990).

[48] DEL. CODE ANN. tit. 30, § 375(g) (1997). *See also* Division of Revenue, Technical Information Mem. 90–1-A (Mar. 1, 1990).

[49] DEL. CODE ANN. tit. 25, §§ 2701 *et seq.* (1989 & Supp. 1998).

[50] *Id.* § 2718.

[51] Masten Lumber & Supply Co. v. Brown, 405 A.2d 101, 106 (Del. 1979).

immunity from suit.[52] When the legislature has granted an agency the power to enter into contracts or to "sue and be sued," a waiver of sovereign immunity will be deemed to have been intended.[53]

[B] Basic Provisions

The Delaware lien statute provides that a statement of lien may be filed by any person having performed or furnished labor or materials, in an amount exceeding $25, in connection with the "erection, alteration or repair" of any structure under an express or an implied contract.[54] The lien statute specifically includes contractors, subcontractors, those providing labor or materials under a contract with or order from any subcontractor, and architects as entities entitled to mechanics' liens.[55] The delivery of materials to a construction site creates an irrebutable presumption that such materials were in fact used in the completed structure and a lien thus established.[56] However, the statutory lien will not extend to materialmen having no direct contractual relationship with either the owner, contractors, or subcontractors on a project.[57]

The term *structure* is defined as including "a building or house,"[58] but has been judicially interpreted to include only houses or other buildings permanently constructed on the land.[59] The lien statute mandates that when a claim for labor or materials is filed by the same person against two or more structures having the same owner, the claimant must apportion its claim among the various structures.[60] This raises practical problems when services or materials have been rendered or supplied to structures such as condominium or townhouse complexes, where a single building may contain many individual units. It also limits the lienor's ability to obtain payment upon the sale of a single structure or unit. When a contractor or subcontractor has supplied labor or materials for the benefit of an entire building (such as common-element improvements), it is entitled to file a single mechanics' lien against the entire building as one "structure," even though the structure may be composed of multiple individual units.[61] However, to the extent that labor and materials are supplied to, and solely for the benefit of, a condominium or town-

---

[52] *See* Department of Community Affairs & Econ. Dev. v. M. Davis & Sons, 412 A.2d 939, 941–42 (Del. 1980).

[53] *See id.* at 943; George & Lynch, Inc. v. State, 197 A.2d 734 (Del. 1964).

[54] Del. Code Ann. tit. 25, § 2702(a) (1989).

[55] *Id.*

[56] *See* Gaster v. Wilmington Plumbing Supply Co., 321 A.2d 504, 506 (Del. 1974); S.G. Williams of Dover, Inc. v. Diamond State Vinyl, Inc., 430 A.2d 794, 795 (Del. Super. 1981).

[57] *See* Gould v. Dynalectric Co., 435 A.2d 730, 731 (Del. Super. 1981).

[58] Del. Code Ann. tit. 25, § 2701(2) (1989).

[59] *See* Pioneer Nat'l Title Ins. Co. v. Exten Assoc., 403 A.2d 283, 286 (Del. 1979).

[60] Del. Code Ann. tit. 25, § 2713 (1989).

[61] *See* Kershaw Excavating Co. v. City Sys., Inc., 581 A.2d 1111, 1114 (Del. 1990); Ramsey v. DiSabatino, 347 A.2d 659, 662 (Del. Super. 1975); Wilmington Trust Co. v. Branmar, Inc., 353 A.2d 212, 215 (Del. Super. 1976).

house, each such condominium or townhouse is a separate "structure" for purposes of filing under the lien statute.[62]

Mechanics' liens may also be obtained in connection with labor performed and materials furnished in the construction or repair of bridges, wharves, piers, and docks.[63] However, it is important for contractors and subcontractors to be aware that, in the case of improvements made to the land alone, no lien right exists unless there is a written contract, signed by the owner of the land, setting forth:

1. The names of all parties to the contract
2. A description by metes and bounds of the land to be affected
3. A statement of the general character of the work to be done
4. The total amount to be paid under the contract and the amount of any partial payments
5. The time when such payments are due and payable.[64]

A mechanics' lien action in Delaware is an *in rem* action and results only in the imposition of a lien on the owner's property, although an in personam action against the owner may be joined in the mechanics' lien complaint. A tenant with a leasehold interest may be considered an "owner" in addition to one holding a fee interest in the property, but a mechanics' lien asserted solely against such a tenant will bind only the leasehold interest.[65] If the prior written consent of the property owner or its agent to the lessee's repair or alteration of a leased structure has been obtained, then the owner's fee interest in that structure may also be made subject to the mechanics' lien.[66]

Because the Delaware lien statute does not expressly provide a remedy for work performed or materials furnished in connection with the demolition of a structure, the Delaware Superior Court held that a mechanic's lien will not lie for removal or demolition work.[67]

[C] Procedural Requirements

The lien statute contains very specific procedural requirements that will be strictly enforced by the courts.[68]

---

[62] *See* Wilmington Trust Co. v. Branmar, Inc., 353 A.2d 212, 215 (Del. Super. 1976).

[63] DEL. CODE ANN. tit. 25, § 2702(b) (1989).

[64] *Id.* § 2703.

[65] *See* Hoffman v. Siegel, Civ. Action Nos. 90L-11-005, 90L-08-008, 1991 WL 113431 (Del. Super. June 13, 1991) (Graves, J.).

[66] DEL. CODE ANN. tit. 25, § 2722 (1989). *See also* Department of Community Affairs & Econ. Dev. v. M. Davis & Sons, 412 A.2d 939 (Del. 1980).

[67] *See* Browning-Ferris, Inc. v. Rockford Enters., Inc., 642 A.2d 820 (Del. Super. 1993).

[68] DEL. CODE ANN. tit. 25, §§ 2712, 2713 (1989 & Supp. 1998). *See, e.g.,* Builder's Choice, Inc. v. Venzon, 672 A.2d 1 (Del. 1995) (mechanics' lien action dismissed for failure to strictly comply with statute; claimant omitted from its statement of claim the requisite reference to a filed

The owner of any structure being built, repaired, or altered by a contractor or subcontractor may from time to time request such contractor or subcontractor to furnish it with a written list of all persons who (1) have furnished labor or material in connection with such construction, and (2) are entitled to avail themselves of the lien statute.[69] It is critical that contractors promptly comply with such requests, because unless the list is provided within 10 days of the request, the contractor is not entitled to any further payments until the list is furnished and is not entitled to avail itself of the benefits of the lien statute.[70] Courts have held that a written response that is not limited to entities entitled to avail themselves of the benefits of the lien statute (that is, those entities providing labor or materials with a value in excess of $25) is legally insufficient, and as a result the contractor cannot maintain a mechanics' lien action.[71]

The lien statute delineates with particularity the information that must be set forth in the mechanics' lien statement of claim filed with the prothonotary of the superior court of the county in which the structure is situated, which statement of claim also serves as a complaint when so designated.[72] The statement of claim, which must be supported by the claimant's affidavit that the facts therein are true and correct,[73] must set forth:

1. The name of the claimant
2. The name of the owner or reputed owner of the structure
3. The name of the contractor and whether the claimant's contract was made with the owner or its agent or with such contractor
4. The amount claimed to be due, the nature and kind of labor done or materials furnished, with a bill of particulars annexed showing the kind and amount of labor done or materials furnished
5. The date of commencement of labor or furnishing of materials
6. The date when the provision of labor or furnishing of materials was finished

construction mortgage, notwithstanding that one could not conclusively determine from documents of record that first mortgage was in fact a construction mortgage). The court in *Builder's Choice* noted that when it is unclear whether a first mortgage is a construction mortage, "artful pleading" stating that the mortgage "may be" a construction mortgage will satisfy the statutory requirements. *Id.*

[69] *Id.* § 2705.

[70] *Id.*

[71] *See* Hoffman v. Siegel, Civ. Action Nos. 90L-11-005, 90L-08-008, 1991 WL 113431 (Del. Super. June 13, 1991) (Graves, J.).

[72] DEL. CODE ANN. tit. 25, § 2712 (1989 & Supp. 1998).

[73] *Id.* § 2712(c). The affidavit may *not* be limited to "knowledge and belief." *See* Construction by Franco v. Reed, C.A. No. 94L-09–20, 1994 WL 750306 (Del. Super. Dec. 12, 1994) (affidavit stating that information in statement of claim was true and correct "to the best of [claimant's] knowledge and belief" was fatal to mechanics' lien action, as statute does not permit affidavit to be limited to knowledge and belief).

7. The location of the structure with a description sufficient to identify the same
8. That the labor was done or the materials furnished on the credit of the structure[74]
9. The amount of the claim (which must be in excess of $25) and that neither that amount nor any part thereof has been paid to claimant
10. The amount the claimant claims to be due on each structure
11. The time of recording of a first mortgage on the structure securing existing indebtedness or future advances, provided at least 50 percent of the loan proceeds are used for the payment of labor or materials for the structure.[75]

The statement of claim must be filed within one of two time periods, depending on whether the claimant is a contractor or a subcontractor. A contractor who (1) has contracted directly with the owner or reputed owner of a building and (2) has furnished both labor and material for such structure, must file its statement of claim not less than 90 nor more than 120 days following the completion of the structure.[76] All other persons must file their statement of claim within 90 days from the completion of the labor performed or from the last delivery of materials furnished by them.[77] The performance of labor or furnishing of materials of a trivial nature following the claimant's initial completion will not extend the time period during which the statement of claim must be filed.[78]

The Delaware Code expressly provides that a successful plaintiff in a mechanics' lien case may recover his reasonable attorneys' fees.[79] However, Delaware courts have determined that, absent an agreement, the statute violated the constitutional right of equal protection.[80]

[D] Waiver and Assignment

Any contract or agreement providing for the waiver of a party's right to file a mechanics' lien action is void and enforceable.[81] However a written waiver may be exchanged contemporaneously with actual payment to the contractor or subcontractor. Also, an entity who has filed a mechanics' lien action may agree to subordinate, release, or satisfy all or a portion of the lien.[82]

---

[74] *See id.* § 2717 (proof by claimant that labor was performed or materials were furnished on or adjacent to a structure constitutes prima facie evidence that the same was performed or furnished for and on the credit of such structure).

[75] *Id.* § 2712(b).

[76] *Id.* § 2711(a).

[77] *Id.* § 2711(b).

[78] *See* Byler v. Suttles, 311 A.2d 872 (Del. 1973); Breeding v. Melson, 143 A. 23 (Del. 1927).

[79] Del. Code Ann. tit. 10, § 3912 (Supp. 1998).

[80] Gaster v. J.R. Coldiron, 297 A.2d 384 (Del. 1972).

[81] Del. Code. Ann. tit. 25, § 2706(b) (Supp. 1998).

[82] *Id.*

Contractors should bear in mind that because there is no authority in the lien statute providing for the alienation of an entity's mechanics' lien rights, an unperfected right to a mechanics' lien may not be assigned.[83]

[E] Lien Priority

Any judgment obtained under a statement of claim made pursuant to the Delaware lien statute becomes a lien on the structure and upon the ground on which the structure is situated, relating back to the day on which the labor was begun or the furnishing of materials commenced or the time immediately following the time of recording of a first mortgage, or a conveyance in the nature of a first mortgage.[84] Before the entering of a judgment on a claim, the statement of claim constitutes only a "cautionary lien" that cannot be executed upon but that must be satisfied or bonded over in the event of a sale of the property before adjudication of the merits of the lien claim.[85] In the case of the erection, construction, and filling in of wharves, piers, and docks, the mechanics' liens extend to the lots or lands in front of which such improvements are made.[86]

The lien priority of mechanics' liens is subordinate to first mortgages in certain circumstances. A judgment obtained on a statement of claim made pursuant to the Delaware lien statute becomes a lien on the structure and on the ground on which the structure is situated, relating back to the last to occur of (1) the day on which the labor was begun or the furnishing of materials commenced, or (2) a conveyance in the nature of a first mortgage on the structure securing existing indebtedness or future advances, provided at least 50 percent of the loan proceeds were used for the payment of labor or materials for the structure.[87]

Additionally, the Delaware lien statute provides a mechanism whereby a mechanics' lien may be discharged as a lien on the structure and property by depositing with the court a sum equal to the amount asserted in the statement of claim.[88] The payment must be accompanied by an affidavit of the owner or other party in interest identifying the disputed and undisputed portions of the claim.[89] The undisputed portion of the lien claim will then be paid to the lienor before the lien will be discharged.[90] If the court later determines that the disputed portion of the claim has been grossly overstated by the affiant, the court may award damages to the claimant in an amount up to twice the figure stated by the affiant to be disputed.[91]

---

[83] *See* Gould v. Dynalectric Co., 435 A.2d 730, 731 (Del. Super. 1981).

[84] DEL. CODE ANN. tit. 25, § 2718 (1989 and Supp. 1998).

[85] *See* Eastern Elec. & Heating, Inc. v. Pike Creek Prof'l Ctr., Inc., Nos. 85L-MY-1, 85L-AP-21, 1986 WL 9031 (Del. Aug. 5, 1986) (Herrman, J.).

[86] DEL. CODE ANN. tit. 25, § 2718(b) (1989).

[87] *Id.* § 2718(a) (Supp. 1998).

[88] *Id.* § 2729(a) (Supp. 1998).

[89] *Id.* § 2729 (Supp. 1998).

[90] *Id.*

[91] *Id.*

When the proceeds realized on a sale in execution of a mechanics' lien judgment are not sufficient to pay all liens, such proceeds will be ratably divided among all persons who have filed statements of claim before the date of the sale, without regard to the priority of the mechanics' liens relating to such claims.[92]

[F] Remedies of Owner

The lien statute provides the owner of the structure or its reputed owner with various protections, not the least of which is the right to assure that all requirements of the lien statute are strictly observed by the claimant. Further, if a claim is filed by one or more subcontractors for labor or materials that were to have been furnished by the contractor under the owner's contract with such contractor, then the owner may retain such amounts under the contract as are necessary to satisfy the subcontractors' claims, which sums when paid to the subcontractors by the owner are treated as a payment pro tanto to the contractor toward the moneys owed to the contractor.[93]

When claims are filed by one or more subcontractors for labor performed or materials furnished in connection with the construction, repair, or improvement of a structure used solely as a personal residence, the owner of the residence may assert as a defense that the owner has made full and final payment to the general contractor in good faith.[94] Any payment made by the owner to the contractor after service of process of a mechanics' lien statement of claim,[95] or after the owner acquires notice that the remote lienholder has not been paid by the contractor,[96] will be a payment that is not made "in good faith," thus depriving the owner of the good-faith defense. If the owner has not made full and final payment to the general contractor, then the subcontractors' liens will be allowed, but only to the extent of the balance of the payment due such contractor, which balance will be divided pro rata among the claimants who perfect their liens.[97] Any amounts that have been or must be expended by the owner to complete construction of the structure may be set off against the subcontractors' claims.[98] Finally, it is irrelevant whether the structure was actually occupied as a residence at the time of the furnishing of labor or materials, as long as the structure was intended to become the future dwelling of the owner for whom the structure was being constructed.[99]

---

[92] *Id.* § 2720.

[93] *Id.* § 2723 (1989).

[94] *Id.* § 2707.

[95] *Id.*

[96] *See* Bedford v. Sussex Elec. Constr. Co., 382 A.2d 246, 247–48 (Del. 1978).

[97] DEL. CODE ANN. tit. 25, § 2707 (1989).

[98] *See* Masten Lumber & Supply Co. v. Brown, 405 A.2d 101, 105 (Del. 1979).

[99] *See* Wyatt v. Dunn, Civ. Action No. 90L-SE-8, 1991 WL 236979 (Del. Super. Oct. 21, 1991) (Steele, J.).

CHAPTER 10

FLORIDA

John S. Vento
John F. Panzarella

§ 10.01 INTRODUCTION

[A] Private Projects

Florida has one principal statute that governs both construction liens and construction surety bonds for improvements to private property. Recognizing that a laborer, contractor or supplier to a private construction project may, of necessity, be required to lien the property on which improvements have been made, the Florida Legislature has enacted (and frequently amends) the Construction Lien Law, Part I of FLA. STAT. ch. 713 (1998). This article includes changes made in the 1999 Legislature, which passed a "glitch bill" to resolve issues raised by the 1998 amendments. This "glitch bill" was signed by the Governor on June 18, 1999 and was effective October 1, 1999.

While Florida law does not require owners or contractors to furnish payment or performance bonds on private projects,[1] if an owner chooses to provide or require a payment bond for a private project to protect the property from a construction lien,[2] the statute sets forth specific requirements that a bond must meet to establish its validity.[3]

[B] Public Works

When a private contractor enters into a contract with the State of Florida or any county, city or other public authority in Florida, the law *requires* the contractor to provide both a performance and a payment bond.[4] Florida exempts public property from construction liens for this reason.[5]

The requirement to provide bonds on public projects is subject to certain monetary restrictions. When the contract is with any county, city, political subdivision, or public authority, and the contract is for less than $200,000, the official or the board awarding the contract may waive the requirement of providing any bond.[6] In addition, certain state agencies have been delegated the authority to waive any bond requirements in projects that are valued between $100,000 and

---

[1] Houdaille Indus., Inc. v. United Bonding Ins. Co., 453 F.2d 1048 (5th Cir. 1972).

[2] FLA. STAT. § 713.02(6) (1997).

[3] *See* FLA. STAT. §§ 713.23 (payment bond), 713.24 (transfer bond), and 713.245 (conditional payment bond) (1998).

[4] FLA. STAT. § 255.05 (1998). This section was amended in 1997 to include unpaid finance charges due under a claimant's contract among charges which may be assessed against certain contractors' bonds; to revise language with respect to the time frame for notice of intent to look to such a bond for recovery; to provide for the time period of notice of nonpayment and to provide forms for waiver or rights to claim against the bond for progress payments and final payments. *See Id.*

[5] *Id.* § 713.01(24).

[6] *Id.* § 255.05(1)(a). In the event any waiver is granted, the official or officer granting such a waiver shall not be personally liable to those who may have sought relief under the bond. *Id.*

$200,000. Nevertheless, no payment or performance bond is required if the contract is with the state and is for $100,000 or less.[7] Notwithstanding any such waiver the public property remains exempt from a construction lien.

However, for all contracts of $200,000 or less the Department of Management Services is to provide procedures for retaining up to 10 percent of each request for payments submitted by the contractor, and procedures for determining disbursements from the amount retained on a *pro rata* basis for laborers, material suppliers, and subcontractors as defined in Fla. Stat. § 713.01. There are also procedures for requiring certification from laborers, material suppliers, and subcontractors. These procedures propagate that prior to final payment to the contractor there are no claims against the contractor resulting from the completion of the work provided for in the contract.[8] Thus, because there are no lien rights against state property and because there may be no bond on a project, the Legislature has mandated the foregoing procedures to ensure that proper payments are made to those performing the work who are not in privity with the state or its entities.

Furthermore, out-of-state contractors doing business in Florida for the first time should also be aware that a bid bond or a bid guaranty may also be required to be provided with the contractor's bids on certain public projects.[9] Moreover, Florida law governs surety bond relationships that have "substantial contacts" with Florida.[10]

§ 10.02 BOND LAW

[A] General Concepts

Florida's Construction Lien statute has not been interpreted to "cover this field" and to exempt all other bonds. In fact, any bond that is not required by statute or surpasses the minimum requirements of a statutory bond is construed as a common law bond.[11] Common law bonds are interpreted by their terms in accordance with the general rules of bond construction. That is, Florida recognizes

---

[7] *Id.*

[8] *See Id.*

[9] *See* FLA. STAT. § 153.10 (1997).

[10] See House of Koscot Dev. Corp. v. American Line Cosmetics, Inc., 468 F.2d 64 (5th Cir. 1972) for a discussion of facts to support contacts with the state sufficient for the applicability of Florida law.

[11] *See* National Fire Ins. Co. v. L.J. Clark Constr. Co., 579 So. 2d 743, 745 (Fla. Dist. Ct. App. 1991); Standard Heating Servs., Inc. v. Guymann Constr., Inc., 459 So. 2d 1103 (Fla. Dist. Ct. App. 1984); Southwest Fla. Water Management Dist. *ex rel.* Thermal Acoustic Corp. v. Miller Constr. Co., 355 So. 2d 1258 (Fla. Dist. Ct. App. 1978); United Bonding Ins. Co. v. City of Holly Hill 249 So. 2d 720 (Fla. Dist. Ct. App. 1971); Fuller Indus., Inc. v. R. Terry Blazier & Son, Inc., 188 So. 2d 2 (Fla. Dist. Ct. App. 1966), *cert. denied,* 194 So. 2d 617 (Fla. 1966); *Cf.* Martin Paving Co. v. United Pac. Inc. Co., 646 So. 2d 268, 270 (Fla. Dist. Ct. App. 1994) (holding that common law bonds continue to exist in connection with public construction). *But cf.* Haskell Co. v. Peeples Constr. Co., 648 So. 2d 883, 834 n.1 (Fla. Dist. Ct. App. 1995) (suggesting, *in dictum,* that *Martin Paving* holding is error).

the prevailing law that a construction surety bond is a contractual relationship.[12] Thus, the liability of a surety on a performance bond is then defined by its contract.[13] Usually, the liability of the surety on its performance bond is commensurate with that of its principal, and the surety is not liable if the principal is not liable.[14] However, as an original party to the contract, the surety is jointly and severally liable to the obligee.[15] Upon default, the obligee may sue either the principal or the surety. As between the surety and the principal, the principal should pay or perform under the contract.[16]

Because a construction surety bond is a contract, it is subject to the general law of contracts.[17] Therefore, many of the basic surety bond rules of construction are contract law principles.[18] The instrument should be viewed as a whole with all of the provisions of the bond considered in their entirety and given the intended effect according to the plain meaning of the document. Thus, the intent of the parties is to be determined from the four corners of the document.[19]

Common law bonds most frequently occur in those situations that are not regulated by statute such as those related to private payment and performance bonds. However, a poorly drafted statutory bond may be interpreted by a court as a common law bond, and in such cases an unsuspecting surety may be responsible for liabilities to parties other than those the statute defines.[20]

Except when the form of bond is prescribed by statute, the surety, the principal, and the obligee are free to contract as they wish and tailor a surety bond to their needs.[21] Moreover, the importance of freedom of contract is that the terms of the agreement should not be rewritten by the courts. Thus, a surety on a bond does not undertake to do more than that expressed in the bond, and has the right to stand upon the strict terms of the obligation.[22] If the surety bond states that its liability is limited to a fixed sum, the surety's obligation should not be extended beyond that amount by implication.[23] However, as a general rule of construction,

---

[12] The relationship involves three parties: a principal, an obligee and a surety. In the typical construction surety bond context, the principal is the general contractor, the surety is the bond or insurance company and the obligee is the owner. Normally, the principal has contracted with the owner/obligee to construct an improvement, and the surety has agreed to perform that same obligation if the principal fails to complete it.

[13] *See* Crabtree v. Aetna Cas. & Sur. Co., 438 So. 2d 102 (Fla. Dist. Ct. App. 1983).

[14] *See* Aetna Cas. & Sur. Co. v. Warren Bros. Co., Div. of Ashland Oil, Inc., 355 So. 2d 785 (Fla. 1978).

[15] *See* Plant City v. Scott, 148 F.2d 953 (5th Cir. 1945).

[16] *See* United States v. Tilleraas, 538 F. Supp. 1, 6 (N.D. Ohio 1981).

[17] *See* Crabtree v. Aetna Cas. & Sur. Co., 438 So. 2d 102 (Fla. Dist. Ct. App. 1983).

[18] *See id.*

[19] *See* Phoenix Indem. Co. v. Board of Pub. Instruction, 114 So. 2d 478, 481 (Fla. Dist. Ct. App. 1959).

[20] *See* United Bonding Ins. Co. v. City of Holly Hill, 249 So. 2d 720 (Fla. Dist. Ct. App. 1971).

[21] *See* Travelers Indem. Co. v. National Gypsum Co., 394 So. 2d 481 (Fla. Dist. Ct. App. 1981).

[22] *See* Crabtree v. Aetna Cas. & Sur. Co., 438 So. 2d 102, 105 (Fla. Dist. Ct. App. 1983).

[23] *See* Fidelity & Deposit Co. v. La Centre Trucking, Inc., 559 So. 2d 1242 (Fla. Dist. Ct. App. 1990).

a surety contract prepared by a surety is construed against the surety and in favor of granting the broadest possible coverage to those intended to benefit by its protection.[24]

Although surety contracts are the subject of regulation as insurance for many purposes,[25] they have been distinguished from contracts of insurance generally, so, for example, rules relating to limitations upon defenses or burdens of proof related to insurance contracts do not apply to contracts of surety.[26]

[B] Statutes Applicable to All Bonds

In addition to the general rules of construction applicable to surety bonds, the Florida Legislature has set out additional bond standards that apply to all bonds. A bond must be in writing and signed by the party to be charged under the agreement.[27] A lawsuit to enforce construction lien claims against a payment bond is subject to a one-year statute of limitations, with the date commencing from the last date of furnishing of labor, services, or materials on the project.[28] A prevailing lienor is entitled to reasonable attorneys' fees as part of the lienor's judgment.[29] Moreover, any surety that issues a bond in Florida must comply with the Florida Insurance Code to be recognized as a surety bond insurer in the State of Florida.[30]

[C] Payment and Performance Bonds

In their most fundamental effect, payment and performance bonds are agreements that protect the owner of real property against two different events.[31] A *payment bond* contains the surety's undertaking to guarantee that all subcontractors and materialmen will be paid, thus exempting the real property from a lien. A *performance bond* guarantees that the contract to construct the improvement will be fully performed, thus protecting the fixed price of the contract.[32]

[1] Private Payment Bonds

A private owner may exempt property from construction liens by requiring a contractor to provide a statutory payment bond.[33] Although the primary purpose

---

[24] *See* United Bonding Ins. Co. v. City of Holly Hill, 249 So. 2d 720 (Fla. Dist. Ct. App. 1971).

[25] *See* FLA. STAT. ch. 624 (1997).

[26] *See* Travelers Indemnity Co. v. National Gypsum Co., 394 So. 2d 481 (Fla. Dist. Ct. App. 1981).

[27] *See* FLA. STAT. § 725.01 (1997). This requirement is subject to some criticism. *See* Clover Interior Systems, Inc. v. General Development Corp., 357 So. 2d 459 (Fla. Dist. Ct. App. 1978).

[28] *See* FLA. STAT. ch. 95.11(5)(e) (1997). If the general contractor is the principal on the bond, then the last furnishing of labor, services or materials by the general contractor, if such a date is later than the first.

[29] *See id.* §§ 627.756 and 627.428(1), (3).

[30] *See id.* ch. 624.

[31] *See* Florida Bd. of Regents v. Fidelity & Deposit Co., 416 So. 2d 30 (Fla. Dist. Ct. App. 1982).

[32] *See id.*

[33] *See* FLA. STAT. § 713.02(6) (1997). The provision of a bond by the contractor does not exempt

of the payment bond is to insure that the owner's property is exempt from any construction liens,[34] the bond insures payment to any person who is a contractor, a subcontractor, a sub-subcontractor, a laborer, a professional, or a materialman who contracts with the owner, a contractor, a subcontractor, or a sub-subcontractor provided there is compliance with the statute.[35] Thus, anyone more remote than a sub-subcontractor or a materialman selling to a sub-subcontractor does not have rights against the bond.

For those protected, the bond assures that they will be paid for their labor, services and materials used to improve the real property. However, as in all statutory bonds either an owner or a person seeking protection under a statutory bond must strictly comply with the statute's requirements.

Thus, the statutory payment bond has two distinct parts. The owner must ensure that all the provisions to establish the statutory bond are fulfilled. The payment bond must be obtained before commencing the construction of the improvement. It must be obtained by the prime contractor who has a direct contract with the owner of the property for at least the amount of the original contract price with the prime contractor. It must be attached to the notice of commencement when the notice is recorded and posted at the jobsite. Furthermore, the bond must be executed by a surety authorized to do business in Florida. The bond shall be conditioned that the contractor shall promptly make payments for labor, services and material to all lienors under the contractor's direct contract.[36]

In addition, the bond shall not contain any provisions restricting the class of persons protected or the venue of any proceeding.[37] Also, the owner, contractor or surety shall furnish a true copy of the bond at the cost of reproduction to any lienor demanding it. Any person who fails or refuses to furnish the copy without justifiable cause shall be liable to the lienor demanding the copy for any damages caused by the refusal or failure.[38]

---

the property from the lien of the contractor who furnishes the bond. If the bond is provided it shall secure all liens *subsequently* accruing under the statute. The failure to attach a copy of the bond to the notice of commencement when the notice is recorded negates the exemption. However, if a bond exists but is not recorded the bond may be used as a lien transfer bond pursuant to FLA. STAT. § 713.24 (1998).

[34] *See* Oolite Indus., Inc. v. Millman Constr. Co., 501 So. 2d 655 (Fla. Dist. Ct. App. 1987), *petition for review denied,* 509 So. 2d (Fla. 1987).

[35] FLA. STAT. § 713.01(16) (1998).

[36] *See id.* § 713.23(1)(a). Any form of bond given by a contractor conditioned to pay for labor, services and material used to improve real property shall be deemed to include the condition of this subsection that the contractor shall make prompt payments to all lienholders under the contractor's direct contract.

[37] *See id.* § 713.23(1)(f). The surety is not entitled to the defense of *pro tanto* discharge as against any lienor because of changes or modifications in the contract to which the surety is not a party; however, the liability of the surety may not be increased beyond the penal sum of the bond. A lienor may not waive in advance its right to bring an action under the bond against the surety.

[38] *See id.* § 713.23(1)(b).

If a payment bond has been provided, a lienor making a claim on a bond must strictly follow the statutory procedures. If the lienor has a direct contract with the prime contractor, it may file its claim on the bond by serving a notice of nonpayment.[39]

However, if the lienor does not have a direct contract with the prime contractor, it must first properly serve in writing a notice to the prime contractor before beginning or within forty-five (45) days after beginning to furnish labor, materials or supplies.[40] This notice states that the lienor will look to the prime contractor's bond for protection on the work, and is in addition to the required notice of nonpayment.

As a condition precedent to recovery under the statutory bond, any lienor, whether or not it has a direct contract with the prime contractor, must serve a written notice of nonpayment to the contractor and the surety within ninety (90) days of the failure to receive any payment that is then due and owed from the delivery date for any labor, services or materials.[41] Effective October 1, 1999 pursuant to HB 681, the time period for serving a written notice of nonpayment may not be determined by the issuance of a certificate of occupancy or the issuance of a certificate of substantial completion.

If the lienor does not comply with both relevant notice provisions, no action will lie against the prime contractor or the surety *on the bond.*[42] In any case, a lienor is time-barred from instituting an action against the surety or the prime contractor on the bond after one year from the performance of the labor or completion of delivery of materials and supplies.[43] Effective October 1, 1999 pursuant to HB 681, the time period for bringing an action against the contractor or surety on the bond may not be determined by the issuance of a certificate of occupancy or the issuance of a certificate of substantial completion.

After a statutory payment bond has been executed and delivered, the property is exempt from every construction lien claim filed, except that of the prime contractor furnishing the bond.[44] All claims of lien filed after the bond was executed and delivered are transferred to the bond.[45] A person having an interest in the property, or the contractor, may effect the transfer of the lien by recording

---

[39] *See id.* § 713.23(1)(d).

[40] *See id.* § 713.23(1)(c). If a notice of commencement is not recorded or a reference to the bond is not given in the notice of commencement, and in either case if the lienor is not otherwise notified in writing of the bond, the lienor not in privity with the contractor shall have forty-five (45) days from the date the lienor is notified of the existence of the bond within which to serve notice. *Id.*

[41] *See id.* § 713.23(1)(d). The failure of a lienor to receive retainage not in excess of 10% of the value of labor, services, or materials furnished by the lienor is not considered a nonpayment requiring service of the notice.

[42] *Id.* § 713.23(1)(e). Note conflict with FLA. STAT. § 95.11(5)(e) (1997).

[43] *See* FLA. STAT. § 713.23(a)(3) (1998).

[44] *See* FLA. STAT. § 713.02(6) (1997).

[45] *See id.* § 713.724.

in the clerk's office a notice of bond. The notice of bond will be verified by the clerk. The clerk will mail the notice to the lienor's address shown on the claim of lien and record it.[46]

A lienor may pursue payment for "labor, services, and materials used to improve the property," on a statutory bond.[47] However, a claim of lien secures payment for *materials* rather than *supplies*.[48] Yet, because the statutory payment bond replaces a lienor's claim of lien, a lienor under a statutory bond should be entitled to the same recovery it would have had if it were a lienor under the Construction Lien Law. The use of differing language appears inadvertent.

[D] Lien Transfer Bond

Even if a private owner did not exempt the property from a construction lien at the beginning of construction by recording a bond with the Notice of Commencement, any lien claimed under the Construction Lien Law may be subsequently transferred[49] from the property to a transfer bond executed by a surety insurer licensed to do business in Florida or to a cash deposit.[50] The transfer may be initiated by the owner or any person having an interest in the real property. Pursuant to the 1998 amendments (effective July 1, 1998), the amount of the bond or cash deposit was increased to an amount equal to the amount of the claim of lien, plus three years' interest at the legal rate (currently 30 percent—10 percent per year) plus the greater of $1,000 or 25 percent of the lien claims as a deposit for costs and attorneys' fees. The bond or cash deposit notice must be conditioned to pay any judgment arising from a foreclosure of the claim of lien. Any number of liens may be transferred to one bond or cash deposit.[51]

The 1998 amendments also provide, however, that a court is required to increase the amount of the cash deposit or bond if the amount of the bond in excess of the lien is found to be insufficient to pay the lienor's attorneys' fees and court costs in the action to enforce the lien. This may be difficult to enforce if the current property owner is not the party who has effected the transfer to the

---

[46] *See id.* All references to *clerk* mean the office of the clerk of the circuit court of the county in which the real property is located. FLA. STAT. § 713.01(3) (1998).

[47] *Id.* § 713.23(1)(a). However, in subsection (1)(e) the term used is "labor or materials or supplies."

[48] *Id.* § 713.06. The lien on the real property improved is for any money owed for labor, services or materials furnished and for any unpaid finance charges due under the lienor's contract. A material supplier or laborer, either of whom is not in privity with the owner, or a sub-subcontractor or a subcontractor who complies with the provisions of this part and is subject to the limitations thereof, also has a lien on the owner's real property for labor services or materials furnished to improved public property if the improvement of the public property is furnished in accordance with the subcontract and the direct contract.

[49] *See id.* § 713.24(1).

[50] *See id.* § 713.24(1)(b).

[51] *See id.*

deposit or bond. Interesting issues are presented by a requirement to make a surety increase a bond without the surety having the right to exercise its discretionary underwriting for any additional amount. It is unknown what will result if the court orders an increase in the bond and the surety exercises credit discretion in refusing to increase the amount of the bond. Will the court then require whoever posted the bond to make up the difference by a cash deposit? Certainly logical, but this remains yet to be determined.

Once the clerk receives the bond or cash deposit, the property is released from the claim of lien and the lien is transferred to the bond. The clerk shall make and record a certificate showing the transfer of the lien from the property to the bond or the cash deposit. A copy of this certificate is mailed to the lienor.[52] The lienor must then foreclose on the transfer bond or deposit. Thus, the filing of the bond or cash deposit frees the property from the lien and it makes the property marketable without consideration of the pending litigation.

[E] Conditional Payment Bond

The Conditional Payment Bond Statute, Fla. Stat. § 713.245, was to be repealed effective July 1, 1993, pursuant to 1990 Florida laws, ch. 90–109, § 13, as amended by 1992 Florida laws, ch. 92–286, § 9. However, these session laws were repealed by 1993 Florida laws, ch. 93–99, § 3. The conditional payment bond statute, therefore, remains in effect. In fact § 713.245 was amended to change a reference in § 713.245(2) to § 713.23(1)(f) when subsection (1)(g) was redesignated.[53]

The conditional payment bond statute[54] is a controversial statute which is somewhat confusing in that it is a combination of the construction lien law and the transfer bond law. The statute shifts the liability for payments to lienors from the owner to the prime contractor. An owner who obtains a conditional payment bond does not exempt its property from liens filed under the Construction Lien Law. Instead, an owner who complies with the conditional payment bond may transfer a construction lien from its property to the prime contractor's surety bond.

The conditional payment bond is subject to many of the same requirements of a statutory payment bond.[55] In addition, the conditional payment bond must

---

[52] *See id.*

[53] *See* 1995 Fla. Laws ch. 95-211 § 58.

[54] *See* FLA. STAT. § 713.245 (1998).

[55] *See id.* § 713.245. The conditional payment **must:**

1. Be executed by a surety insurer qualified to do business in Florida;
2. Be executed in an amount equal to the original contract price;
3. Give any lienor the direct right of action against the surety;
4. Not contain any provisions restricting the venue of any proceeding or the classes of persons protected by bond; or
5. Not require a lienor to waive its rights in advance.

Id.

warn potential lienors with a disclaimer stating that it is not an ordinary payment bond, and that the lienors must proceed under the Construction Lien Law.[56]

In order to protect rights, a lienor must file a claim of lien under the Construction Lien Law and then proceed to seek protection under the bond. Once a claim of lien has been filed against the property, the owner or the prime contractor may file a copy of the bond, a notice of bond as specified in Fla. Stat. § 713.23(2) (1998), and a sworn certificate of payment to the contractor in the form specified in FLA. STAT. § 713.245(4) (1998) within 90 days.[57] Any notice of bond recorded more than 90 days after the recording of the lien is not effective unless the owner, the prime contractor, and the surety all sign the notice of bond.[58] The certificate of payment swears that the owner has paid the prime contractor for any labor, services or materials described in the claim of lien.[59] Upon receipt of the notices and the copy of the bond, the clerk shall serve a copy of the bond, the notice and the certificate on the contractor, the surety and the lienor.

If the prime contractor signs the certificate of payment or the joinder in certificate of payment, or fails to timely record a notice of contest of payment, then the lien transfers to the bond to the extent of the amount specified in the certificate of payment.[60] All outstanding amounts remain a lien on the property.[61]

If the prime contractor disputes the amount set forth in the certificate of payment, the prime contractor must file a notice of contest of payment within 15 days after the clerk certifies service of the certificate.[62] If the notice of contest specifies a portion of the lien has been paid, then that amount is transferred to the bond, and the outstanding amount remains as a lien.[63]

[F] Public Project Payment and Performance Bonds

Effective July 1, 1998 the Florida Legislature made significant changes to the law of public bonds. Because of lobbying by competing interests and the

---

[56] FLA. STAT. § 713.245(1) (1998) requires:

> In at least 10 point type, the following statement must be placed on the bond:
> THIS BOND ONLY COVERS CLAIMS OF SUBCONTRACTORS, SUB-SUBCONTRACTORS, SUPPLIERS AND LABORERS TO THE EXTENT THAT THE CONTRACTOR HAS BEEN PAID FOR THE LABOR, SERVICES, OR MATERIALS PROVIDED BY SUCH PERSONS. THIS BOND DOES NOT PRECLUDE YOU FROM SERVING A NOTICE TO OWNER OR FILING A CLAIM OF LIEN ON THIS PROJECT.

[57] FLA. STAT. § 713.245(4) (1998). The notice of bond is the same notice that is filed under a FLA. STAT. § 723.23(2) (1997) payment bond. Any party making a material misstatement of fact on these notices may be subject to criminal prosecution. FLA. STAT. § 713.245(12) (1998).

[58] *See* FLA. STAT. § 713.245(4) (1998).

[59] *Id.*

[60] *See id.* § 713.245(10).

[61] *See id.*

[62] *See id.*

[63] *See id.*

confusion of the legislative session, there are often errors or omissions in or created by the amendments. These were addressed this year in the "glitch bill," mentioned earlier in this article. The "glitch bill," HB 681, was approved by the Governor on June 18, 1999 and is effective October 1, 1999.

Before beginning work on a *public* project, the person entering into a formal contract in Florida with the state or a public authority must execute and record in the public records of the county where the improvement is located, a payment and performance bond with a surety authorized to do business in Florida.[64] The statutory bond must contain two conditions: the prime contractor must perform the contract in a time and manner designated by the contract, and the prime contractor must make all payments due to persons who would be able to make claims under the Construction Lien Law.[65] In addition, and effective with the 1998 amendments, the bond *must* contain a description of the project sufficient to identify it, including a legal description and street address (if applicable) of the property being improved and a general description of the improvement. Furthermore, it *must* state the names, addresses, and phone numbers of the contractor, surety and the owner of the property.[66] Finally, the statute requires that the bond contain a reference to notice and time limitation provisions of the statute and make specific reference to the statute. Although the statute is very specific as to what must be in a public project bond, all bonds furnished for public works contracts are deemed bonds under this statute regardless of form.[67]

Unlike a statutory private payment bond for which *every* claimant must serve a notice of nonpayment to the contractor and surety, persons in privity with the prime contractor on a public bond project are *not* required to deliver either the preliminary notice to a public owner or a notice of nonpayment as a condition precedent to claim against a public project bond. However, a claimant (except a laborer) who does *not* have a direct contract with the prime contractor shall, before commencing or not later than 45 days after commencing to furnish labor, materials or supplies for the prosecution of the work, furnish the contractor with a notice that he or she intends to look to the bond for protection.[68] A claimant (except a

---

[64] *See id.* § 255.05(1)(a). The statute is remedial in nature. It places a corresponding duty on a public agency to see that a bond is in fact posted for the protection of subcontractors on public projects in excess of $200,000. The public agency is liable for its failure to ensure that the bond is posted. *See* Palm Beach County v. Trinity Indus., Inc., 661 So. 2d 942 (Fla. Dist. Ct. App. 1995).

[65] *See id.*

[66] The 1998 amendments require information on the first page of the bond (to be recorded) as would be put in the notice of commencement posted for private work. Although the statutory language is mandatory, there is no consequence addressed in the statute about the failure to include any of the required information. However, earlier cases had held that the failure to comply with the requirement of recording the bond rendered the bond a common law bond, excusing the claimants from the statutory notices and leaving the parties to comply with the notices in the bond form itself, if any. *See* Houdaille Indus., Inc. v. United Bonding Ins. Co., 453 F.2d 1048 (5th Cir. 1972).

[67] *See* FLA. STAT. § 255.05(4) (1998).

[68] *See id.* § 255.05(2). In Haskell Co. v. Peoples Constr. Co., 648 So. 2d 833 (Fla. Dist. Ct. App.

laborer) who does *not* have a direct contract with the prime contractor and has not received payment for his or her labor, materials or supplies must also deliver to the contractor and to the surety written notice of the performance of the labor or delivery of the materials or supplies and of the nonpayment. The notice of nonpayment may be served at any time during the progress of the work or thereafter but not before 45 days after the first furnishing of labor, services or materials, and not later than 90 days after the final furnishing of the labor, services or materials by the claimant. With respect to rental equipment, notice may not be served later than 90 days after the date that the rental equipment was last on the job site available for use.[69]

If the nonprivity claimant does not comply with the statutory notices, the claimant may not institute an action against the surety or the prime contractor. Moreover, no action, except for an action exclusively for retainage, shall be instituted against a prime contractor or the surety on the bond after one year from the performance of the labor or completion of delivery of the materials or supplies.[70] An action exclusively for recovery of retainage must be instituted against the contractor or surety within one year after the performance of the labor or completion of delivery of the materials or supplies, or within 90 days after the receipt of final payment (or the payment estimate containing the owner's final reconciliation of quantities if no further payment is earned and due as the result of deductive change orders) by the contractor or surety, whichever comes last.[71] Effective October 1, 1999 the time periods for service of a notice of nonpayment or for bringing an action against a contractor or a surety may not be determined by the issuance of a certificate of occupancy or the issuance of a certificate of substantial completion.

Effective July 1, 1998, the contractor can shorten the prescribed time in which to commence an action to enforce any claim against the payment bond by recording and serving a notice of contest of claim against the payment bond in substantially the form set forth in Fla. Stat. § 255.05(2)(a)1 (1998). The claimant has 60 days from the date of service (mailing) to file suit. This can be done only where the claimant is no longer furnishing labor, services or materials on the project.

1995), the court held that the failure to give notice of intent to look to the bond within 45 days after work was commenced prevented a subcontractor from recovering on the bond, even though notice was given within 45 days after the subcontractor was due to be paid. As a reaction to the case, the Legislature changed the statute, effective October 1, 1995, by deleting the words "and who has not received payment for his labor, materials or supplies." The statute now clearly states that a claimant, not in privity with contractor, shall, within 45 days after beginning to furnish labor, materials or supplies, furnish the subcontractor with a notice that it intends to look to the bond for protection. 1997 Florida Laws ch. 95-06, § 25.

[69] *See id.*

[70] *See* FLA. STAT. § 255.05(2) (1998). Note conflict for commencing date with id. § 95.11(2)(b).

[71] *See id.* § 255.05(2)(a)2.

[G] Other Bonds

[1] Bid Bonds

Florida does not have any general statute that regulates bid bonds. There are various statutes requiring bid bonds applicable to some agencies of government in Florida.[72] In the absence of a specific statute for a given agency, the undertakings that insure the principal's obligations under a bid are common law bonds.

[2] Bid Protest Bond

Florida does require a person who protests a Florida Department of Transportation bid solicitation, rejection or award to post a bond.[73] The amount of the bond varies with the amount being protested. If the action is protesting a bid solicitation in an amount greater than $250,000, then the bond shall be $5,000. If the action is protesting a bid rejection or contract award in an amount greater than $250,000, then the bond shall be $5,000 or one percent of the contract price, whichever is greater. A bond of $2,500 is required for the actions protesting bid solicitations, bid rejections, or contracts less than $250,000. The bond is conditioned upon the payment of all costs that may be adjudged against the person filing the protest. The bond will be forfeited if the administrative hearing officer determines that the protest was filed improperly.

§ 10.03 LIEN LAW

[A] General Concepts

The Florida statute providing for construction liens on real property is found in Part I of Fla. Stat. ch. 713 (1998). Effective January 1, 1991, Part I was renamed the Construction Lien Law.[74]

The Florida Construction Lien Law (lien law) was enacted to provide contractors, subcontractors, sub-subcontractors, laborers, materialmen and certain professionals with a mechanism to secure payment on private construction projects

---

[72] *See* FLA. STAT. § 153.10 (1997). This statute requires bid bonds for county water system and sanitary sewer projects.

[73] *See id.* § 337.11.

[74] 1990 Fla. Laws ch. 90–109 (codified at FLA. STAT. § 713.001 (1997)). In 1989, the Mechanics Lien Law Study Commission was appointed by the governor, the president of the Senate and the speaker of the House for the purpose of reviewing the existing Construction Lien Law. The commission authored the "Florida Mechanic's Lien Law Study Commission Report, a Report to the Governor, the President of the Senate, the Speaker of the House (January 1990)," that discussed the confusion existing among the construction industry and public regarding mechanics or construction liens. As a result of that report, substantial statutory changes were made resulting in the current Construction Lien Law.

in Florida. The lien law grants to only these classes of potential "lienors" the right to lien a project for payment for services rendered, materials supplied or work performed to "improve"[75] real property and for unpaid finance charges due under the lienor's contract.[76] Publicly owned property is not subject to construction liens.[77]

Lien rights are statutorily created, and are not subject to liberal construction in favor of any party to whom Part I applies.[78] So long as potential claimants comply with the procedural requirements of the lien law, "lienors" are afforded the right to file a "claim of lien" against real property which will act as an encumbrance against the owner's interest in the property subject to various defenses and owner remedies. Effective January 1, 1991, construction lenders, as defined by the statute, are also subject to potential liability for lienors' claims.[79]

[B] Basic Provisions

The method to perfect a lien under the lien law depends upon the status of the lienor. The lien law provides that a lien may be perfected for specific "professional services,"[80] materials provided or services performed for subdivision improvements,[81] labor, materials and services furnished by one not in privity with an owner,[82] or labor, materials and service furnished by one in privity with the owner and unpaid finance charges due under the lienor's contract.[83] Each category of lienors has a distinct method of attaching the property. Except for those persons directly in privity with the owner, improvements to real property pursuant to a direct contract price for $2,500 or less are exempt from the effect of the lien law.[84]

The lien law provides protection to only specifically identified classes of "lienors." Different pre-lien requirements are imposed on each of these potential classes. The specific classes of lienors include:[85]

---

[75] *See* FLA. STAT. § 713.01(12) (1998).

[76] *See* FLA. STAT. § 713.05 (1997); FLA. STAT. § 713.06(1) (1998).

[77] *See* FLA. STAT. § 713.05 (1997); FLA. STAT. §§ 713.01(24) and 713.06(1) (1998).

[78] *See* FLA. STAT. § 713.37 (1997).

[79] *See* FLA. STAT. § 713.13(6) (1998). For a definition of *lender, see id.* § 713.01(15).

[80] FLA. STAT. § 713.03 (1997). "Professionals" under the statute include architects, landscape architects, interior designers, engineers, surveyors and mappers. These professionals may make a claim against the property irrespective of whether the real property is actually improved. *See id.*

[81] *Id.* § 713.04 (1997). "Subdivision" *improvements* include, but are not limited to, the grading, leveling, excavating and filing of land; the grading and paving of streets, curbs and sidewalks; the construction of ditches; the laying of pipes and conduits for water, gas, electric, sewage and drainage purposes; and the altering, repairing and redoing of all these things. *See id.*

[82] FLA. STAT. § 713.06 (1998).

[83] FLA. STAT. § 713.15 (1997); FLA. STAT. § 713.06(1) (1998).

[84] *See* FLA. STAT. § 713.02(5) (1997).

[85] *See* FLA. STAT. § 713.01(16) (1998).

1. *Contractor,* defined as "a person other than a materialman or laborer who enters into a contract with the owner of real property for improving it, or who takes over from a contractor as so defined the entire remaining work under such contract."[86]
2. *Subcontractor,* defined as "a person other than a materialman or laborer who enters into a contract with the contractor for the performance of any part of such contractor's contract."[87]
3. *Sub-subcontractor,* defined as "a person other than a materialman or laborer who enters into a contract with a subcontractor for the performance of any part of such subcontractor's contract, including the removal of solid waste from real property."[88]
4. *Subdivision improver* is any lienor who performs services or furnishes materials "to real property for the purpose of making it suitable as the site for the construction of an improvement or improvements."[89]
5. *Laborer,* defined as "any person other than an architect, landscape architect, engineer, surveyor or mapper, and the like who, under properly authorized contract, personally performs on the site of the improvement labor or services for improving real property and does not furnish materials or labor service of others."[90]
6. *Materialman,* defined as a person furnishing materials "under contract to the owner, contractor subcontractor or sub-subcontractor on the site of the improvement or for direct delivery to the site of the improvement or, for specially fabricated materials, off the site for the improvement of the particular improvement, and who performs no labor in the installation thereof."[91]
7. *Professional,* defined as a person who performs "services as architect, landscape architect, interior designer, engineer, surveyor or mapper."[92]

Notwithstanding the provisions of the lien law, any contractor, subcontractor, or sub-subcontractor who is not licensed "as a contractor pursuant to the laws of the jurisdiction within which he is doing business" shall have no lien rights.[93]

Lien rights exist only by virtue of contract rights.[94] Thus, lien rights do not exist if the work being performed by the claimant is not part of the "direct contract."[95] *Direct contract* is defined as "a contract between the owner and any

[86] *Id.* § 713.01(7).
[87] *Id.* § 713.01(26).
[88] *Id.* § 713.01(27).
[89] *Id.* § 713.04(1).
[90] *Id.* § 713.01(14).
[91] *Id.* § 713.01(18) (1998).
[92] FLA. STAT. § 713.03 (1997).
[93] FLA. STAT. § 713.02(7) (1998).
[94] *See* Lofter v. Rashide, 523 So. 2d 1230 (Fla. Dist. Ct. App. 1988); Hawaiian Inn, Inc. v. Robert Myers Painting, Inc., 363 So. 2d 125 (Fla. Dist. Ct. App. 1978).
[95] *Id.*

other person."[96] *Owner* is defined to include a person who is the owner of "any legal or equitable interest in real property, which interest can be sold by legal process, and who enters into a contract for the improvement of real property."[97] *Owner* includes within its meaning a condominium association, but only as to improvements made to the association's property or common elements.[98] *Contract* means an agreement for "improving real property, written or unwritten, express or implied, and includes extras or change orders."[99] *Extras or change orders* means "labor, services or materials for improving real property authorized by the owner and added to or deleted from labor, services or materials covered by a previous contract between the same parties."[100] Such extras or change orders are lienable for their reasonable (*quantum meruit*) value.[101]

With one exception, a construction lien extends solely to the right, title and interest of the person who contracts for the improvement "as such right, title and interest exists at the commencement of the improvements or is thereafter acquired in the real property."[102] Thus, a lien may attach to a leasehold interest, but not to the underlying fee simple interest of a lessor.[103]

However, under certain circumstances, both the lessor's and lessee's entire interest are subject to a lien when the improvement is made by the lessee in accordance with an agreement between the lessee and the lessor.[104] However, a lease that contains prohibitive language as to the lienability of the property may prevent the lien from extending beyond the lessee's interest *if it is recorded in the public records.*[105]

---

[96] FLA. STAT. § 713.01(8) (1998).

[97] *Id.* § 713.01(21).

[98] *See id.*

[99] *Id.* § 713.01(5).

[100] *Id.* § 713.01(10).

[101] *See* Mike Henry, Inc. v. Donaldson, 558 So. 2d 1093 (Fla. Dist. Ct. App. 1990).

[102] FLA. STAT. § 713.10 (1997). The statutory exception generally provides that a spouse who contracts for the improvement of real property is deemed to have acted as the agent for the other spouse, thus subjecting both spouses' interest in the property to a potential lien. The noncontracting spouse may avoid the lien as provided by statute. *See id.* § 713.12.

[103] *See id.* § 713.10.

[104] *See* Budget Elec. Co. v. Strauss, 417 So. 2d 1143 (Fla. Dist. Ct. App. 1982) ("[I]f, as part of the consideration for the lease the lessee is required to make improvements under circumstances that the lessor could enforce that promise, then the leased property should be subject to the liens of parties contracting with the lessee to perform such improvements.") *Id. See also* FLA. STAT. § 713.10 (1997).

[105] *See* FLA. STAT. § 713.10 (1997). A short form of the lease or a similar statement setting forth the prohibitive may be used as an alternative to the entire lease. *See id.;* Jones v. Wright, 391 So. 2d 313 (Fla. Dist. Ct. App. 1980) (noting when 50-year lease contained a provision that lessee was not permitted to do anything that would create a lien or claim of lien on the leasehold, and when that lease was recorded, liens for improvements will not lie). Note that if the lessee knowingly or wilfully fails to advise a contractor of a prohibitive lease provision concerning liens, the contract between the lessee and contractor is voidable at the contractor's option. *See* FLA. STAT. § 713.10 (1997).

Because a lien extends to an owner's interest in real property that is "thereafter acquired," a lienor contracting with a lessee will have a claim against the freehold interest when the lessee later acquires the fee simple interest in the property, despite a lien prohibition in a recorded lease.[106] Thus, when a lessee acquires a fee interest in real property subsequent to the attachment of a lien, the lien will attach to the lessee's new interest irrespective of restrictive language in the lease.[107]

Generally speaking, lienable services must constitute part of the improvement under the direct contract. With the exception of "specially fabricated materials" constructed off-site, on-site labor is lienable while off-site labor is not lienable.[108] Obviously, to the extent that the cost of off-site labor is built into the cost of material, off-site labor can be lienable.

Improvement is defined as including any "building, structure, construction, demolition, excavation, solid waste removal, landscaping, or any part thereof existing, built, erected, placed, made or done on land or other real property for its permanent benefit."[109] Thus, labor and services associated with general maintenance of real property do not fall within the definition of improvement and are not lienable.[110] Likewise, a potential lienor performing services outside of the parameters of the direct contract will have no right to lien for those services.[111]

Liens for materials incorporated into the site, including normal wastage, are lienable.[112] The delivery of materials to the site of the improvement, or to a place designated by the person with whom the materialman contracted other than the site of the improvement, is *prima facia* evidence of the incorporation of those materials into the improvement.[113] However, the burden is on the materialman to establish actual delivery,[114] and when materials are picked up over the counter and not shown to have been delivered to the site of the improvements, no such lien will exist.[115]

Lienable material as contemplated by the lien law includes "supplying tools, appliances, or machinery used on the particular improvement to the extent of the reasonable rental value for the period of actual use (not determinable by the contract for rental unless the owner is a party thereto), but does not include

---

[106] L. M. Adamson v. First Fed. Sav. & Loan Ass'n. of Andalusia, 519 So. 2d 1036 (Fla. Dist. Ct. App. 1998).

[107] *See id.* at 1039.

[108] FLA. STAT. § 713.01(14) (1998).

[109] *Id.* § 713.01(13).

[110] *See* Legault v. Sun Coast Lawn Serv., Inc., 486 So. 2d 72 (Fla. Dist. Ct. App. 1986).

[111] *See* Lofter v. Rashide, 523 So. 2d 1230 (Fla. Dist. Ct. App. 1988).

[112] *See* FLA. STAT. § 713.01(11) (1998).

[113] *See id.* § 713.01(11); FLA. STAT. § 713.09 (1997).

[114] *See* Tuttle/White Constructors, Inc. v. Hughes Supply, Inc., 371 So. 2d 559, 565 (Fla. Dist. Ct. App. 1979).

[115] *See* Florida E. Coast Properties, Inc. v. Coastal Constr. Prod., Inc., 553 So. 2d 705 (Fla. Dist. Ct. App. 1989).

supplying handtools."[116] Thus, the rental value of equipment is lienable subject to limitations of "the reasonable rental value" and the period of use.[117]

There is one exception to the general rule that lienable materials must be incorporated into the job. That exception relates to specially fabricated materials. *Specially fabricated material* is defined as material not generally suited or readily adaptable in a similar improvement or one that has little or no value if not used in the contemplated improvement.[118] When the "specially fabricated materials" have not been incorporated into the improvements through no fault of the lienor, a lien for those materials will exist excluding the value of "any design work, submittals, or the like preliminary to actual fabrication of the materials."[119]

Lienable services provided by professional lienors were expanded effective January 1, 1991 to include services used in connection with improving the real property or supervising any portion of the work of improving the real property rendered in accordance with that professional's contract and with the direct contract.[120] The professional's lien exists regardless of whether the real property is actually improved.[121]

Professionals are deemed to include architects, landscape architects, interior designers, engineers, land surveyors and mappers.[122]

[C] Notice Requirements

[1] Generally

Lienors must comply with various strict notice requirements of the lien law to qualify for a potential lien against real property. Generally, these notice requirements are strictly enforced.[123] The types of possible notices include a Notice to Owner,[124] a Contractor's Affidavit.[125] a Claim of Lien[126] and a 15-day Notice of Recordation of Lien.[127] Effective October 1, 1999, HB 681 amended the statute to require that a Notice to Owner form contain all required information. However,

---

[116] Fla. Stat. § 713.01(11) (1998).

[117] *See* Essex Crane Rental Corp. v. Millman Constr. Co., 516 So. 2d 1130 (Fla. Dist. Ct. App. 1987).

[118] *See* Oolite Indus., Inc. v. Millman Constr. Co., 501 So. 2d 655, 656 (Fla. Dist. Ct. App. 1987); *see also* Surf Properties, Inc. v. Markowitz Bros., Inc., 75 So. 2d 298 (Fla. 1954) ("specially fabricated materials" will not include standard equipment or stock items that are "readily adaptable to use in" other similar improvements).

[119] *See* Fla. Stat. § 713.01(11) (1998).

[120] *See* Fla. Stat. § 713.03(1) (1997).

[121] *See id.* § 713.03(2).

[122] *See id.* § 713.03(1).

[123] *See* Fla. Stat. § 713.06(2)(f) (1998).

[124] *See id.* § 713.06(2).

[125] *See id.* § 713.06(3).

[126] *See id.* § 713.08.

[127] *See id.* § 713.08(4)(c).

the Notice to Owner form may differ in format from the statutory form and may contain *additional* information, provided, however, the title of the form, "Notice to Owner," is prominently displayed. The Notice to Owner form must be served on all persons designated in the notice of commencement. In the absence of a recorded Notice of Commencement, a lienor may rely on the information contained in the building permit application to serve the prescribed notice.

Laborers

As the most protected class of potential lienors, laborers need not serve a Notice to Owner regardless of whether the laborer is in privity with the owner.[128] Laborers need only prepare and record a claim of lien within 90 days of the last work performed at the jobsite[129] and serve a copy of that claim of lien on the owner before recording or within 15 days after recording the claim of lien.[130] Failure to serve a copy of the claim of lien within the 15-day deadline renders the claim of lien "voidable to the extent that the failure or delay is shown to have been prejudicial to any person entitled to rely on the service" of the claim of lien.[131] Effective October 1, 1999, HB 681 provides that "the time period for recording a claim of lien may not be determined by the issuance of a certificate of occupancy or the issuance of a certificate of substantial completion."

Contractors

A contractor is defined as one in privity with the owner,[132] so a Notice to Owner form is not required.[133] Similar to a laborer, a contractor must also record a claim of lien within 90 days of the last work performed at the jobsite[134] and must serve a copy of that claim before recording or within 15 days of recording the lien.[135] Again, failure to serve a copy of the claim of lien within the 15-day deadline renders the claim of lien "voidable to the extent that the failure or delay is shown to have been prejudicial to any person entitled to rely on the service" of the claim of lien.[136] Additionally, a contractor must execute and deliver to the owner a Final Contractor's affidavit at least five days before instituting a lien foreclosure action as a prerequisite to instituting that action.[137] The Final Contrac-

---

[128] *See* Fla. Stat. § 713.05 (1997); Fla. Stat. § 713.06(2)(a) (1998).

[129] *See* Fla. Stat. § 713.08(5) (1998).

[130] *See id.* § 713.08(4)(c).

[131] *Id.*

[132] *Id.* § 713.01(7).

[133] *See* Fla. Stat. § 713.05 (1997).

[134] *See* Fla. Stat. § 713.08(5) (1998).

[135] *See id.* § 713.08(4)(c).

[136] *Id.*

[137] *See id.* § 713.06(3)(d)(1). Commencement of an action against a subcontractor by the owner for discharge of a mechanics lien did not result in a waiver of the subcontractor's requirement to file a contractor's final affidavit as a condition precedent to maintenance of a lien foreclosure action. The fact that the lien foreclosure action was filed by the subcontractor as a counterclaim did not

tor's Affidavit must state that all lienors who have timely served a Notice to Owner on the owner and contractor have been paid in full, or if not paid in full, the amount due or to become due for labor, service or material furnished.[138] A contractor who institutes an action before serving the final contractor's affidavit may amend the complaint to show delivery of the affidavit provided the statute of limitations has not run before filing the amended complaint. The filing of the affidavit is a condition precedent to bringing a lien foreclosure action rather than a jurisdictional defect.[139]

Subcontractors

A subcontractor, who by definition enters into a contract with a contractor as opposed to the owner,[140] must serve the owner with a Notice to Owner form within the earliest of the following periods:

1. Before or within 45 days of first commencing to furnish services or materials to the job or within 45 days of commencing to make "specially fabricated materials";[141] or
2. Before the date of the owner's final payment under the owner's contract with the contractor who has furnished the affidavit stating that all lienors under it have been paid.[142]

Subcontractors must record the lien within 90 days of the last work performed, with a copy sent to the owner before recording or within 15 days thereof.

Sub-subcontractors

Sub-subcontractors are subject to the same notice requirements as subcontractors with one exception. A sub-subcontractor must also serve any additional people designated by the owner, usually the prime contractor, with the sub-sub-

---

alter the statutory requirement or excuse noncompliance. *See* Hanley v. Kajak, 661 So. 2d 1248 (Fla. Dist. Ct. App. 1995); FLA. STAT. § 713.21(4) (1997).

[138] *See* FLA. STAT. § 713.06(3)(d)1 (1998).

[139] *See* Holding Elec., Inc. v. Roberts, 530 So. 2d 301, 302 (Fla. 1988).

[140] *See* FLA. STAT. § 713.01(26), (1998).

[141] *Id.* §§ 713.01(11) and 713.06(2)(a). Trees selected by homeowners for installation at their property by a landscaping contractor were not "specially fabricated materials" for purposes of exception to the requirement that a subcontractor give owners notice of a potential mechanics lien within 45 days after services or materials are delivered to a job site. Thus, material suppliers who sell materials over the counter should measure the 45-day period for notifying owners of a potential mechanics lien as running from the date materials were actually delivered at the job site, rather than the exception. *See* Stunkle v. Gazebo Landscaping Design, Inc., 660 So. 2d 623 (Fla. 1995); FLA. STAT. § 713.06(2)(a) (1998).

[142] FLA STAT. § 713.06(3)(d)(1) (1998). The owner may direct in a notice of commencement that other individuals or entities receive a copy of the notice to owner. Those individuals typically include lenders, title companies. or attorneys. Although the lien law requires lienors to mail the notice to owner to the owner's designees, the failure to mail a copy will not invalidate an otherwise valid lien. *See id.* § 713.06(2)(b).

contractor's Notice to Owner as a prerequisite to perfecting and recording a lien.[143] The notice must be served within the earliest of the following periods:

1. Before or within 45 days of commencing to furnish services or materials;[144] or
2. Before the final payment to the subcontractor through whom the sub-subcontractor is working.[145]

Sub-subcontractors must record the lien within 90 days of the last work performed, with a copy sent to the owner before recording or within 15 days thereof.

Materialmen

A materialman dealing directly with an owner must follow the same notice and lien procedures as a contractor, except a materialman need not provide the Final Contractor's Affidavit before initiating suit to foreclose a lien.[146] A materialman dealing directly with the prime contractor should follow the notice and lien procedures of a subcontractor, and a materialman doing business with a subcontractor should follow the notice and lien procedures set forth for a sub-subcontractor. When a materialman is doing business with the sub-subcontractor, the sub-subcontractor notice and lien procedures should be followed with the additional requirement that the materialman serve an additional copy of its Notice to Owner on the subcontractor who has contracted with the materialman's customer (the sub-subcontractor).[147]

Subdivision Improvers

A subdivision improver is only required to record its claim of lien within 90 days after the final furnishing of materials or services or labor to the jobsite. The lienor must also serve a copy of that lien on the owner before recording, or within 15 days after recording that claim of lien.[148]

The lien law grants a subdivision improver certain rights that, under certain circumstances, allow the lienor to attach a lien to property other than the improved

---

[143] *Id.* § 713.06(2)(a).

[144] *See id.* Because delivery of materials is the genesis of the 45-day period, when materials are sold for direct delivery to a jobsite and are picked up at the counter, the pickup date will begin the 45-day countdown. Arlington Lumber & Trim Co. v. Vaughn, 548 So. 2d 727 (Fla. Dist. Ct. App. 1989).

[145] FLA. STAT. § 713.06(2)(a) (1998); *see also* Carter Sand Co. v. Baymeadows, Inc., 320 So. 2d 14, 15 (Fla. Dist. Ct. App. 1975).

[146] *See* FLA. STAT. § 713.05 (1997).

[147] A materialman furnishing materials under the lien law may have a lien for the reasonable value of the actual use of equipment to the extent of the reasonable rental value of that equipment. *See* FLA. STAT. § 713.01(11) (1998).

[148] *See* FLA. STAT. § 713.04(1) (1997), FLA. STAT. § 713.08(4)(c) (1998).

parcel.[149] In some cases, a subdivision improver's lien may be equitably divided among the abutting property.[150]

Professionals

Lienors for professional services are required to record a claim of lien within 90 days of the last work performed at the jobsite and must serve a copy of the claim of lien on the owner subject to the same 15-day period.[151] Neither a Notice to Owner nor a contractor's final affidavit is required from the professional unless the professional functions as a contractor.[152]

[2] Specific Requirements

The lien law specifically provides that a Notice to Owner is not "a lien, cloud, or encumbrance on the real property," nor does the notice serve as actual or constructive notice of a lien, cloud, or encumbrance.[153] The form of the notice to owner must be in substantially the form set forth in the statute.[154] As of January 1, 1991, the form contains a "warning to owner" which advises the owner, among other things, to obtain a written release from the noticing party each time a payment is made to the contractor.[155]

The manner of serving notices and other instruments, including claims of lien and affidavits,[156] is prescribed by the lien law as including one of the following: (1) actual delivery to the person to be served or to one partner of a partnership or to an officer, director, managing agent, or business agent of a corporation; (2) mailing to the same individuals, postage prepaid, by registered or certified mail to that individual's last known address;[157] (3) posting on a premises of the improvements if neither (1) or (2) can be accomplished; (4) by

[149] *See* FLA. STAT § 713.04(1) (1997).

[150] *See id.*

[151] *See* FLA. STAT. § 713.08 (1998).

[152] *See* FLA. STAT. § 713.03 (1997). Hutton v. 3-L Enters., Inc., 431 So. 2d 277 (Fla. Dist. Ct. App. 1983) (court found that an engineer was functional equivalent of contractor).

[153] FLA. STAT. § 713.06(2)(a) (1998).

[154] *See id.* § 713.06(2)(c).

[155] *Id.*

[156] Note that FLA. STAT. § 713.06(3)(d)(1) (1998) does not require "service" of the contractor's affidavit, but merely requires that the affidavit be given to the owner.

[157] If a *notice to owner* (and effective October 1, 1999 pursuant to HB 681, a preliminary notice under § 713.23 or a preliminary notice under § 255.05) is mailed within 40 days after the lienor first furnishes labor, services or materials, service is effective as of the date of mailing, if a registered or certified mail log is kept showing the date set, the registered or certified mail number, the person served, and the postal service date stamp (effective July 1, 1998). FLA. STAT. § 713.18 (Supp. 1999).

If *any instrument* served pursuant to § 713.18(1)(b) is sent to the last address shown in the Notice of Commencement but is returned as "refused," "moved, not forwardable," or "unclaimed" or is otherwise not delivered or deliverable through no fault of the person serving, then service is effective as of the date of mailing. FLA. STAT. § 713.18(1)(b) (1998).

facsimile transmission when the person being served has listed his or her facsimile number in the notice of commencement; or, effective October 1, 1999, pursuant to HB 681, "by overnight delivery or second-day delivery using a delivery service that maintains, in the ordinary course of business, records that specify when and where delivery was made." If real property is owned by one or more people, the lienor may serve any notices or other papers on one of the owners.[158]

When the owner and general contractor are identical and each has a common corporate officer, the notice to owner need not be sent to both the owner and the general contractor.[159] Similarly, a lienor need not serve a Notice to Owner when the lienor is in privity with the owner or the owner's agent.[160] When a Notice to Owner is served upon a lender, it must be in writing and served in accordance with § 713.18, and "shall be addressed to the person designated, if any, and to the place and address designated in the notice of commencement."[161] When the lender receiving notice pays a contractor on behalf of the owner for an improvement and fails to make proper payments as provided by the lien law, the lender shall be liable to the *owner* for damages sustained by the owner as a result of that nonpayment. No other individual has rights against the lender for lender's failure to comply.[162]

As stated, a prospective lienor must record a claim of lien within 90 days after the final furnishing of the labor or services or materials by the lienor except when the original contractor has defaulted or the contract was terminated pursuant to the lien law. In the case of a default or termination, "no claim of lien attaching prior to such default shall be recorded after ninety days from the date of such default or ninety days after the final performance of labor or services or furnishing of materials, whichever occurs first."[163] The claim of lien is to be recorded in the clerk's office in the county or counties in which the real property is situated.[164] The claim of lien may be amended at any time during the period allowed for the original recording, provided that "such amendment shall not cause any person to suffer any detriment by having acted in good faith in reliance upon such claim of lien as originally recorded."[165]

The claim of lien must contain the following information:

[158] *See* FLA. STAT. § 713.18(2) (1998).

[159] *See* Broward Atl. Plumbing v. R.L.P., Inc., 402 So. 2d 464 (Fla. Dist. Ct. App. 1981).

[160] *See* King v. Brickellbanc Sav. Ass'n., 551 So. 2d 604 (Fla. Dist. Ct. App. 1989).

[161] FLA. STAT. § 713.06(d) (1998). Also note that § 713.06(b) (effective October 1, 1997) provides that when the owner, in his notice of commencement, designates a person in addition to himself to receive a copy of a lienor's notice to owner, the lienor shall serve a copy of his notice on the person so designated.

[162] *See id.*

[163] FLA. STAT. § 713.08(5) (1998).

[164] *See id.*

[165] *Id.* § 713.08(4)(b).

1. The name of the lienor and address where notice or process may be served on the lienor;
2. The name of the person with whom the lienor contracted or with whom the person is employed;
3. Thc labor, services or materials furnished and the contract price or value thereof. Specially fabricated materials that have not been incorporated into the site and the contract price or value thereof must be separately stated in the claim of lien;
4. The real property's description;
5. The name of the owner;
6. The time when labor, services or materials were first and last furnished;
7. The balance due the lienor for the labor, services or materials[166] and for unpaid finance charges due under the lienor's contract.
8. If the lien is claimed by one not in privity with the owner, the date and method of service of the notice of owner; if the lien is claimed by one not in privity with the contractor or subcontractor, the date and method of service of the copy of the notice on the contractor or subcontractor must be stated.[167]

The claim of lien must be signed and verified by the lienor or the lienor's agent acquainted with the facts stated in the claim of lien.[168]

The omission of the foregoing details or errors in the claim in lien will not, within the discretion of the trial court, prevent the enforcement of the lien against one who has not been adversely affected by the omission or error.[169] No lien shall exist for a period of longer than one year after the claim has been recorded unless an action to enforce the lien has been commenced within that time period,[170] unless the owner, owner's agent, or attorney has shortened the time for commencing the action by recording in the clerk's office a notice contesting the lien.[171] When a

[166] The amount of the lien should not include overhead and profit which are above and beyond the reasonable value of the labor, services or materials. *See* Broderick v. Overhead Door Co., 117 So. 2d 240 (Fla. Dist. Ct. App. 1959); *see also* Surf Properties, Inc. v. Markowitz Bros., Inc., 75 So. 2d 298 (Fla. 1954). Because recovery for overhead and profit as separate items are not within the purview of the lien law, a contractor who makes that claim in its lien is liable to the homeowner for punitive damages for the filing of a fraudulent lien. *See* Martin v. Jack Yanks Constr. Co., 650 So. 2d 120 (Fla. Dist. Ct. App. 1995). Additionally, the lien should not include attorneys' fees, liquidated damages, or other contract damages directly attributable to the value of the labor, materials or services. C.A. Davis, Inc. v. Yell-for-Penell, Inc., 274 So. 2d 267 (Fla. Dist. Ct. App. 1973).

[167] FLA. STAT. § 713.08(1) (1998).

[168] *See id.* § 713.08(2).

[169] *See id.* § 713.08(4)(a).

[170] *See* FLA. STAT. § 713.22(1) (1997).

[171] *See id.* § 713.22(2).

notice of contest of lien is recorded, the period for instituting an action is shortened to 60 days, after which time the lien is automatically extinguished.[172]

The notice of contest is mailed by the clerk to the lien claimant at the address shown on the claim of lien or the most recent amendment to that claim of lien, and the clerk must certify service on the face of the notice and record the notice.[173] Service is determined to be complete upon mailing.[174] In any event, a lien that is extended as a result of the initiation of an action is good against creditors or subsequent purchasers for valuable consideration and without notice only when a notice of *lis pendens* has been recorded.[175]

[D] Waiver

A right to a claim of lien may not be waived in advance.[176] "A lien right may be waived only to the extent of labor, services, or materials furnished."[177]

However, a prospective lienor may waive, release or satisfy any part of that lienor's lien either for the amount due for labor, services or materials furnished, or for labor, services or materials furnished through a certain date.[178] Additionally, a prospective lienor may waive, release, or satisfy any part of the lien for labor, services or materials furnished as to any part or parcel of the real property.[179] The acceptance by a lienor of an unsecured note for the balance due does not constitute a waiver of the lien, unless expressly stated in writing.[180]

[E] Lien Priority

Professional liens and subdivision improvement liens attach at the time of recording the lien and take priority as of that date.[181] Liens for contractors, subcontractors, sub-subcontractors and materialmen attach and take priority as of the time of the recording of the notice of commencement, if any.[182] If the notice of commencement is not recorded, the liens attach and take priority as of the time of recordation of the claim of lien.[183]

---

[172] *See id.*

[173] *See id.* § 713.22(2).

[174] *See id.*

[175] *See id.* § 713.22(1).

[176] *See id.* § 713.20(2).

[177] *Id.*

[178] *See id.* § 713.20(3).

[179] *See id.*

[180] *See id.* § 713.20(1).

[181] *See* FLA. STAT. § 713.(1) (1998).

[182] *See* FLA. STAT. § 713.07(2) (1997). The provision is important to lenders because a mortgage recorded after the recording of the notice of commencement is subject to all subsequent liens which relate back and take priority as of the earlier time of the recording of the notice of commencement. Lenders therefore must obtain subordination agreements to protect their security.

[183] *See id.* § 713.07(2). The lien law requires an owner to record a notice of commencement

If construction ceases before completion and the owner wishes to recommence construction, the lienor's priority for recommencing construction may supersede the liens of lienors involved in the original construction. The owner's options relating to recommencement are discussed in Fla. Stat. § 713.07(4), (1997). Effective January 1, 1991, before any disbursement of construction funds to a contractor, a lender must also record a copy of the notice of commencement in the clerk's office, the failure of which renders and lender liable to the owner for all damages sustained by the owner as a result of the failure to record.[184]

[F] Remedies of Owner

The lien law provides certain potential remedies for an owner wishing to avoid a lien and potential liability to a lienor. For example, an owner may demand a sworn statement under oath from a lienor stating the nature of the labor or services performed and to be performed, the materials furnished and to be furnished, the amount paid on account to date, the amount due and the amount to become due the lienor.[185] The failure to provide that statement within 30 days will deprive the lienor of the lien.[186]

Additionally, so long as an owner complies with the mandates of the lien law, an owner may make use of the "proper payments defense," which will limit the owner's liability for liens to the amount of the direct contract price.[187] Special procedures are established for an owner faced with abandonment and recommencement of construction.[188] An owner may also terminate the effect of a Notice

---

before starting construction for any improvement for which the direct contract price is $2,500 or more, or for professional services or subdivision improvements. *Id.* §§ 713.02(5), 713.03(2) and 713.04(2). The contents of the notice of commencement are prescribed by statute, and the notice of commencement shall not be filed earlier than 90 days before actual commencement of construction. FLA. STAT. § 713.13(2) (1998). The owner must post at the site either a certified copy of the notice or a notarized statement confirming the recordation of the notice with a copy attached to the statement. *Id.* § 713.13(1)(a).

[184] *See* FLA. STAT. § 713.13(6) (1998).

[185] *See* FLA. STAT. § 713.16(2) (1997).

[186] *See id.* In addition, an owner of real property may request from the contractor a list of all subcontractors and suppliers who have any contract with the contractor to furnish any material or to perform any service for the contractor with respect to the owner's real property or improvements. The contractor's failure to furnish that list within ten days after receipt of the owner's written request, sent by registered or certified mail, will result in a forfeiture of the contractor's right to assert a lien against the owner's property to the extent that the owner is prejudiced by the contractor's failure to furnish that list or by any omissions to the list. A list furnished under this section will not constitute a notice to owner on behalf of the listed contractors and suppliers, however. *See id.* § 713.165.

[187] FLA. STAT. §§ 713.06(3)(a) and 713.13 (1998); *see also* Royal v. Clemons, 394 So. 2d 155 (Fla. Dist. Ct. App. 1981).

[188] *See* FLA. STAT. § 713.22(1)(a) (1997). The notice of commencement must include phone numbers of contractor, surety, lender and persons designated by owner to receive notice and fax number if service by fax is acceptable.

of Commencement[189] or may transfer liens to a bond.[190] Finally, a lien is rendered entirely unenforceable against an owner when the lien has been wilfully exaggerated.[191]

[G] Lender Responsibilities

Effective October 1, 1992, the construction lien law was greatly expanded to increase the liability and responsibility of lenders that make construction loans and secure them with mortgages on improved real property.[192] Section 713.13(6) of the Florida Statutes provides that a lender must, prior to disbursement of any construction funds to the contractor, record the notice of commencement in the clerk's office, provided it has not already been recorded by the owner. The failure of the lender to record the notice of commencement as required by the statute makes the lender liable to the owner for all damages sustained by the owner as a result of the failure to record. The provision provides a right of action for damages to the owner against the lender for failure to record the notice. It excludes a right of action for failure to record from all others. In the commencement notice, the lender must designate itself, in addition to all others, to receive copies of notices to the owner.

Pursuant to Fla. Stat. § 713.06(2)(d) (1998), any lender who, after receiving a notice to the owner, pays a contractor on behalf of the owner for an improvement, shall be required to make proper payments as to each such notice received

---

[189] *See* FLA. STAT. § 713.132 (1998), which provides that a notice of termination is effective to terminate the notice of commencement at the later of thirty (30) days after recording of the notice of termination or the date stated in the notice of termination as the date on which the notice of commencement is terminated, provided that the notice of termination has been served pursuant to section (1)(f) on the contractor and on each lienor who has given notice.

[190] *See id.* § 713.24; *see also* §§ 10.01–10.03 on construction bonds.

[191] *See* FLA. STAT. § 713.31 (1997). A person who wilfully files a fraudulent lien commits a felony of the third degree. *See id.* § 713.31. Moreover, any person, firm or corporation that knowingly and intentionally makes or furnishes to another person a written statement in the form of an affidavit, *whether or not under oath,* containing false information about the payment status of subcontractors, sub-subcontractors or suppliers, knowing that one to whom it was furnished might rely on it, shall be guilty of a felony of the third degree. The statute was amended in 1995 to delete the requirement of an oath and any reference to the crime of perjury as a result of the court's decision in Redding v. State, 666 So. 2d 921 (Fla. Dist. Ct. App. 1995), which held that the state had failed to establish perjury under the statute because, even though the contractor's applications for payment were notarized, the notary testified that she did not administer the oath to the defendant when he signed the applications. *See* FLA. STAT. § 713.35 (1997); 1995 Florida Laws Ch. 95–940, § 9. However, a contractor will not be liable for a civil theft under FLA. STAT. § 772.11 (1997), by reason of a misapplication of construction funds pursuant to FLA. STAT. § 713.345 (1997), because that statute does not denominate the crime as a theft. Rather, it defines the crime as a misapplication, and specifies all applicable penalties. *See* Seabridge, Inc. v. Superior Kitchens, Inc., 672 So. 2d 848 (Fla. Dist. Ct. App. 1996).

[192] *See* FLA. STAT. § 713.01(15) (1998) (a "lender" is one who not only loans money but also secures the loan with a mortgage on improved real property).

by the lender. The failure of the lender to comply with this paragraph renders the lender liable to the owner for all damages sustained by the owner as a result of that failure. Only the owner has a claim or right of action against the lender for failure to make proper payments. Nothing in thc scction prohibits the lender from disbursing construction funds directly to the owner in which event the lender has no obligation to make proper payments under this paragraph.

Finally, Fla. Stat. § 713.3471 (1998) requires that, within five business days after a lender makes a final determination, prior to distribution of all funds available under a construction loan, that the lender will cease further advances, the and lender must serve a written notice of that decision on the contractor and on any other lienor who has given the lender notice. The lender giving such notice is insulated from liability to the contractor based upon the decision to cease further advances if the decision is otherwise permitted under the loan documents. The failure to give notice when required renders the lender liable to the contractor to the extent of the actual value of materials and direct labor costs furnished by the contractor, plus 15 percent for overhead, profit and all other costs, from the date on which the notice of the lender's decision is actually served. The lender's liability is limited to the amount of undisbursed funds at the time the notice should have been given, unless the failure to give notice was for the purposes of defrauding the contractor. The lender will not be liable to the contractor for consequential or punitive damages for failure to give timely notice. Most importantly, the statute grants a cause of action against the lender to the contractor for damages sustained as a result of the lender's failure to give timely notice. However, the separate cause of action may not be used to hinder or delay any foreclosure action; may not be the basis of any claim for an equitable lien or equitable subordination of the mortgage lien; and may not be asserted as an offset or a defense in the foreclosure case.

CHAPTER 11

GEORGIA

Neal J. Sweeney
R. Lee Mann, III
Eugene J. Heady

§ 11.01 INTRODUCTION

On private projects, Georgia law does not require any type of bond. Instead, Georgia's statutory mechanics' and materialmen's lien law provides protection for contractors, subcontractors, laborers, and suppliers that furnish labor and materials for private projects. Georgia's lien law is set forth in §§ 44-14-360 *et seq.* of the Georgia Code. The statutory lien rights granted in §§ 44-14-360 *et seq.* of the Georgia Code cannot be prospectively waived even if a payment bond is provided on a private project.

Public property in Georgia may not be liened. To provide protection to those furnishing materials or labor on public projects, Georgia law requires payment and performance bonds on all public projects in excess of $40,000. The purpose and coverage of these statutorily prescribed bonds are similar to that of the federal Miller Act,[1] but Georgia's payment bond protection extends to more parties and the notice requirements are more liberally construed. There are no general requirements for bid bonds on public works projects, but there are specific requirements for what a bid bond must provide if one is required.

Georgia's "Little Miller Act" is set forth in two separate places in the Georgia Code, §§ 36-82-101 through -105 and § 13-10-1. The Georgia Little Miller Act does not define *public works.*[2] After reviewing a number of court interpretations over the previous twenty years, the Georgia Court of Appeals concluded that "it is clear that the nexus between public works and/or public bodies for purposes of the applicability of [the Little Miller Act] . . . is closely aligned to the provision of essential government services" and not to "any project which may incidentally be the recipient of some public funding."[3] However, downtown development projects authorized under the Georgia Code are public works even though they do not involve providing what would traditionally be considered essential government services.[4]

Georgia's Little Miller Act and the legal principles applicable to private construction bonds are relatively straightforward and, with a few exceptions, are consistent with most other states. Georgia's lien law, however, has been described as a "thicket" by one court.[5] Great caution must be exercised in navigating this "thicket." Georgia's lien law is frequently amended by the Georgia legislature and the Code provisions are very detailed. The Code often provides specific language and forms to be used in connection with liens. Georgia's lien law is strictly construed against the lien claimant, and strict compliance with its Code requirements is required to perfect a mechanics' or materialmen's lien. Any

---

[1] 40 U.S.C. §§ 270a–270f (1988).

[2] Consolidated Elec. Supply v. Bishop Contracting Co., 205 Ga. App. 674, 423 S.E.2d 415 (1992).

[3] 423 S.E.2d at 417.

[4] *See* City of Atlanta v. United Elec. Co., 202 Ga. App. 239, 414 S.E.2d 251 (1991).

[5] Adair Mortgage Co. v. Allied Concrete Enters., 144 Ga. App. 354, 241 S.E.2d 267 (1977).

deviation from the Code requirements, no matter how slight, puts the lien claimant at great risk.

§ 11.02 BOND LAW

[A] General Concepts

Georgia's treatment of the construction surety bond relationship is similar to that of most states. There are three parties: the surety, the principal, and the obligee. The *principal* is a party obtaining the bond and the one owing the duty, typically the contractor or the subcontractor. The *obligee* is a party to whom the obligation is owed, such as the owner. The *surety* binds itself to perform in accordance with the contract and the terms of the surety bond if the principal does not perform. The liability of the surety and the principal is joint and several unless the contract expressly provides otherwise.[6] The obligee, however, is entitled to only one performance. Therefore, if the principal performs, the surety's obligation is discharged.[7]

A surety bond required by statute will be reviewed in light of the statute creating the duty to give the bond, and the provisions of the statutes and applicable regulations will be read into the bond. To the extent a statutory bond contains provisions that do not comply with the statute, they may be eliminated as surplusage.[8]

Surety bonds that are not required by statute are common law bonds.[9] Generally, the liability of the surety under a common law bond will be defined by the plain meaning of the terms of the bond.[10] However, virtually all construction sureties are "compensated" sureties.[11] As such, the bond should be construed most strongly against the surety and in favor of bond coverage.[12] There is a one-year limitation of action under Georgia Little Miller Act payment bonds.[13] Similar time

---

[6] Turner Broad. Sys., Inc. v. Sanyo Elec. Co., 33 B.R. 996 (Bankr. N.D. Ga.), *aff'd,* 742 F.2d 1465 (5th Cir. 1983).

[7] H.J. Kellos Constr. Co. v. Balboa Ins. Co., 495 F. Supp. 408 (S.D. Ga. 1980).

[8] American Cas. Co. v. Irvin, 426 F.2d 647 (5th Cir. 1970).

[9] Sims Crane Serv., Inc. v. Reliance Ins. Co., 514 F. Supp. 1033 (S.D. Ga.), *aff'd,* 667 F.2d 30 (5th Cir. 1981).

[10] American Cas. Co. v. Irvin, 426 F.2d 647 (5th Cir. 1970).

[11] A "compensated" surety is one that regularly engages in the business of executing surety contracts for a premium payment as contrasted with an uncompensated or "gratuitous" surety, which is one that becomes a surety for an obligation in a noncommercial situation. *See* Carl R. Dickey, et al., "Performance Bond Claims" *in* HANDLING FIDELITY, SURETY, AND FINANCIAL RISK CLAIMS 105, 120 (1990) (formerly published by John Wiley & Sons and now published by Aspen Law & Business). Frequently, the courts will distinguish between defenses available to a compensated surety and defenses available to a gratuitous surety. *Id.*

[12] Sims Crane Serv., Inc. v. Reliance Ins. Co., 514 F. Supp. 1033 (S.D. Ga.), *aff'd,* 667 F.2d 30 (5th Cir. 1981); Houston Gen. Ins. Co. v. Brock Constr. Co., 241 Ga. 460, 246 S.E.2d 316 (1978).

[13] GA. CODE ANN. § 36–82–105 (1993).

limitations expressly stated in common law payment bonds are also enforceable and not void on grounds of public policy.[14]

Generally, a surety's liability cannot be more than the stated penal sum of the bond.[15] However, Georgia has a specific statute addressing bad faith on the part of sureties.[16] The refusal of a surety to remedy a default or make payment in accordance with the terms of the bond within 60 days after receipt of a notice of default or demand for payment may subject the surety to a 25-percent penalty *plus* reasonable attorneys' fees.[17] The question of bad faith under the statute is an issue for the jury unless there is, as a matter of law, a reasonable defense that vindicates the surety's good faith.[18]

If the default of the principal is disputed, the surety in good faith may insist on a judicial determination of the sufficiency of any reasonable defense asserted. Because the liability of the surety is contingent on the liability of the principal, a surety is entitled to all of the contractor's defenses under the contract.[19] The surety may also assert its own independent defenses.

In theory, a surety's obligation is discharged if the underlying obligation of the principal is changed without the notice and approval of the surety. In reality, this principle has little application to construction bonds. Georgia's Little Miller Act expressly states that no change in the construction contract shall release the surety of its payment bond obligation: "No agreement, modification, or change in the contract, change in the work covered by the contract, or extension of time for the completion of the contract shall release the surety of such payment bond."[20] In addition, virtually every construction contract expressly anticipates

---

[14] Sam Finley, Inc. v. Interstate Fire Ins. Co., 135 Ga. App. 14, 217 S.E.2d 358 (1975).

[15] Long v. City of Midway, 169 Ga. App. 72, 311 S.E.2d 508 (1983).

[16] GA. CODE ANN. § 10–7–30 (1994). A plaintiff may not recover a bad faith penalty or attorneys' fees under § 10-7-30 in a suit brought under the federal Miller Act. United States v. All Am. Bldg. Sys., Inc., 857 F. Supp. 69, 70 (1994).

[17] Houston Gen. Ins. Co. v. Brock Constr. Co., 241 Ga. 460, 246 S.E.2d 316 (1978); Travelers Indem. Co. v. Sasser & Co., 138 Ga. App. 361, 226 S.E.2d 121 (1976); *see also* Ayers Enters., Ltd. v. Exterior Designing, Inc., 829 F. Supp. 1330 (N.D. Ga. 1993) (holding that § 10-7-30 is plaintiff's exclusive remedy in case where surety refuses in bad faith to pay obligation, and § 13-6-11, which allows recovery of litigation expenses in general contract cases, is not available). *Contra* Congress Re-Insurance Corp. v. Archer-Western Contractors, Ltd., 226 Ga. App. 829, 487 S.E.2d 679 (1997) (holding that under Georgia Code Annotated § 9-12-13 and interpretive case law a general contractor could recover from a surety *either* the 25-percent penalty for bad faith or recover attorney fees and expenses of litigation, but could not recover both; this holding appears contrary to the plain language of Georgia Code Annotated § 10-7-30, which allows for recovery of *both* a 25-percent penalty for bad faith *and* reasonable attorney's fees).

[18] McDevitt & Street Co. v. K-C Air Conditioning Serv., Inc., 203 Ga. App. 640, 646, 418 S.E.2d 87, 93 (1992).

[19] Vickers v. Chrysler Credit Corp., 158 Ga. App. 434, 280 S.E.2d 842 (1981); GA. CODE ANN. § 10-7-2 (1994). A principal's waiver of its claims against a creditor in return for a release does not defeat the surety's right to assert those claims to reduce its liability to the creditor. Hardaway Co. v. Amwest Sur. Ins. Co., 263 Ga. 698, 700, 436 S.E.2d 642, 644-45 (1993).

[20] GA. CODE ANN. § 36-82-102 (1993).

that changes will be made, and the terms of those contracts are in turn incorporated in the bond. Most performance and payment bond forms also expressly provide for the surety's consent to alterations.[21] This consent to changes is generally enforceable.[22]

In addition, the Georgia Supreme Court held that a creditor's release of the principal without the consent of the surety does not discharge the surety if the creditor, in the instrument of release, reserves its rights against the surety. In *Hardaway Co. v. Amwest Surety Insurance Co.,*[23] a prime contractor, Hardaway, brought an action against a subcontractor's surety, Amwest, to recover damages for the default of the subcontractor, B&F Contractors. Previously, B&F had sued Hardaway for additional costs it had incurred before it defaulted; in settlement of that suit, Hardaway released B&F from Hardaway's claims regarding default. Hardaway specifically provided, however, that it retained its rights against Amwest. In the suit against it, Amwest contended that the release of B&F terminated Hardaway's rights against Amwest.

The Georgia Supreme Court, in answering a certified question from the Eleventh Circuit, held that "the release of the principal debtor, without the consent of the surety, releases the surety, unless the right to go against the surety is reserved in the instrument of release, or it appears from the whole transaction that the surety should remain bound."[24] Therefore, Amwest could not escape liability based on Hardaway's release of B&F.

[B] Bid Bonds

Georgia's Little Miller Act does not require bid bonds on public projects. Instead, it describes the requirements for bid bonds if the state or governmental entity requires that bid bonds be provided.[25] For example, the Georgia Department of Transportation has an express statutory requirement for bid bonds.[26] However, lack of specific enabling legislation does not preclude public agencies from requiring bid bonds. If bid bonds are required, the Georgia Little Miller Act requires that the bond must be in an amount of not less than five percent of the total amount payable by the terms of the contract. Instead of a bid bond, a cashier's check, certified check, or cash in the same amount may be accepted. If the amount of the bid bond is under $300,000, an irrevocable letter of credit may be accepted.[27]

Under Georgia common law, if a bidder has made a genuine bid mistake, it

[21] *See, e.g.,* American Institute of Architects (AIA) Document A311.

[22] Bobbitt v. Firestone Tire & Rubber Co., 158 Ga. App. 580, 281 S.E.2d 324 (1981).

[23] 263 Ga. App. 698, 436 S.E.2d 642 (1993).

[24] 263 Ga. App. at 699, 436 S.E.2d at 644 (quoting Schwitzerlet-Seigler Co. v. C&S Bank, 155 Ga. 740, 746, 118 S.E. 365 (1923)).

[25] GA. CODE ANN. § 13-10-1 (Supp. 1998).

[26] *Id.* § 32-2-68.

[27] *Id.* § 13-10-1(d).

may be entitled to withdraw the bid, and both the contractor and the bid bond surety are excused from liability.[28] However, a careful reading of recent statutory amendments and relevant case law concerning public projects is required to understand when the contractor may withdraw such a bid without penalty.

In *Department of Transportation v. American Insurance Co.*,[29] the Supreme Court of Georgia considered a dispute concerning whether a bidder on a Georgia Department of Transportation (GDOT) construction project was obligated to forfeit his bid bond where the bidder first attempted to withdraw his bid after all bids were submitted and opened and where the bidder ultimately declined to execute the contract that GDOT awarded to the bidder. The dispute arose after the bidder discovered an alleged mistake in the bid and attempted to withdraw the bid. The court held that GDOT was not obligated to release the bidder from his $148,000 bid bond even where the bidder documented a clerical, unintentional mistake and notified GDOT promptly after the bid opening. The bidder notified GDOT that his bid was based on an incorrect quantity of concrete and requested a release from his bid bond. GDOT refused. Subsequently, the contractor and its bid bond surety filed a lawsuit seeking a return of the bid bond. The court noted that the Georgia bid statutes were intended to alter common law rules. Although the statute permitted GDOT to release bid bonds, it did not require such a release. The court reasoned that the statutory provisions replaced the normal rules of equity. The statutorily required bid bond was intended to compel the bidder to execute a contract with GDOT if its bid is accepted or to compensate GDOT for the losses incurred if the bidder defaults. Because the statute had no provision for withdrawal of bids for unintentional mistakes, the court refused to imply an equity provision for such withdrawal.

In 1998, the Georgia legislature added Code Section 13-10-1(3)(A) to permit a bidder to withdraw its bid from consideration after the bid opening without penalty for certain bid mistakes. The statute relates to bid, performance, and payment bond requirements for contracts for public works. The statute, however, does "not apply to bids for contracts with any public agency or body which receives funding from the United States Department of Transportation and which is primarily engaged in the business of public transportation."[30] Under § 13-10-1(3)(A), a public bidder is entitled to withdraw its bid after bid opening without forteiture of its bid security if:

(i) The bidder has made an appreciable error in the calculation of his or her bid that can be documented by clear and convincing written evidence;

(ii) Such errors can be clearly shown by objective evidence drawn from

---

[28] First Baptist Church v. Barber Contracting, Inc., 189 Ga. App. 804, 377 S.E.2d 717 (1989) (involving bids taken for a *private* contract).

[29] 288 Ga. 505, 491 S.E.2d 328 (1997).

[30] GA. CODE ANN. § 13-10-1(a)(1).

inspection of the original work papers, documents, or materials used in the preparation of the bid sought to be withdrawn;

(iii) The bidder serves written notice upon the public entity which invited proposals for the work prior to the award of the contract and not later than 48 hours after the opening of bids, excluding Saturdays and Sundays and legal holidays;

(iv) The bid was submitted in good faith and the mistake was due to a calculation or clerical error, an inadvertent omission, or a typographical error as opposed to an error in judgment; and

(v) The withdrawal of the bid will not result in undue prejudice to the public entity or other bidders by placing them in a materially worse position than they would have occupied if the bid had never been submitted.[31]

[C] Performance Bonds

Georgia's Little Miller Act requires performance bonds on all public contracts in excess of $40,000. If the amount of the bond does not exceed $300,000, an irrevocable letter of credit may be accepted.[32]

The value of the bond must at least be the value of the contract. The performance bond is "for the protection" of the governmental entity for which the work is done.[33] A performance bond cannot be considered to have the force and effect of a payment bond.[34]

[D] Payment Bonds

As with performance bonds, Georgia's Little Miller Act requires payment bonds for all public contracts in excess of $40,000, with an irrevocable letter of credit being acceptable if the bond amount does not exceed $300,000.

The payment bond must be in at least the amount of the contract price. The payment bond must be payable to the governmental entity, but be "for the use and protection of all subcontractors and all persons supplying labor, materials, machinery, and equipment" to the project.[35] Additionally, instead of a payment bond, the governmental entity may accept a cashier's check, certified check, or cash in the amount of at least the total contract price.[36]

---

[31] Id. § 13-10-1(3)(A).

[32] GA. CODE ANN. § 13-10-1(d) (Supp. 1998).

[33] *Id.* § 3-10-1(b)(1).

[34] B&B Elec. Supply Co. v. H.J. Russell Constr. Co., 166 Ga. App. 499, 304 S.E.2d 544 (1983).

[35] GA. CODE ANN. § 13-10-1(b)(2)(A) (Supp. 1998). Unlike with bid and performance bonds, the obligee may not maintain an action for the breach of a payment bond. A payment bond is intended to protect laborers and material suppliers rather than the obligee of the bond. Ayers Enters., Ltd. v. Exterior Designing, Inc., 829 F. Supp. 1330, 1332-33 (1993).

[36] *Id.* § 13-10-1(b)(2)(B).

Georgia courts will typically look to the decision of federal courts relating to the federal Miller Act in construing Georgia's Little Miller Act.[37] However, the spectrum of parties protected by Georgia's Little Miller Act is broader than that of the federal Miller Act, with protection extended to third-tier subcontractors and a supplier of a supplier.[38] Note that, in contrast, Georgia lien law does not extend protection to a supplier of a supplier.

The expansive protection of Georgia's Little Miller Act is consistent with the Georgia courts' insistence on liberally construing Georgia's Little Miller Act law for protection of those who furnish labor or materials for public works.[39]

Unlike most other states, Georgia courts do enforce the responsibility of the government entity to require a contractor to obtain a payment bond in accordance with the statute. Thus, a subcontractor has a right to sue the governmental entity for materials furnished because of the government's failure to require the payment bond.[40]

If a surety named in a payment bond fails to obtain authorization to do business in Georgia, its bonds shall not be approved and filed unless the surety makes and files an affidavit with the bonds stating under oath that the surety is the "fee simple owner of real estate equal in value to the amount of bonds over and above any and all liens, encumbrances, and exemption rights allowed by law."[41] Section 36-82-102 of Georgia's Little Miller Act provides a direct right of action by subcontractors and material suppliers against a public owner that fails to obtain the payment bond, together with an affidavit when necessary, required for public works. In *DeKalb County v. J&A Pipeline Co.,*[42] the Georgia Supreme Court ruled that the public owner's duty under § 36-82-102 did not extend to investigating and confirming the solvency of the surety providing the payment bond. Therefore, if the surety provides a payment bond "in the manner and form"

---

[37] TDS Constr., Inc. v. Burke Co., 206 Ga. App. 223, 425 S.E.2d 359 (1992); Amcon, Inc. v. Southern Pipe & Supply Co., 134 Ga. App. 655, 215 S.E.2d 712 (1975).

[38] Barton Malow Co. v. Metro Mfg., Inc., 214 Ga. App. 56, 57, 446 S.E.2d 785, 787 (1994) (holding that definition of *subcontractor* may include supplier of materials as well as supplier of labor or services); Tom Barrow Co. v. St. Paul Fire & Marine Ins. Co., 205 Ga. App. 10, 421 S.E.2d 85 (1992); Home Indem. Co. v. Battey Mach. Co., 109 Ga. App. 322, 136 S.E.2d 193 (1964).

[39] Sims Crane Serv., Inc. v. Reliance Ins. Co., 514 F. Supp. 1033 (S.D. Ga. 1981), *aff'd,* 667 F.2d 30 (11th Cir. 1982); City of Atlanta v. United Elec. Co., 202 Ga. App. 239, 414 S.E.2d 251 (1991); Ingalls Iron Works Co. v. Standard Accident Ins. Co., 107 Ga. App. 454, 130 S.E.2d 606 (1963).

[40] Kelly Energy Sys. v. Board of Comm'rs, 196 Ga. App. 519, 396 S.E.2d 498 (1990); *see also* Hall Cty. Sch. Dist. v. C. Robert Beals & Assocs., Inc., 231 Ga. App. 492, 498 S.E.2d 72 (1998) (holding that a school board qualified as a "public body" within the meaning of Georgia Code Annotated §§ 13-10-1 and 36-82-102 and thus was subject to a direct action for damages sustained by unpaid subcontractors when the school board failed to obtain a payment bond in the manner and form required by the statutes because the school board failed to investigate the solvency of the surety).

[41] GA. CODE ANN. § 36-82-102 (1993).

[42] 263 Ga. 645, 437 S.E.2d 327 (1993).

prescribed by Georgia's Little Miller Act, the public owner has no liability under § 36-82-102 if it turns out that the payment bond is worthless due to the surety's insolvency.[43]

In reaching its conclusion, the supreme court started with the proposition that the public owner, in this case DeKalb County, enjoyed sovereign immunity from any cause of action except as authorized by statute. Here the authorization to bring a cause of action is provided by § 36-82-102. In the Supreme Court's view, the duty imposed by § 36-82-102 was limited to confirming that the payment bond was in the proper form and that there was no additional duty on the part of the public owner to go beyond the form and investigate its accuracy or the solvency of the surety.[44] Therefore, sovereign immunity was not waived for such a claim.

The claimant argued that Georgia's Little Miller Act, including § 36-82-102, should be liberally construed to fulfill its remedial purpose of protecting subcontractors and material suppliers. The court agreed with the purpose of protecting subcontractors and material suppliers, but noted that the Little Miller Act was a substitute for lien rights, which do not exist on public works. Therefore, protection under the Little Miller Act should be no greater than that provided under Georgia lien law.

The court then pointed out that a private owner can defeat subcontractors' and material suppliers' claims of lien by obtaining an affidavit from the prime contractor, as prescribed by § 44-14-361.2(a)(2), swearing that all subcontractors and material suppliers have been paid, even if the affidavit is false.[45] Consequently, the court reasoned that by allowing a public owner to rely on a payment bond or surety's affidavit which was correct in form but was in fact worthless, Georgia

[43] *Id.; see also* Mayer Elec. Supply Co. v. DeKalb Cty., 211 Ga. App. 698, 440 S.E.2d 84 (1994) (holding that county was not required to inquire into surety's solvency when affidavit of surety comported with statutory requirements, even if real estate schedule accompanying affidavit was facially irregular). *But see* Hall Cty. School Dist. v. C. Robert Beals & Assocs., Inc., 231 Ga. App. 492, 498 S.E.2d 72 (1998) (holding that a school board can be held liable under Georgia Code Annotated § 36-82-102 if it fails to approve the solvency of the surety as now required under Georgia Code Annotated § 13-10-1, as amended).

[44] Nor is there any duty that the public body obtain an *additional* payment bond pending the outcome of an arbitration proceeding initiated by a subcontractor to resolve a payment dispute, when the public body had previously accepted a payment bond from a general contractor that met the statutory requirements. Abe Eng'g, Inc. v. Fulton Cty. Bd. of Educ., 214 Ga. App. 514, 515, 448 S.E.2d 221, 223 (1994). In *Abe Engineering,* a dispute arose on a project for the Fulton County Board of Education (FCBE) between the general contractor, Williams Construction Company, and a subcontractor, Abe Engineering, Inc., concerning payment for work performed under the subcontract agreement. The dispute was resolved in arbitration with an award to Abe. Williams completed the project and FCBE made final payment to Williams. Abe sued both Williams's surety for payment under the payment bond and FCBE for failure to satisfy the arbitration award entered against the now insolvent general contractor. The Georgia Court of Appeals held that FCBE was not required to obtain an additional payment bond pending the outcome of the arbitration proceeding and that FCBE could not be held liable for the subcontractor's claim because FCBE had complied with § 36-82-102. *Id.*

[45] *See generally* **§ 11.03[K].**

Little Miller Act claimants were receiving no less protection than they would enjoy under Georgia lien law.

The court in *J&A Pipeline* did not eliminate all hope for payment bond claimants confronted with insolvent sureties. Although no right of action against the public owner can be brought under § 36-82-102, the claimant could assert an *equitable lien* against contract funds earned by the prime contractor but not yet paid by the public owner.[46] Because such a claim is an equitable lien on funds held by the owner and not a cause of action seeking to impose liability on the public owner, it is not barred by sovereign immunity.

In addition, the court in *J&A Pipeline* noted that § 13-10-1, one of the provisions referenced in § 36-82-102, was amended, effective July 1, 1991, to expressly require that the payment bond "be approved as to form *and as to solvency of the surety* by the . . . county" (emphasis supplied). Based on its timing, the amendment did not apply to the payment bond in *J&A Pipeline* and the court expressly refused to consider what impact the amendment might have had on its analysis.

This amended language will likely increase the required scope of the public body's investigation into the solvency of the surety. For example, in *Hall County School District v. C. Robert Beals & Associates, Inc.*,[47] the Court of Appeals of Georgia found that a school district was not entitled to summary judgment against a subcontractor's direct claim where the contractor's bond proved to be invalid. The court ruled that a school board qualified as a "public body" within the meaning of § 13-10-1 and § 36-82-102 and thus was subject to a direct action for damages sustained by unpaid subcontractors when the school board failed to obtain a payment bond in the manner and form required by the statutes because the school board failed to investigate the solvency of the surety. Although the school board was not required to take any further steps than those required by the statute to investigate the propriety of the information provided by the surety, the revisions to § 13-10-1(f) did require the school board to investigate and approve the solvency of the surety, and a failure to do so could render the school board liable.

No action can be brought on a payment bond until at least ninety days after the last labor was performed or material supplied, or when the subcontract or purchase order was completed. In addition, as with the federal Miller Act, formal notice is required from any party not in direct contractual privity with the contractor. This notice must be received by the contractor within the same 90-day period in order to be sufficient.[48] However, as with other elements of Georgia's Little Miller Act, the notice requirement has been liberally construed.[49]

---

[46] *See* Pembroke State Bank v. Balboa Ins. Co., 144 Ga. App. 609, 241 S.E.2d 483 (1978).

[47] 231 Ga. App. 492, 498 S.E.2d 72 (1998).

[48] GA. CODE ANN. § 36-82-104(b)(c) (1993); F.L. Saino Mfg. Co. v. Fireman's Fund Ins., 173 Ga. App. 753, 328 S.E.2d 387 (1985).

[49] *See, e.g.*, Devore & Johnson, Inc. v. Bowen & Watson, Inc., 216 Ga. App. 63, 64-65, 453 S.E.2d 67, 69 (1994) (holding that letter sent by certified mail from material supplier to general

As with the federal Miller Act, no action on a payment bond can be instituted after one year from completion of the contract and acceptance of the public work by the governmental entity.[50]

Although many of the court decisions construing the Georgia Little Miller Act indicate great deference to claimants, such leniency should not be expected. Instead, all requirements associated with the contents and timing of notice should be strictly complied with. Failure to do so can be fatal to a claim.[51]

[1] Waiver of Payment Bond Rights

A 1991 amendment to the Georgia lien law has a direct impact on payment bond rights. The amendment, which became effective on January 1, 1992, declared "null, void and unenforceable" any waiver of payment bond rights "in advance of furnishing labor, services and materials."[52] Subcontract clauses that prospectively waive payment bond rights now appear to be unenforceable. Now, as with liens, bond rights can only be waived through the forms prescribed by statute: interim waivers, for progress or partial payments,[53] and unconditional waivers for final payment.[54]

Interim and unconditional waivers are enforceable against the claimant provided payment is made. However, payment is *presumed unless,* within 30 days of execution of the waiver, the claimant files a claim of lien or the statutorily prescribed affidavit of nonpayment in the county in which the property is located.[55] The affidavit simply swears that the claimant was not paid the amount for which the earlier waiver was executed.

This presumption of payment and the relatively short period in which it becomes effective (30 days) can be a dangerous trap for the trusting or inattentive claimant. Interim waivers are signed on a routine basis as part of the progress

---

contractor that included both name of party to whom materials were furnished and computations of outstanding balances was sufficient to satisfy notice requirement even though it did not state specifically that its purpose was to provide statutory notice); Huddleston Concrete Co. v. Safeco Ins. Co. of Am., 186 Ga. App. 531, 368 S.E.2d 117 (1988).

[50] GA. CODE ANN. § 36-82-105 (1993).

[51] *See* York-Shipley, Inc. v. Air Conditioning Contractors, Inc., 470 F. Supp. 56 (N.D. Ga. 1979) (even a delay of one day in complying with the 90-day notice period bars claim).

[52] GA. CODE ANN. § 44-14-366(a) (Supp. 1998).

[53] *Id.* § 44-14-366(c); *see* Insurance Co. of N. Am. v. Allgood Elec. Co., 229 Ga. App. 715, 494 S.E.2d 728, 730-31 (1997) (holding that subcontractor's certification of anticipated payment advances, plus retainage, for approximately ninety-nine percent of the work and subcontractor's partial lien waiver purporting to release "all claims arising out of said subcontract and the project through December 1991 . . . , including but [not] limited to claims representing mechanics liens," does not evidence an agreement relinquishing the subcontractor's right to recover the entire unpaid balance of its lump-sum performance contract; Georgia Code Annotated § 44-14-366(f) did not appear to be at issue).

[54] *Id.* § 44-14-366(d).

[55] *Id.* § 44-14-366(f).

payment application process. It should also be routine to file the required affidavit of nonpayment if there is a risk that payment will not actually be received within the specified 30 days.

[E] Notice of Commencement and Notice to Contractor

Effective January 1, 1994, Georgia's Little Miller Act was amended to include additional notice requirements that payment bond claimants must satisfy in certain circumstances. Section 36-82-104 has been rewritten. It now allows the contractor to gain additional protection from lower tier subcontractors and suppliers by filing a "Notice of Commencement" for the project within 15 days after the contractor physically commences work. The Notice of Commencement must be filed with the clerk of the superior court in the county in which the project is located. Copies must also be provided within 10 days of a written request from a subcontractor or material supplier, or the protection otherwise provided by the notice is lost as to the requesting party. The Notice of Commencement must include the name, address, and telephone number of the contractor; the name and location or general description of the project; the name and address of the public entity for which the work is being performed; and, if a security deposit is used in lieu of a bond, the holder of the deposit.[56]

If the contractor fails to file the Notice of Commencement, the obligations of bond claimants are unchanged from the existing law.[57] If the contractor properly files the Notice of Commencement, bond claimants who are not in privity with the contractor, must provide a preliminary notice to maintain their rights against the payment bond. To do so, the claimant must give the contractor a "Notice to Contractor" within 30 days of the filing of the Notice of Commencement. The Notice to Contractor must contain the name, address, and telephone number of the claimant; the name, address, and telephone number of each person at whose instance the labor or material is being furnished; the name and location of the project; a description of the labor and materials being provided; and, if known, the contract price or amount claimed to be due, if any.[58]

Effective April 5, 1994, § 10-7-31 was added to extend the Notice of Commencement and Notice to Contractor procedures to private payment bonds. The Notice of Commencement relating to a private payment bond must be filed with the clerk of the superior court in the county in which the property is located not later than 15 days after the contractor physically commences work on the property. This filing requirement is the same as for the Notice of Commencement under Georgia lien law.[59]

---

[56] GA. CODE ANN. § 36-82-104(f) (1993) (effective Jan. 1, 1994).

[57] *Id.* § 36-82-104(b)(1) and (g).

[58] *Id.* § 36-82-104(b)(2).

[59] *See* § 44-14-361.5, discussed in **§ 11.03[E]**.

§ 11.03 LIEN LAW

[A] General Concepts

Georgia lien law serves the "important public interest" of making the owner liable for labor and material that enter into the construction of the improvement of real property.[60] Despite the important public interest served, the lien law is contrary to common law. Therefore, the lien law and all of its technical requirements regarding the form and timing of notice are strictly construed against the party asserting the lien.[61]

Public property in Georgia is not subject to a lien. When a lien is filed on public property, it has no legal effect.[62]

[B] Persons Protected

Georgia lien law specifically identifies a large number of parties that are entitled to a lien against real estate for which they furnish labor, services, or material. These parties include contractors, subcontractors, materialmen, mechanics, laborers, registered architects, registered land surveyors, registered professional engineers, and manufacturers of machinery.[63] In 1991, the lien law was amended to extend coverage to suppliers of rental tools, appliances, machinery, and equipment used for the improvement of property.[64] In addition, the definition of the term "materials" was expanded to include the reasonable value or rental price of these items.[65]

Section 44-14-361 is the operative statute that actually grants lien rights, but it must be referenced to § 44-14-360, which defines the key elements of § 44-14-361 including "contractor," "materials," "materialmen," and "subcontractor."

---

[60] Tucker Door & Trim Corp. v. Fifteenth St. Co., 235 Ga. 727, 221 S.E.2d 433 (1975); Henderson v. Mitchell Eng'g Co., 158 Ga. App. 306, 279 S.E.2d 750 (1981).

[61] Palmer v. Duncan Wholesale, Inc., 262 Ga. 28, 413 S.E.2d 437, 438-39 (1992) ("[W]e have long recognized that statutes involving materialman's liens must be strictly construed in favor of the property owner and against the materialman."); Meco of Atlanta, Inc. v. Super Valu Stores, Inc., 215 Ga. App. 146, 149, 449 S.E.2d 687, 689 (1994); Benning Constr. Co. v. Dykes Paving & Constr. Co., 204 Ga. App. 73, 418 S.E.2d 620 (1992) ("The lien statute is given a strict construction. . . ."), *rev'd on other grounds,* 236 Ga. 16, 426 S.E.2d 564 (1993); L&W Supply Corp. v. Whaley Constr. Co., 197 Ga. App. 680, 399 S.E.2d 272 (1990); Roberts v. Porter, Davis, Saunders & Churchill, 193 Ga. App. 898, 389 S.E.2d 361 (1989). In Consolidated Sys., Inc. v. Amisub, Inc., 261 Ga. 590, 408 S.E.2d 109, 110 (1991), the Supreme Court of Georgia explained: "The creation of liens under § 44-14-361.1 is in derogation of the common law, and strict compliance with the requirements . . . is required."

[62] Dekalb County v. J&A Pipeline Co., 263 Ga. 645, 651, 437 S.E.2d 327, 333 (1993); City of Albany v. Lynch, 119 Ga. 491, 46 S.E. 622 (1904); B&B Elec. Supply Co. v. H.J. Russell Constr. Co., 166 Ga. App. 499, 500, 304 S.E.2d 544, 545 (1983).

[63] GA. CODE ANN. § 44-14-361(a) (Supp. 1998).

[64] *Id.* § 44-14-361(a)(9).

[65] *Id.* § 44-14-360(3).

Lien rights cover "the labor, services, or materials [which] were furnished if they are furnished at the instance of the owner, contractor, or some person acting for the owner or contractor."[66] "A stranger may not order work done upon real estate and thus charge the . . . owner. . . . "[67] Because of this, a lien claimant must prove a contractual link between himself and the owner of the property to be liened. That link need not be direct. The lien claimant can prove a contractual link with the owner by establishing a chain of privity between himself and the property owner.

Ordinarily, any break in this chain of privity, such as a mistake in the name recited in a claim of lien, cuts off the claimant's lien rights.[68] However, in *Underground Festival, Inc. v. McAfee Engineering Co.,*[69] the Georgia Court of Appeals held that a mistake in the name recited in the contract between the material supplier and the lessee did not prevent a lien from attaching to the lessor's property when the lessee ratified the contract and the improvements were made pursuant to a construction allowance from the lessor.

Lien rights extend down the chain of privity to subcontractors to subcontractors and suppliers to subcontractors.[70] The term "subcontractor" as defined in Georgia's lien law has been expansively construed to afford lien rights to lower-tier subcontractors and suppliers to lower-tier subcontractors. The Code states: "Subcontractor means, but is not limited to, subcontractors having privity of contract with the contractor."[71] The Georgia Court of Appeals has seized on this open-ended ("not limited to") definition to extend lien rights beyond second-tier subcontractors. In *Tonn & Blank, Inc. v. D.M. Asphalt, Inc.,*[72] the court interpreted "subcontractor" to mean "one who, pursuant to a contract with the prime contractor or in a direct chain of contracts leading to the prime contractor, performed services or procured another to perform services in furtherance of the goals of the prime contractor."[73] In that case, the court found that a supplier to a second-tier subcontractor could assert a lien. Under the court's analysis, however, lien rights could extend even further, provided a chain of subcontracts reaches up to the prime contractor. Extending protection that far goes beyond the coverage provided under the federal Miller Act and the lien law of most states.

This more expansive interpretation of the definition of subcontractor, and hence those covered under Georgia lien law, was reaffirmed by the Georgia Court

---

[66] GA. CODE ANN. § 44-14-361(b) (Supp. 1998).

[67] D&N Elec., Inc. v. Underground Festival, Inc., 202 Ga. App. 435, 439, 414 S.E.2d 891, 894 (1991).

[68] *See, e.g.,* Georgia N. Contracting, Inc. v. Haney & Haney Constr. & Mgt. Corp., 204 Ga. App. 366, 419 S.E.2d 348 (1992).

[69] 214 Ga. App. 243, 447 S.E.2d 683 (1994); *see* Accurate Constr. Co. v. Dobbs House, 154 Ga. App. 604, 269 S.E.2d 494 (1980).

[70] *Id.* § 44-14-361(a).

[71] *Id.* § 4-14-361(a)(9).

[72] 187 Ga. App. 272, 370 S.E.2d 30 (1988).

[73] 370 S.E.2d at 31.

of Appeals in *Tom Barrow Co. v. St. Paul Fire & Marine Insurance Co.*[74] In that case, the court again allowed a claim by a supplier to a second-tier contractor (a supplier to a subcontractor to a subcontractor to the prime contractor), which is beyond the protection of the federal Miller Act and the lien laws of most states. Relying on *Tonn & Blank, Inc. v. D.M. Asphalt,* the court expressly rejected the argument that the federal Miller Act's limitation of protection only to suppliers of first-tier subcontractors (a supplier to a subcontractor to a prime contractor) should be applied in Georgia lien law.

In *Benning Construction Co. v. Dykes Paving Co.,*[75] however, the Georgia Supreme Court reversed a court of appeals decision allowing the supplier to a second-tier contractor to enforce a lien. Although the supreme court quoted *Tonn & Blank, Inc. v. D.M. Asphalt* with approval, it added an additional requirement not raised in the earlier case: that the direct chain of contracts leading to the prime contractor be "authorized." In *Benning Construction Co.,* the subcontract between the prime contractor and the first-tier subcontractor specifically prohibited assignment without the prime contractor's written consent. The subcontractor nonetheless entered into a sub-subcontract with Lanier Paving. The lien claimant, Dykes Paving, was a supplier to Lanier Paving. The supreme court ruled that the subcontractor's failure to obtain the prime contractor's authorization to further subcontract part of the work to Lanier Paving broke the direct chain of contracts required for Dykes Paving to assert a lien.

The Supreme Court's interpretation of the impact of the anti-assignment clause, which is routine subcontract boilerplate, can substantially restrict the otherwise broad protection afforded lower-tier subcontractors and suppliers under Georgia lien law. The court's discussion suggests, but does not expressly hold, that the anti-assignment clause might be ineffective if a representative of the prime contractor who was authorized to waive the clause was aware of the assignment and did not object to it.

The chain of contracts that establishes lien rights may, in theory, be limitless for subcontractors, but this is not true for suppliers and materialmen. Because of the wording of Georgia Code Annotated § 44-14-361(a), in Georgia, lien rights extend no further than the first supplier in the chain. Suppliers to subcontractors or contractors at any level in the chain are protected, but suppliers to other suppliers are not.[76]

Lien rights accrue to a supplier of materials even if the materials are not ultimately incorporated or used in the improvement.[77] The debt, and hence the

---

[74] 205 Ga. App. 10, 421 S.E.2d 85 (1992).

[75] 263 Ga. 16, 426 S.E.2d 564 (1993).

[76] *See* GA. CODE ANN. § 44-14-361(a)(2) (Supp. 1998); Porter Coatings v. Stein Steel & Supply Co., 157 Ga. App. 260, 277 S.E.2d 272, *aff'd,* 247 Ga. 631, 278 S.E.2d 377 (1981).

[77] United Bonding Ins. Co. v. Good-Wynn Elec. Supply Co., 124 Ga. App. 545, 184 S.E.2d 508 (1971). *Cf.* Troup Enters. v. Mitchell, Carrington, & Rayfield, Inc., 199 Ga. App. 173, 404 S.E.2d 337 (1991) (holding that if work is performed in an improper manner, the lien only extends to the reasonable value of the benefits conferred on the owner).

lien rights, exist if the materials were furnished and not paid for.[78] Evidence of delivery of material to the jobsite creates a rebuttable presumption that materials were received and used by the contractor for the improvement.[79] The burden is on the owner to prove that the materials were not used.[80]

In order to preserve its lien rights, a materialman must maintain a separate account for the property against which a lien is asserted. If the materialman simply uses one general account for a particular contractor and applies all payments from that contractor against that general account, no lien rights can be established.[81] The burden is on the materialman to segregate the materials used on a particular project and to apply payments so that there is no confusion among the separate accounts.[82] If the materialman fails to maintain these separate accounts, it cannot resurrect its lien rights by an after-the-fact effort to segregate invoices and payments.[83]

[C] Property Subject to Liens

Virtually every legal interest in real property can be encumbered under Georgia's lien law.[84] Although the real property of the state, local, and federal government used for the benefit of the public cannot be liened,[85] the real property of private religious and charitable organizations can be liened even if they perform public services.[86] Separate Code provisions limit lien rights that can be asserted against condominium and time-share projects.[87]

If the improvements are made only at the request of a lessee of the property, the lien can only attach to that lease interest. A tenant cannot order work performed on property and thus render the owner-landlord liable for a lien for the cost of that work unless there is some relation between the tenant and the owner-landlord pursuant to which the landlord expressly or impliedly consented

---

[78] *Id.*

[79] Williamscraft Dev., Inc. v. Vulcan Materials Co., 196 Ga. App. 703, 397 S.E.2d 122 (1990); Electrical Distribs. v. Turner Constr. Co., 196 Ga. App. 359, 364, 395 S.E.2d 879, 883-84 (1990).

[80] Maloy v. Planters Warehouse & Lumber Co., 142 Ga. App. 69, 234 S.E.2d 807 (1977).

[81] Atlanta Lighting Fixture Co. v. Peachtree-Sheridan Corp., 113 Ga. App. 313, 147 S.E.2d 847 (1966).

[82] *Id.;* Resurgens Plaza S. Assocs. v. Consolidated Elec. Supply, Inc., 215 Ga. App. 818, 820, 452 S.E.2d 784, 787 (1994).

[83] Grigsby v. Fleming, 96 Ga. App. 664, 101 S.E.2d 217 (1957). *But see* Dallas Bldg. Material, Inc. v. Rose, 191 Ga. App. 783, 383 S.E.2d 151 (1989), in which the owner was required to show actual payment to the supplier even though the supplier had failed in his duty to credit properly various project accounts.

[84] James G. Wilson Mfg. Co. v. Chamberlin-Johnson-Du Bose Co., 140 Ga. 593, 79 S.E. 465 (1913); Meco of Atlanta, Inc. v. Super Valu Stores, Inc., 215 Ga. App. 146, 148, 449 S.E.2d 687, 689 (1994).

[85] B&B Elec. Supply Co. v. H.J. Russell Constr. Co., 166 Ga. App. 499, 500, 304 S.E.2d 544, 545 (1983).

[86] New Ebenezer Ass'n v. Gress Lumber Co., 89 Ga. 125, 14 S.E. 892 (1892).

[87] GA. CODE ANN. §§ 44-3-95 and -160 (1991 Supp. & 1998).

to the contracts under which the improvements are made. Mere knowledge that the improvements are being made by the tenant is not enough; the landlord must expressly or impliedly authorize the tenant to make the improvements for the owner-landlord's benefit.[88] If this authorization does not exist, the lien would not attach to the owner-landlord's interest in the property, but only to the tenant's interest in the lease.[89] The case of *Nunley Contracting Co. v. Four Taylors, Inc.*[90] illustrates the manner in which a contractor's lien rights can be substantially impaired by leasing arrangements between related but separate companies.

In order to lien the tenant's interest in the property, the lien claimant must identify the tenant in its claim of lien as the person whose interest in the premises is being liened.[91] In *Meco of Atlanta, Inc. v. Super Valu Stores, Inc.,*[92] the appellant/material supplier sought to enforce a lien against the leasehold of the appellee. The claim of lien filed pursuant to § 44-14-361, however, failed to assert that the estate being subjected to the lien was that of the appellee. Instead, it named only the landlord, who had not authorized the tenant to make repairs for its benefit. The court held that if the claimant filed a lien solely against the reversionary interest of the landlord, it would "indirectly allow appellee/lessee to subject the landlord's equitable interest in improvements to the leasehold to a lien asserted by appellant/materialman. It is well settled that one cannot do indirectly that which the law does not allow to be done directly."[93] The court further reasoned that this mistake caused the appellant to fail to satisfy § 44-14-361.1(a)(2), because its lien document did not reveal affirmatively the identity of the person whose interest in the premises was being subjected to a lien.[94]

[D] Notice of Commencement and Notice to Contractor

Effective January 1, 1994, Georgia Code Annotated § 44-14-361.5 was added to the Georgia lien law. Section 44-14-361.5 provides owners additional protection against lien claims by lien claimants that are *not* in privity with the contractor (sub-subcontractors and suppliers to subcontractors). The additional protection comes through an additional notice requirement which arises only if the owner of the property, the owner's agent, or the contractor files a "Notice of Commencement" for the project.[95] The Notice of Commencement must include the name, address, and telephone number of the contractor; the name and location of the project, including a legal description of the property; the name and address of the true owner of the property; the name and address of the person other than the true owner at whose instance the improvements are being made, if not the

---

[88] *D&N Electric,* 414 S.E.2d at 892.

[89] *Id.*

[90] 192 Ga. App. 253, 384 S.E.2d 216 (1989).

[91] *Meco of Atlanta, Inc.,* 215 Ga. App. at 148-49, 449 S.E.2d at 689-90.

[92] 215 Ga. App. 146, 449 S.E.2d 687 (1994).

[93] 215 Ga. App. at 148, 449 S.E.2d at 689.

[94] *Id.*

[95] Ga. Code Ann. § 44-14-361.5(d) (Supp. 1998).

true owner; the name and address of the surety for the payment and performance bonds, if any; and the name and address of the construction lender, if any.[96] The Notice of Commencement must be filed with the clerk of the superior court in the county where the property is located not later than 15 days after the contractor physically commences work on the property.[97] A copy of the Notice of Commencement must also be posted at the project site and a copy provided within 10 days of receipt of a written request to anyone requesting a copy.[98] Failure to provide a copy of the notice precludes the owner or contractor from enforcing the additional notice requirement against the requesting party.[99]

If the Notice of Commencement is not provided, the provisions of the existing lien law remain unchanged.[100] If a Notice of Commencement is properly filed and provided, then subcontractors and suppliers that are not in privity with the contractor must provide a "Notice to Contractor" to the owner or agent of the owner and the contractor within 30 days from the filing of the Notice of Commencement, or 30 days following the first delivery of labor, services, or materials to the property, whichever is later.[101] The Notice to Contractor must contain the name, address, and telephone number of the person providing labor, services, or materials; the name and address of each person at whose instance they were furnished; the name and location of the project; a description of the labor, services, and materials being provided; and, if known, the contract price or anticipated value of the services or materials provided and the amount claimed to be due.[102]

Failure to timely file a proper Notice to Contractor in response to a Notice of Commencement will extinguish the lien rights of subcontractors and suppliers.[103]

[E] Preliminary Notice of Lien

Georgia lien law permits, but does not require, the filing of a preliminary notice of lien rights.[104] The preliminary notice of lien is entirely optional. It gives owners and purchasers early notice of potential lien claims and, in many cases, may benefit the claimant by expediting satisfaction of the claim. A preliminary notice of lien can also preserve a subcontractor's or supplier's lien right that might otherwise be dissolved by a subsequent *false* affidavit of payment filed by the owner or contractor, as discussed in **§ 11.03[K]**. Regardless of the filing of a

---

[96] *Id.* § 44-14-361.5(b).

[97] *Id.*

[98] *Id.*

[99] *Id.* § 44-14-361.5(a).

[100] GA. CODE ANN. § 44-14-361.5(d) (Supp. 1998).

[101] *Id.* § 44-14-361.5(c).

[102] *Id.*

[103] *Id.* § 44-14-361.5(a).

[104] GA. CODE ANN. § 44-14-361.3(a) (Supp. 1998); Wachovia Bank v. American Bldg. Consultants, Inc., 138 B.R. 1015 (Bankr. N.D. Ga. 1992).

preliminary notice of lien, the *claimant is still required to file a claim of lien* in full compliance with the lien law to perfect its lien.

The preliminary notice of lien must be filed with the clerk of the superior court of the county in which the project is located.[105] The form and contents of the preliminary lien notice are similar to those required of a claim of lien and are described in Georgia Code Annotated § 44-14-361.3(a)(2) through (5). If the claimant is not in privity with the owner, a copy of the preliminary notice of lien must be sent by registered or certified mail to the contractor or the owner of the property.[106]

The wording of the statute is somewhat ambiguous. It is unclear whether the preliminary notice of lien must be filed within 30 days of when materials or labor were first furnished, within 30 days of when they were last furnished, or within 30 days of any furnishing of labor or materials.[107] To be safe, the preliminary notice should be filed within 30 days of when materials or labor were first furnished.

A preliminary notice of lien expires if the claimant waives the lien in writing or the time for filing a claim of lien expires.[108] It will also be dissolved if the claimant fails to file a notice of lien within ten days of the date the owner mails a demand for filing a claim of lien.[109] On nonresidential property (more than four family units),[110] the demand cannot be sent before substantial completion or abandonment or termination of the contractor's contract with the owner.[111] Upon final payment, the claimant must cancel the preliminary notice of lien in the manner prescribed in § 44-14-362(b). Failure to effect the cancellation of the preliminary notice subjects the claimant to liability to the owner for all actual damages and costs and reasonable attorneys' fees incurred by the owner in having the preliminary notice canceled.[112]

[F] Requirements for Perfecting a Claim of Lien

The five basic requirements for perfecting a lien under Georgia law are set forth in Georgia Code Annotated § 44-14-361.1(a), as follows:

1. The claimant must substantially comply with its contract for furnishing materials or labor for the project;
2. The claimant must record a claim of lien containing the information required by the lien law within three months after last furnishing materials or labor;

---

[105] *Id.* § 44-14-361.3(a)(1).

[106] *Id.* § 44-14-361.3(b).

[107] *Id.* § 44-14-361.3(a)(1).

[108] GA. CODE ANN. § 44-14-361.4(a) (Supp. 1998).

[109] *Id.* § 44-14-361.4(a)(3-4).

[110] *Id.* § 44-14-360(8).

[111] GA. CODE ANN. § 44-14-361.4(a)(4) (Supp. 1998).

[112] *Id.* § 44-14-362(a).

3. At the time of recording the lien, the claimant must send a copy of the claim of lien by registered or certified mail to the owner of the real property or the contractor, as agent of the owner;
4. The claimant must commence an action on the underlying debt secured by the lien within twelve months from the time the debt became due. Note that the date the debt became due is deemed to be the date the claimant last furnished materials or labor, and that this action refers to the suit against the party with whom the lien claimant contracted, *not* the lien foreclosure suit; and
5. Within fourteen days of filing the suit on the underlying debt (not the lien foreclosure action), the claimant must file a sworn notice of commencement of the suit in the property records of the court where the claim of lien was filed.

Strict compliance with these statutory requirements is essential to establish an enforceable lien. To underscore the importance of strict compliance with the lien law, § 44-14-361.1(a) states that the lien "must be created and declared in accordance with [these] provisions, and on failure of any of them, the lien shall not be effective or enforceable."[113]

[1] Substantial Compliance with Contract

To perfect a claim of lien, a lien claimant must establish that it substantially complied with the contract pursuant to which it furnished materials or labor for the project.[114] Although case law defining "substantial completion" is sparse, in one older case, the Georgia Court of Appeals noted that "[m]ere trivial defects or omissions" will not defeat a claimant's right to a lien.[115]

If the lien claimant's completion of the project was prevented by the owner, that interference constitutes the equivalent of substantial completion.[116] However, abandoning the work before completion based upon the "mere apprehension" that the claimant will not be paid defeats the claim of lien.[117]

[2] Filing the Claim of Lien

The claim of lien must be filed in the office of the clerk of the superior court of the county in which the property to be liened is located. Section 44-14-361.1(a)(2) provides sample language for the claim of lien. In essence, the claim of lien must contain the following:

[113] GA. CODE ANN. § 44-14-361.1(a) (Supp. 1998).

[114] GA. CODE ANN. § 44-14-361.1(a)(1); Summit-Top Dev., Inc. v. Williamson Constr., Inc., 203 Ga. App. 460, 416 S.E.2d 889 (1992).

[115] McCrary v. Barberi, 100 Ga. App. 167, 110 S.E.2d 426, 428 (1959).

[116] Summit-Top Dev., Inc. v. Williamson Constr., Inc., 203 Ga. App. 460, 462, 416 S.E.2d 889, 891 (1992).

[117] *Id.*

1. The correct legal name of the person claiming the lien;
2. The amount claimed;
3. The date the claim became due, which is deemed to be the date that the lien claimant last furnished materials or labor for the project;
4. The identity of the project for which the labor, services, or materials were furnished;
5. The correct legal name of the owner of the real property that was improved; and
6. An accurate description and identification of the real estate for which the labor, services, or materials were furnished.

The claim of lien must be filed within 3 months, not 90 days, after last furnishing materials or labor for the project. This limitation applies equally to contractors, subcontractors, materialmen, architects, and engineers. This deadline cannot be excused, relaxed, or extended by actions of the debtor or the creditor. Failure to comply with this three-month deadline will typically result in forfeiture of all lien rights. On the other hand, filing before the work is completed may also invalidate the lien.[118]

If some materials were furnished more than three months before the claim of lien was filed, the lien may still be timely and applied to all materials supplied provided that the claim of lien was filed within three months after the *last* lienable item was furnished.[119] The lien claimant cannot extend the time for filing by voluntarily returning to the project to make sure that its work is complete,[120] but the time for filing *may* be extended if the owner directs the claimant to perform corrective or remedial work.[121] A lien claimant should exercise extreme caution, however, in relying on owner-directed corrective work to extend the time for filing. Whether owner-directed corrective work extends the time for filing is, at best, a jury question.[122]

In many of the cases addressing the issue of when the three-month period begins to run, the date the lien claimant last furnished materials or labor for the project is not in dispute. Instead, a question of fact exists as to whether the last furnishing of materials or labor was part of the original contract pursuant to which the materials or labor were furnished. If that last act was within the original contract, the three-month period does not begin to run until the date of the last

---

[118] *See, e.g.*, Tri-City Constr. Co. v. Sandy Plains Partnership, 206 Ga. App. 506, 426 S.E.2d 57 (1992); Troup Enters. v. Mitchell, Carrington & Rayfield, Inc., 199 Ga. App. 173, 404 S.E.2d 337 (1991).

[119] Downtowner of Atlanta, Inc. v. Dunham-Bush, Inc., 120 Ga. App. 342, 170 S.E.2d 590 (1969).

[120] *See* Womack Indus., Inc. v. B&A Equip. Co., 199 Ga. App. 660, 405 S.E.2d 880 (1991).

[121] *See* Schwan's Sales Enters., Inc. v. Martin Mechanical Contractors, Inc., 202 Ga. App. 510, 414 S.E.2d 727 (1992); *see also* Cumberland Bridge Assocs., Ltd. v. Builders Steel Supply, Inc., 169 Ga. App. 945, 315 S.E.2d 484 (1984) (jury found that statutory period ran from date contractor performed some repair and "minor installation" work).

[122] *See id.*

act.[123] If that last act was outside the original contract, the three-month period begins to run whenever materials or labor were last furnished for the original contract.[124] If the evidence is not conclusive, the issue is decided by the trier of fact.[125]

If the claim of lien is filed on time and the action on the underlying debt is commenced on time, the claim of lien will still be effective against the property owner despite the lien claimant's failure to specify the amount or due date in the claim of lien.[126] However, if a claim of lien contains an erroneous date for when the claim became due, that defect must be corrected through amendment within three months of when the claim actually became due, or the lien will be invalid.[127] In *Tri-City Construction,*[128] the contractor filed a claim of lien on November 27, 1989 for a "claim which became due on July 31, 1989." The lien, on its face, would be invalid, because the claim of lien was filed more than three months after the debt became due. However, the owner and contractor appeared to agree that the project was not completed and the debt not due until sometime in November 1989. The original claim of lien was therefore premature and invalid. The contractor apparently did not recognize the problem until August 16, 1990, when it filed its complaint to enforce the lien along with an "amended" claim of lien which stated that the claim became due on November 8, 1989. The court rejected the original lien as ineffective because it was premature and rejected the "amended" lien because it was filed more than three months after the claim actually became due.

The claim of lien must contain a legally sufficient description of the property to be liened. The sufficiency of a property description is a question of law for the court.[129] "The test for sufficiency of a description in a legal document is whether it makes possible the identification of the real or personal property described."[130] In one older case, the Court of Appeals held that identifying property by only a

[123] *See, e.g.,* Cumberland Bridge Assocs., Ltd. v. Builders Steel Supply, Inc., 169 Ga. App. 945, 315 S.E.2d 484 (1984).

[124] *See, e.g.,* Womack Indus., Inc. v. B&A Equip. Co., 199 Ga. App. 660, 405 S.E.2d 880 (1991); Crane Co. v. Hirsch, 61 Ga. App. 632, 7 S.E.2d 83 (1940).

[125] *See* Resurgens Plaza S. Assocs. v. Consolidated Elec. Supply, Inc., 215 Ga. App. 818, 819-20, 452 S.E.2d 784, 786 (1994); Schwan's Sales Enters., Inc. v. Martin Mechanical Contractors, Inc., 202 Ga. App. 510, 414 S.E.2d 727 (1992); Sears Roebuck & Co. v. Superior Rigging & Erecting Co., 120 Ga. App. 412, 170 S.E.2d 721 (1969).

[126] J.H. Morris Building Supplies v. Brown, 245 Ga. 178, 264 S.E.2d 9 (1980); Georgia N. Contracting, Inc. v. Haney & Haney Constr. & Management Corp., 204 Ga. App. 366, 419 S.E.2d 348 (1992).

[127] Tri-City Constr. Co. v. Sandy Plains Partnership, 206 Ga. App. 506, 426 S.E.2d 57 (1992).

[128] 206 Ga. App. 506, 426 S.E.2d 57 (1992).

[129] Mull v. Mickey's Lumber & Supply Co., 218 Ga. App. 343, 344, 461 S.E.2d 270, 272, cert. *denied* (Ga. 1995); *see* Peoples Bank v. Northwest Ga. Bank, 139 Ga. App. 264, 228 S.E.2d 181, 183-84 (1976) (stating that although it is not completely necessary that the physical description be sufficient in itself to identify the property, it must raise a warning flag providing a key to the identity of the property).

[130] *Mull,* 461 S.E.2d at 273.

street address, without a legal description of the property, was sufficient and would not invalidate a claim of lien.[131]

If, however, the lien claimant makes a mistake in the property description in its claim of lien, whether the lien is enforceable or not depends on the degree of the mistake. In *Grubb v. Woodglenn Properties, Inc.*[132] the court found that the use of an inaccurate property description in a lien did not invalidate the lien, because the deed description contained an incorrect plat book page number but was correct in every other respect.[133] However, in *Mull v. Mickey's Lumber & Supply Co.,*[134] the appellants built a house on Lot 21, which was one of two contiguous lots that they owned. The appellee, a lumber supplier, filed a materialmen's lien but mistakenly described the property as Lot 20, instead of the correct Lot 21. Although the lot number was incorrect, the lien document did reference the warranty deed, which contained an accurate description of both lots. The court noted that statutes involving materialmen's liens must be strictly construed in favor of the property owner.[135] The court found that the error in the property description was a fatal deficiency that could not be remedied by the lien document's reference to the warranty deed, and therefore that the lien was unenforceable.[136]

A claim of lien must include the correct legal name of the owner of the property.[137] Absent a factual dispute about the correct name of the legal owner of the property to be liened, almost any mistake in the name of the legal owner of the property will invalidate a claim of lien.[138] However, in *Federal Deposit Insurance Corp. v. Gray,*[139] the Court of Appeals of Georgia considered a case in which there was conflicting evidence regarding the correct name of the corporation that owned the property when the appellee filed the lien. Some evidence was presented that "Norton Properties, Inc." owned the property, whereas other evidence indicated that "S. Donald Norton Properties, Inc." was the owner.[140] The trial court charged the jury that "[f]or a claim of lien to be valid, the lien claimant must name the correct owner of the property at the time the lien is filed. If the

---

[131] Love v. Hockenhull, 91 Ga. App. 877, 878, 87 S.E.2d 352, 354 (1955).

[132] 220 Ga. App. 902, 470 S.E.2d 455, 458, *cert. denied* (1996).

[133] *Id. Accord* Blanton v. Major, 144 Ga. App. 762, 242 S.E.2d 360 (1978) (rejecting a similar argument and finding a lien description sufficient when it stated the property owner, land lot number, district, county, lot number, block, and subdivision).

[134] 218 Ga. App. 343, 344, 461 S.E.2d 270, 272, *cert. denied* (Ga. 1995).

[135] 461 S.E.2d at 273.

[136] *Id.* at 272-73.

[137] GA. CODE ANN. § 44-14-361.1(a)(2).

[138] *See* Meco of Atlanta, Inc. v. Super Value Stores, Inc., 215 Ga. App. 146, 149, 449 S.E.2d 687, 689-90 (1994); North v. Waffle House, Inc., 177 Ga. App. 162, 163, 338 S.E.2d 750, 751-52 (1985); A&A Heating & Air Conditioning Co. v. Burgess, 148 Ga. App. 859, 859-60, 253 S.E.2d 246, 247 (1979); Fowler v. Roxboro Homes, 98 Ga. App. 829, 829-30, 107 S.E.2d 285, 285-86 (1959).

[139] 255 Ga. App. 415, 484 S.E.2d. 67 (1997).

[140] 484 S.E.2d at 69.

lien claimant fails to name the correct owner of the property in a claim of lien, then the lien is void."[141] The court of appeals indicated that the jury could resolve the conflict in the evidence and determine whether the lien was valid and enforceable.[142]

[3] Notice of the Claim of Lien

In addition to filing the claim of lien with the clerk of the superior court, since 1991 the claimant has been required to send a copy of the claim of lien by registered or certified mail to the owner of the property or the contractor, as agent for the owner.[143] Failure to comply with this notice requirement will presumably render the claim of lien invalid.[144] Wise lien claimants mail the notice to both the owner and the contractor, via certified mail return receipt requested, on the day the lien is filed.

In *Grubb v. Woodglenn Properties, Inc.*,[145] however, the Georgia Court of Appeals rejected an owner's contention that a contractor's lien was unenforceable because the contractor did not mail a copy of the claim of lien to the owner by registered or certified mail as specified in § 44-14-361.1(a)(2). In *Grubb*, the owner had been personally served with a copy of the lien when the contractor filed a complaint against the owner. The court held that personal service of a copy of the lien with the complaint was sufficient to satisfy the notice requirements of § 44-14-361.1(a)(2), because personal service exceeds the statutory requirement of delivering the lien by registered or certified mail.[146]

[4] Commencing Suit on the Underlying Debt

Georgia lien law requires that the claimant commence a lawsuit against the debtor for recovery of the debt underlying the lien within 12 months from the date the debt became due.[147] It is very important to note three things about this requirement for perfecting a claim of lien.

First, the suit on the underlying debt is a breach of contract action against the party with whom the lien claimant contracted, not an *in rem* lien foreclosure action. Thus, if the lien claimant is a subcontractor, unless the contractor has declared bankruptcy,[148] the subcontractor must sue the general contractor within

---

[141] *Id.*

[142] *Id.*

[143] GA. CODE ANN. § 44-14-361.1(a)(2).

[144] *See id.* § 44-14-361.1(a) (providing that any failure to comply with the requirements specified therein renders the lien unenforceable).

[145] 220 Ga. App. 902, 470 S.E.2d 455, *cert. denied* (Ga. 1996).

[146] 470 S.E.2d at 458.

[147] GA. CODE ANN. § 44-14-361.1(a)(3) (Supp. 1998).

[148] If the general contractor has declared bankruptcy, died, absconded, or left the state, the subcontractor could proceed directly against the liened property without first filing suit against the

12 months—not bring a lien foreclosure action against the property owner within twelve months.[149]

Second, because this suit refers to a contract action against the party with whom the lien claimant contracted, the requirement for filing a notice of this suit within fourteen days (discussed in **§ 11.03[F][5]**, *infra*) commences as soon as the lien claimant files a complaint, counterclaim, or cross-claim against the party with whom it contracted.[150] As is evident from the cases discussed in **§ 11.03[F][5]**, a lien claimant may not be thinking about its lien rights when it files a breach of contract action against the party with whom it contracted. If it does not consider its lien rights, and fails to file a notice of commencement of the breach of contract action within 14 days of filing suit, the lien claimant will permanently lose its lien rights.

Third, the date the claim became due is deemed to be the date that the claimant last furnished materials or labor for the property, not the date the work was billed. The claim for payment becomes due upon the *delivery* of the last item constituting a part of the account and not the due date stated in a supplier's invoice.[151] Consequently, this date should be the date of last furnishing labor or materials that is recited in the claim of lien. This date will always be earlier than the date that the claim of lien was filed, so if the claimant waits twelve months from the date the claim of lien was filed to commence a lawsuit, the claimant's lien rights will have already lapsed. If the claimant fails to initiate the action within the statutory twelve-month period, the claim of lien is extinguished and rendered unenforceable.[152]

If the party with whom the lien claimant contracted has declared bankruptcy, the automatic stay provision of the Bankruptcy Code may prevent the lien claimant from suing the bankrupt party in a Georgia state or superior court.[153] Timely filing a claim in the contractor's bankruptcy proceeding will, however, satisfy the

---

general contractor. *See* GA. CODE ANN. § 44-14-361.1(a)(4). In this situation, though, the lien foreclosure action must be filed within twelve months of the time the debt became due, and a notice of commencement of that action must be filed within fourteen days. *See id.;* Calhoun/Johnson Co. v. Houston Family Trust No. 1, 236 Ga. App. 793, 513 S.E.2d 759 (1999); Northside Wood Flooring v. Borst, 232 Ga. App. 569, 502 S.E.2d 506, *cert. denied* (Ga. 1998).

[149] *In re* Harbor Club, 185 B.R. 959, 962 (Bankr. N.D. Ga. 1995); Beall v. F.H.H. Constr., Inc., 193 Ga. App. 544, 388 S.E.2d 342 (1989); Hancor, Inc. v. Fleming Farms, Inc., 155 Ga. App. 579, 580, 271 S.E.2d 712, 712 (1980); Logan Paving Co. v. Liles Constr. Co., 141 Ga. App. 81, 232 S.E.2d 575, 577 (1977).

[150] Metromont Materials Corp. v. Cargill, Inc., 221 Ga. App. 853, 853-54, 473 S.E.2d 498, 499 (1996), *cert. denied* (Ga. 1997); Beall v. F.H.H. Constr., Inc., 193 Ga. App. 544, 388 S.E.2d 342 (1989).

[151] Dixie Lime & Stone Co. v. Ryder Truck Rental, Inc., 140 Ga. App. 188, 230 S.E.2d 322 (1976).

[152] Hancor, Inc. v. Fleming Farms, Inc., 155 Ga. App. 579, 271 S.E.2d 712 (1980).

[153] *See* 11 § U.S.C. 362(a).

requirement for bringing suit on the underlying debt.[154] This is not required, though, because as discussed in **§ 11.03[G]**, infra, if the contractor has declared bankruptcy, the lien claimant may forego suing the contractor and proceed with a lien foreclosure action against the property.[155]

The extensive reliance on arbitration in construction contracts frequently puts lien claimants in the difficult position of having to initiate an action within the twelve-month period to perfect a lien despite the presence of an arbitration clause, which arguably could result in a waiver of the party's right to arbitrate the dispute. The Georgia Court of Appeals has refused to make a lien claimant choose between its lien rights and its arbitration rights. Instead, the lien law and the Georgia Arbitration Code is "interdependent and compatible." If the claimant consistently seeks to enforce its arbitration rights, initiating an action to preserve a lien will not waive its right to arbitration. The correct procedure is to stay the lien action and proceed to arbitration.[156]

[5] Notice of Suit on the Underlying Debt

The claimant must provide yet another notice when it files the action on the underlying debt. This notice of action must be filed with the clerk of the superior court of the county in which the property is located and the lien was filed.[157] Failure to file the required notice in a timely fashion renders the lien unenforceable.[158] Filing this notice is not required, however, if the general contractor or owner has filed a lien removal bond pursuant to Georgia Code Annotated § 44-14-364.[159]

The contents of the notice of action are specifically prescribed by statute. The notice must be executed under oath[160] by the claimant or by the claimant's attorney of record. The notice must (1) contain the name of the owner of the real property involved; (2) refer to a deed or other recorded instrument in the chain

---

[154] *See* Melton v. Pacific Southern Mortgage Trust, 241 Ga. 589, 247 S.E.2d 76 (1978); Newton Lumber & Supply, Inc. v. Crumbley, 161 Ga. App. 741, 290 S.E.2d 114 (1982).

[155] Ga. Code Ann. § 44-14-361.1(a)(4); Underground Festival, Inc. v. McAfee Eng'g Co., 214 Ga. App. 243, 245, 447 S.E.2d 683, 685 (1994); Galbreath v. Vondenkamp, 192 Ga. App. 284, 398 S.E.2d 278 (1990).

[156] H.R.H. Prince Ltc. Faisal M. Saud v. Batson-Cook Co., 161 Ga. App. 219, 291 S.E.2d 249 (1982).

[157] Ga. Code Ann. § 44-14-361.1(3) (Supp. 1998).

[158] Statham Machinery & Equip. Co. v. Howard Constr. Co., 160 Ga. App. 466, 287 S.E.2d 249 (1981), *cert. denied* (Ga. 1982). Unenforceability of the lien for failure to comply with the requirement to file a notice of action will not, however, adversely affect the claimant's underlying contract claim. *See* Consolidated Sys., Inc. v. Amisub, Inc., 261 Ga. 590, 408 S.E.2d 109 (1991).

[159] Hardee v. Spivey, 193 Ga. App. 234, 387 S.E.2d 430 (1989).

[160] Ga. Code Ann. § 44-14-361.1(a)(3) was amended in 1998 to provide that a lien claimant's failure to execute the notice under oath is an amendable defect, and that the amended notice relates back to the original filing of the notice. *See* Ga. Code Ann. § 44-14-361.1(a)(3).

of title of the property; (3) identify the court, style, number, parties, and date of the action filed against the debtor; and (4) identify the book and page number where the claim of lien is recorded.[161] Upon filing of this notice, the clerk adds the book and page reference showing where the notice was recorded.[162]

This notice of action must be filed within 14 days after filing the suit on the underlying debt. The requirement for filing a notice of action within 14 days is fully applicable when the suit on the underlying debt is asserted by a counterclaim or cross-claim.[163] It also applies when the suit on the underlying debt is filed in a bankruptcy proceeding.[164] As long as the action on the underlying debt is filed within 12 months of the time the claim became due, the notice may be timely filed within 14 days thereafter. Therefore, even if notice of action is not filed until more than twelve months after the claim became due, it is still valid.[165]

In *Palmer v. Duncan Wholesale, Inc.*,[166] the Georgia Supreme Court made abundantly clear the need to comply with the requirement of filing a notice of action in order to enforce a claim of lien. In that case, Duncan supplied materials to the contractor for an improvement to property owned by the Palmers. There was no question about the validity of Duncan's claim of lien. Duncan filed suit against the contractor on the underlying debt, but failed to file a notice of commencement of the suit. The contractor then filed for bankruptcy, and Duncan initiated an action pursuant to § 44-14-361.1(a)(4) to enforce its lien directly against the property. The supreme court ruled that when Duncan failed to file the requisite notice of lien within 14 days of filing its breach of contract action against the contractor, Duncan permanently lost its lien rights: "At that moment, Duncan lost its ability to ever enforce its claim of lien against the improved property."

Duncan argued that the contractor's subsequent bankruptcy cured its failure to file a notice of its suit against the contractor, because a suit on the underlying debt was not even required once the contractor declared bankruptcy.[167] The court flatly rejected this argument: "The contractor's subsequent bankruptcy filing could not breathe new life into the extinguished right to a lien so as to give the materialman another bite at the apple it had missed on its first bob."[168]

---

[161] *Id.*

[162] *Id.* § 44-14-361.1(a)(3).

[163] Metromont Materials Corp. v. Cargill, 221 Ga. App. 853, 473 S.E.2d 498, 500 (1996), *cert. denied* (Ga. 1997); Beall v. F.H.H. Constr., Inc., 193 Ga. App. 544, 388 S.E.2d 342 (1989).

[164] Ga. Code Ann. § 44-14-361.1(a)(4); Calhoun/Johnson Co. v. Houston Family Trust No. 1, 236 Ga. App. 793, 513 S.E.2d 759 (1999); Newton Lumber & Supply, Inc. v. Crumbley, 161 Ga. App. 741, 290 S.E.2d 114 (1982).

[165] Abacus, Inc. v. Hebron Baptist Church, Inc., 201 Ga. App. 376, 411 S.E.2d 113 (1991).

[166] 262 Ga. 28, 413 S.E.2d 437 (1992).

[167] Pursuant to Ga. Code Ann. § 44-14-361.1(a)(4), if the party with whom the claimant contracted has declared bankruptcy, died, absconded from the jurisdiction, or left the state, a suit on the underlying debt is not required and the lien claimant can proceed directly against the liened property. *See* Ga. Code Ann. § 44-14-361.1(a)(4) (Supp. 1998).

[168] 413 S.E.2d at 439.

In *Metromont Materials Corp. v. Cargill,*[169] the Georgia Court of Appeals relied on *Palmer* in holding that Metromont, an unpaid concrete supplier, lost its right to enforce its lien by failing to file the requisite notice of lien within 14 days of filing a cross-claim to recover on the underlying debt. Cargill, the owner, had filed an interpleader action against Metromont and many other subcontractors and suppliers. Metromont filed an answer and counterclaim seeking to foreclose on its lien claim and asserted a cross-claim against the general contractor.[170] Metromont, however, failed to file the statutory notice of commencement of the cross-claim within the statutory 14-day window.[171] When notified that its lien claim was defective because of its failure to timely file the requisite notice, Metromont dismissed and refiled its cross-claim against the general contractor and filed a notice of commencement of that action within 14 days.[172]

The trial court granted the owner's motion for partial summary judgment and the court of appeals affirmed, holding that Metromont's failure to file the required statutory notice in the first action against the general contractor permanently extinguished Metromont's lien rights.[173] The court reasoned that because filing notice is a prerequisite to enforcing a lien, Metromont lost its right to enforce its lien rights on the 15th day after it commenced its original action against the general contractor via its cross-claim in the interpleader action.[174] The court stated that the harsh result was consistent with the requirements of the lien statute and "with the long-standing principle that statutes involving material supplier's liens must be strictly construed in favor of the property owner and against the materialman."[175] Accordingly, *Metromont* makes it clear that a counterclaim or a cross-claim will constitute a commencement of a suit on the underlying debt and thus trigger the start of the 14-day period for filing a notice of commencement of action. Unless the notice of commencement of action is timely filed, the claimant's lien rights will be permanently extinguished on the 15th day after the suit is commenced.

The Georgia Legislature added a new Code section to Georgia lien law in 1998. This new Code section, Georgia Code Annotated § 44-14-367, allows the clerk of the court where a lien was filed to void the lien if no notice of commencement of an action on the underlying debt has been filed within 14 months from the time the claim became due.[176] The procedure for voiding the lien is specified in § 44-14-367. This procedure became effective on July 1, 1998, and only applies to liens created on or after that date.[177]

---

[169] 221 Ga. App. 853, 473 S.E.2d 498, 500 (1996), *cert. denied* (Ga. 1997).

[170] 473 S.E.2d at 499.

[171] *Id.*

[172] *Id.*

[173] 473 S.E.2d at 499-500.

[174] *See id.* at 500.

[175] *Id.*

[176] GA. CODE ANN. § 44-14-367.

[177] *See id.*

[G] Impact of Contractor's Bankruptcy and Contractual Pay-When-Paid Provisions on Lien Rights

Since 1989, Georgia lien law has contained a provision which relieves the lien claimant from filing suit on the underlying debt when the party with whom the claimant contracted has declared bankruptcy, died, absconded, or left the state.[178] In these situations, the lien claimant may elect to proceed directly with a lien foreclosure action against the property owner.[179] The lien foreclosure action must be brought within 12 months of the date the debt became due, which is deemed to be the date of last furnishing materials or labor for the project.[180] The lien claimant must file a notice of commencement of the lien foreclosure action within fourteen days of filing it, or it will lose its lien rights.[181]

Effective July 1, 1997, Georgia's lien law was amended to make this provision applicable when the claimant's contract contains a pay-when-paid provision. As amended in 1997, Georgia Code Annotated § 44-14-361.1(a)(4) now provides that if

> the contract between the party claiming the lien and the contractor or subcontractor includes a provision preventing payment to the claimant until after the contractor or subcontractor has received payment, then . . . the person or persons furnishing material, services, labor, and supplies shall be relieved of the necessity of filing an action or obtaining judgment against the contractor or subcontractor as a prerequisite to enforcing a lien against the property improved by the contractor or subcontractor.[182]

This provision recognizes the difficult situation that an unpaid subcontractor or material supplier encounters when forced to wait for payment because the owner has failed to pay the general contractor and the subcontract contains a pay-when-paid provision.[183] Typically, pay-when-paid provisions allow a general contractor to delay payment to the subcontractor for a reasonable time while waiting on payment from the owner.[184] Pay-when-paid provisions are enforceable

---

[178] *See id.*

[179] *Id.* Alternatively the lien claimant may elect to timely file a claim in the contractor's bankruptcy proceeding and file a timely notice of commencement of that action. *See* Melton v. Pacific Southern Mortgage Trust, 241 Ga. 569, 247 S.E.2d 76 (1978); Newton Lumber & Supply, Inc. v. Crumbley, 161 Ga. App. 741, 290 S.E.2d 114 (1982).

[180] *Id.*

[181] *Id.;* Northside Wood Flooring v. Borst, 232 Ga. App. 569, 502 S.E.2d 508, *cert. denied* (Ga. 1998).

[182] GA. CODE ANN. § 44-14-361.1(a)(4).

[183] *See generally* Justin Sweet & Jonathon J. Sweet, SWEET ON CONSTRUCTION INDUSTRY CONTRACTS: MAJOR AIA DOCUMENTS § 17.10 (John Wiley & Sons, Inc., 3d ed. 1996 & Supp. 1997, now published by Aspen Law & Business) (discussing payment condition clauses including pay-if-paid and pay-when-paid clauses).

[184] *See id.* at 139-40.

in Georgia if the contract clearly and expressly makes payment by the owner a condition precedent to payment to the subcontractor.[185]

When the lien claimant's contract contains a pay-when-paid provision and the owner withholds payment from the general contractor, Georgia Code Annotated § 44-14-361.1(4) now allows the subcontractor or material supplier to foreclose a lien directly against the property, without the necessity of first filing suit on the underlying debt. Under the amended Code language, a pay-when-paid clause will not operate as a waiver of the subcontractor's or material supplier's right to file and enforce a lien claim, nor will the pay-when-paid provision serve as a defense to the lien claim. Thus, the general contractor is able to continue using pay-when-paid provisions in its subcontracts, and subcontractors and material suppliers are afforded a direct remedy against the property. As a practical matter, however, the protection afforded the general contractor by the pay-when-paid provision may be lost, because the general contractor usually will be forced to defend the lien action or indemnify the owner for it.

[H] Foreclosure of Liens

A lien claimant that has substantially complied with its contract, filed a timely and proper claim of lien, initiated a timely action on the underlying debt, and provided the required notice of action may bring an action to foreclose on the lien to satisfy the debt.[186] The 12-month time period during which a lien claimant must bring an action on the primary debt usually has no effect on the time for bringing an action to foreclose on the lien. Thus, although a lien claimant must bring an action against the primary debtor within 12 months, the lien statute mandates no similar time limitation for the lien claimant to institute a foreclosure action against the owner—with two exceptions.

First, if the party with whom the claimant contracted has declared bankruptcy, died, absconded, or left the state, or if the lien claimant's contract contains a pay-when-paid provision, the lien claimant can proceed under § 44-14-361.4(a)(4) with a lien foreclosure action against the property. When proceeding under this provision, the lien foreclosure action must be filed within 12 months of the date the debt became due, and the lien claimant must file a notice of commencement of that action within 14 days.[187]

Second, if the lien claimant is a contractor in privity with the owner, the action against the owner on the primary debt must be brought within 12 months,

[185] Georgia Glass & Metal, Inc. v. Arco Chem. Co., 201 Ga. App. 15, 410 S.E.2d 142 (1991); St. Paul Fire & Marine Ins. Co. v. Georgia Interstate Elec. Co., 187 Ga. App. 579, 370 S.E.2d 829 (1988); Jerome Distribs., Inc. v. B.L.I. Constr. Co., 142 Ga. App. 776, 237 S.E.2d 13 (1977); Sasser & Co. v. Griffin, 133 Ga. App. 83, 210 S.E.2d 34 (1974).

[186] GA. CODE ANN. § 44-14-530(a) (Supp. 1998).

[187] *See id.* § 44-14-361.1(a)(4).

and because of the possibility of claim preclusion, the lien foreclosure action should be brought with it.

The owner is only personally liable if the debt secured by the lien is owed to a contractor that is in privity with the owner. In cases in which the lien claimant is a subcontractor, laborer, or materialman who is not in privity with the owner, the foreclosure action is solely *in rem* against the real property, and the owner cannot be held personally liable.[188] In an action by a subcontractor or materialman to foreclose on the liened property, only the lien claimant and the owner of the real property are necessary parties. The contractor in privity with the owner need not be made a party, although the contractor can be joined or can intervene on its own.[189]

[I] Discharging Liens with Bonds

A lien can be discharged by filing a bond with the clerk of the superior court of the county in which the lien is filed.[190] The bond must be either cash or an approved security and double the amount claimed under the lien. The bond requirement for residential property (four family units or less) is limited to the amount claimed. Once the bond is posted, the lien is discharged so far as the owner and the property are concerned, and there is nothing left on which to foreclose. Because the bond is a substitute for the lien, the party against whom the claim is asserted in an action on the bond can present any defense that would have been available in an action to foreclose on the lien, such as failure to comply with the lien law.[191] For instance, even if a bond is posted to discharge a lien, the claimant must still bring a suit on the underlying debt within twelve months as required by Georgia Code Annotated § 44-14-361.1(a)(3).[192] The filing of a bond does, however, relieve the claimant from the requirement of filing a notice of commencement of that suit.[193]

---

[188] Ben O'Callaghan Co. v. Schmincke, 376 F. Supp. 1361 (N.D. Ga. 1974).

[189] GA. CODE ANN. § 44-14-361.1(d) (Supp. 1998).

[190] *Id.* § 44-14-364.

[191] Hoffman Elec. Co. v. Chiyoda Int'l Corp., 203 Ga. App. 731, 417 S.E.2d 371 (1992); Linco Constr. Co. v. Tri-City Concrete, Inc., 161 Ga. App. 174, 288 S.E.2d 125 (1982); Apex Supply Co. v. Commercial Union Ins. Co., 143 Ga. App. 131, 237 S.E.2d 649 (1977).

[192] Stonepecker, Inc. v. Shepherd Constr. Co., 188 Ga. App. 513, 373 S.E.2d 295 (1988). However, if the contractor has declared bankruptcy, under Georgia Code Annotated § 44-14-361.1(a)(4), the lien claimant need not bring a suit on the underlying debt and can proceed directly against the bond. *See* Hendricks v. Blake & Pendleton, Inc., 221 Ga. App. 651, 472 S.E.2d 482, *cert. denied* (Ga. 1996) (holding that a plumbing subcontractor's intervening bankruptcy relieved the material supplier of the necessary prerequisite of filing an action or obtaining judgment against the contractor or subcontractor and that a bond posted to discharge the materialman's lien provided the necessary contractual link to allow the material supplier to proceed directly against the surety).

[193] Hardee v. Spivey, 193 Ga. App. 234, 387 S.E.2d 430 (1989); All Phase Elec. Supply Co. v. Foster & Cooper, Inc., 193 Ga. App. 232, 387 S.E.2d 429 (1989); Burgess v. Travelers Indem. Co., 185 Ga. App. 82, 363 S.E.2d 308 (1987).

In *Benning Construction Co. v. All-Phase Electric Supply Co.*,[194] the Georgia Court of Appeals held that a waiver and release of lien executed by a lien claimant *after* its liens had been discharged by a bond to discharge the liens did not waive the claimant's rights against the bond. The claimant, All-Phase, had filed two liens on a shopping center project for unpaid materials supplied to a subcontractor. Within a week, the prime contractor discharged the liens with a bond pursuant to § 44-14-364. Six weeks and again ten weeks later, All-Phase sold materials to a new subcontractor on the project. All-Phase was paid for each transaction and executed a "Waiver and Release of Lien" which purported to waive all current and future lien rights on the project.

In defending All-Phase's claim against the bond that discharged the liens, the prime contractor and its surety argued that the language of the lien waivers executed by All-Phase dissolved the two liens and all previous liens. The court rejected this argument. The court pointed out that when the bond was posted, under the terms of § 44-14-364(a) the liens were discharged. "Thus, when All-Phase executed the waivers of lien . . . several months later, there was no lien against the property upon which the waiver might act."[195] Instead, "All-Phase's claims were then predicated on the bond, which is subject to contract law."[196]

[J] Lien Waivers

Before 1991, parties could waive their lien rights in advance of furnishing labor, services, or material.[197] This waiver could even be accomplished through a "flowdown" provision in a subcontract.[198] That is no longer the case. Effective January 1, 1992, *prospective lien waivers are invalid.* Any purported waiver or release *in advance of* furnishing labor, services, or materials is "null, void, and unenforceable."[199]

In lieu of waving lien rights, contractors are frequently asked to prospectively subordinate their lien rights to any other security interests granted by the owner to obtain project financing. Although a subordination agreement may substantially diminish or eliminate the value of a claimant's lien rights, the amendment confirms that they continue to be valid and enforceable.

Lien rights for labor, services, or materials that already have been supplied can be waived, but only if the waiver is accomplished pursuant to the lien law. Georgia Code Annotated § 44-14-366 contains verbatim forms for: (1) interim waiver and release upon payment (to be used for progress or partial payments),

---

[194] 206 Ga. App. 279, 424 S.E.2d 830 (1993).

[195] 424 S.E.2d at 832.

[196] *Id.* at 831 (citing Linco Constr. Co. v. Tri-City Concrete, 161 Ga. App. 174, 288 S.E.2d 125 (1982)).

[197] AAA Plastering Co. v. TPM Constructors, Inc., 247 Ga. 601, 277 S.E.2d 910 (1981).

[198] MCC Powers v. Ford Motor Co., 184 Ga. App. 47, 361 S.E.2d 716 (1987).

[199] GA. CODE ANN. § 44-14-366(a) (Supp. 1991).

(2) unconditional waiver and release upon final payment, and (3) affidavits of nonpayment.[200] To be effective, a waiver must be "substantially" in the form set forth in the statute.[201] A lien claimant's oral or written statements cannot adversely affect an otherwise enforceable lien unless made pursuant to a statutory waiver and release form.[202] As previously mentioned, a valid lien waiver, executed after the lien has been discharged by a bond pursuant to § 44-14-364, does not waive the claimant's rights against the bond.[203]

A quick reading of the Georgia Code on lien waivers can give a claimant a false and dangerous sense of security. The statutory forms set forth in the Code state that the waivers are valid and binding against the claimant "*only*" if the amount stated in the waiver is paid.[204] But the Code must be read very carefully. A subsequent subsection of the Code states that *payment is conclusively presumed to have been made* unless the claimant files a claim of lien or an affidavit of nonpayment within thirty days of the execution of the waiver.[205] Thus, even though the statutory lien waiver forms appear to be conditional and not effective until payment is received, by statute the waivers become unconditional in 30 days unless the claimant has filed a claim of lien or affidavit of nonpayment. The filing must take place in the county in which the property is located.[206]

This presumption of payment and the relatively short time frame (30 days) in which it becomes effective can be a dangerous trap for the trusting or inattentive claimant. Interim waivers are signed on a routine basis as part of the progress payment application process. It should also be routine to file the required affidavit of nonpayment or claim of lien if there is a risk payment that will not actually be received within the specified 30 days.

[K] Affidavits of Payment

Pursuant to Georgia Code Annotated § 44-14-361.2, the lien rights of any claimants who have not filed a valid preliminary notice of lien or valid notice of lien can be dissolved by the filing of an affidavit by the contractor in privity with the owner which states that the agreed price or reasonable value of the labor, services, or materials furnished have been paid or waived in writing.[207] To be effective, the affidavit must be given as part of a transaction involving the final disbursement of the contract price by the owner to the contractor.[208] In *CC&B*

---

[200] *Id.* § 44-14-366(c), (d).

[201] *See* **§ 11.02[D][1]**, *supra*.

[202] GA. CODE ANN. § 44-14-366(b).

[203] Benning Constr. Co. v. All-Phase Elec. Supply Co., 206 Ga. App. 279, 424 S.E.2d 830 (1992).

[204] GA. CODE ANN. § 44-14-366 (c), (d).

[205] *Id.* § 44-14-366(f)(2).

[206] *Id.* § 44-14-366(f)(2)(C).

[207] *Id.* § 44-14-361.2(A).

[208] *Id.* § 44-14-361.2(a)(2)(B)(iii).

Industries, Inc. v. Stroud,[209] the Court of Appeals stated: "This statute contemplates a *single* affidavit that the agreed price or reasonable value of *all* the labor, services or materials employed in the *completed* project have been paid and not, as the Owner contends, *periodic* affidavits that the agreed price or reasonable value of *some* of the labor, services, or materials employed to date in the *ongoing* project have been paid."[210]

The owner also can dissolve lien rights with an affidavit when the owner's affidavit is part of a bona fide sale of the property or loan transaction.[211] An unsworn statement by the contractor stating that payment has been made is not sufficient to dissolve a subcontractor's or materialmen's claim of lien.[212]

In *Shockley Plumbing Co. v. NationsBank,*[213] a property owner executed a *false* affidavit along with a warranty deed. The court of appeals held that the *false* affidavit was effective to dissolve a contractor's materialmen's lien absent evidence that the underlying sale was not bona fide. The court noted that there was no evidence that the lender had any actual or constructive knowledge that the property owner was attempting to defraud creditors, nor was there any evidence of collusion.[214]

Affidavits of Payment are frequently the subject of controversy. Even a false affidavit can be effective to dissolve liens that are not the subject of preliminary notice of lien or notice of lien.[215] On the other hand, if there is evidence indicating that the owner was aware of any irregularity or there are allegations or proof of fraud and/or collusion, the effectiveness of a false affidavit can be challenged.[216]

In *Balest v. Simmons,*[217] however, the court found that the owner's knowledge of and involvement in the contractor's execution of a false affidavit did not impair the effectiveness of the affidavit as a bar to the assertion of any claim of lien. The case involved construction and financing of a home. In order to close on a mortgage to pay for the construction, the contractor executed a lien affidavit essential for the closing to take place. The owner then used the proceeds of the mortgage to pay the contractor the original contract price. However, the contractor contended that he was owed extras and should not be bound by the lien affidavit, because he executed it only so that the owner could close on the mortgage. The court was unpersuaded, in part because the contractor received the proceeds from the closing. The court concluded that under these circumstances, the affidavit as a whole was sufficient to dissolve the contractor's rights. Significantly, the court

---

[209] 198 Ga. App. 658, 402 S.E.2d 527, *cert. denied* (Ga. 1991).

[210] 402 S.E.2d at 528 (emphasis in original).

[211] GA. CODE ANN. § 44-14-361.2(a)(2)(B)(i, ii).

[212] Southern Concrete Constr. Co. v. Hall, 205 Ga. App. 516, 422 S.E.2d 663 (1992).

[213] 229 Ga. App. 60, 493 S.E.2d 227, 229 (1997).

[214] *Id.*

[215] Steimer v. Northside Bldg. Supply Co., 202 Ga. App. 243, 415 S.E.2d 688 (1992); Lowe's of Ga., Inc. v. Merwin, 156 Ga. App. 876, 275 S.E.2d 812 (1981).

[216] Walk Softly, Inc. v. Hyzer, 188 Ga. App. 230, 372 S.E.2d 500 (1988).

[217] 201 Ga. App. 605, 411 S.E.2d 576 (1991).

held that the lien affidavit not only dissolved lien rights, but also barred the contractor's breach of contract claim against the owner.

[L] Contract Price as Limit on Aggregate Amount of Liens

At first glance, Georgia lien law appears to protect owners from claims of lien when the owner has paid the full contract price to the general contractor. Section 44-14-361.1(e) states: "In no event shall the aggregate amount of liens set up by § 44-14-361 exceed the contract price of the improvements made or services performed."[218] Carefully read, however, this provision only protects owners when the "aggregate amount of liens"—meaning the total amount of all liens filed on the property, exceeds the contract price.[219] Furthermore, mere payment of the contract price to the contractor is not of itself sufficient to even establish a defense to the "aggregate" of the liens filed on the property:

> [A]n owner's mere payment of the full contract price to the contractor, standing alone, is not and has never been a complete defense to foreclosure of a materialman's lien. "The obvious purpose of the statute is to protect materialmen who comply with its terms. If it is held that mere payments to the contractor in discharge of the contract price would defeat the lien of materialmen, the whole statute which undertakes to authorize liens for materialmen would be avoided."[220]

In order to use payments to a general contractor as a defense to a lien claim, the owner must establish that the "payments were applied as provided by law."[221] This means that the owner must show either that sums paid to the contractor were "properly appropriated" to materialmen and laborers or that the contractor has provided the owner with a statutory Affidavit of Payment (see **§ 11.03[K]**, *supra*).[222]

If no liens have been filed, then payments by the contractor to materialmen and laborers will be considered "properly appropriated" and will protect the owner.[223] However, if liens have been filed before the contractor actually pays

---

[218] Ga. Code Ann. § 44-14-361.1(e).

[219] *See id.;* Mayer Elec. Supply Co. v. Federal Ins. Co., 195 Ga. App. 191, 192-93, 393 S.E.2d 270, 272 (1990) ("[I]t is entirely possible that an owner who has paid the full contract price to the contractor may nevertheless still have his property subjected to enforceable materialmen's liens to the maximum extent of the full contract price.").

[220] Freeman v. Fulton Concrete Co., 204 Ga. App. 465, 466, 419 S.E.2d 536, 537 (1992) (quoting Mayer Elec. Supply Co. v. Federal Ins. Co., 195 Ga. App. 191, 393 S.E.2d 270 (1990)); *accord* D&N Elec., Inc. v. Underground Festival, Inc., 202 Ga. App. 435, 414 S.E.2d 891 (1991).

[221] *See id.*

[222] *See id.*

[223] *See Mayer Elec. Supply Co.,* 393 S.E.2d at 273.

materialmen and laborers, those payments are not a defense to the claims asserted by materialmen and laborers.[224]

In *Browning v. Gaster Lumber Co.,*[225] the Georgia Supreme Court considered the issue of whether "payments were applied as provided by law" when the owner had paid the general contractor before any liens were filed, but the general contractor paid materialmen and laborers after a lien was filed. The court held that these payments could not be used as a defense to claims of materialmen and laborers: "Payments that are made by the owner before any lien is filed and recorded but which are not applied [by the general contractor to materialmen and laborers] until after a lien is filed and recorded may not be set up in defense of a foreclosure action on such lien unless such payments were made to parties with superior-ranking lien claims."[226] The Court also reaffirmed that full payment by the owner to the contractor of the contract price will afford the owner a defense to lien claims only if the general contractor has dispersed all of that payment to materialmen and laborers with valid lien rights at a time when no claim of lien has been filed or recorded, and that it is the owner's burden to prove this.[227]

This burden is applied to the owner even when the contractor has abandoned the contract.[228] However, in the case of abandonment, the extent of the value of the liens that can be asserted against the property is limited to the original contract price *less* the cost of completion.[229]

[M] Lien Priority

The priority of the liens created under § 44-14-361 is ranked according to the date the claim of lien is filed.[230] However, all liens mentioned in § 44-14-361.1 that are properly filed are treated as if filed on the same date.[231] These liens, therefore, share pro rata in the proceeds of the real property in the event that the sale is not sufficient to cover all of the lien claims. The liens that are superior to mechanics' liens are identified in § 44-14-361.1(c), and include tax liens and the general and special liens of laborers.

Mechanics' liens are superior to all other liens not specifically excepted in

---

[224] *See id.*

[225] 267 Ga. 72, 475 S.E.2d 576 (1996).

[226] *Id.,* 475 S.E.2d at 578.

[227] *See id.* at 579.

[228] Gaster Lumber Co. v. Browning, 219 Ga. App. 435, 465 S.E.2d 524 (1995), *aff'd,* 267 Ga. 72, 475 S.E.2d 576 (1996); Bishop v. Forsyth Paving Contractors, Inc., 181 Ga. App. 345, 352 S.E.2d 198 (1986).

[229] Mayer Elec. Supply Co. v. Federal Ins. Co., 195 Ga. App. 191, 393 S.E.2d 270 (1990).

[230] GA. CODE ANN. § 44-14-361.1(b) (Supp. 1998).

[231] *Id.*

§ 44-14-361.1.[232] Inferior liens would therefore cover mortgages. However, if title to the real estate is conveyed to secure a debt, as in a deed to secure debt, § 44-14-361.1(c) does not apply. Instead, if a deed to secure debt is taken without actual knowledge of a mechanics' lien and before a claim of lien has been recorded, the deed to secure debt is superior to the lien.[233] Likewise, a lien cannot be enforced against a bona fide purchaser who acquired title to the real estate without notice of the lien.[234]

[232] *Id.* § 44-14-361.1(c).

[233] Georgia State Sav. Ass'n v. Wilson, 189 Ga. 21, 5 S.E.2d 14 (1939).

[234] Ashmore v. Whatley, 99 Ga. 150, 24 S.E. 941 (1896).

CHAPTER 12

HAWAII

Kenneth R. Kupchak
Michael A. Yoshida
Anna H. Oshiro

§ 12.01 INTRODUCTION

On private projects Hawaii generally does not require that prime contractors furnish a bond.[1]

On private projects Hawaii law does provide certain mechanics' lien rights.

On Hawaii public works, buildings, roads or other site improvement projects in excess of $25,000,[2] prime contractors must furnish a joint performance and payment bond, in the full amount of the contract, including estimates for extra work. Depending upon the date of the Hawaii public contract, Hawaii will follow either the old federal Heard Act, the state procurement code, or the modified state procurement code, each with different timing and notice requirements.[3] Heard Act bonds provide secondary coverage for persons who have furnished labor or materials used in the prosecution of the work.

At a minimum on private projects lien coverage extends below the prime contractor for two tiers—in other words, claimants supplying labor or materials to the prime contractor or to any of its subcontractors.

On public projects Hawaii does not provide contractors with any mechanics' lien rights.

Two chapters of Hawaii's Revised Statutes govern bonds and mechanics' liens. The chapter governing bonds for public projects is Chapter 103D, "Hawaii Public Procurement Code,"[4] particularly § 103D-323, "Bid Security," § 103D-324, "Contract Performance and Payment Bonds," and § 103D-325, "Bond Forms and Copies." In addition, the state procurement office has enacted administrative rules accompanying and enlarging upon Hawaii's procurement statutes, particularly Hawaii Administrative Rules Subchapter 24, §§ 3-122-221 through 229, "Bid Security, Contract Performance and Payment Bonds."

The Hawaii lien law is Chapter 507, "Liens", particularly Part II, "Mechanic's and Materialman's Lien" ("Lien Law").

---

[1] Roof construction with a guaranty over seven years must be accompanied by a replacement bond. HAW. REV. STAT. § 444-25.7 (1985).

[2] Although HAW. REV. STAT. § 103-34 (Supp. 1990), and its revisions under the 1994 Procurement Code (HAW. REV. STAT. § 103D-324) require security for *any* public works contract, the Hawaii Attorney General concludes that security need not accompany "informal bid" contracts. Haw. Op. Att'y Gen. 72-14 (1972).

[3] Territory v. Mellor, 33 Haw. 523 (1935); *see also* Territory v. Pac. Coast Gas Co., 22 Haw. 446 (1915).

[4] Various state and county agencies have adopted regulations which elaborate on the statute and accompanying administrative rules. These are available and include: (i) Interim General Conditions, Div. of Pub. Works, Dep't of Accounting & General Services, State of Hawaii (Aug. 1994); (ii) General Provisions for Construction Projects, Divs. of Air and Water Transportation, State of Hawaii (1977); (iii) Standard Specifications For Road And Bridge Construction, Div. of Highways, Dep't. of Transp., State of Hawaii (1975); (iv) General Conditions of Construction Contracts of the City and County of Honolulu, Dep't of Finance (1998); and (v) General Provisions, Procurement Policy Board, Department of Accounting and General Services (Dec. 1995).

§ 12.02 BOND LAW

[A] General Concepts

Hawaii[5] treats the construction surety bond relationship as tripartite and bonds as tripartite contracts.[6] Each construction surety bond has an obligee, typically an owner or a general contractor, and joint and several obligors, typically the general contractor or subcontractor, and its surety.[7]

Hawaii surety contracts must be written and signed by the surety.[8] Although no Hawaii suretyship case has decided whether an obligee must accept the surety contract within a reasonable period of time, thus providing a surety with the right to revoke before delivery and acceptance, the principles of contract law are applicable to suretyship agreements.[9] Similarly, no Hawaii case has considered if the principal must request or assent to its surety executing and delivering a bond in its behalf. Hawaii recognizes that a reasonable time to act is implied in construction surety relationships.[10]

Several cases address Hawaii rules of law regarding interpretation of surety contracts.[11] No Hawaii decision has established the governing law with respect to surety contracts. Generally, absent an effective choice by the parties, Hawaii follows the modern approach with respect to contracts and looks to the law of the place with the most significant relationship to the parties and the transaction on each issue.[12] The construction and interpretation of a contract is for the Hawaii courts.[13] And the goal of interpretation is to ascertain the intent of the contracting

---

[5] Hawaii adopted certain principles of common law. Allied Amusements, Ltd. v. James W. Glover, Ltd., 40 Haw. 92, 93-95 (1953). HAW. REV. STAT. § 1-1 (1985) provides for the adoption of English common law modified, *inter alia,* by such law as is "established by Hawaiian usage. . . ."

[6] "A surety bond is tripatrite in nature requiring the party insured, the principal obligor, and the surety. Thus 'a person cannot be a surety for himself'." Eastern Star, Inc. v. Union Bldg. Materials Corp., 6 Haw. App. 125, n.12 133, 712 P.2d 1148, 1154 n.12 (1985) (quoting 72 C.J.S. PRINCIPAL AND SURETY § 9, at 518 (1951)).

[7] *See also infra* note 11 for examples.

[8] HAW. REV. STAT. § 656-1(2) (1993).

[9] United States v. Findlay, 4 U.S. Dist. Ct. Haw. 191 (1913).

[10] Honolulu Roofing Co. v. Felix, 49 Haw. 578, 426 P.2d 298 (1967). *See also* Mayer v. Alexander & Baldwin, 56 Haw. 195, 532 P.2d 1007 (1975).

[11] *See e.g.,* Mayer v. Alexander & Baldwin, 56 Haw. 195, 532 P.2d 1007 (1975); Honolulu Roofing Co. v. Felix, 49 Haw. 578, 426 P.2d 298 (1967); Allied Amusements v. Glover, 40 Haw. 92 (1953); Holzinger v. Goo, 36 Haw. 506 (1943); Honolulu Iron Works v. Bigelow, 33 Haw. 607 (1935); Territory v. Mellor, 33 Haw. 523 (1935); Craig v. Uyeoka, 32 Haw. 913 (1933); Hustace v. Davis, 23 Haw. 606 (1917); Territory v. Pac. Coast Gas Co., 22 Haw. 446 (1915); Robinson v. Kaae, 22 Haw. 403 (1915); Hackfeld & Co. v. Medcalf, 20 Haw. 47 (1910); Stanley v. Akoi, 12 Haw. 344 (1900).

[12] Commercial Ins. Co. of Newark v. Pacific-Peru Constr. Corp., 558 F.2d 948 (9th Cir. 1977).

[13] Reed & Martin, Inc. v. City & County of Honolulu, 50 Haw. 347, 348–49, 440 P.2d 526 (1968).

parties from all the words and clauses taken as a whole in connection with the relevant surrounding circumstances.[14]

Providing the language in a surety bond is clear, unambiguous and susceptible of but one meaning, that language controls, and liability may not be imposed beyond the express contractual terms.[15] Hawaii courts construe the contract of a compensated surety against a surety and in favor of the obligations that an obligee has reasonable grounds to expect will be imposed.[16] Because a surety's liability often is predicated upon the underlying contract of its contractor/principal, the surety's liability cannot be greater than that of its contractor/principal.[17] If an obligee has materially breached the underlying contract, thus excusing the contractor's further performance, the surety may well not have any liability.[18]

Hawaii recognizes that a surety may be released "if the security is impaired by the act or negligence of the holder, to injury of the [surety], without his knowledge and consent. . . ."[19] Such release will only occur to the extent of the security released, unless the surety has suffered no detriment or is estopped.[20] A construction surety that is called upon under its bond is entitled to be subrogated *pro tanto* to the rights of the obligee against any security and principal,[21] but only to the extent necessary to reimburse it for its reasonably necessary outlay in completing the work.[22]

Changes in conditions by the obligee, with or without the consent of the principal, (*e.g.*, changes in the work, time of performance or payments to the principal or its subcontractors in contradiction of an assignment in favor of the surety) may not relieve the surety; such relief when granted is only *pro tanto*.[23]

The surety has the burden of proving the defense of material alteration, which defense can be waived by acts and conduct, but can be found to have consented in advance to changes when the underlying construction contract contemplates change orders and the possibility of time extensions.[24]

---

[14] University of Hawaii Prof'l Assembly v. Univ. of Haw., 66 Haw. 214, 649 P.2d 720 (1983); *see also* Hawaiian Pineapple Co. v. Saito, 24 Haw. 787 (1919), *petition denied,* 260 F. 153 (9th Cir. 1919).

[15] Territory v. Howell, 23 Haw. 797 (1917); Territory v. Pacific Coast Gas Co., 22 Haw. 446 (1915); United States v. Findlay, 4 U.S. Dist. Ct. Haw. 191 (1913); Hackfeld & Co. v. Medcalf, 20 Haw. 47 (1910). *But see* Stanley v. Akoi, 12 Haw. 344 (1900).

[16] Honolulu Roofing Co. v. Felix, 49 Haw. 578, 426 P.2d 298 (1967).

[17] Hustace v. Davis, 23 Haw. 606 (1917); Robinson v. Kaae, 22 Haw. 403 (1915). *See also* authorities cited *supra* in note 15.

[18] William W. Bierce Ltd. v. Waterhouse, 19 Haw. 398 (1909), *rev'd on distinguishable grounds,* Bierce v. Waterhouse, 219 U.S. 320 (1911).

[19] Holzinger v. Goo, 36 Haw. 506, 511 (1943).

[20] Honolulu Roofing Co. v. Felix, 49 Haw. at 609, 426 P.2d at 319.

[21] *See supra* note 19 and *infra* note 23.

[22] Honolulu Ironworks Co. v. Bigelow, 33 Haw. 607 (1935).

[23] *See* Honolulu Roofing Co. v. Felix, 49 Haw. 578, 426 P.2d 298 (1967); Hustace v. Davis, 23 Haw. 606 (1917).

[24] *Id.*

[B] Bid Bonds

Hawaii does not require bid bonds on private projects. Hawaii does, however, require bids for public projects which are (1) in excess of $25,000, and (2) awarded pursuant to a competitive bid or competitive sealed proposal, to be accompanied by a deposit which may be a surety bond.[25] Failure to submit a bid with a bid bond renders a construction bid nonresponsive and subject to immediate rejection.[26] In Hawaii, a bid bond typically guarantees that the low, responsive, responsible bidder will enter into the contract upon which it bids. Typically the bond will provide a penal sum in the event the contractor refuses to enter into the contract after an award, or to deliver required performance and payment bonds after an award.[27]

[C] Performance Bonds

While Hawaii does not require contractors to provide performance bonds on private projects, Hawaii's Bond Law requires on public projects in excess of $25,000[28] that the prime contractor shall furnish a joint performance and payment bond in an amount equal to the prime contract price.[29] The Bond Law applies to all state and county agencies that have authority to contract for the construction of any public building or other public work or public improvement, including highway work.[30] All applicable permutations of Hawaii's Bond Law give first priority to the contracting agency on its performance bond, over the payment bond claims of persons supplying materials or labor on a project.[31] Prime contractors are not third-party beneficiaries of other prime contractors' performance bonds because the performance aspects of such bonds are for the benefit of the government.[32]

---

[25] HAW. REV. STAT. § 103D-323 (1993), H.A.R § 3-122-223.

[26] *Id.*

[27] On public works projects the penal sum is 5% of the bid amount. § 103D-323(5)(1993), H.A.R § 3-122-223(b).

[28] *See supra* note 2.

[29] HAW. REV. STAT. § 103-34 (Supp. 1990). *See also* authorities cited in *supra* note 3.

[30] HAW. REV. STAT. § 103D-102, H.A.R. § 3-120-3(a).

[31] Hawaii's laws have undergone numerous changes within the last five years. This has created some confusion, as the state law applicable to each public project may be different depending upon when the contract was awarded. Practitioners must be particularly careful with respect to the timing of performance and payment bond claims. For contracts solicited or entered into prior to July 1, 1994, the old procurement statutes apply (HAW. REV. STAT. § 507-17). For contracts entered into from July 1, 1994 on but before July 3, 1997, the Procurement Code applies (HAW. REV. STAT. § 103D-324(d) (1993); and for contracts entered into from July 2, 1997 on, the Revised Procurement Code applies. (HAW. REV. STAT. § 103D-324(d) (Supp. 1998)). Under each of these statutory forms, the contracting entity's rights under the statutorily mandated performance bond retains priority over third-party payment bond claims. *See* HAW. REV. STAT. §§ 507-17 (1985), 103D-325(d) (1993), 103D-324(d) (Supp. 1998), *supra.*

[32] Territory v. Pac. Coast Gas Co., 22 Haw 446 (1915) (decided under prior law).

The contracting agency, under Hawaii's administrative rules, has discretion to lessen performance/payment bond amounts (i.e. to 50 percent of the contract price), if a written determination is made that is in the best interests of the state to do so.[33] The Hawaii Supreme Court has not considered whether a contracting agency can be held liable for failure to require a prime contractor to furnish a bond in accordance with the Bond Law.

A Hawaii statute of limitation is applicable to suretyship actions relating to the improvement of real property for a private project.[34] The terms of the suretyship contract would still constitute the dominant factor.[35] If the contract is silent, the repose applicable to construction surety issues is two years from discovery, but not later than ten years from completion of construction.[36]

On a public works project entered into prior to July 1, 1994, the government has an exclusive period of two months from the completion and final settlement of any contract (as opposed to completion of the work) within which to file an action on the performance portion of the bond. Thereafter the payment beneficiaries may institute an action on the bond in the name of the government.[37] This section was repealed as of July 1, 1994. However, there are still construction contracts remaining to which it may apply.

[D] Payment Bonds

For private projects, Hawaii law does not require contractors to furnish payment bonds.

There are no lien rights on public projects. In lieu of lien rights, Hawaii's Bond Laws require that prime contractors furnish a joint performance and payment bond.[38] For many years, i.e. up through July 1, 1994, Hawaii's payment bond law (§ 507-17) tracked the long-repealed federal Heard Act, and state courts construing and interpreting § 507-17 relied upon Heard Act decisions by analogy.[39] In 1993, Hawaii's legislature enacted a comprehensive public procurement code ("Procurement Code"), applicable to all public contracts entered into from July 1, 1994.[40] The payment bond provisions of the Procurement Code are set forth in § 103D-324. This section was subsequently revised in 1997, for all contracts awarded after July 1, 1997.[41] Thus, for purposes of determining the claim requirements for payment bonds on public projects, there are three potentially applicable statutes: (1) the "Heard Act" code applicable to public contracts

[33] H.A.R. § 3-122-225.

[34] HAW. REV. STAT. § 657-8 (1985).

[35] Robinson v. Kaae, 22 Haw. 403 (1916) and authorities cited *supra* note 15.

[36] HAW. REV. STAT. § 657-8 (1994).

[37] HAW. REV. STAT. § 507-17 (1985); Territory v. Mellor, 33 Haw. 523 (1935).

[38] HAW. REV. STAT. § 103D-324 (Supp. 1998).

[39] *See* authorities cited in *supra* note 3 and *infra* notes 41 and 42.

[40] Chapter 103D, "Hawaii Public Procurement Code," HAW. REV. STAT. § 103D-102, Op. Atty Gen. No. 94-4 (1994).

[41] HAW. REV. STAT. § 103D-324 (1998 Supp.).

entered into prior to July 1, 1994; (2) the "Procurement Code" applicable to public contracts entered into from July 1, 1994 through July 1, 1997; and (3) the "Revised Procurement Code," applicable to public contracts entered into from July 1, 1997, and on.

[1] Who Is Covered

Hawaii's "Heard Act" payment bond statute (applicable to pre-July 1, 1994 public contracts), afforded secondary coverage for persons furnishing labor and materials *to the contractor,* which were *used* in the prosecution of the work provided for in the public contract.[42] Hawaii Revised Statutes § 103-4 stated "[t]he bond shall also by its terms inure to the benefit of any and all persons entitled to file claims for labor performed or materials furnished in the work so as to give them a right of action as contemplated by section 507-17." Section 507-17, now repealed in light of the enactment of the 1994 Procurement Code, defined "labor" or "furnishing materials" or words of similar context as having the broad meaning set forth in the Lien Law (see discussion below).

Under the Procurement Code and Revised Procurement Code (applicable to public contracts awarded from July 1, 1994), the payment bond statutes afford protection to every person who has furnished labor or material to the contractor for work provided in the contract.[43]

No Hawaii decisions interpreting Hawaii's Bond Laws have considered whether a prime contractor furnishing a bond with greater coverage than the Bond Law requires, will, nevertheless, be held to the expanded coverage. Under common law, however, the surety's obligation is as set forth in its contract.[44] Yet, courts do not extend the coverage of the bond beyond its clear and unambiguous terms.[45] When common sense dictates, however, the courts have found the surety responsible or release it only *pro tanto,* looking to the substance.[46]

The issue of what tiers of subcontractors or material suppliers may claim under any version of Hawaii's Bond Law payment bond rights has not reached the Hawaii Supreme Court.[47]

---

[42] HAW. REV. STAT. § 103-34 (1990 Supp.)

[43] HAW. REV. STAT. § 103D-324(d) (1993); HAW. REV. STAT. § 103D-324(d) (1998 Supp.), H.A.R. § 3-122-227 (1998).

[44] *See* authorities cited in *supra* note 15.

[45] *Id.;* Territory v. Mellor, 33 Haw. 523 (1935); Hustace v. Davis, 23 Haw. 606 (1917).

[46] Honolulu Roofing Co. v. Felix, 49 Haw. 578, 426 P.2d 298 (1967); Allied Amusements Ltd. v. James W. Glover Ltd., 40 Haw. 92 (1953); Holzinger v. Goo, 36 Haw. 506 (1943); Hustace v. Davis, 23 Haw. 606 (1917).

[47] Although HAW. REV. STAT. § 507-17 (1985) states the bond is for those that supply labor and materials to the person who enters into the contract with the State, thus cutting off subsequent tiers, the terms "labor" and "furnishing materials" are incorporated from § 507-41, the mechanic's lien law, which affords much broader protection. *See* H. Hackfeld & Co. v. Hilo R.R., 14 Haw. 448 (1902). In contrast, under the Procurement Code and Revised Procurement Code, protection is

[2] Notice and Timing Requirements

For persons seeking to file public project payment bond claims in Hawaii, it is crucial to ascertain the date the general contract was entered into in order to determine the notice and timing requirements of the applicable bond statute. There are three potentially applicable statutes. For pre-Procurement Code contracts, (applicable to public contracts entered into prior to July 1, 1994), there are no notice requirements. Under § 507-17, notice was required only *after* institution of a bond action. As the law restricts all claims to one action, the notice is to inform of intervention rights. Pursuant to § 507-17, the government has a two month exclusive window from completion and final settlement within which to file its performance claims against the bond. The government has no standing to bring payment claims on behalf of subcontractors or suppliers.[48]

"Final settlement" is established by the contracting officer's publication of his determination of the amount to be due after the contract, as opposed to the work, is fully completed (although full payment is not then made and the amount is subject to change).[49] All payment claimants may intervene in the government's action.[50]

If the government does not file within said two months, any payment claiment may institute an action within four months of contract performance and final settlement and *not later.*[51] As only one action is permitted, other payment claimants must intervene within five months after performance and final settlement, and *not later.*[52] Claimants are required first to apply with the government for the right of action with an accompanying affidavit "that labor or materials for prosecution of the work have been furnished by him, and that payment therefor has not been made."[53]

---

afforded only to those that supply labor and materials to "the contractor." "Contractor" is defined in both the Procurement Code and its accompanying administrative rules, as the person having a contract with the State. *See* HAW. REV. STAT. § 103D-104 (1993) and H.A.R. § 3-120-2. This implies that second and third tier subcontractors and material suppliers cannot institute payment bond claims under Hawaii's current payment bond statutes. This is buttressed by the fact that, in contrast to the old form (applicable to pre-July 1994 contracts), the new versions of the procurement code do *not* link payment bond claims to the broad definitions afforded in Hawaii's mechanic's lien statutes. On the other hand, the latest version of the payment bond statute (applicable to all public contracts entered into after July 1, 1997), is very similar to the Federal Miller Act. To the extent the Hawaii courts apply the reasoning of federal case law on the Miller Act, protection may be afforded to second, but not to third-tier subcontractors and material suppliers.

[48] Territory v. Pac. Coast Gas Co., 22 Haw. 446 (1915).

[49] Territory v. Mellor, 33 Haw 523 (1935); HAW. REV. STAT. § 507-17 (1985).

[50] *Id.*

[51] HAW. REV. STAT. § 507-17 (1985) (now repealed but technically applicable to public contracts awarded prior to July 1, 1994).

[52] HAW. REV. STAT. § 507-17 (1985).

[53] *Id.* § 507-17.

The second potentially applicable statute is the Procurement Code, applicable to public contracts entered into from *July 1, 1994, until July 1, 1997.* Pursuant to same, every person who has furnished labor or material to the general contractor for work on a public contract in excess of $25,000, who has not been paid in full *after two months from the completion and final settlement of any contract,* may institute an action against the contractor and its sureties.[54]

Each suit must be brought in the circuit in which the contract has to be performed *prior to the expiration of one year* after the completion and final settlement of the contract.[55] Under the Procurement Code there is still no notice requirement, and the named obligee need not be joined.

The Revised Procurement Code applies to contracts awarded *after July 1, 1997.* The Revised Procurement Code contains requirements similar to the federal Miller Act. Thus, cases interpreting same may be instructive in interpreting Hawaii's current public project payment bond statute. Under this latest version, a suit on a payment bond must be brought within one year after *the last delivery of labor or materials to the project site.* This eliminates the ambiguous and often hard to determine "final settlement" timing provision. However, the Revised Procurement Code payment bond statute contains a strict notice requirement. Written notice of bond claims must be sent both to the contractor *and* surety within 90 days from the last provision of materials or labor to a project.[56] The claim must state the amount claimed and the name of the party to whom the material was furnished or supplied or for whom the labor was done or performed. The notice must be served by registered or certified mail, or by any manner authorized by law to serve summons.[57]

[3] Priority of Payment

Other provisions of the various versions of Hawaii's payment bond statutes are for the most part uniform. If "the bond is insufficient to pay the full amount of the claims, then, after paying the full amount due the State, the remainder shall be distributed pro rata among the intervenors."[58]

Should an insurer wrongfully deny coverage, attorneys' fees are recoverable under Hawaii's insurance statutes.[59] However, Hawaii's courts do not charge the

---

[54] Haw. Rev. Stat. § 103D-324(d) (1993).

[55] *Id.* § 103D-324(e).

[56] Haw. Rev. Stat. § 103D-324(e) (Supp. 1998).

[57] *Id.*

[58] Haw. Rev. Stat. § 507-17 (1985); H.A.R. § 3-122-227(b) (1998).

[59] Haw. Rev. Stat. § 431:10-242 (1988 Supp.); *see also* Haw. Rev. Stat. §§ 431:1-201, 431:1-203, and 210(3) (1988 Supp.), which bring surety bonds under the purview of Hawaii's attorney fee statute. *See also* Elliot Megdal & Associates v. Hawaii Planning Mill, Ltd., 797 F. Supp. 832 (D. Haw. 1992).

surety with delay damages where the bond specifically exculpates delay damages.[60]

Hawaii claimants on surety bonds are not entitled to recover attorneys' fees, unless there are express provisions in the bond so providing; modest attorney commissions are permitted by statutory formula.[61]

[E] Additional Bond Issues

Hawaii has a two tier court system. An appeal may be taken from the general jurisdiction circuit court to the Supreme Court, which in its discretion may assign the matter to the Intermediate Court of Appeals.[62] In Hawaii the issue of a claim for bad faith against a surety has not been resolved.

§ 12.03 LIEN LAW

[A] General Concepts

Generally speaking, the purpose of the Lien Law is to provide any person or association of persons furnishing labor or material in the improvement of real property pursuant to a contract with a security mechanism on private construction projects in Hawaii, providing they have not waived their lien rights and comply with the detailed procedural requirements. A mechanics' lien right is a significant security device because it places a lien against and operates as an encumbrance on the property. Because mechanics' lien rights are created entirely by statute, and in derogation of common law, the procedural requirements including the all important notice requirements of the Lien Laws, are strictly construed.[63]

[B] Basic Provisions

Hawaii's Lien Law provides that:

> Any person . . . furnishing labor or material in the improvement of real property shall have a lien upon the improvement as well as upon the interest of the owner of the improvement in the real property upon which the same is situated, or for the benefit of which the same was constructed, for the price agreed to be paid (if the price does not exceed the value of the labor and materials), or if the price exceeds the value thereof or if no price is agreed

---

[60] Mayer v. Alexander & Baldwin, 56 Haw. 195, 532 P.2d 1007 (1975).

[61] Honolulu Roofing Co. v. Felix, 49 Haw. 578, 426 P.2d 298 (1967); Allied Amusement Ltd. v. James W. Glover Ltd., 40 Haw. 92 (1953).

[62] HAW. REV. STAT. tit. 32, 35 (1985 & Supp. 1990).

[63] Hopper v. Lincoln, 12 Haw. 352 (1900); Allen & Robinson v. F.H. Redward & Hawaiian Lodge, No. 21, 10 Haw. 151 (1895); Lucas v. Redward, 9 Haw. 23 (1893).

> upon . . . for the fair and reasonable value for all labor and materials covered by their contract, express or implied. . . .[64]

The definition of "person" includes "natural persons, partnerships, corporations, firms, unincorporated associations, joint ventures, and any other party recognized at law as a person."[65] Thus, Hawaii's Lien Laws broadly define those entitled to protection, unlike many states which limit protection to only contractors and subcontractors.[66] However, somewhere in the chain there must be an express or implied contract to furnish labor or material.[67] Therefore, labor or materials furnished by a trespasser cannot be the subject of a lien claim.[68]

Lien applicants providing engineering and/or architectural services may also assert lien claims in certain situations. For example, if an architect's or engineer's labor was incorporated into the improvement of real property as defined in the Lien Law,[69] a lien may attach.[70]

The Lien Law actually is an *in rem* action and results in a lien upon "the improvement as well as upon the interest of the owner of the improvement in the real property upon which the same is situated, or for the benefit of which the same was constructed. . . ."[71] An "owner" can be a fee owner, a lessee for a term of years, or a vendee under a contract for the purchase of the real property.[72] A lien claim not only binds the interest of the owner of the improvement in real property, but the improvement as well.[73] The fee simple interest of an owner-lessor can also be the subject of a lien claim brought by a claimant who contracted with the lessee if the lease requires the improvement of the real property.[74]

Hawaii's Lien Law does not provide mechanic's or materialman's lien rights on state, public works or public property.[75] However, when the public property is subject to a leasehold interest in favor of a private entity, the leasehold estate may be the subject of a lien.[76]

The Lien Law contains certain prerequisites for lienable work. In addition to the requirements mentioned previously, the person asserting the lien must have

---

[64] HAW. REV. STAT. § 507-42 (1985).

[65] *Id.* § 507-41.

[66] H. Hackfeld & Co. v. Hilo R.R., 14 Haw. 448 (1902).

[67] *Id.;* Lucas v. Hustace, 20 Haw. 693 (1911); Allen & Robinson, Ltd. v. Reist, 16 Haw. 23 (1904).

[68] Lucas v. Hustace, 20 Haw. 693 (1911); Allen & Robinson, Ltd. v. Reist, 16 Haw. 23 (1904).

[69] HAW. REV. STAT. § 507-41 (1993).

[70] Haines v. Maalaea Land Corp., 62 Haw. 13, 608 P.2d 405 (1980); Nakashima Assoc. v. Pac. Beach Corp., 3 Haw. App. 58, 641 P.2d 337 (1982).

[71] HAW. REV. STAT. § 507-42 (1993).

[72] *Id.* § 507-41.

[73] *Id.* § 507-42.

[74] *Id.;* Lewers & Cooke, Ltd. v. Wong, 22 Haw. 765 (1915); Media Five Ltd. v. Yakimetz, 2 Haw. App. 339, 631 P.2d 1211 (1981).

[75] Haw. Op. Att'y Gen. 72-13 (1972).

[76] Tropic Builders, Ltd. v. United States, 52 Haw. 298, 475 P.2d 362 (1970).

furnished "labor" or "materials" in the "improvement" of real property.[77] *Improvement* is defined broadly to include:

> [T]he construction, repair, alteration of or addition to any building, structure, road, utility, railroad, or other undertaking or appurtenances thereto, and includes any building, construction, erection, demolition, excavation, grading, paving, filling in, landscaping, seeding, sodding, and planting, or any part thereof existing, built, erected, placed, made, or done on real property, or removed therefrom, for its benefit.[78]

Labor is defined to include "professional services rendered in furnishing the plans for or in the supervision of the improvement."[79] In addition, *furnishing of materials* is broadly defined to include the supplying of:

> [M]aterials incorporated in the improvement or substantially consumed in the construction operations or specially fabricated for incorporation in the improvement; building materials used during construction but not remaining in the improvement, diminished by the salvage value of the materials; transportation to bring the materials to the site of the improvement; tools, appliances, or machinery (but not including hand tools), used during the construction but not in excess of the reasonable rental value for the period of actual use.[80]

The delivery of materials to the improvement site or to a different site based upon the written instructions of the general contractor that the materials are for a particular improvement, shall be *prima facie* evidence the materials were incorporated into the improvement.[81]

[C] Notice Requirements

The Lien Law contains various notice requirements, which are strictly enforced.[82]

All lien claimants must file and serve a formal Application For A Lien and Notice Of Lien ("Application"). A copy of the filed Application and Notice must be served upon the "owner of the property and any person with an interest therein and upon the party or parties who contracted for the improvement if other than the owner of the property or any person with an interest therein."[83]

---

[77] HAW. REV. STAT. § 507-42 (1993).

[78] *Id.* § 507-41.

[79] *Id.*

[80] *Id.*

[81] *Id.*

[82] *Id.* § 507-43; State Sav. & Loan Ass'n. v. Kauaian Dev. Co., Inc., 50 Haw. 540, 445 P.2d 109 (1968); Lewers & Cooke, Ltd. v. Wong, 22 Haw. 765 (1915); Allen & Robinson v. F. H. Redward & Hawaiian Lodge, No. 21, 10 Haw. 151 (1895).

[83] HAW. REV. STAT. § 507-43(a) (1993).

The Application must set forth the following: (1) the amount of the claim; (2) the labor or material furnished; (3) a description of the property sufficient to identify the same; (4) names of the parties who contracted for the improvement; (5) the name of the general contractor; (6) the names of the owners of the property; (7) the name of any person with an interest in the property, and any other matter necessary to a clear understanding of the claim.[84] The Application can also (but need not) specify the names of the mortgages or other encumbrances of the property, if any, and the name of the surety of the general contractor, if any.[85]

In the event a required party is not named and served, the lien action is not void; the interest of the excluded party, however, is not subject to the asserted lien.[86]

The Application and Notice must be properly served in the manner prescribed for service of a summons.[87] Service may be made personally in the manner prescribed by the Hawaii Rules of Civil Procedure,[88] or if such service is not attainable, by publication or registered mail.[89]

The Application and Notice must be filed no later than forty-five days after the date of completion of the improvement.[90] The date of completion is the time when the owner or the general contractor for the improvement completes a publication of a notice that the improvement has been completed or abandoned, and an affidavit of publication from the newspaper attesting to the date of publication, along with a copy of the notice, are filed in the office of the clerk of the circuit court where the property is situated.[91]

Published notice is not effective unless there has been substantial completion or the improvement has been actually abandoned.[92] In the event the required notice is not published and filed within one year of the actual completion or abandonment of the improvement, the date of completion is, by statute, deemed to be one year after the actual completion or abandonment.[93]

A hearing is held not less than three nor more than ten days after service of the Application and Notice.[94] At this hearing the court determines whether probable cause exists to permit the lien to attach.[95] Any person required to receive the Application and Notice can offer testimony and documentary evidence contesting

---

[84] *Id.*

[85] *Id.*

[86] Jack Endo Elec. Co. v. Lear Siegler, Inc., 59 Haw. 612, 585 P.2d 1265 (1968).

[87] HAW. REV. STAT. § 507-43(a) (1993).

[88] HAW. R. CIV. P. 4(a).

[89] HAW. REV. STAT. §§ 634-23 -25 (1993).

[90] *Id.* § 507-43(b).

[91] *Id.* § 507-43(f).

[92] *Id.*

[93] *Id.* § 507-43(g).

[94] *Id.* § 507-43(a) (1985); Moore v. Tablada, 68 Haw. 228, 708 P.2d 140 (1985).

[95] HAW. REV. STAT. § 507-43(a) (1993).

the Application and Notice.[96] The hearing can be continued by the court so the entire controversy need not be determined on the originally scheduled day.[97] The lien will not attach to the property until the court orders probable cause exists.[98] Following attachment, the lien expires three months after entry of the court's order finding probable cause and directing attachment of the lien unless proceedings are commenced within that time to foreclose upon the lien.[99]

An action to foreclose upon the lien and collect the amounts owed must be filed in the circuit court where the property is located.[100] Applications concerning the same improvement may be consolidated and any person having an interest in the property may be named as a party or be permitted to intervene.[101]

[D] Waiver

The Lien Law does not contain specific waiver provisions.

[E] Lien Priority

The Lien Law provides different rules as to priority depending upon whether one is dealing with a mechanics' and materialmen's lien *vis-a-vis* other mechanics' and materialmen's liens or a mechanics' and materialmen's lien *vis-a-vis* other encumbrances.[102]

The Lien Law provides that the lien shall have priority over all other liens of any nature, *except* liens in favor of any branch of government and mortgages, liens or judgments recorded or filed prior to the time of visible commencement of the work.[103] However, when a mortgage is recorded prior to the date of completion, the mortgage will have priority if: (1) all or portion of the money advanced under and secured by the mortgage is used for the purpose of paying for the improvement; and (2) the mortgage recites that the purpose of the mortgage is to secure the moneys advanced for the purpose of paying for the improvement.[104] Also, under the Lien law, even if a mortgage meets the foregoing requirements, interest owed on the principal amount secured by the mortgage would not have priority.[105]

Mechanics' and materialmen's liens on the same improvement rank equally

[96] *Id.*
[97] *Id.*
[98] *Id.*
[99] *Id.* §§ 507-43(e), 507-47.
[100] *Id.* § 507-47.
[101] *Id.*
[102] *Id.* §§ 507-46, 507-47.
[103] *Id.* § 507-46.
[104] *Id.*
[105] Strouss v. Simmons, 66 Haw. 32, 657 P.2d 1004 (1982).

in priority *vis-a-vis* each other and relate to and take effect from the time of the visible commencement of the improvement.[106] In the event the proceeds of the foreclosure sale are insufficient to pay all mechanics' and materialmen's liens filed against the property, the proceeds are distributed *pro rata* based on the lienor's respective principal amounts.[107]

[F] Remedies of the Owner

The Lien Law provides the owner with various forms of protection, including the right to assure that all of the provisions of the Lien Law have been complied with, the right to retain funds,[108] and the right to bond off a claim.[109]

---

[106] Haw. Rev. Stat. § 507-46 (Supp. 1998).
[107] *Id.* § 507-47.
[108] *Id.* § 507-48.
[109] *Id.* § 507-45.

CHAPTER 13

IDAHO

Paige Alan Parker
Kimbell D. Gourley

§ 13.01 INTRODUCTION

In Idaho, one furnishing labor or materials to a private project can secure the outstanding obligation and protect himself against non-payment by filing a lien as provided in Idaho Code §§ 45-501 *et seq.* To be valid, the claim of lien must substantially comply with the statutory requirements, be timely filed in the county where the work was performed and be served on the owner of the property no later than 24 hours following the filing of the claim.

The Idaho Legislature has determined that in the public sector such remedies are either unavailable or would be unseemly, and thus has enacted the Public Contracts Bond Act, Idaho Code §§ 54-1925 *et seq.*, as a substitute for the lien remedies available in the private sector. The Public Contracts Bond Act does not have any threshold amount and applies to "*any* contract for the construction, alteration, or repair of *any* public building or public work or improvement of the State of Idaho, or of any county, city, town, municipal corporation, township, school district, public educational institution, or other political subdivision, public authority, or public instrumentality, or of any officer, board, commission, institution, or agency of the foregoing. . . ." The payment bond is set at no less than 85 percent of the contract amount. The payment bond's protection extends to the subcontractor of the contractor furnishing the payment bond and also to persons furnishing labor, material, or rented, leased, or otherwise supplied equipment to the subcontractor but having no contractual relationship, expressed or implied, with the contractor.

In addition, a performance bond in an amount of not less than 85 percent of the contract amount is required for the protection of the public body awarding the contract. The Public Contracts Bond Act does not limit the authority of the State of Idaho or other public body to require a performance bond or other security in addition to that required in the Act.

§ 13.02 BOND LAW

[A] General Concepts

The Idaho Public Contracts Bond Act is modeled after the federal Miller Act, 40 U.S.C. §§ 270(a) *et seq.* The Act is intended to protect persons who furnish labor and materials to public works by obligating the prime contractor on his bond to satisfy their unpaid claims.[1] The Act is deemed remedial in purpose.[2]

Because the federal Miller Act is the model for the Idaho Public Contracts Bond Act, the Idaho courts look to the federal cases interpreting the Miller Act for guidance.[3]

---

[1] School Dist. No. 91, Bonneville County v. Tayson, 94 Idaho 599, 603, 495 P.2d 5, 9 (1972).

[2] LeGrand Steel v. A.S.C. Constructors, Inc., 108 Idaho 817, 818, 702 P.2d 855, 856 (Ct. App. 1985).

[3] Beco Corp. v. Roberts & Sons Constr. Co., Inc., 114 Idaho 704, 712, 760 P.2d 1120, 1128 (1988).

The exact form of performance or payment bond is not specified by statute. The only statutory requirement is that "[e]ach bond shall be executed by a surety company or companies duly authorized to do business in this state . . ."[4] In the alternative, in lieu of a surety bond, the contractor may give a *government obligation*[5] defined as "a public debt obligation of the United States government or the State of Idaho and an obligation whose principal and interest is unconditionally guaranteed by the United States government or the State of Idaho."[6] If a government obligation is used, it is given to the official having the authority to approve the surety bond or its authorized custodian; it must be in an amount at par value to the amount of the required surety bond; and it must authorize the official receiving the obligation to collect or sell the obligation if the person defaults on the required condition.[7]

If the State of Idaho, or a department, board, commission, institution, or agency thereof is the public entity awarding the contract, the performance and the payment bonds must be payable to the State of Idaho or the particular authorized state agency. On all other contract, the bonds are payable to the public body concerned.[8] A government obligation, permitted in lieu of a surety bond, must "be in an amount equal at fair market value to the penal sum of the required surety bond."

[B] Bid Bonds

Security, which may take the form of a bid bond, is required on bids presented to a county,[9] a highway project by a county or highway district,[10] a municipal corporation,[11] or a local improvement district.[12] In each situation, a bidder may present security in the form of cash, a cashier's check made payable to the public body, a certified check made payable to the public body, or a bidder's bond executed by a qualified surety company, made payable to the public body.[13] In all cases in which a bidder's security is required, the security must be at least five percent of the amount bid. The bid will not be considered unless one of the acceptable forms of bidder security is enclosed with the bid and submitted in a form which substantially complies with the form provided by the public entity.[14]

---

[4] IDAHO CODE § 54-1926.

[5] IDAHO CODE § 54-1926A(a) (1988).

[6] IDAHO CODE § 54-1901(h).

[7] *Id.*

[8] *Id.* § 54-1926.

[9] IDAHO CODE § 31-4005 (1996).

[10] IDAHO CODE § 40-908.

[11] *Id.* § 50-341(E).

[12] IDAHO CODE § 50-1710 (1988).

[13] *See* authorities cited in footnotes, 9 through 12, *supra.*

[14] *Id.;* IDAHO CODE § 31-4006 (1983).

In the event that the lowest responsible bidder fails to execute the contract, the lowest responsible bidder's security is forfeited to the public body.[15]

In the case of a county, municipal corporation, or local improvement district, if the county commission, the city council, or district commission awards the contract to the next lowest responsible bidder, the amount of the lowest responsible bidder's security is applied to the difference between the lowest responsible bid and the next responsible bid, and the surplus, if any, is returned to the lowest responsible bidder if cash or a check is used, or to the surety on the bidder's bond if a bond is used.[16]

[C] Performance Bonds

In Idaho, the performance bond requirement applies only to public projects. There is no threshold amount which triggers the bond requirement. Idaho Code § 54-1926 applies to "any contract for the construction, alteration, or repair of any public building or public work or improvement" of any state or local governmental body. The performance bond is fixed by the contracting body but must be no less than 85 percent of the contract amount.[17] The bond penalty sum is conditioned upon the faithful performance of the contract in accordance with the plans, specifications, and the conditions thereof.[18]

If the public body requires a performance bond in excess of 50 percent of the total contract amount, the public body is prohibited from withholding from the contractor any amount exceeding five percent of the total amount payable to the contractor as retainage.[19] Further, the public body is required to release to the contractor any retainage for those portions of the project accepted by the contracting body and the contractors as complete within 30 days after such acceptance.[20] Subcontractors are included within the protection of the five-percent limit withheld as retainage by a public body requiring a performance or payment bond in excess of 50 percent.

The public body may require a performance bond in addition to that prescribed by the Public Contracts Bond Act.[21]

Public body is inclusive of the State of Idaho; any county, city, town, municipal corporation, township, school district, public educational institution, or other policy subdivision, public authority, or public instrumentality; and any officer, board, institution, or agency thereof.[22] The performance bond is made

---

[15] *Id.* § 31-4008; IDAHO CODE §§ 40-911, 50-341(H).
[16] *Id.* §§ 31-4010, 50-341(I), 56-1710.
[17] *Id.* § 54-1926.
[18] *Id.*
[19] *Id.*
[20] *Id.*
[21] *Id.*
[22] *Id.*

payable to the public body concerned.[23] The performance bond is solely for the protection of the public body awarding the contract.[24]

In lieu of a performance bond, the contractor may give a government obligation.[25] A *government obligation* is defined as "a public debt obligation of the United States government or the State of Idaho and an obligation whose principal and interest is unconditionally guaranteed by the United States Government or the State of Idaho."[26] If a government obligation is used, it is given to the official having the authority to approve the surety bond or its authorized custodian, must be in an amount at par value to the amount of the required surety bond, and must authorize the official receiving the obligation to collect or sell the obligation if the person defaults on the required condition.[27] The Idaho Code provides that using a government obligation instead of a surety bond for security is the same as using a corporate surety bond, a certified check, a bank draft, a post office money order, or cash.[28]

Idaho Code § 54-1926A, authorizing the use of government obligations instead of surety bonds, was enacted by the Idaho Legislature in 1986. In the 1978 case of *McKay Construction Company v. Ada County Board of County Commissioners,*[29] the Idaho Supreme Court held that the requirement for a performance bond was mandatory and that time certificates restrictively endorsed to prevent the contractor from negotiating the certificates without the consent of the public body was insufficient. The Idaho Code provision permitting the use of government obligations in lieu of a surety bond has certainly expanded the options available to a public works contractor. However, even with this modification, the security must still be either a performance bond executed by a security company duly authorized to do business in Idaho or be a government obligation meeting the requirements of Idaho Code § 54-1926(A).

There is a sparsity of case law interpreting the performance bond provisions of the Public Contracts Bond Act. In the absence of State authority, the Idaho courts consistently look to the case law interpreting the federal Miller Act, upon which the Idaho Public Contracts Bond Act is derived, for guidance.[30]

[D] Payment Bonds

The payment bond provisions of the Idaho Public Contracts Bond Act are applicable to "contracts for the construction, alternation, or repair of any public building or public work or public improvement of the State of Idaho, or of any

[23] *Id.*

[24] *Id.*

[25] *Id.; id.* § 54-1926A(A).

[26] *Id.* § 54-1901(h).

[27] *Id.* § 54-1926A(a).

[28] *Id.* § 54-1926A(c).

[29] 99 Idaho 235, 580 P.2d 412 (1978).

[30] Beco Corp. v. Roberts & Sons Constr. Co., Inc., 114 Idaho 704, 712, 760 P.2d 1120, 1128 (1988).

county, city, town, municipal corporation, township, school district, public educational institution, or other political subdivision, public authority, or public instrumentality, or of any officer, board, commission, institution or agency of the foregoing. . . ."[31] As so specified, that act does not apply to private projects.

The payment bond provisions of the Idaho Public Contracts Bond Act are also derived from the federal Miller Act, 40, U.S.C. § 270(a) and are substantively identical. Idaho public courts have held that the purpose both of the federal Miller Act and the Idaho Public Contractors Bond Act is "to protect persons who furnish labor or materials to public works."[32]

The scope of the protection afforded under the payment bond provisions of the Idaho Public Contractors Act is limited to those who have a direct contractual relationship with the prime contractor and those who have a direct contractual relationship with one of the prime contractor's subcontractors.[33] The Idaho Court of Appeals has defined a subcontractor as "one who performs for or takes from the prime contractor a specific part of the labor or material requirements of the original contract. . . ."[34] On this definition, the Idaho Court of Appeals in *LeGrand Steel v. ASC Constructors, Inc.,*[35] determined that a major materialman on a project with direct contractual relationships with the prime contractor was a "subcontractor" under the terms of Idaho Code § 54-1927, permitting a submaterialman to sue on the prime contractor's payment bond.

The payment bond must be in an amount fixed by the contracting body but in no event less than 85 percent of the contract amount.[36] The payment bond is solely for the protection of persons supplying labor or materials, or renting, leasing or otherwise supplying equipment to the contractor or his subcontractors in the prosecution of the work provided for in the contract.[37] If the public body requires a payment bond in excess of 50 percent of the total contract amount, the public body is limited to withholding 5 percent of the total amount payable to the contractor as retainage, and this retainage must be released to the contractor for those portions of the project accepted by the contracting public body and the contractor as complete within 30 days after such acceptance.[38]

Subcontractors are included within the protection of the 5 percent limit withheld as retainage by a public body requiring a performance or payment bond in excess of 50 percent. The retainage withheld by a contractor pursuant to a contract with a subcontractor is limited to an amount not exceeding 5 percent of

[31] IDAHO CODE § 54-1926.

[32] LeGrand Steel v. A.S.C. Constructors, Inc., 108 Idaho 817, 818, 702 P.2d 855, 856 (Ct. App. 1985).

[33] *Id.*

[34] *Id., quoting* Clifford E. MacEvoy Co. v. United States, 332 U.S. 102, 109, 64 S. Ct. 890, 88 L. Ed. 1163 (1944).

[35] 108 Idaho 817, 702 P.2d 855 (Ct. App. 1985).

[36] IDAHO CODE § 54-1926.

[37] *Id.*

[38] *Id.*

the total amount payable to the subcontractor. The contractor is required to remit the retainage to the subcontractor within 30 days after completion of the subcontract.

The payment bond must be executed by a surety company or companies duly authorized in the State of Idaho and must be payable to the public body concerned.[39] As in the case of performance bonds, a government obligation may be furnished in lieu of a payment bond.[40] If the claim is made against the contractor, the public contracting body may not return the government obligation to the contractor unless the 90 days period for bringing a civil suit under Idaho Code § 54-1927 has lapsed.[41] If a civil action is brought in the 90 day period, the public contracting body is required to hold the government obligation or the proceeds thereof subject to the order of the court having jurisdiction of the action.[42]

The right to sue on the payment bond accrues when a claimant who has furnished labor or materials or rented, leased or otherwise supplied equipment in the prosecution of the work has not been paid in full before the expiration of 90 days after the day on which the last labor was done or performed by him or material or equipment was furnished or supplied by him for which such claim is made.[43]

For a subcontractor in privity of contract with the prime contractor, the suit must be commenced before the expiration of one year from the date on which final payment under the subcontract became due.[44] Suit must be brought in the appropriate court in any county in which the contract was to be performed.[45]

For claimants not in privity of contract with the contractor, written notice must be given to the contractor within 90 days from the date on which the claimant performed the last labor or furnished or supplied the last material for which the claim is made.[46] The written notice must state with substantial accuracy the amount claimed and the amount of the person to whom the material or equipment was furnished or supplied or for whom the labor was done or performed. The notice must be served by registered or certified mail, postage prepaid, and addressed to the contractor at any place he maintains an office or conducts his business or at his residence.[47] Suit against the contractor must be commenced prior to the expiration of one year from the date on which the claimant performed the last of the labor or furnished or supplied the last of the material or equipment

---

[39] *Id.*

[40] *See* footnotes 25 through 28 *supra* and the textual material referenced to therein.

[41] IDAHO CODE § 54-1926A(d).

[42] *Id.*

[43] *Id.* § 54-1927.

[44] *Id.*

[45] *Id.*

[46] *Id.*

[47] *Id.*

for which suit is brought.[48] Again, the suit must be brought in the appropriate court in any county in which the contract was to be performed.[49]

The time periods prescribed in Idaho Code § 54-1927 may be subject to contractual modification.[50] In *Consolidated Supply Company v. Babbitt,*[51] the Idaho Supreme Court found that a provision in the payment bond which set an expiration date of two years following the date on which the principal ceased work on the contract governed the time in which the contractor could file suit rather than the one year provision specified in Idaho Code § 54-1927.[52]

The time for filing suit by a subcontractor of the prime contract is determined by the date on which final payment became due the subcontractor pursuant to the terms of the parties' contract. The Idaho Court of Appeals in *Eimco Division, Envirotech v. United Pacific Insurance Co.,*[53] involving a "battle of the forums" dispute, found that a letter from a materialman to the general contractor insisting upon full payment not later than 120 days from the date of shipment became the controlling bench mark for the beginning of the one-year period in which suit could be brought.[54]

Due to the remedial nature of the Idaho Public Contracts Bond Act, the Idaho Courts have liberally applied the act to protect the laborers and materialmen. Thus failure of a materialman to give written notice by registered or certified mail to a contractor is not fatal since the registered or certified mail requirement is intended "to assure receipt of the notice not to make the described method mandatory so as to deny right of suit when the required written notice within the specified time has actually been given and received."[55] The Idaho Supreme Court has also held that substantial compliance with a requirement that the amount claimed to be stated with substantial accuracy will preserve a claim.[56]

As noted above, the payment bond exists for the benefit of a claimant who has furnished labor or material or rented, leased, or otherwise supplied equipment in the prosecution of work provided in such contract in respect of which a payment bond is furnished. The Idaho Supreme Court in *City of Weippe v.*

---

[48] *Id.*

[49] *Id.; see also* Interform Co. v. Mitchell, 575 P.2d 1970, 1280 (9th Cir. 1987) (interpreting Idaho law) ("[A] furnisher of rental equipment continues to supply such equipment through the entire rental period; the date of last supply occurs not at the beginning of a job but at the end or at the time the equipment is last available for use on the job.").

[50] City of Weippe v. Yarno, 96 Idaho 319, 323, 528 P.2d 201, 205 (1974).

[51] 96 Idaho 636, 534 P.2d 466 (1975).

[52] *Id.* at 641; 534 P.2d at 471.

[53] 109 Idaho 762, 710 P.2d 672 (1985).

[54] *Id.* at 764, 710 P.2d at 674.

[55] Consolidated Concrete v. Empire West Constr. Co., 100 Idaho 234, 236, 596 P.2d 106, 108 (1979), *quoting* Fleisher Eng'g & Constr. Co. v. United States, 311 U.S. 15, 19, 61 S. Ct. 81, 83, 85 L. Ed. 12,15, (1940).

[56] School Dist. No. 91, Bonneville County v. Tayson, 94 Idaho 599, 603, 495 P.2d 5, 9 (1972).

Yarno,[57] addressed the issue of whether materials provided to a public works contractor had to be incorporated in the public works before a claim could be made on the payment bond. Citing cases interpreting the federal Miller Act, the Idaho Supreme Court held that no showing of substantial consumption need be made.[58] Thus, tires and antifreeze supplied at the insistence and request of the contractor were deemed to be materials within the definition of that term under the Idaho Public Contracts Bond Act.

The Idaho Public Contracts Bond Act provides that in the event a public body fails or neglects to obtain the delivery of a payment bond, that public body is required to promptly make payment to all persons who have supplied materials and performed labor in the prosecution of the work under the contract. Suit must be commenced within one year after the furnishing of the materials or labor and must be brought in any court having jurisdiction in any county in which the contract was to be performed.[59]

If suit is brought, a reasonable attorneys' fee may be recovered by the prevailing party.[60] The Idaho Court of Appeals, however, has held that the attorneys' fees statute under the Idaho Public Contracts Bond Act is not applicable for appeals.[61] Of course, attorneys' fees may be awarded pursuant to Idaho Code § 12-121 if an appeal is pursued or defended frivolously, unreasonably, or without foundation.[62]

[E] Additional Bond Issues

The Idaho Supreme Court has recognized the tort of bad faith in the first party insurance context.[63] However, the tort of bad faith has been rejected with regards to debtor-credit relationships.[64] There have been no applications of these bad faith principles to the provision of the Idaho Public Contracts Bond Act. Idaho does, however, allow punitive damages in connection with breach of contract claims, but only when it is shown that the defendant acted in a manner that was an extreme deviation of reasonable standards of conduct and the act was performed by the defendant with an understanding of or disregard of its likely

---

[57] 96 Idaho 319, 528 P.2d 201 (1974).

[58] *Id.* at 322, 528 P.2d at 203, *citing* Montgomery v. Unity Elec. Co., 155 F. Supp. 179, 180 (D.C.P.R. 1957); United States v. National Sur. Corp., 179 F. Supp. 598, 604 (E.D. Pa. 1959); United States v. Fire Ass'n of Philadelphia, 260 F.2d 541, 544 (2d Cir. 1958).

[59] IDAHO CODE § 54-1928.

[60] IDAHO CODE § 54-1929 (1988).

[61] LeGrand Steel Prods. Co. v. A.S.C. Constructors, Inc., 108 Idaho 817, 819, 702 P.2d 855, 857 (Ct. App. 1985).

[62] *Id.*

[63] White v. Unigard Mut. Ins. Co., 112 Idaho 94, 98, 730 P.2d 1014, 1018 (1986).

[64] Black Canyon Racquetball Club, Inc. v. Idaho First Nat'l Bank, 119 Idaho 171, 176, 804 P.2d 900 (1991).

consequences.[65] The Idaho Public Contract Bond Act does not apply to an out-of-state bond on an out-of-state project.[66]

§ 13.03 LIEN LAW

[A] General Concepts

Idaho has had a mechanics' and materialmen's lien since 1893. The purpose of these lien statutes is to compensate persons who perform labor upon or furnish materials to be used in construction or alteration or repair of a structure.[67] These lien statutes are liberally construed so as to affect their objects and to promote justice.[68]

"Substantial compliance" is the standard to which the Idaho Courts look in determining whether such a lien is valid.[69] The lien statutes operate *in rem,*[70] and a foreclosure of the lien lies in equity.[71]

Because the lien statute does not operate *in personam,* the claimant must look to the property, and not the owner thereof, for satisfaction absent a direct contractual relationship with the owner.[72] However, the Idaho Court of Appeals in *Idaho Lumber, Inc. v. Buck,*[73] held that when a materialman or subcontractor furnishes labor and materials that benefit the property of a person with whom there is no privity of contract, an action in *quantum meruit* may lie against the landowner to recover the reasonable value of the labor and materials so furnished.[74]

[B] Basic Provisions

The Idaho mechanics' and materialmen's liens cover laborers, materialmen, professional engineers and licensed surveyors. Laborers and materialmen are covered if they perform labor upon, or furnish materials to be used in, the construction, alteration or repair of any mining claim, building, wharf, bridge, ditch, dike, flume, tunnel, fence, machinery, railroad, wagon road, aqueduct to create hydraulic power, or any other structure, or who grades, fills in, levels, surfaces or otherwise improves any land, or who performs labor in any mined or mining claim.[75] Also protected are persons who survey, grade, fill in, or otherwise

---

[65] Cheney v. Palos Verdes Inv. Corp., 104 Idaho 897, 905, 665 P.2d 661, 669 (1983).

[66] Seubert Excavators, Inc. v. Eucon Corp., 93.5 ICAR 266, 270 n.7, (Ct. App. Mar. 3, 1993).

[67] Barber v. Honorof, 116 Idaho 767, 768–69, 780 P.2d 89, 90–91 (1989).

[68] *Id.* at 768, 780 P.2d at 90.

[69] Chief Indus., Inc. v. Schwendiman, 99 Idaho 682, 685, 587 P.2d 823, 826 (1978).

[70] *Id.*

[71] Jensen v. Bumgarner, 25 Idaho 355, 360, 137 P. 529, 530 (1913).

[72] Pierson v. Sewell, 97 Idaho 38, 44–45, 539 P.2d 590, 595–96 (1975).

[73] 109 Idaho 737, 710 P.2d 647 (Ct. App. 1985).

[74] *Id.* at 745, 710 P.2d at 655–56.

[75] Idaho Code § 45-501.

improve a lot or the street in front or adjoining the lot in any incorporated municipality at the request of the owner.[76]

The lien claimant must be "otherwise unsecured in whole or in part" to be eligible under the lien statute.[77] Idaho's mechanics' lien law was never intended to be an additional layer of non-consensual security for creditors who are already secured.[78]

Professional engineers and licensed surveyors are covered if, under contract, they prepare or furnish designs, plans, plats, maps, specifications, drawings, surveys, estimates of cost, on site observation or supervision, or render any professional service whatsoever for which the professional engineer or licensed surveyor is legally authorized to perform in connection with any land or building development or improvement, or to establish boundaries.[79]

The substantive requirement is that the work, materials, or services performed must be at the insistence of the owner of the building or improvement, or his agent.[80] The Code provides that every contractor, subcontractor, architect, builder, or any person having charge of the project is deemed to be the agent of the owner for the purposes of the mechanics' and materialmen's lien.[81] However, a lessee of a mining claim is not considered to be the agent of the owner for lien purposes.[82]

The land subject to the lien includes the land upon which the services are performed together with a convenience space about the same as may be required for the convenient use and occupation thereof, to be determined by the court.[83] Of course, if a person owns less than a fee simple estate in the land, only his interest therein is subject to such a lien.[84]

A timely filed mechanics' or materialmen's lien relates back to the time the building, improvement, or structure was commenced, the work was done, or the materials or professional services were first commenced to be furnished.[85] For materials, the lien does not attach until the construction materials are delivered to the construction site.[86] Although there is no lien in which the labor is not used or the materials are not incorporated into the building, structure or improvement,[87] there is no requirement that all the materials furnished be incorporated into the

---

[76] *Id.* § 45-504.

[77] *Id.* § 45-501.

[78] Statement of Purpose to Senate Bill No. 1410.

[79] Idaho Code § 45-501.

[80] *Id.*

[81] *Id.*

[82] *Id.*

[83] *Id.* § 5-505.

[84] *Id.*

[85] Idaho Code § 45-506 (1977); Beall Pipe & Tank Corp. v. Tumac Intermountain, 108 Idaho 487, 492, 700 P.2d 109, 114 (Ct. App. 1985).

[86] 108 Idaho at 492, 700 P.2d at 115.

[87] Chief Indus, Inc. v. Schwendiman, 99 Idaho 682, 687, 587 P.2d 823, 828 (1978).

project.[88] When materials are delivered to the work site, a rebuttable presumption arises that such materials were incorporated into the structure or improvement.[89]

The mechanics' and materialmen's liens are preferred and take preference over any other lien, mortgage, or other encumbrance which the mechanics or materialmen's lien holder had no notice and which was unrecorded at the time the building, improvements, or structure was commenced, the work was done, or materials or professional services were commenced to be furnished.[90] Because Idaho is a "race-notice" state, notice of a lien, mortgage or encumbrance upon land prior to when the project was commenced may affect the priority of the mechanics' and materialmen's liens.

Nothing in the mechanics' and materialmen's lien laws affects the rights of a person to maintain a personal action to recover for the debt against the person liable therefor.[91] Thus, a claimant may collect the debt both through a foreclosure of lien and a personal action against the contractor.[92] However, a lien claimant need not seek payment from the original contractor before enforcing his lien against the real property.[93]

The cost of filing and recording the claim along with a reasonable attorneys' fee is recoverable as part of the foreclosure of the lien.[94] The recovery of attorneys' fees and costs upon a successful foreclosure is mandatory under Idaho Code § 45-513 (1971), subject to the discretion of the court as to amount.[95] The mechanics' and materialmen's lien attorneys' fees statute has been determined not to permit attorneys' fees on appeal.[96] However, attorneys' fees may be awarded on appeal pursuant to Idaho Code § 12-121 if the Appellate Court is left with the abiding belief that an appeal has been brought or defended frivolously, unreasonably or without foundation.[97]

As a general rule, a tenant or lessee is not considered the agent of the owner or lessor within the interpretation of the mechanics' and materialmen's lien statute merely by virtue of that relationship.[98] However, there are two major exceptions. First, a landlord's interest in real property may be subject to a lien for work performed by agreement with the tenant if the lease specifically requires the tenant

---

[88] Idaho Lumber & Hardware Co. v. Digiacomo, 61 Idaho 383, 386, 109 P.2d 637, 638 (1940).

[89] 99 Idaho at 688, 587 P.2d at 828.

[90] *Id.*

[91] IDAHO CODE § 45-515.

[92] Acoustic Specialties, Inc. v. Wright, 103 Idaho 595, 602, 651 P.2d 529, 536 (1982).

[93] *Id.*

[94] IDAHO CODE § 45-513.

[95] Olsen v. Rowe, 125 Idaho 686, 873 P.2d 1340 (Ct. App. 1994).

[96] Weber v. Eastern Idaho Packing Corp., 94 Idaho 694, 698-99, 496 P.2d 693, 698 (1972), *overruled on other grounds,* Pierson v. Sewell, 97 Idaho 38, 45, 539 P.2d 590, 597(1975).

[97] W.F. Constr. Co., Inc. v. Kalik, 103 Idaho 713, 716, 652 P.2d 661, 664 (Ct. App. 1982).

[98] Bunt v. Roberts, 70 Idaho 158, 161, 279 P.2d 629, 630 (1955).

to see that the work is done.[99] If the lease or a real estate sale agreement requires the lessee or vendee to make certain improvements, the Idaho courts have held that the lessee/vendee is an agent of the owner, subjecting the interest of the owner, as well as the interest of the lessee/vendee in the real estate, to the lien.[100] However, when the agreement only gives the lessee/vendee the right to make improvements but does not require any particular improvement, the owner's interest in the real property is not subject to a mechanics' or materialmen's lien.[101]

Second, the landlord's interest may be subject to a lien if he requests the work be done or where the landlord has, by some act in ratification or consent, authorized the work done and the furnishing of the material and labor.[102] Thus, work authorized by a tenant to bring a building in compliance with the city electrical code after the landlord forwarded a letter from the city chief electrical inspector outlining electrical violations and deficiencies, may be deemed a specification of work to be done or a consent for such work, subjecting the property to lien.[103]

The Idaho Court of Appeals has held that the lien claimant must have relied upon the credit of the land for payment and not simply on the personal credit of the purchaser before the lien attaches.[104] Whether there was such reliance is a question of fact.[105]

Materials furnished for use in the construction, alteration or repair or other improvement are not subject to attachment, execution or other legal process to enforce any debt due by the purchaser of such materials.[106] However, such materials may be subject to attachment, execution or other legal process due for the purchase money thereof so long as the same are being applied to the construction, alteration or repair, or improvement in good faith.[107]

[C] Notice Requirements

There is no differentiation in notice requirements between original contractors, professional engineers, and licensed surveyors and all other individual, including subcontractors, laborers, and material suppliers. The statute reads that

---

[99] Christensen v. Idaho Land Developers, Inc., 104 Idaho 458, 459, 660 P.2d 70, 71 (Ct. App. 1983).

[100] Idaho Lumber, Inc. v. Buck, 109 Idaho 737, 741-42, 710 P.2d 647, 651-52 (Ct. App. 1985).

[101] *Id.*

[102] Christensen v. Idaho Land Developers, Inc., 104 Idaho at 459, 660 P.2d at 71.

[103] *Id.*

[104] Beall Pipe & Tank Corp. v. Tumac Intermountain, 108 Idaho 487, 492, 700 P.2d 109, 114 (Ct. App. 1985).

[105] *Id.*

[106] IDAHO CODE § 45-514 (1977).

[107] *Id.*

"any person" claiming a lien must file for record with the county recorder for the county in which the property is located a claim "within ninety (90) days after the completion of the labor or services or furnishing of materials, or the cessation of the labor, services or furnishing of materials for any cause."[108]

Of crucial importance is the requirement that a true and correct copy of the claim of lien must be served on the owner or reputed owner of the property no later than 24 hours following the filing of the claim of lien.[109] Service may be made by either delivering a copy to the owner or by mailing a copy of the claim of lien to the owner by certified mail to the owner's last-known address.[110] The Idaho Supreme Court ruled that oral notification is not sufficient.

Trivial work done or materials furnished after the contract has been substantially completed will not extend the time in which a lien claim can be filed under Idaho Code § 45-507. Thus, the time period is not extended where an article is furnished or a service is rendered after a substantial completion of the contract and the article or service is not expressly required by the terms of the contract.[111] The issue of whether the work is substantial or trivial is fact sensitive and the appellate court will defer to the trial court's characterization.[112] The general rule is that the date on which the last item of material was furnished or of the last work performed is the date of substantial completion of the contract and that new items added thereafter to the account will not extend the time in which to claim a lien or revive a lien already expired.[113]

When additional material or labor is relied upon to extend the time for filing the claim of lien, the claimant must show that the material or labor was actually used in the project and that such labor or material was reasonably necessary to compete construction according to the terms of the contract.[114] The date on which the contract was completed is to be ascertained by the conditions of the contract, the conduct of the parties in relation thereto, and the surrounding facts and circumstances.[115]

[D] Release of Lien

In order to remove the lien while a claim is pending the debtor of the lien claimant or a party in interest in the premises subject to the lien must obtain a

---

[108] *Id.* § 45-507.

[109] *Id.;* Ashley Glass Co. v. Bithell, 123 Idaho 544, 547, 850 P.2d 193 (1993).

[110] *Id.*

[111] 129 Idaho at 895.

[112] Baker dba K.B. Indus. v. Boren, 129 Idaho 885, 895, 934 P.2d 951 (Ct. App. 1997).

[113] Baker dba K.B. Indus. v. Boren, 129 Idaho 885, 896, 934 P.2d 951 (Ct. App. 1997), *quoting* Gem State Lumber Co. v. Whitty, 37 Idaho 489, 499, 217 P. 1027, 1030 (1923).

[114] *Id.; see also* Barlow's, Inc. v. Bannock Cleaning Corp., 103 Idaho 310, 313, 647 P.2d 766, 769 (Ct. App. 1982).

[115] 129 Idaho at 896.

surety bond with that party as principal and executed by a corporation authorized to transact surety business in the state as a surety. The form of the bond is prescribed in the statute and calls for a penalty sum of one and one-half times the claim.[116] The party seeking to release the mechanics' lien by positing a surety bond must then file a petition in the district court of the county where the property is located setting forth the title of the cause; an allegation of the purchase and payment of the premium of the bond, along with the dates of the purchase and payments; an allegation incorporating by reference a true copy of the bond, with a copy of the bond attached to the petition; the name or names of the owner or reputed owners of the land subject to the lien; a description of the real property subject to the lien, along with the instrument number of the lien; and a prayer for an order releasing the lien. The district court then issues an order setting the time and date of a hearing not less than five and not more than ten days from the date of the order.

A copy of the petition and of the order must be served on the lien claimant at least two days prior to the date set for hearing in the manner provided by law for service of summons.[117] The lien claimant may file an objection with the clerk of the court and serve the petitioner or the petitioner's attorney excepting to the efficiency of the surety within two days after having been served a copy of the petition for release of the lien. Failure to file such an exception within two days is deemed to be a waiver of any objection to the justification and sufficiency of the surety.[118]

At the hearing on the petition, the court will enter an order releasing the mechanics' lien upon the petitioner's filing of the original bond and introducing into evidence a receipt for payment of the premium. There is no appeal from the entry of that order.[119]

The lien claimant is then entitled to bring an action against the debtor and to join the surety and recover the amount found due the lien claimant by the court; the costs of preparing the filing of the lien claim, including attorneys' fees, if any; the cost of the proceedings; attorneys' fees incurred in the proceedings; and interest at the rate of seven percent per annum from the date found by the court that the sum was due and payable. This proceeding is second in priority only to criminal hearings, and the plaintiff may serve upon the adverse party a demand for a 30-day trial setting. The priority of the setting is lost, however, if the hearing date is vacated due to stipulation.[120]

By posting the bond, the surety submits to the jurisdiction of the court and irrevocably appoints the clerk of the court as its agent upon whom any papers may be served. The surety's liability may be enforced on motion without the

---

[116] IDAHO CODE § 45-519.
[117] *Id.* § 45-520.
[118] *Id.* § 45-524.
[119] *Id.* § 45-521.
[120] *Id.* § 45-522.

necessity of an independent action. The motion is served on the clerk, who shall mail copies to the surety if the surety's address is known. The motion on the bond cannot be instituted until 30 days following notice of entry of judgment in the action against the lien claimant's debtor if no appeal is filed. If an appeal is filed, the motion may not be instituted until 30 days following the filing of the remitter from the court of appeals or the supreme court.[121]

[E] Foreclosure of Lien

Once a lien has been filed, the claimant must initiate a foreclosure action within six months of the filing.[122] When a number of persons are claiming liens against the same property, they may join in the same action or, if separate actions have been commenced, the court may consolidate them.[123]

The only exception to the six-month limitation on filing the foreclosure action is when there has been a payment on account or an extension of credit given with an expiration date. If such payment or credit with expiration date is endorsed on the record of a lien, then the time period in which to file the foreclosure action is extended six months from the date of such payment or the expiration of the extension.[124] The Idaho Supreme Court has held that this is a one-time only exception. Additional or successive payments on account, even though endorsed on lien of record, no matter when made, will not extend the duration of the lien beyond the six-month period following the first payment.[125]

The six-month period cannot be waived and is an absolute limitation on the right to sue.[126] However, Idaho Rule of Civil Procedure 6(a), which provides that if the last day of a period is a Saturday, Sunday, or legal holiday, the period runs until the end of the next day which is neither a Saturday, Sunday or holiday, applies to determining when the six-month period has run.[127]

When foreclosing, the claimant should file a *lis pendens*. The Idaho Supreme Court has held that a subsequent purchaser or encumbrancer will not be put on constructive notice of the foreclosure of a mechanic's lien unless a *lis pendens* is filed.[128]

The court has the power to determine the amount of land subject to foreclosure. As noted above, a claim of lien is not defective if it describes more property than which may be charged with the lien. The court has the power to call witnesses to ascertain the amount of land necessary for the convenient use

---

[121] *Id.* § 45-523.

[122] *Id.* § 45-510.

[123] IDAHO CODE § 45-513 (1977).

[124] *Id.*

[125] Palmer v. Bradford, 86 Idaho 395, 401, 388 P.2d 96, 99 (1963).

[126] Cather v. Kelso, 103 Idaho 684, 686-87, 652 P.2d 188, 190-91 (1982).

[127] *Id.* at 688, 652 P.2d at 192.

[128] Credit Bureau of Lewiston-Clarkston, Inc. v. Idaho First Nat'l Bank, 117 Idaho 29, 31, 784 P.2d 885, 887 (1989).

and occupation of the property to be sold under the terms and conditions of the lien and judgment.[129] Because this duty is on the court, the claimant need not even allege in this complaint the amount of land required.[130]

[F] Priority of Liens

Among the covered lien claimants, a rank of priority is provided as follows: (1) all laborers, other than contractors or subcontractors; (2) all materialmen, other than contractors or subcontractors; (3) subcontractors; (4) the original contractor; and (5) all professional engineers and licensed surveyors.[131] All lien holders within a class must be paid in full from the proceeds of the sale of the property subject to the lien before members of the next lowest priority class are paid.[132] If there are insufficient proceeds to pay all the members of a class in full, the members of that class share pro rata.[133]

[G] Remedies of Owner

In a foreclosure action, the original contractor is only entitled to recover the amount due under the contract after deducting all claims of all other parties for work done or materials furnished to him.[134] The owner may withhold during the pendency of the action any sums due a contractor in the amount for which the claim or claims have been filed.[135] In the case of a judgment is entered against the owner, the owner is entitled to deduct from any amount due to a contractor the amount of the judgment and costs.[136] If the amount of judgment and costs exceeds the amount due the contractor and if the owner has settled with the contractor in full, the owner is entitled to recover back from the contractor any amounts paid by the owner in excess of the contract price and for which the contractor was originally liable.[137] As noted above, if the owner has counterclaims exceeding the amount of the claim of lien, the lien is extinguished.[138]

Pursuant to Idaho Code § 45-511, the contractor may be held liable for costs and attorneys' fees incurred by an owner in defense of claims made against the

---

[129] Robertson v. Moore, 10 Idaho 115, 128, 77 P. 218, 222 (1904), *overruled on other grounds,* Dover Lumber Co. v. Case, 31 Idaho 276, 170 P. 108 (1918).

[130] Beall Pipe & Tank Corp. v. Tumac Intermountain, Inc., 108 Idaho 487, 491, 700 P.2d 109, 113 (Ct. App. 1985).

[131] Idaho Code § 45-512.

[132] *Id.*

[133] *Id.*

[134] *Id.* § 45-511.

[135] *Id.*

[136] *Id.*

[137] *Id.*

[138] *See* footnote 115, *supra* and textual material referenced therein.

owner by subcontractors.[139] However, if the contractor admits that the subcontractors are entitled to the monies claimed due and owing and the owner fails to pay the subcontractors without cause, the owner may be forced to pay the attorneys' fees and costs of the subcontractors.[140]

[H] Waiver

Any waiver of lien rights signed by a party protected by the Idaho Mechanics and Materialmen's Lien statute is unenforceable unless supported by consideration.[141] A lien waiver that releases lien rights against the property and acknowledges payment in full for labor and material costs as of a date certain does not release the owner from labor and material cost claims subsequent to that date.[142] If the owner deals directly with subcontractors, a lien waiver signed by the contractor will not hold the owner harmless for obligations owed by the owner to the subcontractors.[143]

[139] Bouten Constr. Co. v. M&L Land Co., 125 Idaho 95, 877 P.2d 928 (Ct. App. 1994).
[140] Acoustic Specialties, Inc. v. Wright, 103 Idaho 595, 651 P.2d 529 (1982).
[141] Pierson v. Sewell, 97 Idaho 38, 42-43, 539 P.2d 590, 594-95 (1975).
[142] Baker dba K.B. Indus. v. Boren, 129 Idaho 885, 896, 934 P.2d 951 (Ct. App. 1997).
[143] *Id.* at 897.

CHAPTER 14

ILLINOIS

Stanley P. Sklar[1]

[1] The author gratefully acknowledges the assistance of Ania M. Domagala, an associate in the Construction Practice Group at Bell, Boyd & Lloyd.

§ 14.01 LIEN LAW

[A] General Concepts

The state of Illinois has completed a recodification of its statutes, and, although the sections of the Illinois Mechanics' Lien Act ("Act") have not changed, the chapter designation has. The Act is now referred to as Chapter 770, Act 60 of the Illinois Compiled Statutes. The official designation is 770 ILCS 60/0.01 *et. seq.* The object and purpose of the Mechanics' Lien Act is to protect those who in good faith furnish material or labor for the construction of buildings.[2] However, a lien is valid only if each of the statutory requirements is scrupulously observed. The failure to strictly comply with the requirements of the Act will result in the loss of lien rights.[3] The remedies provided in the Act (in § 30) are available to contractors, subcontractors, and material suppliers who have not been paid, as well as to owners whose property is subject to mechanics' liens in excess of funds available for payments.

The Act provides a remedy for unpaid subcontractors and material suppliers, which permits them to assert their rights against property owned by a party with whom they have no contractual relationship. It also protects general contractors who have a direct contractual relationship with the owner of property by permitting them to lien the property to the extent of the improvement made to the property. However, failure by the contractor to provide to the owner a sworn statement listing all subcontractors, subcontract amounts, and balances due, as required by § 5 of the Act, will result in the loss of the contractor's rights under the Act *and* the contract.[4]

With respect to the form and contents of the claim for lien, the general contractor is guided by § 7 of the Act, and the subcontractor is guided by § 24. Under § 7, overcharges will not defeat the lien so long as there is no intent to defraud.[5] Thus, this section provides a safe haven for the careless contractor who makes an honest mistake or error.[6] Another requirement that should be noted is inclusion of a sufficiently correct legal description of the property. The cautious

[2] Daily v. Mid-America Bank & Trust Co., 130 Ill. App. 3d 639, 474 N.E.2d 788 (1985). *See also* First Bank v. Rinaldi, 262 Ill. App. 3d 179, 634 N.E.2d 1204 (1994); Contract Dev. Corp. v. Beck, 255 Ill. App. 3d 660, 627 N.E.2d 760 (1994) (both holding that a claimant may recover under the Act when the value of the property has been increased by furnishing labor or materials).

[3] Niles Constr. Co. v. LaSalle Nat'l Bank, 119 Ill. App. 2d 1, 254 N.E.2d 535 (1969); *accord* Hill Behan Lumber Co. v. Marchese, 1 Ill. App. 3d 789, 275 N.E.2d 451 (1971).

[4] Malesa v. Royal Harbour Management Corp., 187 Ill. App. 3d 655, 543 N.E.2d 591 (1989).

[5] Midwest Concrete Prod. Co. v. LaSalle Nat'l Bank, 94 Ill. App. 3d 394, 418 N.E.2d 988 (1981) (holding attorneys' fees to be recoverable only when authorized by contract or statute); Hemenover v. DePatis, 86 Ill. App. 3d 586, 408 N.E.2d 387 (1980). *See also* Plepel v. Nied, 106 Ill. App. 3d 282, 435 N.E.2d 1169 (1982); Fedco Elec. Co. v. Stunkel, 77 Ill. App. 3d 48, 395 N.E.2d 1116 (1979).

[6] United Cork Co. v. Volland, 365 Ill. 564, 572, 7 N.E.2d 301 (1937); Atlee Elec. Co. v. Johnson Constr. Co., 14 Ill. App. 3d 716, 303 N.E.2d 192 (1973). *Compare* Fedco Elec. Co. v. Stunkel, 77

practitioner will include not only the property's legal description but also its common address[7] and real estate tax number (permanent index number (PIN)). An often overlooked but nonetheless important inclusion in the lien is the name of the lien's preparer.

Effective July 25, 1997, a new section was added to the Act: Construction Trust Funds [770 ILCS 60/21.02]. This section imposes a duty on any person who requests or requires a waiver of mechanics' lien from the party furnishing labor or materials, to hold as trustee, such funds as may be received on behalf of such party. Failure to hold such money in trust will render the obligated party liable for all damages.

[B] Basic Provisions of General Contractor's Lien

The first inquiry is whether the client is a general contractor or subcontractor. Section 1 of the Act sets forth an elaborate definition of *contractor.* A general contractor may be any person, individual, corporation, or body politic whose work falls within one of the § 1 categories. [Note that the definition of *person* is found in § 105 of Chapter 131.] In *Levey Film, Inc. v. Cosmopolitan Bank & Trust,*[8] *the court held that a contractor* need not be an architect, structural engineer, professional engineer, land surveyor, or property manager. Thus, it allowed a tenant to claim a mechanics' lien when the owner authorized the tenant to perform repairs and improvements to leased premises.

Once it is established that the party seeking a lien is a general contractor under at least one of the categories of § 1, the following requirements must be met in order to prevail on the lien.

1. There must be a valid contract (which may be express, implied, partially implied, partially oral, or partially written) between the parties.[9]
2. The contract may be with the owner,[10] the owner's authorized agent,[11] or one "knowingly permitted" by the owner to improve the real estate.[12]

Ill. App. 3d 48, 395 N.E.2d 1116 (1979) (dismissing electrical contractor's lien claim because contractor knowingly, not mistakenly, overstated amount in lien).

[7] *In re* Argonne Constr. Co., 10 B.R. 570 (N.D. Ill. 1981).

[8] 247 Ill. App. 3d 348, 653 N.E.2d 875 (1995).

[9] Rittenhouse v. Warren Constr. Co., 264 Ill. 619, 106 N.E. 466 (1914); B & C Elec., Inc. v. Pullman Bank & Trust Co., 96 Ill. App. 3d 321, 421 N.E.2d 206 (1981); Bleck v. Stepanich, 64 Ill. App. 3d 436, 381 N.E.2d 363 (1978); Excellent Builders, Inc. v. Pioneer Trust & Sav. Bank, 15 Ill. App. 3d 832, 305 N.E.2d 273 (1973).

[10] Edward Hines Lumber v. Dell Corp., 49 Ill. App. 3d 873, 364 N.E.2d 368 (1977); Dunlop v. McAtee, 31 Ill. App. 3d 56, 333 N.E.2d 76 (1975). *But see* M. Ecker & Co. v. LaSalle Nat'l Bank, 268 Ill. App. 3d 874, 645 N.E.2d 335 (1994) (ruling that assignment-of-rents provision contained in mortgage as additional security for the mortgage did not create an "ownership" interest in the mortgagee within the meaning of the Act).

[11] Fischer v. McHenry State Bank, 74 Ill. App. 3d 509, 392 N.E.2d 995 (1979); Fettes, Love & Sieben, Inc. v. Simon, 46 Ill. App. 2d 232, 196 N.E.2d 700 (1964).

[12] Hacken v. Isenberg, 288 Ill. 589, 124 N.E. 306 (1919); Miller v. Reed, 13 Ill. App. 3d 1074,

3. The contractor must furnish lienable fixtures, services, or materials. *Furnishing of materials* refers to the ordinary type of building materials that go into and become a component or integral part of the building[13] and that are delivered to the jobsite.[14] *Furnishing of fixtures, apparatus, or machinery* refers to those fixtures, apparatus, or machinery that are so attached to the real estate as to become an integral part thereof.[15] *Furnishing of services* generally refers to the services of the architect or structural engineer, even though the statute clearly intends it to extend to the mechanic, laborer, or otherwise.[16]
4. The contractor must complete performance of the contract or have a valid excuse for nonperformance. Performance needs no explanation. However, a valid excuse for nonperformance refers to the owner's breach of contract, owner's abandonment of the project, owner's prevention of performance, or owner's failure to pay when payment is due.[17]

---

302 N.E.2d 131 (1974); Philip S. Linder Co., Inc. v. Edwards, 13 Ill. App. 3d 365, 300 N.E.2d 283 (1973); Wertz v. Mullay, 144 Ill. App. 329 (1908). *See, e.g.,* L.J. Keefe Co., Inc. v. Chicago & Northwestern Transp. Co., 287 Ill. App. 3d 119, 678 N.E.2d 41 (1997) (disallowing lien where work performed benefited a licensee rather than the property itself [i.e. work performed benefited an electric company (which was granted a license to install its equipment on the land) rather than the land]).

[13] Levyfilem, Inc. v. Cosmopolitan Bank Trust, 274 Ill. App. 3d 348, 653 N.E.2d 875 (1995); Verplank Concrete & Supply, Inc. v. Marsh, 40 Ill. App. 3d 742, 353 N.E.2d 27 (1976); Atlee Electric Co. v. Johson Constr. Co., 14 Ill. App. 3d 716, 303 N.E.2d 192 (1973); Johns-Mansville Corp. of Delaware v. LaTour D'Argent Corp., 277 Ill. App. 503 (1934).

[14] Rittenhouse & Embree Co. v. FE Brown & Co., 254 Ill. 549, 98 N.E. 971 (1912).

[15] Owings v. Estes, 256 Ill. 553, 100 N.E. 205 (1912); Norman A. Koglin Assoc. v. Valenz Oro, Inc., 277 Ill. App. 3d 142, 659 N.E.2d 971 (1996); Airtite v. DPR Ltd. Partnership, 265 Ill. App. 3d 214, 638 N.E.2d 241 (1994). *See also* Flader Plumbing & Heating Co. v. Callas, 171 Ill. App. 3d 74, 524 N.E.2d 1097 (1988) (ruling that contractor must ascertain its burden of proof as to what is lienable and with is non-lienable as to its claim; if contractor is unable to do so, court will not do it for him); Crane Erectors & Riggers, Inc. v. LaSalle Nat'l Bank, 125 Ill. App. 3d 658, 466 N.E.2d 397 (1984) (holding that intention of parties as to whether they considered equipment to be part of realty is key factor in determining if equipment is fixture and thus lienable).

[16] First Bank of Roscoe v. Rinaldi, 262 Ill. App. 3d 179, 634 N.E.2d 1204 (1994) (holding that while the services of a "property manager" are lienable, claimant's labor was not lienable because it was "developer" not "property manager"); BRL Carpenters, Ltd. v. American Nat'l Bank & Trust Co., 126 Ill. App. 3d 137, 466 N.E.2d 1166 (1984) (holding that services of construction superintendent qualified as lienable labor); D. M. Foley Co. v. North West Fed. Sav. & Loan Ass'n, 122 Ill. App. 3d 411, 461 N.E.2d 500 (1984) (holding that maintenance landscaping services were not lienable); Stepuncik v. Michalek, 67 Ill. App. 3d 440, 384 N.E.2d 526 (1978) (holding that labor of employee of general contractor performed in building's construction was lienable). *See also* Lyons Sav. v. Gash Assoc., 279 Ill. App. 3d 742, 665 N.E.2d 326 (1996) (holding that, while maintenance of property is non-lienable, cleaning mess of construction or demolition is lienable); National Wrecking Co. v. Midwest Terminal Corp., 234 Ill. App. 3d 750, 601 N.E.2d 999 (1992) (ruling that services involving removal or demolition of structures from property are lienable).

[17] Wilmette Partners v. Hamel, 230 Ill. App. 3d 248, 594 N.E.2d 1177 (1992) (excusing contractor from performance of demolition contract because developer prevented contractor's perfor-

[C] Enforcing General Contractor's Lien

The following is a summary of conditions necessary to enforce a general contractor's lien:

1. The claim for mechanics' lien must be filed in the office of the recorder of deeds for the county in which the improvement is located.[18]
2. The original contractor's lien should be verified, contain a brief statement of the contract, state the net balance due, sufficiently describe the real estate, include the date of the contract, and claim a lien for a specific amount.[19] Verification is a statement under oath.[20] The brief statement of the contract should be sufficient to inform third persons of the value, character, and extent of the lien.[21] The net balance due is the balance due after allowing all credits.[22] A sufficient description is generally the legal description.[23]
3. The original contractor's lien must be recorded within four months after completion of the work in order to prevail over the owner and third parties. However, the contractor will prevail over the original owner as long as the lien is filed within two years after completion where the property was not conveyed to a third party or where there was an intervening encumbrancer within such two years. If the lien is recorded within four months, it will be

mance by ejecting contractor from property); J. E. Milligan Steel Erectors Inc. v. Garbe Iron Works, Inc. 139 Ill. App. 3d 303, 486 N.E.2d 945 (1985) (excusing subcontractor's abandonment of work site after making good-faith effort to cooperate with general contractor who refuse to pay); Gottschalk Constr. Co. v. Carlson, 253 Ill. App. 520 (1929). *See also* Whalen v. K-Mart Corp., 166 Ill. App. 3d 339, 519 N.E.2d 991 (1988) (ruling that owner's or general contractor's failure to demand certificates of insurance from subcontractor constitutes a waiver of such contract requirement and therefore subcontractor's failure to provide such certificates of insurance will not be valid defense to subcontractor's claim). *But see* Harmon v. Dawson, 175 Ill. App. 3d 846, 530 N.E.2d 564 (1988) (ruling that contractor's failure to perform in reasonably workmanlike manner constitutes breach of contract).

[18] 770 ILCS 60/7.

[19] *Id. See, e.g.,* Candice Co., Inc. v. Ricketts, 281 Ill. App. 3d 359, 666 N.E.2d 722 (1996) (holding lien to be defective for failure to accurately describe underlying contract where lien merely stated that plaintiff was claimant and it had contract with defendants)

[20] MacDonald v. Rosengarten, 134 Ill. 126, 25 N.E. 429 (1890); Braun-Skiba v. LaSalle Nat'l Bank, 279 Ill. App. 3d 912, 665 N.E.2d 485 (1996).

[21] Schmidt v. Anderson, 253 Ill. 29, 97 N.E. 291 (1911).

[22] Hayes v. Hammond, 162 Ill. 133, 44 N.E. 422 (1896); Fedco Elec. Co. v. Stunkel, 77 Ill. App. 3d 48, 395 N.E.2d 1116 (1979).

[23] Springer v. Kroeschell, 161 Ill. 358, 43 N.E. 1084 (1896). *See* Steinberg v. Chicago Title & Trust Co., 142 Ill. App. 3d 601, 491 N.E.2d 1294 (1986) (perimeter metes and bounds descriptions of land were not proper descriptions to be used in mechanics lien clam when, at time lien was filed, land to which lien sought to attach had changed from raw tract of land identified by perimeter metes and bounds descriptions to subdivided land recorded by plat and sold to, or encumbered by, third parties).

enforced against subsequent purchasers of the property, creditors and encumbrancers, subject, however, to questions of priority.[24]

4. The complaint to foreclose a mechanics' lien must be filed in the circuit court of the county where the property is located within two years after the completion of the work for which the lien was originally recorded. Such enforcement may be accomplished by one of the following:

   a. Filing a petition to intervene and filing a counterclaim in the mechanics' lien foreclosure action of another claimant; or
   b. Filing an answer and counterclaim in the mechanics' lien foreclosure action of another claimant who has made you a party; or
   c. Filing an answer and counterclaim in a mortgage foreclosure suit that was filed by a mortgagee against the property; or
   d. Filing an original complaint to foreclose the lien in the circuit court of the county where the improvement is located.

Although a mechanics' lien suit may be instituted by filing an answer and a counterclaim in the listed conditions, it is important to note that the answer and counterclaim are distinguishable and that both are required under the Act.[25] In some instances, however, the answer will qualify as a "counterclaim." This is so where the claimant sets forth all of the elements necessary to establish its right to foreclose the lien and specifically prays for such relief in the answer. In other words, a counterclaim does not necessarily have to be filed separately under certain circumstances.[26] Further, § 11 mandates that all parties interested in the property must be joined and made a part of the proceedings. The failure to do join a party causes the judgment of foreclosure to be unbinding on the party not joined.[27]

[D] Basic Provisions of Subcontractor's Lien

Where a claimant is not a general contractor, § 21 of the Act must be analyzed.[28] A subcontractor is one who contracts with the general contractor to do a portion of the work and has no privity of contract with the owner.[29] Unlike

---

[24] *In re* Saberman, 3 B.R. 316 (Bankr. N.D. Ill. 1980); Application of Bickel, 301 Ill. 484, 134 N.E. 76 (1922); Schaeffer v. Weed, 8 Ill. (3 Gilm.) 511 (1846); Apollo Heating & Air Conditioning Corp. v. American Nat'l Bank & Trust Co., 135 Ill. App. 3d 976, 482 N.E.2d 690 (1985).

[25] Norman A. Koglin Assocs. v. Valenz Oro, Inc., 223 Ill. 2d 385, 680 N.E.2d 283 (1997).

[26] Norman A. Koglin Assoc. v. Valenz Oro, Inc., 277 Ill. App. 3d 142, 659 N.E.2d 971 (1995) (holding that a mechanics' lien claimant already named as a defendant in a foreclosure action brought by another contractor need not "file a separate counterclaim to preserve its rights, where its answer incorporated its lien and sought affirmative relief.").

[27] Interstate Elec. Supply Co. v. Contractors & Eng'r, Inc., 149 Ill. App. 3d 1080, 501 N.E.2d 866 (1986).

[28] 770 ILCS 60/21; Stepuncik v. Michalek, 67 Ill. App. 3d 440, 384 N.E.2d 526 (1978).

[29] Dunlop v. McAtee, 31 Ill. App. 3d 56, 333 N.E.2d 76 (1975).

the general contractor who only has a lien on the real estate, the subcontractor has a lien on the real estate as well as on the money due or to become due the general contractor from the owner *and* on the fixtures incorporated into the real estate during the job.[30] The prerequisites to a subcontractor's lien are similar to those of a general contractor's lien. Except that a subcontractor must wait for a period of 10 days after it has served its 90-day notice (discussed below) before it may record its claim for lien.[31]

[E] Basic Provisions of Subcontractor's Notice and Claim for Lien

Under § 5 of the Act, a subcontractor performing services or delivering materials to a single-family, owner-occupied residence must, within 60 days from the first furnishing of labor or materials, notify the occupant, personally or by certified mail, that it is supplying labor or materials.[32] This notice must be served in addition to the 90-day notice under § 24 described below.[33]

Under § 24, the subcontractor must, within 90 days after completion of the work, serve a written notice of the claim, personally or by certified or registered mail, return receipt requested and delivery limited to addressee only, on the owner, the owner's agent, the owner's architect, or the owner's superintendent,[34] and the mortgagee.[35] In the event the owner's agent or superintendent cannot be located, the 90-day notice should be recorded with the office of the Recorder of Deeds of the county in which the property is located.[36]

[F] Enforcing Subcontractor's Lien

The rights of the subcontractor may be enforced in a number of ways:

1. An action at law may be filed directly against the general contractor based upon the subcontract between the contractor and the subcontractor. This is not a lien enforcement procedure.

---

[30] Brady Brick & Supply Co. v. Lotito, 43 Ill. App. 3d 69, 356 N.E.2d 1126 (1976). *See also* Struebing Constr. Co., Inc. v. Golub-Lake Shore Place Corp., 281 Ill. App. 3d 689, 666 N.E.2d 846 (1996) (ruling that subcontractor is entitled to a lien not only to the extent of payments owed the general contractor, but also to extent of wrongful payments); *cf.* Kupferschmid, Inc. v. Rodeghero, 139 Ill. App. 3d 975, 488 N.E.2d 305 (1986) (holding that it is not necessary for item to have been actually installed or "incorporated" for there to be valid claim for lien).

[31] 770 ILCS 60/28.

[32] Hill Behan Lumber Co. v. American Nat'l Bank & Trust Co., 101 Ill. App. 3d 268, 427 N.E.2d 1325 (1981).

[33] Hill Behan Lumber Co. v. Marchese, 1 Ill. App. 3d 789, 275 N.E.2d 451 (1971).

[34] Caruso v. Kafka, 265 Ill. App. 3d 310, 638 N.E.2d 663 (1994); Lundy v. Boyle Indus., Inc., 46 Ill. App. 3d 809, 361 N.E.2d 321 (1977).

[35] Hill Behan Lumber Co. v. Irving Fed. Sav. & Loan Ass'n, 121 Ill. App. 3d 511, 459 N.E.2d 1066 (1984). *But see* Swansea Concrete Prod., Inc. v. Distler, 126 Ill. App. 3d 927, 467 N.E.2d 388 (1984) (holding that subcontractor who failed to comply with notice requirements of § 24 could nonetheless recover money damages based on doctrine of promissory estoppel).

[36] 770 ILCS 60/21.

2. An action at law may be filed against the general contractor and the owner to impose joint and several liability under §28 of the Act. This, however, is subject to otherwise perfecting the subcontractor's lien rights under the Act.
3. An action at law may be filed against the general contractor's surety if it furnished a bond or letter of credit under Illinois 30 ILCS 60/1 and 2.
4. An action in equity may be filed to enforce the mechanics' lien within two years after the date of completion of work.[37]
5. The subcontractor may file a petition to intervene in a pending action by the general contractor against the owner. However, the intervening subcontractor must also file its action to foreclose its mechanics' lien in the nature of a counterclaim in that action.[38]
6. Like a general contractor, the subcontractor may also file a petition to intervene in a pending mortgage foreclosure action.

[G] Calculating Time Periods

The time period within which to record the claim for lien must be calculated by counting four calendar months, *not 120 days,* from substantial completion of the work.[39] One must record or register no later than the last day following completion of the fourth calendar month. "Substantial" completion is the key; cosmetic work or touch-up or punch-list work will not help to revive the lien if the four-month period has expired.[40]

The Act does not require the general contractor to serve any notices because the contract between the owner and general contractor is considered sufficient notice to the owner. All that needs to be done to preserve the lien rights of the general contractor is to record the claim for lien in the county in which the property is located within the allotted four-month period.[41] The subcontractor, on the other hand, must serve the § 24 notice within 90 days, *not three months.*

Finally, the notice a subcontractor performing work on a single-family,

---

[37] 770 ILCS 60/9, 28.

[38] *Id.*

[39] *See In re* Saberman, 3 B.R. 316 (N.D. Ill. 1980); Waldbiling Woodworking, Inc. v. King Arthur's N., Ltd., 104 Ill. App. 3d 417, 432 N.E.2d 1048 (1982).

[40] Miller Bros. Indus. Sheet Metal Corp. v. LaSalle Nat'l Bank, 119 Ill. App. 2d 23, 255 N.E.2d 755 (1969). *See also* Lyons Sav., *supra* (holding that work on a single project performed in two phases, where each phase resulted from separate proposals and was assigned separate job numbers by the contractor, was actually two separate jobs and therefore calculation of four-month period for work performed during phase 1 must be made from date of completion of phase 1 and not phase 2). *But cf.* DeAnguera v. Arreguin, 92 Ill. App. 2d 381, 234 N.E.2d 808 (1968) (holding that removal of leveling blocks, installation of clamps, lock handles and rubbing parafis, and making of minor adjustments was essential to completion of materialman's contract and, therefore, four-month period calculated from completion of such work, rather than delivery date of windows 11 months prior).

[41] Component, Inc. v. Walter Kassuba Realty Corp., 64 Ill. App. 3d 140, 381 N.E.2d 42 (1978).

owner-occupied, residence must serve per §§ 5 and 21, must be served within 60 days, not two months, from the date the subcontractor first furnishes material or labor.[42]

[H] No-Lien Contracts

The addition of § 1.1 and the amendment of § 21 have rendered no-lien contracts entered into after January 1, 1992 invalid and unenforceable where such agreement was made in anticipation of and in consideration for the awarding of a contract. While the Illinois Supreme Court has upheld the constitutionality of this provision,[43] the full impact of this provision upon existing contracts and pending lawsuits is unknown at this time. However, it is believed that the customary rules of constitutional law should govern the applicability of the Act on existing cases and contracts entered into before the effective date of the Act.

[I] Waivers of Liens

Waivers of lien are not defined under the Mechanics' Lien Act. A waiver is the intentional relinquishment of a legal right.[44] Under § 21.01 of Chapter 770, Act 60, fraudulently obtaining a waiver of lien from a subcontractor and failing to pay therefor within 30 days after receiving a final payment is a Class A misdemeanor.[45]

The format and language of the waiver of lien should always be analyzed because a waiver may be a final waiver as to all moneys for labor or materials furnished or to be furnished, a waiver as to the extent of payment received (partial money waiver), or a waiver as to the labor or materials furnished to a specific date (partial date waiver).

Partial waivers of lien that are issued by the various title companies are commonly known as *date waivers*. In other words, lien rights as to labor or materials furnished to the date that the waiver bears are waived. Other commercially prepared waivers may be money waivers, which waive a specific amount regardless of the date on the waiver.[46]

For example, in *Country Service & Supply Co. v. Harris Trust & Savings Bank*,[47] the court construed the waiver language as a clear and unambiguous waiver by the plaintiff of all mechanics' lien claims for services or materials when it stated plaintiff does "hereby waive and release any and all lien or claim [for]

---

[42] Hill Behan Lumber Co. v. American Nat'l Bank & Trust Co., 101 Ill. App. 3d 268, 427 N.E.2d 1325 (1981).

[43] R.W. Dunteman Co. v. C/G Enterprises, Inc., 181 Ill. 2d 153, 692 N.E.2d 306 (1998).

[44] Fisher v. Harris Bank & Trust Co., 154 Ill. App. 3d 79, 506 N.E.2d 418 (1987).

[45] *See* State Capital Dev. Bd. *ex rel.* P. J. Gallas Elec. Contractors, Inc. v. G. A. Rafel & Co., 143 Ill. App. 3d 553, 493 N.E.2d 348 (1986); Premier Elec. Constr. Co. v. LaSalle Nat'l Bank, 132 Ill. App. 3d 485, 477 N.E.2d 1249 (1984).

[46] Country Serv. & Supply Co. v. Harris Trust, 103 Ill. App. 3d 161, 430 N.E.2d 631 (1981).

[47] 130 Ill. App. 3d 161, 430 N.E.2d 631 (1981).

labor or services, material, fixtures or apparatus heretofore *furnished to this date.*" [Emphasis in original.] The court held that an innocent party, like a lending agency, has a right to rely on the signed and written waiver so long as there was no evidence of fraud.

Country Service illustrates the importance of making sure that the date on a partial waiver coincides with the last date of work for which the request for payment is submitted. The date on the waiver should not be the date payment is received, nor the date that the waiver is tendered, nor the date of the payment request. If a date waiver is submitted, the lien rights will be waived to the date on the waiver.

A waiver of lien may not be repudiated after the contractor accepts valuable consideration, even where a check, for example, is subsequently dishonored.[48] Furthermore, a waiver of lien may not be repudiated even when the check obtained is less than the amount shown on the waiver.[49]

In connection with the above issue, it should be noted that the question of whether the industry practice of subcontractors tendering claim-for-lien waivers prior to receiving payment creates valid and binding waivers is unresolved. The cases on this issue suggest that the validity of a waiver of lien is no longer strictly interpreted on the face of the lien, but, rather, in consideration of the facts of each case.[50]

Effective July 25, 1997, § 21.02 was added to the Mechanics' Lien Act, creating a new civil remedy for lien-holders who issued lien waivers but who subsequently were not paid. This section provides that an owner, contractor, subcontractor or supplier who requires a lien waiver from a person furnishing labor, services or materials in exchange for payment or the promise of payment is deemed to hold the "unpaid sums subject to the waiver" in trust for such person who furnished labor, services or materials.[51]

Finally, under 770 ILCS 60/1, taking additional security does not destroy the right to a mechanics lien.

[J] Priority of Liens

In general, as between conflicting liens or claims that may affect the property, the claim or lien that is first in time is first in right,[52] and the order of priority

48 Decatur Lumber & Mfg. Co. v. Crail, 350 Ill. 319, 183 N.E.2d 228 (1932).

49 Capitol Plumbing v. Snyder, 104 Ill. App. 2d 431, 244 N.E.2d 856 (1969).

50 *See* Edward Hines Lumber Co. v. Dell Corp., 49 Ill. App. 3d 873, 364 N.E.2d 368, 7 Ill. Dec. 207 (1st Dist. 1977); Chicago Bridge & Iron v. Reliance Ins. Co., 46 Ill. 2d 522, 264 N.E.2d 134 (1970); Premier Elec. Constr. Co. v. LaSalle Nat'l Bank, *supra. See also* Fisher v. Harris Bank & Trust Co., 154 Ill. App. 3d 79, 506 N.E.2d 418, 106 Ill. Dec. 711 (2d Dist. 1987) (holding that receipt by owner of subcontractor's waiver of lien bars future subcontractor foreclosure action if it can be shown that owner in fact relied on waiver).

51 *See generally* Judith Landesman, *Construction Trust Fund Provisions of the Mechanics Lien Act,* Real Est. Law Newsl. (ISBA, Springfield, IL), Vol. 44, No. 1, Nov. 1998.

52 Halo Am. Nat'l Union v. Mead Cycle Co., 12 Ill. App. 2d 479, 139 N.E.2d 865 (1957). *See*

depends upon the dates of recording rather than the dates of execution.[53] Under Chapter 770, Act 60, § 16, the priority rights of the lien claimants protect the claimant to the extent of the enhanced value resulting from the labor or materials furnished by the claimant.

If a mechanics' lien is inferior to a prior lien, the mechanics' lien claimant has a right to share in the proceeds of sale of the property only after the prior lien has been paid in full.[54] If there are several lien claimants of equal priority, the proceeds of the sale available to pay them are divided proportionately.

Under § 1 of the Act, the encumbrance created by the mechanics' lien dates back to the date of the original contract between the general contractor and the owner.[55] It should also be noted that the subcontractor's lien dates back to the date of the original contractor's contract.[56]

When the contract for work is made before the date a mortgage is recorded, the lien claim is superior to the mortgage claim.[57] Section 16 of the Act establishes that when the mortgage is recorded before the date of the contract, the mortgagee has a prior lien to the extent of the value of the land and improvements before the contract,[58] and the contractor has priority to the extent of the enhancement in value of the property resulting from work performed under the contract.[59] If no enhancement is shown, the mortgagee has priority.[60]

A judgment is not a lien on the premises until it or a memorandum of same is recorded with the recorder of deeds.

[K] Remedies of Owner

If there are several liens filed against the owner's property, and the owner, for whatever reason, has insufficient funds to pay the amounts owed to the general contractor and its subcontractors, the owner may, under § 30, file suit for general

---

also Capitol Indem. Corp. v. United States, 41 F.3d 320 (7th Cir. 1994) (exemplifying how good business planning and cooperation between owner, contractor, subcontractors, and surety, will fall to juggernaut of Internal Revenue Service enforcing its claim for back taxes on unrelated projects).

[53] Glen Ellyn Sav. & Loan Ass'n v. Bank of Geneva, 65 Ill. App. 3d 916, 382 N.E.2d 1267 (1978).

[54] Cochran v. Malick, 271 Ill. App. 476 (1933).

[55] Boyer v. Keller, 258 Ill. 106, 101 N.E. 237 (1913).

[56] Pittsburgh Plate Glass Co. v. Kranz, 291 Ill. 84, 125 N.E. 730 (1919).

[57] Interstate Bldg. & Loan Ass'n v. Ayers, 177 Ill. 9, 52 N.E. 342 (1898).

[58] Croskey v. Northwestern Mfg. Co., 48 Ill. 481 (1868); Metropolitan Life Ins. Co. v. Ohlhaver, 284 Ill. App. 477, 1 N.E.2d 259 (1936); Huebner v. Kornajzer, 259 Ill. App. 540 (1931).

[59] North Presbyterian Church v. Jeven, 32 Ill. 214 (1863); Moulding-Brownell Corp. v. E.C. Delfosse Constr. Co., 304 Ill. App. 491, 26 N.E.2d 709 (1940); Abhau v. Grassie , 191 Ill. App. 577 (1915); Langford v. Mackay, 12 Ill. App. 223 (1882); Miller v. Ticknor, 7 Ill. App. 393 (1880). *See also* Lyons Sav. v. Gash Assocs., et al., 665 N.E.2d 326 (Ill. Ct. App. 1996) (holding that contract price was appropriate measure of "improvement" where cost of improvements was less than ten percent of value of realty; thus, contractor was entitled to priority over mortgagee to extent of contract price).

[60] Metropolitan Life Ins. Co. v. Ohlhaver, 284 Ill. App. 477, 1 N.E.2d 259 (1936).

settlement of mechanics' liens.[61] What is due from the owner to the contractor and from the contractor to each lienor is the primary inquiry. Under § 34, an owner may also serve written demand on a lien claimant requiring suit to enforce the lien to be commenced or an answer in a pending suit to be filed within 30 days of such demand. If such demand is not complied with in such 30 days, the lien is deemed forfeited.[62]

It must be remembered that the owner has a duty to refrain from paying the contractor until the owner receives the contractor's sworn statement.[63] This is a duty owed to the subcontractors, and a breach can result in liability to the subcontractors under § 32 of the Act. The Act does not require the owner to make a request for a § 5 sworn statement (the duty is on the contractor to supply one), but the owner will be potentially liable to a subcontractor without one.[64] Common owners' defenses are:

1. Failure of subcontractor to serve notice within 90 days of completion (or improper service or service upon wrong parties);
2. Failure of general contractor and subcontractor to record within four months after completion;
3. Failure of general contractor and subcontractor to foreclose claim within two years from date of completion;
4. Failure to allocate as to date of completion or amount on multi-parcel or multi-unit developments;
5. Failure to accurately state the nature of the contract in the claim for lien;
6. Failure to state nature of services or materials to show that they are lienable;
7. Incorrect names of parties or owners;
8. Inaccurate legal descriptions;
9. Failure to file *lis pendens* notices after filing suit and failure to name each party on the *lis pendens* notice;
10. Filing claim for work completed more than three years after commencement (§ 6) when contract fails to state completion date;
11. Failure to comply with 60-day notice requirement by subcontractor on single-family, owner-occupied residential real estate;
12. Claiming a lien for nonlienable services or materials.

[L] Lien on Public Improvements

Section 23 of the Act governs mechanics' lien on public projects. The lien is only a subcontractor's lien limited to the unpaid money due the general

---

[61] 770 ILCS 60/30. Vernon Hills III LP v. St. Paul Fire & Marine Ins., 278 Ill. App. 3d 303, 678 N.E.2d 374 (1997).

[62] 770 ILCS 60/34.

[63] 770 ILCS 60/5.

[64] Malesa v. Royal Harbour Management Corp., 187 Ill. App. 3d 655, 543 N.E.2d 591 (1989).

contractor, and the bonds or warrants issued for the project. It does not attach to the improvement. In other words, a general contractor has no mechanics' lien to enforce against the real estate owned by the public body and its rights are limited to only those under the contract (usually enforceable in the Illinois Court of Claims). The subcontractor's right against the funds due or to become due the general contractor is enforced by filing suit against the general contractor for an accounting in the circuit court of the county where the project is located.

If the subcontractor follows the required procedure, the public body is required to preserve the funds for the benefit of the lien claimant in the amount claimed. If any officer of the state or municipality violates this duty, § 23(d) of the Act provides that he will be liable to the claimant on his official bond in the amount of damages caused by his violation. This is not a suit on the lien, but is a separate nonexclusive, cumulative right the Act gives the subcontractor.[65]

Suit for an accounting must be filed within 90 days after service of the notice of lien claim on the public body.[66] Failure to file a complaint within the 90-day period will result in termination of the lien, which may not be reasserted. A certified copy of the filed complaint must be served on the clerk or secretary of the state or municipal body within the 90-day time period.[67]

[M] Conditional Payment Provisions

Section 21 (770 ILCS 60/21) was amended effective September 23, 1992, to provide as follows:

> Any provision, in a contract, agreement, or understanding, when payment from a contractor to a subcontractor or supplier is conditioned upon receipt of the payment from any other party including a private or public owner, shall not be a defense by the party responsible for payment to a claim brought under Section 21, 22, 23, or 28 of this Act against the party. For the purpose of this Section, "contractor" also includes subcontractor or supplier. The provisions of this amendatory Act of 1992 shall not be construed as declarative of existing law [but] as a new enactment.

§ 14.02 BOND LAW

[A] Bid Bonds

Illinois statutes do not require contractors to furnish bid bonds on either private or public construction projects. However, bid bonds may be required by contract. They protect the owner/obligee from damages resulting from the bidding

---

65 West Chicago Park Dist. v. Western Granite Co., 200 Ill. 527, 66 N.E. 37 (1902); Walker Process Equip. v. Advance Mechanical Sys., 282 Ill. App. 3d 452, 668 N.E.2d (1996).

66 770 ILCS 60/23.

67 *Id.*

contractor's failure to execute the awarded contract or failure to furnish the performance and payment bonds required by statute or contract.

The normal measure of damages to the owner is the difference between the principal's bid price and the next acceptable bid.[68] Upon payment by the surety to the owner, the surety is subrogated to the rights of the owner to claim damages against the defaulted bidder.[69] If the owner is unable to obtain a commitment from the next lowest bidder and is required to reopen the bidding, the additional expenses incurred, as well as delay damages, may also be recovered by the owner.[70]

[B] Performance Bonds

The Public Construction Bond Act, Illinois Compiled Statutes, Chapter 30, Act 550, §§ 1 and 2, imposes a statutory obligation on every contractor in Illinois who enters into a contract with a public entity for public construction work to furnish a performance bond to the public entity. In certain situations, the law authorizes a bank letter of credit to be furnished in lieu of a bond. The public entity looks to the performance bond as an assurance or guaranty that the contract will be completed and that all of the terms, conditions, covenants, undertakings, and agreements of the contract will be performed. In essence, the law requires that all of the obligations placed on the bond principal by the terms of the underlying contract will be undertaken and completed by the surety in the event that the principal cannot or does not complete such obligations.[71]

The bond required by the Public Construction Bond Act may be obtained from the company, agent, or broker of the contractor's choice. The bond and surety are subject to the reasonable approval or disapproval of the state or political subdivision concerned.[72]

The liability of the surety, within the limit of the penal amount of the bond, is coextensive with that of the contractor. The courts have limited the surety's liability to the penal sum of the bond even when the principal's liability was greater.[73]

When a bond incorporates by reference a construction contract, as § 1 of

---

[68] Village of Woodridge v. Bohren Int'l, Inc., 60 Ill. App. 3d 692, 377 N.E.2d 121 (1978).

[69] Anna Nat'l Bank v. Wingate, 63 Ill. App. 3d 676, 381 N.E.2d 19 (1978); Seaboard Sur. Co. v. Glenayre Estates, Inc., 114 Ill. App. 2d 341, 252 N.E.2d 712 (1969).

[70] *See* R. Heyne, *The Basics of Performance and Payment Bonds* (June 1987) (unpublished paper delivered to Ill. State Bar Ass'n real estate seminar).

[71] *Cf.* People *ex rel.* Skinner v. Hellmuth, Obata & Kassabaum, Inc., 114 Ill. 2d 252, 500 N.E.2d 34 (1986) (holding that, while cause of action against principal barred by statute of limitations, surety may not use that defense when bond issued under separate statute with different applicable limitations period).

[72] 30 ILCS 550/1.

[73] Turk v. United States Fidelity & Guar. Co., 361 Ill. 206, 197 N.E. 765 (1935); Griffin Wellpoint Corp. v. Engelhardt, Inc., 92 Ill. App. 3d 252, 414 N.E.2d 941 (1980).

the Public Construction Bond Act requires, the provisions of the contract are the provisions of the bond.[74]

The surety will not be discharged from its performance bond obligations when the essentials of the original contract have not been changed and the performance of the principal is not materially different from that first contemplated.[75]

It has been held that, in the absence of any prohibitory statute, the time within which a suit may be brought upon a bond may be limited by a contractual provision in the bond. Contractual provisions shortening the period of time in which an action may be brought upon a bond to secure public, as well as private, construction contracts have been upheld to the extent that the period fixed is reasonable.[76]

[C] Payment Bonds

In addition to a performance bond, every contractor in Illinois who enters into a contract with a public entity for public construction work is required to furnish a bond to the public entity assuring payment for material used and for all labor performed in such work, whether by subcontract or otherwise.[77] The failure of the public body to obtain a payment bond from the contractor will not necessarily result in the public body being liable to unpaid suppliers on the project.[78]

Pursuant to the express provisions of the Public Construction Bond Act, each bond is deemed to require that the principal and surety agree to pay all persons, firms, and corporations having contracts with the principal or with subcontractors all just claims due them under the provisions of the contracts for labor performed or material furnished in the performance of the contract when such claims are not satisfied out of the contract price.[79]

The Public Construction Bond Act provides an alternative remedy to that afforded by the Mechanics' Lien Act.[80] The purpose of the Public Construction Bond Act is to protect those individuals or entities who furnish labor or materials on public projects for whom no right of mechanics' lien exists against a public body.[81] When an obligee attempts to claim against the payment bond for perfor-

---

[74] Fisher v. Fidelity & Deposit Co., 125 Ill. App. 3d 632, 466 N.E.2d 332 (1984).

[75] Claude S. Corp. v. Henry's Drive-In, Inc., 51 Ill. App. 2d 289, 201 N.E.2d 127 (1964).

[76] Board of Educ. v. Hartford Accident & Indem. Co., 152 Ill. App. 3d 745, 504 N.E.2d 1000 (1987).

[77] Board of Educ. v. Hartford Accident & Indem. Co., 152 Ill. App. 3d 745, 504 N.E.2d 1000 (1987).

[78] Emulsicoat, Inc. v. City of Hoopeston, 99 Ill. App. 3d 835, 425 N.E.2d 1349 (1981).

[79] 30 ILCS 550/1.

[80] Decatur Hous. Auth. v. Christy-Foltz, Inc., 117 Ill. App. 3d 1077, 454 N.E.2d 379 (1983).

[81] Housing Auth. v. Holtzman, 120 Ill. App. 2d 226, 256 N.E.2d 873 (1970).

mance obligations, its claim is usually denied because the obligee seeking performance is not an intended third-party beneficiary.[82]

The protections of 30 ILCS 550/2, are limited to subcontractors and materialmen. The public body does not have standing under the Act to compel the surety to pay lien claims.[83] The statute gives to the subcontractor's suppliers a right to sue upon the bond given by the contractor to the public body under the Act.[84]

A claimant is entitled to recover the amount due for labor or materials furnished for incorporation into the project. The amount due might also include interest from the date of the suit's commencement.[85] Although a contractor on a public project is required to post a bond to assure payments for labor performed and material used on the job, the contractor and its surety are free to contract with the public entity for additional liability.[86] Unless an ambiguity exists and the contract is construed against the surety, it is not bound beyond the express terms of its undertakings. Unless covered expressly by the language of the bond, insurance premiums, costs of equipment repair, and equipment rental are not covered by the bond because these items are not incorporated into the project.[87]

The Illinois Public Construction Bond Act states that any action under the statute shall be brought in the circuit court of Illinois in the judicial circuit in which the contract is to be performed.[88]

Chapter 30, Act 550, § 2, requires that any person having a claim for labor and materials must file a verified notice of its claim with the officer, board, bureau, or department awarding the contract within 180 days after the date of the last item of work or the furnishing of the last item of materials. The statute also requires that the claimant furnish a copy of the verified notice to the contractor within 10 days of filing of such notice. However, notwithstanding the requirements of § 16, the notice requirements may be sufficiently satisfied where written notice was served upon the surety within the 180-day period.[89] Yet, as a practical matter, compliance with the express language of the statute will eliminate any potential defenses to the claim. Section 16 also provides that no action shall be brought under the statute until the expiration of 120 days after the date of the last item

---

[82] Board of Educ. v. Hartford Accident & Indem. Co., 152 Ill. App. 3d 745, 504 N.E.2d 1000 (1987).

[83] Northwest Water Comm'n v. Santucci, Inc., 162 Ill. App. 3d 877, 516 N.E.2d 287 (1988).

[84] Housing Auth. v. Holtzman, 120 Ill. App. 2d 226, 256 N.E.2d 873 (1970).

[85] County of Will v. Woodhill Enter., Inc., 4 Ill. App. 3d 68, 274 N.E.2d 476 (1971).

[86] Illinois State Toll Highway Comm'n v. M.J. Boyle & Co., 38 Ill. App. 2d 38, 186 N.E. 390 (1962).

[87] Board of Local Improvements v. St. Paul Fire Ins. Co., 39 Ill. App. 3d 255, 350 N.E.2d 36 (1976); Arrow Contractors Equip. Co. v. Siegel, 68 Ill. App. 2d 447, 216 N.E.2d 181 (1966).

[88] 30 ILCS 550/2.

[89] City of Dekalb v. Sornsin, 32 Ill. 2d 284, 205 N.E.2d 254 (1965).

of work or the furnishing of the last item of materials. In addition, no action of any kind can be brought later than six months after the acceptance by the state or political subdivision of the building project or work. Determining the date on which "acceptance" occurred is often the center of dispute when determining whether the statutory requirements have been satisfied.

CHAPTER 15

INDIANA

Terrence L. Brookie

§ 15.01 INTRODUCTION

On private projects, Indiana does not require prime contractors to furnish any kind of bond. However, Indiana does provide mechanics' lien rights to a designated class of claimants on private projects.

Depending on the type of public project, a prime contractor may be required to post a bid bond, performance bond, payment bond, or combination payment/performance bond.

On public projects, Indiana does not provide contractors with mechanics' lien rights, but special remedies do exist that allow certain claimants performing work upon state and local government public works projects the right to impound contract proceeds due the general contractor. Generally, this is in addition to the right to bring claim on the payment bond.

In Indiana, there is one principal statute concerning mechanics' liens, which is set forth at Indiana Code § 32-8-3-1 to -18. Depending on the type of public works projects, there are several statutes pertaining to the bonds.

§ 15.02 BOND LAW

[A] General Concepts

A contract of surety creates a tripartite relationship among the party secured, the principal obligor, and the parties secondarily liable.[1] A surety is one who undertakes to do that which the principal is bound to do in the event that the principal fails to comply with its obligations.[2]

Liability of a surety cannot exceed the amount of liability expressly assumed in the contract of surety.[3] As a general rule, a contract of suretyship is construed most strongly against a surety for hire and in favor of the person or entity to be protected. Any contractual ambiguities are resolved in favor of the beneficiary.[4]

If the contract that the surety has guaranteed is altered without the surety's consent, the surety is discharged on the theory that the surety insured only the original contract.[5]

[B] Bid Bonds

Indiana does not require contractors to furnish bid bonds on private projects.

Depending on the type of public project, contractors may be required to furnish bid bonds or other security. Title 4 projects involve the construction or improvement of certain state public works projects solicited by the Indiana

---

[1] Meyer v. Building & Realty Serv. Co., 196 N.E. 250 (Ind. 1935).

[2] Indiana Univ. v. Indiana Bonding & Sur. Co., 416 N.E.2d 1275 (Ind. Ct. App. 1981).

[3] Simmons, Inc. v. Pinkerton's, Inc., 762 F.2d 591 (7th Cir. 1985).

[4] Garco Indus. Equip. Co. v. Mallory, 485 N.E.2d 652 (Ind. Ct. App. 1985).

[5] Argonaut Ins. Co. v. Town of Cloverdale, Inc., 699 F.2d 417 (7th Cir. 1983).

Department of Administration after June 30, 1985. Title 4 projects are address at Indiana Code § 4-13.6-1-1 to -20. *Public works* means the process of altering, building, constructing, demolishing, improving, or repairing any public structure or building or other public improvement to real property owned by, or leased in the name of the state of Indiana and includes the preparation of drawings, plans, and specifications therefor.[6] Title 4 projects do not include the following:

1. Indiana Commission for Higher Education,
2. State educational institutions,
3. Military officers and military and armory boards of the state,
4. State Fair Commission,
5. Any entity established by the general assembly as a body corporate and political having the authority and power to issue bonds to be secured and repaid solely by revenues pledged for that purpose (however, such an entity shall comply with Title 4 if the law creating the entity requires it to do so), and
6. Indiana Department of Transportation.[7]

The director of the Indiana Department of Administration may require a contractor to submit a bid bond on Title 4 projects. The bid bond may equal any percentage of the estimated cost of the public works project that the director requires.[8]

The statute governing Title 5 projects is found at Indiana Code § 5-16-1-1 to -8. Title 5 projects are restricted to those state public works projects not covered by Indiana Code § 4-13.6-1-1 to -20. There is no requirement for a bid bond. The bidder on Title 5 projects need only submit as a part of its bid a statement of the bidder's financial status.

Projects involving the construction of a highway or bridge in the state highway system or the construction or repair of a building or other structure for the Department of Transportation (formerly Department of Highways) are governed by Indiana Code § 8-23-9-1 to -57. Each bidder must submit a bid guarantee (and a performance bond) payable to the state. On contracts of $100,000 or less, the commissioner of the department may waive the bond requirements.[9] The bid guaranty must be in an amount equal to five percent of the bid price.[10]

Title 36 projects involve local government projects and include all public works projects performed or contracted for by a political subdivision or their agencies regardless of whether the projects are performed on property owned or leased by the political subdivision or agency.[11] *Public work* is defined as the construction, reconstruction, alteration, or renovation of a public building, airport

[6] Ind. Code § 4-13.6-1-13 (West 1991).

[7] *Id.* § 4-13.6-2-3.

[8] *Id.* § 4-13.6-7-5.

[9] *Id.* § 8-23-9-8 (West Supp. 1998).

[10] *Id.* § 8-23-9-9.

[11] *Id.* § 36-1-12-1.

facility, or other structure that is paid for out of a public fund or out of a special assessment. It includes construction, alteration, or repair of a highway, street, alley, bridge, sewer, drain, or other improvement that is paid for out of a public fund or out of a special assessment.[12] The statute governing Title 36 projects is found at Indiana Code § 36-1-12-1 to -21. A bond and certified check is to be filed with each bid in an amount determined and specified by the political subdivision or agency in the notice of letting the contract. The amount of the bond or certified check may not be set at more than ten percent of the contract price and shall be payable to the political subdivision or agency.[13]

[C] Performance Bonds

Indiana does not require contractors to provide performance bonds on private projects.

If the estimated cost of a Title 4 public works project is at least $150,000, a performance bond is required in an amount equal to 100 percent of the total contract price. The bond shall contain the following provisions: (1) the contractor shall well and faithfully perform the contract; (2) no change, modification, omission, or addition in or to the terms of the conditions of the contract, plans, specifications, drawings, or profile or any irregularity or defect in the contract or in the procedures preliminary to the letting and awarding of the contract shall affect or operate to release or discharge the surety in any way; and (3) the provisions and conditions of Indiana Code § 4-13.6-7 shall be a part of the terms of the contract and bond.[14] A surety is not released until the expiration of one year after final settlement with the contractor.[15]

Unless the bond provides a greater period of time, all suits must be brought against a surety on a bond required under Title 4 within one year after final settlement with the contractor. All suits against the surety after that period of time are expressly barred by statute.[16]

On a Title 5 project in excess of $100,000, Indiana Code § 5-16-5.5-4 calls for a performance bond equal to the total contract price. The surety is not released for a period of one year after final settlement with the contractor.[17]

On Title 8 Department of Transportation projects, each bidder must submit a performance bond with its bid guaranty payable to the state. On contracts of $100,000 or less, the commissioner of the Department of Transportation may waive the performance bond requirement.[18] The performance bond must be in a penal sum set by the commissioner, but may not be less than the amount equal

---

[12] *Id.* § 36-1-12-2 (West 1997).

[13] *Id.* § 36-1-12-4.5.

[14] *Id.* § 4-13.6-7-7(a) (West Supp. 1998).

[15] *Id.* § 4-13.6-7-7(d).

[16] *Id.* § 4-13.6-7-11 (West 1991).

[17] *Id.*

[18] *Id.* § 8-23-9-8 (West Supp. 1998).

to the bidder's proposal or the contract price.[19] This performance bond insures not only the completion of the project by the general contractor, but also the payment of subcontractors as well.

On Title 36 projects in excess of $100,000, other than those for highways, roads, streets, alleys, bridges, and pertinent structures situated on the streets, alleys, and dedicated highway right-of-ways, the contractor must furnish the local political subdivision or agency with a performance bond equal to the contract price. The surety on the performance bond is not released until one year after the date of the political subdivision or agency's final settlement with the contractor. The performance bond must specify that (1) a modification, omission, or addition to the terms and conditions of the public works contract, plans, specifications, drawings, or profile; (2) a defect in the public works contract; or (3) a defect in the proceedings preliminary to the letting and awarding of the public works contract does not discharge the surety.[20]

[D] Payment Bonds

Indiana does not require payment bonds on private projects.

On Title 4 projects with an estimated cost of at least $150,000, the contractor must post a payment bond with the Public Works Division of the Department of Administration equal to 100 percent of the total contract price. The bond shall include language that (1) the contractor, its successors and assigns, whether by operation of law or otherwise, and all subcontractors, their successors and assigns, whether by operation of law or otherwise, shall pay all indebtedness that may accrue to any person on account of any labor or service performed or materials furnished in relation to the public work; (2) the bond shall directly inure to the benefit of the subcontractors, laborers, suppliers, and those performing service or who may have furnished or supplied labor, material, or service in relation to the public work; (3) no change, modification, omission, or addition in or to the terms or conditions of the contract, plans, specifications, drawings, or profile or any irregularity or defect in the contract or in the procedures preliminary to the letting and awarding of the contract shall affect or operate to release or discharge the surety in any way; and (4) the provisions and conditions of Indiana Code § 4-13.6-7 shall be a part of the terms of the contract and bond.[21]

If the estimated cost of the public works project is less than $150,000, the director may require that the contractor either execute a payment bond equal to any percentage (but not more than 100 percent) of the cost of the project, or the division will withhold retainage in an amount of 10 percent of the dollar value of all payments made to the contractor until the project is substantially completed.[22]

---

[19] *Id.* § 8-23-9-9.

[20] *Id.* § 36-1-12-14(e) (West 1997).

[21] *Id.* § 4-13.6-7-6(a) (West Supp. 1998).

[22] *Id.* § 4-13.6-7-6(f).

The division can make a final settlement with the contractor within 61 days following the date of substantial completion if the contractor has materially fulfilled all of its obligations under the public works contract, the division has not received any claims from subcontractors or suppliers, and the contractor has furnished satisfactory evidence showing full payment of all subcontractors and suppliers.[23]

In order to make a claim upon the payment bond on Title 4 projects, a "subcontractor" or "supplier" must file a verified claim with the division within 60 days from the last labor performed, last material furnished, or last service provided. The claim must state the amount due and owing to that claimant and shall give as much detail explaining the claim as possible.[24] The claimant must also notify the surety of the contractor by sending a copy of the claim to the surety. The claimant must also inform the division that the surety has been notified.[25] A suit against the surety cannot be filed until the expiration of 30 days after filing of the claim with the division. If the claim is not paid in full at the expiration of 30 days, the claimant may bring a lawsuit in its own name upon the bond.[26]

Unless the bond provides a greater period of time, all suits must be brought against the surety within one year after final settlement with the contractor, and all suits against the surety after this time are barred.[27] As an alternate remedy on certain Title 4 projects, a protected claimant may impound contract proceeds due the general contractor, as discussed further in **§ 15.04[A].**

A payment bond must be provided by the contractor in an amount equal to the total contract price on Title 5 projects. The bond directly inures to the benefit of subcontractors, laborers, materialmen, and those performing service who have furnished or supplied labor, material, or service for the construction of any public work or improvement.[28] The bond must provide that any change, modification, omission, or addition in or to the terms of the contract, plans, specifications, drawings, or profiles, and any irregularity or defect in the contract or in the proceedings preliminary to the letting and awarding of the contract shall not operate to release or discharge the surety.[29] Within 60 days after the completion of labor or within 60 days after the last item of material has been furnished, the payment bond claimant may file a verified statement of claim of the amount owed in duplicate with the state agency or commission that entered into the contract. The state shall deliver to the surety one of the duplicate statements. The state's failure to deliver a duplicate statement does not serve as a defense for the surety.[30]

---

[23] *Id.* § 4-13.6-7-8(a) (West 1991).
[24] *Id.* § 4-13.6-7-10(a).
[25] *Id.* § 4-13.6-7-10(b).
[26] *Id.* § 4-13.6-7-10(c).
[27] *Id.* § 4-13.6-7-11.
[28] *Id.* § 5-16-5-2(a) (West Supp. 1998).
[29] *Id.* § 5-16-5-2(b) (West Supp. 1999).
[30] *Id.* § 5-16-5-2(d).

If the claimant proceeds by filing a verified claim, it may not bring suit against the surety until 30 days after filing the claim. The suit must be brought against the surety within 60 days from the date of final completion and acceptance of the project. The failure to bring suit within 60 days bars any action against the surety.[31] The surety is not released from its obligation until one year after final settlement between the state and the contractor.[32]

An older case held a claimant may elect not to proceed by filing a verified claim as a precondition to bringing suit against the surety on a payment bond on a Title 5 project. The court held if a claimant does not file a duplicate statement with the state entity, the claimant must commence its suit against the surety within one year after the agency or board's full, final, and complete settlement upon the contract with the bonded contractor.[33] The validity of this case has been questioned.

The contractor must post a combination performance and payment bond payable to the state on Title 8 projects with an estimated cost in excess of $100,000. The commissioner of the Department of Transportation may waive the bond requirements on contracts of $100,000 or less. Instead, the department may establish requirements necessary to assure payment of subcontractors, suppliers, and employees by the contractor.[34] The combined bond, which is designated a performance bond, must be at least equal to the contract price.[35]

A Title 8 claimant may pursue the surety on the payment bond and, alternatively, may pursue the contractor by filing a claim with the department, as discussed further in **§ 15.04[C]**[36] In order to make a claim on the payment bond, the claimant must, within one year after acceptance of labor, material, or services by the commissioner of the department, furnish the surety on the bond a statement of the amount due.[37] Suit cannot be brought against the surety on the payment bond until 60 days after the furnishing of the statement, and if the indebtedness is not paid in full at the expiration of 60 days, the claimant can file an action against the surety in its own name. The claimant must bring its action within 18 months from the date of final acceptance of the project.[38]

On Title 36 projects, the contractor is required to furnish a payment bond on projects whose costs are more than $100,000.[39] The bond must be an amount equal to the contract price and must state it is for the benefit of subcontractors, laborers, material suppliers, and those performing services.[40] The payment bond

[31] *Id.* § 5-16-5-2(e).
[32] *Id.* § 5-16-5-1 (West 1989).
[33] American States Ins. Co. v. Floyd I. Staub, Inc., 370 N.E.2d 989 (1977).
[34] IND. CODE § 8-23-9-8 (West Supp. 1999).
[35] *Id.* § 8-23-9-9.
[36] *Id.* §§ 8-23-9-33, -39.
[37] *Id.* § 8-23-9-10.
[38] *Id.* § 8-23-9-11.
[39] *Id.* § 36-1-12-13.1(a) (West 1997).
[40] *Id.* § 36-1-12-13.1(b).

must further state that a modification, omission, or addition to the terms of the contract, plans, specifications, drawings, or profiles; a defect in the public works contract; or a defect in the proceedings preliminary to the letting and awarding of the contract does not discharge the surety.[41] The claimant may also pursue the alternate remedy against contract proceeds under Title 36, as set forth in **§ 15.04[D].** The claimant may file a signed duplicate statement of the amount due with the contracting political subdivision or agency within 60 days after the last labor was performed, the later material furnished, or last service provided. The contracting entity is to forward one of the signed duplicate statements to the surety on the payment bond. However, the failure of the contracting entity to forward the statement does not affect the rights of the claimant and does not operate as a defense for the surety.[42] A lawsuit may not be brought against the surety until 30 days after the filing of the signed duplicate statement with the contracting entity. If the claim is not paid in full at the end of the 30-day period, the claimant may bring an action against the surety. The lawsuit must be brought within 60 days after the date of the final completion and acceptance of the public work.[43]

In *Indiana Carpenters Pension Fund v. Seaboard Surety Co.,*[44] the Indiana Court of Appeals distinguished between the claim under I.C. § 36-1-12-12(b) required to impound contract proceeds on local government projects (see **§ 15.04[D]**) and the claim seeking recovery from a surety on a payment bond under I.C. § 36-1-12-13.1. A claim to impound contract proceeds is not a condition precedent to recovering against the payment bond, so a separate duplicate statement *must* be filed to maintain an action against a surety on the payment bond. In order to proceed against the surety on the payment bond, if payment has not been made or is not made in full, the claimant has until 60 days after the last labor or service is performed or last item of material furnished by any subcontractor, material provider or laborer to seek payment by filing the duplicate statements of amount due with the Public Works Board, and then must wait 30 days before initiating an action against the surety upon the payment bond. However, the action against a surety must be filed within 60 days of the date the public works project is finally completed and accepted.

By statute, a surety remains liable on its payment bond until one year following the Board's final settlement with the Contractor.[45] This particular statutory provision was not addressed in *Indiana Carpenters* and would appear to conflict with that decision, as *Indiana Carpenters* holds that a duplicate statement of the amount due in order to assert a bond claim *must* be filed with the appropriate public works board within 60 days after the last item or service is provided by any subcontractor, supplier, service provider, or laborer. In the event a claimant

---

[41] *Id.* § 36-1-12-13.1(c).

[42] *Id.* § 36-1-12-13.1(d).

[43] *Id.* § 36-1-12-13.1(e).

[44] 601 N.E.2d 352 (Ind. Ct. App. 1992), *transfer denied,* 615 N.E.2d 892 (Ind. 1993).

[45] IND. CODE § 36-1-12-13.1(c) (West 1997).

does not timely file its statement within 60 days but made a bond claim within 1 year, a conflict exists.

Indiana Code § 36-1-12-13.1, the statute requiring bonds on local government public projects, does not provide coverage to a lessor of equipment to a subcontractor.[46] In this case, the payment bond contained language stating that the amount of the bond would be reduced to the extent of payment or payments made in good faith. This prevented a lessor of equipment to a subcontractor on a public works project from recovering the amount owed, as the contractor had already paid the full contract price to the subcontractor, thus extinguishing the lessor's claim, even though the equipment lessor was a proper claimant under the language of the bond in question.[47]

ERISA does not preempt a state common law claim under Title 36 against a payment bond surety to recover a delinquent fringe benefit contribution under the payment bond.[48] The date of "final completion and acceptance" for the purpose of the statute requiring an action against a payment bond surety to be brought within 60 days of that date, occurs when the project is at its end; meaning all work under the original project contract must be finished before final completion and acceptance can occur.[49]

§ 15.03 LIEN LAW

[A] General Concepts

The Indiana legislature made several significant changes to Indiana's mechanics' lien laws (effective July 1, 1999) for all contracts and subcontracts for the improvement of real estate located in Indiana entered into after June 30, 1999. The major changes are as follows: the time period for filing a mechanics' lien has been increased to 90 days on most projects; lender priority over liens in certain situations; the demise, in most cases, of the no-lien contract; and the demise of any construction contract provision making the contract subject to the laws of another state or requiring that the dispute be resolved in another state.

The primary purpose of Indiana's mechanics' lien statute is to protect the contractor and those claiming under the contractor from the failure of the owner to provide compensation due under the contract. The second purpose is to protect real estate from secret liens that could cloud alienability of real estate.[50] As a right created solely by statute, and in derogation of common law, the provisions relating

[46] Dow-Parr, Inc. v. Lee Corp., 644 N.E.2d 150 (Ind. Ct. App. 1994).

[47] *Id.* at 157.

[48] Seaboard Sur. Co. v. Indiana State Dist. Council, 645 N.E.2d 1121 (Ind. Ct. App. 1995), *transfer denied.*

[49] Moduform, Inc. v. Harry H. Verkler Contractor, Inc., 681 N.E.2d 243 (Ind. Ct. App. 1997), *transfer denied,* 690 N.E.2d 1186.

[50] *In re* Hull, 19 B.R. 501 (Bankr. N.D. Ind. 1982).

to the creation, existence, or persons entitled to the lien are strictly construed.[51] Once the lien has successfully attached, the provisions relating to the enforcement of the lien should be liberally construed to effect the purpose of the statute.[52]

However, recent Indiana cases have held that the protection and enforcement provisions of Indiana's mechanics' lien statute should require only "substantial compliance" by the lien claimant.[53]

[B] Basic Provisions

The mechanics' lien statute provides that provides that contractors, subcontractors, mechanics, lessors leasing construction and other equipment and tools, journeymen, laborers, and all other persons performing labor or furnishing materials or machinery possess mechanics' lien rights.[54] A subcontractor of a subcontractor is also considered to be a "subcontractor" under the statute.[55] A materials supplier who directly supplies the owner is afforded lien rights.[56] A supplier to a general contractor also has lien rights,[57] as does a supplier to a subcontractor.[58] A supplier to a materialman is outside the protection of the statute.[59] Professional engineers, land surveyors, and architects who are registered in the state of Indiana are also afforded lien rights.[60]

A real estate developer performing supervisory services, but not physical labor, in the construction of a hotel was not a "contractor" under the Indiana mechanics' lien statute, and therefore, did not have standing to assert a mechanics' lien.[61]

The mechanics' lien remedy is an in rem remedy against real estate and results in a lien on the owner's property. It arises against the interest of the owner upon the owner's consent to the furnishing of labor or materials, notwithstanding the fact that the owner did not contract with the lien claimant.[62] For the mechanics' lien to attach to the interest of the underlying property owner, the labor performed

---

[51] Miles Homes of Ind., Inc. v. Harrah Plumbing & Heating Serv. Co., 408 N.E.2d 597 (Ind. Ct. App. 1980).

[52] Lafayette Tennis Club, Inc. v. C.W. Ellison Builders, Inc., 406 N.E.2d 1211 (Ind. Ct. App. 1980).

[53] O.J. Shoemaker, Inc. v. Board of Trustees, 479 N.E.2d 1349 (Ind. Ct. App. 1985).

[54] 1999 Ind. Acts 99-53 § 1 (codified as amended at IND. CODE § 32-8-3-1).

[55] Nash Eng'g Co. v. Marcy Realty Corp., 54 N.E.2d 263 (1944).

[56] Van Wells v. Stanray Corp., 341 N.E.2d 198 (1976).

[57] Waverly Co. v. Moran Elec. Serv., Inc., 26 N.E.2d 55 (1940).

[58] Indianapolis Power & Light Co. v. Southeastern Supply Co., 257 N.E.2d 722 (1970).

[59] City of Evansville v. Verplanck Concrete & Supply, Inc., 400 N.E.2d 812 (Ind. Ct. App. 1980).

[60] IND. CODE § 32-8-25-1 (West Supp. 1999).

[61] Premier Invs. v. Suites of Am., Inc., 644 N.E.2d 124 (Ind. 1994).

[62] Mann v. Schnarr, 95 N.E.2d 138 (1950).

and materials furnished must be pursuant to the owner's authority and active assent. Mere passive or inactive consent is insufficient to bind the owner.[63]

A lien is permitted on the improvements and the entire land upon which the improvements are situated.[64]

A mechanics' lien cannot be enforced against public property held for public use.[65] The public use and necessity exception did not apply to prevent a contractor that entered into a contract with a public utility to construct a natural gas pipeline from acquiring a mechanics' lien against the utility's facilities.[66]

In order to claim a lien for materials, a claimant must show (1) the materials were furnished for the purpose of being used in constructing a particular improvement; (2) the materials were sold to the property owner or agent for that purpose; (3) the improvements were authorized by or consented to by the property owner; and (4) the materials were actually used in the construction.[67] However, when it is established that the materials were actually delivered to the jobsite, a presumption arises that they were used in the improvement.[68] Indiana permits a lien for labor involved in "erecting, altering, repairing or removing" improvements.[69]

An unpaid supplier of fuel products, whose products were used to power labor-saving material utilized by the contractor at the job site, is not within the class of persons protected by the mechanics' lien statute.[70] Property owners were not denied due process by the mechanics' lien statute, which allows attachment of a lien without prior hearing or bond.[71] Indiana's mechanics' lien statute is not preempted by the Natural Gas Act.[72]

[C] Notice Requirements

In order to claim the lien, the claimant must file a notice of intention to hold a mechanics' lien. The notice of intention must be a sworn statement in writing and must set forth the following elements:

1. The amount claimed,
2. The name and address of the claimant,
3. The name of the owner,

---

[63] Stern & Son, Inc. v. Gary Joint Venture, 530 N.E.2d 306 (Ind. Ct. App. 1988).

[64] IND. CODE. § 32-8-3-2 (West 1979).

[65] American States Ins. Co. v. Floyd I. Staub, Inc., 370 N.E.2d 989 (1977).

[66] McCartin McAuliffe Mechanical v. Midwest, 685 N.E.2d 165, 171 (Ind. Ct. App. 1997), *reh'g denied.*

[67] Stanray Corp. v. Horizon Constr., Inc., 342 N.E.2d 645 (1976).

[68] Van Wells v. Stanray Corp., 341 N.E.2d 198 (1976).

[69] IND. CODE § 32-8-3-1 (West Supp. 1999).

[70] P&P Oil Service Co. v. Bethlehem Steel, 643 N.E.2d 9 (Ind. Ct. App. 1994).

[71] Haimbaugh Landscaping, Inc. v. Jegen, 653 N.E.2d 95 (Ind. Ct. App. 1995), *reh'g denied, transfer denied.*

[72] McCartin McAuliffe Mechanical v. Midwest, 685 N.E.2d 165, 170 (Ind. Ct. App. 1997), *reh'g denied.*

4. The latest address of the owner as shown on the property tax records of the county where the property is located, and
5. The legal description and street number, if any, of the property.[73]

Effective July 1, 1999, the time period for filing a notice of intention to hold a mechanics' lien is extended from 60 days to 90 days after last performing labor or furnishing material machinery, except for residential property which remains 60 days.[74]

The time for filing begins from the date of the last act performed by the claimant.[75] The period for filing the lien may not be extended by performing some act incidental to the original work.[76] A subcontractor commences work at a job site when it actually begins performing the task for which it was hired, rather than when it moves its equipment to the location. It finishes its work, so as to commence the 60-day period for filing its mechanics' lien notice, when it finishes the task for which it was hired, not when it removes its equipment used in performing its tasks from the site.[77]

The sworn statement may be verified and filed on behalf of the lien claimant by an attorney registered to practice in the state of Indiana and in good standing.[78] The notice of the claimant's intention to hold the lien upon the property must be filed in duplicate, as the county recorded is required by statute to mail one of the duplicates to the owner named in the notice within three business days after recording the notice.[79] The failure of the recorder to mail a duplicate does not affect the validity of the lien.[80] The notice must be filed with the county recorder in the county where the property sought to be liened is located.[81]

A pre-lien notice must be given in order to establish the right to require the mechanics' lien for single- and double-family dwellings that are owner occupied. If the work performed is for alteration or repair work of owner-occupied single- or double-family dwellings, within 30 days from the date of the first delivery or labor performed the claimant must provide written notice to the owner or its legal representative that (1) the claimant has performed labor or supplied materials or delivered machinery; and (2) the claimant is asserting lien rights against the property. This need not be recorded, but failure to serve this notice on the owner will defeat the lien even though the claimant subsequently files a timely notice of intention to hold the lien. If the work is for original construction rather than

[73] IND. CODE § 32-8-3-3(c) (West Supp. 1999).

[74] *Id.* § 32-8-3-3.

[75] Gooch v. Hiatt, 337 N.E.2d 585 (1975).

[76] Display Fixtures Co., Div. of Stein Indus., Inc. v. R. L. Hatcher, Inc., 438 N.E.2d 26 (Ind. Ct. App. 1982).

[77] Riddle v. Newton Crane Serv., Inc., 661 N.E.2d 6 (Ind. Ct. App. 1996).

[78] IND. CODE § 32-8-3-3(d) (West Supp. 1999).

[79] *Id.* § 32-8-3-3(a).

[80] Brownsburg Lumber Co. v. Mann, 537 N.E.2d 1386 (Ind. Ct. App. 1989).

[81] IND. CODE § 32-8-3-3) (West Supp. 1999).

alteration or repair, the notice must be given within 60 days from the date of the first delivery of materials or labor performed and this pre-lien notice must be recorded.[82]

In addition, as a condition precedent to acquiring a mechanics' lien for the original construction of a single- or double-family dwelling, anyone who provides on credit any material, labor, or machinery for such construction must serve the owner of the real estate on which the construction is taking place with written notice of the delivery or labor and the existence of the lien right, within 60 days from the date of the first delivery or labor performed, *and* must also file a copy of such written notice in the county recorder's office for the county in which the property is located, also within the 60-day period.[83] Persons such as a general contractor who deal directly with the owner are not required to file the pre-lien notice.

The mechanics' lien will be barred unless suit is filed within one year after the notice of intention to hold a lien is filed.[84] An owner can send written notice to the claimant to commence suit within 30 days after receiving the notice of intention to hold a lien.[85] If the claimant fails to file suit within 30 days from receipt of the notice, the mechanics' lien will be lost.

When the general contractor's contract with the owner gives it the duty to clear liens from the property and the financial responsibility for any liens that are not cleared, the general contractor has standing to issue written notice to the claimant to commence suit within 30 days.[86]

[D] Amount of Lien

When no contract exists between the lien claimant and the property owner, damages are based upon the reasonable value of the labor and materials provided.[87] Reasonable value is not necessarily identical to cost.[88] In the case of a mechanics' lien asserted by a subcontractor of a general contractor, when a contract exists between the contractor and subcontractor but not between the subcontractor and the property owner, although the amount of the contract may be prima facie evidence of reasonable value, the lien is for the reasonable value of the work and materials provided and not for the price as fixed by contract.[89]

When a contract with a fixed price exists between the contractor and the property owner, the lien amount is measured and limited by the agreed contract

---

[82] *Id.* § 32-8-3-1.

[83] *Id.*

[84] *Id.* § 32-8-3-6 (West 1979).

[85] *Id.* § 32-8-3-10.

[86] Controlled Demolition, Inc. v. F.A. Wilhelm Constr., Inc., 84 F.3d 263 (7th Cir. 1996).

[87] Korellis Roofing, Inc. v. Stolman, 645 N.E.2d 29 (Ind. Ct. App. 1995).

[88] Wilson v. Jenga Corp., 490 N.E.2d 375, 376 (Ind. Ct. App. 1986).

[89] *Korellis,* 645 N.E.2d at 31.

price, subject to claims of defect in the workmanship or other damage to the property asserted by the owner.[90]

[E] No-Lien Contract and Lien Waivers

For contracts and subcontractors entered into after June 30, 1999, a no-lien agreement is void in Indiana except with respect to the following projects:

1. A Class 2 structure (as defined in I.C. § 22-12-1-5) (residential or improvement to residential property); and
2. Property owned, operated, managed or controlled by a public utility, municipally owned utility, joint agency, rural electric membership corporation, or not-for-profit utility; and intended to be used and useful for the production, transmission, delivery, or furnishing of heat, light, water or power to the public.[91]

On those projects still subject to a no-lien agreement, five requirements must be met to bind those potential lien claimants who are not parties to the construction contract:

1. The no-lien contract between an owner and general contractor containing the no-lien provision or stipulation must be in writing,
2. It must contain specific reference, by legal description, of the real estate to be improved,
3. It must be acknowledged as provided in the case of deeds,
4. The contract must be filed and recorded in the recorder's office in the county where the construction project is located, and
5. The contract must be recorded within five days after the date of execution of the contract.[92]

A no-lien contract is not valid toward claimants who provide labor or material before the recording of said contract.[93]

Effective July 1, 1999, except for the residential construction or those public utility projects stated above, any provision in the contract for the improvement of real estate which requires one who is a valid lien claimant to waive any right to lien the real estate or make a claim against a payment bond, before the claimant is paid for labor and materials furnished, is void.[94] Also effective July 1, 1999, but not applying to residential construction or those public utility projects stated above, any provision in a contract where one or more persons agree not to file a notice of intention to hold a lien is void.[95]

---

[90] *Id.* at 32-33.

[91] Ind. Code § 32-8-3-1 (West Supp. 1999).

[92] *Id.* § 32-8-3-1(c).

[93] Imperial House of Ind., Inc. v. Eagle Sav. Ass'n, 376 N.E.2d 537 (1978).

[94] Ind. Code § 32-8-3-16(b) (West Supp. 1999).

[95] *Id.* § 32-8-3-16(c).

For contracts and subcontracts entered into after June 30, 1999 (except for residential construction or those public utility projects stated above), a "pay when paid" clause does not operate as a defense to a mechanics' lien. The obligor's receipt of payment from a third party is not a condition precedent to the provider's right to record or foreclose a lien. Nor does the obligor's receipt of payment limit or provide a defense to the provider's right to record or foreclose a lien.[96]

[F] Lien Priority

A properly recorded mechanics' lien relates back in priority to the time when the mechanic began to perform labor or furnish materials. The lien takes priority over any other types of liens created thereafter. However, effective July 1, 1999, the mortgage of a lender has priority over all mechanics' liens recorded after the date the mortgage was recorded to the extent of the funds actually owed to the lender for the specific project to which the lien rights relate, except for residential construction and those public utility projects stated above.[97] All properly recorded mechanics' liens have equal priority regardless of the date of filing or performance.[98]

[G] Remedies of the Owner

In addition to the limited application of the no-lien contract, the owner or any person having an interest in the property, including mortgagees and other lienholders, may obtain a bond to remove a claim and cover prospective costs and attorneys' fees. Upon the filing of the bond, the court is to enter an order releasing the property from the lien, and thereafter the property is discharged from said lien.[99]

[H] Attorneys' Fees

Should the lienholder recover a judgment in any sum on the mechanics' lien claim, the claimant is also entitled to recover reasonable attorneys' fees.[100] However, when the net recovery in a mechanics' lien action favors the owner—for example, when the lien claimant's judgment is exceeded by the owner's counterclaim against the claimant—the contractor is not entitled to an award of attorneys' fees.[101]

---

[96] *Id.* § 32-8-3-18.

[97] *Id.* § 32-8-3-5(c).

[98] *Id.* § 32-8-3-5.

[99] *Id.* § 32-8-3-11 (West 1979).

[100] *Id.* § 32-8-3-14 (West Supp. 1999).

[101] Complete Elec. Co. v. Liberty Nat'l Bank, 530 N.E.2d 1216 (Ind. Ct. App. 1988); Clark's Pork Farms v. Sand Livestock Sys., Inc., 563 N.E.2d 1292 (Ind. Ct. App. 1990).

[I] Forum Selection and Choice of Laws

For contracts and subcontracts entered into after June 30, 1999, any contractual provision which makes the contract for the improvement of real estate located in Indiana subject to the laws of another state is void.[102] Also void is any provision that requires any litigation, arbitration or other dispute resolution process on the contract to occur in another state.[103]

[J] Personal Liability Notice to Owner

A claimant is entitled to put the owner on notice in writing that the claimant has a claim against funds that are retained by the owner on a private construction project.[104] This does not place a mechanics' lien on the property, but creates the right to bring an action against the owner for the amount claimed.[105] This statute allows a person furnishing services, labor or materials to a contractor to acquire a lien on the accounts receivable of the contractor due from the owner.[106] This remedy, sometimes referred to as the *stop notice remedy* or personal liability notice to owner, affords protection to those who are entitled to assert claims under the mechanics' lien statute.[107]

In order to perfect this claim, the notice must:

1. Be in writing,
2. Be delivered to the owner's agent in the owner's absence,
3. State the amount of the claim,
4. Describe services rendered or materials supplied, and
5. Contain a statement that the claimant holds the owner responsible for the amount of the claim.[108]

Unlike the mechanics' lien remedy, there is no 60-day or 90-day limitation period for issuing the notice, and there is no time period to bring suit other than the underlying cause of action's statute of limitations. The only time limit faced by the claimant is that the notice must be provided before the owner has already disbursed all of the contract funds to the general contractor.

Once the notice is received by the owner, the owner is then liable to the extent of funds then due the general contractor which the owner has on hand. In the event the owner has paid all the money due the general contractor, the owner

---

[102] IND. CODE § 32-8-3-17 (West Supp. 1999).

[103] *Id.* § 32-8-3-17.

[104] *Id.* § 32-8-3-9 (West 1979).

[105] *In re* Hull, 19 B.R. 501 (Bankr. N.D. Ind. 1982).

[106] Zeigler Bldg. Materials, Inc. v. Parkinson, 398 N.E.2d 1330 (Ind. Ct. App. 1980).

[107] Lee & Mayfields, Inc. v. Lykowski House Moving Eng'rs, Inc., 489 N.E.2d 603 (Ind. Ct. App. 1986).

[108] IND. CODE § 32-8-3-9 (West 1979).

cannot be forced to pay a second time.[109] The owner has the right to set off claims arising out of the general contractor's breach from the retained funds, after receipt of a stop notice.[110] Multiple claimants share on a pro rata basis if insufficient funds exist.[111] No-lien contracts do not defeat the remedy.[112]

Recovery based on this remedy does not constitute a mechanics' lien; therefore, attorneys' fees are not recoverable by a successful claimant.[113] The owner is liable to the subcontractor or supplier asserting this remedy only to the extent of funds owed to the general contractor.[114]

This remedy does not apply to retainages held by a government agency on public construction contracts.[115]

§ 15.04 CLAIMS ON STATE AND LOCAL PUBLIC PROJECTS

As a general rule, a claimant may not file a lien against public property, whether the property is owned by the local, state or federal government. Special statutory remedies do exist in Indiana that offer protection to certain claimants performing work upon state and local government public works projects. These remedies provide the right to impound contract proceeds in addition to the payment bond remedies discussed. There is no statutory right to attorneys' fees.

The unpaid subcontractor, laborer, material supplier, or person performing services can elect to proceed against the surety or impound contract proceeds. The two remedies are cumulative and not exclusive remedies.[116]

[A] Title 4 State Projects

Claimants can impound or "lien" contract proceeds due a general contractor which are retained by the state on a Title 4 project by filing a verified statement of claim with the applicable agency. This remedy under Title 4 applies to public works contracts in excess of $150,000.[117] The public works contract must contain provisions for the retainage of portions of payments by the Public Works Division to the contractor, by the subcontractors, and for the payment of subcontractors and suppliers by the contractor.[118]

---

[109] Indianapolis Power & Light Co. v. Todd, 485 N.E.2d 632 (Ind. Ct. App. 1985).

[110] Blade Corp. v. American Drywall, Inc., 400 N.E.2d 1183 (Ind. Ct. App. 1980).

[111] IND. CODE § 32-8-3-9 (West 1979).

[112] *In re* Hull, 19 B.R. 501 (Bankr. N.D.Ind. 1982).

[113] McCorry v. G. Cowser Constr., Inc., 644 N.E.2d 550 (Ind. 1994).

[114] Coplay Cement Co. v. Willis & Paul Group, 983 F.2d 1435 (7th Cir. 1993).

[115] Secrist v. Board of Comm'rs, 100 Ind. 59 (1885).

[116] Indiana Carpenters Pension Fund v. Seaboard Sur. Co., 601 N.E.2d 352 (Ind. Ct. App. 1992), *transfer denied,* 615 N.E.2d 892 (Ind. 1993).

[117] IND. CODE § 4-13.6-7-2(a) (West Supp. 1999).

[118] *Id.*

Only subcontractors and suppliers are provided this remedy.[119] *Subcontractor* means any person entering into a contract with a contractor to furnish labor and materials used in the actual construction of the public works project. Labor used in delivery and unloading of materials at a project site is not considered to be labor used in actual construction.[120] *Supplier* means any person supplying materials, but not on-site labor to a contractor or a subcontractor.[121]

The requirements for filing a verified statement of claim with the Public Works Division have been previously set forth in **§ 15.02[D].**

If a subcontractor or supplier files a claim with the division and the claim is undisputed, the division is to (1) pay the claimant from the amounts retained from the contractor; (2) take a receipt for each payment; and (3) deduct the total amount paid to subcontractors and suppliers from the balance due to the contractor.[122] If there is not a sufficient amount held in the contractor's retainage to pay all the subcontractors and suppliers making undisputed claims, the claimants share on a pro rata basis. If there is a dispute among the contractor, subcontractors and suppliers to the funds, it is the responsibility of the division to retain sufficient funds until the dispute is settled and the correct amount is determined.[123] After the division makes the final settlement with the contractor, any verified statements against retainage are barred.[124]

[B] Title 5 State Projects

In addition to the payment bond remedy, a claimant may file a verified claim for all amounts owing on Title 5 projects with the appropriate public agency. If a claimant timely files its verified statement of claim, it becomes the duty of the public agency administering the project to withhold from payment to the general contractor sufficient funds to satisfy the claim.[125]

Coverage is provided to subcontractors, materialmen, laborers, and those furnishing services to the project.[126] The claim must (1) be filed with the board, commission, trustee, officer, clerk, or agent of the state or commission that entered into the contract; (2) be a verified statement filed in duplicate; (3) be filed within 60 days from the date of last work or service performed or the last item of materials furnished to the project; and (4) contain a statement of the amount due the subcontractor.[127] After the claim is filed, if there is no dispute, the public

[119] *Id.* § 4-13.6-7-10(a) (West 1991).
[120] *Id.* § 4-13.6-1-18.
[121] *Id.* § 4-13.6-1-20.
[122] *Id.* § 4-13.6-7-9(a).
[123] *Id.* § 4-13.6-7-9(c).
[124] *Id.* § 4-13.6-7-8.
[125] *Id.* § 5-16-5-1 (West 1989).
[126] *Id.*
[127] *Id.* § 5-16-5-2(d) (West Supp. 1999).

agency is to pay the claim out of the funds due the contractor and take receipt, and then deduct that sum from the contract price. If there is a dispute over any of the parties' claims to the funds so withheld, sufficient funds are to be retained by the state agency until the dispute is settled and the correct amount is determined. In the event there are insufficient funds to satisfy all claimants, those claimants having complied with the above receive a prorated share.[128]

[C] Title 8 Indiana Department of Transportation Projects

The remedy of impounding contract proceeds is provided to any person, firm or corporation to whom any money is owed for having performed labor or furnished material or other service in the construction of a highway or bridge in the state highway system or in the construction or repair of a building or other structure for the Department of Transportation.[129] In order to make a claim to contract proceeds on a Department of Transportation project under Title 8, a notice of claim is necessary. The notice of claim must:

1. Be a verified itemized statement,
2. Be filed with the department,
3. Include the amount due the person, firm or corporation,
4. State whether the labor or materials were performed or furnished to a contractor or subcontractor,
5. Give the name of the contractor or subcontractor,
6. Provide the dates the labor or material was performed or furnished,
7. Provide the rate or cost and the character of the labor, material or service, and
8. Include the post office address of the claimant.[130]

The claim must be filed in triplicate, and the department is to send a copy by certified mail to the contractor and to the surety of the contractor. Failure to mail these copies does not affect the validity of the claim.[131] This notice must be filed within 60 days of the performance of the last labor or the furnishing of the last of the materials or other service and within 30 days after final acceptance of the improvement by the department.[132]

After receipt of the claim, the department is to retain the amount of the claim out of the amount due the contractor.[133] The contractor is to either allow or reject the claim within 20 days and must notify the department in writing.[134] If the claim is rejected in whole or in part, the department is to immediately notify

[128] *Id.* § 5-16-5-1 (West 1989).

[129] *Id.* § 8-23-9-26 (West Supp. 1999).

[130] *Id.*

[131] *Id.* § 8-23-9-27.

[132] *Id.* § 8-23-9-26.

[133] *Id.* § 8-23-9-28.

[134] *Id.* § 8-23-9-29.

the claimant of this action by certified mail. Within 90 days after receiving notice of rejection, the claimant *must* commence a suit against the contractor or the surety on the bond (in the event claim is made upon the bond) to recover the amount of the claim.[135]

[D] Title 36 Local Government Projects

An unpaid subcontractor or material supplier, laborer, or those furnishing services can file a statement of claim with the political subdivision or agency to impound contract proceeds.[136] Also included are materialmen who supply contractors or subcontractors.[137] The claimant must file with the contracting entity a signed duplicate statement of the amount due. This remedy applies to contracts for which the cost is estimated to be more than $100,000.[138] The claim form also must be signed by an individual from the contracting entity who is directly responsible for the project and who can verify (1) the quantity of a purchased item, or (2) the weight or volume of the material applied, in the case of a road, street or bridge project.[139]

The claim must be filed within 60 days after the date of last labor performed, last materials furnished, or last service rendered by the claimant.[140] Any court action must be brought within 60 days after the date of the final completion and acceptance of the public work.[141]

A claim to impound contract proceeds under Title 36 must be filed with the board within 60 days from the last date on which that claimant last supplied materials or performed services.[142] Though not required, it is recommended the signed duplicate statement be verified.

---

[135] *Id.* § 8-23-9-30.

[136] *Id.* § 36-1-12-12 (West 1997).

[137] *Id.* § 36-1-12-1.2(3) (West Supp. 1999).

[138] *Id.* § 36-1-12-13.1 (West 1997).

[139] *Id.* § 36-1-12-12(e).

[140] *Id.* § 36-1-12-13.1(d).

[141] *Id.* § 36-1-12-13.1(e).

[142] Indiana Carpenters Pension Fund v. Seaboard Sur. Co., 601 N.E.2d 352 (Ind. Ct. App. 1992), *transfer denied,* 615 N.E.2d 892 (Ind. 1993).

CHAPTER 16

IOWA

Jeffrey D. Stone[1]

[1] This chapter is adapted from the Iowa chapter in the First Edition, written by James C. Fifield, Esq. and Thomas A. Finley, Esq.

§ 16.01 INTRODUCTION

On private projects, Iowa does not require prime contractors or subcontractors to furnish any kind of bond. However, on private projects, but not on public projects, Iowa law provides contractors and their subcontractors with certain mechanics' lien rights.

On public projects of $25,000 or more (and some smaller county projects), Iowa requires prime contractors to either furnish a bond securing performance and payment or deposit other appropriate security in an amount ranging from 75 to 100 percent of the contract price. The payment benefits of the bond extend to subcontractors and those contracting with subcontractors, but not to a person furnishing only materials to a subcontractor furnishing only materials.[2]

The principal Iowa statute governing public improvement project bonds is Chapter 573, Code of Iowa (bond law). The bond law does not apply "[i]f the public corporation has entered into a contract with the federal government or accepted a federal grant which is governed by federal law or rules that are contrary to the provisions of [the bond law]."[3] The principal Iowa mechanics' lien statute is Chapter 572, Code of Iowa (lien law).

§ 16.02 BOND LAW

[A] General Concepts

As in other jurisdictions, Iowa treats the construction surety bond relationship as a tripartite relationship and treats bonds as tripartite contracts. Each construction surety bond has an obligee, which is typically an owner or a general contractor, and joint and several obligors, which are typically the general contractor or subcontractor and its surety.

Iowa surety contracts ordinarily must be in writing and signed by the surety against whom one is making a bond claim.[4] Regarding governing law, Iowa generally follows the modern approach and looks to the law of the place with the most significant relationship to the parties and the transaction on each issue, absent an express choice of law by the parties.[5]

When the contract of a paid surety on a private construction project is involved, Iowa applies the same rules of construction and interpretation as govern

---

[2] Iowa Code §§ 573.6–7 (1995).

[3] Iowa Code § 573.14 (1995).

[4] Iowa's Statute of Frauds, Iowa Code § 622.32 (1995), generally prohibits introduction of any evidence of an unwritten, unsigned contract "wherein one person promises to answer for the debt, default, or miscarriage of another," unless the oral contract is not denied or when the other party's foreseeable detrimental reliance on the unwritten contract renders it unjust not to enforce the contract. *See* Meylor v. Brown, 281 N.W.2d 632, 634–35 (Iowa 1979).

[5] Cole v. State Auto & Cas. Underwriters, 296 N.W.2d 779, 781–82 (Iowa 1980).

insurance contracts.[6] Providing the language in a private construction surety bond is clear, unambiguous, and susceptible of but one meaning, that language controls, and liability may not be imposed beyond the express contractual terms.[7] As elsewhere, Iowa courts construe the contract of a compensated surety strongly against the surety and in favor of the obligations that an obligee has reasonable grounds to expect will be imposed upon the surety.[8] Because a surety's liability often is predicated upon the underlying contract of its contractor/principal, the surety's liability cannot be greater than that of its contractor/principal.[9] Similarly, a surety may assert against the obligee any defense that would be available to the contractor/principal.[10]

The terms of bonds furnished to comply with statutory requirements, such as those described in the following sections, are deemed identical with the statutory terms.[11] If the bond omits terms required by statute, those terms will be read into the bond, notwithstanding any express provisions in the bond to the contrary.[12] Any provisions in a statutory bond beyond those required by the statute will be deemed "mere surplusage" and of no effect.[13]

[B] Bid Bonds

Iowa does not require prime contractors to furnish bid bonds on either public or private projects. Iowa law generally does require bidders on public projects to furnish bid security in cash or cash equivalent form, usually in an amount between 5 and 10 percent of the estimated total contract cost of the public improvement.[14] A optional bid bond is expressly permitted in lieu of other bid security in some instances.[15]

In Iowa, a bid bond typically guarantees the owner that the low, responsive, responsible bidder will enter into the contract upon which it bids. Typically, the bid bond will provide a penal sum in a set amount in the event the contractor refuses to actually enter into the contract after an award is made or refuses to deliver a statutorily required bond after an award is made.

---

[6] United States v. Tyler, 220 F. Supp. 386 (N.D. Iowa 1963).

[7] New Amsterdam Cas. Co. v. Central Nat'l Fire Ins. Co., 4 F.2d 203 (8th Cir. 1925).

[8] Bankers Life Co. v. Aetna Cas. & Sur. Co., 366 N.W.2d 166 (Iowa 1985).

[9] Benson v. Alleman, 220 Iowa 731, 263 N.W. 305 (1935).

[10] State v. Bi-States Constr. Co., 269 N.W.2d 455 (Iowa 1978).

[11] Schisel v. Marvill, 198 Iowa 725, 728–29, 197 N.W. 662, 662-63 (1924).

[12] State Sur. Co. v. Lensing, 249 N.W.2d 608, 611 (Iowa 1977).

[13] Philip Carey Co. v. Maryland Cas. Co., 201 Iowa 1063, 1070–71, 206 N.W. 808, 810-11 (1926).

[14] *See, e.g.*, Iowa Code §§ 18.6(9), 73A.18, 331.341(1), and 384.97(5)-.98 (1995) (5 to 10 percent on state, city, county, township, state fair board, and regents projects).

[15] *Id.* §§ 73A.20, 384.97(5).

[C] Performance Bonds

Although Iowa does not require contractors to provide performance bonds on private projects, the bond law requires that prime contractors on public projects of at least $25,000 ($5,000 in the case of a county public improvement project not to be paid for from the secondary road fund)[16] must furnish "a bond, with surety, conditioned for the faithful performance of the contract, and for the fulfillment of other requirements as provided by law (Contractor's Bond)."[17] On public projects, other than those funded in whole or in part by the use of city or county funds, the contractor's bond shall be in an amount not less than 75 percent of the contract price; except that, in contracts in which no part of the contract price is to be paid until after the public improvement's completion, the bond amount may be fixed at not less than 25 percent of the contract price.[18] Cash or specified cash equivalents may be deposited in lieu of a contractor's bond.[19] With respect to city- or county-funded projects, a corporate surety bond in an amount equal to 100 percent of the contract price is required.[20]

Certain "targeted small businesses" are excepted from the otherwise non-waivable requirement of a bond or equivalent security in the case of projects or individual transactions of no more than $50,000.[21] The bond law's remedies remain available to persons contracting with the targeted small business or with subcontractors of the targeted small business.[22]

Notwithstanding any provision in the bond to the contrary, Iowa's bond law deems every contractor's bond surety to have consented without notice to any extension of time to the contractor in which to perform the contract.[23] Similarly, the bond law invalidates any bond provision purporting to limit to less than one year from the work's acceptance the right to sue on the contractor's bond for defects of which the obligee did not know or which were not discovered at the time the work was accepted.[24] As explained in **§ 16.02[D],** Iowa's bond law also implies payment bond provisions into every contractor's bond.

[D] Payment Bonds

On private projects, Iowa law does not require contractors to furnish payment bonds.

On public improvement projects, the bond law automatically implies specific

[16] *Id.* § 331.341(4).
[17] *Id.* § 573.2.
[18] *Id.* § 573.5.
[19] *Id.* § 573.4.
[20] *Id.* §§ 331.341(1), 384.97(5).
[21] *Id.* § 12.44.
[22] *Id.* § 573.2.
[23] *Id.* § 573.6(2)(a).
[24] *Id.* § 573.6(2)(c).

payment bond terms into any contractor's bond, "whether said provisions be inserted in such bond or not."[25] Those implied terms oblige the principal and sureties to pay all subcontractors and persons having contracts directly with subcontractors "all just claims due them for labor performed or materials furnished in the performance of the [public improvement] contract . . . when the same are not satisfied out of the portion of the contract price which the public corporation is required to retain until completion of the public improvement," but only as to those claims that have been duly established against that retainage.[26] The bond law also deems every contractor's bond surety to have consented without notice to any change in the contract, plans, or specifications, "when such change does not involve an increase of more than 20 percent of the total contract price, and shall then be released only as to such excess increase."[27] Contractor's bond payment benefits do not extend to a person furnishing only materials to a subcontractor furnishing only materials.[28]

[1] Retainage Fund

The bond law generally mandates that progress payments be made monthly within 14 days of the public corporation's receipt of an approved request for payment.[29] With the exception of regents' projects,[30] the bond law also requires that not more than five percent of the amount determined due by the project architect or engineer be retained from each such payment by the public corporation.[31] The retainage constitutes a "fund for the payment of claims for materials furnished and labor performed on the improvement."[32] The retainage funds are held by the public corporation for 30 days after the improvement's completion and final acceptance.[33] If no claims are on file at the end of that 30-day period and the contractor has submitted all certificates, materials, and documents required by the contract, then the retainage sum due under the contract is to be paid over to the contractor and, if not paid over within 10 days (or up to 20 days if specified in the contract documents) following the end of that 30-day period, interest shall accrue in favor of the contractor from the end of the 30-day period.[34]

If claims are on file at the end of the 30-day period, the public corporation

[25] *Id.* § 573.6.

[26] *Id.* § 573.6(1).

[27] *Id.* § 573.6(2)(b).

[28] *Id.* § 573.7.

[29] *Id.* § 573.12(2)(a)(1).

[30] *Id.* § 573.12(1) (allowing regents' institutions to make progress payments without retention, until 95 percent of the contract amount has been paid, with the remaining 5 percent treated as a retainage fund).

[31] *Id.* § 573.12(1).

[32] *Id.* § 573.13.

[33] *Id.* § 573.14.

[34] *Id.*

must continue to retain from the retainage funds "a sum equal to double the total amount of all claims on file."[35] To the extent that there are retainage funds in excess of the doubled claim amount, those excess funds are to be paid out as though there were no claims on file.[36] No claims for material furnished to a nonsupplier subcontractor will cause any part of the retainage funds to be withheld from the contractor, unless the claims are "supported by a certified statement that the general contractor had been notified within 30 days after the materials are furnished or by itemized invoices rendered to contractor during the progress of the work, of the amount, kind, and value of the material furnished."[37] The phrase "during the progress of the work" has been construed to mean during the "progress of that portion of the work in which the materials for which claim is made [are] utilized," and not to mean during the progress of the work on the *entire* public improvement project.[38]

[2] Claims for Payment

Anyone who has "performed labor, or furnished material, service, or transportation, in the construction of a public improvement," pursuant to a contract with the principal contractor or with a subcontractor, may file a written, sworn, itemized statement of claim for payment.[39] *Construction* includes "repair, alteration and demolition," in addition to its ordinary meaning.[40] For purposes of the bond law, *material* includes, in addition to its ordinary meaning, "feed, gasoline, kerosene, lubricating oils and greases, provisions and fuel, and the use of forms, accessories, and equipment, but shall not include personal expenses or personal purchases of employees for their individual use."[41] The bond law defines *service* to include, in addition to its ordinary meaning, "the furnishing to the contractor of worker's compensation insurance, and premiums and charges for such insurance shall be considered a claim for service."[42] *Labor* has been interpreted to include payment obligations of subcontractors to union health, welfare, and pension trusts arising as a result of labor performed by union members on the project.[43]

The claim must be filed with the "officer, board or commission" authorized by law to let contracts for the improvement.[44] The claim may be filed at any time

[35] *Id.*

[36] *Id.* The constitutionality of this and other provisions of the bond law was upheld in Economy Forms Corp. v. City of Cedar Rapids, 340 N.W.2d 259 (Iowa 1983).

[37] Iowa Code § 573.15 (1995).

[38] Lumberman's Wholesale Co. v. Ohio Farmers Ins., 402 N.W.2d 413, 416 (Iowa 1987).

[39] Iowa Code § 573.7 (1995).

[40] *Id.* § 573.1(1).

[41] *Id.* § 573.1(2).

[42] *Id.* § 573.1(5).

[43] Dobbs v. Knudson, Inc., 292 N.W.2d 692, 694-95 (Iowa 1980).

[44] Iowa Code § 573.7 (1995).

within 30 days of the improvement's completion and final acceptance.[45] A claim may be filed after that 30-day period, if the full contract price has not been paid by the public corporation and "no action is pending to adjudicate rights in and to the unpaid portion of the contract price,"[46] unless the court is satisfied that a claim will not materially delay such a pending action and allows a belated filing to be made in the action.[47] The allowance of such "piggyback" claims is limited to claims of persons who have directly contracted with the general contractor.[48]

[3] Actions to Adjudicate Claims Against Retainage Funds or Liability on Contractor's Bond

The bond law authorizes the public corporation, the principal contractor, the surety, or a labor or material claimant who has filed a claim to bring an action in equity "to adjudicate all rights to [the retainage] fund or to enforce liability on [the] bond."[49] Such an action may be brought in the county in which the public improvement is situated and must be filed "at any time after the expiration of thirty days, and not later than sixty days, following the completion and final acceptance of said improvement."[50]

When a claim has been filed, the contractor may serve upon the claimant, in the same manner as an original notice, a written demand requiring the claimant to commence suit to enforce the claim.[51] If suit is not commenced within 30 days after service of the demand, "the retained and unpaid funds due the contractor shall be released."[52] The public corporation's failure to pay the funds within 20 days following the funds' release by the claimant's failure to commence suit causes interest to run.[53]

If such an action is commenced, the general contractor may bond off the claim(s) by filing with the public corporation or person withholding the funds a surety bond in double the amount of the claim(s), securing payment of any final judgment rendered for such claim(s).[54] Once such a bond is posted, the withheld funds must be paid to the contractor, if owed.[55]

The bond law provides that all claimants who have filed claims, the principal contractor, the contract-letting board or officer, and the contractor's bond surety must be joined as parties to any action to adjudicate claims or enforce liability.[56]

---

[45] *Id.* § 573.10(a).
[46] *Id.* § 573.10(2).
[47] *Id.* § 573.11.
[48] Lumberman's Wholesale Co. v. Ohio Farmers Ins., 402 N.W.2d 413, 415 (Iowa 1987).
[49] IOWA CODE § 573.16 (1995).
[50] *Id.*
[51] *Id.*
[52] *Id.*
[53] *Id.*
[54] *Id.*
[55] *Id.* § 573.16.
[56] *Id.* § 573.17.

Once the claims have been adjudicated by the court, the retainage funds held by the public corporation are to be paid out in the following sequence: (1) costs of the action; (2) claims for labor; (3) claims for materials; and (4) claims of the public corporation.[57] The court may award as costs a partially or wholly successful labor or materials claimant's reasonable attorneys' fees.[58] If the retainage funds are insufficient to pay all of the claims in the second or third category for labor or materials, respectively, then the claims within the particular category are to be paid in order of their filing until the funds are exhausted.[59] Once the retainage funds have been fully paid out, any remaining duly filed and established claims shall give rise to entry of a judgment against the principal and surety in the amount of those claims.[60] Once the public corporation receives evidence of a claim's settlement or of entry of judgment on the claim, any remaining retainage funds not needed to pay the claim are to be paid out to the contractor within 20 days, or else interest will begin to run.[61]

[4] Contractor's Payment Obligations

The contractor may retain the lesser of the retainage authorized by the subcontract or five percent.[62] Upon satisfactory performance of the subcontractor's work, the contractor must pay the subcontractor within seven days following the contractor's receipt of a progress payment or a final payment for that work.[63] If the contractor could have received payment for the subcontractor's work, but has not due to causes other than any fault of the subcontractor, then the contractor must pay the subcontractor within a "reasonable time" after the contractor could have received the payment.[64] If the contractor receives interest for late final payment, then the contractor must pay the subcontractor a proportionate share of that interest.[65]

[E] Additional Bond Issues

For county highway improvements and farm-to-market fund highway system improvements, claims must be filed with the county auditor and the auditor of the state Department of Transportation, respectively.[66]

For purposes of filing claims, if a contractor abandons or is legally excluded from work on the improvement, the improvement is deemed "completed" on the

---

[57] *Id.* § 573.18.
[58] *Id.* § 573.21.
[59] *Id.* § 573.19.
[60] *Id.* § 573.22.
[61] *Id.* § 573.18.
[62] *Id.* § 573.12(1).
[63] *Id.* § 573.12(2)(a).
[64] *Id.* § 573.12(2)(b)(2).
[65] *Id.* § 573.12(3)(a).
[66] *Id.* § 573.8.

date of the contract's official cancellation.[67] Only funds then due the contractor, if any, are available for the payment of claims in such an abandonment or exclusion situation.[68] If those funds are insufficient to cover the claims, then the claimants may sue on the contractor's bond.[69]

§ 16.03 LIEN LAW

[A] General Concepts

The Iowa statute providing for mechanics' liens is embodied in Chapter 572, Code of Iowa (lien law). Generally, the purpose of the lien law is to provide contractors and subcontractors with a security mechanism in private construction projects in Iowa, providing they have not waived their lien rights and comply with the detailed procedural requirements. A mechanics' lien right is a significant security device because it places a lien against the owner's property to ensure payment for value-enhancing labor or materials and operates as an encumbrance on the owner's interest in its property. Iowa's lien law will be "liberally construed with a view to promote its objects and assist the parties in obtaining justice."[70]

Iowa's lien law draws key distinctions between "owner-occupied dwellings" and other private construction projects. In general, mechanics' lien rights are more limited when the lien relates to material or labor concerning an "owner-occupied dwelling."

[B] Basic Provisions

Iowa's lien law provides that "[e]very person who shall furnish any material or labor for, or perform any labor upon, any building or land for improvement, alteration, or repair thereof . . . by virtue of any contract with the owner, the owner's agent, trustee, contractor, or subcontractor shall have a [mechanics'] lien." Thus, in Iowa, contractors and subcontractor possess mechanics' lien rights. Persons who contract with subcontractors also possess mechanics' lien rights, but only if they provide the principal contractor with a one-time written notice within 30 days of the first furnishing of labor or materials containing the name, mailing address, and telephone number of the person furnishing the labor or materials, and the name of the subcontractor to whom the labor or materials were furnished.[71] This notice requirement does not apply to single-family or two-family residential dwellings.[72] The lien claim must be supported with a certified statement

---

[67] *Id.* § 573.23.

[68] *Id.*

[69] *Id.*

[70] Gollehon, Schemmer & Assoc., Inc. v. Fairway-Bettendorf Assoc., 268 N.W.2d 200, 210 (Iowa 1978).

[71] Iowa Code § 572.33(1)(a) (1999).

[72] *Id.* § 572.33(2).

that the principal contractor was so notified.[73] This notice covers additional labor or materials furnished by the same person to the same subcontractor for use in the same construction project.[74] This means that if the person fails to give timely notice, mechanics' lien rights are lost for any labor or materials furnished on a particular project to the same subcontractor. In order to allow the principal contractor access to payment information, the statute also provides that the principal contractor is not prohibited from requesting information regarding payments to the person furnishing labor or materials to a subcontractor.[75]

A mechanics' lien claim must arise out of a contract for furnishing either labor or materials.[76] Therefore, labor or materials furnished or supplied before the date of the contract cannot be included in a mechanics' lien claim. Express contracts, whether written or oral, as well as implied contracts are covered by the lien law, so long as there is a contract with the owner of an interest in the real estate, or with the owner's agent, trustee, contractor, or subcontractor.[77]

The lien law defines *owner* to "include every person for whose use or benefit any building, erection, or other improvement is made, having the capacity to contract."[78] An "owner" can be a fee owner, vendor, vendee, lessor, or lessee, but the mechanics' lien extends only to the "owner's" interest in the property.

It is important to remember that in Iowa the lien law does not provide for mechanics' lien rights on public projects.

The lien law provides certain prerequisites for lienable work. The work must be for "improvement, alteration, or repair" of any "building or land."[79] *Building* is construed as if followed by the words "erection, or other improvement upon land."[80] In addition to those broad descriptions, Iowa's lien law specifically extends coverage to work in the nature of "construction or repair of any work of internal or external improvement" and to "grading, sodding, installing nursery stock, landscaping, sidewalk building, [and] fencing on any land or lot."[81] Iowa's lien law defines *material* broadly to include not only its ordinary meaning, but also "machinery, fixtures, trees, evergreens, vines, plants, shrubs, tubers, bulbs, hedges, bushes, sod, soil, dirt, mulch, peat, fertilizer, fence wire, fence material, fence posts, tile, and the use of forms, accessories, and equipment."[82]

[C] Notice Requirements

The lien law contains strict notice and filing requirements, which must be observed in order for mechanics' lien rights to be enforceable.

---

[73] *Id.* § 572.33(1)(b).
[74] *Id.* § 572.33(1)(a).
[75] *Id.* § 572.33(3).
[76] *Id.* § 572.2.
[77] *Id.*
[78] *Id.* § 572.1(3).
[79] *Id.* § 572.2.
[80] *Id.* § 572.1(3).
[81] *Id.* § 572.2.
[82] *Id.* § 572.1(2).

[1] General Rules

A mechanics' lien cannot be enforced until it has been "perfected." To perfect a mechanics' lien, the lien claimant must file a verified mechanics' lien statement with the clerk of the district court for the county in which the building, land, or improvement is located. The notarized lien statement must set forth the following information: (1) a statement or account of the amount claimed owed, after giving due allowance for all credits; (2) the times when the material was furnished or labor performed and when completed; (3) the description of the property to be charged with the lien; and (4) the name and last known mailing address of the owner, agent, or trustee of the property.[83]

If the lien statement is filed by a subcontractor within 90 days from the date on which the last of the material was furnished or the last of the labor was performed by the subcontractor or if the lien statement is filed by a contractor, the clerk of court will mail a copy of the lien to the owner, agent, or trustee, and the mechanics' lien claimant does not need to send notice to the owner, agent, or trustee.[84] If a subcontractor files a lien statement after the 90-day period has elapsed, then the subcontractor must serve notice of the lien to the owner, the owner's agent, or trustee in the same manner as for service of original notice.[85] In the case of such late-filed subcontractor's liens, the subcontractor may enforce the lien against the property, or against a bond given by the owner, only to the extent of the balance due from the owner to the contractor at the time of service of the subcontractor's notice.[86] However, if the bond was given by the contractor or by the person contracting with the subcontractor, then the bond will be enforced to full extent of the amount due the subcontractor.[87]

An action in equity to enforce a perfected mechanics' lien must be commenced in the county in which all or part of the affected property is situated within two years from the expiration of the 90-day lien-filing period, or else it will be barred under Iowa's lien law.[88] However, if the lienholder is served with a written demand of the owner, the owner's agent, or contractor, then the lienholder must either commence an action to enforce the lien within 30 days following service of the demand or lose the lien and its benefits.[89] Attorneys' fees may be recovered in a successful action to enforce a mechanics' lien, if the plaintiff lienholder furnished labor or materials directly to the defendant.[90]

---

[83] *Id.* § 572.8.

[84] *Id.*

[85] *Id.* § 572.10.

[86] *Id.* § 572.11.

[87] *Id.* § 572.11.

[88] *Id.* §§ 572.24, -.25, -.27.

[89] *Id.* § 572.28.

[90] *Id.* § 572.32.

A mechanics' lien may be assigned and "follows the assignment of the debt for which it is claimed."[91]

Special rules apply to liens for railway, canal, viaduct, or similar work.[92]

[2] Special Rules for Owner-Occupied Dwellings

In an effort to protect homeowners from hardship flowing from contractors' failure to pay subcontractors, special rules apply to mechanics' liens for "owner-occupied dwellings." Iowa's lien law defines *owner-occupied dwelling* to mean "the homestead of an owner . . . and actually occupied by the owner or the spouse of the owner, or both," and includes "a newly constructed dwelling to be occupied by the owner as a homestead, or a dwelling that is under construction and being built by or for an owner who will occupy the dwelling as a homestead."[93] In Iowa, *homestead* means, if within a city, up to one-half acre of contiguous land and the home and related structures used in connection with the homestead.[94] *Homestead,* if in a rural area, includes up to 40 acres of contiguous land.[95] For purposes of the "owner-occupied dwelling" provisions of the Iowa lien law, a vendee buying a house on contract from the building contractor has been recognized as the "owner," when the house "was under construction and was being built for the buyer, . . . [who] intended to occupy the dwelling as a homestead," even though the contractor was the record title holder at the time it contracted with the supplier.[96]

An original contractor, who is using or plans to use labor or material from any subcontractors in conjunction with "a contract for an owner-occupied dwelling," must take special steps to avoid losing mechanics' lien rights and remedies otherwise afforded by Iowa's lien laws. If the contractor has a written contract with the owner, that contract must include a notice stating, "Persons or companies furnishing labor or material for the improvement of real property may enforce a lien upon the improved property if they are not paid for their contributions, even if the parties have no direct contractual relationship with the owner," and a copy of the written contract must be given to the owner.[97] If the original contractor and the owner have no written contract, then the contractor must, within 10 days of commencement of work on the dwelling, provide the owner written notice "stating the name and address of all subcontractors that the contractor intends to use for the construction and that the subcontractors may have lien rights in the event they are not paid for their labor or material used on [the] site."[98] The contractor must

---

[91] *Id.* § 572.29.

[92] *Id.* §§ 572.7, -.11.

[93] *Id.* § 572.1(4).

[94] *Id.* §§ 561.1, -.2.

[95] *Id.* § 561.2.

[96] Louie's Floor Covering v. DePhillips Interest, Ltd., 378 N.W.2d 923, 925 (Iowa 1985).

[97] Iowa Code § 572.13(2) (1995).

[98] *Id.* § 572.13(2).

update the notice as additional subcontractors and suppliers are used beyond the names disclosed on earlier notices.[99]

An original contractor who fails to provide the appropriate notice to the dwelling owner is not entitled to the lien and remedies afforded by the lien law "as they pertain to any labor performed or material furnished by a subcontractor not included in the notice."[100] It should be noted that it is unclear whether these special notice provisions of Iowa's lien law apply only to new owner-occupied dwellings or extend as well to improvements or repairs to existing owner-occupied dwellings. Finally, a principal contractor, who has been paid in full for more than 30 days by the owner but who fails to pay a subcontractor for work performed or materials furnished for a specific owner-occupied dwelling, may be subjected to liability for actual and punitive damages under Iowa's lien law, absent prompt cure or posting of a bond.[101]

Ordinarily, the lien rights of a subcontractor, who perfects a mechanics' lien during the 90-day perfection period following the date of the last work performed or material supplied by the subcontractor, are not affected by the owner's payment to the contractor of any or all of the contract price within that 90-day period.[102] However, when an owner-occupied dwelling is involved, the subcontractor's lien rights extend only to the balance due from the owner to the principal contractor at the time special written notice is served on the owner.[103] This special notice must contain the owner's name, the address of the lienable property, and the lien claimant's name, address, and telephone number.[104] The notice must also contain the following language:

> The person named in this notice is providing labor or materials or both in connection with improvements to your residence or real property. Chapter 572 of the Code of Iowa may permit the enforcement of a lien against this property to secure payment for labor and materials supplied. You are not required to pay more to the person claiming the lien than the amount of money due from you to the person with whom you contracted to perform the improvements. You should not make further payments to your contractor until the contractor presents you with a waiver of the lien claimed by the person named in this notice. If you have any questions regarding this notice you should call the person

---

[99] *Id.*

[100] *Id.* Frontier Properties Corp. v. Swanberg, 488 N.W.2d 146, 147–48 (Iowa 1992) (finding that failure to give appropriate notice, while depriving contractor of lien law remedies, does not preclude contractor from asserting common law actions against owner for work and materials furnished by subcontractors).

[101] Iowa Code § 572.30 (1995).

[102] *Id.* § 572.14.

[103] *Id.* § 572.14(2) (1995). Carson v. Roediger, 513 N.W.2d 713 (Iowa 1994).

[104] Iowa Code § 572.14(3) (1995).

named in this notice at the phone number listed in this notice or contact an attorney. You should obtain answers to your questions before you make any payments to the contractor.[105]

The special notice may be served (1) via personal delivery to the owner or spouse; (2) via certified mail with delivery restricted to the owner and return receipt requested; or (3) by personal service as if the notice were a summons.[106]

[3] Special Rules for Condominiums and Cooperative Apartments

Iowa's lien law grants occupying owners of condominium units and of cooperative apartment units protection analogous to that accorded homeowners. A mechanics' lien arising as a result of the construction of a cooperatively owned apartment building or a condominium "is not enforceable . . . as against the interests of an owner in an owner-occupied dwelling unit contained in [that building] acquired in good faith and for valuable consideration, unless a lien statement specifically describing the dwelling unit is filed" in timely fashion.[107] With the exception of the specific dwelling unit description requirement, the lien filing requirements for cooperative and condominium units are essentially the same as for ordinary mechanics' liens with respect to form and place of filing.[108] However, the 90-day filing period for perfecting a mechanics' lien on such units runs "from the date on which the last of the material was supplied or the last of the labor was performed in the construction of that dwelling unit."[109]

[D] Waiver

A lien claimant may waive the mechanics' lien rights and remedies afforded by the lien law. Such a waiver may be express or implied. Any doubts about the waiver will be resolved in favor of the lien.[110] No mechanics' lien rights arise in favor of a person who, at the time of contracting to provide lienable work or materials or during the progress of the work, takes any collateral security on that contract.[111] However, new security taken after completion of the work does not impair a person's mechanics' lien rights, unless expressly given and received in lieu of a mechanics' lien.[112]

---

[105] *Id.*

[106] *Id.*

[107] *Id.* § 572.31.

[108] *Id.* §§ 572.8, -.9, -.31.

[109] *Id.* § 572.31.

[110] Metropolitan Fed. Bank v. Allen, 477 N.W.2d 668, 673 (Iowa 1991) (lien waiver must be "clear, satisfactory, unambiguous, and free from doubt").

[111] Iowa Code § 572.3 (1995).

[112] *Id.* § 572.4.

[E] Lien Priority

The lien law provides specific rules of priority among conflicting liens. The order of filing the verified mechanics' lien statements determines the priority among mechanics' lien claimants.[113] With two important exceptions, mechanics' liens are prior to all other liens, "except for liens of record prior to the time of the original commencement of the work or improvements."[114] The first exception to that rule is that "purchasers, encumbrancers, and other persons who acquire interest in good faith and for a valuable consideration and without notice" are accorded priority over the mechanics' liens filed beyond the 90-day period following the completion of the work or improvements.[115] The second exception to the rule is that construction mortgage liens of record are prior to "mechanics' liens of claimants who commenced their particular work or improvement subsequent to the date of the recording of the construction mortgage lien."[116] The lien law phrase "their particular work or improvement" has been construed to mean any work or material supplied by the particular lien claimant, not just the particular work or material for which the lien claimant remains unpaid.[117]

Under the lien law, a prior lien, mortgage, or encumbrance upon the land is deprived of its priority with respect to a building or improvement constructed on that land, as against a mechanics' lien upon the building or improvement for which the lienable material or labor was furnished or done.[118]

[F] Remedies of Owner

The lien law provides the owner with various forms of protection against mechanics' liens, including the right to retain funds[119] and the right to bond off a claim.[120]

§ 16.04 PUBLIC PROJECTS—TIMING

The Iowa legislature enacted a new section to Chapter 573 affecting the time frame in which retained funds may be released on a public project. The new law, Iowa Code § 573.15A, provides the governmental body with an option to release the retained funds earlier than the existing time period of 30 days after completion and final acceptance of the project. This would allow the prime contractor to pay its subcontractors and suppliers their respective retainages earlier than had pre-

---

[113] *Id.* § 572.17.

[114] *Id.* § 572.18.

[115] *Id.*

[116] *Id.*

[117] Metropolitan Fed. Bank v. Allen, 477 N.W.2d 668, 671 (Iowa 1991).

[118] Iowa Code § 572.20 (1995).

[119] *Id.* § 572.13(1).

[120] *Id.* § 572.15.

viously been allowed under the law. At the option of the governmental body, the retained funds may now be released 30 days after completion of 95 percent of the contract. Once a governmental body elects to release the retained funds 30 days after completion of 95 percent of the contract (presumably by formal resolution or some other form of public notice), then the time period for filing claims would end at the expiration of 30 days after completion of 95 percent of the contract, and the time period for filing suit to enforce any such claim is any time after the expiration of 30 days, and not later than 60 days after completion of 95 percent of the contract. Although it is unclear from the statute, one would assume that the shortened time period for filing claims, and suit to enforce same, would apply only to subcontractors and suppliers who have completed their contractual obligations at the time of the deadlines tied to 95 percent completion. In any event, the bond would remain in place to pay any claims for work not finished at the point of 95 percent completion, to which the existing deadlines for filing claims and suits tied to completion and final acceptance would apply.

This new law was promulgated by the Iowa Department of Transportation (IDOT) to allow it to release retainage on highway projects if just 5 percent or less of the work remained to be completed, but could not be completed for several months due to winter weather. Previously, if IDOT wanted to release the retained funds under those circumstances, it had to close out the original contract and issue a supplemental contract for the uncompleted work—a cumbersome process.

It is too soon to tell what other governmental authorities will use this new optional time frame for the early release of retained funds. It would appear that the governmental authorities more familiar with and that more often let construction contracts will be more comfortable with its implementation. It will be up to the prime contractor not only to make the governmental authority aware of this new provision, but also to make the governmental authority comfortable with its implementation on a particular project.

CHAPTER 17

KANSAS

Keith Witten

§ 17.01 CONSTRUCTION BONDS

The most commonly encountered construction bonds in Kansas consist of three different types of bond, each serving its own distinct function. Bid bonds provide a means of assuring that the bidder will execute a satisfactory contract and file proper payment or performance bonds, or both, as required by a construction contract. Performance bonds assist in assuring the complete performance of a construction contract. Payment bonds help to assure that those who provide labor and materials to be incorporated into a project will receive payment.

§ 17.02 BID BONDS

Kansas does not by statute require prime contractors to furnish bid bonds on either public or private projects. However, the statutes presuppose that such bonds may be required on public projects.[1] Administrative regulations sometimes specifically require bid bonds. For example, regulations of the Kansas Department of Transportation provide that the Standard Specifications for State Road and Bridge Construction govern the bidding procedure for contracts let by the secretary of transportation.[2] The Standard Specifications for State Road and Bridge Construction require that each bid be accompanied by a bid bond.[3] As a practical matter, all public contract bid solicitations and most substantial private contract bid solicitations require the furnishing of a bid bond.

§ 17.03 PERFORMANCE BONDS

Kansas law does not require contractors to furnish performance bonds on private projects. However, pursuant to statute the Kansas secretary of administration has adopted a standard contract for construction or repair of public buildings prescribing that a bond be given for the faithful performance of a contract in the amount of the contract price.[4] The Kansas director of purchases has the authority

---

[1] KAN. STAT. ANN. § 75-3738 (1997).

[2] KAN. ADMIN. REGS. § 36-30-2 (1997).

[3] Standard Specifications for State Road and Bridge Construction § 102.12 (1990).

[4] KAN. STAT. ANN. § 75-3741(b)(4) (1997). Furthermore, pursuant to KAN. STAT. ANN. § 68-410 (1992), the person or persons to whom a contract is awarded for the construction, improvement, reconstruction, and maintenance of the highway system the cost of which exceeds $1,000 are required to give good and sufficient surety bond in an amount not less than the contract price, conditioned upon the faithful performance of the contract and the payment by the contractor and subcontractors of all indebtedness incurred for supplies, materials or labor furnished, used or consumed in connection with the construction of the project, including gasoline, lubricating oils, fuel oils, greases, coal and similar items used or consumed directly in carrying out the provisions of the contract. Upon the filing with and approval of the bond by the secretary of transportation, no mechanic's lien will attach. No action may be brought on such a bond after one year from the completion date of the contract. The provisions of KAN. STAT. ANN. § 60-1111 do not apply to contracts made by the secretary of transportation. Finally, pursuant to KAN. STAT. ANN. § 68-521

to prescribe the amount and form of any bond given for the faithful performance of a public contract.[5] As an alternative to payment and performance bonds a bidder or contractor may furnish a certificate of deposit payable to the state in an amount at least equal to the contract price.[6]

§ 17.04 PAYMENT BONDS

[A] Statutory Payment Bonds

Payment bonds in Kansas take several different forms. Kansas law does not require contractors to provide payment bonds on private projects. However, on a private project, the contractor may furnish a statutory payment bond.[7] By filing a bond conditioned for the payment of all claims that might be the basis of liens in a sum not less than the contract price with the clerk of the district court (presumably in the county in which the property is located) and obtaining approval of the bond by a judge of the district court, the owner of the project gains the comfort of knowing that no mechanics' lien can attach to the property and that any liens that have already been filed against the project are discharged.[8] If no payment bond is filed, contractors and their subcontractors and suppliers on private projects may file mechanics' liens.

By statute, any public official who enters into a contract for in excess of $40,000 for the purpose of making public improvements, constructing public buildings, or making repairs on public buildings shall obtain a payment bond in at least the amount of the contract.[9] The statute does not define public official, but the legislature probably intended to include officials of political subdivisions, such as municipalities.[10] Also, the party to whom a contract has been awarded on all county projects for the construction of any courthouse, jail or any other county building, or the construction of any bridge in excess of $10,000 is required to furnish a payment bond in the amount of the contract conditioned upon the faithful performance of the contract.[11]

Finally, there is a special statute[12] applying solely to contracts for the

(Supp. 1998), no contract let by the board of county commissioners for the construction, surfacing, repairing or maintaining of any road, the estimated cost of which exceeds $10,000, may be considered as awarded unless the contractor within ten days after the letting gives a bond as required by KAN. STAT. ANN. § 60-1111 and a performance bond conditioned upon the faithful performance of the contract in a penal sum equal to the amount of the contract, payable to the county upon failure to comply with the terms of the contract.

[5] KAN. STAT. ANN. § 75-3738(g).

[6] *Id.* § 60-1112 (1983). In practice, this alternative has found little use.

[7] *Id.* § 60-1110 (1994).

[8] *Id.*

[9] *Id.* § 60-1111(a).

[10] *See, e.g., id.* § 60-459(d).

[11] *Id.* § 19-214 (1995).

[12] *Id.* § 68-410 (1992).

construction, improvement, reconstruction, and maintenance of the highway system the cost of which exceeds $1,000 that requires the contractor to give a combination payment and performance surety bond in an amount not less than the contract price, conditioned upon the faithful performance of the contract and the payment by the contractor and subcontractors of all indebtedness incurred for supplies, materials or labor furnished, used or consumed in connection with the construction of the project, including gasoline, lubricating oils, fuel oils, greases, coal and similar items used or consumed directly in carrying out the provisions of the contract.

Upon the filing with and approval of the bond by the secretary of transportation, no mechanics' lien will attach.[13] No action may be brought on such a bond after one year from the completion date of the contract. Furthermore, the action may be brought in any county where any part of the contract has been performed.[14] However, no action on the bond may be brought unless within six months after the completion date of the contract, according to the records of the secretary of transportation, an itemized statement of the amount of the indebtedness, sworn to and acknowledged before a notary or other officer authorized to administer oaths, is filed with the secretary of transportation.[15]

On a public project, a public works payment bond covers "all indebtedness incurred for labor furnished, materials, equipment or supplies, used or consumed in connection with or in or about the construction of [a] public building or in making [a] public improvement."[16] On Kansas public projects, contractors apparently have mechanics' lien rights if no public works payment bond has been provided.[17] The liability of a governmental officer or entity for failing to require a contractor on a public works project to furnish a payment bond has never been adjudicated in Kansas.[18]

[B] Common Law Payment Bonds

If the contractor on a private project furnishes a payment bond that is not filed with the district court as allowed by the statute, the bond would be a common law payment bond. It would not have the effect of discharging mechanics' liens against the property, but the surety would be liable for any claims, including mechanics' liens, that come within its terms.

---

[13] *Id.*

[14] *Id.*

[15] *Id.*

[16] *Id.* § 60-1111(a) (1994).

[17] Huttig Mill Work Co. v. Randel, 125 Kan. 744, 745, 266 P. 106, 107 (Kan. 1928). However, rather than selling the public improvement to satisfy the lien, mandamus will lie to compel payment or the imposition of a levy to raise the money to pay the lien. *Id.*

[18] In view of the fact that a mechanics' lien can attach to public property under Kansas law if public officials fail to require the filing of a public works payment bond, it is likely that a governmental officer or entity would not be liable because the claimant would have an adequate alternative remedy. Huttig Millwork Co. v. Randel, 125 Kan. 744, 745-46, 266 P. 106, 107 (Kan. 1928).

§ 17.05 COMPLETION BONDS

A performance bond is to be distinguished from a completion bond because a completion bond provides only one option for a surety—completion of the project. In a typical performance bond, the surety has no absolute duty to complete the project, but may instead remedy the default or arrange for performance of the principal's contract, with the balance of the contract price to be credited against the reasonable cost of completing performance of the contract. Because completion bonds limit the options for the surety, they are less commonly written than performance bonds.

§ 17.06 GENERAL PRINCIPLES OF BOND LAW

[A] Tripartite Relationship

Kansas, like most other jurisdictions, treats the construction surety bond relationship as a tripartite relationship and treats bonds as tripartite contracts.[19] Each construction surety bond has an obligee, typically an owner or a general contractor, and joint and several obligors, which are typically the general contractor or subcontractor and its surety.

[B] Formal Requirements

In Kansas, as in other jurisdictions, a surety contract must be in writing and signed by or on behalf of the surety against whom the claim is made in order to be valid.[20] No Kansas cases discuss whether an obligee must accept a surety contract within a reasonable time, whether a surety may revoke a surety contract before the obligation is delivered and accepted, or whether the principal must request or assent to the surety executing and delivering a bond on its behalf.[21]

[C] Liability of Principal as Measure of Liability of Surety

The liability of a surety is coextensive with that of its principal. Therefore, a discharge of the principal discharges the surety, unless the surety has consented to remain liable or the creditor reserves its rights against the surety.[22]

---

[19] *See* Alexander v. Young, 65 F.2d 752, 756 (10th Cir. 1933).

[20] Kan. Stat. Ann. § 33-106 (1986) provides:

> No action shall be brought whereby to charge a party upon any special promise to answer for the debt, default or miscarriage of another person; . . . unless the agreement upon which such action shall be brought, or some memorandum or note thereof, shall be in writing and signed by the party to be charged therewith, or some other person thereunto by him or her lawfully authorized in writing.

See United States v. Gonzales, 541 F. Supp. 783, 785 (D. Kan. 1982).

[21] 72 C.J.S. *Principal and Surety* §§ 57-60 (1951). Acceptance by the obligee and assent by the principal are likely to be inferred from the circumstances. *But see* Alexander v. Young, 65 F.2d 752, 756 (10th Cir. 1933).

[22] Security Nat'l Bank v. Continental Ins. Co., 586 F. Supp. 139, 146-48 (D. Kan. 1982).

[D] Statutes of Limitation

Any action in Kansas upon a surety bond (other than a public works payment bond)[23] must be brought within five years of the date the cause of action accrued.[24] Thus, an action upon a performance bond must be brought within five years of the date the cause of action accrued, unless the bond provides a different time within which suit must be brought.[25] An action on a public works bond must be brought within six months from the completion of the public improvements or public works.[26] However, Kansas law recognizes the validity of reasonable contractual limitations of the time within which suit on a surety bond may be brought.[27]

[E] Principles of Contract Construction Apply

The meaning of a surety contract is to be ascertained in the same manner as that of any other contract.[28] The construction of an unambiguous contract is a matter for the court.[29] The cardinal goal of a court in the interpretation of a contract is to ascertain the intention of the parties and give effect to that intention.[30] In reaching that goal, a court will look to the four corners of the document in striving to harmonize all of its provisions.[31] However, an ambiguous contract will be construed strictly against the party who drafted it, generally the surety.[32] A compensated or corporate surety is not entitled to receive a strict construction of the bond in its favor.[33] On the other hand, the surety's liability may not be extended by implication beyond the terms of the bond.[34]

[F] Choice of Law

Kansas follows the traditional rule that the law of the place where the contract was made governs the interpretation of a contract.[35] A contract is considered to have been made where the last act necessary to its formation occurred.[36]

---

[23] KAN. STAT. ANN. § 60-1111(b) (1983).

[24] *Id.* § 60-511; Bob Eldridge Constr. Co., Inc. v. Pioneer Materials, Inc., 235 Kan. 599, 606, 684 P.2d 355, 361 (Kan. 1984).

[25] KAN. STAT. ANN. § 60-511 (1983); Bob Eldridge Constr. Co., Inc. v. Pioneer Materials, Inc., 235 Kan. 599, 606, 684 P.2d 355, 361 (Kan. 1984).

[26] KAN. STAT. ANN. § 60-1111 (1994).

[27] Coates v. Metropolitan Life Ins. Co., 515 F. Supp. 647, 649-50 (D. Kan. 1981).

[28] Stevens v. Farmers Elevator Mut. Ins. Co., 197 Kan. 74, 76, 415 P.2d 236, 239 (Kan. 1966).

[29] United States v. Ables, 739 F. Supp. 1439, 1445 (D. Kan. 1990).

[30] Garvey Ctr., Inc. v. Food Specialties, Inc., 214 Kan. 224, 229, 519 P.2d 646, 650 (Kan. 1974).

[31] Short v. Wise, 239 Kan. 171, 173-74, 718 P.2d 604, 606 (Kan. 1986).

[32] Desbien v. Penokee Farmers Union Coop. Ass'n, 220 Kan. 358, 363, 552 P.2d 917, 923 (Kan. 1976).

[33] Stevens v. Farmers Elevator Mut. Ins. Co., 197 Kan. 74, 76, 415 P.2d 236, 239 (Kan. 1966).

[34] Koch v. Merchants Mut. Bonding Co., 211 Kan. 397, 400, 507 P.2d 189, 192 (Kan. 1973).

[35] Simms v. Metropolitan Life Ins. Co., 9 Kan. App. 2d 640, 642-43, 685 P.2d 321, 324 (Kan. Ct. App. 1984).

[36] *Id.*

[G] Statutory Bonds

When a statute requires a bond to be given, the provisions of the statute are read into the bond and the bond cannot be extended beyond the fair import of the statutory terms.[37] There are two exceptions to this rule. First, even though a bond is given pursuant to a statute, if the bond shows an intention to guarantee compliance with the terms of the contract pursuant to which the bond was given, the bond covers the full performance of all of the terms of the contract.[38] Second, the protection required by the statute controls over the language of the bond only when the bond purports to provide less protection than the statute requires.[39]

[H] Bonds on Federal Projects—Miller Act

Miller Act[40] bonds are discussed in Chapter 1 of this text. However, because one case construing Kansas law has explicitly analogized the Kansas public works payment bond statute to the Miller Act,[41] and Kansas courts frequently look to the interpretation given to similar federal statutes,[42] it is always helpful to keep in mind how a given issue has been treated by federal courts under the Miller Act.

§ 17.07 LIABILITY OF SURETY

[A] Bid Bonds

The purpose of a bid bond is to require the bidder to go forward with the construction contract regardless of errors it may have made in preparation of its bid.[43] At one time, case law clearly provided that a unilateral error by the contractor was not grounds for relief from its bid, even if it sought to withdraw its bid before its acceptance by the owner on the basis of that error.[44] Under the then prevailing rules, the contractor did not have to perform the underlying construction contract, but if it refused to do so, it forfeited the bid bond in a known amount and was relieved of its obligations under the construction contract.[45]

---

[37] Wells v. Mehl, 25 Kan. 205, 206 (Kan. 1881).

[38] Thompson Transp. Co. v. Middlestates Constr. Co., 194 Kan. 52, 59, 397 P.2d 368, 374 (Kan. 1964).

[39] Wichita Sheet Metal Supply, Inc. v. Dahlstrom & Ferrell Constr. Co., 246 Kan. 557, 560-61, 792 P.2d 1043, 1046 (Kan. 1990).

[40] 40 U.S.C. §§ 270a and 270b (1986).

[41] Blinne Contracting Co. v. Bobby Goins Enters., Inc., 715 F. Supp. 1044, 1048 (D. Kan. 1989).

[42] *See, e.g.,* Wright v. State, 5 Kan. App. 2d 494, 496, 619 P.2d 155, 159 (Kan. 1980).

[43] Triple A Contractors, Inc. v. Rural Water Dist. No. 4, 226 Kan. 626, 629, 603 P.2d 184, 186 (Kan. 1979).

[44] *Id.*

[45] *Id.*

In the absence of fraud, Kansas courts held that a unilateral mistake would not excuse the nonperformance of a contract such as a bid.[46] Consequently, a unilateral mistake in a bid excused neither the bidder nor its surety under a bid bond from liability under that bond. Whether the surety on a contract that was void because it was let without compliance with mandatory competitive bidding statutes[47] was relieved of liability has not been passed upon by Kansas courts.

However, in 1995 the Kansas legislature enacted comprehensive legislation dealing with errors in bids.[48] That legislation allowed any bidder to correct any mistakes in its bid before the time and date set by the awarding authority for bid opening by withdrawing or correcting its bid.[49] On the other hand, a bid containing an error in judgment cannot be withdrawn after the time and date set for bid opening.[50]

When the awarding authority has reason to believe that nonjudgmental mistakes have been made, it may request a verification of the bid calling attention to the suspected nonjudgmental mistake. The bidder may either verify the bid as submitted or withdraw it if a request for verification has been made. If the bidder does not respond within two business days after the bidder receives a request for verification the bid shall be considered verified. Once a bid has been verified, it is considered submitted as verified.[51]

Furthermore, a bidder may seek to withdraw its bid on the basis of a nonjudgmental mistake by notifying the awarding authority within two business days after the bids have been opened that there is a nonjudgmental mistake in its bid. The awarding authority must allow withdrawal of the bid without penalty or forfeiture of bid security if a nonjudgmental mistake is evident on the face of the bid or the bidder establishes by clear and convincing evidence that it made a nonjudgmental mistake.[52] If a bidder is allowed to withdraw its bid, the awarding authority may require that the bidder not be allowed to perform any work on the project through subcontract agreements or by any other means including rebids.[53]

Whenever it appears that an awarding authority is attempting to enforce any contract based on a bid in which a nonjudgmental mistake has been made, the bidder, the attorney general or any county or district attorney may bring an action in the district court of the county in which the contract was awarded to enjoin

---

[46] *Id.*

[47] Kaw Valley Drainage Dist. v. Board of County Comm'rs, 117 Kan. 634, 637-38, 232 P. 1056, 1057 (Kan. 1925).

[48] The legislation does not, however, apply to the Kansas Turnpike Authority. KAN. STAT. ANN. § 75-6908 (1997).

[49] *Id.* § 75-6902.

[50] *Id.* § 75-6903.

[51] *Id.* § 75-6904.

[52] *Id.* § 75-6905.

[53] *Id.* § 75-6906.

enforcement of the contract.[54] Upon a proper showing, the court may grant a temporary or permanent injunction, restraining order or other equitable relief.[55]

Presumably, it would still be true under the new legislation regarding errors in bids that the contractor does not have to perform the underlying construction contract, but if it refuses to do so, it may forfeit the bid bond in a known amount and be relieved of its obligations under the construction contract.[56]

[B] Performance Bonds

Generally, construction contracts between a contractor and a state or other public body for highway repair or construction are not considered to be for the benefit of third persons.[57] Presumably, it would follow that a materialman would not be considered a third-party beneficiary of a prime contractor's performance bond, nor would one prime contractor be considered a third-party beneficiary of another prime contractor's performance bond.

Although no reported Kansas case has considered whether a contracting body could be liable for its failure to require a contractor to furnish a performance bond, liability would seem unlikely because the performance bond is solely for the benefit of the contracting body as obligee. An action in Kansas upon a performance bond must be brought within five years of the date the cause of action accrued, unless the bond provides a different time within which suit must be brought.[58]

[C] Payment Bonds

[1] Relationship to Mechanics' Liens

A payment bond on either a public work or a private project is a substitute for a mechanics' lien.[59] Accordingly, it is fair to analogize the rules applicable to mechanics' liens to public works payment bonds.[60]

---

[54] *Id.* § 75-6907.

[55] *Id.*

[56] Triple A Contractors, Inc. v. Rural Water Dist. No. 4, 226 Kan. 626, 629, 603 P.2d 184, 186 (Kan. 1979).

[57] Lewis v. Globe Constr. Co., 6 Kan. App. 2d 478, 486, 630 P.2d 179, 185 (Kan. 1981).

[58] KAN. STAT. ANN. § 60-511 (1983); Bob Eldridge Constr. Co., Inc. v. Pioneer Materials, Inc., 235 Kan. 599, 606, 684 P.2d 355, 361 (Kan. 1984).

[59] J.W. Thompson Co. v. Welles Prods. Corp., 243 Kan. 503, 509, 758 P.2d 738, 742 (Kan. 1988). KAN. STAT. ANN. § 60-1110 (1983) provides that when a private payment bond is filed with and approved by the clerk of the district court, no lien attaches and any liens already filed are discharged. KAN. STAT. ANN. § 60-1111(b) provides that when a public works payment bond is filed with the clerk of the district court, no lien attaches and any liens already filed are discharged. BRB Contractors, Inc. v. Akkerman Equip., Inc., 935 F. Supp. 1156 (D. Kan. 1996).

[60] Cedar Vale Co-Op Exch., Inc. v. Allen Utils., Inc., 10 Kan. App. 2d 129, 132, 694 P.2d 903, 906 (Kan. Ct. App. 1985).

[2] Remoteness

Privity with either the owner, the general contractor, or a subcontractor is a requirement to the assertion of a claim against a public works payment bond.[61] Thus, suppliers of equipment and materials to contractors and subcontractors on a public works project come within the protection of the public works payment bond.[62] On the other hand, a supplier to a supplier is too remote to assert a claim against a public works payment bond, either directly or by virtue of a theory of unjust enrichment.[63]

[3] Elements of Recovery

A public works payment bond covers "all indebtedness incurred for labor furnished, materials, equipment or supplies, used or consumed in connection with or in or about the construction of [a] public building or in making [a] public improvement."[64] Few Kansas cases provide much guidance beyond the words of the statute itself as to what indebtedness the statute covers.

In 1989, a federal district court applying Kansas law held that costs of transportation and equipment rental are recoverable, but that the rental value of idle equipment and increased expenses represent damages for breach of contract that are not recoverable.[65] More recently, another United States District Court opinion reaffirmed that equipment rental is a proper element of recovery.[66] An earlier Kansas decision had held that rental charges for equipment used in the construction are not recoverable under a statutory public works payment bond.[67] However, at that time, the mechanics' lien law, for which the public works payment bond provides a substitute remedy, did not include "equipment" as one of the covered elements.

It is clear, though, that if the bond provides more expansive protection than the statute requires, the bond language controls.[68] On the other hand, Kansas courts will not extend the coverage of a bond beyond its clear and unambiguous terms.[69]

---

[61] Wichita Sheet Metal Supply, Inc. v. Dahlstrom & Ferrell Constr. Co., 246 Kan. 557, 564, 792 P.2d 1043, 1048 (Kan. 1990), *rev'g* 14 Kan. App. 2d 111, 783 P.2d 353 (Kan. Ct. App. 1989).

[62] J.W. Thompson Co. v. Welles Prods. Corp., 243 Kan. 503, 510, 758 P.2d 738, 743-44 (Kan. 1988).

[63] *Id.*

[64] KAN. STAT. ANN. § 60-1111(a) (1994).

[65] Blinne Contracting Co. v. Bobby Goins Enters., Inc., 715 F. Supp. 1044, 1046-47 (D. Kan. 1989).

[66] Trestle & Tower Eng'g, Inc. v. Star Ins. Co., 13 F. Supp. 2d 1166, 1170-71 (D. Kan. 1998).

[67] Road Supply & Metal Co. v. Bechtelheimer, 119 Kan. 560, 563, 240 P. 846, 847–48 (Kan. 1925).

[68] Wichita Sheet Metal Supply, Inc. v. Dahlstrom & Ferrell Constr. Co., 246 Kan. 557, 560–61, 792 P.2d 1043, 1046 (Kan. 1990).

[69] Koch v. Merchants Mut. Bonding Co., 211 Kan. 397, 400, 507 P.2d 189, 192 (Kan. 1973).

[4] Elements Not Recoverable

In Kansas, claimants under a public works payment bond are not entitled to recover damages for breach of contract, such as for lost profits or additional expenses incurred as a result of another's breach of contract.[70] Thus, a claimant would presumably not be able to recover delay damages.[71] However, a claimant can recover a reasonable profit on items actually supplied, as opposed to profits that would have been earned if the claimant had been allowed to complete its contract.[72] In addition, a claimant may recover pre-judgment interest when its claim is liquidated.[73]

Materials or supplies that are stolen or converted are not recoverable.[74] When equipment, supplies or materials are stolen, they cannot be said to have been used or consumed in connection with the project.[75]

[5] Notice Requirements

A claimant on a public works or private payment bond need not give any notice before filing suit, unless the bond itself imposes such a requirement. However, any suit on a public works payment bond must be brought within six months from the completion of the public building or improvement.[76] Kansas recognizes the validity of reasonable contractual limitations of the time within which suit on a surety bond may be brought.[77]

[6] Problems of Proof

Proof of delivery of construction materials to a building site constitutes prima facie evidence or creates a presumption of their use in the improvement, unless there is well-grounded suspicion that the contractor used the materials for some other building or purpose.[78]

[7] Recovery of Attorneys' Fees

Kansas follows the American rule that attorneys' fees are not recoverable in the absence of a contractual or statutory provision authorizing their recov-

---

[70] Blinne Contracting Co. v. Bobby Goins Enters., Inc., 715 F. Supp. 1044, 1046–47 (D. Kan. 1989).

[71] *Id.* at 1047.

[72] *Id.*

[73] *Id.*

[74] Trestle & Tower Eng'g, Inc. v. Star Ins. Co., 13 F. Supp. 2d 1166, 1171 (D. Kan. 1998).

[75] *Id.* In addition, damages for stolen equipment would seem more akin to damages for breach of contract.

[76] KAN. STAT. ANN. § 60-1111(b) (1983).

[77] Coates v. Metropolitan Life Ins. Co., 515 F. Supp. 647, 649-50 (D. Kan. 1981).

[78] Seyb-Tucker Lumber & Implement Co. v. Hartley, 197 Kan. 58, 63, 415 P.2d 217, 221 (Kan. 1966); Cedar Vale Co-Op Exch., Inc. v. Allen Utils., Inc., 10 Kan. App. 2d 129, 132, 694 P.2d 903,

ery.[79] However, by statute, an insurer that refuses without just cause or excuse to pay the full amount of the loss under an insurance policy or surety bond is required to pay the insured's reasonable attorneys' fees in a suit against the insurer.[80] That statute applies to sureties.[81]

[8] Extra-contractual Liability

Under Kansas law, in an action for breach of an insurance contract only contractual damages are available, and such damages ordinarily do not include damages for mental anguish.[82] In the absence of an independent tort causing additional damages, punitive damages are not recoverable.[83] Moreover, Kansas law does not recognize the tort of bad faith in first-party insurance claims.[84]

Furthermore, there is no private right of action for monetary damages for an insurer's failure to comply with the Unfair Claims Settlement Practices Act under Kansas law.[85] Therefore, it appears that bad faith would not be recognized in the context of claims against payment or performance bonds either. However, a Kansas statute that penalizes an insurer for refusing without just cause or excuse to pay the full amount of the loss by requiring it to pay the insured's reasonable attorneys' fees in the action against the insurer[86] has been held to apply to sureties.[87]

§ 17.08 MECHANICS' LIENS

The purpose of a mechanics' lien is to provide a mechanics' lien claimant with security for its debt by providing an encumbrance in the nature of a statutory

---

906–07 (Kan. 1985). Even if it makes specially fabricated materials for a project, which fit only that project, a manufacturer may not proceed against a public works bond unless the materials were actually used or consumed in the project. Hope's Architectural Prods., Inc. v. Lundy's Constr., Inc., 762 F. Supp. 1430, 1433 (D. Kan. 1991).

[79] Iola State Bank v. Briggs, 233 Kan. 450, 459, 662 P.2d 563, 572 (Kan. 1983).

[80] KAN. STAT. ANN. § 40-256 (1993); Russell v. Phoenix Assurance Co., 188 Kan. 424, 426, 362 P.2d 430, 431 (Kan. 1961).

[81] Russell v. Phoenix Assurance Co., 188 Kan. 424, 426, 362 P.2d 430, 431 (Kan. 1961).

[82] Moffet v. Kansas City Fire & Marine Ins. Co., 173 Kan. 52, 57, 244 P.2d 228, 233 (Kan. 1952).

[83] Hess v. Jarboe, 201 Kan. 705, 709, 443 P.2d 294, 297 (Kan. 1968); Moffet v. Kansas City Fire & Marine Ins. Co., 173 Kan. 52, 57, 244 P.2d 228, 233 (Kan. 1952). Independent torts that could justify the imposition of punitive damages in an appropriate case include the torts of outrage and malicious prosecution. Weathers v. American Family Mut. Ins. Co., 793 F. Supp. 1002 (D. Kan. 1992).

[84] Spencer v. Aetna Life & Casualty Ins. Co., 227 Kan. 914, 926, 611 P.2d 149, 155 (Kan. 1980); Resolution Trust Corp. v. Fidelity & Deposit Co., 885 F. Supp. 228 (D. Kan. 1995).

[85] Earth Scientists (Petro Servs.), Ltd. v. United States Fidelity & Guar. Co., 619 F. Supp. 1465, 1468-72 (D. Kan. 1985).

[86] KAN. STAT. ANN. § 40-256 (1993).

[87] Russell v. Phoenix Assurance Co., 188 Kan. 424, 426, 362 P.2d 430, 431 (Kan. 1961).

mortgage founded upon consent[88] based upon the principle that the improvements to the land made by the claimant add to its value.[89] Although Kansas pays lip service to the rule that mechanics' lien laws are to be construed liberally as remedial in nature, nevertheless, because they are solely creatures of statute, many cases hold that all of the requirements for imposition of a lien provided by those statutes must be strictly followed.[90]

§ 17.09 REQUIREMENT OF CONTRACT

An essential prerequisite to a mechanics' lien is a contract between an owner and another person for the furnishing of labor, equipment, material, or supplies.[91] Such a contract may be written, oral, or implied.[92] Whether labor furnished or materials supplied before a contract exists can be the subject of a mechanics' lien is not clear.[93]

§ 17.10 WHO IS ENTITLED TO FILE A MECHANICS' LIEN

Any person furnishing labor, equipment, material, or supplies used or consumed for the improvement of real property under a contract with the owner or someone on its behalf[94] and any supplier, subcontractor, or other person furnishing labor, equipment, material, or supplies used or consumed at the site of the property subject to a mechanics' lien, under an agreement with the contractor, or a subcontractor of the contractor, may have a lien for the amount due for such labor, equipment, material, or supplies.[95] Accordingly, in Kansas contractors, subcontractors, and subcontractors and suppliers of subcontractors may obtain a mechanics' lien. On the other hand, suppliers to a sub-subcontractor are not in privity with the owner, contractor, or subcontractor and, therefore, have no lien rights.[96]

---

[88] Davis-Wellcome Mortgage Co. v. Long-Bell Lumber Co., 184 Kan. 202, 207, 336 P.2d 463, 467 (Kan. 1959).

[89] Brohan v. Nafziger, 206 Kan. 58, 61, 476 P.2d 649, 652 (Kan. 1970).

[90] Schwaller Lumber Co. v. Watson, 211 Kan. 141, 143-44, 505 P.2d 640, 643 (Kan. 1973).

[91] Construction Materials, Inc. v. Becker, 8 Kan. App. 2d 394, 397, 659 P.2d 243, 246 (Kan. 1983).

[92] T.M. Deal Lumber Co. v. Vieux, 179 Kan. 760, 765, 298 P.2d 339, 343 (Kan. 1956).

[93] Star Lumber & Supply Co. v. Capital Constr. Co., 238 Kan. 743, 750, 715 P.2d 11, 17 (Kan. 1986).

[94] KAN. STAT. ANN. § 60-1101 (1994).

[95] *Id.* § 60-1103. Kansas law also authorizes mechanics' liens against personal property in favor of those who perform work, make repairs or improvements, or replace, add, or install equipment for the full amount and reasonable value of the services performed, including the reasonable value of all material used in the performance of such services and the reasonable value of all equipment replaced, added, or installed. KAN. STAT. ANN. § 58-201 (1994). Such a lien takes priority over a perfected security interest. Security Benefit Life Ins. Corp. v. Fleming Cos., 21 Kan. App. 2d 833, 908 P.2d 1315 (Kan. Ct. App. 1995).

[96] Wichita Sheet Metal Supply, Inc. v. Dahlstrom & Ferrell Constr. Co., 246 Kan. 557, 564, 792 P.2d 1043, 1048 (Kan. 1990), *rev'g* 14 Kan. App. 2d 111, 783 P.2d 353 (Kan. Ct. App. 1989).

§ 17.11 ARCHITECTURAL AND ENGINEERING SERVICES

The term labor is broad enough to include either mental or physical toil, bodily or intellectual exertion.[97] However, no mechanics' lien will attach for such labor when no visible construction ever takes place.[98] Thus, architectural and engineering services provided by contractors did not constitute lienable labor resulting in an improvement to the property within the meaning of the mechanics' lien statute where the construction never commenced and no visible or physical manifestation of the contractors' work ever appeared on the property.[99] The court expressly left open what it termed the "troublesome issues" of whether a mechanics' lien could attach for off-site architectural and engineering services if construction had been commenced.[100]

§ 17.12 ENVIRONMENTAL REMEDIATION

Hazardous waste removal necessary in the normal course of the owner's business, not done as a part of an overall plan to improve the property, that would not necessarily enhance the value of the property or adapt the property for new or further purposes, but would merely allow the owner's business to continue as before, does not constitute an improvement to the property and, therefore, is not subject to a mechanics' lien.[101] On the other hand, the court left open the possibility that if a claimant performed hazardous waste removal as a part of an overall plan to improve the property, and could show that its work would enhance the value of the property or adapt the property for new or further purposes, it might be entitled to a mechanics' lien.

§ 17.13 WAIVER

The right of a materialman to assert and perfect a mechanics' lien is a statutory privilege that may be lost by the materialman's conduct and neglect.[102] For example, by recovering a personal judgment against the owner without foreclosing its mechanics' lien, a contractor is precluded from later attempting to foreclose the lien.[103] However, to be effective, an agreement to waive a mechanics' lien must be certain in its terms and clearly and unequivocally established.[104]

Furthermore, if no action to foreclose or adjudicate a mechanics' lien is

[97] Mark Twain Kansas City Bank v. Kroh Bros. Dev. Co., 14 Kan. App. 2d 714, 719, 798 P.2d 511, 515 (Kan. Ct. App. 1990).

[98] *Id.*

[99] *Id.*

[100] *Id.*

[101] Haz-Mat Response, Inc. v. Certified Serv. Ltd., 259 Kan. 166, 910 P.2d 839 (Kan. 1996), *rev'g* 21 Kan. App. 2d 56, 896 P.2d 393 (Kan. Ct. App. 1995).

[102] Benner-Williams, Inc. v. Romine, 200 Kan. 483, 485, 437 P.2d 312, 314 (Kan. 1968).

[103] Home State Bank v. P.B. Hoidale Co., 239 Kan. 165, 169, 718 P.2d 292, 295 (Kan. 1986).

[104] Benner-Williams, Inc. v. Romine, 200 Kan. 483, 485, 437 P.2d 312, 314 (Kan. 1968).

brought within one year, the lien expires.[105] Thus, even though a mortgagee files a foreclosure action against real estate within one year of the filing of a mechanics' lien against that same real estate, the mechanics' lienholder will lose its lien unless it takes affirmative steps to foreclose or defend its mechanics' lien within the one-year period, such as by filing an answer or cross-claim asserting its claim against the property owner.[106]

§ 17.14 ELEMENTS RECOVERABLE BY A MECHANICS' LIEN CLAIMANT

A mechanics' lien may be imposed only for labor, equipment, material, or supplies "used or consumed for the improvement of real property."[107] The labor, equipment, material, or supplies must actually be used in the construction and become part of the realty itself;[108] it is not sufficient that they were furnished for or delivered to the site of the particular building.[109] An improvement includes any physical addition made to real property that enhances its value.[110] The mechanics' lien statute expressly allows the recovery of the cost of transporting materials and supplies to the construction site,[111] which includes mileage and travel time.[112]

[A] Prejudgment Interest

Mechanics' lien claimants are entitled to prejudgment interest on the amount due, provided that the amount is liquidated.[113]

[B] Rental Charges

The question whether rental charges for equipment used in the construction[114] and charges for the use of machinery, tools, and equipment retained by the contractor are lienable under Kansas law is not clearly settled. Early case law held that rental charges for equipment were neither labor nor materials.[115] How-

---

[105] KAN. STAT. ANN. § 60-1108 (1994).

[106] Columbia Savings Ass'n, F.A. v. McPheeters, 21 Kan. App. 2d 919, 911 P.2d 187 (Kan. Ct. App. 1996).

[107] KAN. STAT. ANN. § 60-1101 (1994).

[108] Benner-Williams, Inc. v. Romine, 200 Kan. 483, 485, 437 P.2d 312, 314 (Kan. 1968).

[109] Seyb-Tucker Lumber & Implement Co. v. Hartley, 197 Kan. 58, 63, 415 P.2d 217, 221 (Kan. 1966). The reason for this requirement is that property should not be burdened with a lien to secure the price of materials that never entered into its construction or improvement. *Id.*

[110] Mark Twain Kansas City Bank v. Kroh Bros. Dev. Co., 14 Kan. App. 2d 714, 719, 798 P.2d 511, 516 (Kan. Ct. App. 1990).

[111] KAN. STAT. ANN. § 60-1101 (1994).

[112] Geis Irrigation Co. v. Satanta Feed Yards, Inc., 214 Kan. 373, 378, 521 P.2d 272, 276-77 (Kan. 1974).

[113] J. Walters Constr. Co. v. Greystone South Partnership, Ltd. Partnership, 15 Kan. App. 2d 689, 700, 817 P.2d 201, 209-10 (Kan. Ct. App. 1991).

[114] Wilkinson v. Pacific Mid-West Oil Co., 152 Kan. 712, 714, 107 P.2d 726, 727 (Kan. 1940).

[115] *Id.;* Bridgeport Mach. Co. v. McKnab, 136 Kan. 781, 786, 18 P.2d 186, 188 (Kan. 1933).

ever, at that time the statute did not include "equipment" as one of the items which were lienable.

A federal district court in a case involving the closely analogous public works payment bond statute concluded that the costs of equipment rental, so long as it was actually incurred during performance and not for idle equipment would be recoverable.[116] Given the addition of "equipment" to the list of lienable items, it is likely that equipment rental for equipment actually used in the construction project will be recoverable.

[C] Labor

The mechanics' lien statute allows a lien to be imposed for "labor" furnished. As mentioned above, the term labor may include either mental or physical toil, bodily or intellectual exertion.[117] However, a mechanics' lien may attach for an improvement, even where it is not visible, although in most instances it will be.[118]

Under Kansas law, a mechanics' lien claimant is entitled to include in its lien claim the actual cost of items supplied under its contract along with a reasonable profit.[119] In addition, mechanics' lien claimants are entitled to prejudgment interest on the amount due, provided that the amount is liquidated.[120]

§ 17.15 ELEMENTS NOT RECOVERABLE BY A MECHANICS' LIEN CLAIMANT

Profits that would have been earned if the claimant had been allowed to complete its contract are not recoverable.[121]

§ 17.16 ISSUES RELATING TO THE FORM OF A MECHANICS' LIEN STATEMENT

[A] Verification

The mechanics' lien statement filed with the clerk of the district court must be "verified" i.e., contain a declaration that it is true made by a person under oath or affirmation.[122] Effective July 1, 1990, mechanics' liens need only be signed under penalty of perjury under the laws of the state of Kansas.[123]

[116] Blinne Contracting Co. v. Bobby Goins Enters., Inc., 715 F. Supp. 1044, 1046 n.1 (D. Kan. 1989).

[117] Mark Twain Kansas City Bank v. Kroh Bros. Dev. Co., 14 Kan. App. 2d 714, 719, 798 P.2d 511, 515 (Kan. Ct. App. 1990).

[118] Haz-Mat Response, Inc. v. Certified Waste Serv. Ltd., 259 Kan. 166, 910 P.2d 839 (Kan. 1996).

[119] Elder Mercantile Co. v. Ottawa Inv. Co., 100 Kan. 597, 607-08, 165 P. 279, 283 (Kan. 1917).

[120] J. Walters Constr. Co. v. Greystone South Partnership, Ltd. Partnership, 15 Kan. App. 2d 689, 700, 817 P.2d 201, 209-10 (Kan. Ct. App. 1991).

[121] *Id.*

[122] Kan. Stat. Ann. § 53-502(c) (1994).

[123] *Id.* § 53-601.

A mechanics' lien claimant should take great care to comply with the requirement of verification because a defective verification of a mechanics' lien statement may invalidate the lien.[124] For example, if the claimant is a corporation but the verification does not show that the signer is an agent of the corporation, the verification is improper.[125] A verification that does not verify the truth of the statement but only acknowledges the signing of the statement is insufficient.[126] Finally, a verification that is qualified will not pass muster.[127]

[B] Itemization

A mechanics' lien claimant must file a reasonably itemized statement and the amount of the claim.[128] If the amount of the lien is evidenced by a written instrument or if a promissory note has been given, a copy of the instrument or note may be attached in lieu of the itemized statement.[129] The statement must be sufficiently itemized to inform the landowner of the claim and allow the landowner to ascertain whether the work was completed and whether the amount charged is fair.[130]

[C] Description of Claimant

A mechanics' lien statement must show the name and address of the claimant sufficient for service of process of the claimant.[131] Generally, this requirement should present less opportunity for blunders than some of the other provisions of the statute. However, a claimant that does business under a trade name should refer to itself by its actual name rather than its trade name in the mechanics' lien statement.[132] Because the address of the claimant should be sufficient for service of process on the claimant, the address shown should be a street address rather than merely a post office box.

[D] Description of Real Property

A mechanics' lien statement must show a description of the real property against which the lien is claimed.[133] A legal description is best and may generally

---

[124] Lewis v. Wanamaker Baptist Church, 10 Kan. App. 2d 99, 692 P.2d 397 (Kan. Ct. App. 1984).

[125] Ekstrom United Supply Co. v. Ash Grove Lime & Portland Cement Co., 194 Kan. 634, 636, 400 P.2d 707, 709-10 (Kan. 1965).

[126] D.J. Fair Lumber Co. v. Karlin, 199 Kan. 366, 369-70 (Kan. 1967).

[127] DaMac Drilling, Inc. v. Shoemake, 11 Kan. App. 2d 38, 42, 713 P.2d 480, 484 (Kan. Ct. App. 1986).

[128] KAN. STAT. ANN. § 60-1102(a) (1994).

[129] *Id.*

[130] Kopp's Rug Co., Inc. v. Talbot, 5 Kan. App. 2d 565, 571, 620 P.2d 1157, 1172 (Kan. Ct. App. 1980).

[131] KAN. STAT. ANN. § 60-1102(a) (1994).

[132] M & B Investment, Inc. v. Smith, 9 Kan. App. 2d 31, 34, 670 P.2d 534, 535-36 (Kan. Ct. App. 1983).

[133] KAN. STAT. ANN. § 60-1102(a) (1994).

be obtained by consulting a title company. However, so long as the description is sufficient to enable a person familiar with the locality to identify the premises with certainty, to the exclusion of others, it will be adequate.[134] A description of the property as "[O]ne barn and the surrounding tract of land belonging to Mr. and Mrs. L. E. Due of Rural Route 1, Centerville, Kansas," was inadequate.[135]

Keep in mind that the amount of property the mechanics' lien statement claims a lien against is not necessarily determinative of how much property is covered.[136] Also, even though the claimant only supplied labor or material on a portion of the property, the lien will attach to all of the property, at least where it is contiguous and not separated by roadways or in any other manner.[137]

[E] Description of Owner

A mechanics' lien statement must show the name of the owner of the property.[138] Several wrinkles in regard to the naming of the owner can occur that bear noting. First, the identity of the owner may change between the time the subcontractor or supplier entered into contract and the time the lien statement will be filed. This sometimes happens when a developer builds a house on land he owns and then sells it. Under these circumstances, a claimant who entered into a contract with the original owner may be able to file a lien statement either as an original contractor, naming the original holder of title as owner, or as a subcontractor, naming as owners both the original owner and the subsequent owners and naming the original owner and the construction company as contractor.[139]

Second, owners who own less than the entire interest in the real estate may nevertheless enter into contracts for improvements of the property that can lead to the filing of a mechanics' lien.[140] Thus, the interest of the owner of an equitable title to the land in question may be subject to a mechanics' lien.

For example, when a contractor agrees to purchase a lot, construct a house on the lot and convey title to the property to a home buyer, the home buyer has an equitable interest in the property even prior to conveyance of the property to him, and when the home buyer receives fee simple title, any mechanics' liens that have been filed attach to the full extent of the home buyer's ownership.[141]

---

[134] Sutherland Lumber Co. v. Due, 212 Kan. 658, 660, 512 P.2d 525, 527-529 (Kan. 1973).

[135] *Id.*

[136] Golden Belt Lumber Co. v. McLean, 138 Kan. 351, 26 P.2d 274 (Kan. 1933).

[137] Confinement Specialists, Inc. v. Schlatter, 6 Kan. App. 2d 1, 626 P.2d 223 (Kan. Ct. App. 1981), *rev. denied,* 229 Kan. 669 (Kan. 1981).

[138] KAN. STAT. ANN. § 60-1102(a) (1994).

[139] Star Lumber & Supply Co. v. Capital Constr. Co., 238 Kan. 743, 750, 715 P.2d 11, 17 (Kan. 1986). *But see* KAN. STAT. ANN. § 60-1103 (1994), with respect to claimants whose contract is with an "owner contractor."

[140] Schwaller Lumber Co. v. Watson, 211 Kan. 141, 146, 505 P.2d 640, 645 (Kan. 1973) (mechanics' lien may be enforced against interest of one joint tenant even though interest of other joint tenant not subject to lien).

[141] Toler v. Satterthwaite, 200 Kan. 103, 110-111, 434 P.2d 814, 820 (Kan. 1967).

However, when a mechanics' lien arises under a contract with a tenant, it will ordinarily attach only to the leasehold.[142]

[F] Original Contractor

A mechanics' lien statement of a supplier, subcontractor or other person furnishing labor, equipment, material or supplies used or consumed at the site of the property subject to the lien must state the name of the original contractor.[143]

[G] Subcontractor, Supplier, Etc.

A mechanics' lien statement of a supplier, subcontractor or other person should include the name of the party claiming the mechanics' lien. Just as is true in regard to claims of original contractors, the claimant should take care to list its actual name as the name of the claimant, even though it uses a trade name.[144]

§ 17.17 AMENDMENT OF A MECHANICS' LIEN STATEMENT

A mechanics' lien claimant may amend his or her lien statement by obtaining leave of court.[145] However, any amendment may not increase the amount claimed.[146]

§ 17.18 ASSIGNMENT OF A MECHANICS' LIEN

A mechanics' lien may be assigned, subject to any defenses that might have been made if there had been no assignment.[147]

§ 17.19 PROCEDURAL ISSUES

[A] Notice Requirements

[1] Original Contractor

A mechanics' lien claimant who has a contract with the owner of real property or with the trustee, agent, or spouse of the owner, must file with the

[142] Lentz Plumbing Co. v. Fee, 235 Kan. 266, 274, 679 P.2d 736, 744 (1984). An exception to this rule exists when the lease allows the lessee to make improvements to the property and deduct its expenses for the improvements from rental payments, in which case the lessee may be regarded as the agent of the lessor. *Id.* at 272-73, 679 P.2d at 743. Kansas City Heartland Constr. Co. v. Maggie Jones Southport Cafe, Inc., 250 Kan. 32, 35, 824 P.2d 926, 929 (1992). Implied agency may arise from manifestations between the principal and the agent, not the appearance to a third party or what the third party should have known. *Id.* at 41, 824 P.2d at 930. Agency will not be inferred because a third party assumed it existed. *Id.*

[143] KAN. STAT. ANN. § 60-1103(a)(1) (1994).

[144] M & B Inv., Inc. v. Smith, 9 Kan. App. 2d 31, 34, 670 P.2d 534, 535-36 (Kan. Ct. App. 1983).

[145] KAN. STAT. ANN. § 60-1105(b) (1994).

[146] *Id.*

[147] *Id.* § 60-1104.

clerk of the district court of the county in which the real estate is located within four months of the date material, equipment, or supplies were last used or consumed or labor was last performed, a verified[148] statement showing the names of the owner and claimant, a description of the real property, and a reasonably itemized statement and the amount of the claim.[149] If the amount of the lien is evidenced by a written instrument or if a promissory note has been given, a copy of the instrument or note may be attached in lieu of the itemized statement.[150]

[2] Subcontractor, Supplier, Etc.

A supplier, subcontractor, or other person supplying labor, equipment, material, or supplies used or consumed at the site of the property subject to the lien under an agreement with the contractor, subcontractor, or owner contractor may obtain a lien by filing a verified lien statement with the clerk of the district court of the county in which the real estate is located within three months of the date material, equipment, or supplies were last used or consumed or labor was last performed.[151]

The verified lien statement must also state the name of the contractor and include (1) an attached affidavit of the supplier or subcontractor that a warning statement was properly given[152] and (2) a notice of intent to perform must have been filed.[153] The statute defines an owner contractor as one who owns fee title to the real estate subject to the lien and enters into contracts with more than one person, firm, or corporation for labor, equipment, material, or supplies used or consumed for the improvement of the real property.[154]

A supplier, subcontractor, or other person supplying labor, equipment, material, or supplies used or consumed at the site of the property subject to the lien under an agreement with the contractor, subcontractor, or owner contractor must (1) cause a copy of the lien statement to be served personally upon any one owner and any party obligated to pay the lien in the manner required for service of a summons,[155] (2) mail a copy of the lien statement to any one owner and any party obligated to pay the lien by restricted mail, or (3) if the address of any one owner or any party obligated to pay the lien is unknown and cannot be ascertained with reasonable diligence, post a copy of the lien statement in a conspicuous place on the premises.[156]

When any claimant who has filed a notice of intent to perform has been paid

---

[148] Effective July 1, 1990, mechanics' liens need only be signed under penalty of perjury under the laws of the state of Kansas. KAN. STAT. ANN. § 53-601 (1994).

[149] *Id.* § 60-1102(a).

[150] *Id.*

[151] *Id.* § 60-1103(a).

[152] If required by KAN. STAT. ANN. § 60-1103a.

[153] If required by KAN. STAT. ANN. § 60-1103b (Supp. 1998).

[154] KAN. STAT. ANN. § 60-1103 (1994).

[155] *See id.* §§ 60-304 and -308.

[156] *Id.* § 60-1103(c).

in full, the claimant must execute and file a release of that notice and waiver of lien in a form substantially similar to a statutorily prescribed form in the same office in which the claimant filed the notice of intent to perform and pay any required filing fee. The form must identify the property as set forth in the notice of intent to perform and state that the claimant intends to waive or relinquish any statutory right to a lien.

The filing of a release of notice of intent to perform and waiver of lien makes the notice of intent to perform of no further effect and extinguishes the claimant's right to a lien.[157] An owner of real estate on which a notice of intent to perform was filed, the owner's heirs, or one acting for the owner or the owner's heirs may make demand upon the claimant after payment in full to the claimant for the filing of a release of notice of intent to perform and waiver of lien. In any event, the effectiveness of a notice of intent to perform expires 18 months from the date of its filing unless within that time the claimant has filed a mechanics' lien.

The owner of the property that is subject to the mechanics' lien claim will not be liable for anything more than it has agreed to pay the original contractor, except for payments to the contractor made (1) before the expiration of the three-month period for filing lien claims, if no warning statement is required, or (2) subsequent to the date the owner received the warning statement, if one was required. If the owner discharges any lien that the contractor fails to discharge, that payment may be credited against the amount due the contractor.[158]

A subcontractor or supplier who has a claim that exceeds $250[159] for the improvement of residential property must (1) mail to any one of the owners of the property a warning statement,[160] or (2) have in its possession a copy of a statement signed by any one owner of the property stating that the general contractor or claimant had given the warning statement to one of the owners of the property.[161] The statute contains a specific definition of the phrase "improvement of residential property."[162]

---

[157] *Id.* § 60-1103b (Supp. 1998).

[158] *Id.* § 60-1103(d) (1994).

[159] *Id.* § 60-1103a(d).

[160] Under KAN. STAT. ANN. § 60-1103a(c), the warning statement must contain substantially the following statement in order to be effective: Notice to owner: (name of supplier or subcontractor) is a supplier or subcontractor providing materials or labor on Job No. _______ at (residence address) under an agreement with (name of contractor). Kansas law will allow this supplier or subcontractor to file a lien against your property for materials or labor not paid for by your contractor unless you have a waiver of lien signed by this supplier or subcontractor. If you receive a notice of filing of a lien statement by this supplier or subcontractor, you may withhold from your contractor the amount claimed until the dispute is settled.

[161] *Id.* § 60-1103a(b) (1994).

[162] KAN. STAT. ANN. § 60-1103a(a) (1994) defines *improvement of residential property* as "(1) improvement of a preexisting structure in which the owner resides at the time the claimant first furnishes labor, equipment, materials, or supplies and which is not used or intended for use as a residence for more than two families or for commercial purposes or improvement or construction

A subcontractor or supplier may obtain a mechanics' lien upon "new residential property"[163] after the passage of title to a good-faith purchaser for value only if it filed a "notice of intent to perform"[164] with the clerk of the district court of the county where the property is located before the recording of the deed effecting passage of title to the new residential property.

[B] Where to File

A mechanics' lien claimant must file its mechanics' lien statement with the clerk of the district court of the county in which the real estate is located.[165]

[C] When to File

An original contractor must file a mechanics' lien statement within four months of the date material, equipment, or supplies were last used or consumed or labor was last performed.[166] A supplier, subcontractor or other person furnishing labor, equipment, material or supplies used or consumed at the site of the property subject to the lien, must file a mechanics' lien statement within three months of the date material, equipment, or supplies were last used or consumed or labor was last performed.[167]

---

of any addition, garage, fence, swimming pool, outbuilding, or other improvement appurtenant to such a structure; or (2) any construction upon real property which is (A) owned or acquired by an individual at the time the claimant first furnishes labor, equipment, materials or supplies; (B) intended to become and does become the principal personal residence of that individual upon completion; and (C) not used or intended for use as a residence for more than two families or for commercial purposes."

[163] KAN. STAT. ANN. § 60-1103b(a) defines *new residential property* as a new structure that is constructed for use as a residence and that is not used or intended for use as a residence for more than two families or for commercial purposes. "New residential property" does not include any improvement of a preexisting structure or construction of any addition, garage, or outbuilding appurtenant to a preexisting structure.

[164] Under KAN. STAT. ANN. § 60-1103b(c), the "notice to perform" must contain substantially the following statement in order to be effective:

NOTICE OF INTENT TO PERFORM

I ______________________________ of (name of supplier, subcontractor, or contractor) ______________________________ (address of supplier, subcontractor, or contractor) ______________________________ do hereby give notice that I am a supplier, subcontractor, or contractor or other person providing materials or labor on property owned by ______________________________ (name of property owner) and having the legal description as follows:

____

____

______________________________.

[165] KAN. STAT. ANN. § 60-1102(a) (1994).

[166] *Id.* § 60-1102(a).

[167] *Id.* § 60-1103(a).

Minor work necessary in good faith to complete a project may extend the time for filing a mechanics' lien statement.[168] However, isolated orders for materials may not be enough to give a claimant additional time to file.[169]

When a supplier furnishes material to a contractor that later delivers those materials to the job site, the time for filing the supplier's mechanics' lien begins to run on the last day the supplier furnishes the materials; later delivery by the contractor to the job site does not enlarge the time allowed, even though the supplier will not have a valid lien unless the material is used or consumed at the site of the property subject to the lien.[170]

The test as to when work has been completed so as to start the running of the time for filing the lien statement is whether any later-performed work was a part of the work necessary to be performed under the terms of the original contract to complete the job and comply in good faith with the requirements of the contract.[171] A subsequent gratuitous furnishing of material in the nature of a substitution or replacement to remedy a defect in the material originally delivered will not extend the time within which to file the lien statement.[172] The trial court must examine all facts surrounding the question of whether a lien was timely filed, and is not required to accept a contractor's statements concerning the last work date if they are contradicted by the evidence.[173]

§ 17.20 FORECLOSURE OF A MECHANICS' LIEN

[A] Time Limit for Filing Suit

An action to foreclose a mechanics' lien must be brought within one year from the filing of the lien statement or one year from the maturity date of a promissory note attached to the lien statement in lieu of an itemized statement.[174]

[B] Where Suit Must be Filed

Suits to enforce mechanics' lien should be brought in the district court of the county in which the property is located.[175]

---

[168] Benner-Williams, Inc. v. Romine, 200 Kan. 483, 485, 437 P.2d 312, 314 (Kan. 1968).

[169] Star Lumber & Supply Co. v. Mills, 186 Kan. 204, 208, 349 P.2d 892, 896 (Kan. 1960).

[170] Bethlehem Steel Corp. v. National Cooperative Refinery Ass'n, 19 Kan. App. 2d 330, 332–33, 871 P.2d 1282, 1284–85 (Kan. Ct. App. 1994).

[171] Manhattan Mall Co. v. Shult, 254 Kan. 257, 864 P.2d 1136, 1141 (Kan. 1993).

[172] *Id.*

[173] *Id.*

[174] KAN. STAT. ANN. § 60-1105(a) (1994).

[175] *Id.* § 60-1102(a).

§ 17.21 PRIORITY ISSUES

A mechanics' lien has priority over all other liens and encumbrances that are subsequent to the commencement of the furnishing of labor, equipment, material, or supplies at the site of the property subject to the lien.[176] A claimant's mechanics' lien relates back to the first date of any work on the premises by the holder of any unsatisfied lien, regardless of who performed that work.[177]

Subcontractor's mechanics' liens attach at the time the general contractor began work or construction; accordingly, their priority relates back to that date.[178] A purchase money mortgage loses its priority to a mechanics' lien that attaches after execution of the mortgage but before the mortgage is recorded, when the mechanics' lienholder has no actual notice of the prior mortgage.[179]

§ 17.22 SPECIAL RULES WHEN MORE THAN ONE MECHANICS' LIEN OR CLAIM ASSERTED

In cases in which more than one lien has been filed against the property or there are other encumbrances against it, Kansas statutes provide special rules to deal with those situations. First, the statute requires that in an action to foreclose a mechanics' lien, all persons who have filed mechanics' liens, and any other persons who have encumbrances of record, should be joined as parties.[180] Second, if the building or other improvement is still under construction, the judge, on application of any party engaged in furnishing labor or materials for such building or improvement, may stay the trial of a pending action to foreclose a mechanics' lien on the property for a reasonable time to permit the filing of a mechanics' lien statement by that party.[181] Finally, if the proceeds of the mechanics' lien foreclosure sale are insufficient to pay all the claimants, then the court shall order them to be paid in proportion to the amount due each.[182]

§ 17.23 REMEDIES OF OWNERS

Kansas law provides an owner with several rights designed to protect the owner from mechanics' liens. First, an owner may require the contractor to file a

---

[176] *Id.* § 60-1101. However, under KAN. STAT. ANN. § 58-2336 (1994), a mechanics' lien may have priority over a mortgage securing future advances that was recorded prior to the commencement of the furnishing of labor, equipment, material, or supplies, to the extent such advances exceed the maximum amount stated in the mortgage. Old Colony Ventures v. SMWNPF Holdings, Inc., 924 F. Supp. 1076 (D. Kan. 1996).

[177] *Id.*

[178] J. Walters Constr. Co. v. Greystone South Partnership, Ltd. Partnership, 15 Kan. App. 2d 689, 701–04, 817 P.2d 201, 210-12 (Kan. Ct. App. 1991).

[179] Shade v. Wheatcraft Indus., Inc., 248 Kan. 531, 537, 809 P.2d 538, 543 (Kan. 1991).

[180] KAN. STAT. ANN. § 60-1106 (1994).

[181] *Id.* § 60-1107.

[182] *Id.* § 60-1109.

payment bond for at least the contract price with the clerk of the district court (presumably in the county in which the project is located).[183] Upon approval of the bond, lien claims do not attach to the real estate, and the claimant's sole remedy is against the bond.[184]

Second, if the owner does not require the contractor to file a payment bond, the owner has additional rights to protect against mechanics' liens. Where such an action is brought by a subcontractor, or person other than the original contractor, the plaintiff must join the original contractor as a party defendant, and the original contractor is required to defend against the claim of every subcontractor, or other person claiming a mechanics' lien at his or her own expense.[185] If the original contractor fails to defend against those claims, the owner may defend against them at the expense of the original contractor.[186]

Until all mechanics' lien claims, costs and expenses are finally adjudicated, and defeated or satisfied, the owner may retain from the original contractor the amount of all mechanics' lien claims, costs and expenses that the original contractor may be required to pay.[187] If the sheriff of the county in which the action to foreclose a mechanics' lien is pending cannot make service of process on the original contractor, the court may proceed to adjudicate the liens upon the land and render judgment to enforce them with costs.[188]

Third, if any mechanics' lien or liens are filed but no action to foreclose any of such liens is commenced, the owner of the land may file a petition in the district court of the county in which the land is situated, naming the lien claimants as defendants, and asking for an adjudication of those liens.[189] If any lien claimant fails to establish its mechanics' lien, the court may tax against that claimant all or any portion of the costs of the action as is just.[190] If no action to foreclose or adjudicate any mechanics' lien is filed within one year from the time of filing the lien statement, or one year from the maturity date of a promissory note attached to the lien statement in lieu of an itemized statement, the lien is considered canceled.[191]

Finally, an owner may further protect itself by various contractual provisions, such as those requiring the general contractor to furnish it with satisfactory evidence that the general contractor has fully paid the claims of subcontractors, suppliers, and materialmen before the owner has any duty to disburse funds to the general contractor.

---

[183] *Id.* § 60-1110.

[184] *Id.*

[185] *Id.*

[186] *Id.*

[187] *Id.*

[188] *Id*

[189] *Id.* § 60-1108.

[190] *Id.*

[191] *Id.*

§ 17.24 CLAIM AGAINST OWNER BY ONE NOT IN PRIVITY WITH OWNER

Generally, a subcontractor or materialman may not obtain a personal judgment against the owner of real estate whose property has benefited from the labor or materials supplied, on the basis of quasi-contract or unjust enrichment, in the absence of privity of contract with the owner or a direct promise to pay by the owner.[192] However, a subcontractor may recover against an owner on a claim for unjust enrichment, even though it lacks privity with the owner, when special circumstances exist.

An essential prerequisite to recovery is the owner's acceptance of the benefits rendered under circumstances reasonably notifying the owner that the subcontractor expects to be compensated for those services by the owner. In the absence of evidence that the owner misled the contractor to its detriment, that the owner in some way induced the subcontractor to change its position to its detriment, or that the owner committed a fraud on the subcontractor, an action for unjust enrichment will not lie.[193]

---

[192] Holiday Dev. Co. v. J.A. Tobin Constr. Co., 219 Kan. 701, 708–09, 549 P.2d 1376, 1383 (Kan. 1976).

[193] Haz-Mat Response, Inc. v. Certified Waste Serv. Ltd., 259 Kan. 166, 910 P.2d 839 (Kan. 1996), *rev'g* 21 Kan. App. 2d 56, 896 P.2d 393 (Kan. Ct. App. 1995).

Chapter 18

KENTUCKY

Buckner Hinkle, Jr.[1]

[1] This chapter is adapted from the First Edition chapter written by James W. Smirz, who is the founding partner of Smirz & Tolver, P.L.C., a Lexington, Kentucky law firm.

§ 18.01 INTRODUCTION

Kentucky law grants certain mechanics' lien rights to any person who performs labor or who furnishes material on public and private projects.

Kentucky requires that the successful bidder on public projects in excess of $25,000 furnish both performance and payment bonds. The performance bond must be for 100 percent of the contract price as it may be increased. The payment bond must be in the full amount of the original contract price and at a minimum must provide coverage for the protection of all persons furnishing labor or materials to the contractor or its subcontractors.

Two principal statutes govern bonds and mechanics' liens. The principal Kentucky statute governing bonds is known as the Kentucky Model Procurement Code, Kentucky Revised Statutes Annotated §§ 45A.005 *et seq.,* and is further amplified at 200 Kentucky Administrative Regulations 5:020–5:317 (bond law). The principal Kentucky mechanics' lien law for both public and private work is found at Title XXXI, "Debtor-Creditor Relations," Kentucky Revised Statutes Annotated §§ 376.010 *et seq.* (statutory liens).

§ 18.02 BOND LAW

[A] General Concepts

Kentucky treats the contract surety bond relationship as a tripartite relationship and treats bonds as tripartite contracts. Each contract surety bond has an obligee, which is typically an owner or a general contractor, and joint and several obligors, which are typically the general contractor or subcontractor and its surety. A definition appears in the Kentucky Administrative Regulations,[2] in which it is required that the Commonwealth shall be the obligee, the contractor shall be the principal, and the surety shall perform the contract.[3] Surety contracts in Kentucky must be in writing and signed by the surety.[4]

The Kentucky Model Procurement Code provides that the principles of law and equity, including the Uniform Commercial Code (UCC), the law merchant, and law relative to the capacity to contract, and the law of agency, fraud, misrepresentation, duress, coercion, mistake, and bankruptcy shall supplement its provision.[5] Regarding jurisdiction and venue, Kentucky generally looks to the law

---

[2] 200 Ky. Admin. Regs. 5:305, § 1(1) (1979) (amended 1992).

[3] *Id.*

[4] The relevant Kentucky statute of frauds is found at Ky. Rev. Stat. Ann. § 371.010(4) (Baldwin 1950) (amended 1990), which provides in pertinent part as follows:

> No action shall be brought to charge any person: . . . (4) upon any promise to answer for the debt, default or misdoing of another unless the promise, contract, agreement, representation, assurance or ratification, or some memorandum or note, be in writing, and signed by the party to be charged therewith, or by his authorized agent.

[5] *Id.* § 45A.015(1).

of the place with the most significant relationship to the parties and the transaction on each issue.[6] In Kentucky the construction and interpretation of a surety contract is for the court,[7] and the goal of any such construction and interpretation is to ascertain the intent of the contracting parties from all the words and clauses taken as a whole in connection with the relevant surrounding circumstances.[8]

The rule of *strictissimi juris* (strict interpretation) does not apply to a surety for compensation, but such a surety is entitled to have its contract interpreted by ordinary rules of law, and its liability cannot be enlarged beyond the scope of the contract.[9] Kentucky courts have construed the compensated surety contract strongly against a surety and in favor of the obligees or beneficiaries under the bond.[10] A surety is liable when the principal is liable, [11] and the surety's liability cannot be greater than that of its (contractor) principal.[12] If an obligee has materially breached the underlying contract, thus excusing the contractor's further performance, the surety may well not have any liability.

[B] Bid Bonds

Kentucky requires bidders to furnish a five-percent bid bond on competitive sealed bidding for public or private projects with an estimated cost exceeding $25,000. No bid bond is required for private construction. The bid bond must guarantee the public owner that the bidder will enter into the contract upon which it bids. The bid bond must be for a penal sum equal to at least five percent of the bid amount payable if the contractor refuses actually to enter into the contract after an award is made or refuses to deliver the required performance and payment bonds after an award is made.[13]

The successful bidder must be the responsive and responsible bidder whose bid offers the best value.[14] A bidder may be allowed to withdraw its bid under the Kentucky statute before award; then both the contractor and its bid bond surety

---

[6] T.C. Young Constr. Co. v. Hartford Accident & Indem. Co., 441 S.W.2d 781 (Ky. 1969).

[7] Standard Oil Co. of N.J. v. National Sur. Co., 234 Ky. 764, 29 S.W.2d 29 (Ky. 1930); Union Indem. Co. v. Pennsylvania Boiler Works, 246 Ky. 473, 55 S.W.2d 367 (Ky. 1933).

[8] Standard Oil Co. of N.J. v. National Sur. Co., 29 S.W.2d 29 (Ky. 1930); Union Indem. Co. v. Pennsylvania Boiler Works, 55 S.W.2d 367 (Ky. 1933).

[9] American Bonding Co. v. Anderson, 20 F. Supp. 217 (W.D. Ky. 1937), *rev'd,* 110 F.2d 961 (6th Cir. 1940); American Radiator & Standard Sanitary Corp. v. Albany Mun. Hous. Corp., 441 S.W.2d 433 (Ky. 1969); Kentucky Rock Asphalt Co. v. Fidelity & Cas. Co., 37 F.2d 279 (6th Cir. 1930); Commissioners of Sinking Fund v. Anderson, 20 F. Supp. 217 (W.D. Ky. 1937), *aff'd,* 110 F.2d 961 (6th Cir.), *cert. denied,* 311 U.S. 669 (1940).

[10] American Radiator & Standard Sanitary Corp. v. Albany Mun. Hous. Corp., 441 S.W.2d 433 (Ky. 1969).

[11] United States Fidelity & Guar. Co. v. Travelers' Ins. Mach. Co., 167 Ky. 382, 180 S.W. 815, *reh'g denied,* 183 S.W. 482 (Ky. 1915).

[12] Calhoun v. City of Paducah, 6 Ky. Op. 482 (1872).

[13] KY. REV. STAT. ANN. §§ 45A.185 (1), (2), (3) (Baldwin 1979).

[14] *Id.* § 45A.080(5) (amended effective July 15, 1998).

may be able to avoid liability.[15] If a bidder's bid is not responsive because it does not provide a bid bond, the bid is required to be rejected; however, the secretary of the cabinet may establish regulations (Kentucky Administrative Regulations) providing for exceptions to this requirement, if there has been substantial compliance.[16]

After opening of bids, but before award, a bidder who has made a unilateral mistake through inadvertence may be allowed to withdraw its bid and bid bond.[17] When the low bidder provided a five-percent bond to the public owner when the bid invitation called for a ten-percent bid bond, which was corrected after opening of bids, the owner's waiver of the flaw did not give the second low bidder a cause of action against either the owner or the low bidder.[18]

Terms such as "evaluated," "responsive," "responsible" and "best value" are defined in the Model Procurement Code.[19]

[C] Performance Bonds

Performance bonds on private projects are not statutorily required. However, the bond law requires that on public projects in excess of $25,000, the contractor shall furnish a performance bond in an amount equal to 100 percent of the contract as it may be increased.[20] This requirement applies to all expenditures of "public funds by the Commonwealth[21] under any contract or like business agreement." The applicable definition of public funds expended by the Commonwealth includes any "governmental body," which also includes any board, bureau, commission, department, agency, institution, department, council, legislative body, government corporation, or other establishment of the executive or legislative branch of the state government.[22]

Bonds designated as performance bonds for public projects may actually be combination performance and labor and material payment bonds,[23] although

---

[15] *Id.* § 45A.185(6). The amendment was effective July 15, 1994.

[16] *Id.* § 45A.185(3).

[17] Board of Educ. v. Hooper, 350 S.W.2d 629 (Ky. 1961). *See also* Harry Harris, Inc. v. Quality Constr. Co., 593 S.W.2d 872, 874 (Ky. Ct. App. 1979) (discretionary review denied), in which a subcontractor was not allowed to withdraw an erroneous bid after it was included in the general's bid accepted by the owner.

[18] Shannon J. Holloway Constr. v. Louisville & Jefferson County Metro. Sewer Dist., 674 S.W.2d 523 (Ky. 1983).

[19] Ky. Rev. Stat. Ann. §§ 45A.070 (3), (6), (7) (Baldwin amended 1990).

[20] Ky. Rev. Stat. Ann. §§ 45A.190(1)(a), (2). 200 Ky. Admin. Regs. 5:30, § 1(2) requires a bond on contracts less than $25,000 when the requirement is contained in the bid invitation per Ky. Rev. Stat. § 45A.080 or an advertisement and solicitations for proposals for competitive negotiations pursuant to Ky. Rev. Stat. §§ 45A.085 and 45A.090.

[21] Ky. Rev. Stat. § 45A.020.

[22] *Id.* § 45A.030(11) (amended 1982).

[23] United States Fidelity & Guar. Co. v. Miller, 549 S.W.2d 316 (Ky. Ct. App. 1977); Henry A. Peter Supply Co. v. Hal Perry Constr. Co., 563 S.W.2d 749 (Ky. Ct. App. 1978).

Kentucky jurisprudence distinguishes between a performance bond and a labor and material payment bond.[24] The Kentucky Administrative Regulations only require that the bond name the Commonwealth of Kentucky as the obligee, when required by the terms of the bid invitation.[25] The regulations would seem to permit a single performance and payment bond for 100 percent of the contract price as it may be increased.[26] These regulations apparently contravene the statutory mandate requiring separate performance and payment bonds.[27]

The limitation period for actions on a contract bond is the same as the limitation period for contracts, that is, 15 years after the accrual of the cause of action.[28] The Kentucky courts will recognize and enforce a shorter contractual limitation period when such is not prohibited by statute.[29] Contractual limitations longer than that prescribed by the statute may not be enforced.[30]

[D] Payment Bonds

Kentucky law does not require payment bonds for private sector projects.

Kentucky's Model Procurement Code requires contractors to furnish a payment bond in an amount equal to 100 percent of the original contract price for public projects in excess of $25,000.[31] The Federal Miller Act[32] case law has been used by analogy by the Kentucky courts in interpreting the bond statute when the case is one of first impression.[33] The bond statute requires that, at a minimum, the payment bond afford coverage to two tiers, in other words, claimants supplying materials to the prime contractor to whom the contract was awarded, or to any of its subcontractors providing labor.[34]

The Kentucky Administrative Regulations expressly include labor, material, equipment, taxes, supplies, or other proper expenses incurred or to be incurred in the performance of the contract as payment bond obligation.[35] The surety's liability is measured by the terms of its contract.[36]

---

[24] Standard Accident Ins. Co. v. Rose, 234 S.W.2d 728 (Ky. Ct. App. 1950).

[25] 200 Ky. Admin. Regs. 5:305, § 2 (1979) (amended effective January 10, 1992).

[26] *Id.* § 1(1) (amended effective January 10, 1992).

[27] Ky. Rev. Stat. Ann. §§ 45A.190(1)(a), (b) (Baldwin 1979).

[28] *Id.* § 413.090(2) (amended 1988). *See also* Ky. Rev. Stat. § 413.220 (statute may be seven years if within defined circumstances).

[29] Webb v. Kentucky Farm Bureau Ins. Co., 577 S.W.2d 17 (Ky. Ct. App. 1978).

[30] Burlew v. Fidelity & Cas. Co., 276 Ky. 132, 122 S.W.2d 990 (Ky. 1938).

[31] Ky. Rev. Stat. Ann. §§ 45A.190(1)(a), (b) (Baldwin 1979).

[32] 40 U.S.C. § 270a (1986), amended Oct. 13, 1994, Pub. L. No. 103-355, Title IV, § 4104(b)(1)(B), 108 Stat. 3342.

[33] Reliance Ins. Co. v. Commonwealth Dep't of Transp., 576 S.W.2d 231, 235 (Ky. Ct. App. 1978).

[34] Ky. Rev. Stat. Ann. § 45A.190(1)(b) (Baldwin 1979) and 200 Ky. Admin. Regs. 5:305, § 1(1) (1979).

[35] 200 Ky. Admin. Regs. 5:305, § 1(1) (1979).

[36] Standard Oil Co. of N.J. v. National Sur. Co., 234 Ky. 764, 29 S.W.2d 29 (Ky. 1930).

A materialman of a materialman who supplies goods to a general contractor is not within the purview of the statute.[37]

Kentucky's bond statute does not address the question of notice. However, notice provisions in contracts and/or bonds will be generally enforced according to their terms. It is imperative that the one asserting a payment bond claim comply with any notice requirements contained in the bond.[38] When a bond does not contain an express notice provision, the surety will not be able to assert the defenses of laches or estoppel. The courts place an affirmative burden on the surety to ascertain the status of the principal's performance.[39]

It is settled Kentucky law that a contractor may not be assessed liquidated damages unless there is a showing of actual damages.[40]

Kentucky courts and the Sixth Circuit have held that insurance premiums are neither labor, materials, nor supplies as such terms are used in the Kentucky statutes providing a lien in favor of persons who furnish labor, materials, or supplies for the construction of a public improvement.[41] The Kentucky courts have further held that "the presence or absence of a right to assert a mechanic's lien can be a guide to the interpretation of a payment bond."[42] Kentucky follows the "American rule" concerning attorneys' fees. Unless they are provided for in the contract, they generally will not be awarded.

[E] Additional Bond Issues

The Insurance Code of Kentucky[43] defines an insurer to include sureties.[44] *Surety insurer* is also defined in the statute.[45] In Kentucky, sureties are covered by the Unfair Claims Settlement Practices Act.[46]

---

[37] Safeco Ins. Co. of Am. v. W.B. Browning Constr. Co., 886 F.2d 807 (6th Cir. 1989).

[38] Wehr Constr. v. Steel Fabricators, 769 S.W.2d 51, 56 (Ky. Ct. App. 1988).

[39] Florida Steel Corp. v. Indiana Lumberman's Mut. Ins. Co., 794 S.W.2d 175 (Ky. Ct. App. 1990) (citing with approval National Union Indem. Co. v. Standard Oil Co., 90 S.W.2d 375 (Ky. Ct. App. 1936)).

[40] Wehr Constr. v. Steel Fabricators, 769 S.W.2d 51, 54 (Ky. Ct. App. 1988) (citing with approval Fidelity & Deposit Co. v. Jones, 256 Ky. 181, 75 S.W.2d 1057 (Ky. 1934)).

[41] *In re* Zaepfel & Russell, Inc., 49 F. Supp. 709 (W.D. Ky. 1941), *aff'd sub nom.* Farmers State Bank v. Jones, 135 F.2d 215 (6th Cir. 1943); Charles E. Channel Co. v. D&D Millwork Co., 288 Ky. 319, 156 S.W.2d 170 (Ky. 1941).

[42] United States Fidelity & Guar. Co. v. Miller, 549 S.W.2d 316, 319 (Ky. Ct. App. 1977).

[43] KY. REV. STAT. ANN. §§ 304.1-010 *et seq.* (Baldwin 1984).

[44] *Id.* § 304.1-040; *see also id.* § 304.21-010.

[45] *Id.* § 304.5-060(2).

[46] *Id.* § 304.12-230; 806 KY. ADMIN. REGS. 12:095 (1993), overruled by Curry v. Fireman's Fund Ins. Co., 784 S.W.2d 176 (Ky. 1989). *See also* Federal Kemper Ins. Co. v. Hornback, 711 S.W.2d 844, 75 Ky. L.J. 539 (1986-7) (first-party bad faith in Kentucky); Curry v. Firemans Fund Ins. Co. 784 S.W.2d 176 (Ky. 1989). *Federal Kemper* was overruled, but Curry v. Firemans Fund Ins. Co. adopted the dissent in *Federal Kemper. See also* First Nat'l Bank v. Lustig, 832 Supp. 1065 (E.D. La. 1993); Whittmer v. Jones, 864 S.W.2d 885 (Ky. 1993); Empire Fire & Marine v.

§ 18.03 LIEN LAW

[A] General Concepts

Mechanics' liens are statutorily created.[47] Generally speaking, the purpose of the lien law is to provide contractors and subcontractors with a security mechanism on private construction projects in Kentucky, providing they have not waived their lien rights and comply with the detailed procedural requirements. A mechanics' lien right is a significant security device because it places a lien against the owner's property for the debt of the owner and operates as an encumbrance on the owner's interest in its property. Because mechanics' lien rights are created entirely by statute, the lien law is strictly enforced, particularly the procedural requirements including the all-important notice requirements. Kentucky also provides a lien for labor, materials, or supplies furnished on a public improvement.[48]

[B] Basic Provisions

The mechanics' lien in private projects benefits

> any person who performs labor or furnishes materials, for the erection, altering or repairing of a house or other structure or for any fixture or machinery therein . . . by contract with or with the written consent of the owner, contractor, subcontractor, architect, or authorized agent with interest as provided in KRS 360.040 and costs.[49]

In Kentucky, every person who performs work (labor) or furnishes material under contract with the owner or has the owner's written consent possesses mechanics' lien rights. The lien law does not define the term *person;* however, it does require a contract or the written consent of the owner.[50] Provision is made for persons who do not contract directly with the owner; however, strict notice provisions must be complied with. These notice provisions vary according to the amount claimed and whether the lien is upon a single or double owner-occupied family dwelling.[51] The private lien law defines *labor.*[52] A licensed architect, landscape architect, engineer or land surveyor who performs professional services or serv-

---

Simpsonville Wrecker, 880 S.W.2d 886 (Ky. 1994); Sculimbrene v. Paul Revere Ins., 925 F. Supp. 505 (E.D. Ky. 1996).

[47] KY. REV. STAT. ANN. § 376.010(1) (Baldwin 1978) (amended 1994).

[48] *Id.* § 376.210.

[49] *Id.* § 376.010(1).

[50] *Id.*

[51] *Id.* §§ 376.010(3), (4).

[52] *Id.* § 376.010(5) (amended 1994). This appears to nullify Dirt & Rock Rentals v. Irwin & Powell Constr. Inc., 838 S.W.2d 412 (Ky. Ct. App. 1992) (holding that KY. REV. STAT. § 376.010(5)

ices as defined in the statute shall have a lien on the building, structure, land, or project where the services were performed.[53]

The lien on property held by an owner under an executory contract shall follow the property to the extent of the actual value of the improvement.[54] If labor is performed by contract for a lessee, and if the lessor refused to pay for the labor, the improvements may be removed, if such can be done without damage to the premises and before the term of the lease expires.[55]

The lien law does not expressly state that its remedy is either sole or exclusive, nor does it alter the duty of a party to pay for an improvement to its property; the remedy established by the lien law is cumulative.[56] When a property owner contracts with a builder to improve property and fails to pay, the property is potentially subject to a mechanics' lien and the owner to a personal judgment.[57] A preexisting obligation is not lienable.[58] The term *authorized agent* embraces an ostensible agent by estoppel.[59] Protection is provided by the lien law to a materialman who provides material to a remote subcontractor, away from the jobsite, as long as the material is ultimately used to improve the property.[60]

Further, a lien will be upheld for profit on a cost-plus contract.[61] However, the right to a mechanics' lien is purely statutory, and unless facts bring the claim reasonably within the statute, no lien exists.[62] A properly perfected lien relates back to the date of first labor or material supplied or furnished and will be superior to a judgment and attachment of a general creditor.[63] When several materialmen and laborers file and perfect liens, they will share equally and are not ranked.[64]

[C] Notice Requirements

The lien law contains various strict notice requirements that are strictly enforced.[65]

---

defines "labor" as including work actually done by machinery, but not including the leasing of machinery to another who performs the work with the machinery).

[53] KY. REV. STAT. ANN. § 376.075 (amended 1998).

[54] *Id.* § 376.020.

[55] *Id.* § 376.040 (Baldwin 1978).

[56] Guaranty Elec. Co. v. Big Rivers Elec. Corp., 669 F. Supp. 1371 (W.D. Ky. 1987).

[57] Dersch v. Miller, 137 Ky. 89, 124 S.W. 362 (Ky. 1909).

[58] Cardinal Kitchens, Inc. v. Home Supply Co., 467 S.W.2d 775 (Ky. 1971).

[59] Ohio Oil Co. v. Smith-Haggard Lumber Co., 156 S.W.2d 111 (Ky. 1981).

[60] Woodsen Bend, Inc. v. Masters' Supply, Inc., 571 S.W.2d 95 (Ky. Ct. App. 1978).

[61] Bond v. W.T. Congleton Co., 278 Ky. 829, 129 S.W.2d 570 (Ky. 1939).

[62] *In re* Louisville Daily News & Enquirer, 20 F. Supp. 465 (W.D. Ky. 1937).

[63] Finck & Schmidt Lumber Co. v. Mehler, 102 Ky. 111, 43 S.W. 766 (1897); KY. REV. STAT. ANN. § 376.010 (Baldwin 1978) (amended 1994).

[64] Charles White Co. v. Percy Galbreath & Sons, Inc., 563 S.W.2d 478 (Ky. Ct. App. 1978).

[65] Laferty v. Wickes Lumber Co., 708 S.W.2d 107 (Ky. Ct. App. 1986); Middletown Eng'g v. Main St. Realty, 839 S.W.2d 274, 275, 276 (Ky. 1992).

All potential lien claimants must serve a formal notice on the owner by regular mail at the owner's last known address within seven days of the filing of a lien statement with the county clerk of the county where the improvement is built.[66] In addition, persons who have not directly contracted with the owner, in order to acquire a valid lien, must notify the owner in writing, on contracts of $1,000 or less, within 75 days after the last item of material was furnished or labor performed and within 120 days for contracts exceeding $1,000.[67] When owner-occupied single- or double-family dwellings are involved, notice to the owner must be within 45 days.[68]

The statement of lien must be filed with the clerk of the county in which the building or property is situated within six months of the last furnishing of labor or material and must set forth the following elements:

1. The name and address of the claimant
2. The name of the owner
3. The amount it claims minus any credits
4. Whether the material or labor was furnished by contract to the owner, a contractor, or subcontractor
5. The date the work was completed
6. A description of the property sufficient to identify it
7. If the claimant is a corporation, its agent for service of process.

The statement of lien also must be a sworn statement. Failure to mail a copy to the owner within seven days of its being filed with the clerk shall cause the lien to be dissolved.[69] The filing of a complaint without the separate mailing of the prelitigation notice does not satisfy the notice provision of the statute.[70] If the statement of lien is not subscribed and sworn to, the court will dismiss claims under mechanics' liens.[71]

If an action is not brought to enforce the lien within 12 months from the day it is filed with the clerk, it shall be deemed to have been dissolved.[72] Actions to enforce a lien shall be an equitable proceeding. The petition shall allege the facts necessary to secure a lien. It shall also describe the property charged and the interest the plaintiff seeks to subject. Several lienholders may wish to unite

---

[66] KY. REV. STAT. ANN. § 376.080(1) (Baldwin 1978) (amended 1990).

[67] *Id.* § 376.010(3). *See also* Middleton Eng'g Co. v. Main St. Realty, Inc., 839 S.W.2d 274 (Ky. 1992) (holding that when contractor is not the agent of the owner, a lien must be perfected by satisfying the requirements of both KY. REV. STAT. § 376.010(3) and KY. REV. STAT. § 376.080(1). Actual notice of the owner does not serve as a substitute for the statutory requirements of KY. REV. STAT. § 376.010(3)).

[68] *Id.* § 376.010(4). This provision was amended to exclude new construction of residences in 1994, at ch. 167, § 1, effective July 1, 1994.

[69] *Id.* § 376.080(1) (amended 1990).

[70] Laferty v. Wickes Lumber Co., 708 S.W.2d 107 (Ky. Ct. App. 1986).

[71] Hub City Wholesale Elec., Inc. v. Mik-Beth Elec. Co., 621 S.W.2d 242 (Ky. Ct. App. 1981).

[72] KY. REV. STAT. ANN. § 376.090 (Baldwin 1978).

as plaintiffs, and the remainder shall be named as defendants. The debtor and all other persons having an interest in the property to be subjected shall also be made defendants. The matter will be heard by a master commissioner.[73]

[D] Waiver

In Kentucky, the right to file a mechanics' lien may be waived in writing.[74] Waivers are commonly used in ordinary construction contracts to protect the person who pays for the labor, material, or supplies furnished to the project. A mechanics' lien may also be waived by implication. However, an express waiver must be supported by consideration and an implied waiver arises only when there is detrimental reliance by one party.[75] The Kentucky courts will recognize a release of lien.[76]

[E] Lien Priority

The lien law provides for different rules as to priority.[77] When a notice of mechanics' lien was filed before a mortgage was recorded, but after it was executed, the mechanics' lien had priority. When a notice of mechanics' lien was filed after the mortgage was recorded and it appeared that the mortgagee had no notice that work was in progress, the mortgage had priority.[78] The liens of subcontractors are of equal rank and take precedence over the lien of the main contractor under proper circumstances.[79]

[F] Remedies of Owner

The lien law provides the owner with various forms of protection, including the right to assure that all of the provisions of the lien law have been complied with, the right to retain funds,[80] and the right to bond off a claim,[81] as well as the right to have the contractor apply payments to the claim.[82]

---

[73] *Id.* § 376.110(1).

[74] *Id.* § 376.070.

[75] Greensburg Deposit Bank v. GGC-Goff Motors, 851 S.W.2d 476 (Ky. 1993).

[76] Merchants Nat'l Bank v. Professional, Inc., 579 S.W.2d 100 (Ky. 1979).

[77] Ky. Rev. Stat. Ann. §§ 376.010(1), .090(2), .160.

[78] Gordon v. House, 201 Ky. 45, 255 S.W. 846 (Ky. 1923); Higgins Lumber Co. v. Cunningham, 216 Ky. 298, 288 S.W. 334 (Ky. 1926); Staton Springs Park Co. v. Keesee, 217 Ky. 329, 289 S.W. 292 (Ky. 1926); Weil v. B.E. Buffaloe & Co., 251 Ky. 673, 65 S.W.2d 704 (Ky. Ct. App. 1933).

[79] Schnute Holtman Co. v. Sweeney, 136 Ky. 773, 125 S.W. 180 (Ky. 1933). *See also* Doll v. Young, 149 S.W. 854 (Ky. 1912), in which subcontractors' liens were denied when the general contractor's building collapsed before completion. The subs had no right to liens when the general failed to complete the contract after the collapse.

[80] Merchants Nat'l Bank v. Professional, Inc., 579 S.W.2d 100, 103 (Ky. 1979).

[81] Ky. Rev. Stat. Ann. § 376.100 (Baldwin 1978) (amended 1986).

[82] *Id.* § 376.070.

In order to charge the surety under a release of lien bond, the underlying lien must in all respects be valid.[83] The owner's execution of a release of lien bond does not discharge the contractor and its surety from a bond executed by them to protect the owner against mechanics' liens. [84] A contractor is required to pay a materialman from money received from the owner for materials furnished and labor performed when a lien on the property is involved.[85]

[G] Public Contract Lien

Kentucky statutes provide any person who performs labor or furnishes materials or supplies for the construction of a public improvement owned by the state or any of its political subdivisions with a lien on the funds due the contractor.[86] The public contract portion of the Kentucky lien law defines *labor, materials,* and *supplies.*[87]

Equipment rentals are lienable, but subordinate to other claims provided for by statute.[88] However, the statute does not cover the purchase price of equipment purchased under a conditional sales contract.[89] Insurance premiums are neither labor, materials, nor supplies as those terms are defined in the statute.[90]

The person who is claiming a public contract lien must file a statement of lien in the clerk's office of the county where the seat of the government owning the property improved is located.[91] When the statement of lien is filed with the county clerk, an attested copy thereof must be delivered to the public authority making the contract for the public improvement.[92] Additionally, there must be filed with such public authority a signed copy of a letter addressed to the contractor or subcontractor at the address in the contract, with a post office receipt showing that an attested copy of the lien statement has been sent by the lien claimant to the contractor or subcontractor by certified mail, return receipt requested, or by registered mail.[93]

The statute provides that upon compliance with the filing requirements, the public authority shall deduct and withhold the amount of the lien claim, plus a

---

[83] Jungbert v. Marret, 313 Ky. 338, 231 S.W.2d 84 (Ky. 1950).

[84] Aetna Cas. & Sur. v. United States Gypsum Co., 239 Ky. 247, 39 S.W.2d 234 (Ky. 1931).

[85] Henry A. Peter Supply Co. v. Hal Perry Constr. Co., 563 S.W.2d 749 (Ky. Ct. App. 1978).

[86] Ky. Rev. Stat. Ann. § 376.210 (Baldwin 1966).

[87] *Id.* § 376.195 (amended 1986).

[88] Whayne Supply Co. v. Morgan Constr. Co., 440 S.W.2d 779 (Ky. 1969); Ky. Rev. Stat. Ann. § 376.195(4)(a) (Baldwin 1978) (amended 1986).

[89] Traylor Bros., Inc. v. Indiana Equip. Co., 336 S.W.2d 590 (Ky. 1960).

[90] *In re* Zaepfel & Russell, Inc., 49 F. Supp. 709 (W.D. Ky. 1941), *aff'd sub nom.* Farmers State Bank v. Jones, 135 F.2d 215 (6th Cir. 1943).

[91] Ky. Rev. Stat. Ann. § 376.210(3) (Baldwin 1966).

[92] *Id.* §§ 376.230(1), (2). Section 376.230(1) requires a sworn affidavit from the claimant setting forth the amount due, last date of furnishing material, labor, or supplies, and the name of the public improvement upon which the lien is claimed.

[93] *Id.* § 376.240.

fee, from any amount then due the contractor, and if a sufficient amount is not then due the contractor, the remaining amounts shall be withheld from the next payments that become due.[94]

If the contractor fails to file with the public authority a written protest putting in issue the amount of or its liability for the lien within 30 days from receipt of the attested copy of the statement of lien, the amount withheld shall be paid by the public authority to the lien claimant and charged to the account of the contractor.[95]

When the contractor files a written protest, the money will be withheld and not disbursed until the contractor authorizes the public authority to do so or unless the public authority is ordered to do so by a court.[96]

When a protest has been properly filed, the lien claimant must file a suit (summons) within 30 days against the public authority. If the lien claimant fails to file a suit, then the lien is automatically released, and the funds withheld are likewise to be released and promptly paid to the contractor.[97]

The lien, and suit to enforce it, must be filed in the circuit court of the county where the seat of the government owning the improvement is located, and that court has exclusive jurisdiction over the action.[98]

The lien of a subcontractor working on a public building attaches only to such funds due to and actually earned by the contractor at the time of filing of its lien.[99]

In one case, when the contractor went bankrupt, the public owner called upon a subcontractor to complete its subcontract. The subcontractor did so and then timely filed its lien. The bankrupt prime contractor's surety bond protected the owner against the line even though the owner did not notify the surety that it had requested the subcontractor to complete its own contract.[100] Fringe benefits are part of labor and may be the subject of a lien on a public project.[101]

If a public works contractor fails to protest a lien as required by the statute, the contractor will lose all defenses to the lien claim. Filing the protest is a condition precedent to voicing any objection to the lien, including an objection to the public authority paying the lien claimant.

---

[94] *Id.* § 376.250(1).
[95] *Id.* § 376.250(2).
[96] *Id.* § 376.250(3).
[97] *Id.* § 376.250(4) (Baldwin 1978).
[98] *Id.* § 376.250(5).
[99] McLean County v. Meuth Carpet Supply, 573 S.W.2d 340 (Ky. 1978).
[100] Fidelity & Cas. Co. v. Board of Regents, 287 Ky. 439, 152 S.W.2d 581 (Ky. 1941).
[101] Reliance Ins. Co. v. Commonwealth Dep't of Transp., 576 S.W.2d 231 (Ky. Ct. App. 1978).

CHAPTER 19

LOUISIANA

Harvey C. Koch[1]

[1] The author gratefully acknowledges the efforts of Ronald L. Riggle and Katharine Levy in helping to prepare this chapter.

§ 19.01 INTRODUCTION

There are two separate Louisiana statutes that govern bonds furnished in conjunction with construction projects. The first, covering public works projects, can be found at West's Louisiana Revised Statutes Annotated (La. Rev. Stat. Ann.) §§ 38:2241 *et seq.* The second, addressing private projects, can be found at §§ 9:4801 *et seq.* and is entitled the Private Works Act.

General contractors on public projects in excess of $25,000 are required to furnish a bond.[2]

On private projects in Louisiana, general contractors are not required to furnish any kind of bond. If a bond is not furnished, the law provides contractors, laborers, and furnishers of materials with certain lien rights. The owner may be relieved of all claims against him and the privileges securing them by requiring the general contractor to furnish and maintain a bond.[3]

§ 19.02 BOND LAW

[A] General Concepts

Suretyship in Louisiana is an accessory promise or obligation by which one party binds itself to a creditor to fulfill the obligation of another if the latter fails to do so.[4] The law requires that suretyship be express and in writing.[5] Implicit in suretyship's accessorial nature is the idea that the extinction of the principal obligation extinguishes the suretyship.[6]

As in most jurisdictions, Louisiana courts will construe ambiguous bond language against the surety.[7] This policy does not take priority over the rule that a contract of suretyship cannot be presumed.[8] It should, however, be noted that while the contract for suretyship is not presumed, the creditor's acceptance is presumed upon his receipt of the writing evidencing the surety's obligation and he need not give formal acceptance.[9] The comment following Louisana Civil Code Annotated (La. Civ. Code. Ann.) art. 3039 points out that the surety may withdraw up until the creditor receives the writing evidencing his obligation. It is only after an obligation of suretyship is found to exist that the construction rule will come into play.

Bonds furnished by general contractors in conjunction with the construction

---

[2] La. Rev. Stat. Ann. § 38:2241(A)(2) (1999 La. Sess. Law Serv. Act 673 (S.B. 802) (West)).

[3] La. Rev. Stat. Ann. § 9:4802(C) (West 1991).

[4] La. Civ. Code. Ann. art. 3035 (West 1994).

[5] *Id.* art. 3038.

[6] *Id.* art. 3059.

[7] Bossier Med. Properties v. Abbott & Williams Constr. Co., 557 So. 2d 1131, 1133 (La. App. 2d Cir. 1990).

[8] McKesson Chem. Co. v. Tideland Chem. Co., 471 So. 2d 812 (La. App. 3d Cir. 1985).

[9] La. Civ. Code Ann. art. 3039 (West 1994).

of public projects are subject to the "read in, read out" rule. In other words, any statutory requirements not contained in the bond are read into it, and any coverage beyond what is required by statute is read out of it.[10]

A surety's liability can be no greater than that of the principal.[11] Therefore, if the contractor's liability is reduced, the surety's liability will be reduced pro tanto. Modifications, omissions, or additions to the contract terms, plans, and specifications or manner and mode of payment cannot diminish or enlarge the obligations of a public works bond.[12] Similarly, the surety on a private works bond is not released from its obligations because of such changes, but is entitled to indemnification from the owner if the changes materially prejudice the surety.[13] There is a slight ambiguity as to the meaning contained within the term "indemnification" as between La. Rev. Stat. Ann. § 9:4812(E) and La. Civ. Code. Ann. art. 3035. The statute discusses indemnification under the original terms of the contract as provided by the Code article, and the Code article, revised in 1987, has substituted the term "security" for the term "indemnification" in an effort to more accurately reflect the surety's right. The old term was understood to include both "reimbursement" and security".[14]

[B] Bid Bonds

Louisiana Revised Statutes Annotated (La. Rev. Stat. Ann.) § 38:2218(A) was amended July 18, 1991, to require bidders on public works to provide a certified check, cashier's check or bid bond for not more than five percent of the contract price of work to be done. Former law made this requirement optional with the contracting body. It should be noted from the language within the statute that while the requirement is mandatory for bidders bidding on the contract price of work to be done, it remains an optional requirement, at the discretion of the public entity, for bidders bidding on the estimated price of supplies or material.[15] Prior to the 1991 amendment and reenactment of both La. Rev. Stat. Ann. § 38:2214 and § 38:2215, case law held that all formal requirements of the bidding statues be strictly complied with or the bid would be considered void.[16] Following the amendment and reenactment of the statues, the Louisiana Supreme Court recognized that the two statutes had to be reconciled in such a manner as to give full force and effect to each as amended. The court went on to point out that La. Rev. Stat. Ann. §§ 38:2214 and 38:2215 should be interpreted together

[10] Bowles & Edens Co. v. H & H Sewer Sys., Inc., 324 So. 2d 528 (La. App. 1st Cir. 1975); La. Rev. Stat. Ann. § 38:2241(C) (West 1989).

[11] Pacific Lining Co. v. Algernon-Blair Constr. Co. 812 F.2d 237, 241 (5th Cir. 1987).

[12] La. Rev. Stat. Ann. § 38:2241(A)(2) (1999 La. Sess. Law Serv. Act 673 (S.B. 802) (West)).

[13] La. Rev. Stat. Ann. § 9:4812(E) (West 1991).

[14] *Id.;* La. Civ. Code Ann. art. 3053 Comment b (West 1994).

[15] La. Rev. Stat. Ann. § 38: 2218(A) (West 1991 & Supp. 1999).

[16] Thigpen Const. Co. v. Parish of Jefferson, 560 So. 2d 947 (La. App. 5th Cir. 1990), *overruled by* New Orleans Rosenbush Claims Serv., Inc. v. City of New Orleans, 653 So. 2d 538 (La. 1995).

to provide that "a public entity has 30 days to do one of the following: (1) award a contract to the lowest responsible bidder; (2) reject all bids for just cause; or (3) extend the deadline by mutual consent with the lowest responsible bidder."[17] Prior court holdings, that the bid bond requirements could be waived, were based on the permissive nature of the statute. With bid bonds now mandatory, such cases are no longer controlling.[18]

If a bidder makes a mistake in calculating a bid, it may be able to withdraw the bid without forfeiting the bid security. For this to occur, the public entity must determine that "the error is a patently obvious mechanical, clerical, or mathematical error, or unintentional omission of a substantial quantity of work, labor, material, or services, as opposed to a judgment error, and that the bid was submitted in good faith" and the bidder has submitted sworn evidence of such mistake to the public entity within 48 hours of the bid opening.[19]

[C] Performance Bonds

A performance bond guarantees that the contractor will perform the contract.[20] Although Louisiana law does not mandate that a bond be furnished for a private construction project, requiring the general contractor to furnish a bond is the method by which an owner is protected from personal liability and the property from liens.[21] A bond furnished by a general contractor on a private project will be presumed to include both a payment and a performance provision unless the latter is expressly excluded.[22]

It has been held that the Private Works Act does not govern the performance provision of the bond, and, accordingly, the one-year prescriptive period provided by the Act for bringing an action against the surety does not apply to an action brought by an owner under the performance provision of the bond.[23] Therefore, the applicable prescriptive period for bringing an action on a performance bond will be either the 10-year period for bringing actions on a contract, or a shorter period as may be designated in the bond.[24]

Prior to 1985 a performance and payment bond was required on public works projects in Louisiana. The relevant passage was found in the second and third sentences of La. Rev. Stat. Ann. § 38:2241(A), which read, "He shall require of

---

[17] New Orleans Rosenbush Claims Serv. Inc. v. City of New Orleans, 653 So. 2d 538, 546 (La. 1995).

[18] F. H. Myers Constr. Corp. v. City of New Orleans, 570 So. 2d 84 (La. App. 4th Cir. 1986).

[19] La. Rev. Stat. Ann. § 38: 2214(C) (West Supp. 1992); Terrebonne Parish Police Jury v. A. L. Sizeler Constr. Co., 491 So. 2d 409 (La. App. 1st Cir. 1986).

[20] Congregation of St. Peter's v. Simon, 497 So. 2d 409, 412 (La. App. 3d Cir. 1986).

[21] La. Rev. Stat. Ann. § 9:4812(A) (West 1991).

[22] *Id.* § 9:4812(C)(2).

[23] Congregation of St. Peter's v. Simon, 497 So. 2d 409 (La. App. 3d Cir. 1986).

[24] Kiva Constr. & Eng'g, Inc. v. International Fidelity Ins. Co., 749 F. Supp. 753 (W.D. La. 1990).

the contractor a bond with good solvent, and sufficient surety in a sum not less than fifty percent of the contract price for the faithful performance of the contract with an additional obligation for the payment by the contractor or subcontractor for all work done, labor performed, or material or supplies furnished for the construction, alteration, or repair of any public works, or for transportation and delivery of such materials or supplies to the site of the job by a for-hire-carrier, or for furnishing materials or supplies for use in machines used in the construction, alteration, or repair of any public works. No modification, omissions, additions in or to the terms of the contract, in the plans or specifications, or in the manner and mode of payment, shall in any manner affect the obligation of the surety."[25] The statutory requirement of furnishing a payment and performance bond has been reinforced by jurisprudence. The Louisiana Court of Appeals, later affirmed by the Louisiana Supreme Court, found that "Louisiana public works bonds are statutory in nature and not only guarantee performance of the construction work but also payment of laborers and materialmen."[26]

The 1985 amendment of La. Rev. Stat. Ann. § 38:2241 has created a difference of opinion, stemming from a disparity in language between sections (A) and (D), as to whether or not a performance bond is required on public works projects in the state. Subsection (A)(2) now reads (with 1999 amendment), "For each contract in excess of $25,000 per project, the public entity shall require of the contractor a bond with good, solvent, and sufficient surety in a sum of not less than fifty percent of the contract price for the payment by the contractor or subcontractor to claimants as defined in R.S. § 38:2242. The bond furnished shall be a statutory bond and no modification, omissions, additions in or to the terms of the contract, in the plans or specifications, or in the manner and mode of payment shall in any manner diminish, enlarge, or otherwise modify the obligations of the bond. . . ."[27] What is unreconciled is a provision in (D) stating, "A bond issued pursuant to this Section shall not create, nor shall such bond be construed to create, any cause of action in favor of the public entity, or any third party, for personal injury or property damages sustained by any third party during the effective period of the bond. Nothing contained herein shall in any way limit the liability on the bond for the performance of the work pursuant to the contract in question. . . ."[28] This has been interpreted as requiring a performance bond as well as a payment bond. As the situation now stands, if a surety only provides a payment bond for a contractor under the provisions of § 38:2241(A), the "read in, read out" rule could conceivably be applied to read into the bond the performance requirement mentioned in § 38:2241(D).

---

[25] La. Rev. Stat. Ann. § 38:2241(A) (prior to the 1985 amendment and reenactment).

[26] Lambert v. Maryland Cas. Co., 403 So. 2d 739, 753 (La. App. 4th Cir. 1981), *aff'd,* 418 So. 2d 553 (La. 1982).

[27] La. Rev. Stat. Ann. § 38:2241(A)(2) (1999 La. Sess. Law Serv. Act 673 (S.B. 802) (West)).

[28] *Id.* § 38:2241(D).

The normal time period for a claimant asserting an action on the bond is one year.[29] Nevertheless, when the claimant bringing a claim against either the contractor or the surety is the state or one of its agencies, the applicable time period is five years.[30] The five-year period begins to run upon "the substantial completion of the project, as defined in R.S. § 38:2241.1, or acceptance of such work, whichever occurs first, or of notice of default of the contractor unless otherwise limited in" the Chapter containing this statute.[31] It should be noted that in 1997 the Louisiana Supreme Court found that the time period provided by R.S. § 38:2189 was peremptive and not prescriptive, stating that the statute erected a "peremptive time limitation on the State's ability to bring suits against the contractor or the surety on a public works contract" and therefore was not "susceptible of suspension, interruption, or renunciation. . . ."[32]

[D] Payment Bonds

A payment bond guarantees that those who supply materials, services, and/or labor on a private project will be paid should the contractor fail to make payment.[33] A surety's liability is limited to the amount of the bond, and if the aggregate of outstanding claims is greater than the amount of the bond, the statute sets forth a scheme for the discharge of the surety's liability.[34]

The purpose of the bond is to protect the owner from liability that otherwise might be incurred and to protect creditors seeking payment for materials supplied to and labor performed for a contractor or subcontractor.[35]

Louisiana law requires that a contractor on every public project in excess of $25,000 furnish a payment bond.[36] All requirements contained in the statute will be read into the bond, and any obligations beyond the requirements of the statute will be deemed surplusage and read out of the bond.[37]

Louisiana does not require contractors to furnish payment bonds on private projects. If the owner wishes to protect itself and its property from liability and liens that may arise from private construction, the necessary amount of the bond will vary depending on the amount of the construction contract.[38] Also, a surety

---

[29] LA. REV. STAT. ANN. § 38:2247 (West 1989).

[30] *Id.* § 38:2189.

[31] *Id.* § 38:2189.

[32] State Through Div. of Admin. v. McInnis Bros. Constr. 701 So. 2d 937, 948 (La. 1997).

[33] Congregation of St. Peter's v. Simon, 497 So. 2d 409, 412 (La. App. 3d Cir. 1986).

[34] LA. REV. STAT. ANN. § 9:4813(B) (West 1991).

[35] Town of Winnsboro v. Barnard & Burk, Inc., 294 So. 2d 867 (La. App. 2d Cir. 1974), *distinguished on other grounds in* D & O Contractors, Inc. v. Terrebonne Parish Sch. Bd., 545 So. 2d 588 (La. App. 1st Cir. 1989).

[36] LA. REV. STAT. ANN. § 38:2241(A)(2) (1999 La. Sess. Law Serv. Act 673 (S.B. 802) (West)).

[37] *Id.* § 38:2241 (C) (West 1989).

[38] *Id.* § 9:4812 (West 1991).

bond filed with the notice of a private works contract is deemed to be a statutory bond, and all requirements of the statute will be read into it.[39]

In order to bring an action on a public works bond, a claimant must preserve its right by filing a sworn statement of the amount due with the governing authority having the work done and also record it in the office of the recorder of mortgages for the parish in which the work was performed or materials supplied within 45 days after the recordation of acceptance by the governing authority or notice of default of the contractor or subcontractor.[40] The 45-day period is a strict requirement. In a 1989 case, it was held that filing a statement of account one day beyond the 45-day period barred a subsequent action brought against the surety.[41] Notice is given via registered or certified mail to any place the general contractor maintains an office in Louisiana.[42] Although the 45-day period is still a strict requirement, the actual method of notifying the contractor may be somewhat less strict than the statute requires. It has been held that personal delivery of notice to the contractor within the 45-day period is sufficient in order to comply with the notice provision of the statute.[43] Furthermore, in order for a claimant who has a direct contractual relationship with a subcontractor but no contractual relationship with the general contractor to preserve its claim against the surety, the claimant must not only fulfill the notice requirements, but must also give written notice to the contractor within the same 45-day period.[44] And, it has been specifically held that a general contractor who was retained by the surety to complete a public building project when the initial contractor defaulted was NOT able to recover from the parish for his services when the surety was declared insolvent because (1) there was no privity of contract as between the two parties, and (2) the general contractor was not a "claimant" under R.S. § 38:2242(A)(1).[45] When the notice requirements have been satisfied, an action must be brought within one year of the registry of acceptance of the work, or the notice of default of the contractor.[46]

In order to bring a claim on a private works bond, a sub-subcontractor, laborer, or furnisher of materials must deliver written notice of its claim to the contractor as required by the statute.[47] The notice requirements for perfecting a lien and thus establishing priority are discussed further in **§ 19.03[C].**

---

[39] *Id.* cmt. (e).

[40] *Id.* § 38:2242(B) (West 1989 & Supp. 1999)

[41] Interstate Sch. Supply Co. v. Guitreau's Constr. & Consulting Co., 542 So. 2d 138, 139 (La. App. 1st Cir. 1989), *called into doubt in* "K" Constr., Inc. v. Burko Constr., Inc. 629 So. 2d 1370, 1373 (La. App. 4th Cir. 1993) (4th circuit noted that Interstate was distinguishable from the current case and that it seemed to undermine the purpose of the Private Works Act).

[42] LA. REV. STAT. ANN. § 38:2247 (West 1989).

[43] Daigle v. Donald M. Clement Contractors, 533 So. 2d 1064, 1066 (La. App. 4th Cir. 1988).

[44] LA. REV. STAT. ANN. § 38:2247 (West 1989).

[45] *See* Louisiana Ins. Guar. Assoc. v. Rapides Parish Police Jury, 182 F.3d 326 (5th Cir. 1999).

[46] LA. REV. STAT. ANN. § 38:2247 (West 1989).

[47] *Id.* § 9:4822(J) (West 1991).

[E] Additional Bond Issues

If, after amicable demand for payment has been made on the principal and surety and 30 days elapse without payment being made, any claimant recovering the full amount of the recorded claim, whether by a concursus proceeding or by separate suit, will be allowed 10-percent attorneys' fees.[48] An amendment to this section in 1991 added subsection B which provides, "If the trial court finds that such an action was brought by any claimant without just cause or in bad faith, the trial judge shall award the principal or surety a reasonable amount as attorney's fees for defending such action."[49] The purpose of this law is to promote the amicable resolution and settlement of claims arising out of public works contracts.

§ 19.03 LIEN LAW

[A] General Concepts

The Louisiana law providing for the establishment of liens in favor of laborers, furnishers of materials, contractors, and subcontractors is entitled the Private Works Act.[50] This is the same statute discussed in **§ 19.02[C]** in relation to payment and performance bonds issued for private projects. As stated, an owner can protect its property from liens by requiring the general contractor to furnish a bond. If the owner does not require the general contractor to furnish a bond, however, the Private Works Act governs lien rights that various parties may have against an owner's property. One of the objectives of the Private Works Act is to protect the claims of those who contribute labor, materials, or equipment to the construction or improvement of an immovable by creating privileges in their favor on the immovable.[51]

[B] Basic Provisions

The law of Louisiana grants lien rights to those who fit into either one of two categories. Generally, these categories are first, those who deal with the owner,[52] and second, those who deal with the general contractor or a subcontractor.[53] The first category includes the general prime contractor, laborers employed directly by the owner, sellers or movables to the owner, lessors of equipment to the owner, and surveyors, engineers, and architects employed by the owner.[54] The

---

[48] *Id.* § 38:2246(A) (West 1991 & Supp. 1999)

[49] *Id.* § 38:2246(B) (West Supp. 1999).

[50] *Id.* §§ 9:4801 *et seq.* (West 1991 & Supp. 1999).

[51] Fruge v. Muffoletto, 242 La. 569, 137 So. 2d 336 (1961).

[52] La. Rev. Stat. Ann. § 9:4801 (West 1991).

[53] *Id.* § 9:4802 (West 1991 & Supp. 1999); Cirlot Co. v. Lake Forest, Inc., 475 So. 2d 799, 800 (La. App. 4th Cir. 1985).

[54] La. Rev. Stat. Ann. § 9:4801 (West 1991).

second category includes subcontractors, laborers of the prime contractor or a subcontractor, sellers of movables to the prime contractor or a subcontractor, lessors of movables to the prime contractor or subcontractor, and engineers, architects, and consultants hired by the prime contractor or a subcontractor.[55] Also, in order for a lessor of movables to the prime contractor or a subcontractor to be entitled to later perfect a lien and assert a claim, a copy of the lease agreement must be delivered to the owner and to the contractor within 10 days of the movable being placed at the site of the project.[56]

Under both categories of claimants, the privilege given under the statute is accessory to and is given only in order to secure the personal liability of the owner.[57]

[C] Notice Requirements

The time period for filing a statement of claim and delivering the same to the owner differs for the contractor and other claimants, and also depends on whether or not a notice of the contract was originally filed.[58] The written notice of the contract should be filed before the work begins and should contain a legal property description of the immovable, the identification of the parties and their respective mailing addresses, the price of the work, when payment is to be made, and a description of the type of work involved. The owner and the contractor should sign the notice.[59]

If the contract amount is over $25,000 and a notice of the contract has been properly filed, a laborer, subcontractor, or furnisher or materials has 30 days after the owner and contractor sign and file a notice of acceptance to file a statement of claim asserting a lien against the property and deliver such statement to the owner. The general contractor has 60 days to file a claim.[60]

If notice of the contract has not been filed, however, a laborer, subcontractor, or furnisher of materials has 60 days from the later of either the filing of a notice of termination or the substantial completion or abandonment of the work to file a claim.[61] Also, when the notice of contract has not been filed, a prime contractor will only be able to assert the privilege granted by the statute against the owner if the contract amount is less than $25,000. In such a case, the contractor has 60 days to file a claim. On the other hand, if the contract amount is over $25,000

---

[55] *Id.* § 9:4802 (West 1991 & Supp. 1999).

[56] *Id.* § 9:4802(G) (West Supp. 1999).

[57] *Id.* § 9:4802 cmt. (c) (West 1991).

[58] *Id.* § 9:4822 (West 1991 & Supp. 1999).

[59] *Id.* § 9:4811 (West 1991).

[60] *Id.* § 9:4822 (West 1991 & Supp. 1999).

[61] *Id.*

and the notice of the contract is not filed, the prime contractor will not be able to assert the privilege otherwise granted by the statute.[62]

[D] Waiver

Louisiana recognizes the validity of lien waivers.[63] Waiver may occur by payment of the secured claim or by express waiver. Waiver may be implied from the particular facts and circumstances of the case.[64] Under appropriate factual circumstances, the courts will also allow the invocation of equitable estoppel to prevent a lien from being enforced.[65]

[E] Lien Priority

The privileges granted to contractors, laborers, and furnishers of materials will take priority over the claims of third persons when one of two things occurs. First, if the notice of contract is filed, as previously discussed, the date of filing will be the effective date of the privileges granted by the statute to third parties. If no notice of contract is filed, the effective date will be the date the work is begun by either placing materials at the site or conducting work that, from a simple inspection, would indicate that the work has actually begun.[66] In the objective determination of whether or not work has begun such things as the services rendered by an architect, engineer or surveyor, or the driving of test piling, cutting or removal of trees and debris, placing of fill dirt, or the leveling of the land surface will not be considered as indicators in the determination of whether work has begun, nor will the placing of materials having an aggregate price of less than one hundred dollars be considered an adequate indicator.[67] It should be noted that the examples given in the statute as not constituting the beginning of the work must be analyzed in relation to the type of construction to be performed. For example, what might appear to be the simple placing of fill dirt, which would not trigger the effective date for privileges, could actually be considered as work activating the effective date for privileges if the dirt work is performed for the construction of a golf course.[68] The list in the statute should be viewed as illustrative, and not exclusive, the real test being whether or not the work is an integral part of the construction and not simply preparatory in nature.[69]

Also, if the work being performed is for the addition to, or the modification

---

62 *Id.* § 9:4811(D) (West 1991).

63 Executive Office Ctrs., Inc. V. Cournoyer, 433 So. 2d 324, 327 (La. App. 4th Cir. 1983).

64 Babineaux v. Grisaffi, 180 So. 2d 888, 889 (La. App. 3d Cir. 1984).

65 Concrete Post-Tensioning, Inc. v. Armco, Inc., 449 So. 2d 712 (La. App. 3d Cir. 1984).

66 LA. REV. STAT. ANN. § 9:4820(A)(1), (2) (West 1991 & Supp. 1999).

67 *Id.* § 9:4820(A)(2) (West 1991 & Supp. 1999).

68 C & J Contractors v. American Bank & Trust, 559, So. 2d 810 (La. App. 1st Cir. 1990).

69 *Id.* at 815.

of, or repairs to an existing building, or other construction, and a notice of contract has not been filed, a 30-day lapse in construction will, as to third parties acquiring rights in the immovable during the lapse, be deemed a separate work from that conducted subsequent to the 30-day lapse. As a result, privileges acquired before such a lapse will not cover work performed thereafter. Consequently, third-party rights acquired during the lapse period will prime the contractor's lien for subsequently performed work.[70]

[70] LA. REV. STAT. ANN. § 9:4820 cmt. (b) (West 1991 & Supp 1999).

CHAPTER 20

MAINE

Jotham D. Pierce, Jr.
Debra L. Brown[1]

[1] The authors of this chapter thank Eileen J. Griffin for her contributions on the prior edition.

§ 20.01 INTRODUCTION

On private projects, Maine does not require contractors to furnish any kind of bond.

On public projects in excess of $100,000, Maine requires contractors to provide both performance and payment bonds in the full amount of the contract. The payment bond must protect claimants supplying labor or materials to the contractor or its subcontractor. The public contracting authority, at its discretion, may require contractors to furnish bid security in one of various possible forms. The Public Works Surety Bond Law of 1971[2] governs bond requirements for public projects. In addition, the surety contract is treated as an insurance contract and governed by applicable statutes.[3]

For both private and public projects (except with the state or United States government), contractors, subcontractors, and other parties supplying labor, materials, or services are provided mechanics' lien rights. Maine's mechanics' liens are governed by Maine Revised Statutes Annotated title 10, §§ 3251 *et seq.*

Finally, Maine has its own "Prompt Pay" statute, at Maine Revised Statutes Annotated title 10, §§ 1111–1120, which sets out payment requirements on both private and public (other than DOT) projects, and provides remedies for nonpayment.

§ 20.02 BOND LAW

[A] General Concepts

The Public Works Surety Bond Law of 1971, Maine Revised Statutes Annotated title 14, § 871, governs bond requirements for public projects. The statute is modeled after the federal Miller Act.[4] Therefore, Maine courts consider that the use of federal precedent is appropriate as an aid in interpreting Maine's statute.[5]

The majority of Maine cases addressing surety bonds date to the nineteenth or early twentieth century. Because surety bonds are furnished by compensated sureties, nineteenth-century case law is not a reliable guide as to how today's construction surety bond will be interpreted. There is no reason to believe, however, that Maine courts would diverge from the general common law principles applied by other states in construing bonds. Also, Maine's general contract principles will apply when interpreting a surety contract.

It has long been the established rule of law in Maine that the paramount

---

[2] ME. REV. STAT. ANN. tit. 14, §§ 871 *et seq.* (West 1980).

[3] *See id.* at tit. 24-A, §§ 3101 *et seq.*

[4] *See* L.D. 375, Statement of Fact (105th Legis. 1971) ("The proposed legislation is intended to provide limitation of action on state work similar to that which is provided on federal contracts which are covered by the so-called Miller Act.").

[5] Vacuum Sys., Inc. v. Washburn, 651 A.2d 377, 379 (Me. 1994).

principle in the construction of contracts is to give effect to the intention of the parties as gathered from the language of the agreement viewed in the light of all the circumstances under which it was made.[6] The intention of the parties must be gathered from the written instrument, construed in respect to the subject-matter, the motive and purpose of making the agreement, and the object to be accomplished.[7] The intent of the parties to a bond is determined by the expressions therein, inevitable implications, and conclusions of law.[8]

The obligations of a surety must be drawn from the obligations of the principal in the underlying construction contract. Unless the language or specifications of performance required of the contractor are to be disregarded as mere surplusage, the contract and bond are indissolubly tied together.[9] The condition that the principal shall faithfully perform the contract incorporates the contract into the bond. What the contractor has agreed to perform is what the bond assumes.[10] However, a court cannot import into a bond an obligation not covered by its terms.[11] At the same time, a bond agreement made by a bonding company, agreeing for consideration to act as surety, will be construed most strongly against the surety.[12]

When determining what law to apply to contracts generally, Maine has adopted the doctrine found in the Restatement (Second) of the Law, Conflict of Laws 2d (1971) § 188: in the absence of an express effective choice of applicable state law by the parties, the rights and duties of the parties with respect to an issue in contract are to be determined at the forum level by the local law of the state which, with respect to that particular issue, has the most significant relationship to the transaction and the parties.[13] Specifically, in an insurance contract (in Maine, a surety contract is treated as an insurance contract), the validity of the contract and the rights and duties created thereby, are to be determined, in the absence of an express effective choice of law by the parties, by the local law of the state which the parties understood was to be the principal location of the insured risk during the term of the policy, unless with respect to the particular issue involved, some other state has a more significant relationship to the transaction and the parties, in which event the local law of the other state will be applied.[14]

Surety contracts in Maine are governed specifically by the provisions set

---

[6] Forbes v. Wells Beach Casino, Inc., 307 A.2d 210, 216 (Me. 1973); Bell v. Jordan, 102 Me. 67, 70, 65 A. 759 (1906).

[7] Roberts v. McIntire, 84 Me. 362, 364, 24 A. 867 (1892).

[8] Foster v. Kerr & Houston, 133 Me. 389, 394, 179 A. 297, 299 (1936).

[9] *Id.*

[10] *Id.*, 133 Me. at 396.

[11] McFarland v. Rogers, 134 Me. 228, 184 A. 391 (1936).

[12] *Id.*

[13] Baybutt Constr. Corp. v. Commercial Union Ins. Co., 455 A.2d 914, 918 (1983).

[14] *Id.* (citing Restatement (Second) of the Law, Conflict of Laws 2d (1971), § 193).

forth at Maine Revised Statutes Annotated title 24-A, §§ 3101–3105. Additionally, the surety contract is treated as an insurance contract under the statutory scheme governing insurance contracts.[15] Pursuant to this statutory scheme, all sureties transacting business in Maine must appoint an agent to receive service of legal process issued against the surety in the state.[16] Additionally, no surety bond may deprive Maine courts of jurisdiction over foreign insurers or limit the time for commencing actions against foreign insurers to a period of less than two years from the time when the cause of action accrues.[17] Also pursuant to statutory provisions governing insurance contracts, sureties may be liable for unfair claims settlement practices, including failing to acknowledge and review claims within a reasonable time after receipt of written notice.[18]

[B] Bid Bonds

Bid security is not required on private projects. Bid security may be required by public contracting authorities to guarantee that, if the work is awarded to the contractor, the contractor will contract with the contracting agency.[19] The contracting authority sets the amount of the bid security with that goal in mind. Bid security also may be required at the discretion of the contracting authority to assure that the contractor is bondable. The bid security must be payable to and deposited with the state or other contracting body.

A bid security may take many forms, including United States postal money order, official bank checks, cashier's checks, certificates of deposit, certified checks, money in escrow, and bonds from surety companies or other parties with documented adequate financial standing.[20] The bid securities are returned to unsuccessful bidders.

Upon satisfactory execution and delivery of the contract and performance and payment bonds, the bid security of the successful bidder is returned.

[C] Performance Bonds

Maine does not require contractors to provide performance bonds on private projects, but for any contract exceeding $100,000 involving public projects, the

---

[15] ME. REV. STAT. ANN. tit. 24-A, § 3101 (West 1990).

[16] *Id.* § 421 (West Supp. 1998).

[17] *Id.* § 2433.

[18] *Id.* § 2436-A (West. Supp. 1998); *but see* John J. Aromando, *The Surety's Liability for "Bad Faith": Claims for Extra-Contractual Damages by an Obligee Under the Payment Bond,* 47 Me. L. Rev. 390 (1995) (arguing that Maine's law on bad faith should have no applicability to the relationship between the surety and the payment bond claimant).

[19] ME. REV. STAT. ANN. tit. 14, § 871(3) (West Supp. 1998).

[20] *Id.*

general contractor must furnish a performance bond.[21] The performance bond is required for any contracts awarded by the state or a contracting body such as a political subdivision, quasi-municipal corporation, or any public authority. Projects covered include the construction, alteration, or repair of any public building or other public improvement or public work, including highways. The performance bond must be payable to and deposited with the state or other contracting body.

The performance bond must be for an amount equal to the full contract amount, conditioned upon the faithful performance of the contract in accordance with the plans, specifications, and conditions.[22] The performance bond shall be solely for the protection of the state or the contracting body awarding the contract.

[D] Payment Bonds

Contractors need not provide payment bonds on private projects. Payment bonds are required for public projects when the contract amount exceeds $100,000.[23] The statute serves as a replacement for a materialman's right to obtain a mechanic's lien because one cannot secure a mechanic's lien on state property.

As with performance bonds, the payment bond is required for any contract awarded by the state, any political subdivision, quasi-municipal corporation, or any public authority. Projects requiring payment bonds are the same as those requiring performance bonds: the construction, alteration, or repair of any public building or other public improvement or public work, including highways. The payment bond must be payable to and deposited with the state or other contracting body.

The payment bond must be for an amount equal to the full contract amount, and must be solely for the protection of claimants supplying labor or materials to the contractor or its subcontractor for work done under the contract. The term *materials* includes the rental of equipment.[24]

If a party in contract with the contractor or subcontractor has not been paid in full before the expiration of 90 days after labor or materials were last furnished, that party may bring an action on the payment bond.[25] If the claimant has a contract with a subcontractor of the prime contractor, but no contractual relationship, express or implied, with the prime contractor, that claimant must give written notice to the prime contractor within 90 days of completion of work or lose the right of action. The written notice must state the amount claimed with substantial accuracy, and the name of the party to whom the material or labor was supplied. Additionally, the notice must be addressed to the contractor at any place it

---

[21] *Id.*

[22] *Id.* § 871(3)(A).

[23] *Id.* § 871(3).

[24] *Id.* § 871(3)(B).

[25] *Id.* § 871(4) (West 1980).

maintains an office or conducts its business or at the contractor's residence. Finally, the notice must be served by registered or certified mail, postage prepaid. However, in *Vacuum Systems, Inc. v. Washburn,*[26] the court held that notice served by first-class mail which is actually received is sufficient to satisfy the statutory notice requirements.

Actions on the payment bond must be brought in the county in which the principal or surety has its principal place of business.[27] This poorly drafted provision, read literally, could require a payment bond action to be brought in California, if that were the home office of the surety. In practice, an action most commonly would be brought against both the contractor and the surety. It is likely that the contractor would not have its business located in the same state as an out of state surety, and therefore the contractor would not be subject to the jurisdiction of the state of the location of the surety. Lawsuits in Maine involving a payment bond typically are filed in the county where either the claimant or the contractor has an established place of business, or where the construction project is located.[28] Presumably, however, an out of state surety technically could raise the defense that an action against it is not properly brought in Maine because the surety has no principal place of business in Maine. Apparently, this quirky venue issue has not been raised in court, and no Maine case law addresses how to resolve the conflict.

No action may be commenced after the expiration of one year from the date on which the unpaid labor or materials were last supplied. The one year limitations period is strictly enforced.[29] If the amount due is unknown because of the unavailability of final quantity estimates for materials supplied, the one-year statute of limitations begins with the determination of the final quantity estimates by the contracting authority.[30] The material supplier must file notice of claim with the contractor/principal within 90 days following the determination of final quantity estimates.

A supplier's recovery under the Public Works Surety Bond law may not include costs and attorneys' fees.[31] Furthermore, a claim for payment pursuant to a payment bond does not incorporate all the contractual remedies, such as recovery of attorneys' fees, a supplier may have against a subcontractor, but merely seeks payment for materials supplied for the job.[32]

---

[26] 651 A.2d 377 (Me. 1994).

[27] Me. Rev. Stat. Ann. tit. 14, § 871(3) (West Supp. 1998).

[28] *Id.* §§ 505, 501 (West 1980).

[29] *See* Vacuum Sys., Inc. v. The Bridge Constr. Co., 632 A.2d 442, 444 (1993) (holding that contractor and surety were permitted to assert a statute of limitations defense when supplier failed to file lawsuit within one year of last providing materials, even though supplier participated informally in arbitration proceeding with contractor).

[30] Me. Rev. Stat. Ann. tit. 14, § 871(4) (West 1980).

[31] Chadwick-BaRoss, Inc. v. T. Buck Constr., Inc., 627 A.2d 532, 536 (Me. 1993).

[32] *Id.*

§ 20.03 LIEN LAW

[A] General Concepts

The Maine statutory provisions governing mechanics' liens are contained in Maine Revised Statutes Annotated title 10, §§ 3251 through 3269, and provisions governing liens for road work and landscaping are contained in Maine Revised Statutes Annotated title 10, § 3501. The lien statute is designed to protect the rights of the owner as well as to afford security for those performing labor or furnishing labor or materials.[33] Maine courts apply a "dual standard" to the interpretation of mechanics' liens.[34] On the one hand, courts will strictly require that every jurisdictional requirement and all conditions as prescribed by statute be met.[35] For example, failure to comply with the requirement that the lien claim be under oath will render the lien fatally deficient.[36] However, "when it is clear that the lien has been honestly earned *and the lien claimant is within the statute,*" the statute will be construed liberally in favor of the claimant "to further [its] equity and efficacy."[37] Thus, the lien claimant should comply strictly with claim and notice requirements.

The lien law applies liberally to anyone who supplies labor or materials or services used in "erecting, altering, moving or repairing" a structure fixed upon land.[38] The statutes specifically extend to property owned by public authorities other than the state of Maine.[39] It does not matter whether the owner owns the property free and clear: the lien attaches to whatever interest the owner has. The claimant need not have contracted directly with the owner or the general contractor.

[B] Lienable Work

In Maine, mechanics' lien rights are available to contractors generally, including whoever (1) performs labor; (2) furnishes labor; (3) furnishes materials (including repair parts of machines used); (4) performs services as a surveyor, architect, or engineer; (5) performs services as a real estate licensee; or (5) leases or supplies equipment used on the project in question.[40]

---

[33] Pineland Lumber Co. v. Robinsons, 382 A.2d 33, 38 (Me. 1982).

[34] *Id.* at 36 (citing Wescott v. Bunker, 83 Me. 499, 506, 22 A. 388 (1891); Expanded Metal Fire-Proofing Co. v. Delp, 247 Pa. 337, 93 A. 496 (1915)).

[35] Pineland Lumber Co. v. Robinsons, 382 A.2d at 36.

[36] *Id.* at 39.

[37] *Id.* (emphasis added) (quoting Shaw v. Young, 87 Me. 271, 32 A. 897 (1895)); *see also* John W. Goodwin, Inc. v. Fox, 642 A.2d 1339, 1341 (Me. 1994); Twin Island Dev. Corp. v. Winchester, 512 A.2d 319, 323 (Me.1986); Shaw v. Young, 87 Me. 271, 274, 32 A. 897 (1895).

[38] ME. REV. STAT. ANN. tit. 10, § 3251 (West Supp. 1998).

[39] *Id.*

[40] *Id.* § 3251.

The labor, services, or materials must be furnished in "erecting, altering, moving or repairing a house, building or appurtenances, including any public building erected or owned by any city, town, county, school district or other municipal corporation."[41] A lien also may arise by virtue of "constructing, altering or repairing a wharf or pier, or any building thereon."[42] Further, a lien arises for the "surveying, clearing, grading, draining, excavating or landscaping of the ground adjacent to and upon which" a house, building or appurtenances, or wharf or pier are constructed.[43] Under a separate statute, work performed "in the laying out or construction of any road, path or walk, or in improving or beautifying any land in a manner commonly known as landscape gardening" will give rise to a lien "on the lot of land over which such road, path or walk is laid out or constructed or on the land so improved and beautified."[44]

When claiming a lien for labor, the labor performed must qualify as lienable work under the statute. For example, in *Dufour v. Silsby,*[45] the court found that the claimant was not entitled to a security lien for snowplowing because that work was not lienable under the statute.

With respect to materials, the party claiming a lien has the burden of proving that materials furnished actually were incorporated into the building.[46] The materials must have been furnished for and identifiable to a particular building, and relying in part upon the credit of the building, and not sold on open account for general use, relying solely on the credit of the purchaser.[47] The fact of delivery permits but does not compel a finding of incorporation.[48] When there is delivery but no evidence of incorporation, and unrefuted evidence that some of the materials were removed from the site, a finding of incorporation is erroneous.[49]

To qualify as lienable work, the items supplied and installed must be "so connected with and attached to the building, so adapted to and necessary for the use for which it was . . . [designed], as to lead to the conclusion that it was intended to be permanently . . . a part of the realty."[50] The theory of the lien statutes is that the work has been a benefit to the realty and enhanced its value.[51] When a tenant installs items which are not affixed to the building, but are subject

[41] *Id.*

[42] *Id.*

[43] *Id.*

[44] *Id.* § 3501.

[45] 411 A.2d 383 (Me. 1980).

[46] LaPointe Bros., Inc. v. Farrell, 363 A.2d 225 (Me. 1976); Thompson Lumber Co. v. Heald, 157 Me. 78, 170 A.2d 156 (1961).

[47] Mutual Lumber Co. v. Gero, 244 A.2d 564, 567–68 (1968); J.W. White Co. v. Griffith, 127 Me. 516, 145 A. 134, 136 (1929).

[48] LaPointe Bros., Inc. v. Farrell, 363 A.2d at 228.

[49] *Id.*

[50] Fischbach & Moore, Inc. v. Presteel Corp., 398 A.2d 397, 399 (Me. 1979) (quoting Baker v. Fessenden, 71 Me. 292, 299 (1880)).

[51] Hanson v. News Publishing Co., 97 Me. 99, 53 A. 990 (1902).

to removal by the tenant, and are not essential to the purpose for which the building was designed, those items are not lienable.[52]

When a particular project concerns such things as sewer lines, or refrigeration lines, or water, gas or electric lines, Maine follows the majority rule that a valid mechanics' lien can attach to, and be enforceable against, one particular parcel of land as security for labor and materials furnished, and work performed, on a different and separate parcel of land, if the work has a physical or beneficial connection with the liened premises and is essential to the convenient and comfortable use of those premises.[53] For example, a contractor may assert a lien against the property of a paper mill for work performed in installing sewage and water pipelines leading to the mill, even though the pipelines are not on the property owned by the mill.[54] Maine courts will allow this type of lien without regard to the nature of the defendant's interests in the outlying property on which the work was done.

In some instances, portions of the work performed by a contractor may be lienable work and portions of the work not lienable. In those cases, a lien may stand only if it is possible to distinguish between the amount of lienable work and the amount of non-lienable work.[55] The lien is valid only to the extent that the labor or materials are incorporated into the building, although the contractor may be entitled to a personal judgment for the nonlienable items not incorporated.[56] When a laborer so intermingles his lien claim with nonlienable items that the exact amount for which he is entitled to a lien cannot be ascertained, the whole lien must fail.[57]

[C] Owner Consent

For the lien to attach, Maine law requires that the labor, materials, or services be provided "by virtue of a contract with or by consent of the owner."[58] The word *owner* includes the possessor of both legal and equitable titles to the real estate. This is important when the property has been mortgaged, because both the possessory owner (equitable title) and the mortgagee (legal title) are considered owners within the meaning of the statute.[59] Although consent of the possessory owner usually is easy to prove, consent of a mortgagee bank is not so simple, especially when the mortgagee is not the construction lender.

---

[52] *Id.*

[53] *See* Newell v. Carlow, Newell & Smith, Inc, 403 A.2d 1209, 1213 (1979).

[54] *Id.* at 1214.

[55] *See* Fischbach & Moore, Inc. v. Presteel Corp., 398 A.2d at 401.

[56] E.A. Thompson Lumber Co. v. Heald, 157 Me. 78, 170 A.2d 156 (1961); Andrew v. Dubeau, 154 Me. 254, 146 A.2d 761 (1958).

[57] *See* Baker v. Fessenden, 71 Me. 292, 293 (1880).

[58] Me. Rev. Stat. Ann. tit. 10, § 3251 (West Supp. 1998).

[59] Bateman v. F.D.I.C., 970 F.2d 924, 927 (1st Cir. 1992) (interpreting Maine's lien statute); Carey v. Boulette, 158 Me. 204, 213, 182 A.2d 473, 475 (1962).

To show that an owner has consented, the party asserting the lien must show (1) that the owner had knowledge of the nature and extent of the work being performed, and (2) conduct on the part of the owner justifying the expectation that it had consented to the making of the alterations on the credit of the property.[60] A lienholder can demonstrate mortgagee consent by showing that the bank knew about the work on the property and failed to object, and perhaps by showing the absence of other special circumstances suggesting lack of consent.[61]

In those cases in which a tenant has contracted with the lien claimant, the landlord's consent can be inferred from the language of a lease permitting the tenant to make alterations, the landlord's knowledge of what was contemplated and what was actually done, and the landlord's conduct.[62] In *Fischbach & Moore, Inc. v. Presteel Corp.,*[63] a lease authorized the tenant to obtain electrical installation work without special permission from the landlord. The landlord knew that the work was in progress and never objected. Consent was inferred.

If an owner who leaves property in the hands of a tenant knows that repairs will necessarily be made from time to time, but makes no provision for them, consent to those repairs will be inferred absent dissent.[64]

Consent can be inferred from the actions of an agent. Knowledge of the work is imputed to the owner when the agent has actual knowledge.[65] If the owner does not object based upon this imputed knowledge, consent is inferred.[66] An owner can negate a claim of "consent" by giving written notice that it will not be responsible for the labor, materials, or services furnished.[67]

The mechanics' lien can attach only to that interest the owner has in the property.[68] The lien does not attach to the land if the owner's interest only extends to the building upon the land.[69] If the contracting party has no interest in the land or its improvements, or has failed to procure the owner's consent, the lien has nothing to attach to and becomes a nullity.[70] It is, therefore, incumbent upon a materialman seeking to establish a lien to determine the extent of the contracting party's interest in the land or the consent of the owner.[71]

Ownership is determined at the time services giving rise to the lien are first rendered.[72]

---

[60] Carey v. Boulette, 158 Me. at 213, 182 A.2d at 475.

[61] Bateman v. F.D.I.C., 970 F.2d at 927.

[62] Fischbach & Moore, Inc. v. Presteel Corp., 398 A.2d at 400 (Me. 1979) (citing Maxim v. Thibault, 124 Me. 201, 126 A. 869 (1924)).

[63] *Id.*

[64] Shaw v. Young, 87 Me. 271, 32 A. 897 (1895).

[65] Parker-Danner Co. v. Nickerson, 554 A.2d 1193 (Me. 1989).

[66] *Id.*

[67] ME. REV. STAT. ANN. tit. 10, § 3252 (West 1997).

[68] *Id.* § 3251 (West Supp. 1998).

[69] *Id.*

[70] Lyon v. Dunn, 402 A.2d 461, 463 (Me. 1979).

[71] *Id.*

[72] *Id.*

[D] Residential Homeowner Protection

In Maine, special protection against double payment is provided to residential owners.[73] Enforcement of a lien against an owner of commercial or industrial property may result in that owner paying twice—once to the contractor and then to the unpaid subcontractor. However, for owners of residential property, the lien can only be enforced to the extent of the balance due to the general contractor upon commencement of the action or upon written notice from the subcontracting party.[74]

Written notice to the owner must set forth (1) a description of the property sufficiently accurate to identify it; (2) names of the owners; (3) that the person giving notice will, is in the process of, or has provided labor, supplies, or services; (4) that the person giving notice may claim a lien; and (5) the following warning: "Under Maine law, your failure to assure that ____________________ (name of the claimant giving notice) is paid before further payment by you to ____________________ (name of contractor) may result in your paying twice."[75] This written notice does not negate the need for filing the lien claim statement required under § 3253.[76]

[E] Time Limitations for Enforcing Liens

A mechanics' lien arises from the moment the first materials, labor, or services are furnished[77] and requires no pre-work notification or filing. However, the lien cannot be enforced without further action from the holder of the lien.[78] What action is required will depend upon whether the work was provided pursuant to a direct contract with the owner.

Under § 3255(1) of the Maine Revised Statutes Annotated, if a contractor furnishes labor, materials, or services pursuant to a contract *directly with the owner,* and that contractor claimant wants to preserve his lien, a lien statement need not be filed in the Registry of Deeds,[79] but "*within 120 days after the last of the labor or services are performed or labor, materials or services are so furnished*" the claimant must commence an action in the county in which the property is located.[80] The claimant must file his action against the debtor and the

---

[73] ME. REV. STAT. ANN. tit. 10, § 3255(3) (West 1997).

[74] *Id.* The amount "due" the contractor is subject to deduction or setoffs in favor of the homeowner for improperly performed work. Pond Cove Millwork Co. v. Steeves, 598 A.2d 1181 (Me. 1991).

[75] *Id.*

[76] *Id.*

[77] Lyon v. Dunn, 402 A.2d at 463.

[78] *Id.*

[79] ME. REV. STAT. ANN. tit. 10, § 3253 (West 1997).

[80] *Id.* § 3255(1).

owner of the property affected, and all other parties who have an interest in the property.[81]

Under § 3253 of the Maine Revised Statutes Annotated, if a contractor *does not have a contract directly with the owner,* then to preserve his lien the contractor claimant must record a lien claim statement in the office of the Registry of Deeds in the county in which the property is situated.[82] This lien claim statement must be filed "*within 90 days after he ceases to labor, furnish materials or perform services.*"[83] The claimant then must also file a civil action within 120 days after the last of the labor or services are performed or labor, materials or services are furnished, as specified in § 3255, and the action must list as defendants the debtor and the owner of the property affected, and all other parties who have an interest in the property.[84]

When filing the civil action in court, the claimant should be sure to remember the broad meaning of "owner" as described in **§ 20.03[C].** Whenever the property is mortgaged, the claimant may have a contract with the person regarded as the owner, but the claimant will rarely have a direct contract with the mortgagee. The claimant in this typical situation must file the 90-day lien notice in the Registry of Deeds and the 120-day civil action in court if the lien is to take priority over the interest of the mortgagee.

Courts must liberally interpret the description of property to validate the lien, so long as the property can be reasonably recognized. Inaccuracy as to the amount due is not fatal so long as it does not appear that the claimant "willfully claims more than his due."[85]

The notice requirements for preserving a lien are strictly enforced, but even if a lien claimant fails to preserve and perfect his lien as required under the lien statute, that failure does not bar an action for breach of contract or unjust enrichment.[86] Further, the fact that the owner is a governmental entity that has received a benefit without payment, does not necessarily bar recovery for unjust enrichment based on governmental immunity.[87]

To preserve a lien, there can be no overstating the importance of filing the lien statement in the Registry of Deeds within 90 days of the completion of work (when the contractor does not have a contract directly with the owner) and filing the civil action within 120 days of completion of work (in all cases). If the 90th

---

[81] *Id.*

[82] *Id.* § 3253.

[83] *Id.*

[84] *Id.* § 3255.

[85] *Id.* § 3254.

[86] A.F.A.B., Inc. v. Town of Old Orchard Beach, 610 A.2d 747, 749-50 (Me. 1992) (*A.F.A.B. I*).

[87] A.F.A.B., Inc. v. Town of Old Orchard Beach, 639 A.2d 103, 105-06 & n.4 (Me. 1994) (*A.F.A.B. II*). In determining damages for unjust enrichment, the contractor's bill is relevant but not dispositive in determining the value of the benefit the owner actually received and retained. A.F.A.B., Inc. v. Town of Old Orchard Beach, 657 A.2d 323, 325 (Me. 1995) (*A.F.A.B. III*).

or 120th day falls on a Saturday, Sunday, or holiday, the period for filing is extended to the next day that is not a Saturday, Sunday, or holiday.[88]

[F] Completion of Work

Because the time period for commencing a lien action is based on the completion of the work, and because there is no statutorily prescribed method for establishing the completion of the work, determining when work is "completed" generates considerable uncertainty. The 90-day and 120-day time limits are created to give the owner assurance that, after that time expires, it will be free to pay the contractor without fear of double liability. In general, when the claimant's work is "completed" depends on the nature of the last work. Unfortunately, this issue has been interpreted infrequently within the last century by the Maine Supreme Court, so there is little case law guidance.

It is clear that "trifling services" will not extend or revive a lien period: "The laborer ought not to be encouraged to leave some trifling matter incomplete and wait to see if payment is made, if that fails, complete the trifling work to revive and continue the lien."[89] However, if the minor service was an unintentionally omitted detail of a contract, but was an item for which the owner had an absolute right to demand delivery before payment of the contract price, the work may be considered incomplete until that delivery.[90] In general, the value of the material last furnished is not controlling so long as the contractor furnished the service in good faith, and not as a mere accommodation for which no charge was intended.[91] Thus, the status of punch-list work is unclear, and the claimant should be conservative in its assessment of last work.

A lien claimant must distinguish between work done pursuant to more than one contract and work under one continuing contract. If a claimant performed work under one contract, for the benefit of the owner, the fact that the materials were furnished at different times has no relevance: the lien is effective for all work. However, one lien cannot cover a series of distinct contracts, even if they relate to one building.[92] In one case, a supplier had entered into a contract with a builder to supply materials to build a house.[93] When the builder canceled the contract with the owner, the supplier contracted directly with the owner. The

---

[88] ME. REV. STAT. ANN. tit. 1, § 71(12). Although the Law Court held in Bellegarde Custom Kitchens v. Leavitt, 295 A.2d 909, 912 (Me. 1972) that the time period for filing a lien or lien action is not extended even if the 90th or 120th day falls on a weekend or holiday, this holding was legislatively overruled in 1973 by ME. REV. STAT. ANN. tit. 1, § 71(12), which specifically provides that the statutory computation period for civil actions shall be in accordance with Rule 6(a) of the Maine Rules of Civil Procedure.

[89] Hartley v. Richardson, 91 Me. 424, 430, 40 A. 336, 337 (1898).

[90] Delano Mill Co. v. Warren, 123 Me. 408, 123 A. 417, 418 (1924).

[91] *Id.* (citing Cole v. Clark, 85 Me. 336, 27 A. 186 (1893); Hartley v. Richardson, 91 Me. 424, 40 A. 336 (1898)).

[92] Van Wart v. Reed, 112 Me. 404, 92 A. 328 (1914).

[93] Baker v. Fessenden, 71 Me. 292 (1880).

second contract, although it continued the work performed under the first, did not extend the lien period of the first contract.[94] Because the owner had paid under its contract with the supplier, and the lien period arising under the contract with the builder had expired, the supplier was without remedy under the lien statute.[95]

If the lien period does expire, the contractor cannot revive it by fictitiously trying to extend the date of the completion of the work.[96]

[G] Form and Content of Lien Statement

The lien claim statement required to be filed in the Registry of Deeds under § 3253 must state (1) the amount due the lien claimant, with all just credits given; (2) a description of the property intended to be covered by the lien sufficiently accurate to identify it; and (3) the names of the owners, if known.[97] The statement must be signed and sworn to.[98]

Failure to file the notice with the Registry of Deeds under § 3253, if the lien claimant is not in direct contract with the owner, will result in the dissolution of the lien.[99] The subcontractor lien claimant will have no lien to enforce by commencing action under § 3255 if § 3253 is not complied with.[100]

Failure to swear to the truth of the facts contained in the lien statement will render the statement statutorily deficient.[101] A claimant's oath stating only that the foregoing statement was its "free act and deed" is fatally deficient.[102] On the other hand, personal knowledge of the facts asserted is not required.[103]

[H] Form and Content of Complaint

The complaint to enforce a lien may be filed in superior or district court[104] in the county or division where the property affected is located.[105] The complaint itself must state:

---

[94] *Id.*

[95] *Id.*

[96] *See* Morin v. H. W. Maxim Co., 146 Me. 421, 82 A.2d 789 (1951); Marshall v. Mathieu, 143 Me. 167, 57 A.2d 400 (1948).

[97] ME. REV. STAT. ANN. tit. 10, § 3253 (West 1997).

[98] *Id.*

[99] Lyon v. Dunn, 402 A.2d 461, 463 (Me. 1979).

[100] *Id.* at 466.

[101] Pineland Lumber Co. v. Robinsons, 382 A.2d 33, 37 (Me. 1982).

[102] *Id.*

[103] HCI Corp. v. Voikos Constr. Co., 581 A.2d 795, 798 (Me. 1990) (holding that, for a person swearing to the truth of the contents of a lien statement, it is sufficient for that person to swear to the truth of the statements based on that person's best knowledge, information or belief).

[104] In 1981, ME. REV. STAT. ANN. tit. 10, § 3255(1) (West 1965) was revised to expressly permit lien actions to be filed in district court in addition to superior court, thus overruling cases such as Choate v. Adams, 387 A.2d 227, 228 (Me. 1978) (holding that only the superior court had jurisdiction to entertain actions for the enforcement of liens).

[105] ME. REV. STAT. ANN. tit. 10, § 3255(1) (West 1997).

1. The plaintiff claims a lien on the building and land upon which it stands for labor, materials, or services furnished in erecting, altering, moving, or repairing the building;
2. Whether the plaintiff had a contract with the owner or consent of the owner;
3. If there is no contract directly with the owner, that the plaintiff has complied with § 3253;
4. That the property should be sold and the proceeds applied to the discharge of the lien;[106]
5. The date on which the last item of work was furnished;[107]
6. Whether a jury trial is demanded;[108] and
7. The caption must include the phrase "Title to Real Estate Affected."

The debtor and the owner(s) *must* be parties.[109] The court in *John W. Goodwin, Inc. v. Fox,*[110] however, held that the subcontractor could amend its complaint to add the debtor contractor in the early stages of the litigation, even though it was after the 120-day statutory period. If the debtor is a subcontractor, the contractor need not be joined, even if the owner has paid the contractor, who then failed to pay the subcontractor.[111] The lien claimant may join tenants, mortgagees, other lienors, and other parties with interests in the property.[112]

The practice in Maine is to perform a title search in the Registry of Deeds before filing to determine the identities of all "owners" so that they may be named as defendants in the civil action. Failure to name an owner as a defendant within the 120 days may result in loss of priority as against that owner.

If the owner or contractor wrongfully withheld payments due, the claimant may want to consider including a count in the lien complaint for violation of Maine's "Prompt Pay" statute.[113] The statute provides for interest, a one percent per month penalty, and attorneys' fees to the "substantially prevailing party."[114]

[I] Bona Fide Purchasers

A bona fide purchaser can take title free of the lien unless the lien claimant has filed a lien claim in the Registry of Deeds under § 3253 *or* filed a special

[106] *Id.* § 3257.

[107] Pendleton v. Sard, 297 A.2d 889, 896 (Me. 1972) (noting that the plaintiff failed to follow the form of complaint set out in Field, McKusick and Wroth, MAINE CIVIL PRACTICE, Vol. 1, Sec. 8.28, p. 213).

[108] ME. REV. STAT. ANN. tit. 10, § 3258 (West 1997).

[109] Andrew v. Bishop, 132 Me. 447, 172 A. 752 (1934). *See also* T.A. Napolitano Elec. Contractors, Inc. v. Direnzo, 602 A.2d 1149 (Me. 1992) (debtor contractor must be joined even when judgment-proof).

[110] 642 A.2d 1339, 1341 (Me. 1994).

[111] *Id.*

[112] ME. REV. STAT. ANN. tit. 10, § 3257 (West 1997).

[113] *Id.* §§ 1111-1120.

[114] *Id.* § 1120.

notice (its "I may file a lien" notice) with the Registry of Deeds pursuant to § 3255, setting forth (1) a description of the property; (2) the names of the owners; (3) that the claimant is going to, is, or has provided labor, materials, or services; (4) that the claimant *may* claim a lien therefor.[115] To preserve the lien, the claimant must then satisfy the notice requirements under § 3253 and commence an action under § 3255(1). This notice must be refiled every 120 days to remain effective.[116]

The purpose of this special notice is to give notice as early as possible to the world that a contractor is working on a project, that the work has not yet been completed, and that the contractor may file a lien if necessary. The existence of the "I may file a lien" notice is sufficient to give the lien claimant priority over a bona fide purchaser. In the absence of this special notice, in theory an owner could sell a partially completed building free of all liens accruing before the sale.

This special notice may be filed before any labor, materials, or services are actually provided.

[J] Waiver

A general arbitration clause will not constitute a waiver of a lien claimant's statutory right to a mechanics' lien, nor will assertion of the lien invalidate the arbitration clause. A lienor may be required to arbitrate the issue of entitlement but may still enforce that debt by means of a mechanics' lien.[117] Typically, upon request the court will stay the mechanics' lien action during the arbitration, retaining jurisdiction to enforce the award.

[K] Lien Priority

A valid lien claim, when reduced to judgment, is entitled to priority over the interest of the owner and all mortgagees who have consented to the work. The court is authorized to sell the property and distribute the proceeds to the successful lien claimant. Lienholders generally share in the proceeds on a pro rata basis, regardless of the filing date of the lien notices or complaints.

A lienholder even may take priority over a mortgage given subsequent to the making of the contract, though the labor and materials may actually be furnished after the mortgage is given.[118]

[L] Remedies of Owner

The owner may petition the court for release of the lien. The petition must set forth:

1. The name of the lienor;
2. The court and county in which the action is pending;

---

[115] *Id.* § 3255(2).

[116] *Id.*

[117] Buckminster v. Acadia Village Resort, Inc., 565 A.2d 313 (Me. 1989).

[118] Saucier v. Maine Supply & Garage Co., 109 Me. 342, 84 A. 461 (1912).

3. The fact that a lien is claimed;
4. The particular structure upon which the lien is claimed;
5. The owner's interest in the structure;
6. The structure's value; and
7. The owner's desire to have the property released from the lien.[119]

The court may and almost universally does order the owner to give bond to the lienor in the full amount of the lien claim as a condition of releasing the property from the lien, and the practice typically is to provide the bond at the time of the petition for the release of the lien.[120] The release of lien section of the lien statute was not designed as a vehicle for challenging procedural deficiencies in securing the lien.[121]

---

[119] ME. REV. STAT. ANN. tit. 10, § 3263 (West 1997).

[120] *See* LaPointe Lumber Co. v. Tanist Broad. Corp., 482 A.2d 1265, 1267-68 (Me. 1984) (finding that the plaintiff's interest was not protected when the court purported to release its lien without requiring a bond).

[121] *Id.* at 1268.

CHAPTER 21

MARYLAND

Robert M. Wright

§ 21.01 INTRODUCTION

There is no requirement in Maryland to provide bonds on private work. Contractors, subcontractors, laborers, and material suppliers are granted mechanics' lien rights on most construction projects. The mechanics' lien law is contained in the Real Property Code, §§ 9-101 *et seq.* of the Annotated Code of Maryland.

With respect to public projects, there is no available mechanics' lien. The Maryland State Finance and Procurement Code, §§ 17-101 *et seq.*, provides that for contracts exceeding $100,000 awarded by a public body, the contractor must provide payment and performance security either by a bond executed by a surety company authorized to do business in the state or cash in an amount equivalent to a bond or other securities satisfactory to the public body awarding the contract. The amount of the performance security is an amount that the public body considers adequate, and payment security must be at least 50 percent of the total amount payable under the contract. A public body other than the state or unit of state government may require payment or performance security if the contract exceeds $25,000 but does not exceed $100,000 and the amount of the security does not exceed 50 percent of the contract amount.

§ 21.02 BOND LAW

[A] General Concepts

Maryland's law applicable to private surety bonds is in general fairly standard. A contract of suretyship is a tripartite agreement among principal, obligor, obligee, and surety. The surety is primarily or jointly liable with the principal once the principal fails to perform.[1] Absent limitations or restrictions contained in the bond instrument, the surety's liability is coextensive with that of the principal.[2] As a general rule, the surety's maximum liability is the penal sum of the bond.[3]

In Maryland, surety contracts are governed by the same rules of construction as other contracts. The surety's contractual burdens are limited to the provisions of the bond and cannot be extended by implication beyond the bond provisions.[4] If the construction contract is incorporated into the bond, the bond agreement will be construed together with the contract to determine the extent and scope of the surety's liability.[5]

---

[1] General Motors Acceptance Corp. v. Daniels, 303 Md. 254, 492 A.2d 1306 (1985).

[2] President & Directors v. Madden, 505 F. Supp. 557 (D. Md. 1980), *aff'd in part and dismissed in part,* 660 F.2d 91 (4th Cir. 1981).

[3] Republic Ins. Co. v. Board of County Comm'r, 68 Md. App. 428, 511 A.2d 1136 (1986).

[4] State Highway Admin. v. Transamerica Ins. Co., 278 Md. 690, 367 A.2d 509 (1976); Burdette v. Lascola, 40 Md. App. 720, 395 A.2d 169 (1978).

[5] President & Directors v. Madden, 505 F. Supp. 557 (D. Md. 1980), *aff'd in part and dismissed in part,* 660 F.2d 91 (4th Cir. 1981).

The surety's liability for damages, in the absence of a contractual limitation, is measured by the loss or damage directly resulting from the default of the principal.[6] The surety is subject to liability for interest claims made by laborers, materialmen, subcontractors, and the owner. In general, interest is computed from the time of demand or notice.[7]

Maryland recognizes that absent a waiver by the surety in the bond, any material change, modification, or variance of the surety's obligation without the surety's consent releases it from liability.[8] A modification or change that does not materially increase the risk of the surety will not discharge the surety but will only reduce the extent of its loss due to the modification.[9] Likewise, an extension to the principal of the time for payment or performance of the principal's obligation without the consent of surety, absent a contractual waiver provision, will also discharge the surety to the extent that the surety is harmed by the extension.[10]

The obligee's neglect to proceed against the principal on the bond will not discharge the surety's obligation.[11] The surety's obligation is direct and primary, and it cannot require the obligee to proceed against the principal because the obligee has a choice of action against the surety or the principal or both.[12]

[B] Statutes of Limitation on Bonds for Private Work

The Maryland Insurance Code contains a provision voiding limitations contained in surety bonds that are shorter than the applicable limitations under Maryland law.[13] The applicable period of limitations for suits on a bond given on a private project is 12 years.[14] The right of action on the bond may, however, be affected by the state statute of repose which, in general, eliminates a cause of

---

[6] *Id.;* General Builders Supply Co. v. MacArthur, 228 Md. 320, 179 A.2d 868 (1962).

[7] Peerless Ins. Co. v. Board of County Comm'rs, 248 Md. 439, 237 A.2d 15 (1968).

[8] Burdette v. Lascola, 40 Md. App. 720, 395 A.2d 169 (1978).

[9] Fidelity & Deposit Co. v. Olney Assocs., Inc., 72 Md. App. 367, 539 A.2d 1 (1987).

[10] *Id.;* A/C Elec. Co. v. Aetna Ins. Co., 251 Md. 410, 247 A.2d 708 (1967).

[11] President & Directors v. Madden, 505 F. Supp. 557 (D. Md. 1980), *aff'd in part and dismissed in part,* 660 F.2d 91 (4th Cir. 1981).

[12] General Motors Acceptance Corp. v. Daniels, 303 Md. 254, 492 A.2d 1306 (1985).

[13] MD. CODE ANN., INS. § 12-104 (Repl. Vol. 1997). In General Ins. Co. of Am. v. Interstate Serv. Co., Inc., 118 Md. App. 126 (1997), suit was filed in Maryland on bonds issued for work done in the District of Columbia and Virginia. The bonds were not issued in Maryland and none of the parties were residents of Maryland. Each bond contained a one (1) year time for suit provision. Contrary to Maryland's law, neither the District of Columbia nor Virginia prohibited a provision in a bond fixing a shorter time limit for suit than that fixed by statute. The Court found that the law of the District of Columbia and Virginia should be applied validating the contractual statute of limitations contained in the bond instruments notwithstanding the fact that the limitation violated Maryland public policy. The Court found that Maryland did not have a materially greater interest in the determination of the issue than did the District of Columbia or Virginia.

[14] MD. CODE ANN., CTS. & JUD. PROC. § 5-102(a)(2) (Repl. Vol. 1998). *See also* President & Directors v. Madden, 505 F. Supp. 557 (D. Md. 1980), *aff'd in part and dismissed in part,* 660 F.2d 91 (4th Cir. 1981).

action against a contractor resulting from the defective or unsafe condition of an improvement to real property occurring more than 10 years after the date the entire improvement first became available for its intended use.[15]

[C] Bid Bonds

Bid bonds are not required by state law on any private project. However, on public projects, if the price is expected to exceed $100,000, bid security is required.[16] Bid security is also required for contracts under $100,000 if federal law or a condition of federal assistance requires bid security. The amount of bid security required for a construction contract is at least five percent of the bid price or price proposal. If the proposal states a rate but not a total price, the amount is in the amount determined by the procurement officer. The required bid security is a bond provided by a surety company authorized to do business in the state of Maryland or cash or any other form of security allowed by regulation. With some exceptions, if bid security is required, the procurement officer must reject a bid or proposal that is not accompanied by proper security.[17] Whenever a bidder or offeror withdraws a bid or proposal, action may be taken against the bid security unless there is a mistake in the bid or proposal and the procurement officer allows the bidder or offeror to withdraw before the procurement contract is awarded.[18]

The bid security's purpose is to assure the owner that the prospective contractor, if awarded the contract, will execute the contract documents and furnish the required bonds. The bid bond's legal effect ends once the contract documents are executed and the required bonds are posted. It does not guarantee the performance of the project or the payment of the contractor's bills.[19]

[D] Public Works Bonds

Other than the statutory requirements for performance security previously described in **§ 21.01**, there are no statutory terms and conditions regarding the contractor's performance security. The Code of Maryland Regulations, however, does prescribe the terms and conditions of the performance security.[20] The bond form provides for either the principal or surety to be sued severally as well as

[15] Md. Code Ann., Cts. & Jud. Proc. § 5-108 (Repl. Vol. 1998). If there is no substantiative cause of action against the contractor by reason of the statute of repose, then there may be no action on the bond. President & Directors v. Madde, 505 F. Supp. 557, 590 (D. Md. 1980), *aff'd in part and dismissed in part,* 660 F.2d 91 (4th Cir. 1981). The Maryland statute of repose has been applied to contract actions. Hilliard & Bartko v. Fedco Sys., 309 Md. 147 (1987); Rouse-Teachers Properties, Inc. v. Maryland Cas. Co., No. 572 Sept. Term 1995 (Ct. Spec. App. (unreported) Jan. 4, 1996). Similar statutes in other states have been applied only to tort actions.

[16] Md. Code Ann., State Fin. & Proc. § 13-207 (Repl. Vol. 1995).

[17] *Id.* § 13-208.

[18] *Id.* § 13-209.

[19] Kennedy Temporaries v. Comptroller of the Treasury, 57 Md. App. 22, 468 A.2d 1026 (1986).

[20] Md. Regs. Code tit. 21, § 21.07.02.10 (1985).

jointly and incorporates the construction contract by reference. The bond states that it stays in effect during any guaranty or warranty period. The surety's obligations commence when the principal is declared to be in default and gives the surety 15 days to either remedy the default or to proceed to complete the contract. If the surety does not act within 15 days, the obligee has a right to proceed to have the remaining contract work completed, with the surety remaining liable for all expenses of completion up to but not exceeding the penal sum of the bond. The bond contains the standard agreement that no change, extension of time, alteration, or addition to the terms of the contract or to the work to be performed shall affect the surety's obligations and contains a stipulation that the surety waives notice of any such action.

Payment security provided under the State Finance and Procurement Code is liberally construed to protect those who supply labor and materials to public construction projects.[21] The Maryland courts generally look to federal decisions under the Miller Act for assistance in interpreting the Maryland statute.[22] However, Miller Act cases are not followed when inconsistent with the intention of the Maryland legislation.[23]

The Maryland statute is by its terms broader than the Miller Act in the tiers of suppliers who are protected. The statute specifically protects a supplier who has a direct contractual relationship with a subcontractor or sub-subcontractor.[24] Maryland law follows federal authority in defining what constitutes a subcontractor.[25] For purposes of the statute, a *subcontractor* is one who performs for and takes from prime contractors a specific part of the labor or material requirements of the original contract. A *subsubcontractor* is one who performs for and takes from a subcontractor a specific part of the labor or material requirements of the subcontract.[26]

Coverage under the payment security includes all labor or materials used in the prosecution of the work provided for in the contract even when a small portion is provided after the notice required by statute.[27] Coverage is also provided for rental equipment to the extent that the equipment is used in the completion of the bonded work.[28] Interest is generally recoverable as a matter of right on the bond when demand has been made to the surety and the surety refuses to pay, or if no demand is made, from the date when suit is filed.[29] Engineering, surveying, and

---

[21] Viscount Constr. Co. v. Dorman Elec. Supply Co., 68 Md. App. 362, 511 A.2d 1102 (1986).

[22] 40 U.S.C.A. § 270(a) (1988); Montgomery County Bd. of Educ. v. Glassman Constr. Co., 245 Md. 192, 225 A.2d 448 (1967); Anne Arundel County v. Fidelity & Deposit Co., 336 Md. 282, 648 A.2d 193 (1994).

[23] General Fed. Constr., Inc. v. D.R. Thomas, Inc., 52 Md. App. 700, 451 A.2d 1250 (1982).

[24] MD. CODE ANN., STATE FIN. & PROC. § 17-108 (1988).

[25] Atlantic Sea-Con, Ltd. v. Robert Dann Co., 321 Md. 275, 582 A.2d 981 (1990).

[26] *Id.*

[27] Stauffer Constr. Co. v. Tate Eng'g, 44 Md. App. 240, 407 A.2d 1191 (1979).

[28] State *ex rel.* Gwynns Falls Quarry Co. v. National Sur. Co., 148 Md. 221, 128 A. 916 (1925).

[29] Mullan Contracting Co. v. IBM Corp., 220 Md. 248, 151 A.2d 906 (1959); Peerless Ins. Co. v. Board of County Comm'rs, 248 Md. 439, 237 A.2d 15 (1968).

architectural services necessary to the construction of the project are recoverable under the bond.[30]

[E] Notice Requirements

A claimant who has a direct contractual relationship with a subcontractor or a sub-subcontractor of a contractor who has provided payment security but who has no contractual relationship with the contractor must give written notice to the contractor within 90 days after the labor or materials for which claim is made were last supplied in the prosecution of the work.[31] The purpose of the notice is to protect the prime contractor.[32] The statute requires that the notice shall (1) state with substantial accuracy the amount claimed and the person to whom the labor or material was supplied; and (2) be sent by certified mail to the contractor at the contractor's residence or a place where the contractor has an office or does business. The court of appeals held that delivery by a supplier to a subcontractor of materials used to correct work defectively done or to replace a defective product or to cure an omitted performance will extend the time limit for the 90-day notice even though the work was completed prior to the deliveries.[33]

There are no cases under the Maryland statute indicating whether the notice merely has to be mailed within 90 days or must be received within 90 days. Under the Maryland mechanics' lien law, notice sent by registered mail within the 90-day period but received in the ordinary course of the mail after the 90-day period is effective.[34] However, in *Pepper Burns Insulation, Inc. v. Artco Corp.*,[35] the Fourth Circuit held that service was untimely under the federal Miller Act when the notice was mailed within 90 days but not received until more than 90 days after the date of last work. In this connection, the wording of both the federal Act and the Maryland Act with respect to the sending of notice is identical. Counsel should ensure that notice is sent and received within the 90-day period, as the Maryland court may follow the federal decisions under its public bond statute.

When there is a series of deliveries on open account, there are no decisions under the State Finance and Procurement Code as to when a notice must be given. However, cases under the Maryland Mechanics' Lien Law may be applied to this statute by analogy.[36] Under the lien law, the time of notice runs from the date of last delivery when there are continuous deliveries of similar products without any lengthy intervals. Maryland courts look to see if the appearance of the transaction

---

[30] Peerless Ins. Co. v. Board of County Comm'rs, 248 Md. 439, 237 A.2d 15 (1968); Caton Ridge, Inc. v. Bonnett, 245 Md. 268, 225 A.2d 853 (1967).

[31] MD. CODE ANN., STATE FIN. & PROC. § 17-108 (Repl. Vol. 1995).

[32] Stauffer Constr. Co. v. Tate Eng'g, 44 Md. App. 240, 407 A.2d 1191 (1979).

[33] Insurance Co. of N. Am. v. Genstar Stone Prods. Co., 338 Md. 161, 656 A.2d 1232 (1995). An agreement between the prime contractor and the subcontractor that the prime will pay the supplier of the subcontractor directly may not excuse the notice requirement.

[34] Reiley v. Abrams, 287 Md. 348, 412 A.2d 996 (1980).

[35] 970 F.2d 1340 (4th Cir. 1992).

[36] Caton Ridge, Inc. v. Bonnett, 245 Md. 268, 225 A.2d 853 (1967).

reflects an express or implied understanding that the supplier should furnish the materials as needed in the construction process so as to view the open account as a single contract.[37] As a practical matter, suppliers furnishing on an open account generally prevail under this theory.

[F] Requirements for and Limitations on Filing Suit

Under both performance and payment security bonds given under the State Finance and Procurement Code, the statute requires that suit be filed in the appropriate court of the county where the contract was executed and performed or where the contractor has its principal place of business.[38] Unless a longer period is provided in the bond instrument, suit must be commenced on the payment bond within one year after the public body finally accepts the work performed under the contract. There is no specified limitation for the public body to file suit under the performance bond. Section 17-109(b) was amended, effective October 1994, to provide that an action *on a payment bond* required by this subtitle shall be filed within one year after the public body finally accepts the work performed under the contract.[39] There are no Maryland cases establishing the time limit for the public obligee to file suit on the performance bond.

When final acceptance has occurred is a mixed question of law and fact. In general terms, the court of appeals has held that the acceptance of the work is the date when the contractor's responsibility to the owner and the owner's liability to the contractor are at an end. This date has been held in particular cases to be the date of release of final payment to the contractor;[40] the date when the last inspection certificate was obtained;[41] or the date of the architect's certificate of completion.[42]

[G] Waiver of Rights

Only a clear and express waiver terminates rights under a public bond. Joint check agreements do not waive the right to claim under a bond nor does the taking of additional security.[43]

Section 9-113 of the Real Property Article provides that an executory

---

[37] Back v. Reisterstown Lumber Co., 24 Md. App. 415, 332 A.2d 30, *cert. denied,* 275 Md. 745 (1975).

[38] Md. Code Ann., State Fin. & Proc. § 17-109 (1988).

[39] *See* discussion in Anne Arundel County v. Fidelity & Deposit Co., 336 Md. 282, 648 A.2d 193 (1994).

[40] Joseph J. Hock, Inc. v. Baltimore Contractors, Inc., 252 Md. 61, 249 A.2d 135 (1969).

[41] General Fed. Constr., Inc. v. D.R. Thomas, Inc., 59 Md. App. 700, 451 A.2d 1250 (1982).

[42] USF&G v. Hamilton & Spiegel, Inc., 241 Md. 133, 215 A.2d 735 (1966).

[43] Allied Bldg. Prods. Corp. v. United Pac. Ins. Co., 77 Md. App. 220, 549 A.2d 1163 (1988). As to circumstances where an etoppel may be raised, *see* Green's Partnership vs. Rollin Bldg. Supply Co., 87 Md App. 220, 589 A.2d 536 (1991).

contract may not require a subcontractor to waive the right to claim on a contractor's bond. Section 9-113, as amended, passed by the legislature in 1994, further provides that a "pay when paid" clause does not abrogate or waive the right of the subcontractor to sue on a contractor's bond.

[H] Effect of Arbitration Clause on Bond Claims

Maryland's Court of Appeals has ruled that when the principal's contract contains an arbitration clause, and the contract is incorporated by reference in the performance bond, the arbitration clause in the underlying contract does not apply to claims on the bond unless it so states specifically in its terms. The court stated that absent an indication of a contrary intention, the incorporation of one contract into another involving different parties does not automatically transform the incorporated document into an agreement between the parties to the second contract.[44]

§ 21.03 LIEN LAW

Maryland's mechanics' lien law was enacted in 1791 and was the first such law in the country. It was enacted to encourage the construction of the District of Columbia. It is one of the more procedurally complex mechanics' lien laws in existence. Although there are many statements in the cases that the law is to be liberally construed in favor of lien claimants, the principal of liberal construction is not applicable to the procedural requirements of the statute, and all statutory requirements must be strictly met.

[A] Property Subject to Mechanics' Lien

Every building erected and every building repaired, rebuilt, or improved to the extent of 15 percent of its value is subject to a mechanics' lien for the payment of all debts without regard to the amount contracted for work done or materials supplied for or about the building. It is not necessary for the individual lien claimant to have done work or supplied materials to the extent of 15 percent of the value of the building so long as the work is a part of a general undertaking (the general contract), the total value of which is not less than 15 percent. The statute does not contain a definition of what constitutes a *building*. The term has been defined to mean an erection intended for use and occupancy as a habitation, or for some purpose of trade, manufacture, ornament, or use such as a house, store, or church but does not include every type of structure on land.[45] The value

[44] Hartford Accident & Indem. Co. v. Scarlett Harbor Associated Ltd. Partnership, 346 Md. 122, 695 A.2d 153 (1997).

[45] Freeform Pools, Inc. v. Strawbridge Home for Boys, Inc., 228 Md. 297, 179 A.2d 683 (1962).

of the work and not the contract price is determinative as to the valuation of the improvement.[46]

The statute specifically includes the drilling and installation of wells to supply water, the construction or installation of any swimming pool or fencing, the sodding, seeding, or planting in or about the premises of any shrubs, trees, plants, flowers, or nursery products, and the grading, filling, landscaping, and paving of the premises.[47]

The statute also grants a lien for the installation of water lines, sewers, drains, and the streets in a development if the owner of the land or the owner's agent contracts for these services to service all lots in a development. Each lot and its improvements are subject on a pro rata basis with the establishment of a lien for all debts for work and material provided in connection with the installation.[48]

Machines, wharves, and bridges are also subjected to a lien in the same manner as a building. There is no lien on a machine that becomes a permanent fixture in a building. To be lienable under this section, the machine must not have lost its character as a movable chattel, but it must be stationary and not movable in its use.[49]

The statute also defines the term *building* for purposes of a mechanics' lien to include any unit of a nonresidential building that is leased or separately sold as a unit. This allows for a lien to be established for work in a tenant space in a shopping mall or other commercial structure. The space must still be improved to the extent of 15 percent of its value, or, if the work is done under contract with a tenant, to 25 percent of its value.[50]

Residential condominium mechanics' liens are covered by the Maryland Horizontal Property Act.[51] This statute grants a mechanics' lien arising as a result of repairs to or improvements to a unit by a unit owner, which shall be a lien only against the unit. A lien is also granted as a result of repairs to or improvements of the common elements if authorized in writing by the council of unit owners. Until the contract price is paid, there is a lien against each unit in proportion to its percentage interest in the common elements. Upon payment of the proportionate amount by any unit owner to the lien claimant or on the posting of a bond, an individual unit owner is entitled to a recordable release of the unit

---

[46] Schacks v. Ford, 128 Md. 287, 97 A. 511 (1960); as to the valuation of the structure, *see* E.L. Gardner, Inc. v. Bowie Joint Venture, 64 Md. App. 302, 494 A.2d 988 (1985).

[47] MD. CODE ANN., REAL PROP. § 9-102(a) (Repl. Vol. 1996).

[48] *Id.* § 9-102(b). As to the method of applying the pro rata allocation, *see* Celta Corp. v. AG Parrott Co., No. 1907 (Md. Jan. 4, 1993).

[49] Stebbins v. Culbreth, 86 Md. 656, 39 A. 321 (1898); New England Car Spring Co. v. Baltimore & Ohio R.R., 11 Md. 81 (1857).

[50] MD. CODE ANN., REAL PROP. § 9-101(b) (Repl. Vol. 1996); § 9-103(c)(2) requires 25 percent improvement on leased propoerty.

[51] *Id.* § 11-118.

from the mechanics' lien, and the council of unit owners is not entitled to assess that unit for payment of the remaining amount due for the repairs or improvements.

There is no mechanics' lien for work done or materials supplied for or about public buildings.[52]

[B] Extent of Lien

The lien extends to the land covered by the building and to as much other land immediately adjacent thereto as may be necessary for the ordinary and useful purposes of the building. There is a statutory procedure for the court to set boundaries if necessary. However, if the building is erected, repaired, or rebuilt by a tenant for life or for years, the mechanics' lien applies only to the extent of the tenant's interest.[53] There is no distinction between a completed building and an unfinished building so long as construction has commenced.[54] Additionally, when the contractor or supplier has an entire contract for work and materials on more than one building (for example, apartment buildings, row houses, or single houses in a subdivision), the lien extends to all of the properties without regard to how much material went into any one building.[55]

The mechanics' lien attaches to the land only in the county in which it was established. If any part of the land is located in another county, the lien claimant can file a certified copy of the docket entries, court order, and any required bond with the circuit court for that other county.[56]

[C] Property Purchased by Bona Fide Purchaser

The mechanics' lien statute exempts from a lien a building and the land upon which it is erected if before the establishment of a lien in accordance with the statute, legal title has been granted to a bona fide purchaser for value.[57] However, the filing of a petition to establish a lien constitutes notice to a purchaser of the possibility of a lien being subsequently perfected.[58] On the other hand, if before

---

[52] Williams Constr. Co. v. Construction Equip., Inc., 253 Md. 60, 251 A.2d 864 (1969); Darling v. Baltimore, 51 Md. 1 (1879).

[53] MD. CODE ANN., REAL PROP. § 9-103 (Repl. Vol. 1996).

[54] *Id.* § 9-103(c).

[55] District Heights v. Noland, 202 Md. 43, 95 A.2d 90 (1953); Fulton v. Parklett, 104 Md. 62, 64 A. 58 (1906); Maryland Brick v. Dunkerly, 85 Md. 199, 36 A. 761 (1897).

[56] MD. CODE ANN., REAL PROP. § 9-107 (Repl. Vol. 1996).

[57] *Id.* § 9-102(d). When legal title passes to a mortgagee prior to the filing of a lien petition, the mortgagee who buys in at the foreclosure sale after a lien is established takes free and clear of the mechanics' lien action and is a bona fide purchaser. This is true even if the mortgagee controlled the entity owning the property and knew of the owner's inability to pay for the work for which the claim was made. I.A. Constr. Corp. v. Carney, 104 Md. App. 378, 656 A.2d 369 (1995).

[58] *Id.* § 9-102(e). National Glass, Inc. v. J.C. Penney, 336 Md. 606, 616, 336 A.2d 606 (1994)

the filing of a petition to establish a mechanics' lien the owner contracts to sell the land, equitable title is deemed to have passed to the contract purchaser, and the lien established against the contract seller is inferior to the buyer's equitable title.[59] Conversely, if the holder of equitable title contracts with a builder or material supplier, the equitable interest is subject to a mechanics' lien.[60] A mechanics' lien is granted on whatever interest the person who contracts for the improvements has in the property.[61]

After equitable title to the property has passed to a contract purchaser, no lien can be established on the property, even if the contract purchaser had knowledge that laborers and material suppliers had not been paid for their labor and materials.[62]

[D] Persons Entitled to Lien

Any person furnishing work or materials or both, for or about the building pursuant to a contract, may establish a lien. There is no requirement for contractual privity with the owner or with the general contractor or any specific subcontractor or supplier. The person furnishing the work and materials need not be within a specific tier of contractual relationships with either the general contractor or the owner.[63]

When a materialman delivers materials to the construction site, it does not have to affirmatively prove that the materials were actually used on the project as long as they were purchased for and delivered to the site of the work.[64] It is sufficient to establish a prima facie case for the material supplier to produce delivery tickets designating the place of delivery even when the materials had been picked up at the material supplier's place of business by the contractor.[65] If

---

(stating that once the petition to establish a Mechanics' Lien is filed, there is notice to subsequent purchasers. Subsequent purchasers must be promptly joined in the lien proceeding to establish the lien against them). Caretti, Inc. v. Colonnade Ltd. Partnership, 104 Md. App. 131, 655 A.2d 64 (1995).

[59] Himmighoefer v. Medallion Indus., 302 Md. 270, 487 A.2d 282 (1985). Contract purchasers are not "owners" for purposes of the mechanic's lien law. Consequently, giving notice to a contract purchaser who subsequently settles on the property prior to the filing of a Petition to Establish a Lien is ineffective to prevent the contract purchaser from being considered a bona fide purchaser taking free of any lien rights. To be an "owner" under the statute, the alleged owner must be a party to the agreement for the doing of work or furnishing of material for or about the building. Wolf Org., Inc. v. Oles, *et al.,* 119 Md. App. 357 (1998). *See also* Sterling Mirror v. Rahbar, 90 Md. App. 193, 600 A.2d 899 (1992).

[60] Coldheim v. Clark & Co., 68 Md. 498, 13 A. 363 (1888).

[61] Grinnell Co. v. City of Crisfield, 264 Md. 552, 287 A.2d 486 (1972).

[62] York Roofing v. Adcock, 333 Md. 158, 634 A.2d 39 (1995).

[63] Diener v. Cubbage, 259 Md. 555, 270 A.2d 471 (1970); MD. CODE ANN., REAL PROP. § 9-101(f) (Repl. Vol. 1988).

[64] District Heights v. Noland, 202 Md. 43, 95 A.2d 90 (1953).

[65] *Id.*

the owner can affirmatively prove that the materials were not used on the project, the presumption is rebutted and a lien cannot be established.[66]

The work does not have to be performed at the jobsite but may be performed off site if the work product is used in the building.[67] The lien rights apply to architects and engineers preparing plans and specifications that are used to construct the building even when jobsite supervision is not provided.[68] However, items not incorporated in the building structure are generally not lienable unless attached to services required for the construction of the building. For example, a bare rental of equipment with no operator is not lienable, whereas a rental with an operator is lienable.[69]

Note that any work or materials provided must be incidental to the construction of a "building" unless otherwise specifically stated in the statute. Therefore, drilling and installation of wells, construction of a swimming pool, or fencing, landscaping, sodding, or seeding is not lienable unless it is incidental to the construction of a building.[70] There is no necessity for a "building" with respect to the installation of water lines, sewers, drains, and streets in a development.[71]

Section 9-113 of the lien law provides that a "pay when paid" clause does not abrogate or waive the right of a subcontractor to claim a mechanic's lien.

[E] Amount of Lien

With the exception of single-family dwellings erected on the owner's own land, the amount of the lien is for the entire amount unpaid to the lien claimant. It makes no difference how much of the contract balance remains unpaid to the contractor. The Maryland mechanics' lien law puts the owner at risk of having to pay twice if the contractor does not pay its subcontractors and suppliers.

When the contract is with the owner and establishes a lump-sum price for the work, the lien claimant is entitled to a lien to the extent of the unpaid contract price due.[72] If the contract with the owner is cost plus, the lien claimant is entitled to a lien for direct costs for labor, materials, and supplies furnished, to include premiums for workers' compensation liability insurance, hauling, storage, and other operating expenses for equipment, and for the claimant's profit.[73] However,

---

[66] Holcomb v. Fender, 203 Md. 480, 101 A.2d 814 (1954).

[67] 5500 Coastal Highway Ltd. Partnership v. Electrical Equip. Co., 305 Md. 532, 505 A.2d 533 (1986).

[68] Liebergott v. Investment Bldg. Corp., 249 Md. 584, 241 A.2d 138 (1968).

[69] Giles & Ransome, Inc. v. First Nat'l Realty, 238 Md. 203, 208 A.2d 582 (1965). Effective October 1, 1996, a mechanic's lien became available for the leasing of equipment, with or without an operator, for use for or about the building or premises. House Bill No. 255, amending § 9-102(a) of the lien law.

[70] MD. CODE ANN., REAL PROP. § 9-102 (Repl. Vol. 1996); *cf.* Freeform Pools, Inc. v. Strawbridge Home for Boys, Inc., 228 Md. 297, 179 A.2d 683 (1962).

[71] MD. CODE ANN., REAL PROP. § 9-102(b) (Repl. Vol. 1996).

[72] Gambell v. Woodlea Co., 246 Md. 260, 228 A.2d 243 (1967).

[73] House v. Fissell, 188 Md. 160, 51 A.2d 669 (1947).

the contractor may not make claim for general overhead expenses incurred in connection with the general operation of its business and not charged exclusively to the project. These items would include executive salaries, rent, interest charges, depreciation, taxes, and general office expenses.[74] If the contract with the owner does not provide for any price or method of determining price, the contractor is entitled to the reasonable value of its labor and materials.[75]

When the claimant is a subcontractor having no direct contract with the owner, the owner is not bound by the contract price. The subcontractor is entitled to the reasonable value of the labor performed or materials supplied. However, the contract price is prima facie proof of reasonable value, and the owner has the burden of introducing evidence to show unreasonableness. The contract price establishes a ceiling upon the lien claim in the event that reasonable value would be in excess of the contract price.[76]

[F] Limitation on Amount Recoverable from Owner by Subcontractor on Single-Family Dwelling

Although in most cases the lien law puts the owner at risk of having to pay twice if the contractor does not pay its bills, the statute contains an exception with respect to single-family dwellings erected on the owner's own land. In this circumstance, the lien is limited to that amount of money remaining in the owner's hands that has not been paid to the contractor at the time of receiving a copy of the lien notice.[77] In addition, the lien extends only to the amount by which the owner is "indebted under the contract" at the time the notice is given. Therefore, if the homeowner has a legitimate offset against the balance remaining, the lien claimant may be entitled to no funds.[78]

A subcontractor seeking to establish a lien against a single-family residence has the burden of proof to establish the amount by which the homeowner was indebted to the general contractor at the time of the lien notice.[79]

[G] Interest

Prejudgment interest is allowed at the contract rate from the date when the original payments were due to the lien claimant. Interest rates specified on the

---

[74] 188 Md. at 164.

[75] Diener v. Cubbage, 259 Md. 555, 270 A.2d 471 (1970).

[76] *Id.*

[77] MD. CODE ANN., REAL PROP. § 9-104(f) (Repl. Vol. 1996); Ridge Sheet Metal Co. v. Morrell, 69 Md. App. 364, 517 A.2d 1133 (1986).

[78] For the definition of a single-family dwelling, *see* Grubb Contractors v. Abbot, 84 Md. 384, 579 A.2d 1185 (1990); Reisterstown Lumber v. TSAO, 319 Md. 623, 574 A.2d 307 (1990). A vacation home is also considered a "residence" for purposes of the mechanics' liens statute. Best Tri-Wall v. Berry, 108 Md. App. 381, 672 A.2d 116 (1996).

[79] F. Scott Jay & Co. v. Vargo, 112 Md. App. 354, 685 A.2d 799 (1996).

supplier's delivery tickets and invoices will be enforced. If there is no contract rate, interest will probably be allowed at the legal rate from the date when payment was due.[80] The legal rate in Maryland is six percent.

[H] Procedure to Establish Lien

In Maryland, there is no advance filing that may be made before construction to establish entitlement to a mechanics' lien. A lien is not established except by court order and after the owner has an opportunity to be heard. Procedurally, a lien claimant who does not have a direct contract with the owner must send the appropriate lien notice and must thereafter file a "Petition to Establish a Mechanics' Lien," which is served upon the owner and upon which the court will act to establish either an interlocutory or final lien as appropriate. Because the filing of such petition is notice to potential purchasers, it is recommended that it be filed as soon as possible.

[I] Notice of Lien

A contractor who has a contract directly with the owner does not have to send a lien notice. However, anyone who has a contract with anyone except the owner or its agent must comply with the notice provisions of the statute, and failure to do so will result in no entitlement to a lien.[81] Notice must be personally delivered to the owner by the claimant or its agent or mailed by the lien claimant within 120 days after claimant has performed the last work or furnished the last of its materials. The notice is timely if mailed within 120 days and received by the owner in the ordinary course of the mail after 120 days.[82] If the notice is mailed within 120 days but is returned unclaimed and not served within the 120-day period, the notice is ineffective.[83] Oral notice is insufficient.

When materials are sold on open account and there are continuous deliveries without any lengthy intervals between deliveries, the courts will generally rule that there is a single contract, and notice must be given within 120 days of the last delivery.[84] If the contract is completed and the materialman or contractor delivers goods or does work for the purpose of extending time within which notice may be given, no lien will be established.[85] However, if work in the nature of

---

[80] AMI v. JAD Enters., Inc., 77 Md. App. 654, 551 A.2d 888 (1989).

[81] Md. Code Ann., Real Prop. § 9-104 (Repl. Vol. 1996).

[82] Riley v. Abram, 287 Md. 348, 412 A.2d 996 (1980); Mardirossian Family Enters. v. Clearail, Inc., 324 Md. 191, 596 A.2d 1018 (1991).

[83] Mardirossian Family Enters. v. Clearail, Inc., 324 Md. 191, 596 A.2d 1018 (1991); Bukowitz v. Maryland Lumber Co., 210 Md. 148, 122 A.2d 486 (1956); William Penn Supply Corp. v. Watterson, 218 Md. 291, 146 A.2d 420 (1958).

[84] Back v. Reisterstown Lumber Co., 24 Md. App. 415, 332 A.2d 30, *cert. denied,* 275 Md. 745 (1975).

[85] T. Dan Kolker, Inc. v. Shure, 209 Md. 290, 121 A.2d 223 (1956).

punch-list or warranty work is done, the time for delivering notice may be measured from the date of that work.[86] With respect to warranty work, the court of appeals has observed that the lien statute makes no exception with respect to items necessary for the completion of the contract, as opposed to replacement items or items substituted for previously delivered but defective items.[87]

As to the form of the notice, the statute sets out the notice form in detail.[88] The notice requires:

1. A physical description of the building sufficient to identify it
2. A description of the work done and materials furnished
3. The time when the work was done or the materials furnished
4. The name of the person for whom the work was done or to whom the materials were furnished
5. The total amount earned under the claimant's contract to the date of the notice and the total amount that is due and unpaid as of the date of the notice.

Finally, the notice must state that the lien claimant does solemnly declare and affirm under the penalties of perjury that the contents of the foregoing notice are true to the best of the affiant's knowledge, information, and belief. The full name and address of the lien claimant should be given.

If notice cannot be given on account of absence or other causes, the lien claimant, in the presence of a competent witness and *within 120 days,* may place the notice on the door or other front part of the building. Notice by posting is sufficient in all cases in which the owner of the property has died and the successors in title do not appear on the public records of the county.[89] It is recommended that when posting is done, the claimant should photograph the posted notice to eliminate disputes over proper posting.

When there is more than one owner, the lien claimant may give notice to any one of the owners.[90] The notice of lien may be amended within the 120-day period but may not be amended after the 120-day period has expired.[91] Note that when the lien is being sought against the interest of a tenant, for life or for years, the "owner" for purposes of service of notice is the tenant.[92]

Once the owner receives the notice, the owner has a statutory right to withhold from sums due the contractor the amount the owner ascertains to be due to the party giving the notice.[93]

---

[86] Reisterstown Lumber Co. v. Reeder, 224 Md. 499, 168 A.2d 385 (1961).

[87] *Id.;* Insurance Co. of N. Am. v. Genstar Stone Prods. Co., 338 Md 161, 656 A.2d 1232 (1995).

[88] Md. Code Ann., Real Prop. § 9-104(b) (Repl. Vol. 1996).

[89] *Id.* § 9-104(e).

[90] *Id.* § 9-104(d).

[91] Kenly v. Sisters of Charity, 63 Md. 306 (1885).

[92] Md. Code Ann., Real Prop. § 9-101(e) (Repl. Vol. 1996).

[93] *Id.* § 9-104(f).

[J] Instituting Lien Action

The lien action is commenced by the filing of a "Petition to Establish a Mechanics' Lien." The action must be instituted within 180 days after the work has been finished or the material furnished.[94] In light of the effect of contracts of sale, the petition should be filed as soon as possible. The filing of the lien petition within 120 days does not substitute for a proper lien notice.[95] All owners of the property against which the lien is sought are necessary party defendants.[96]

If the claimant is a foreign corporation and does business in Maryland, it may not maintain an action to establish a mechanics' lien unless it registers or qualifies to do business in the state.[97] If this has not been done, there are procedures to retroactively qualify the foreign corporation at any time before the initial interlocutory lien hearing.

The petition must be supported by an affidavit by the lien claimant or some person on the claimant's behalf and shall contain at least the following:

1. The name and address of the lien claimant
2. The name and address of the owner
3. The nature or kind of work done or kind or amount of materials furnished
4. The time when work was done or materials furnished
5. The name of the person for whom the work was done or to whom the materials were furnished and the amount or sum claimed to be due, less any credit recognized by the claimant
6. A description of the land, including a statement as to whether a part of the lien is located in another county, and a description adequate to identify the building
7. If the petitioner is a subcontractor, facts showing that the notice required was properly mailed or served or posted.

If the lien is not to be established against two or more buildings on separate lots or parcels owned by the same person, the lien will be postponed to other mechanics' liens unless the petitioner designates the amount it claims to be due on each building. The petition must have attached copies of all material papers that constitute the basis of the lien claim unless their absence is explained by affidavit. The *material papers* in general are the written contract, all change orders, a breakdown of all payment requisitions, all invoices, and an itemized

---

[94] *Id.* § 9-105(a).

[95] William Penn Supply Corp. v. Watterson, 218 Md. 291, 146 A.2d 420 (1958).

[96] Md. Rules 12-302 (Repl. Vol. 1999). Caretti, Inc. v. Colonnade Ltd. Partnership, 104 Md. App. 131, 655 A.2d 64 (1995) (if after Petition is filed, property is sold, new owner must be promptly joined).

[97] Snavely, Inc. v. Wheeler, 74 Md. App. 428, 538 A.2d 324 (1988).

statement of account so that the owner can examine the principal evidence upon which the claim is founded.[98]

The statute also requires that a petition to enforce the lien must be filed within one year after the date upon which the "Petition to Establish the Lien" was filed.[99] It is recommended that the petition be titled "Petition to Establish and Enforce Mechanics' Lien" and include a request for enforcement. This procedure eliminates the necessity of filing a separate petition to enforce.

Once the petition is filed, a judge reviews the petition. If the judge finds that there are reasonable grounds for the lien to attach, the judge will issue a show cause order requiring the owner to respond by counter affidavit on or before a designated date and setting a hearing within 45 days from the date of the show cause order.[100] If no response is filed, the court may issue a final lien order. Otherwise, an interlocutory lien hearing is held, which is similar to motion for summary judgment proceedings. If there is no legal defense to the lien but only a dispute of fact, a1n interlocutory order establishing the mechanics' lien is entered, with the matter set for trial on the merits within six months. If the court determines that there is no genuine dispute of any material fact and the petitioner is entitled to a lien, then a final lien order will be entered.[101]

In connection with the interlocutory lien order, the court may require the claimant to file a bond in an amount the court believes sufficient for damages that may accrue to the owner, including reasonable attorneys' fees.[102] In many cases, the court will decline to require this bond. If this bond is required, the lien does not attach until the bond is filed. The owner may file a bond or cash security to discharge the lien and clear title on the property.[103]

In 1992, Maryland's Court of Special Appeals held that, in connection with the interlocutory lien hearing, an interlocutory lien would not necessarily be entered in all cases in which there was a dispute of fact. The court held that the lien claimant must show by a preponderance of the evidence that probable cause exists justifying the establishment of the interlocutory lien. The court at this stage must make a fact finding that the facts as a whole would lead a reasonably cautious person to believe that the petitioner is entitled to an interlocutory lien hearing beyond the affidavit supporting the lien petition.[104]

The lien petition should assert that the building was improved to the extent of 15 percent of its value or that the work done was part of an overall undertaking improving the building to the extent of 15 percent of its value.[105]

---

[98] AMI v. JAD Enters., Inc., 77 Md. App. 654, 551 A.2d 888 (1989).

[99] Md. Rules 12-305 (Repl. Vol. 1999).

[100] Md. Code Ann., Real Prop. § 9-106 (Repl. Vol. 1996); Md. Rules 12-304 (Repl. Vol. 1999).

[101] *Id.* § 9-106; E.L. Gardner, Inc. v. Bowie Joint Venture, 64 Md. App. 302, 494 A.2d 988 (1985); Tyson v. Masten Lumber & Supply, 44 Md. App. 293, 408 A.2d 1051 (1979).

[102] Md. Rules 12-304 (Repl. Vol. 1999).

[103] Md. Code Ann., Real Prop. § 9-106 (Repl. Vol. 1996).

[104] Reistertown Lumber Co. v. Royer, 91 Md. App. 746, 605 A.2d 980 (1992).

[105] Westpointe v. Kalkruth, 109 Md. App. 569, 675 A.2d 571 (1996).

At trial on the merits, if the lien claimant prevails, a final lien order is entered, which has the effect of continuing the original interlocutory lien. If the claimant does not prevail, the interlocutory lien is terminated.[106]

[K] Effect of Arbitration Clause

If the lien claimant is a contractor having a direct contract with the owner, which contract contains an arbitration clause, the court may conduct a probable cause hearing and enter an interlocutory lien order. At that time, the case may be stayed and referred to arbitration on the merits. If the arbitrators find in favor of the lien claimant, the court may then enter a final lien.[107]

[L] Priorities Between Mechanics' Liens and Other Liens

Because a mechanics' lien does not attach to the property until it is established by judicial order, all other types of intervening liens and encumbrances that attached before the date of establishment of a mechanics' lien have priority and are satisfied in accordance with their priority in any foreclosure proceeding. If the proceeds of sale are insufficient to satisfy all mechanics' liens that have been established, then all of the proceeds of sale that are available to satisfy mechanics' liens are distributed pro rata to all mechanics' lienors.[108]

[M] Amendments

Pleadings in an action filed to establish a lien may be amended provided the amendments do not increase the amount of the claim or materially alter the description of the land if the amendments are requested after the expiration of the period within which notice of lien must be given or the period in which the "Petition to Establish a Mechanics' Lien" must be filed.[109]

[N] Waiver of Lien Rights

There is no waiver of mechanics' lien rights by granting a credit or receiving a note or other security unless it is received as payment or the lien right is expressly waived.[110] In addition, the lien law provides that an executory contract between a contractor and any subcontractor or material supplier may not waive or require the subcontractor or material supplier to waive the right to claim a

---

[106] MD. RULES 12-304 (Repl. Vol. 1999).

[107] Caretti, Inc. v. Colonnade Ltd. Partnership, 104 Md. App. 131, 655 A.2d 64 (1995) (distinguishing and reversing by implication McCormick Constr. Co. v. 9690 Deereco Road Ltd. Partnership, 79 Md. App. 177, 556 A.2d 292 (1989)).

[108] MD. CODE ANN., REAL PROP. § 9-108 (Repl. Vol. 1996).

[109] *Id.* § 9-112; MD. RULES BG72 (Repl. Vol. 1992).

[110] MD. CODE ANN., REAL PROP. § 9-110 (Repl. Vol. 1996).

mechanics' lien or to sue on a contractor's bond. Any such waiver is void.[111] Lien waivers given either during or after construction are valid. Lien waivers contained in an executory contract between the owner and any contractor are also valid.

[O] Lien Releases

The statute provides that at the time of final payment, the contractor shall give to the owner a signed release of lien from each material supplier and subcontractor who provided work or materials under the contract. The statute also provides that the owner is not subject to a lien and is not otherwise liable for any work or materials included in the release given under this section.[112] There are no decisions indicating whether the owner would still be liable for a forged mechanics' lien release given by the contractor. Nonetheless, this statute gives the owner the right to demand mechanics' lien releases if it has omitted to place such a requirement in its contract.

[P] Other Personal Actions

Nothing in the mechanics' lien law affects the right of any person to maintain any personal action against either the owner of the building or any other person, such as the contractor, who is liable for the debt claimed.[113]

---

[111] *Id.* § 9-113. National Glass, Inc. v. J.C. Penney, 336 Md. 606, 336 A.2d 606 (1994) (contract calling for application of Pennsylvania law, with a waiver of right to file mechanics' lien on Maryland property, held unenforceable as violating Maryland public policy).

[112] MD. CODE ANN., REAL PROP. § 9-114 (Repl. Vol. 1996).

[113] *Id.* § 9-111.

CHAPTER 22

MASSACHUSETTS

David J. Hatem
Maura A. Greene[1]

[1] The authors wish to acknowledge the assistance of Northeastern University Law student Bethanni Forbush-Moss.

§ 22.01 INTRODUCTION

Massachusetts does not require general contractors to furnish any kind of bond in connection with contracts performed for private entities. Massachusetts does, however, provide contractors and their subcontractors with mechanics' lien rights in connection with work performed for private entities.

Massachusetts does require general contractors to furnish payment bonds in connection with public works projects and has established a two-tiered system for such payment bonds. For public works projects performed directly for the Commonwealth, general contractors are required to furnish payment bonds in an amount equal to not less than one-half of the total contract price for all projects in excess of $5,000. General contractors must also furnish payments bonds in an amount equal to not less than one-half of the total contract price for all other public works projects in excess of $2,000. In each instance, the payment bond must provide coverage for claimants supplying labor or materials to the contractor or to any of its subcontractors.

Massachusetts law prohibits the imposition of mechanics' liens upon any public building or other type of public work.

In Massachusetts, the statutory provision that governs payment bonds for all public works projects is set forth in one of the two Massachusetts competitive bidding statutes, General Laws of the Commonwealth of Massachusetts, Chapter 149, §§ 1 *et seq.* Sections 29 and 29A of Chapter 149 are the statutory provisions that govern bonds for public works projects and private construction, respectively (bond law). The Massachusetts Mechanics' Lien Law is set forth in Chapter 254, §§ 1 *et seq.* (lien law).

§ 22.02 BOND LAW

[A] General Concepts

Massachusetts bond law developed as an "outgrowth of mechanics' lien statutes."[2] Because Massachusetts law prohibits the imposition of liens upon public buildings or other public works, the Massachusetts legislature enacted the bond law in 1935 to provide security to subcontractors, laborers, and materialmen who furnish labor and materials on public works projects.[3] Because of the remedial nature of the bond law, Massachusetts courts have held that it "should be broadly construed to effectuate its self-evident policies."[4]

Although the protection afforded subcontractors, laborers, and materialmen

---

[2] Massachusetts Gas & Elec. Light Supply Co. v. Rugo Constr. Co., 321 Mass. 20, 21, 71 N.E.2d 408, 410 (1947).

[3] *See* Lessard v. Revere, 171 Mass. 294, 50 N.E. 533 (1898); Manganaro Drywall, Inc. v. White Constr. Co., 372 Mass. 661, 664, 363 N.E.2d 669, 671 (1977).

[4] M. Lasden, Inc. v. Decker Elec. Corp., 372 Mass. 179, 182, 360 N.E.2d 1068, 1070 (1977).

by the bond law is similar in nature to that offered by mechanics' lien rights, the bond law represents an improvement over the mechanics' lien statutory scheme. It streamlines the process by which claims may be made and by ensuring that progress on the work itself is not delayed or hindered by the competing rights and obligations represented by the lien law system.[5]

Under Massachusetts law, a construction surety bond is in essence a contract between the general contractor and the surety for the benefit of both the owner and any subcontractors or suppliers (or other creditors) of the general contractor.[6] At the time of its enactment, the bond law represented a statutory exception to the Massachusetts rule of law that precluded recovery under a contract by a third-party beneficiary.[7] For this reason, a statutory provision was made for surety bonds on private construction projects, although the use of such bonds is permissive rather than mandatory.[8]

Under Massachusetts law, a surety contract will be governed by the law of the jurisdiction where it was made.[9] A surety contract made in Massachusetts is governed by the statute of frauds and must be in writing and signed by the party from whom payment or performance is sought.[10] The terms and conditions under which a suretyship relationship is created are to be ascertained by the court "from the instrument creating that undertaking construed in reference to the usages of business, the object sought to be accomplished, the relationship of the parties to each other, and the attending circumstances."[11]

The surety contract is typically only one part of the suretyship relationship; most surety contracts either expressly or impliedly reference and incorporate the contracts between the principal and the obligee or other creditors because the

[5] The relative simplicity of the bond law in relationship to the lien law is indicated by the comparative sizes of the respective statutory provisions; the bond law consists of one relatively short provision in the competitive bidding statute, while the lien law is set forth in its own chapter, comprising 32 separate sections.

[6] *See, e.g.,* American Air Filter Co. v. Innamorati Bros., Inc., 358 Mass. 146, 260 N.E.2d 718 (1970).

[7] *See* Bernhard, *Third Party Beneficiary Rights in Massachusetts,* 49 Mass. L.Q. 159 (1964).

[8] Powers Regulator Co. v. United States Fidelity & Guar. Co., 7 Mass. App. Ct. 913, 388 N.E.2d 1205 (1979) (rescript).

[9] *See* Kearsarge Metallurgical Corp. v. Peerless Ins. Co., 383 Mass. 162, 418 N.E.2d 580, 583 (1981).

[10] MASS. GEN. LAWS ch. 259, §§ 1 *et seq.* (1959 & Supp. 1991) is the Massachusetts statute of frauds and provides in pertinent part:

> No action shall be brought . . . to charge a person upon a special promise to answer for the debt, default or misdoings of another . . . unless the promise, contract or agreement upon which such action is brought, or some memorandum or note thereof, is in writing and signed by the party to be charged therewith or by some person thereunto by him lawfully authorized.

[11] Miller v. Perry, 333 Mass. 155, 129 N.E.2d 143, 144–45 (1955).

surety is not obligated unless the obligee or creditors have performed satisfactorily.[12]

[B] Bid Deposits

Massachusetts has two distinct but parallel public bidding statutes.[13] Both statutes are covered by the bond law, and both statutes require that each bid be accompanied by a bid deposit.[14] The purpose of the bid deposit is to provide security to the awarding authority in the event that the bidder fails to perform its agreement to execute a contract and furnish payment and performance bonds.[15] The bid deposit requirement is strictly enforced, and the failure to make a correct deposit is grounds for rejection of the bid.[16] Bid deposits may be made in the form of a bid bond, cash, certified check, or treasurer's or cashier's check payable to the awarding authority.[17] The amount of the deposit must be equal to five percent of the value of the bid.[18] All bid deposits except those of the three lowest responsible bidders must be returned within five days after the opening of the bids.[19] The bid deposits of the three lowest responsible bidders shall be returned upon the execution and delivery of a contract.[20]

In the event of forfeiture due to the failure of the bidder to perform, the awarding authority is entitled to no more than the difference between the forfeiting bidder's price and the price of the next lowest, responsible, eligible bidder.[21] The forfeiting bidder is entitled to the return of its bid deposit if its failure to perform is because of "death, disability, bona fide clerical or mechanical error of a substantial nature, or other similar unforeseen circumstances affecting the general bidder."[22]

[C] Performance Bonds

Massachusetts law does not require contractors to furnish performance bonds in connection with construction work performed for either public or private entities. General contractors, however, are authorized to require performance bonds from subcontractors on public projects involving the construction of build-

---

[12] *See* Albre Marble & Tile Co. v. Goverman, 353 Mass. 546, 233 N.E.2d 533 (1968).

[13] Mass. Gen. Laws ch. 149 and ch. 30, § 39M (1982).

[14] *See id.* at ch. 149, § 44B(2); ch. 30, § 39M(a).

[15] *Id.* at ch. 149, § 44B(3).

[16] J. D'Amico, Inc. v. City of Worcester, 19 Mass. App. Ct. 112, 472 N.E.2d 665 (1984).

[17] Mass. Gen. Laws ch. 30, § 39M(a); *id.* at ch. 149, § 44B(2)

[18] *See id.* at ch. 149, § 44B(2); ch. 30, § 39M(a) (1982).

[19] *Id.* at ch. 149, § 44B(3).

[20] *Id.*

[21] *Id.*

[22] *Id.*

ings.[23] Statutory performance bonds are solely for the benefit of the general contractor and are intended to secure to the general contractor the performance of the subcontractor's work.[24] In the event of the subcontractor's failure to perform, the surety is obligated to reimburse the general contractor for costs incurred to hire another subcontractor.[25]

[D] Payment Bonds

Massachusetts law does not require contractors to furnish payment bonds in connection with construction work performed for private entities.

The bond law establishes a two-tiered system of mandatory payment bonds on public projects. A general contractor entering into a contract with the Commonwealth for the construction, reconstruction, alteration, remodeling, repair, or demolition of a public building or other public work must furnish a payment bond in an amount not less than one-half of the total contract price if the amount of contract is in excess of $5,000.[26] When the contracting authority is a political subdivision other than the Commonwealth, the general contractor must furnish a payment bond in an amount not less than one-half the total contract price if the amount of the contract is in excess of $2,000.[27]

The bond law may be conveniently divided into three basic parts. The first part establishes definitional criteria for a claimant under the bond law. The second part sets forth the procedures that must be followed by any claimant seeking to recover an amount under the bond. The third part sets forth the enforcement procedures and remedies available to a successful claimant.

The bond law expressly states that the requisite payment bond is to be used "for payment by the contractor and subcontractors for labor performed or furnished and materials used or employed" in the construction project.[28] Massachusetts courts have held that the security afforded by the bond extends to any subcontractor or supplier, provided that the subcontractor or supplier seeks payment for work and/or materials supplied or furnished to perform a portion of the work required under the general contract.[29]

The bond law provides security for all labor performed or furnished and materials used or employed in the construction project.[30] This includes all skilled and unskilled labor, monies due for the rental or hire of vehicles and machinery,

---

[23] *Id.* at ch. 149, § 44F (1982).

[24] *Id.;* Continental Bronze Co. v. Salvo & Armstrong Co., 8 Mass. App. Ct. 799, 397 N.E.2d 1143 (1979).

[25] Continental Bronze Co. v. Salvo & Armstrong Co., 8 Mass. App. Ct. 799, 397 N.E.2d 1143 (1979).

[26] MASS. GEN. LAWS ch. 149, § 29 (1982).

[27] *Id.*

[28] *Id.*

[29] Peters v. Hartford Accident & Indem. Co., 377 Mass. 863, 867, 389 N.E.2d 63 (1979).

[30] MASS. GEN. LAWS ch. 149, § 29 (1982).

and transportation charges for any materials used for the construction project.[31] Security is also afforded to the supplier of lumber and specially fabricated materials that are not actually incorporated into the project and that are no longer fit for any other use.[32] The supplier's recovery is limited, however, to the extent of the purchase price of the lumber or specially fabricated materials less the fair salvage value.[33] The supplier's recovery for specially fabricated materials is contingent on the material being in conformity with the contract, plans and specifications for the construction project.[34] The bond must also provide coverage for certain transportation and permanent equipment repair or capital costs that will survive the particular project.[35] No coverage is afforded, however, for equipment repair costs.[36] Finally, the bond also secures payments for certain labor-related costs, including costs for health and welfare plans, supplementary unemployment benefit plans, and other fringe benefits which are payable in cash and provided for in collective bargaining agreements between organized labor and the general contractor or subcontractors.[37] Trustee actions to collect such benefits are, however, preempted by the Employee Retirement Income Security Act of 1974 (ERISA), 29 U.S.C. §§ 1001-1461 (1988).[38]

The second part of the bond law sets forth the procedures that must be followed to perfect a claim on the bond. A claimant having a contractual relationship with the general contractor furnishing the bond who has not been paid in full for any amounts due for covered labor, materials, or equipment, appliances or transportation within 65 days after the due date for payment must do the following: file a petition in superior court within one year after the day on which the claimant last performed labor or furnished the labor, or materials, equipment, appliances or transportation for which payment is sought; and prosecute the claim by trial through final adjudication and execution for the payments justly due the claimant.[39] Any claimant having a contractual relationship with a subcontractor performing labor or both performing labor and furnishing materials, but no contractual relationship with the general contractor furnishing the bond must give written notice to the general contractor within 65 days after the date on which the claimant last performed the covered labor or furnished the labor, and materials, equipment, appliances or transportation to enforce his rights under the bond.[40] In order to be effective, the notice must state with substantial accuracy the amount

---

[31] Look v. City of Springfield, 292 Mass. 515, 517, 198 N.E. 661 (1935).

[32] MASS. GEN. LAWS ch. 149, § 29; Dix Lumber Co. v. City of Boston, 289 Mass. 291, 294, 194 N.E. 117 (1935).

[33] MASS. GEN. LAWS ch. 149, § 29 (1982).

[34] *Id.*

[35] *Id.*

[36] Cohen v. Henry N. Worthington Co., 334 Mass. 509, 515, 136 N.E.2d 237 (1956).

[37] MASS. GEN. LAWS ch. 149, § 29 (1982).

[38] Williams v. Ashland Eng'g Co., 45 F.3d 588 (1st Cir. 1995), *cert. denied,* 516 U.S. 807 (1995).

[39] MASS. GEN. LAWS ch. 149, § 29.

[40] *Id.*

claimed and the name of the party for whom the labor was performed or the labor, materials, equipment, appliances, or transportation that materials were furnished. The notice must be mailed by registered or certified mail, postage prepaid, to the business office or principal residence of the general contractor or in any manner in which civil process may be served.[41] If any part of the claim is for specially fabricated material, the claimant must give the general contractor written notice of the placement and cost of the order no later than 20 days after receiving the final approval in writing for the use of the material.[42]

Apart from issues of contract compliance, the issue most often litigated under the bond law is whether the statutory notice requirements were complied with fully by the claimant. So long as actual notice is received by the general contractor within the prescribed statutory period, the failure of the claimant to send the notice by registered mail or to the correct address will be waived by the courts.[43] The notice letter need not be lengthy or involved; a brief letter setting forth the amount of the claim and the name of the party for whom the labor was performed or the labor, materials, equipment, appliances, or transportation were furnished is sufficient to satisfy the statutory requirements.[44]

The third part of the bond law deals with judicial enforcement of bond claims and the remedies available to a successful claimant. In order to ensure the expeditious processing of bond claims, actions to enforce claims under the bond law are subject to General Laws of the Commonwealth of Massachusetts, Chapter 231, §§ 59 and 59B, which provide for the expedited trial of certain enumerated types of actions.

Although the bond law contains language that suggests that a claim filed before the expiration of 65 days after the date on which the claimant last furnished the labor, materials, equipment, appliances or transportation is premature, the statute expressly provides that the court shall not dismiss any petition on the grounds that it was filed before the 65th day.[45] The court is prohibited, however, from entering a decree upon any claim before the 70th day after the date on which the claimant last performed the labor or furnished the labor, materials, equipment, appliances or transportation included in the claim.[46]

The bond law provides for the mandatory award of reasonable legal fees to any successful claimant.[47] The award for legal fees must under no circumstances be less than the published rate of any recommended fee schedule for a statewide

---

[41] *Id.;* Bastianelli v. National Union Fire Ins. Co., 36 Mass. App. Ct. 367, 631 N.E.2d 566 (1994).

[42] MASS. GEN. LAWS ch. 149, § 29.

[43] Cinder Prods. Corp. v. Schena Constr. Co., 22 Mass. App. Ct. 927, 492 N.E.2d 744 (1986).

[44] Barboza v. Aetna Cas. & Sur. Co., 18 Mass. App. Ct. 323, 465 N.E.2d 290, *review denied,* 393 Mass. 1101, 469 N.E.2d 830 (1984).

[45] MASS. GEN. LAWS ch. 149, § 29 (1982).

[46] *Id.*

[47] *Id.*

bar association or for a bar association in which the office of the counsel for the claimant is located, whichever is higher.[48] The legal fees component of the bond law has, inevitably perhaps, been attacked on constitutional grounds.[49] Such attacks have historically focused upon the failure of the bond law to provide for an award of legal fees to a successful defendant of a claim. The Massachusetts courts, however, have held that the failure to provide for such an award is rationally related to the underlying purpose of the bond law, which is to ensure prompt payment of subcontractors on public works.[50]

§ 22.03 LIEN LAW

[A] General Concepts

The Massachusetts mechanics' lien law is set forth in Chapter 254 of the Massachusetts General Laws.[51] That statute allows contractors, subcontractors, suppliers, and laborers to obtain security for unpaid construction debts by providing for mechanics' liens against property on which construction is being performed.[52] Massachusetts mechanics' liens cannot, however, be obtained on public construction projects,[53] and cannot be obtained by professional service providers such as architects or engineers.[54]

To obtain a lien under Chapter 254 and for it to be enforced, a claimant must strictly comply with a series of detailed procedural requirements.[55] Many of the procedures, in turn, are new, and have not yet been interpreted by any courts, as a result of a 1996 amendment that substantially rewrote the Massachusetts mechanics' lien law for the first time since 1915.[56] These new procedures, along with lien priorities, prohibited practices, lien bonds, and required forms, are described in **§§ 22.03[B]–[I].**

[B] Basic Provisions

The Massachusetts lien law allows liens to be established for the value of labor, materials, general and subcontractor services, and tools, appliances, or rental equipment used in the erection, alteration, repair, or removal of a building,

---

[48] *Id.* Although the statute provides for use of statewide fee schedules, no such schedules exist in Massachusetts.

[49] Manganaro Drywall, Inc. v. White Constr. Co., 372 Mass. 661, 663, 363 N.E.2d 669 (1977).

[50] *Id.*

[51] MASS. GEN. LAWS ch. 254, §§ 1–33.

[52] *Id.* at ch. 254, §§ 1, 2, and 4.

[53] *Id.* at ch. 254, § 6.

[54] Libbey v. Tidden, 192 Mass. 175, 78 N.E. 313 (1906).

[55] Volpe Constr. Co. v. First National Bank, 30 Mass. App. Ct. 249, 567 N.E.2d 1244 (1991).

[56] 1996 Mass. Acts ch. 364.

structure, or other improvement, or alteration to real property.[57] Liens can be obtained by general contractors, by direct or lower-tier subcontractors, by suppliers, and by laborers.[58] The procedures by which these different entities obtain liens, however, vary. In general, all liens except for laborer liens require a written contract, a recorded notice of contract, a recorded statement of account, and a verified complaint.[59] Laborer liens do not require a written contract or notice of contract, but do require a statement of account, and verified complaint.[60] Separate provisions also exist for liens based upon work performed in dredging or otherwise reclaiming submerged land, but are not addressed here.

The procedural discussion in **§§ 22.03[C]** and **22.03[D]** spells out the general contractor's lien procedures, followed by the variations applicable to direct and lower-tier subcontractors and suppliers. The laborer's lien is then addressed separately in **§ 22.03[E].**

[C] General Contractor Mechanics' Lien Procedures

A general contractor may obtain a lien for all labor, materials, rental equipment, appliances, tools, or construction management and general contractor services.[61] To do so, a general contractor must satisfy four basic requirements: (a) a written contract, (b) a notice of contract, (c) a statement of account, and (d) a lawsuit.

The written contract need not be in any particular form, as long as it is in a form otherwise enforceable by Massachusetts law.[62] A credit application is probably insufficient to establish a written contract.[63] The written contract may be between a general contractor and the owner of "any interest in real property," or with any person acting "for, on behalf of, or with the consent of such owner. . . ."[64] In other words, the contract can be between the general contractor and the owner, the general contractor and a lessee, or the general contractor and any entity operating with the consent of the owner, such as a managing agent or trust. Provided that such a written contract exists, the next step required for a general contractor to establish a mechanics' lien is the recording of a "notice of contract." That notice of contract must be substantially in the form set out in the statute, as shown in **Volume 3.** The notice of contract must be recorded in the land records of the county where the property is located, no later than the earliest of (1) 60

[57] MASS. GEN. LAWS ch. 254, §§ 1, 2, and 4.

[58] *Id.*

[59] *Id.* at ch. 254, §§ 2, 4, 5, 8, and 11.

[60] *Id.* at ch. 254, § 1.

[61] *Id.* at ch. 254, § 2.

[62] *Id.* at ch. 254, § 2A.

[63] *See* National Lumber Co. v. Suburban Builders Corp., Mass. App. Div. 152, 1996 WL 521253 (1996).

[64] MASS. GEN. LAWS ch. 254, § 2.

days after the filing of a notice of substantial completion; (2) 90 days after the filing of a notice of termination; or (3) 90 days after the last furnishing of labor and/or materials for the project.[65] The notice of substantial completion and notice of termination are also requirements under the mechanics' lien statute.[66] Both notices will be discussed in **§ 22.03[F].**

A mechanics' lien must then be perfected by two additional steps: (1) the recording of a statement of account and (2) the filing and recording of a verified complaint. The statement of account need not be in any particular form, but is required to include "a just and true account of the amount due," minus all just credits, along with the name of the owner and a brief description of the property.[67] That statement of account must then be recorded in the land records of the county where the property is located, no later than the earliest of (1) 90 days after the filing of a notice of substantial completion; (2) 120 days after the filing of a notice of termination; or (3) 120 days after the last furnishing of labor or materials.[68] A recommended form for the statement of account is shown in **Volume 3.**

Finally, a lien will dissolve unless a lawsuit to enforce the mechanics' lien is commenced within 90 days after the recording of the statement of account.[69] The complaint must be verified; must contain a brief description sufficient to identify the property, along with a statement of the amount due; and must be recorded within 30 days in the land records for the county where the property is located.[70]

[D] Subcontractor, Supplier, and Material Supplier Liens

Direct and lower-tier subcontractors and suppliers are also permitted mechanics' liens under Massachusetts law, and can establish them by very similar procedures. Liens may be obtained for labor, material, rental equipment, appliances, tools, or subcontractor construction management services.[71] Any subcontractor or supplier may establish a lien by way of (1) a written contract, (2) a notice of contract, (3) a statement of account, and (4) filing and recording a complaint.

The time limits applicable to these filing requirements are the same as are applicable to general contractors, as described in **§ 22.03[C].** A subcontractor or supplier's notice of contract must be filed no later than the earliest of (1) 60 days

---

[65] *Id.*
[66] *Id.* at ch. 254, §§ 2A, 2B.
[67] *Id.* at ch. 254, § 8.
[68] *Id.*
[69] *Id.* at ch. 254, § 11.
[70] *Id.* at ch. 254, § 5.
[71] *Id.* at ch. 254, § 4.

after the filing or recording of the notice of substantial completion; (2) 90 days after the filing or recording of the notice of termination; or (3) 90 days after the last furnishing of labor, or materials, rental equipment, appliances or tools for the project.[72] A subcontractor's or supplier's statement of account must be filed no later than the earliest of (1) 90 days after the filing or recording of the notice of substantial completion; (2) 120 days after the filing or recording of the notice of termination; or (3) 120 days after the last furnishing of labor, or materials, rental equipment, appliances, or tools.[73] The complaint must then be filed in court within 90 days thereafter, and recorded within 30 days.[74] The different procedures applicable to subcontractors and suppliers are as follows.

First, a subcontractor or supplier must give actual notice of the filing of its notice of contract to the owner of the real property.[75] Second, the form of notice of contract required by the statute is different, and requires far more detail than the general contractor's form.

Finally, for lower-tier subcontractors or suppliers (with no direct contractual relationship with the general contractor), there is one further requirement which, if not complied with, can substantially limit the amount of a lien. Specifically, such parties cannot obtain or enforce liens in amounts in excess of the unpaid balance of the subcontract between the general contractor and the intermediate subcontractor at the time of recording of the notice of contract, unless the lower-tier subcontractor or supplier sends a "Notice of Identification" to the general contractor within 30 days after commencing work.[76] That notice is discussed in **§ 22.03[F].**

Other differences between general contractor and subcontractor/supplier mechanics' liens arise in terms of the types of lien waivers that may be allowed, and the types of priority that can be established for mechanics' liens. Those issues are discussed in **§§ 22.03[F]–[I].**

[E] Laborers' Liens

Unlike those of contractors, subcontractors, and suppliers, laborer mechanics' liens do not require a written contract and do not require the filing of a notice of contract.[77] Instead, any person due for personal labor can establish a lien simply by recording a statement of account in the land records in the county where the property is located within 90 days after completing the work, by filing a lawsuit within 90 days thereafter, and by recording the complaint within 30 days thereafter.[78]

---

[72] *Id.*

[73] *Id.* at ch. 254, § 8.

[74] *Id.* at ch. 254, §§ 5, 11.

[75] *Id.* at ch. 254, § 4.

[76] *Id.*

[77] *Id.* at ch. 254, §§ 1, 5, 8, 11.

[78] *Id.* at ch. 254 §§ 5, 8, 11.

Like the other statements of account under this statute, there is no statutorily required form for the laborer's statement of account. The statement must, however, contain a just and true account of the sums due, minus applicable credits, along with a brief description of the property and the name of the owner of the property.[79] In addition, a laborer's lien is limited to the value of "not more than 30 days work actually performed for the 90 days next prior to his filing a statement [of account]."[80] Finally, like other lawsuits commenced under this statute, a lawsuit for a laborer's lien must be commenced by verified complaint, and must contain the property description and amount due. The complaint must be filed in court within 90 days after filing of the statement of claim, and must be recorded in the land records within 30 days after its filing.[81]

Section One expressly allows third-party beneficiaries to seek laborer liens. This provision is generally construed to allow unions and benefit trustees to assert lien claims on behalf of laborers. Trustees, however, are preempted by ERISA from recovering employee benefits.[82]

[F] Additional Filings

In addition to the filings described in **§§ 22.03[C]–[E],** the Massachusetts mechanics' lien law provides three other notices: the notice of substantial completion, the notice of termination, and the notice of identification.

A *notice of substantial completion* may be filed by the owner and/or the general contractor.[83] Substantial completion includes work under the written contract that is sufficiently complete so that it can be occupied or utilized for its intended use.[84] It is filed for the purpose of limiting the time during which mechanics' liens can be asserted. The owner must send a copy of that notice by certified mail, along with the date of filing or recording, to every person who has filed a notice of contract.[85] The general contractor must also send that notice by certified mail to every person who has entered into a written contract directly with the contractor, and to every person who has sent a written notice of identification to the general contractor.[86] If the general contractor refuses to execute a notice of substantial completion, the owner can go to court to obtain an order to remedy that refusal.[87]

---

[79] *Id.* at ch. 254, § 8.

[80] *Id.* at ch. 254, § 1.

[81] *Id.* at ch. 254, §§ 5, 11.

[82] McCoy v. Massachusetts Institute of Tech., 950 F.2d 13 (1st Cir. 1991); Chestnut Adams Ltd. Partnership v. Bricklayers and Masons Trust Funds of Boston, 415 Mass. 87, 612 N.E.2d 236 (1993), *cert. denied,* 504 U.S. 910 (1992).

[83] Mass. Gen. Laws ch. 254, § 2A.

[84] *Id.*

[85] *Id.*

[86] *Id.*

[87] *Id.* at ch. 254, § 15A.

A *notice of termination* is a document that may be filed by the owner if a contract is terminated prior to filing or recording of a notice of substantial completion.[88] Similar to a notice of substantial completion, the notice of termination cuts off the time during which mechanics' liens can be filed. The notice of termination must be sent by certified mail by the owner to the general contractor and to any persons who have filed notices of contract.[89] After the notice of termination is served by the owner upon the general contractor, the general contractor must deliver that notice to every person with whom it has entered into a contract, and to every person who has served upon the general contractor a written notice of identification.[90]

A *notice of identification* may be sent to the general contractor by any party performing work or supplying materials or furnishes rental equipment who has a written contract but does *not* have a direct contractual relationship with the general contractor.[91] Such notice must be sent by certified mail within 30 days of commencement of the work by the lower-tier subcontractor or supplier to the general contractor.[92]

The notice of identification secures the lower-tier subcontractor's right to recover an amount that may be greater than that owed by the general contractor to the intermediate subcontractor.[93] If a lower-tier contractor fails to send a notice of identification to the general contractor, any lien that the lower-tier subcontractor obtains will be capped by the amount owed by the general contractor to the intermediate subcontractor at the time the lower-tier subcontractor filed its notice of contract.[94]

[G] Lien Priority

Massachusetts mechanics' liens take priority over any later filed encumbrances, but under some circumstances may have priority over previously recorded mortgages as well.[95]

First, liens established by laborers have priority over previously recorded mortgages if the labor performed is in the erection, alteration, repair or removal of a building, structure, or other improvement at issue which began before the recording of the mortgage.[96] Second, subcontractor mechanics' liens have priority over previously recorded mortgages, but only as to amounts "actually advanced

---

[88] *Id.* at ch. 254, § 2B.
[89] *Id.*
[90] *Id.*
[91] *Id.* at ch. 254, § 4.
[92] *Id.*
[93] *Id.*
[94] *Id.*
[95] *Id.* at ch. 254, § 7.
[96] *Id.* at ch. 254, § 7(a).

or unconditionally committed" after the recording of a notice of contract.[97] Third, neither general contractor nor subcontractor liens can have priority against a purchaser of the property, other than one acting in concert with the previous owner, if the purchaser's deed is recorded prior to the filing of the applicable lien documents.[98]

Finally, previously recorded mortgages have priority over general contractor liens to the extent of "amounts actually advanced or unconditionally committed" (1) prior to the filing or recording of a notice of contract and (2) after the filing or recording of a notice of contract, but within 25 days after the last day of a period stated in an accurate waiver and subordination of lien executed in a prescribed statutory partial waiver form, except for retainage.[99] This provision allows a contractor's retainage to take lien priority over mortgage funds advanced after the filing of a notice of contract, provided that a statutory form waiver and subordination of liens is executed.

[H] Lien Bonds

The Massachusetts lien statute also establishes procedures by which a party can either prevent liens from attaching to real property or dissolve liens once they have attached.[100]

First, in terms of preventing liens, the statute provides for a lien prevention bond.[101] The lien prevention bond allows any person to record a bond to prevent lien filings.[102] When such a bond is recorded, instead of following all of the procedures spelled out earlier in this chapter, the claimant must commence suit under the bond within 90 days after last performing or furnishing labor or materials.[103] Under the prior version of this statute, a party seeking to enforce a claim against a lien prevention bond may also need to file a notice of contract before filing its claim against the bond.[104]

The second type of lien bond is recorded in order to remove a lien after the lien has been filed.[105] If such a bond is posted, it must be in the form specified in the statute. Such a bond must be filed or recorded in the applicable land records, and notice of that recording must be given to the lien claimant.[106] Actions to enforce the lien and collect under the bond must then be commenced within 90

[97] *Id.* at ch. 254, § 7(c).
[98] *Id.* at ch. 254, § 7(d).
[99] *Id.* at ch. 254, § 7(b).
[100] *Id.* at ch. 254, §§ 12, 14.
[101] *Id.* at ch. 254, § 12.
[102] *Id.*
[103] *Id.*
[104] Warren Bros. Co. v. Peerless Ins. Co., 8 Mass. App. Ct. 719, 397 N.E.2d 329 (1979).
[105] Mass. Gen. Laws ch. 254, § 14.
[106] *Id.*

days after a claimant has received notice of the recording of the bond.[107] No new rights for a claimant are, however, created by the recording of a lien bond.[108] In other words, if there is a defect in the lien, the filing of the bond does not cure the defect, and merely substitutes the bond for the real estate as security for any amounts otherwise recoverable under the lien statute.

[I] Prohibited Practices, Lien Waivers, and Mandatory Funding

Under the prior version of the Massachusetts mechanics' lien law, the filing of mechanics' lien documents were generally regarded as a hostile act, and often led to disruptions in the performance of work, payment of requisitions, and bank funding of construction. One of the goals in amending the statute was to curtail that adversary aspect of Massachusetts mechanics' liens, so that the filing of mechanics' lien documents would be a routine matter and would not disrupt construction. To accomplish this goal, Chapter 254 prohibits certain construction and lending practices relating to mechanics' liens, and allows parties to seek expedited relief in court for conduct that runs afoul of these prohibitions.[109] Those prohibited activities include the following:

1. Refusal to continue to provide financing or payments solely because of the filing of a notice of contract or statement of claim.[110] (This prohibition is not, however, applicable to construction projects containing from one to four dwelling units.)[111]
2. Filing of a notice of contract or statement of claim for an invalid reason.
3. The taking of any action under the statute which is foreclosed by a judgment or release.[112]
4. The refusal of any party to execute a notice of substantial completion or the improper filing of a notice of termination.[113]

Any person aggrieved by one of these actions may seek expedited relief in either the state superior court or state district court where the land is located. The relief may include (1) a prompt ruling on the matter or (2) a prompt discharge of the lien.[114] An action to obtain such relief may be commenced by any person in interest, including but not limited to owners, contractors, subcontractors, and mortgage holders, and must include notice to the holders of any recorded mortgages, who are allowed to appear and be heard in any proceeding.[115] The statute

[107] *Id.*
[108] *Id.*
[109] *Id.* at ch. 254, § 15A, 32, 33.
[110] *Id.* at ch. 254, § 15A(a).
[111] *Id.* at ch. 254, § 33.
[112] *Id.* at ch. 254, § 15A(e).
[113] *Id.* at ch. 254, § 15A(f).
[114] *Id.* at ch. 254, § 15A.
[115] *Id.*

allows for short orders of notice and for hearings within seven days after the filing of the complaint.[116] The application for relief under § 15A shall be made on a verified complaint accompanied by other written proof of the facts upon which the application was made.[117]

The statute also prohibits and makes unenforceable any covenants, promises, or agreements that waive lien rights.[118] Specifically, the statute provides that any agreement, promise, or covenant that purports to bar the taking of any steps to establish or enforce a lien, or that purports to subordinate lien rights under the statute, is against public policy and is void and unenforceable, with few exceptions.[119] The exceptions include: (1) waivers of liens given by persons named as principals on lien bonds in connection with interim or final payments, (2) statements by persons "entitled to file documents under this chapter of amounts due or paid to them," (3) lien dissolutions, and (4) partial waivers and subordination of liens by general contractors who have recorded notices of contract, provided that the waivers and subordinations are in a statutorily required form.[120] Subcontractors and suppliers therefore cannot be asked to sign a waiver or subordination of lien forms, although they can be asked to sign statements regarding amounts of money that are due and amounts of money that have been paid to them.

The "Partial Waiver and Subordination of Lien" form provided in the statute works with the new anti-retaliatory and mortgage priority provisions of the statute. Together, these provisions facilitate the continuation of payments to contractors or subcontractors, despite the prior filing of a notice of contract, circumstances under which further payments were often not made under the prior version of this statute. By executing the form, the contractor waives all lien rights, *except* as to retainage, in order to obtain payment for undisputed amounts, but does not waive its right to disputed claims in order to obtain such payment.

---

[116] *Id.*
[117] *Id.*
[118] *Id.* at ch. 254, § 32.
[119] *Id.*
[120] *Id.*

CHAPTER 23

MICHIGAN

Patrick J. Keating
David M. Hayes
Mary C. Dirkes

§ 23.01 INTRODUCTION

On private projects, Michigan does not require principal contractors to furnish any kind of bond. However, Michigan law does provide contractors and their subcontractors with certain lien rights, termed "construction liens," rather than "mechanics' liens." The Michigan construction lien law is known as the Michigan Construction Lien Act.[1]

Conversely, on public projects, Michigan law does not provide contractors with any construction lien rights.[2] There are, however, two principal statutes governing bonds with respect to public projects.

The first bond statute governs nonhighway public projects in excess of $50,000, and is known as the Contractor's Bond For Public Buildings or Works Act (the "Michigan Public Works Bond Act").[3] The Michigan Public Works Bond Act requires principal contractors to furnish both performance and payment bonds in amounts set by the contracting agency, but the bonds may not be less than 25 percent of the contract amount. The performance bond must name the public owner as obligee, while the payment bond must be for the benefit of persons furnishing labor, material, or both, used or reasonably required for use in the performance of the contract.[4] If, however, the principal contractor is a common carrier as defined in § 3 of Act No. 300 of the Public Acts of 1909, as amended, or the designated operator of a state-subsidized railroad, the principal contractor may provide an irrevocable letter of credit from a state or national bank or a state or federally chartered savings and loan association instead of a bond.[5]

The second bond statute governs state highway projects, and is known as the Public Buildings and Public Works Act (the "State Highway Public Works Bond Act").[6] Under the State Highway Public Works Bond Act, contractors are not required to post performance bonds but must provide payment bonds in an amount providing "sufficient security" for subcontractors, suppliers, and laborers on the project. The statute provides that "claimants," i.e., persons furnishing labor and materials used in connection with or consumed in the project, are afforded protection under the payment bond. Similar to the statute governing nonhighway projects, if the contractor on a state highway project is a common carrier as defined in § 3 of Act No. 300 of the Public Acts of 1909, as amended, or the designated operator of a state-subsidized railroad, the contractor may provide an

---

[1] M.C.L.A. §§ 570.1101 *et seq.;* M.S.A. §§ 26.316(101) *et seq.*

[2] Kammer Asphalt Paving Co., Inc. v. East China Township Schs., 443 Mich. 176, 181, 504 N.W.2d 635, 638 (1993); Adamo Equip. Rental Co. v. Mack Dev. Co., 122 Mich. App. 233, 236, 333 N.W.2d 40, 41(1982).

[3] M.C.L.A. §§ 129.201 *et seq.*; M.S.A. §§ 5.2321(1) *et seq.*

[4] The purpose and intent of the Michigan Public Works Bond Act is to safeguard and protect contractors and material suppliers in the public sector. Skyline Steel Corp. v. A.J. Dupuis Co., 648 F. Supp. 360, 370 (E.D. Mich. 1986).

[5] M.C.L.A. § 129.201; M.S.A. § 5.2321(1).

[6] M.C.L.A. §§ 570.101 *et seq.*; M.S.A. §§ 26.321 *et seq.*

irrevocable letter of credit from a state or national bank or a state or federally chartered savings and loan association instead of a bond.[7]

§ 23.02 BOND LAW

[A] General Concepts

Michigan treats the construction surety bond relationship as a tripartite relationship and treats bonds as tripartite contracts. Each construction surety bond has an obligee, which is typically an owner or general contractor, and joint and several obligors, which are typically the general contractor or subcontractor and its surety. A good definition appears in *Ellis v. Phillips,*[8] in which the Michigan Supreme Court defined "suretyship" as "a contractual relation resulting from an agreement where one person, the surety, engages to be answerable for the debt, default or miscarriage of another, the principal."[9]

Michigan surety contracts must be in writing and signed by the surety against whom one is making a bond claim.[10] In Michigan, the construction and interpretation of a surety contract is for the court.[11] The goal of any such construction and interpretation is to ascertain the intent of the contracting parties.[12] Ambiguities are strictly construed against the surety.[13] In construing ambiguous terms, courts will give great weight to the manner in which the parties have treated the contract.[14]

The language in a construction surety bond will control as long as it is clear and unambiguous.[15] A surety's liability is limited by both the terms of the surety agreement and the scope of liability of the contractor/principal.[16] Thus, the surety's liability generally cannot be greater than that of its contractor/principal.[17]

---

[7] M.C.L.A. § 570.101; M.S.A. § 26.321.

[8] 363 Mich. 587, 110 N.W.2d 772 (1961).

[9] *Id.* at 596, 110 N.W.2d at 776.

[10] The relevant Michigan statute of frauds is found at M.C.L.A. § 566.132(1); M.S.A. § 26.922(1), which provides in pertinent part as follows:

> In the following cases an agreement, contract, or promise is void, unless that agreement, contract, or promise, or a note or memorandum of the agreement, contract, or promise is in writing and signed with an authorized signature by the party to be charged with the agreement, contract, or promise:
>
> . . . (b) A special promise to answer for the debt, default or misdoings of another person.

[11] *See* William C. Roney & Co. v. The Federal Ins. Co., 674 F.2d 587 (6th Cir. 1982).

[12] *Id.* at 590.

[13] *Id.*

[14] *Id.*

[15] *Id.* at 589.

[16] Board of Governors of Wayne State Univ. v. Building Sys. Hous. Corp., 62 Mich. App. 77, 85, 233 N.W.2d 195, 199 (1975).

[17] Grand Blanc Cement Prod., Inc. v. Insurance Co. of N. Am., 225 Mich. App. 138, 144, 571

Furthermore, the surety may insist upon compliance with all unambiguous terms of the surety contract that limit the surety's liability.[18]

A judgment against the principal is *prima facie* evidence in a suit against a surety, even if the surety was not a party to the action against the principal and had no notice of that action.[19] The effect of such a presumption is to require the surety to come forward with evidence to rebut its liability for the judgment against the principal.[20] The surety may assert any defenses that are available to the principal in an action against the surety on the underlying obligation, in addition to any personal defenses that the surety may have.[21] If no action can be maintained against the principal, then no action can be maintained against the surety.[22]

If a surety is required to pay the principal's obligation, Michigan courts have found it to be fundamental that the surety is entitled to reimbursement from the principal.[23] The surety also has the right to call upon co-sureties for contribution.[24]

Generally, a surety will be released or discharged if its risk is materially increased by some action of the principal.[25] For example, if the principal changes without the consent of the surety, the surety will be discharged under the rationale that a change in the obligation by the substitution of principals has the effect of creating a new contract for which the surety never intended to become liable.[26] Similarly, when a substitution of the obligee occurs, such a change typically operates to release the surety from its obligation.[27] In order for the surety to be discharged, however, a change in the obligations or duties must be prejudicial to the surety.[28] Mere immaterial or technical departures from the contract, not resulting in any damage to the surety, will not release the surety.[29]

N.W.2d 221, 227 (1997). *See also* In re MacDonald's Estate, 341 Mich. 382, 387, 67 N.W.2d 227, 229 (1954).

[18] Board of Governors of Wayne State Univ. v. Building Sys. Hous. Corp., 62 Mich. App. 77, 85, 233 N.W.2d 195, 199 (1975).

[19] P.R. Post Corp. v. Maryland Cas. Co., 403 Mich. 543, 547–48, 271 N.W.2d 521, 523–24 (1978).

[20] *Id.* at 552, 271 N.W.2d at 525.

[21] *See* In re MacDonald's Estate, 341 Mich. 382, 387, 67 N.W.2d 227, 229 (1954).

[22] Ackron Contracting Co. v. Oakland County, 108 Mich. App. 767, 772, 310 N.W.2d 874, 876 (1981).

[23] Michigan Nat'l Bank of Detroit v. Kellam, 107 Mich. App. 669, 683–84, 309 N.W.2d 700, 706 (1981); Ellis v. Phillips, 363 Mich. 587, 596, 110 N.W.2d 772, 776 (1961).

[24] Ellis v. Phillips, 363 Mich. 587, 597, 110 N.W.2d 772, 777 (1961).

[25] Howard v. Lud, 119 Mich. App. 55, 60, 325 N.W.2d 623, 626 (1982).

[26] *Id.*

[27] Reichert v. State Sav. Bank of Royal Oak, 261 Mich. 227, 229, 246 N.W. 95, 96 (1933).

[28] Hunters Pointe Partners Ltd. Partnership v. United States Fidelity & Guar. Co., 177 Mich. App. 745, 749–50, 442 N.W.2d 778, 779–80 (1989); Chris Nelson & Sons, Inc. v. Michigan Corp., 84 Mich. App. 29, 32–33, 269 N.W.2d 295, 297 (1978).

[29] Ramada Dev. Co. v. United States Fidelity & Guar. Co., 626 F.2d 517, 521 (6th Cir. 1980).

[B] Bid Bonds

In Michigan, a bid bond typically guarantees the owner that the low, responsive, responsible bidder will enter into the contract upon which it bid. Michigan does not require contractors to furnish bid bonds on either public or private projects. Nevertheless, the contracting agency can require a bid bond. On the local level, all bids submitted to counties for the construction of facilities, drains, or other contracts, and all bids for construction services with school districts, must be accompanied by a bond, certified check, or other security as the contracting entity may require.[30] Typically, the bid bond will provide a penal sum in a set amount in the event the contractor refuses to actually enter into the contract after an award is made, or refuses to deliver required performance and payment bonds after an award is made.[31]

It is critical in Michigan that the bidder actually be the low, responsive, responsible bidder. If a bidder has made a genuine bid mistake that entitles it to withdraw its bid, then both the contractor and its bid bond surety may be able to avoid liability.[32]

[C] Performance Bonds

A performance bond assures completion of a project in the event of a default by the general contractor, thus protecting the owner of the property.[33] Performance bonds are conditioned upon the faithful performance of the contract in accordance with the contract plans, specifications and terms.[34]

Michigan does not require contractors to provide performance bonds on private projects. In addition, there is no performance bond requirement under the State Highway Public Works Bond Act. For nonhighway public projects in excess of $50,000, however, the Michigan Public Works Bond Act does require the prime contractor to furnish a performance bond in an amount to be set by the contracting agency for not less than 25 percent of the contract sum.[35] Although the Michigan Public Works Bond Act uses the term "governmental unit," which is the contracting agency, it is defined broadly to include "the state or a county, city, village, township, school district, public educational institution, other political subdivi-

---

[30] M.C.L.A. § 45.86; M.S.A. § 5.1156 (county purchases); M.C.L.A. § 280.223; M.S.A. § 11.1223 (county drains); M.C.L.A. § 380.1267(3); M.S.A. § 15.41267(3) (school districts).

[31] *See* Adamo Equip. Co. v. Alexander & Alexander of Michigan, Inc., 821 F.2d 649 (6th Cir. 1987) (unpublished opinion); Fraser Public Schs. Dist. v. Kolon, 35 Mich. App. 441, 445–46, 193 N.W.2d 64, 67 (1971).

[32] Clinton County Dep't of Public Works v. American Bank & Trust Co., 406 Mich. 85, 87–88, 276 N.W.2d 7, 8 (1979); Fraser Public Schs. Dist. v. Kolon, 35 Mich. App. 441, 445–46, 193 N.W.2d 64, 66–67 (1971).

[33] Kammer Asphalt Paving Co., Inc. v. East China Township Sch., 443 Mich. 176, 179, n.4, 504 N.W.2d 635, 637, n.4 (1993).

[34] M.C.L.A. § 129.202; M.S.A. § 5.2321(2).

[35] *Id.*

sion, public authority or public agency."[36] The Michigan Public Works Bond Act expressly provides that performance bonds shall be solely for the protection of the governmental agency that awarded the contract.[37] The claimant under a performance bond generally is entitled to recover its direct and consequential damages that are incurred as a result of the contractor's default, unless, of course, such damages are precluded under either the bond or the contract at issue.

The Michigan Public Bonds Work Act was intended to cover only situations in which a governmental unit hires a private contractor to perform work on government property.[38] When a building is being constructed for a governmental unit, but the land is privately owned, the statute does not apply.[39] Interestingly, however, the Michigan Supreme Court has held that a university chartered under the Michigan Constitution (The University of Michigan) is subject to Michigan's public bonding statute as a valid exercise of the Michigan legislature's police power, despite the fact that the University is considered separate from the government of the state of Michigan.[40] This decision reflects a growing trend in the Michigan Supreme Court to liberally construe the Michigan Public Works Bond Act.[41]

[D] Payment Bonds

Under the Michigan Public Bonds Work Act, payment bonds are "solely for the protection of claimants . . . supplying labor or materials to the principal contractor or his [or her] subcontractors in the prosecution of the work provided for in the contract."[42] The bond, therefore, must be "executed by a surety company authorized to do business in this state."[43]

On private projects, Michigan law does not require contractors to furnish payment bonds. On public projects, however, the Michigan Public Works Bond Act requires contractors to furnish a payment bond in the amount fixed by the governmental unit (but not less than 25 percent of the contract).[44] The State

[36] M.C.L.A. § 129.201; M.S.A. § 5.2321(1).

[37] M.C.L.A. § 129.202; M.S.A. § 5.2321(2).

[38] Modern Transit-Mix, Inc. v. Michigan Bell Telephone Co., 130 Mich. App. 300, 303, 342 N.W.2d 14, 15 (1983).

[39] The Milbrand Co. v. Department of Social Servs., 117 Mich. App. 437, 440–41, 324 N.W.2d 41, 43 (1982)

[40] W.T. Andrew Co., Inc. v. Mid-State Sur. Corp., 450 Mich. 655, 662, 545 N.W.2d 351, 354 (1996), *on remand,* 221 Mich. App. 438, 562 N.W.2d 206 (1997), *leave to appeal granted,* 586 N.W.2d 746 (1998).

[41] *See* Trustees for Michigan Laborers' Health Care Fund v. Warranty Builders, Inc., 921 F. Supp. 471, 473–75 (E.D. Mich. 1996), *aff'd,* Trustees for Michigan Laborers' Health Care Fund v. Seaboard Sur. Co., 137 F.3d 427 (6th Cir. 1998).

[42] M.C.L.A. § 129.203; M.S.A. § 5.2321(3).

[43] M.C.L.A. § 129.204; M.S.A. § 5.2321(4); Kammer Asphalt Paving Co., Inc. v. East China Township Schs., 443 Mich. 176, 182, 504 N.W.2d 635, 639 (1993).

[44] M.C.L.A. § 129.203; M.S.A. § 5.2321(3).

Highway Public Works Bond Act also requires contractors to obtain payment bonds in an undetermined amount providing "sufficient security" for subcontractors, suppliers, and laborers on the project.[45]

The Michigan Public Works Bond Act requires the *contractor to furnish* the bonds rather than stating that the *governmental entity should require* the bonds.[46] Based upon this language, the Michigan Court of Appeals has held that the contracting governmental unit has no duty to ensure that payment bonds are kept current or to warn subcontractors or material suppliers of the expiration of the bond.[47] Accordingly, suppliers can be precluded from recovering from the governmental entity when the general contractor defaults on payments and the bond has expired. The Michigan Court of Appeals also has held that the Michigan Public Works Bond Act does not place an affirmative duty on the governmental unit to require a prime contractor to furnish a payment bond in accordance with the statute or otherwise face liability to the subcontractor or supplier.[48]

The Michigan Public Works Bond Act, however, does mandate that public units provide subcontractors, material suppliers, and laborers with a certified copy of a payment bond if they submit an affidavit that they have not been paid for services or materials.[49] Such a certified copy "shall be prima facie evidence of the contents, execution, and delivery of the original."[50] The Michigan Supreme Court has held that a governmental entity verifies the validity of a payment bond when it provides a certified copy of the bond at the request of a subcontractor, material supplier, or laborer.[51] The Court insisted that to hold otherwise would render the statutory requirement of payment bonds meaningless.[52] The statute, therefore, places the risk of the invalidity of bonds on the government.[53] However, if subcontractors are willing to work after nonpayment by a general contractor, without at least requesting copies of the bonds, then they are held to have assumed the risk that no bonds (or invalid bonds) exist.[54]

---

[45] M.C.L.A. § 570.101; M.S.A. § 26.321.

[46] M.C.L.A. § 129.201; M.S.A. § 5.2321(1).

[47] Barnes & Sweeney Enters., Inc. v. City of Hazel Park, 169 Mich. App. 422, 427, 425 N.W.2d 572, 574 (1988).

[48] ABC Supply Co. v. City of River Rouge, 216 Mich. App. 396, 399–402, 549 N.W.2d 73, 75–76 (1996), *appeal denied,* 454 Mich. 858, 558 N.W.2d 727 (1997).

[49] M.C.L.A. § 129.208; M.S.A. § 5.2321(8).

[50] *Id.*

[51] Kammer Asphalt Paving Co., Inc. v. East China Township Schs., 443 Mich. 176, 184, 504 N.W.2d 635, 639 (1993). This holding was construed by the court in ABC Supply Co. v. City of River Rouge, 216 Mich. App. 396, 548 N.W.2d 73 (1996), *appeal denied,* 454 Mich. 858, 558 N.W.2d 727 (1997), to be limited to situations where the governmental unit actually supplied certified copies of the bond to a subcontractor or supplier.

[52] Kammer Asphalt Paving Co., Inc. v. East China Township Schs., 443 Mich. 176, 184–85, 504 N.W.2d 635, 640 (1993).

[53] Michigan Tractor & Machinery Co. v. Detroit Concrete & Constr., Inc., 1994 WL 209450, *2 (E.D. Mich. 1994).

[54] Kammer Asphalt Paving Co., Inc. v. East China Township Schs., 443 Mich. 176, 185, n.19, 504 N.W.2d 635, 640, n.19.

The Michigan Public Works Bond Act clarifies that the payment bond is solely for the protection of claimants supplying labor or materials to the principal contractor or its subcontractors in the prosecution of the work provided for in the contract.[55] "Claimant" is defined as a person furnishing labor, material, or both, used or reasonably required for use in the performance of the contract.[56] As defined, "labor and material" specifically includes that part of water, gas, power, light, heat, oil, gasoline, telephone service, and rental of equipment directly applicable to the contract.[57]

The State Highway Public Works Bond Act requires a bond for the payment of subcontractors and for the payment for all labor performed and materials and certain supplies furnished and used on the highway project.[58] "Materials" and "supplies" are defined as including coal, wood, form lumber, gasoline, kerosene and lubricating and fuel oils necessarily used in connection with or consumed in the state highway project. "Labor" includes the hauling, other than by steam or electric railway, to or away from the project any refuse, materials or dirt accumulated or used in connection with or consumed in the state highway project.[59]

[1] Enforcing Payment Bonds

The general theory on which subcontractors, material suppliers, and laborers are permitted to recover on a bond executed in connection with public works and improvements is third-party-beneficiary contract law.[60] Decisions interpreting the Michigan Public Works Bond Act have held that if a prime contractor furnishes a bond with provisions that include more expansive coverage than the bond law requires, claimants will be able to take advantage of the expanded bond coverage.[61] Yet, as with general Michigan law on construction surety bonds, courts cannot extend the coverage of the bond beyond its clear and unambiguous terms.

With respect to bonds issued on nonhighway public projects, suits on payment bonds cannot be filed before 90 days after last supplying labor or materials to the project.[62] Additionally, a suit must be filed within one year from

---

[55] M.C.L.A. § 129.203; M.S.A. § 5.2321(3).

[56] M.C.L.A. § 129.206; M.S.A. § 5.2321(6). "Claimant" has been interpreted broadly by one court to include trust funds seeking unpaid fringe benefits owed to its union employees. Trustees for Michigan Laborers' Health Care Fund v. Seaboard Sur. Co., 137 F.3d 427, 430 (6th Cir. 1998).

[57] M.C.L.A. § 129.206; M.S.A. § 5.2321(6).

[58] M.C.L.A. § 570.101; M.S.A. § 26.321.

[59] M.C.L.A. § 570.105; M.S.A. § 26.325.

[60] Skyline Steel Corp. v. A.J. Dupuis Co., 648 F. Supp. 360, 369 (E.D. Mich. 1986).

[61] Trustees for Michigan Laborers' Health Care Fund v. Warranty Builders, Inc., 921 F. Supp. 471, 476–77 (E.D. Mich. 1996), *aff'd,* Trustees for Michigan Laborers' Health Care Fund v. Seaboard Sur. Co., 137 F.3d 417 (6th Cir. 1998); Royalite Co. v. Federal Ins. Co., 184 Mich. App. 69, 74–75, 457 N.W.2d 96, 98 (1990). *But see* W.T. Andrew Co. v. Mid-State Sur. Co., 221 Mich. App. 438, 442, 562 N.W.2d 206, 208 (1997), *on remand,* 221 Mich. App. 438, 562 N.W.2d 206 (1997), *leave to appeal granted,* 586 N.W.2d 746 (1998).

[62] M.C.L.A. § 129.207; M.S.A. § 5.2321(7).

the date on which final payment was made to the principal contractor.[63] An action instituted on a payment bond may be brought only "in the appropriate court in the political subdivision in which the contract was to be performed."[64]

A party contracting directly with the principal on the bond is not required to furnish any notice.[65] Thus, direct subcontractors and suppliers are not required to formally notify the contractor or the governmental unit.[66]

Conversely, a claimant with no direct contract with the prime contractor must give two written notices. [67] The initial notice must be sent to the principal contractor furnishing the payment bond within 30 days from the date on which the claimant first performed labor or first furnished the materials for which it may claim payment.[68] This notice must state the nature of the materials or labor furnished, the name of the person for whom the work was performed or to whom the material was furnished, and the site for performance.[69] This notice provision ensures that the principal contractor is formally made aware of all potential claimants, either through direct contract or prompt notice.[70]

These indirect parties also must send a second notice within 90 days from furnishing the last labor or materials that states the amount claimed and the party to whom the material was furnished or the labor was provided.[71] This second notice must be sent to the principal contractor furnishing the bond *and* to the governmental unit involved.[72] Although the statute unequivocally requires both notices to be sent by certified mail,[73] the Michigan Supreme Court has held that

---

[63] M.C.L.A. § 129.209; M.S.A. § 5.2321(9).

[64] *Id.*

[65] M.C.L.A. § 129.207; M.S.A. § 5.2321(7).

[66] *Id.*

[67] *Id.*

[68] *Id. See also* Tempco Heating & Cooling, Inc. v. A. Rea Constr., Inc., 178 Mich. App. 181, 190, 443 N.W.2d 486, 490 (1989). The 30-day notice period is specific to each new and independent contractual arrangement. Therefore, if a subcontractor or materialman failed to timely file notice under an earlier agreement on a public project, the subcontractor or materialman could still protect itself under a new and independent agreement on the same project by notifying the principal contractor within thirty days of beginning the new contract. This notification, however, applies only to the new contract. Grand Blanc Cement Prods., Inc. v. Insurance Co. of N. Am., 225 Mich. App. 138, 142, 571 N.W.2d 221, 226 (1997).

[69] M.C.L.A. § 129.207; M.S.A. § 5.2321(7). The statute requires the written notice to be "served" on the principal contractor. One court interpreted the use of the term *served* as requiring a more formal presentation of notice. In Thomas Indus., Inc. v. C&L Elec., Inc., 216 Mich. App. 603, 609, 550 N.W.2d 558, 561–62 (1996), *appeal denied,* 558 N.W.2d 734 (1997), the court held that packing slips delivered to the job site, even though the slips contained the necessary information, did not fulfill the purpose of the notice provision under the statute.

[70] *See* Pi-Con, Inc. v. A.J. Anderson Constr. Co., 435 Mich. 375, 383–84, 458 N.W.2d 639, 642 (1990).

[71] M.C.L.A. § 129.207; M.S.A. § 5.2321(7); Tempco Heating & Cooling, Inc. v. A. Rea Constr., Inc., 178 Mich. App. 181, 190, 443 N.W.2d 486, 490 (1989).

[72] *Id.*

[73] M.C.L.A. § 129.207; M.S.A. § 5.2321(7).

regular mail is sufficient if there is evidence of actual receipt of the notice.[74] Furthermore, although the statute requires an aggrieved party to send out both a 30-day and a 90-day notice, the Michigan Court of Appeals has held that the 30-day notice requirement may be excused if there is no reference to such a requirement within the bond itself.[75]

Although written notification is required to protect the rights of public contractors, material suppliers, and laborers who are not in contract directly with the principal, such notification alone is not sufficient to enforce those rights. The mechanism established by statute to execute payment under the bond is that the claimant file suit against the bonded entities.[76]

Mailing a notice of claim under the Michigan Public Works Bond Act does not represent an election to collect only from the bonded entities, to the exclusion of any direct claims against the obligor.[77] Furthermore, Michigan law provides that a constructive trust may also be imposed when there is a breach of a fiduciary or confidential relationship, misrepresentation, concealment, mistake, undue influence, duress, or fraud, even though the Michigan Public Works Bond Act provides a legal remedy to aggrieved subcontractors, material suppliers, and laborers.[78] There is no election of remedies until one of the remedies is pursued to a final judgment.[79]

With respect to payment bonds issued on highway projects, the State Highway Public Works Bond Act requires that subcontractors serve written notice in duplicate upon the state highway department within 60 days after furnishing the last materials or supplies or performing the last work.[80] All others, except those providing labor, must also provide notice to the state highway department within 60 days after furnishing the last materials or supplies.[81] The notice must specify the project, the claimant's work or goods, and the fact that the claimant will rely upon the security of the bond.[82] Suit must be commenced within one year after completion *and acceptance* of the project.[83]

---

[74] Pi-Con, Inc. v. A.J. Anderson Constr. Co., 435 Mich. 375, 387, 458 N.W.2d 639, 644 (1990); Thomas Indus., Inc. v. C&L Elec., Inc., 216 Mich. App. 603, 608, 550 N.W.2d 558, 561 (1996), *appeal denied,* 558 N.W.2d 734 (1997); W.T. Andrew Co., Inc. v. Mid-State Sur. Corp., 221 Mich. App. 438, 441, 562 N.W.2d 206, 207 (1997).

[75] Royalite Co. v. Federal Ins. Co., 184 Mich. App. 69, 74–75, 457 N.W.2d 96, 98 (1990). *But see* W.T. Andrew Co., Inc. v. Mid-State Sur. Corp., 221 Mich. App. 438, 562 N.W.2d 206 (1997).

[76] M.C.L.A. § 129.209; M.S.A. § 5.2321(9); Skyline Steel Corp. v. A.J. Dupuis Co., 648 F. Supp. 360, 371 (E.D. Mich. 1986).

[77] Skyline Steel Corp. v. A.J. Dupuis Co., 648 F. Supp. 360, 371 (E.D. Mich. 1986).

[78] *See* Michigan Tractor & Machinery Co. v. Detroit Concrete & Constr., Inc., 1994 WL 209450, *2 (E.D. Mich. 1994).

[79] *See* Rutter v. King, 57 Mich. App. 152, 157–58, 226 N.W.2d 79, 82 (1974).

[80] M.C.L.A. § 570.102; M.S.A. § 26.322.

[81] *Id.;* the statute reads in relevant part: "All others, excepting those furnishing labor, shall . . . serve a written notice. . . . "

[82] *Id.*

[83] M.C.L.A. § 570.104; M.S.A. § 26.324.

The statutory notice provisions traditionally have been strictly construed by the Michigan Court of Appeals.[84] However, the Michigan Supreme Court has in the past liberally construed the statutory notice provisions.[85] In addition, many Michigan courts have held that when the bonding contract itself provides for less stringent notice provisions than does the statute, the bond provisions control.[86]

In Michigan, payment bond claimants have tried unsuccessfully to recover damages that are in addition to damages solely for the labor furnished or materials supplied. It remains unclear whether Michigan courts will hold sureties liable for claimants' delay damages, finance charges, lost profits, cancellation charges, or interest on claims which themselves are not recoverable (one court, however, did allow a pension fund to sue under the Michigan Public Works Bond Act for unpaid fringe benefits owed pursuant to a collective bargaining agreement[87]). Similarly, claimants on surety bonds are not entitled to recover attorneys' fees unless there are express contractual provisions in the bond providing for such fees.[88]

Finally, in Michigan, punitive or exemplary damages are not available in connection with a breach of contract claim,[89] and there is no independent cause of action for bad faith against an insurer.[90]

§ 23.03 LIEN LAW

[A] General Concepts

The Michigan statute providing for construction liens is known as the Michigan Construction Lien Act (the "Construction Lien Act"). Generally speak-

---

[84] *See* W.T. Andrew Co. v. Mid-State Sur. Corp., 221 Mich. App. 438, 440, 562 N.W.2d 206, 207 (1997); Tempco Heating & Cooling, Inc. v. A. Rea Constr., Inc., 178 Mich. App. 181, 190–91, 443 N.W.2d 486, 490 (1989); Skyline Steel Corp. v. A.J. Dupuis Co., 648 F. Supp. 360, 370–71 (E.D. Mich. 1986).

[85] *See* Pi-Con, Inc. v. A.J. Anderson Constr. Co., 435 Mich. 375, 380–84, 458 N.W.2d 639, 640–42 (1990).

[86] Trustees for Michigan Laborers' Health Care Fund v. Warranty Builders, Inc., 921 F. Supp. 471, 476–77 (E.D. Mich. 1996), *aff'd,* Trustees for Michigan Laborers' Health Care Fund v. Seaboard Sur. Co., 137 F.3d 427 (6th Cir. 1998); Royalite Co. v. Federal Ins. Co., 184 Mich. App. 69, 74–75, 457 N.W.2d 96, 98 (1990).

[87] Trustees for Michigan Laborers' Health Care Fund v. Warranty Builders, Inc., 921 F. Supp. 471 (E.D. Mich. 1996), *aff'd,* Trustees for Michigan Laborers' Health Care Fund v. Seaboard Sur. Co., 137 F.3d 427 (6th Cir. 1998).

[88] *See* Trustees for Michigan Laborers' Health Care Fund v. Seaboard Sur. Co., 137 F.3d 427, 430–31 (6th Cir. 1998). *See also* Sentry Insurance v. Lardner Elevator Company, 153 Mich. App. 317, 326, 395 N.W.2d 31, 35 (1986).

[89] Sullivan Indus., Inc. v. Double Seal Glass Co., Inc., 192 Mich. App. 333, 351, 480 N.W.2d 623, 632 (1991), *leave to appeal denied,* 441 Mich. 931, 498 N.W.2d 737 (1993); American Central Corp. v. Stevens Van Lines, Inc., 103 Mich. App. 507, 515–16, 303 N.W.2d 234, 237–38 (1981); Isagholian v. Carnegie Institute of Detroit, Inc., 51 Mich. App. 220, 222, 214 N.W.2d 864, 865 (1974).

[90] Roberts v. Auto-Owners Ins. Co., 422 Mich. 594, 604, 374 N.W.2d 905, 909 (1985); Kewin v. Massachusetts Mut. Life Ins. Co., 409 Mich. 401, 423, 295 N.W.2d 50, 56 (1980).

ing, the purpose of the act is to provide contractors, subcontractors, and suppliers with a security mechanism on private construction projects in Michigan.[91] This is accomplished by virtue of a purely statutory procedure designed to protect those who have granted credit to an owner or lessee in the form of labor, material, or equipment furnished to the property. This procedure does not expand or reduce the contractual rights of the parties. A second purpose of the Construction Lien Act is to protect owners from paying twice for services performed.[92]

A construction lien is a significant security device because it grants the lien claimant an interest in the real property of the owner or lessee for the value of the labor, material, or equipment provided, to the full extent of the contract with the owner or lessee.

The Construction Lien Act specifically declares that it is to be "liberally construed to secure the beneficial results, intents and purposes of this act."[93] Substantial compliance with the act is generally sufficient, except for the requirement that the lien be recorded within 90 days after furnishing the last work or material.

As mentioned above, the Construction Lien Act does not provide for construction lien rights on public projects.[94]

[B] Basic Provisions

The Construction Lien Act provides that a lien may be perfected "upon the interest of the owner or lessee who contracted for the improvement to the real property, . . . the interest of an owner who has subordinated his or her interest to the mortgage for the improvement of the real property, and the interest of an owner who has required the improvement."[95] The act specifically provides that "each contractor, subcontractor, supplier or laborer who provides an improvement to real property shall have a construction lien."[96] The act defines the terms "contractor," "subcontractor," "supplier," and "laborer," in a manner sometimes inconsistent with their general usage in the construction industry.[97] For example, one who contracts with an owner to supply only material or equipment is a "contractor" and not a "supplier"; furthermore, because a "supplier" is one who furnishes material or equipment "pursuant to contract with a contractor or a

---

[91] Vugterveen Sys., Inc. v. Olde Millpond Corp., 454 Mich. 119, 121, 560 N.W.2d 43, 44 (1997).

[92] Old Kent Bank of Kalamazoo v. Whitaker Constr. Co., 222 Mich. App. 436, 438, 566 N.W.2d 1, 2 (1997), *appeal denied,* in Old Kent Bank of Kalamazoo v. Delisle, 457 Mich. 858, 581 N.W.2d 729 (1998).

[93] M.C.L.A. § 570.1302(1); M.S.A. § 26.316(302)(1). *See also* Vugterveen Sys., Inc. v. Olde Millpond Corp., 454 Mich. 119, 121, 560 N.W.2d 43, 44 (1997).

[94] Adamo Equip. Rental Co. v. Mack Dev. Co., 122 Mich. App. 233, 236, 333 N.W.2d 40, 41 (1982).

[95] M.C.L.A. § 570.1107(1); M.S.A. § 26.316(107)(1).

[96] *Id.*

[97] M.C.L.A. §§ 570.1103, .1104, .1106; M.S.A. §§ 26.316(103), (104), (106).

subcontractor," one who furnishes material or equipment to a "supplier" has no lien protection. Simply stated, a supplier to a supplier has no lien.

A construction lien claim must arise out of a contract for furnishing either labor or supplying materials or equipment; however, there is no requirement that a contract for an improvement relating to other than residential property be in writing. Although the lien "shall not exceed the amount of the lien claimant's contract less payments made on the contract,"[98] the term "contract" is defined as "a contract of whatever nature, for the providing of improvements to real property, including any and all additions to, deletions from, and amendments to the contract."[99]

The Construction Lien Act actually is an in rem action and results in a lien on the owner's or lessee's interest in the real property, although the lien claim is asserted against the owner or lessee.[100] An "owner" is a person holding a fee interest in real property or an equitable interest arising out of a land contract, and a "lessee" is a person, other than the owner, who holds an interest, other than a security interest, in the real property.[101] The lien attaches to the interest of the owner or lessee who contracted for the improvement, including any subsequently acquired legal or equitable interest.[102] The activation and perfection of construction lien rights dates from the time a claimant first furnishes labor and material and from the last furnishing of labor and material.[103] The act specifically provides a rebuttable presumption that a co-owner or co-lessee consented to an improvement made pursuant to a contract entered into by an owner/lessee.[104] If, upon foreclosure, the court finds such consent by the nonconsenting co-owner or co-lessee, the entire interest of that co-owner or co-lessee, including any subsequently acquired interest, is subject to the construction lien.[105] However, a deficiency judgment may not be entered against a noncontracting co-owner or co-lessee.[106]

Because the lien law creates an action in rem, it is separate and distinct from a breach of contract action.[107] Thus, an action for breach of contract that does not seek to foreclose a lien will not perfect the lien.[108] In addition, possession of a

[98] M.C.L.A. § 570.1107(1); M.S.A. § 26.316(107)(1).

[99] M.C.L.A. § 570.1103(4); M.S.A. § 26.316(103)(4). *See also* M.D. Marinich, Inc. v. Michigan Nat'l Bank, 193 Mich. App. 447, 457, 484 N.W.2d 738, 743 (1992), *leave to appeal denied,* 441 Mich. 921, 497 N.W.2d 184, *reconsideration denied,* 500 N.W.2d 472 (1993).

[100] *See* Republic Bank v. Modular One LLC, 232 Mich. App. 444, 447, 591 N.W.2d 335, 337 (1999).

[101] M.C.L.A. § 570.1105; M.S.A. § 26.316(105).

[102] M.C.L.A. § 570.1107(2); M.S.A. § 26.316(107)(2).

[103] *In re Crane,* 154 B.R. 60, 64 (E.D. Mich. 1993).

[104] M.C.L.A. § 570.1107(5); M.S.A. § 26.316(107)(5).

[105] *Id.*

[106] *Id.*

[107] M.C.L.A. § 570.1302(2); M.S.A. § 26.316(302)(2).

[108] *See* Ruggeri Elec. Contracting Co., Inc. v. City of Algonac, 196 Mich. App. 12, 17, 492 N.W.2d 469, 471 (1992), *leave to appeal denied,* 441 Mich. 928, 497 N.W.2d 189 (1993).

lien does not preclude the lien claimant from pursuing a contract action.[109] Similarly, the acceptance by a lien claimant of a promissory note does not waive or discharge an otherwise valid lien.[110] Therefore, a lien claimant can pursue both recovery on a promissory note and foreclosure on a construction lien. The fact that a lien claimant accepts a judgment and a settlement with respect to the promissory note action does not necessarily waive and discharge the lien claimant's construction lien on the property.[111]

The only prerequisite for lienable work is to provide an improvement to the real property. An "improvement" is defined very broadly as "the result of labor or material provided by a contractor, subcontractor, supplier or laborer, . . . pursuant to a contract."[112] An "improvement" includes surveying and engineering and architectural planning, as well as landscaping services.[113] The term "improvement" in the Construction Lien Act does not fix or define the extent of the lien, but instead identifies the parties that are eligible to seek a lien.[114]

Once a lien has arisen, that lien will not be defeated by the forfeiture, surrender, or termination of any title or interest to which the lien attached. If the person contracting for the improvement had no legal title to the real property, the lien attaches to the improvement and the lien may be enforced by foreclosure against the improvement as it is described in the notice of commencement.[115] If a land contract vendee or a lessee contracted for the improvement and that interest is forfeited, surrendered, or otherwise terminated, a lien claimant may be subrogated to the rights of the contracting vendee or lessee as those rights existed immediately before the property interest was terminated.[116] In order to be subrogated, the lien claimant must have provided a notice of furnishing or be statutorily excused from doing so, and must perform the covenants of the land contract or lease within 30 days after receiving actual notice of the forfeiture, surrender, or termination.[117] The Michigan Court of Appeals has stated that the subrogation right is not the exclusive remedy in the event of forfeiture, "but one of several rights granted to lienholders."[118]

Construction liens on condominiums are expressly subject to the definitions

---

[109] M.C.L.A. § 570.1302(2); M.S.A. § 26.316(302)(2); *See also* Old Kent Bank of Kalamazoo v. Whitaker Constr. Co., 222 Mich. App. 436, 439, 566 N.W.2d 1, 2 (1997), *appeal denied,* Old Kent Bank of Kalamazoo v. Delisle, 457 Mich. 858, 581 N.W.2d 729 (1998).

[110] M.C.L.A. § 570.1115(1); M.S.A. § 26.316(115)(1).

[111] Old Kent Bank of Kalamazoo v. Whitaker Constr. Co., 222 Mich. App. 436, 439–40, 566 N.W.2d 1, 2–3 (1997), *appeal denied,* Old Kent Bank of Kalamazoo v. Delisle, 457 Mich. 858, 581 N.W.2d 729 (1998).

[112] M.C.L.A. § 570.1104(7); M.S.A. § 26.316(104)(7).

[113] *Id.*

[114] Erb Lumber Co. v. Homeowner Constr. Lien Recovery Fund, 206 Mich. App. 716, 720, 522 N.W.2d 917, 919 (1994), *leave to appeal denied,* 448 Mich. 922, 533 N.W.2d 585 (1995).

[115] M.C.L.A. § 570.1121(1); M.S.A. § 26.316(121)(1).

[116] M.C.L.A. § 570.1107(4); M.S.A. § 26.316(107)(4).

[117] *Id.*

[118] Norcross Co. v. Turner-Fisher Assoc., 165 Mich. App. 170, 180, 418 N.W.2d 418, 422 (1987).

and limitations set forth in the Condominium Act of 1978, as amended.[119] In addition to those limitations, the lien law provides four more of its own: (1) a lien for an improvement furnished to a condominium unit or to a limited common element attaches *only* to that condominium unit to which the improvement was furnished; (2) a lien for an improvement performed upon the common elements and authorized by the developer attaches only to those units owned by the developer at the time of *recording* the lien (not at the time of attachment); (3) a lien for any improvement authorized by the condominium association attaches to each condominium unit *only* to the proportional extent mandated under the condominium documents for each unit's contribution to the administrative expenses; and (4) no lien attaches for work performed on the common elements if the work was not contracted for by the developer or the condominium association.[120]

A residential owner, like any owner, may subject his or her property interest to liens. The Construction Lien Act includes a section dealing with residential structures which carves out, in certain restricted circumstances, exemptions to the general lienability of the residential homeowner's property interest.[121] Under this section of the act, lien claimants must first determine if the project is a residential structure. If so, the claimant must meet several additional requirements to secure recovery of valid lien amounts.[122]

The Construction Lien Act mandates that the construction lien amount not exceed the claimant's contract amount less payments made on that contract.[123] Again, a "contract" is defined in the act as "a contract, of whatever nature, for the providing of improvements to real property, including any and all additions to, deletions from, and amendments to the contract." [124] When there are disputes over whether the lien amount, which includes disputed extras, interest on the claim, and other costs, is excessive, the courts have long held that when the amount of lien is in fact found to be excessive, the entire lien is lost only if bad faith is evident.[125] If the error in the amount was due to a good faith mistake, the

[119] M.C.L.A. § 570.1126(2); M.S.A. § 26.316(126)(2). The Condominium Act is found at M.C.L.A. §§ 559.101 *et seq.;* M.S.A. §§ 26.50(101) *et seq.*

[120] M.C.L.A. § 570.1126(1); M.S.A. § 26.316(126)(1).

[121] M.C.L.A. §§ 570.1201 *et seq.;* M.S.A. §§ 26.316(201) *et seq.*

[122] M.C.L.A. § 570.1203; M.S.A. § 26.316(203).

[123] M.C.L.A. § 570.1107(1); M.S.A. § 26.316(107)(1). *See* Erb Lumber Co. v. Homeowner Constr. Lien Recovery Fund, 206 Mich. App. 716, 720, 522 N.W.2d 917, 919 (1994), *leave to appeal denied,* 448 Mich. 922, 533 N.W.2d 585 (1995). The *Erb Lumber Company* court also held that the construction lien amount for supply contracts may include a sum representing the time-price differential when the time-price differential is considered part of the contract price. *Id.* at 721, 522 N.W.2d at 920.

[124] M.C.L.A. § 570.1103(4); M.S.A. § 26.316(103)(4).

[125] *See e.g.,* Georgia-Pacific Corp. v. Central Park North Co., 394 Mich. 59, 63–64, 228 N.W.2d 380, 382 (1975), and the numerous cases cited therein; *see also* Tempo, Inc. v. Rapid Elec. Sales & Serv., Inc., 132 Mich. App. 93, 104, 347 N.W.2d 728, 733 (1984).

appropriate remedy is to instead reduce the amount of the lien accordingly.[126] The lien law also provides the owner or lessee (who follows the payment procedures mandated by the law) the protection of its contract by specifically providing that the sum of the construction liens cannot exceed the amount that the owner or lessee agreed to pay the contractor, less payments made pursuant to sworn statements or waivers.[127]

If the lien claimant, due to the failure of the owner or lessee to perform the contract, and without fault on its part, has been prevented from completely performing the contract, the claimant is entitled to a lien for partial compensation.[128] Under these circumstances, the lien claimant is entitled to compensation for the work performed under the contract in proportion to the price stipulated for complete performance, less any payments made to the lien claimant, plus any additional damages to which the lien claimant is entitled as a matter of law.[129]

[C] Notice Requirements

Before the commencement of any "actual physical improvement," a contracting owner or lessee is required to record a notice of commencement in each county in which the subject real property is located. The primary function of this notice is to set out for the benefit of lien claimants all information necessary to permit the lien claimant to prepare the lien and other notices required by statute.[130] The Construction Lien Act sets forth a procedure whereby a lien claimant can request a notice of commencement, and the act provides for penalties for the failure to provide such notice.[131]

Every subcontractor, supplier, or laborer who contracts to provide an improvement to real property must provide a notice of furnishing to the owner and

---

[126] Tempo, Inc. v. Rapid Elec. Sales & Serv., Inc., 132 Mich. App. 93, 104, 347 N.W.2d 728, 733 (1984); Georgia-Pacific. Corp. v. Central Park North Co., 394 Mich. 59, 63–64, 228 N.W.2d 380, 382 (1975).

[127] M.C.L.A. § 570.1107(6); M.S.A. § 26.316(107)(6). The purposes of the Construction Lien Act are served only if the phrase "payments made" found in subsection 107(6) refers to payments made on the specific contract between the owner and the person with whom the owner contracted. Thus, in Vugterveen Systems, Inc. v. Olde Millpond Corp., 454 Mich. 119, 129, 560 N.W.2d 43, 47 (1997), the court held that the owner, who terminated its first general contractor and subcontractor midway through the project, could use all payments made on the contract with the first contractor as a defense to the first subcontractor's construction lien. The owner could not, however, use payments made on a second general contract with a new general contractor as a defense to the first subcontractor's lien, because such payments were not made on the relevant contract.

[128] M.C.L.A. § 570.1120; M.S.A. § 26.316(120).

[129] *Id.*

[130] *See* Vugterveen Sys., Inc. v. Olde Millpond Corp., 454 Mich. 119, 121, 560 N.W.2d 43, 44 (1997).

[131] M.C.L.A. § 570.1108(9)-(17); M.S.A. § 26.316(108)(9)-(17) (nonresidential structures); M.C.L.A. § 570.1108a(9)-(13); M.S.A. § 26.316(108a)(9)-(13) (residential structures).

the general contractor, if any.[132] A subcontractor or supplier must serve the notice of furnishing within 20 days after furnishing the first labor or material.[133] If the claimant is a laborer, the notice of furnishing must be served within 30 days after wages were contractually due but were not paid,[134] or by the fifth day of the second month following the month in which fringe benefits or withholdings from wages were contractually due but were not paid.[135] If a designee has not been named or has died, service must be made on the owner or lessee.[136]

The primary function of the notice is to advise an owner of the fact that a person with whom the owner has not contracted is providing an improvement to the property. Such person, as a subcontractor, supplier, or laborer, may subsequently claim a lien, and the owner, armed with that knowledge, may take steps to protect itself from such liens. Because a contractor has a direct contract with the owner, the contractor is not required to serve a notice of furnishing.

The time for serving the notice of furnishing may be extended if the notice of commencement is not properly recorded or provided.[137] Service may be made before the actual furnishing of the first materials or labor.[138] Further, the notice contents, as well as the penalty provisions for failure to serve, apply differently to laborers than to subcontractors and suppliers.[139]

The failure of a lien claimant to provide a notice of furnishing within the time specified does not defeat a claimant's right to a lien for work or materials furnished after the service of the notice of furnishing.[140] Moreover, the failure to provide a notice of furnishing only defeats a claimant's right to a lien for work or materials furnished before the service of the notice to the extent that payments were made by or on behalf of the owner or lessee to the contractor pursuant to either a sworn statement or a waiver of lien.[141]

With respect to laborers, the failure to provide a notice of furnishing to the owner's representative will defeat the laborer's lien for wages, fringe benefits, and withholdings for which the notice is required. A laborer's failure to timely provide

[132] M.C.L.A. § 570.1109; M.S.A. § 26.316(109). *See also* Vugterveen Sys., Inc. v. Olde Millpond Corp., 454 Mich. 119, 122, 560 N.W.2d 43, 45 (1997). The Construction Lien Act is remedial in nature—substantial compliance is sufficient to meet the requirements of part one of the act. Consequently, the failure to provide a notice of furnishing was excused when the owner and the contractor met prior to the beginning of construction and the owner knew all the information that is required to be provided in a notice of furnishing. *Id.* at 130–31, 560 N.W.2d at 48.

[133] M.C.L.A. § 570.1109(1); M.S.A. § 26.316(109)(1).

[134] M.C.L.A. § 570.1109(2); M.S.A. § 26.316(109)(2).

[135] M.C.L.A. § 570.1109(3); M.S.A. § 26.316(109)(3).

[136] M.C.L.A. § 570.1109(1) and (2); M.S.A. § 26.316(109)(1) and (2).

[137] M.C.L.A. § 570.1108; M.S.A. § 26.316(108).

[138] Fischer-Flack, Inc. v. Churchfield, 180 Mich. App. 606, 613, 447 N.W.2d 813, 815 (1989).

[139] M.C.L.A. § 570.1109; M.S.A. § 26.316(109).

[140] M.C.L.A. § 570.1109(5); M.S.A. § 26.316(109)(5). *See also* Vugterveen Sys., Inc. v. Olde Millpond Corp., 454 Mich. 119, 122–23, 560 N.W.2d 43, 45 (1997).

[141] M.C.L.A. § 570.1109(6); M.S.A. § 26.316(109)(6). *See also* Vugterveen Sys., Inc. v. Olde Millpond Corp., 454 Mich. 119, 123, 560 N.W.2d 43, 45 (1997), where the court stated that a "delay

the notice to the general contractor will not defeat the laborer's construction lien, but will render the laborer liable to the general contractor for any damages the general contractor incurs as a result of the laborer's untimely notice of furnishing.[142]

Every contractor or subcontractor also must provide a sworn statement that lists each of its subcontractors and suppliers, the type of improvement each provided, all unpaid laborers, the amounts paid, and the amount currently owing to each listed party. The proper form for such a sworn statement is set out in the Construction Lien Act.[143] Suppliers and laborers are not required to provide sworn statements.

With respect to the sworn statement, contractors and subcontractors are treated separately under the Construction Lien Act. Each, however, must provide a sworn statement when payment is due, when requesting a payment, or when the owner or lessee has demanded a sworn statement.[144] The contractor will always provide the statement to the owner. A subcontractor, on the other hand, is required to provide a statement to the owner or lessee only when a demand for the statement has been made.[145] When a subcontractor requests payment, it must provide a sworn statement to the contractor.[146]

The failure to provide a required sworn statement before recording a claim of lien will not invalidate the lien,[147] but an action may not be filed to enforce the lien until the sworn statement has been provided,[148] and no payment on the contract need be made until the sworn statement is provided.[149] The rights and obligations of the recipient of the sworn statement are set forth at length in the act.[150]

In order to retain any construction lien rights afforded under the Construction Lien Act, a claim of lien must be recorded in the office of the register of deeds for each county where the improved real property is located.[151] The act sets out the form, the information to be included, the procedure for providing and record-

---

in providing the notice of furnishing will reduce the lien by the amount that the owner had already paid for the subcontractor's work before the notice was provided. . . . However, these payments must have been pursuant to a contractor's sworn statement or waiver of lien."

[142] M.C.L.A. § 570.1109(7)-(9); M.S.A. § 26.316 (109)(7)-(9).

[143] M.C.L.A. § 570.1110(4); M.S.A. § 26.316(110)(4).

[144] M.C.L.A. § 570.1110(1), (2), (3); M.S.A. § 26.316(110)(1), (2), (3). *See also* Vugterveen Sys., Inc. v. Olde Millpond Corp., 454 Mich. 119, 123, 560 N.W.2d 43, 45 (1997).

[145] M.C.L.A. § 570.1110(2); M.S.A. § 26.316(110)(2). *See also* Vugterveen Sys., Inc. v. Olde Millpond Corp., 454 Mich. 119, 123, 560 N.W.2d 43, 45 (1997).

[146] M.C.L.A. § 570.1110(3); M.S.A. § 26.316(110)(3). *See also* Vugterveen Sys., Inc. v. Olde Millpond Corp., 454 Mich. 119, 123, 560 N.W.2d 43, 45 (1997).

[147] M.C.L.A. § 570.1110(8), (9); M.S.A. § 26.316(110)(8), (9).

[148] *Id. See also* Vugterveen Sys., Inc. v. Olde Millpond Corp., 454 Mich. 119, 124, 560 N.W.2d 43, 45 (1997).

[149] M.C.L.A. § 570.1110(8); M.S.A. § 26.316(110)(8).

[150] M.C.L.A. § 570.1110(6); M.S.A. § 26.316(110)(6).

[151] M.C.L.A. § 570.1111(1); M.S.A. § 26.316(111)(1).

ing the claim of lien, and the express provision that lien rights are extinguished if these procedures are not followed.[152]

The claim of lien *must* be recorded within 90 days from the date the lien claimant last furnished labor or material for the improvement[153] and must include a proof of service of the notice of furnishing unless such notice was not required.[154] The Michigan Court of Appeals has held that the 90-day period commences on the date the original installation work is completed and that the time period is not extended by later performance of warranty work.[155]

Within 15 days after recording the claim of lien, the lien must be served on the owner's designee either personally or by certified mail, return receipt requested, or, if a designee has not been named or has died, service must be made on the owner or lessee.[156] Proof of such service must be attached to any complaint to enforce the lien.[157]

Once properly recorded and served, the lien is effective for a one-year period.[158] Proceedings for the enforcement must be brought within that year or the lien rights are extinguished.[159]

[D] Waiver and Discharge of Liens

The protection afforded by the Construction Lien Act may be waived by a written instrument substantially in accord with the four forms set forth in the act.[160] There is no Michigan authority that provides for a waiver of lien other than in writing. Furthermore, a contract provision requiring the right to a construction lien to be waived in advance of work performed is invalid except to the extent payment is made, and a lien claimant's acceptance of a promissory note or other evidence of indebtedness from an owner, lessee, or contractor does not, by itself, serve to waive or discharge the claimant's lien rights.[161] The act establishes four types of valid waivers, two of which are optional, one that is required if requested, and one that must be provided if the specified event occurs.

A lien claimant who receives full payment, including retention, must provide the owner a full unconditional waiver of lien.[162] A lien claimant who receives partial payment must, if requested, provide a partial unconditional waiver of lien for the amount that the lien claimant has received.[163] Conditional waivers, effective

[152] M.C.L.A. § 570.1111; M.S.A. § 26.316(111).
[153] M.C.L.A. § 570.1111(1); M.S.A. § 26.316(111)(1).
[154] M.C.L.A. § 570.1111(4); M.S.A. § 26.316(111)(4).
[155] Woodman v. Walter, 204 Mich. App. 68, 70, 514 N.W.2d 190, 191 (1994).
[156] M.C.L.A. § 570.1111(5); M.S.A. § 26.316(111)(5).
[157] *Id.*
[158] M.C.L.A. § 570.1117(1); M.S.A. § 26.316(117)(1).
[159] M.C.L.A. § 570.1128; M.S.A. § 26.316(128).
[160] M.C.L.A. § 570.1115; M.S.A. § 26.316(115).
[161] M.C.L.A. § 570.1115(1); M.S.A. § 26.316(115)(1).
[162] M.C.L.A. § 570.1115(2); M.S.A. § 26.316(115)(2).
[163] M.C.L.A. § 570.1115(3); M.S.A. § 26.316(115)(3).

only upon payment of the amount indicated in the waiver, are not required by law, but they are identified in the act and may be required by the contract between the parties.[164]

The Construction Lien Act provides that retainage that is not yet payable is not considered "due" for purposes of the lien law.[165] Thus, partial waivers that purport to waive lien rights for amounts due through a certain date do not waive the claimant's right to a lien for retainage. Once waived, a construction lien cannot be resuscitated absent an express agreement binding upon those whose interests are affected.

[E] Lien Priority

All construction liens have equal priority, attaching to the real estate as of the date of the first actual physical improvement, and are subject only to interests recorded before the first actual physical improvement.[166] "Actual physical improvement" is the physical change in, or alteration of, real property by a contractor, subcontractor, or laborer that is readily visible and of a kind that would alert a person upon reasonable inspection of the existence of an improvement.[167] The Construction Lien Act defines an "improvement" (as distinguished from an "actual physical improvement") to include, among other things, surveying, engineering, architectural planning, construction management, demolishing and repairing, leasing equipment or affixing a fixture;[168] therefore, architects, engineers, and others who furnish labor, materials, or equipment may claim a lien, even though there may have been no "actual physical improvement" as defined by the act. However, because labor provided in preparation for actual physical improvement, such as surveying, or architectural or engineering planning, is specifically excluded as "actual physical change," a lien for such labor would not have priority over a mortgage recorded before an "actual physical improvement" is made.

The priority of a general contractor's construction lien is not affected by changes made to a construction project, if all the general contractor's work related to the same building project and the contractual modifications all related to the

[164] M.C.L.A. § 570.1115(4); M.S.A. § 26.316(115)(4).

[165] M.C.L.A. §§ 570.1115(5), 570.1119(5); M.S.A. §§ 26.316(115)(5), 26.316(119)(5).

[166] M.C.L.A. § 570.1119(4); M.S.A. § 26.316(119)(4). *See* M.D. Marinich, Inc. v. Michigan Nat'l Bank, 193 Mich. App. 447, 454, 484 N.W.2d 738, 741 (1992), *appeal denied,* 441 Mich. 921, 497 N.W.2d 184, *reconsideration denied,* 500 N.W.2d 472 (1993). *See also* LePore v. Parker-Woodward Corp., 818 F. Supp. 1029, 1035 (E.D. Mich. 1993) (liens based on first actual physical improvement that occurred prior to recording of mortgage took priority over mortgage, even though lien claimants had knowledge of mortgage prior to first actual physical improvement). Construction liens can be subordinate to "superpriority liens" such as those liens created under the Natural Resources and Environmental Protection Act, M.C.L.A. §§ 324.101 *et seq. See In re* Approximately Forty Acres in Tallmadge Township, 223 Mich. App. 454, 464, 566 N.W.2d 652, 657 (1997), *appeal denied,* 457 Mich. 885, 586 N.W.2d 231 (1998).

[167] M.C.L.A. § 570.1103(1); M.S.A. § 26.316(103)(1).

[168] M.C.L.A. § 570.1104(7); M.S.A. § 26.316(104)(7).

project as originally contemplated.[169] Moreover, when a general contractor is hired to take over the work of another general contractor, the second general contractor's lien attaches to the real estate as of the date of the first actual physical improvement performed by the first general contractor.[170]

An advance made pursuant to the mortgage, but after the first actual physical improvement, has priority over a construction lien if, for that advance: (1) the mortgagee has received a contractor's sworn statement; (2) the mortgagee has made disbursements pursuant to the contractor's sworn statement; and (3) the mortgagee has received waivers of lien from the contractor and all subcontractors, laborers, and suppliers who have provided notices of furnishing.[171]

[F] Remedies of Owner

The lien law is intended not only to ensure that lien claimants are paid for the improvements they make to property, but also to protect owners from paying twice for such improvements.[172] Thus, an owner may rely on a sworn statement prepared by another party to avoid the claim of a subcontractor, supplier, or laborer, unless the subcontractor, supplier, or laborer has provided a notice of furnishing or is excused from providing a notice of furnishing.[173] If a sworn statement does not list the subcontractors, suppliers, or laborers that have provided the owner with a notice of furnishing, the owner may withhold payment from the contractor to pay these parties.[174] Additionally, the owner may directly pay subcontractors, suppliers, and laborers the amount they are due as shown by the sworn statement.[175]

Once a lien is filed, the owner is further protected from paying twice for the same labor and materials by the act's requirement that a construction lien cannot exceed the amount of the lien claimant's contract, less payments made on the contract.[176] Moreover, if it is determined that a lien was excessive and filed in bad faith, the entire lien will be lost.[177] A clerical error, however, will not deprive a lien claimant of its construction lien.[178]

---

[169] *See* M.D. Marinich, Inc. v. Michigan Nat'l Bank, 193 Mich. App. 447, 457–58, 484 N.W.2d 738, 742 (1992), *appeal denied,* 441 Mich. 921, 497 N.W.2d 184, *reconsideration denied,* 500 N.W.2d 472 (1993).

[170] *Id.*

[171] M.C.L.A. § 570.1119(4); M.S.A. § 26.316(119)(4).

[172] M.D. Marinich, Inc. v. Michigan Nat'l Bank, 193 Mich. App. 447, 453, 484 N.W.2d 738, 741 (1992), *leave to appeal denied,* 441 Mich. 921, 497 N.W.2d 184, *reconsideration denied,* 500 N.W.2d 472 (1993).

[173] M.C.L.A. § 570.1110(7); M.S.A. § 26.316(110)(7).

[174] M.C.L.A. § 570.1110(6); M.S.A. § 26.316(110)(6)

[175] *Id.*

[176] M.C.L.A. § 570.1107(1); M.S.A. § 36.316(107)(1).

[177] Tempo, Inc. v. Rapid Elec. Sales & Serv., Inc., 132 Mich. App. 93, 104, 347 N.W.2d 728, 733 (1984).

[178] Superior Prods. Co. v. Merucci Bros., Inc., 107 Mich. App. 153, 158, 309 N.W.2d 188, 190 (1981).

Even after a lien is filed, the lien may be vacated and discharged from the owner's property if a bond in twice the amount of the lien claim, with the lien claimant as obligee, is filed with the county clerk and a copy is given to the obligee.[179]

Although the court in its discretion may award reasonable attorneys' fees to a prevailing lien claimant, the court may award reasonable attorneys' fees to a prevailing defendant only if the court determines that the lien claimant's action to enforce the construction lien was vexatious.[180]

[G] Homeowner Construction Lien Recovery Fund

The Construction Lien Act includes a section regarding residential structures which carves out, in certain restricted circumstances, exemptions to the general lienability of a residential homeowner's property interest.[181] Under this section, the legislature created the Homeowner Construction Lien Recovery Fund to provide a self-supporting governmental fund to pay validly created and enforced liens against residential structures statutorily exempt from such liens. The purpose of the statute is twofold: (1) to provide for payment of subcontractors and suppliers; and (2) to protect homeowners from paying twice for improvements to their property if the contractor, who receives payment from the homeowner, fails to pay the subcontractor or supplier.[182]

Under the act, a lien cannot attach to a residential structure, to the extent payments have been made, if the homeowner files an affidavit with the court indicating that the homeowner: (1) has paid the contractor; (2) has not colluded with any person to obtain a payment from the lien fund; and (3) has cooperated, and will cooperate, with the Department of Licensing and Regulation in defense of the lien fund.[183]

A "residential structure" is specifically defined by statute.[184] Thus, before asserting a claim against the fund, the lien claimants must first determine if the project is a residential structure. If so, the claimant then must meet several additional requirements to secure recovery of the valid lien amount from the fund.[185]

First, to obtain payment from the fund, a lien claimant must establish: that the lien claimant is licensed, if so required; that the owner or lessee paid the contractor, but the contractor did not pay the lien claimant; that the lien claimant

---

[179] M.C.L.A. § 570.1116(1); M.S.A. § 26.316(116)(1).

[180] M.C.L.A. § 570.1118(2); M.S.A. § 26.316(118)(2). *See also* Vugterveen Sys., Inc. v. Olde Millpond Corp., 454 Mich. 119, 133, 560 N.W.2d 43, 49 (1997).

[181] M.C.L.A. §§ 570.1201 *et seq.;* M.S.A. §§ 26.316(201) *et seq.*

[182] Erb Lumber, Inc. v. Gidley, 234 Mich. App. 387, 594 N.W.2d 81, 85 (1999).

[183] M.C.L.A. § 570.1203(1); M.S.A. § 26.316(203)(1); Horton v. Verhelle, 231 Mich. App. 667, 672–73, 588 N.W.2d 144, 146–47 (1998), *overruled on other grounds,* Smith v. Globe Life Ins. Co., 1999 WL 493901.

[184] M.C.L.A. § 570.1106(3); M.S.A. § 26.316(106)(3).

[185] *See* M.C.L.A. §§ 570.1203(2)-(6); M.S.A. §§ 26.316(203)(2)-(6).

has made a reasonable effort to obtain payment from the contractor; that the lien claimant has not colluded with anyone to obtain payment from the fund; and that the contractor is licensed, if required to be licensed.[186] It is unclear what efforts to collect from a contractor are required. However, a lien claimant was found to have made a reasonable effort when it obtained a default judgment against the contractor and filed the default judgment in the contractor's bankruptcy proceedings, even though the claimant did not seek an exemption order or seek to have the debt declared nondischargeable in bankruptcy.[187] As for the requirement that the delinquent contractor be licensed, a lien claimant may not rely upon the contractor's representations of licensure.[188]

In addition, a claimant who has not paid into the fund as required under the assessment provisions may not recover from the fund.[189] Further, total recovery per residential structure is limited to $75,000; total claims exceeding this amount will be paid pro rata.[190]

The Attorney General, who defends the fund, may assert any defense to a lien claim that would have been available to the owner.[191]

---

[186] M.C.L.A. § 570.1203(3); M.S.A. 26.316(203)(3).

[187] Abode Bldg. Materials, Inc. v. Webster, 185 Mich. App. 655, 661, 462 N.W.2d 806, 809 (1990).

[188] Brown Plumbing & Heating, Inc. v. Homeowner Constr. Lien Recovery Fund, 442 Mich. 179, 186, 500 N.W.2d 733, 736 (1993).

[189] M.C.L.A. § 570.1201(3); M.S.A. § 26.316(201)(3); Horton v. Verhelle, 231 Mich. App. 667, 678–79, 588 N.W.2d 144, 149 (1998), *overruled on other grounds,* Smith v. Globe Life Ins. Co., 1999 WL 493901.

[190] M.C.L.A. § 570.1204; M.S.A. § 26.316(204).

[191] M.C.L.A. § 570.1203(5); M.S.A. § 26.316(203)(5). *See, e.g.,* Horton v. Verhelle, 231 Mich. App. 667, 588 N.W.2d 144 (1998), *overruled on other grounds,* Smith v. Globe Life Ins. Co., 1999 WL 493901, where the lien claimants failed to timely serve their notices of furnishing. To the extent the homeowners made payments to the contractor pursuant to valid sworn statements or waivers of lien prior to the service of the notices of furnishing, the lien claimants' right to collect such payments from the fund would be defeated. (Because the sworn statements at issue were not dated, signed or notarized, the court ultimately held that the homeowner's payments were not made pursuant to a contractor's sworn statement, and thus the payments did not defeat the subcontractors' lien rights.)

CHAPTER 24

MINNESOTA

Dean B. Thomson
Jocelyn L. Knoll

§ 24.01 INTRODUCTION

Minnesota's mechanics' lien statutes (Minn. Stat. §§ 514.01 *et seq.*) and public payment bond statutes (Minn. Stat. §§ 574.26–.32) have the same purpose: to ensure that most contractors and suppliers who provide labor or materials to a construction project are paid for their work. One major difference between liens and bonds, however, is that liens may only be filed against privately owned projects.[1] Minnesota's public payment bond statutes apply only to public projects undertaken by Minnesota state or local governments. The same statute requires prime contractors to provide performance bonds to ensure that the contractor completes its work according to the terms of its contract with the owner. Of course, the owner of a private project is free to require payment and performance bonds from contractors and suppliers; however, these types of bonds would be treated as private contracts not governed by the public payment and performance bond statutes.[2]

§ 24.02 BOND LAW

[A] General Requirements

Except for some relatively arcane exceptions, Minnesota's Public Contractors Performance and Payment Bond Act (the "Act")[3] provides that a public contract for more than $10,000 is not valid unless a contractor supplies (1) a performance bond to the public body with whom the contractor entered into the contract ensuring that the contractor will complete the contract according to its terms; and (2) a payment bond for the use and benefit of all persons furnishing labor and material engaged under, or to perform the contract.[4] Subdivision 1(b) of the Act defines certain terms so that they are consistently used and understood throughout the Act. *Public body* is defined as any public board or body, and *contract* means a contract with a public body for the doing of public work.[5] For the purposes of payment bond claims, *labor and materials* means work, skill, tools, machinery, materials, insurance premiums, equipment, supplies or certain taxes.[6] Thus, the requirement for payment and performance bonds applies to a wide variety of public projects and the coverage provided under the bonds is quite expansive.

The penal sum of each payment and performance bond must not be less than

---

[1] *See, e.g.,* GME Consultants, Inc. v. Oak Grove Dev., Inc., 515 N.W.2d 74 (Minn. Ct. App. 1994) (school district's interest in undeveloped real property held for possible school use is exempt from Minnesota's mechanics' lien statute).

[2] Union Sewer Pipe Co. v. Olson, 84 N.W. 756 (Minn. 1901).

[3] MINN. STAT. § 574.26-.32.

[4] *Id.* § 574.26, subd. 2.

[5] *Id.* § 574.26, subd. 1(b).

[6] *Id.*

the contract price.[7] Nevertheless, for contracts made with the Minnesota Department of Administration or the Department of Transportation, the commissioners of each Department may fix the amount of the bond penalty but not at less than three quarters of the contract price.[8] For projects under $5,000, the contractor may post security, such as certified or cashier's checks, in place of the required bonds.[9] Letters of credit may be used in lieu of performance bonds on contracts under $50,000.[10]

The Minnesota Commissioner of Natural Resources also has the discretion not to require payment and performance bonds on forestry development projects. If the commissioner decides to utilize payment and performance bonds, however, they cannot be less than five percent of the value of the work. In addition, the commissioner also has discretion to decide whether securities may be posted in place of a payment bond for forestry development projects less than $50,000. In place of performance bonds, the commissioner may also allow a deposit of securities, at the time of the bid, which may not be less than five percent of the contract price.[11]

Before beginning any work on the contract, the contractor must file the payment and performance bonds with the treasurer or officer having financial management of the public body named in the bonds. The payment and performance bonds must list the address of the contractor on whose behalf the bonds were issued and of the surety providing the bonds.[12] If the contractor does not file the bonds or they fail to contain this statutorily required information, then a claimant under the payment bond need not provide the surety or the prime contractor written notice of the claimant's claim prior to commencing the lawsuit.[13] For the convenience of the claimant, the public body must make the payment and performance bonds available for inspection and copying upon request. The Act also rejects certain surety defenses by stating that any assignment, modification or change to the contract or its scope, or an extension of time to complete the contract, does not relieve the surety of liability on the bonds.[14]

If the public body fails to obtain and approve a valid payment bond, that public body will be liable to all persons furnishing labor and material under the contract for any loss resulting to them from that failure.[15] As a condition precedent to recovery against the public body, however, the claimant must first exhaust its collection efforts against the contractor that should have provided the bond.[16] The

---

[7] *Id.* § 574.26, subd. 3.
[8] *Id.*
[9] *Id.* § 574.261.
[10] *Id.*, subd. 1(a).
[11] *Id.* §§ 574.263 and 574.264.
[12] *Id.* § 574.28.
[13] *Id.* § 574.31(b).
[14] *Id.* § 574.28.
[15] *Id.* § 574.29.
[16] Green Elec. Sys., Inc. v. Metropolitan Airports Comm'n, 486 N.W.2d 819 (Minn. Ct. App. 1992), *review denied* (Minn. Aug. 27, 1992).

public body is not liable if the bond does not list the proper address of the contractor or the surety.[17]

[B] Time Limits to Bring Bond Action

In regard to a claim on a payment bond, no action may be maintained unless, within 120 days after completion, delivery or provision of a claimant's last item of labor or material for the public work, the claimant serves a written notice personally or by certified mail upon the surety and the contractor-principal on whose behalf the bond was issued at their addresses as stated in the bond.[18] The notice must state, among other things, the nature and amount of the claim and the date the claimant furnished its last item of labor and materials for the public work; the statute provides an acceptable form of notice for use by claimants.[19]

Any action to enforce a payment bond claim must be commenced within one year from the date of the completion, delivery or provision of the claimant's last item of labor or material stated in its notice of claim. If the contractor providing the payment bond failed to state the required information on the bonds it filed with the public body,[20] then the claimant does not have to file a notice of a claim within 120 days of its last item of labor and materials, but the claimant still has to commence an action under the bond within one year from the claimant's actual last delivery of labor and materials.[21]

Any other person having a cause of action on a payment bond may be joined on motion as a party to the action and the court shall then determine the rights of all parties. If the amount realized from the bond is insufficient to discharge all the claims in full, the amount recovered must be prorated among the parties by the court.[22]

On multi-year projects, some subcontractors may complete their work early in the project but still may be owed retention years later at final completion. To prevent subcontractors in this unique situation from having to start a lawsuit merely to preserve their payment bond rights, the Act allows the claimant to extend the deadline for bringing an action on a payment bond claim either by stipulation with the surety or by notice to the surety to which the surety does not object. If the surety does object to extending the deadline for an action on a payment bond claim, then the claimant must start an action, but the Act requires that the action be then continued until any payment, such as retention, is contractually due. The ability of parties to negotiate a new deadline for suit under the Act should avoid needless suits filed merely to preserve potential claims.[23]

---

[17] *Id.*

[18] MINN. STAT. § 574.31, subd. 2(a).

[19] *Id.*

[20] *See id.* § 574.28 for a listing of the information required to be included with a bond filed with a public body.

[21] *Id.* § 574.31, subd. 2(c).

[22] *Id.*

[23] *Id.* § 574.31, subd. 2(d).

In regard to claims on performance bonds, no action shall be maintained later than permitted under the statute of limitations applicable to the claim.[24] This is consistent with prior case law which was the basis for this particular provision.[25] There is no statutory pre-suit notice requirement for claims against the performance bond surety.

[C] Payment Bonds

[1] Who is Covered

Minnesota's Act identifies those who can make a claim under a payment bond as follows:

> A payment bond [is] for the benefit of all persons furnishing labor and materials engaged under, or to perform the contract, [and is] conditioned for payment, as they become due, of all just claims for the labor and materials.[26]

The term "contract" is defined as a contract with a public body for the doing of public work.[27] No case has yet interpreted the relatively new language of this portion of the Act, but a plain reading of the text indicates that at least those with a direct contract with the public body and those engaged under that contract, such as subcontractors, have a claim against the payment bond. To what extent lower tier sub-subcontractors and vendors have a payment bond claim is an open question.

Cases interpreting an earlier, but similar, version of the Act suggest that Minnesota courts might expand coverage beyond the plain language of the Act. In one case, the Minnesota Supreme Court declared that each payment bond claim "must hinge on the totality of the surrounding circumstances and [no case] lends itself to hard-and-fast rules which may be inflexibly applied."[28] The case involved a prime contractor that hired a self-described vendor to supply doors to a project, and the vendor subsequently subcontracted the order to a door manufacturer who, eventually, made a payment bond claim. After stating that the "almost universal rule permits protection to materialmen who sell to subcontractors, but does not allow recovery by those who sell standard products to materialmen,"[29] the court then focused on whether the self-described vendor was really a subcontractor or a materialman for purposes of the Act. The court undertook an extensive review of federal and other states' law on the topic, but then announced, "Whatever may be the rule elsewhere, Minnesota is committed to a liberal interpretation of both statutes which govern contractors, bonds, and laws dealing with mechanic's

[24] *Id.* § 574.31, subd. 1.

[25] *See* Travelers Indem. Co. v. Hennepin County, 918 F.2d 66, 68 (8th Cir. 1990).

[26] Minn. Stat. § 574.26, subd. 2.

[27] *Id.,* subd. 1(3).

[28] Weyerhaeuser Co. v. Twin City Millwork Co., 191 N.W.2d 401, 402 (Minn. 1971).

[29] *Id.* at 403.

liens."[30] Accordingly, after considering a variety of factors, the court found the self-described vendor to be a "subcontractor" for purposes of the Act, which resulted in the door manufacturer's having a valid payment bond claim.[31]

A subsequent, unpublished Minnesota Court of Appeals decision extended payment bond coverage to a supplier of wallboard and related materials to a sub-subcontractor. Under a typical Miller Act analysis, such a claimant would not be covered, but the court found Minnesota's Act to be "broader than the federal statute."[32] Although the case relies on an earlier version of the Act and elides several phrases of the Act in its analysis, it nevertheless reflects an expansive definition of payment bond claimants in the state. Whether the current Act will receive a similar interpretation remains to be seen.

The distinction between public and private projects can have important consequences for determining who is entitled to payment bond protection under the Act. If a public body fails to obtain a valid payment bond for a public project as required by the Act, then the public body is liable to all persons furnishing labor and materials for any loss resulting from the failure to obtain the bond.[33] The Minnesota Court of Appeals has adopted the following factors for determining whether a contract is for "public work" for which a payment bond is required:

1. Ownership of the project;
2. Funding of the project;
3. The scope of the municipalities participation in the project; and
4. The extent the project is put to a public use.[34]

An otherwise private payment bond provided by a subcontractor will be treated as one granting coverage under the Act when the subcontract obligates the subcontractor to undertake all obligations toward the general contractor that the general contractor has toward the public owner.[35]

[2] What Claims are Covered

The Act allows a payment bond claim for "all persons furnishing labor and materials,"[36] and the Act defines *labor and materials* as "work, skill, tools,

---

[30] *Id.* at 406–07.

[31] *Id.* at 407.

[32] Tamarack v. New Mech Coms., Inc., 1993 WL 121255 (Minn. Ct. App. 1993) (unpublished).

[33] MINN. STAT. § 574.28.

[34] Green Elec. Sys. Inc. v. Metropolitan Airports Comm'n, 486 N.W.2d 819, 822 (Minn. Ct. App. 1992) (finding that a kiosk in an airport terminal is "public work"); *cf.* Judd Supply Co. v. Merchants and Manufacturers Ins. Co., 448 N.W.2d 895, 897-99 (Minn. Ct. App. 1989) (holding that a privately owned project is not converted into one for public work requiring a payment bond merely because financing the project is provided or facilitated by a public entity).

[35] Iowa Concrete Breaking Corp. v. Jewat Trucking, Inc., 444 N.W.2d 865, 871 (Minn. Ct. App. 1989) (allowing claimant to recover attorneys' fees pursuant to the Act against the subcontractor's bond).

[36] MINN. STAT. § 574.26, subd. 2.

machinery, materials, insurance premiums, equipment or supplies, or [certain types of] taxes. . . . "[37] Therefore, once a claimant is determined to be within the class of persons protected by the Act, the statute is liberally construed in regard to which items of work are covered claims.[38]

Examples of typically covered items include hourly wages for labor performed at the project site,[39] materials actually incorporated into the project, and fuel used or consumed in connection with the project.[40] On the other hand, an employee's claim for a commission for procuring a project was found to be unrelated to any contribution of labor and materials and, therefore, not covered by the payment bond.[41] Freight and transportation costs are allowed if they can be allocated specifically to the bonded project.[42] It is not dispositive whether the supplier of materials specifically intended them for the bonded project at the time the materials were manufactured or fabricated.[43]

Wages of workers producing materials off site are covered,[44] although an exception might be made when the principal on the payment bond had no reason to know about the off-site work.[45] When no records were kept of the actual time spent by off-site workers producing materials for the bonded project, the amount for which the surety is liable to each worker can be based on a retrospective analysis of how much product was produced during the time period in question, how much product went to other projects, and how many hours each laborer worked during the time period.[46]

A general exception to payment bond coverage is for a contractor's "capital" or "plant" expenses, unless these types of expenses were entirely consumed on the single project.[47] Thus, rent for temporary leases of equipment is covered, even if under a general lease without regard to the specific bonded project.[48] The surety may be liable for minor equipment repairs, when the necessity for the repair reasonably might be attributed entirely to performance of the bonded work.[49]

On the other hand, major equipment repairs, such as a new engine, typically

---

[37] *Id.* § 574.26, subd. 1(2).

[38] Healy Plumbing & Heating Co. v. Minneapolis-St. Paul Sanitary Dist., 169 N.W.2d 50, 55 (Minn. 1969).

[39] General Motors Truck Co. v. Phillips, 254 N.W. 580, 581 (Minn. 1934) (wages of a mechanic, who spent all of his time repairing equipment used on the bonded project, were covered by the bond).

[40] Bartles Scott Oil Co. v. Western Sur. Co., 200 N.W. 937, 938 (Minn. 1924) (gasoline and lubricating oil used by contractor's construction equipment).

[41] Hames v. McBride Agency, Inc., 193 WL 7666 (Minn. Ct. App. 1993) (unpublished).

[42] Bartles Scott Oil Co. v. Western Sur. Co., 200 N.W. 937, 938 (Minn. 1924) .

[43] Combs v. Jackson, 72 N.W. 565, 567 (Minn. 1897).

[44] *Id.*

[45] Weyerhaeuser Co. v. Twin City Millwork Co., 191 N.W.2d 401, 405–06 (Minn. 1971).

[46] Combs v. Jackson, 72 N.W. 565, 567–68 (Minn. 1897).

[47] Clifton v. Norden, 226 N.W. 940, 940–42 (Minn. 1929).

[48] Miller v. American Bonding Co., 158 N.W. 940, 432, 433 (Minn. 1916).

[49] General Motors Truck Co. v. Phillips, 254 N.W. 580, 583 (Minn. 1934).

are treated as capital expenses, and not covered by the payment bond.[50] Likewise, the bond will not recover the purchase price of new equipment[51] or equipment rentals under a lease with a "purchase option," which is a sale in disguise.[52]

Payment for changed or extra work on a project will be covered by the payment bond, so long as the additional work is fairly within the scope of the original contract.[53] Conversely, a material change that constituted a new and independent contract could release a surety from liability for claims regarding that work.[54] There is no reported Minnesota appellate decision on whether the Act covers claims for delay damages or lost profits; there is a split in other jurisdictions as to whether such claims are covered.[55] According to a case apparently based on an earlier and different version of the Act, a vendor of materials is not required, as a condition precedent to an action on a payment bond, to show that the materials delivered to the prime contractor were actually employed or incorporated into the public contract.[56]

The Minnesota payment bond statute expressly provides that unpaid state income withholding, unemployment, and sales taxes are within bond coverage.[57] Because the statute mentions Minnesota but not federal taxes, it is arguable that federal income tax and social security withholding are not covered. Nevertheless, there is no reported Minnesota case addressing this issue.

The payment bond statute expressly states that insurance premiums are covered. The general rule developed by Minnesota courts, however, is that the statute includes only premiums for those specific insurance coverages required by contract or by law in connection with a project. Accordingly, premiums for workers' compensation insurance, a form of coverage mandated by Minnesota law, are covered.[58] Automobile and other vehicle insurance to the extent required by Minnesota law would be covered as well. In the absence of a contractual provision obligating a contractor to provide specific insurance, premiums for property damage, liability, fire, theft, or tornado insurance are not cov-

---

[50] Clifton v. Norden, 226 N.W. 940, 940–42 (Minn. 1929).

[51] *Id.*

[52] Motor Power Equip. Co. v. Park Transfer Co., 247 N.W. 244, 244–45 (Minn. 1933).

[53] American Druggists Ins. v. Thompson Lumber Co., 349 N.W.2d 569, 574 (Minn. Ct. App. 1984).

[54] *Id.* at 574.

[55] *Compare* L.P. Friestedt Co. v. U.S. Fireproofing Co., 125 F.2d 1010, 1012 (10th Cir., 1942) *and* Braude, *The Surety's Liability under the Miller Act for "Delay Damages,"* 36 Fed. B.J. 86, 90 (1977) *with* Seaboard Surety Co. v. United States, 355 F.2d 139 (9th Cir. 1966); Steenburg Constr. Co. v. Prepakt Concrete Co., 381 F.2d 768 (10th Cir. 1967); United States *ex rel* Carter v. Ross Corp., 385 F.2d 564 (6th Cir. 1967); Weyher Constr. Co. v. Cox Constr. Co., 453 P.2d 161 (Utah 1969).

[56] Red Wing Sewer Pipe Co. v. Donnelly, 113 N.W. 1, 2 (Minn. 1907).

[57] MINN. STAT. § 574.26, subd. 1 (1994) ("Labor and materials" means . . . taxes incurred under section 290.92 [income tax withholding], chapter 268 [unemployment taxes], or 297A [sales taxes]").

[58] Guaranteed Gravel & Sand Co. v. Aetna Cas. & Sur. Co., 219 N.W. 546, 548–49 (Minn. 1928); *see* Kunz Ins. Agency v. Phillips, 255 N.W. 90, 91 (Minn. 1934).

ered.[59] Although Minnesota payment bonds cover some types of insurance premiums, a bond itself is not an insurance policy. The payment bond does not afford coverage to claims for damage to persons or property caused by a contractor's or supplier's negligent work product.[60]

Occasionally, material suppliers will take payments received from a public project and apply them to unrelated accounts. By allocating payments in this way, material suppliers can satisfy an unrelated bad debt and still maintain a secured claim against the prime contractor's surety for the full amount of material supplied for the public project.[61] To discourage such application of payments, § 574.32 of the Act provides that if a claimant on a payment bond had actual knowledge or should have known that a payment it received was for labor and materials supplied on a public project, the claimant must prove that it applied the payment to its account for that public work. The claimant's claim will be reduced to the extent it cannot supply this proof. Once a dispute has arisen between a prime contractor and a bond claimant, the claimant is no longer in a position to claim it can apply payments so as to prejudice the rights of the prime contractor or its surety.[62]

Reasonable attorneys' fees, costs and disbursements may be awarded by a court in an action to enforce claims under the Act if the action is successfully maintained or successfully appealed.[63] Interest will accrue at the legal rate[64] unless a different rate was provided in the claimant's contract.[65]

[D] Performance Bonds

The Act requires that a prime contractor provide a public body with a performance bond "for the use and benefit of the public body to complete the contract according to its terms, and conditioned on saving the public body harmless from all costs and charges that may accrue on account of completing the specified work. . . . "[66] There are few cases interpreting this provision of the Act, but the text alone leads one to conclude that the scope of coverage provided public bodies by a performance bond is quite broad. Not only is a surety liable for "all costs and charges," but the penal sum of the bond also may not limit the

---

[59] Kunz Ins. Agency v. Phillips, 255 N.W. 90 (Minn. 1934).

[60] DeVries v. City of Austin, 110 N.W.2d 529, 538–39 (Minn. 1961).

[61] *See* Elk River Concrete Prods. Co. v. American Cas. Co., 129 N.W.2d 309 (Minn. 1964) (permitting such a practice under an earlier version of the Act).

[62] Western Insulation Servs., Inc. v. Central Nat'l Ins. Co., 460 N.W.2d 355, 357 (Minn. Ct. App. 1990).

[63] MINN. STAT. § 574.26, subd. 3; Schultz v. Interstate Mechanical Contractors Co., 265 N.W.2d 296 (Minn. 1936) (allowing fees only if claimant pursues claim to judgment); K.W. Insulation, Inc. v. United States Fidelity & Guar. Co., 1994 WL 638093 (Minn. Ct. App. 1994) (unpublished) (criticizing but following *Schultz*).

[64] MINN. STAT. § 549.09, subd. 1(b).

[65] American Druggists Ins. v. Thompson Lumber Co., 349 N.W.2d 569, 573 (Minn. Ct. App. 1984); Monarch Turf Supply v. Reliance Ins. Co., 1996 WL 363404 (Minn. Ct. App. 1996) (unpublished) (18 percent interest awarded pursuant to claimant's contract).

[66] MINN. STAT. § 574.26, subd. 2.

surety's liability. It has been held that where a bond covers both a penal sum and attorneys' fees, the surety is liable for attorneys' fees in addition to the penal sum of the bond.[67]

As mentioned earlier, the Act does not expressly require notice to the surety as a condition precedent to bringing a suit on a performance bond. Instead, the requirement of reasonable notice to the surety is considered to be one of the traditional legal or equitable defenses available to the surety and these defenses are expressly preserved by the Act as well as the common law or equitable rights of the principal and the obligee.[68]

The Minnesota Supreme Court has held that even if a performance bond surety's breach of contract is willful or malicious, in the absence of a specific statutory provision, punitive damages are not available for the surety's breach of contract, except in exceptional cases where the breach is accompanied by an independent tort.[69]

Performance bonds are not transmogrified into payment bonds merely because the performance bond incorporates the principal's contract with the obligee in which the principal promises to pay its subcontractors and materialmen. The Minnesota Supreme Court has held that the distinction between performance bonds and payment bonds is well recognized in the construction industry and that a performance bond's incorporation of the underlying construction contract does not evidence "an intent to benefit" unpaid materialmen.[70] Material suppliers may maintain an action directly against the performance bond only if the building contract that is incorporated in the performance bond "specifically required a bond conditioned to pay laborers and material supplier."[71]

[E] Bid Bonds

As elsewhere, most Minnesota public and private invitations for bid require each contractor to furnish acceptable bid security.[72] This security assures that the contractor, if selected for award, will enter into the contract or have the capacity to compensate the owner for damages resulting from the contractor's refusal to accept the award.[73] Traditionally, the amount of the bid security has been five percent of the contractor's bid. The form of the security may be a cash deposit, bid bond, or certified check.[74]

---

[67] Iowa Concrete Breaking Corp.v. Jewat Trucking, Inc., 444 N.W.2d 872, 872 (Minn. Ct. App. 1989).

[68] MINN. STAT. § 574.31, subd. 1.

[69] Barr/Nelson, Inc. v. Tontos, Inc., 336 N.W.2d 46, 52 (Minn. 1983).

[70] Cretex Companies v. Construction Leaders, 342 N.W.2d 135, 140 (Minn. 1984).

[71] Green Elec. Sys., Inc. v. Metropolitan Airports Comm'n, 486 N.W.2d 819, 823 (Minn. Ct. App. 1992).

[72] MINN. STAT. § 574.27 (1994); *see, e.g.*, Minn. Dept. of Transp., STANDARD SPECIFICATIONS FOR CONSTRUCTION 1208 (1988).

[73] Johnson v. City of Jordan, 352 N.W.2d 500 (Minn. Ct. App. 1984); Federal Contracting Co. v. City of St. Paul, 225 N.W. 149 (Minn. 1929).

[74] Sutton v. City of St. Paul, 48 N.W.2d 436 (Minn. 1951).

Although most bid bonds are conditioned to pay the owner actual damages (the difference between the contractor's bid and the next low bid,)[75] some bonds are conditioned to pay the owner liquidated damages. A low bidder may avoid forfeiture of its bid security for failure to enter into a contract with the owner if the bidder makes a material mistake in its bid and the owner is notified of the mistake before it is prejudiced.[76] The Act requires that bid security be returned to the bidder after execution of the contract or if the contract is awarded to another bidder.[77]

Sureties generally disclaim in the bid bond or bid bond application any obligation to issue performance or payment bonds upon award of the contract to the contractor. This language protects sureties against claims by contractors for lost profits on contracts that would have been awarded to them but for their failure to obtain required bonds.[78] Nevertheless, behavior by the surety may raise a jury question as to whether the surety is bound by an implied contract to issue the payment and performance bonds.[79]

§ 24.03 MECHANICS' LIENS

[A] Overview

Minnesota's mechanics' lien statute creates an equitable lien interest in real estate and improvements on private construction projects to secure payment of contractors, subcontractors, and others that furnish labor or materials to build, repair, or improve real property.[80] Mechanics' liens are entirely creatures of statute and exist only according to the statute's terms.[81] Minnesota's mechanics' lien statute is premised on the principle that a person whose property is enhanced by others' labor and/or materials should pay for the improvements to the property.[82]

In most cases, lien claimants must satisfy certain early notice requirements in order to file and foreclose a valid mechanics' lien on certain kinds of projects.[83] Failure to provide proper prelien notice is one of the primary reasons why many claimants lose their right to enforce their liens.

Generally, a mechanics' lien attaches and takes effect when the first item of material or labor is furnished upon the premises for the beginning of the improve-

---

[75] Den Mar Constr. Co. v. American Ins. Co., 290 N.W.2d 737 (Minn. 1979).

[76] St. Nicholas Church v. Kropp, 160 N.W. 500 (Minn. 1916).

[77] MINN. STAT. § 574.27.

[78] Independent Sch. Dist. No. 24 v. Weinmann, 68 N.W.2d 248 (Minn. 1955); Elk River Concrete Prods. v. American Cas. Co., 129 N.W.2d 309 (Minn. 1964).

[79] Den Mar Constr. Co. v. American Ins. Co., 290 N.W.2d 737 (Minn. 1979).

[80] MINN. STAT. §§ 514.0 *et seq.*

[81] *See* Kirkwold Constr. v. M.G.A. Constr., 513 N.W.2d 241 (Minn. 1994); Automated Building Components, Inc. v. New Horizon Homes, Inc., 514 N.W.2d 826 (Minn. Ct. App. 1994), *review denied* (Minn. June 15, 1994).

[82] MINN. STAT. § 514.01.

[83] *Id.* § 514.011.

ment and has priority over any mortgage or other encumbrance not then of record unless the lien claimant had actual notice of the other encumbrances.[84] A mechanics' lien claimant must file its lien statement within 120 days of the date on which the lien claimant last furnished its work or material to the project.[85] The lien claimant must file its lien statement with either the county recorder or, if registered (torrens) property, with the registrar of titles of the county in which the improved property is situated, or with the Minnesota Secretary of State if the lien is filed on any telegraph, telephone, electric light, pipeline, or similar project.[86] In addition, a copy of the lien statement must be served personally or by certified mail on the owner, the owner's authorized agent, or the person who entered into the contract with the contractor.[87]

A lien claimant must enforce its lien by commencing a lawsuit that seeks a court order directing that the improved property be sold by foreclosure within one year after the claimant performs its last item of work or furnishes its last item of material.[88] The foreclosure action may be filed in the district court in the county where the improved property or some part of it is located.[89] Upon the successful conclusion of the lien claimant's lawsuit, the county sheriff must sell the property and satisfy the claimant's lien out of the sale proceeds.[90]

[B] Who May File

Minn. Stat. § 514.01 identifies those who are entitled to claim a mechanics' lien as follows:

> Whoever performs engineering or land surveying services with respect to real estate, or contributes to the improvement of real estate by performing labor, or furnishing skill, material or machinery for any of the purposes hereinafter stated, whether under contract with the owner of such real estate or at the instance of any agent, trustee, contractor or subcontractor of such owner, shall have a lien upon the improvement, and upon the land on which it is situated or to which it may be removed, that is to say, for the erection, alteration, repair or removal of any building, fixture, bridge, wharf, fence, or other structure thereon, or for grading, filling in, or excavating the same, or for clearing, grubbing or first breaking, or for furnishing and planting of trees, shrubs, or plant materials, or for labor performed in placing soil or sod or for labor performed in planting trees, shrubs, or plant materials, or for digging or repairing any ditch, drain, well, fountain, cistern, reservoir, or vault thereon,

[84] *Id.* § 514.05, subd. 1.

[85] *Id.* § 514.08, subd. 1.

[86] *Id.* § 514.04. *See* David-Thomas Cos. v. Voss, 517 N.W.2d 341 (Minn. Ct. App. 1994) (lien invalid because it was filed with county recorder, who was in charge of abstract property, rather than registrar of titles, who was in charge of registered property).

[87] MINN. STAT. § 514.08, subd. 1(2).

[88] *Id.* § 514.12, subd. 3.

[89] *Id.* § 514.10.

[90] *Id.* § 514.15.

> or for laying, altering or repairing any sidewalk, curb, gutter, paving, sewer, pipe, or conduit in or upon the same, or in or upon the adjoining half of any highway, street, or alley upon which the same abuts.[91]

In determining who is entitled to assert a lien, Minnesota courts have consistently held that the mechanics' lien statute is remedial in nature and should be liberally construed in order to protect the rights of workers and material suppliers who furnish labor and/or material for the improvement of real property.[92] Although the lien statute is liberally construed after the lien has been found to exist, the courts strictly enforce all the statutory requirements necessary to create and enforce the lien.[93] Strict compliance with the statutory requirements is necessary to protect against a lien being foreclosed on property owned by people who have no notice of the lien.[94]

Courts construing the language of Minn. Stat. § 514.01 have held that the following persons may claim a mechanics' lien: architects (even if no physical or visible work is done on the property);[95] engineers and surveyors;[96] excavators;[97] certain material suppliers;[98] construction managers;[99] and persons furnishing delivery services.[100]

---

[91] MINN. STAT. § 514.01.

[92] *See, e.g.,* Rochester's Suburban Lumber Co. v. Slocumb, 163 N.W.2d 303 (Minn. 1968); Armco Steel Corp. Metal Prods. Div. v. Chicago & N.W. Ry. Co., 149 N.W.2d 23 (Minn. 1967); O.B. Thompson Elec. Co. v. Milliman & Larson, Inc., 128 N.W.2d 751 (Minn. 1964); Aaby v. Better Builders, Inc., 37 N.W.2d 234 (Minn. 1949); Johnson v. Starret, 149 N.W. 6 (Minn. 1914).

[93] David-Thomas Coms., Inc. v. Voss, 517 N.W.2d 341 (Minn. Ct. App. 1994) (although mechanics' lien statute is liberally construed after lien has been created, it is strictly construed as to creation of lien).

[94] *See, e.g.,* Christle v. Marberg, 421 N.W.2d 748 (Minn. Ct. App. 1988).

[95] Korsunsky Krank Erickson Architects, Inc. v. Walsh, 370 N.W.2d 29 (Minn. 1985).

[96] *See* Kirkwold Constr. Co. v. M.G.A. Constr., Inc., 513 N.W.2d 241 (Minn. Ct. App. 1994). *See also* Dunham Assoc., Inc. v. Group Inv., Inc., 223 N.W.2d 376 (Minn. 1974). Even though engineers and surveyors may claim a mechanics' lien under MINN. STAT. § 514.01, "[v]isible staking, engineering, land surveying, and soil testing services do not constitute the actual and visible beginning of the improvement" upon which all liens shall take effect. MINN. STAT.§ 514.05, subd. 2.

[97] MINN. STAT. § 514.01.

[98] Suppliers who deliver materials to the property or who specially manufacture items are generally protected under MINN. STAT. § 514.01 by the courts. *See, e.g.,* Stravs v. Steckbauer, 161 N.W. 259 (Minn. 1917) (specifically manufactured wood forms furnished, but not incorporated into the structure were held to be necessary for the improvement and lienable). The right to a mechanics' lien is lost if the materials are prepared or delivered fraudulently. Thompson-McDonald Lumber Co. v. Morawetz, 149 N.W. 300 (Minn. 1914).

[99] Applying an earlier version of Minnesota's mechanics' lien law, the Minnesota Supreme Court has held that a person hired to supervise work that improves real property was entitled to a mechanics' lien. *See, e.g.,* Lindquist v. Young, 138 N.W. 28 (Minn. 1912) (the owner hired a mechanic to supervise work done on the premises); Wanganstein v. Jones, 63 N.W. 717 (Minn. 1895) (the owner hired an architect to supervise installation of a heating system). Whether the Minnesota Supreme Court would rule this way today is unknown.

[100] Transportation and freight costs for delivery of materials or equipment to the job site are

Conversely, the following persons have been found not to have a right to claim a mechanics' lien: attorneys;[101] persons who provide services such as locating and obtaining finances, obtaining zoning variances, and coordinating leasing agreements;[102] unlicensed residential contractors;[103] and developers.[104]

Under Minn. Stat. § 514.01, persons who furnish services or materials toward the improvement of real estate must do so "under contract with the owner of such real estate or at the instance of the owner's agent, trustee, contractor or subcontractor."[105] As interpreted by the courts, the word *owner* includes any equitable or legal owners of the real estate.[106] Accordingly, a person in possession of land or who holds legal title is an owner under Minn. Stat. § 514.01.[107]

The requirement that a provider of services or materials must be under contract with an owner or furnish the services or materials or at the instance of "any agent, trustee, contractor or subcontractor of such owner" arguably precludes some lower tier sub-subcontractors and vendors from asserting a valid mechanics' lien because they are not in contract with a "contractor" or "subcontractor."[108] Despite this arguable limitation in the scope of the statute, the Minnesota Supreme Court has held that it is immaterial whether the subcontractor was a first or second tier subcontractor: "[i]t is the opinion of the majority of the court that the law was intended to apply to subcontractors generally, and not merely to those standing in direct contract relation with the first or original contractor."[109] It remains an open question as to what tier of subcontractor or vendor lien protection will extend before the courts will consider the claimant too remote to qualify for lien rights.

---

protected by Minn. Stat. § 514.01. *See, e.g.,* McKeen v. Haseltine, 49 N.W. 195 (Minn. 1891) (a charge for the transportation of mill machinery that needed to be repaired was held to be lienable).

[101] London Constr. Co. v. Roseville Townhomes, Inc., 473 N.W.2d 917 (Minn. Ct. App. 1991) (attorneys do not provide the types of services articulated in Minn. Stat. § 514.01, and the mechanics' lien statute's plain meaning excludes attorneys from its protection).

[102] Phillips-Klein Cos., Inc. v. Tiffany Partnership, 474 N.W.2d 370 (Minn. Ct. App. 1991).

[103] Pongratz v. Brunz, 1998 WL 113988 (Minn. Ct. App.) (unpublished) (a contractor waived his right to file a mechanics' lien because he failed to file prelien notice pursuant to Minn. Stat. § 514.011 and he failed to obtain a residential contractor's license pursuant to Minn. Stat. § 326.84).

[104] Nelson v. Nelson, 415 N.W.2d 694 (Minn. Ct. App. 1987) (developer was an owner of the property and Minn. Stat. § 514.01 precludes an owner from filing a lien against the owner's property).

[105] Minn. Stat. § 514.01.

[106] Geissinger v. Robins, 143 N.W.2d 50 (Minn. 1966) (construing an earlier version of Minnesota's mechanics' lien law); Benjamin v. Wilson, 26 N.W. 725 (1886); Nelson v. Nelson, 415 N.W.2d 694 (Minn. Ct. App. 1987).

[107] Lindholm v. Hamilton, 198 N.W. 289 (Minn. 1924).

[108] Minn. Stat. § 514.01.

[109] Spafford v. Duluth, R.W. & S.R. Co., 51 N.W. 469, 470 (Minn. 1892).

[C] What Work and Materials Are Covered

The work or materials furnished must be provided for one of the purposes enumerated in Minn. Stat. § 514.01. These purposes include the following:

- Erecting, altering, repairing, or removing any building, fixture, bridge, wharf, fence, or other structure
- Grading, filling in, or excavating the same
- Clearing, grubbing, or first breaking ground
- Furnishing or placing soil or sod
- Performing labor in placing soil or sod or planting trees, shrubs, or plant materials
- Digging or repairing any ditch, drain, well, fountain, cistern, reservoir, or vault
- Laying, altering, or repairing any sidewalk, curb, gutter, paving, sewer, pipe, or conduit in or on the land or in or on the adjoining half of any highway, street, or alley on which the land borders
- Performing engineering or land surveying services.[110]

To be eligible for a mechanics' lien, the party's services, labor or materials must have improved the real property.[111] An improvement, for the purposes of the mechanics' lien statute, is "a permanent addition to or betterment of real property that enhances its capital value and that involves the expenditure of labor or money and is designed to make the property more useful or valuable as distinguished from ordinary repairs."[112] Accordingly, work that is classified as repair work (i.e., routine maintenance that maintains the property's value as opposed to increasing it) is not an improvement under the mechanics' lien statute.

Examples of lienable improvements are as follows: lumber, cement, brick, roofing materials, paint, hardware, windows and doors, and the labor necessary for them;[113] coal and gas delivered to a contractor to run equipment on the job site, and fuel, dynamite, lubricants, and temporary lighting fixtures and materials for a temporary tool house;[114] and fence erected to protect a tree during construction.[115]

---

[110] MINN. STAT. § 514.01.

[111] *Id.*

[112] Kloster-Madsen, Inc. v. Tafi's, Inc., 226 N.W.2d 603, 607 (Minn. 1975).

[113] Knoff Woodwork Co. v. Zontalis, 6 N.W.2d 264 (Minn. 1942); Sandberg v. Burns, 270 N.W. 575 (Minn. 1936).

[114] Johnson v. Starett, 149 N.W. 6 (Minn. 1914); *see also* Kloster-Madsen, Inc. v. Tafi's, Inc., 226 N.W.2d 603 (Minn. 1975) (removal of light fixtures from and cutting crawl space in ceiling held lienable).

[115] National Lumber Co. v. Farmer & Son, Inc., 87 N.W.2d 32 (Minn. 1957).

[D] Pre-Lien Notice Requirement

One of the most important parts of Minnesota's mechanics' lien statute is its pre-lien notice requirements. Minn. Stat. § 514.011 requires potential lien claimants such as general contractors, subcontractors and material suppliers to serve formal notices of their lien rights on the property's owner in order to perfect their liens.[116] The primary purpose of these requirements is to avoid surprising an unwary property owner or mortgagee with service of a mechanics' lien statement by an unpaid subcontractor or material supplier after the general contractor has been paid the last available construction funds or mortgage proceeds.

Every person who enters into a contract with an owner for the improvement of real property, and who has contracted or will contract with any subcontractors or material suppliers to provide labor, skill, or materials for the improvement must give the owner the notice required in Minn. Stat. § 514.011, subd. 1. This notice is commonly referred to as the *general contractor's notice.* Any person who fails to give the general contractor's notice is barred from seeking and enforcing a mechanics' lien, unless that person is covered by one of the exceptions to the general contractor's notice requirement.[117]

The general contractor's pre-lien notice *must* contain the language set forth in Minn. Stat. § 514.011, subd. 1(a)-(b). Section 514.011 expressly provides that "[a] person [contractor] who fails to provide the notice shall not have the lien and remedy provided by this chapter."[118] The general contractor's pre-lien notice must be included in any written contract with the owner.[119] The general contractor must give the owner a copy of the written contract.[120] If there is not a written contract, the pre-lien notice must be prepared separately and delivered personally or by certified mail to the owner or the owner's authorized agent "within 10 days after the work or improvement is agreed upon."[121] The pre-lien notice, whether included in a written contract or separately given to the owner or the owner's representative, must be in at least 10-point bold type if printed, or in capital letters if typewritten.[122]

In order to perfect their lien rights, persons who contributes to the improvement of real property and who did not contract with the owner directly, such as

[116] For purposes of the pre-lien notice section, MINN. STAT. § 514.011, "owner" means the owner of any legal or equitable interest in real property whose interest in the property (1) is known to one who contributes to the improvement of the real property or (2) has been recorded or filed for record if registered land, and who enters into a contract for the improvement of the real property. MINN. STAT. § 514.011, subd. 5.

[117] MINN. STAT. § 514.011, subd. 1; Emison v. J. Paul Stearns Co., 488 N.W.2d 336 (Minn. Ct. App. 1992).

[118] *Id.*

[119] *Id.*

[120] *Id.*

[121] *Id.*

[122] *Id.*

subcontractors and material suppliers must satisfy the pre-lien notice requirements contained in Minn. Stat. § 514.011, subd. 2.

Subcontractors, material suppliers, and other lien claimants who are not excepted from giving pre-lien notice *must* give the owner or the owner's authorized agent a very detailed and lengthy pre-lien notice. This pre-lien notice is distinctly different than the general contractor's pre-lien notice. Minn. Stat. § 514.011, subd. 2 sets forth the precise language that subcontractors, material suppliers, and other lien claimants must use in their pre-lien notices.

This pre-lien notice must be personally served on or sent by certified mail to the owner or the owner's authorized agent within 45 days after the claimant's first item of labor, skill or material is furnished for the improvement.[123] Although the statute provides this 45-day grace period, a potential lien claimant should serve the pre-lien notice immediately.[124] The pre-lien notice must be in at least 10-point bold type, if printed, or in capital letters, if typewritten.[125]

There are important exceptions to the pre-lien notice requirements. Generally, for the exceptions to apply, the predominant use of the property must be commercial and not residential. For example, pre-lien notice is not required where the improved property is not in agricultural use and is wholly or partially nonresidential in use, provided the work or improvement:

(a) is to provide or add more than 5,000 total usable square feet of floor space; or
(b) is an improvement to real property where the existing property contains more than 5,000 total usable square feet of space; or
(c) is an improvement to real property which contains more than 5,000 square feet and does not involve the construction of a new building or add to the improvement of an existing building.[126]

Historically, courts have strictly construed pre-lien notice requirements, holding that if a lien claimant does not give the owner or the owner's agent a pre-lien notice, the lien claimant cannot enforce a mechanics' lien against the improved property.[127] In 1989, the Minnesota legislature amended Minn. Stat.

[123] *Id.*

[124] Minnesota's mechanics' lien statute provides that the total amount of all liens on an owner's property will be reduced by payments made by the owner or the owner's agent to the contractor *prior* to receiving the required pre-lien notices. MINN. STAT. § 514.03, subd. 2(c)(i). Accordingly, a subcontractor or material supplier may be barred from asserting part or all of its lien claim if the owner pays the general contractor before the owner receives a lien claimant's pre-lien notice.

[125] MINN. STAT. § 514.011, subd. 2.

[126] *Id.* § 514.011, subd. 4c (a)-(c). Other exceptions to the pre-lien notice requirement are set forth in MINN. STAT. § 514.011, subdivisions 1, 4a and 4c.

[127] Merle Constr. Co. v. Berg, 442 N.W.2d 300 (Minn. 1989); Christie v. Marberg, 421 N.W.2d 748 (Minn. Ct. App. 1989); Marquee Plumbing, Inc. v. Barris, 380 N.W.2d 174 (Minn. Ct. App. 1986); Diethelm v. Cavanaugh, 349 N.W.2d 608 (Minn. Ct. App. 1984).

§ 514.011, subd. 2 and gave subcontractors and material suppliers some latitude by expressly providing that a lien claimant does not lose its lien rights by failing to strictly comply with the pre-lien requirements "if a good faith effort is made to comply, unless the owner or another lien claimant proves damage as a direct result of the failure to comply."[128] The Minnesota Supreme Court has intimated that this good faith exception applies only to subcontractors and material suppliers and general contractors must strictly adhere to the pre-lien requirements.[129]

[E] Serving the Lien Statement

Assuming that the lien claimant has given proper notice (when required), the lien claimant must perfect its mechanics' lien by filing a mechanic's lien statement within 120 days after the lien claimant has furnished its last work, material or machinery to the property.[130] In Minnesota, this time requirement is strictly construed by the courts and cannot be extended by a trial court under Rule 6.02 of the Minnesota Rules of Civil Procedure.[131] The lien claimant must file the mechanics' lien statement with the appropriate county recorder or registrar or, in limited circumstances, with the Minnesota Secretary of State.[132]

Minn. Stat. § 514.08, subd. 2 provides that the mechanics' lien statement must be made by or at the instance of the lien claim and "be verified by the oath of some person shown by such verification to have knowledge of the facts stated."[133] The statute describes the core requirements for the mechanics' lien statement.[134] Minn. Stat. § 514.08 also requires a lien claimant to serve personally or by certified mail a copy of the mechanics' lien statement on the owner, the owner's authorized agent, or the person who entered into the contract with the contractor.[135] Personal or certified mail service of a lien statement occurs upon

---

[128] MINN. STAT. § 514.011, subd. 2.

[129] Merle's Constr. Co., Inc. v. Berg, 442 N.W.2d 300, 302 n.1 (Minn. 1989).

[130] MINN. STAT. § 514.08, subd. 1.

[131] Guillame & Assocs., Inc. v. Don-John Co., 336 N.W.2d 262 (Minn. 1983); David-Thomas Cos., Inc. v. Voss, 517 N.W.2d 341 (Minn. Ct. App. 1994).

[132] MINN. STAT. § 514.08, subd. 1(1).

[133] *Id.* § 514.08, subd. 2.

[134] Owners and other defendants in a mechanics' lien foreclosure action frequently contest the accuracy of the amount claimed on the mechanics' lien statement. A lien claimant may lose its lien rights if the amount claimed on the lien statement is inaccurate because of fraud, bad faith, or an intentional demand for an amount in excess of the amount owed. MINN. STAT. § 514.74; Delyea v. Turner, 118 N.W.2d 436 (Minn. 1963); Standard Lumber Co. v. Alsaker, 289 N.W. 827 (Minn. 1940). On the other hand, an honest mistake in the amount demanded or a lien claimant's failure to prove entitlement to the entire amount demanded will not void an otherwise valid lien. Aaby v. Better Builders, 37 N.W.2d 234 (Minn. 1949); Witcher Constr. Co. v. Estes II Ltd. Partnership, 465 N.W.2d 404 (Minn. Ct. App. 1991), *review denied* (Minn. Mar. 15, 1991); Cox v. First Nat'l Bank of Aitkin, 415 N.W.2d 385 (Minn. Ct. App. 1987). Although a lien claimant's overstatement of its lien can be evidence of bad faith, determination of motive is a question of fact. *Id.*

[135] MINN. STAT. § 514.08, subd. 1(2). It is important to note that if a lien claimant serves the

delivery or willful refusal to accept delivery; if certified mail is sent to the intended recipient's last available address and the intended recipient refuses or neglects to accept the mail, "constructive delivery" is deemed to have occurred at the recipient's address.[136]

[F] Enforcing the Lien: Lien Foreclosure

In order to enforce its mechanics' lien, the lien claimant must foreclose its lien by action in the district court in the county where the improved property is situated.[137] A lien claimant must commence foreclosure of its lien within one year from the date of its last item of labor, skill or material furnished to improve the property.[138] A lien claimant may foreclose its lien claim either by filing a complaint or an answer with the district court.[139] It is critical to note that an otherwise valid mechanics' lien will expire unless foreclosure is commenced within one year from the date of the last item furnished by the lien claimant.[140] This does not mean, however, that the mechanics' lien must be reduced to judgment within the one year period.[141]

A mechanics' lien may be foreclosed in either a mechanics' lien foreclosure action or by an action commenced by the owner or other interested party to determine adverse claims against the property. A mechanics' lien foreclosure action must be commenced and conducted in the same manner as actions to

---

mechanics' lien statement by first-class mail (as opposed to serving the statement personally or by certified mail), the service is invalid. Pella Prods., Inc. v. Arvig Tel. Co., 488 N.W.2d 316 (Minn. Ct. App. 1992), *review denied* (Minn. Sept. 30, 1992) (although recipient acknowledged that it received the mechanics' lien statement, the court held that service by first-class mail was ineffective under MINN. STAT. § 514.08, subd. 1(2)).

[136] Rouse Mechanical, Inc. v. Dahl, 489 N.W.2d 272 (Minn. Ct. App. 1992).

[137] MINN. STAT. § 514.10. While the lien foreclosure must ordinarily be venued in the district court for the county in which at least a portion of the improved property is situated, if the case is commenced in federal district court under federal diversity jurisdiction, 28 U.S.C. § 1332, the action must be venued in the district court where at least a portion of the improved premises is situated within the court's jurisdictional boundaries.

[138] MINN. STAT. § 514.12, subd. 3. Additionally, if arbitration is provided for in the contract, an owner may be entitled to stay a mechanics' lien foreclosure action pending arbitration. Even if arbitration is required under the contract, the lien claimant *must* commence foreclosure of its lien in a district court action within one year from furnishing its last item of labor, skill, or material in order to preserve its lien foreclosure rights. After commencing its foreclosure action in district court, the action can be stayed and the lien claimant can proceed with the arbitration process knowing its lien foreclosure rights have been preserved.

[139] *Id.*

[140] *Id.* § 514.74 ("the lien shall be concluded by the dates therein given, showing the first and last items of the claimant's account"); *cf.* Doyle v. Wagner, 111 N.W. 275 (Minn. 1907) (the actual date of last work governs this deadline, not the date in the lien statement).

[141] North Star Iron Works v. Strong, 21 N.W. 740 (Minn. 1884).

foreclose mortgages upon real estate, unless the mechanics' lien statute provides otherwise.[142]

Minn. Stat. § 514.14 grants courts the authority to take any action that is just, including postponement of the trial or delaying judgment, if at any time before the execution of judgment it is brought to the court's attention that a proper party has not been joined or a party entitled to answer has failed to appear.[143] Additionally, when in good faith more than one lien action is commenced, the actions will be consolidated and tried as one action.[144] In order to avoid multiple actions, before commencing its foreclosure action, a lien claimant should first check with the county recorder or, if registered land, with the registrar of titles where the property is located to determine whether a notice of lis pendens has been recorded previously.

Whether asserted in its complaint or answer, the lien claimant should plead all of its causes of action. In addition to the foreclosure of its mechanics' lien against the property, a lien claimant may have claims for breach of contract, breach of warranty, unjust enrichment, negligence, misrepresentation, or fraud. Further, the lien claimant may have a cause of action against a payment bond if one was provided as security for payment to subcontractors and material suppliers on the project. The lien claimant's remedies under Minnesota's mechanics' lien statute are cumulative, not exclusive of other available remedies.[145]

The lien claimant must also file a notice of lis pendens with the county recorder or, if registered land, with the registrar of titles of the county in which the foreclosure action is brought.[146] If the notice of lis pendens is not filed for record within one year from the date of the last item furnished by the claimant, the lien cannot be enforced against any bona fide purchaser, mortgagee, or encumbrancer who was not notified of the action.[147]

A lien foreclosure action is generally tried to the court. The court, however,

---

[142] MINN. STAT. § 514.10.

[143] *Id.* § 514.14.

[144] *Id.* § 514.12, subd. 2.

[145] MINN. STAT. § 514.13 provides that "[t]he rights granted by this chapter are nonexclusive. No failure to comply with any of the provisions of this chapter shall affect the right of any person to recover, in an ordinary civil action, from the party with who a contract was made." MINN. STAT. § 514.13. These two simple sentences have important consequences. Prior to this provision being added to the Minnesota mechanics' lien statute, the Minnesota Court of Appeals held that failure to enforce one's lien rights precluded making an equitable claim for unjust enrichment. *See* Southtown Plumbing, Inc. v. Har-Ned Lumber Co., 493 N.W.2d 137 (Minn. Ct. App. 1992). The court of appeals in *Southtown Plumbing* determined that the mechanics' lien was intended to be an exclusive remedy barring other theories of recovery unspecified by the statute. This new provision should effectively reverse this decision, clearing the way for claims for equitable liens, constructive trusts, and unjust enrichment. In cases in which lien rights have expired or are of little practical value because the lien is subordinate to the mortgage, these types of equitable claims are sometimes the only means by which a contractor may recover the value of its work.

[146] MINN. STAT. § 514.12, subd. 1.

[147] *Id.* § 514.12, subd. 3.

with the consent of the parties, may order that all or part of the lawsuit be tried to the court with an advisory jury.[148] In a mechanics' lien foreclosure action, the lien claimant has the burden of proof.[149] In most cases, the plaintiff will proceed with proving its claim, with the owner and mortgagee following with proving their defenses. The trial court has discretion to alter any order of proof and bifurcate the trial so as to resolve issues of priority before the validity of any liens and the amounts are established.

The judgment is based on the trial court's findings of facts and conclusions of law. The findings of fact must recite all facts which establish ownership of the property, the legal description of the property, the validity and enforceability of the liens, the amount of each lien, and the priority of the claims. Further, the judgment must "direct a sale of the property for the satisfaction of all liens charged thereon, and the manner of such sale, subject to the rights of all persons who are paramount to such liens or any of them."[150] The judgment must also require "the officer making such sale to pay over and distribute the proceeds of the sale, after deducting all lawful charges and expenses, to and among the lienors to the amount of their respective claims."[151] If there are insufficient proceeds from the sale to pay the claims in full, then the officer must pay over and distribute the proceeds among the lien claimants in proportion to the amount due each, without priority among them.[152]

A trial court has discretion to award reasonable attorneys' fees as part of the foreclosure costs.[153] It is important to note, however, that the "right" to recover attorneys' fees probably does not vest until judgment is entered. Thus, if the lien claimant is paid prior to entry of judgment, the lien claimant probably waives any "right" to recover attorneys' fees.[154] Additionally, if the property owner successfully reduces the amount of the recoverable lien, attorneys' fees may be reduced on appeal if they are excessive when compared to the lien amount.[155]

The mechanics' lien foreclosure sale is conducted in the same manner as the sale of real estate upon execution as set forth in Minn. Stat. § 550.175-550.22. The sale must also comply with selected statutory provisions pertaining to mortgage foreclosure sales.

---

[148] *See* Sievert v. LaMarca, 367 N.W.2d 580 (Minn. Ct. App. 1985).

[149] Klingelhutz v. Grover, 236 N.W.2d 610 (Minn. 1975).

[150] MINN. STAT. § 514.15.

[151] *Id.*

[152] *Id.*

[153] *See* MINN. STAT. § 514.14; *see also* Automated Bldg. Components, Inc. v. New Horizon Homes, Inc., 514 N.W.2d 826 (Minn. Ct. App. 1994), *review denied* (Minn. June 15, 1994); Bloomington Elec. Co. v. Freeman's, Inc., 394 N.W.2d 605 (Minn. Ct .App. 1986).

[154] Schutz v. Interstate Contracting Co., 265 N.W. 296 (Minn. 1936). *Cf.* Hilltop Constr. Co. v. Lou Park Apartments, 324 N.W.2d 236 (Minn. 1982) (in a mechanics' lien foreclosure action, in which the court stayed proceedings pending a court ordered arbitration, the general contractor did not lose its right to attorneys' fees).

[155] Northwest Wholesale Lumber, Inc. v. Citadel Co., 457 N.W.2d 244 (Minn. Ct. App. 1990), *review denied* (Minn. Feb. 12, 1988), *appeal after remand,* 457 N.W.2d 244 (Minn. Ct. App. 1990).

The owner has a six-month period from the date the sale is confirmed by the court, not the date of sale, within which to redeem the property.[156] In the event that the owner fails to redeem the property during this period, each creditor, in order of priority, is allowed five days to redeem the property. If no one redeems the property, the recorded sheriff's certificate of sale operates as a conveyance of the property to the purchaser.

During the six-month redemption period, the owner is entitled to possession of the property and to all rents and profits derived from the property. As a safeguard, during this period, a lien claimant should purchase fire and general liability insurance policies to protect its interest in the property. The lien claimant may also pay delinquent taxes and other costs and add these amounts to the amount of the bid at the foreclosure sale.[157]

[G] Lien Priorities

Minn. Stat. § 514.05 provides the basic rules for determining priority among competing interest holders. All mechanics' liens on the same project (whether the claimants are architects, engineers, subcontractors, or material suppliers) have equal priority *vis-a-vis* each other and, generally, establish priority over unrecorded interests in the property as of the date of "the actual and visible beginning of the improvement of the ground."[158] A claimant with a contract to furnish labor, skill, material, or machinery can also establish lien priority over an interest recorded before the actual and visible beginning of the improvement on the ground if the claimant records a brief statement describing the nature of its contract, which statement shall be notice of that person's lien only.[159]

If the statement described in Minn. Stat. § 514.05 is not filed, the priority issue will usually be decided by answering the following question: did the lien claimant begin an "actual and visible improvement to the ground" prior to a bona fide purchaser, mortgagee, or encumbrancer recording or registering its interest? If the answer is yes, then the claimant's lien has priority over the other, later recorded encumbrance. To constitute an "actual and visible improvement," the work must represent an actual beginning of the improvement on the ground and a person using reasonable diligence in examining the property must be able to see that something is being done.[160] Reasonable diligence usually requires more than a "perimeter walk."[161] For purposes of determining priority, a claimant's lien can relate back to the first visible improvement performed by any contractor

[156] MINN. STAT. § 514.15.

[157] *Id.* § 550.24.

[158] *Id.* § 514.05, subd. 1.

[159] *Id.*

[160] Kloster-Madsen, Inc. v. Tafi's, Inc., 226 N.W.2d 603 (Minn. 1975).

[161] Lampert Yards, Inc. v. Thompson-Wetterling Constr. & Realty, Inc., 223 N.W.2d 418 (Minn. 1974); Jesco, Inc. v. Home Life Ins. Co., 357 N.W.2d 123 (Minn. Ct. App. 1984).

or subcontractor as long as the work in question was part of the same general improvement to property.[162]

[H] Lien Waivers

A subcontractor may execute a partial express waiver of all lien rights acquired to date in exchange for a progress payment.[163] Also, in exchange for final payment, a subcontractor may issue an express final waiver of its lien rights regarding all work contemplated by the parties.

Waiver also may be implied by a lien claimant's actions. For example, when a lien claimant accepts a promissory note that sets a repayment date beyond the statutory period for enforcing the lien, all rights under the lien are waived.[164] If the due date on the promissory note is within the time period to file the lien, waiver is not implied.[165]

Waiver by estoppel may occur when an owner reasonably relies on a subcontractor's lien waiver provided to the owner by a contractor in order to secure progress payments from the owner. Under these circumstances, the subcontractor is estopped from arguing that there is no consideration to support the waiver.[166]

In Minnesota, a lien waiver must be based on consideration, and to this end, basic contract law principles apply.[167] Receipt of payment in exchange for work completed is adequate consideration for a partial lien waiver relating to that work. Payment for past work does not serve as sufficient consideration for a waiver of future lien rights.[168] When the amount due is in dispute, a subsequent settlement is valid consideration for a lien waiver.[169] Finally, the consideration requirement may be satisfied by promissory estoppel, as discussed.

Taking additional security in lieu of payment does not waive lien rights except when the agreement states that the additional security is intended to replace the security provided by the lien or states that the potential lien claimant is waiving those rights.[170] Likewise, securing a personal judgment against the owner does not waive lien rights.[171]

---

[162] MINN. STAT. § 514.05; Thompson Plumbing Co., Inc. v. McGlynn Cos., 486 N.W.2d 781 (Minn. Ct. App. 1992).

[163] Engler Bros. Constr. Co. v. L'Allier, 159 N.W.2d 183 (Minn. 1968).

[164] MINN. STAT. § 514.75.

[165] *Id.;* McKeen v. Haseltine, 49 N.W. 195 (Minn. 1891).

[166] Sussel Co. v. First Fed. Sav. & Loan Ass'n, 232 N.W.2d 88, *appeal after remand,* 238 N.W.2d 625 (Minn. 1975); McLellan v. Hamernick, 118 N.W.2d 791 (Minn. 1962).

[167] Sussel Co. v. First Fed. Sav. & Loan Ass'n, 232 N.W.2d 88, *appeal after remand,* 238 N.W.2d 625 (Minn. 1975).

[168] *Id.*

[169] *Id.*

[170] McKeen v. Haseltine, 49 N.W. 195 (Minn. 1891).

[171] Kinzel v. Joslyn, 197 N.W. 217 (Minn. 1924).

Under Minnesota law any provision in a contract requiring a lien waiver before being paid for the work covered by the waiver is void and unenforceable.[172] Many third parties rely on lien waivers, however, without knowing whether or not the contractor, subcontractor, or material supplier has been paid for the work covered by the waiver. Accordingly, this law does "not affect the validity of a waiver as to any third party who detrimentally relies upon the waiver.[173]

[I] Defending Against Liens

In addition to the traditional defenses to construction contract actions, there are several defenses to mechanics' lien actions that are unique and often more compelling than standard construction defenses. These defenses include:

- lack of lienable improvement to the property
- failure to give proper pre-lien notice
- owner issued payment to general contractor prior to receiving pre-lien notice from subcontractor or material supplier
- failure to timely serve or file the lien statement
- intentional overstatement of lien amount in the lien statement
- failure to commence foreclosure of lien within one year from the lien claimant furnishing the last item of work, skill, material, or machinery
- property is public property and not subject to Minnesota's mechanics' lien statute
- lien rights were waived by lien claimant
- property was posted pursuant to Minn. Stat. § 514.05
- lien claimant was paid in full or owner has right of setoff for defective work
- lien has been satisfied, removed, or released
- failure to comply with the requirements of Minn. Stat. §§ 514.01-514.17.

Thus, although the lien statute is liberally constructed in Minnesota, the owner is also not without its defenses.

---

[172] MINN. STAT. § 337.10, subd. 2.
[173] *Id.*

CHAPTER 25

MISSISSIPPI

Ron A. Yarbrough

§ 25.01 INTRODUCTION

Under Mississippi law, there are no lien rights on public property, and unpaid subcontractors, laborers, and material suppliers must look to other remedies to enforce their payment rights. On public projects in excess of $25,000 (other than those involving highway construction), both a payment and a performance bond are required in the full amount of the contract. On highway projects in excess of $1,500, a single performance/payment bond in the amount of the contract is required.

On private projects in Mississippi, the right to file a construction lien is limited to those having a direct contractual relationship with the owner or, in certain instances, the owner's authorized representative. Although they have no right to file a construction lien, first-tier subcontractors and material suppliers of the prime contractor may file a stop notice with the owner that binds the funds in the owner's hands for the benefit of the unpaid subcontractor or supplier. However, if a contract bond is given by the prime contractor, the stop notice is inoperative, and the bond stands as security for the indebtedness.

It is significant that there is no statutory requirement that any bond be given covering work on private projects. However, if a performance bond is given, it is deemed by law to have a payment bond feature, but this "payment" feature is subordinate to the "performance" obligation.

§ 25.02 BOND LAW

[A] General Concepts

To comply with Mississippi's statute of frauds, surety contracts must be in writing and be signed by the surety's authorized representative.[1] As in many other jurisdictions, the language in a contract surety bond is given its ordinary and usual meaning and nothing is to be read into the bond that is not implicit in the language used by the parties.[2] However, in construing the contract of suretyship, Mississippi courts give less deference to compensated sureties.[3] Moreover, Mississippi follows the general rule that a surety's liability is predicated upon the underlying contract of its principal. Therefore, when the principal has no liability on a cause of action, no liability will be imputed to the surety.[4]

As noted in **§ 25.01,** there are three separate bond provisions recognized by Mississippi law. First, there are those relating to contracts entered into with the state, county, city, political subdivision, or other public authority for the construction, alteration, or repair of any public building or public work other than highway

---

[1] MISS. CODE ANN. § 15-3-1 (1972).

[2] Alexander v. Fidelity & Cas. Co., 232 Miss. 629, 100 So. 2d 347, 349 (1958).

[3] Metropolitan Cas. Ins. Co. v. Koelling, 57 So. 2d 562, 563 (Miss. 1952).

[4] State *ex rel.* Brazaele v. Lewis, 498 So. 2d 321, 324 (Miss. 1986).

improvements. These requirements are set out in Mississippi Code Annotated §§ 31-5-51 through 31-5-57 (Supp. 1998), popularly known as the Little Miller Act.[5] Next are bonding requirements for highway projects, which are found at § 65-1-85. This statute relates to all contracts entered into by or on behalf of the Mississippi Department of Transportation for construction, reconstruction, or other public work of a nonmaintenance character. Finally, provisions dealing with bonds covering private construction contracts are governed by a separate statute.[6]

[B] Bid Bonds

A bid bond or other bid security must accompany a bid by any contractor seeking to enter into a contract with the Mississippi Department of Transportation. The bond (or security) must be in the principal amount of not less than five percent of the bid, guaranteeing that the bidder will give a final bond and enter into a contract for faithful performance of the contract, according to the project's plans and specifications.[7] Mississippi statutory law does not require a bid bond for either private projects or nonhighway public projects, but such a bond or other bid security is often required. However, a contractor will not forfeit its bid bond upon withdrawal of a bid if it has made an honest bid mistake and is otherwise entitled to withdraw its bid according to Mississippi law.[8]

[C] Performance and Payment Bonds on Public Projects

[1] Little Miller Act

Under the Little Miller Act, a prime contractor on a public works project is required to furnish a performance bond and a payment bond, both of which must be in the full amount of the contract.[9] The only exception is when the contract is less than $25,000 and is to be paid in a lump sum at the completion of the contract.[10]

The performance bond is payable to and "in favor of or for the protection of" the public body that enters into the contract.[11] *Public body* is defined as "the state or any county, city or political subdivision thereof, or other public author-

---

[5] Since the Little Miller Act became effective April 1, 1981, there are very few reported cases decided under the statute. There are, however, a number of decisions under prior law, and those decisions may likely be persuasive on the issue of which labor and materials are covered, though not necessarily persuasive on other issues, such as which parties are covered and the means of perfecting coverage.

[6] MISS. CODE ANN. §§ 85-7-185 *et seq.* (1972).

[7] *Id.* § 65-1-85 (Supp. 1998).

[8] Mississippi State Bldg. Comm'n v. Becknell Constr., Inc., 329 So. 2d 57, 62 (Miss. 1976).

[9] MISS. CODE ANN. § 31-5-51(1) (Supp. 1998).

[10] *Id.* § 31-5-51(5).

[11] *Id.* § 31-5-51(1)(a).

ity."[12] Because the performance bond is provided expressly for the "public body" who awards the contract, subcontractors and others similarly situated are generally not allowed to recover on the performance bond.[13] However, in *Hanberry Corp. v. State Building Commission,*[14] the court allowed a co-prime to recover from the performance bond surety of another co-prime as a result of delays encountered during construction.

The payment bond required under the Little Miller Act does not protect *every* person who furnishes labor and materials for a public project. Instead, coverage extends to (1) subcontractors and material suppliers of the prime contractor; (2) subcontractors and material suppliers of the prime's subcontractors; and (3) persons who perform work on the site.[15] In order to obtain a certified copy of the bond, a claimant need only request a copy from the owner/public agency.[16]

Under the Little Miller Act, coverage questions typically turn on whether the party for whom the labor was performed or to whom the materials were supplied is a "subcontractor." In *Frazier v. O'Neal Steel, Inc.,*[17] the Mississippi Supreme Court said:

> In order to constitute a subcontractor . . . it is necessary that there be a contract to construct a part or all of the building contract undertaken by the contractor, and the mere fabrication of material furnished to the general contractor is not enough to constitute a materialman to be a subcontractor.

Although there is no Mississippi case on point, the term *labor,* as used in the Act, appears to cover wages earned by workers directly involved on a construction project. However, money loaned to a prime contractor and actually used to make payroll is not covered.[18]

The meaning of the term *materials* is more elusive. No case has been decided construing the exact meaning of the term *materials* under the Little Miller Act, but the traditional rule in Mississippi has been that the materials must have either entered into or become a permanent part of the improvement, or be naturally and necessarily consumed in the course of performance of the work.[19] For many years, the court strictly applied this standard. A decision by the court just before passage of the Little Miller Act appears to signal a more liberal interpretation of the meaning of *materials.*[20]

Under the Little Miller Act, material suppliers, laborers, and subcontractors

---

[12] *Id.* § 31-5-51(1).

[13] Continental Ins. Co. v. Harrison County, 153 F.2d 671, 676 (5th Cir. 1946).

[14] 390 So. 2d 277, 281 (Miss. 1980).

[15] MISS. CODE ANN. § 31-5-51(4) (Supp. 1998).

[16] *Id.* § 31-5-55.

[17] 223 So. 2d 661, 665 (Miss. 1969).

[18] McElrath & Rogers v. W.G. Kimmons & Sons, 146 Miss. 775, 112 So. 164, 165 (1927).

[19] USF&G v. Yazoo County *ex rel.* Rings, 145 Miss. 378, 110 So. 780, 781 (1927).

[20] Houston Gen. Ins. Co. v. Maples, 375 So. 2d 1012, 1016 (Miss. 1979).

who deal directly with the prime contractor are not required to give notice in order to perfect their claim. The rationale, of course, is that the contractor is presumed to know with whom it deals and to whom it owes money. All other claimants are required to give the prime contractor or its surety written notice of the fact of nonpayment, by certified mail or personal delivery, within 90 days from the date on which the claimant performed the last of the labor or supplied the last of the materials for which the claim is made.

The notice must set forth with substantial accuracy the amount of the claim and the identity of the party for whom the labor was performed or materials were supplied.[21] Compliance with other types of "notice" provisions under the predecessor statute to the Little Miller Act was considered an absolute requirement for suit to be proper.[22] However, a federal court in Mississippi has held that failure to comply strictly with the notice requirements of the Little Miller Act will not bar recovery when actual notice was received by the prime contractor.[23] The case turned on its own facts, and a claimant should not assume that it can ignore the notice requirement of the statute.

Interest on a claim brought under the Little Miller Act will be allowed if it is "liquidated," or fixed, in terms of amount. In determining the rate of interest allowable, the court looks to whether there is a written agreement providing for interest. If there is no such agreement between the claimant and the bond principal, the "legal rate" of interest is allowed. Otherwise, the amount specified in the agreement between claimant and prime contractor will control.[24]

The Little Miller Act also allows the trial judge to impose an award of attorneys' fees if the court finds that the prime contractor or surety raised an unreasonable defense to the claim, refused in bad faith to pay the claim, or purposely delayed payment of the claim. Similarly, the trial judge may require a claimant to pay attorneys' fees of the contractor or surety if the court finds the claim was brought without just cause or in bad faith.[25]

A claimant's right to sue under the Little Miller Act accrues following the 90th day after the last labor was performed or materials were provided for which payment has not been made.[26] Suit must be brought within one year after performance and final settlement of the contract or abandonment of the contract before completion. However, this time limitation is measured from the earlier of (1) the date the government authority publishes notice of the final settlement or aban-

---

[21] MISS. CODE ANN. § 31-5-51(3) (Supp. 1998).

[22] USF&G v. Plumbing Wholesale Co., 175 Miss. 675, 166 So. 529, 531 (1936).

[23] Brothers in Christ, Inc. v. American Fidelity Fire Ins. Co., 692 F. Supp. 701, 703 (S.D. Miss. 1988).

[24] Faulkner Concrete Pipe Co. v. USF&G, 218 So. 2d 1, 3–4 (Miss. 1968).

[25] MISS. CODE ANN. § 31-5-57 (1981).

[26] *Id.* § 31-5-53 (Supp. 1998).

donment of the contract; (2) written acceptance of the project by the owner; (3) actual occupancy or use by the owner.[27]

A suit on the bond may be brought in the county in which the contract or some part of the contract was performed, or wherever process may be served on the surety or the prime contractor.[28] In addition, the Little Miller Act provides that any suit on the bond shall be abated when the amount claimed is subject to unperformed contractual provisions or conditions between the parties involved, until those provisions or conditions are performed.[29]

[2] Highway Construction Bonds

Unlike the Little Miller Act, the highway bond statute does not designate the classes of persons who are covered by the payment feature of the bond or the manner in which the protection may be claimed on the bond. The Mississippi Supreme Court has held that the same procedural requirements for perfecting a payment claim under the *general* public works act are to be read into and applied to claims arising under the highway bond.[30] The court's pronouncement occurred before the passage of the Little Miller Act, and one can only assume that the same procedures in the Little Miller Act would likewise apply to the highway bond statute.

If this analysis is correct, those persons covered by the highway bond would be (1) subcontractors and material suppliers of the prime's contractor; (2) subcontractors and material suppliers of the first-tier subcontractors; and (3) laborers who perform work on the project site.[31] By the same reasoning, the 90-day notice requirement and its accompanying procedures would also apply to those not having a direct contract with the prime contractor.[32] In addition, the one-year statute of limitation allows the claimant a 12-month period for bringing suit, marked from the earlier of (1) publication of final settlement or abandonment; (2) written acceptance of the project by the owner; or (3) actual occupancy or use by the owner.[33]

As with claims under the Little Miller Act, prejudgment interest on the claim is allowed if the claim is liquidated. Otherwise, a claimant is entitled to interest only from the date of any judgment until the claim is paid in full. Absent an agreement between the claimant and the prime contractor, interest will be allowed on the claim at the legal rate.

---

[27] *Id.*

[28] *Id.*

[29] *Id.* § 31-5-51(2).

[30] Dixie Contractors, Inc. v. Ballard, 249 So. 2d 653, 654 (Miss. 1971).

[31] Miss. Code Ann. § 31-5-51(4) (Supp. 1998).

[32] *Id.* § 31-5-51(3).

[33] *Id.* § 31-5-53.

Attorneys' fees are allowed by the terms of the highway bond, and a claimant is entitled to "all of the expense and cost and attorney's fees" incurred in enforcing the conditions and obligations of the bond.[34] Consequently, unlike suits brought under the Little Miller Act, a claimant is entitled to recover expenses and attorneys' fees without showing that the prime contractor or surety unreasonably delayed payment or refused in bad faith to pay the claim.

The performance and payment coverage provided by the highway construction bond is by far the broadest of any other bond required in Mississippi. Coverage extends to "labor, material, equipment and supplies therefor."[35] The statute stops there, but the language of the bond presently used by the Mississippi Department of Transportation also includes coverage for premiums incurred for surety bonds, liability insurance, and workers' compensation insurance, among other things.[36]

The same general rules respecting coverage for labor, as they relate to the Little Miller Act, apply to the highway bond, except that the statute specifically defines *labor* as including "all work performed in repairing equipment used in carrying out the performance of the contract, which repair labor is reasonably necessary to the efficient operation of said equipment."[37]

With regard to equipment, the traditional rule that continues to be followed is that purchases of equipment, even if "disguised" as rental agreements, are not covered, and the surety is not liable if the equipment is capable of use on other projects. It would appear from a literal reading of the statute and the case law that purchases of equipment that are fully and totally consumed in prosecuting the work are arguably covered by the bond.[38]

As for repairs to equipment, the general rule is that "day to day repairs to keep the equipment operating on the job are covered. . . . Yet where major replacements or improvements to machinery are involved, these may take on the characteristics of new equipment acquisitions, inconsistent with the concept of operating repairs for which liability exists."[39]

As used in the statute, the term *materials* not only has the traditional meaning of the word, but it is also read together with the term *supplies* as including "all repair parts installed in or on equipment used in carrying out the performance of the contract, which repair parts are reasonably necessary to the efficient operation of said equipment."[40] Therefore, materials that are actually

---

[34] Section 903 bond form of the Current Standard Specifications for Road and Bridge Construction (1990). Presently prescribed by the Mississippi Department of Transportation.

[35] Miss. Code Ann. § 65-1-85 (Supp. 1998).

[36] Section 903 bond form of the Current Standard Specifications for Road and Bridge Construction (1990).

[37] Miss. Code Ann. § 65-1-85 (Supp. 1998).

[38] Euclid-Miss. v. Western Cas. & Sur. Co., 249 Miss. 779, 163 So. 2d 904, 906 (1964); Transamerica Ins. Co. v. Carter Equip. Co., 206 So. 2d 632, 635 (Miss. 1968).

[39] Euclid-Miss. v. Western Cas. & Sur. Co., 249 Miss. 779, 163 So. 2d 904, 908 (1964).

[40] Miss. Code Ann. § 65-1-85 (Supp. 1998).

consumed during performance of the work or that are incorporated into the project are covered, as are those repair parts specified in the statute.

[D] Performance and Payment Bonds on Private Projects

Neither a performance nor a payment bond is required for private construction projects in Mississippi. However, if a performance bond is given, the provisions of Mississippi Code Annotated §§ 85-7-185 *et seq.* will govern, unless the terms of the bond allow broader coverage than provided by the statute.[41]

Unlike bonds on public construction projects, the private works bond statute does not dictate the dollar amount required for a performance bond, and the bond amount may be small relative to the obligations undertaken. As a practical matter, the owner (or its representative who selects the bond form) usually requires the performance bond to be the same amount as the dollar value of the contract.

The essence of Mississippi's private construction bond statute is that if only a performance bond is given, a payment bond feature is read into the bond to protect those who provide labor and materials for the project. However, that does not necessarily mean that all persons who provide labor and materials will be paid. This is because the performance obligee, that is, the party to whom the bond is given, has a prior right to claim on the bond, and the performance obligee may exhaust the amount of the bond before any others are paid.

When a claim is made on the bond, the performance obligee is entitled to be paid first. Once the performance obligee has been fully satisfied, all other claimants are paid pro rata from any amount remaining on the bond. More often than not, when a bond is required, the private owner requires the prime contractor (and, when applicable, the prime contractor requires its subcontractor) to provide *both* a performance bond and a payment bond in the full amount of the contract. In those instances, there is less reason to be concerned over a potential pro rata distribution to unpaid laborers and material suppliers.

It is important to note that the provisions of the private bond statute apply not only to what are typically considered to be private projects, but also to subcontracts on public projects because the bond, in that instance, covers a contract between private parties.[42]

A bond given according to the private works statute provides coverage to "all persons furnishing labor or material under said contract."[43] However, this statute has been construed to mean that only those persons having a direct contract with the person who gives the bond (prime or sub) have a right to claim on the bond.[44] Therefore, unless additional coverage is provided by the express terms of the bond, a bond construed in accordance with Mississippi's private works statute

---

[41] Linde Air Prods. Co. v. American Sur. Co., 168 Miss. 863, 152 So. 292, 293 (1934).

[42] Davis Co. v. D'Lo Guar. Bank, 162 Miss. 829, 138 So. 802, 805 (1932).

[43] Miss. Code Ann. § 85-7-185 (1972).

[44] Alabama Marble Co. v. USF&G, 146 Miss. 414, 111 So. 573, 574 (1927).

extends protection only to those parties having a direct contract with the bond principal and does not protect those beyond the second tier.

As used in the context of private work bonds, the Mississippi Supreme Court has interpreted the terms *labor and material* more narrowly than in cases involving public work bonds. For example, claims for equipment rental and transportation costs have been denied under the private works payment bond statute, and one is left to wonder whether the court's apparent liberalization in the public works cases will apply to private bond disputes.[45]

Unless otherwise provided by the terms of the bond, only the obligee on a performance bond may bring suit during the first six months after completion and final settlement of the contract.[46] If after six months the obligee has not brought suit, any claimant may do so. Only one action, however, is allowed on the bond, and all others claiming to be entitled to be paid must join in the suit that is first filed.[47] The Mississippi Supreme Court, however, has held that when there are multiple claimants, all claimants are entitled to be given "constitutionally adequate notice" of the filing of the first suit.[48] The statute of limitation for filing suit runs one year after the earlier of (1) publication of notice of final settlement or abandonment of the contract; (2) written acceptance of the project by the owner; or (3) actual occupancy or use by the owner.[49]

The same rules with respect to the recovery of interest under the Little Miller Act and the highway bond statute apply to actions brought under the private construction bond statute. The statute also refers to "reasonable attorney's fees in an amount to be set by the judge," but the statute fails to give any guidelines for an award of attorneys' fees.[50] There are no reported cases in Mississippi allowing an award of attorneys' fees based upon a finding of bad faith or oppressive action on the part of the bond principal or surety on a private project.

§ 25.03 LIEN LAW

[A] General Concepts

Mississippi does not recognize lien rights on public construction projects.[51] Lien rights only apply to private projects, and the right to file a construction lien is granted only to one who has a direct contract with the owner or its repre-

---

[45] Great Am. Ins. Co. v. Busby, 247 Miss. 39, 150 So. 2d 131, 137 (1963); Western Cas. & Sur. Co. v. Stribling Bros. Mach. Co., 162 Miss. 581, 139 So. 2d 838, 841 (1962).

[46] Miss. Code Ann. § 85-7-187 (1972).

[47] *Id.* § 85-7-191.

[48] American Fidelity Fire Ins. Co. v. Athens Stove Works, Inc., 481 So. 2d 292, 295 (Miss. 1985).

[49] Miss. Code Ann. § 85-7-193 (1987).

[50] *Id.* § 85-7-189.

[51] Mississippi Fire Ins. Co. v. Evans, 153 Miss. 635, 120 So. 738, 744 (1929); National Sur. Co. v. Hall-Miller Decorating Co., 104 Miss. 626, 61 So. 700, 702 (1913).

sentative. This statutory lien provides a mechanism for a contractor to pursue payment for construction or other services or materials that have been supplied in the course of improving the property.

Liens can be used to enforce payment rights by having a court-ordered sale of the property that has been improved by the construction, service, or materials, with subsequent payment of the proceeds of this sale going to the lienor. Often, enforcing payment rights through a lien can be time-consuming and expensive, and liens may derive their greatest value from forcing the owner of the property to pay the contractor to remove the lien so that construction financing can be converted to permanent financing. Despite its limitations, a lien can be a significant weapon in the arsenal of an unpaid contractor.

[B] Basic Provisions

As noted in **§ 25.03[A],** a construction lien in Mississippi runs only in favor of those persons with a direct contractual relationship with the owner of the property, a duly authorized agent of the owner, a representative or guardian of the owner, or a tenant.[52] In cases involving guardians or tenants, lien rights are particularly limited.[53] Lien rights are available to architects, laborers, materialmen, contractors, engineers, and surveyors, provided they have a direct contractual relationship with the owner.[54] Subcontractors, laborers, materialmen, or others who have a contractual relationship only with the prime contractor do not have lien rights in Mississippi.[55]

It is important to understand these limitations on lien rights because a lien that is filed falsely, knowingly, and without just cause may subject the party filing the lien to liability for the full amount claimed.[56] A federal district court has held that this statute, being penal in nature, should be strictly construed. Specifically, that court found that the "knowing" element of the statute requires the plaintiff to show that the filing was done with "evil or bad" purpose.[57] In addition, the improper filing of a lien or lien notice, if it is false and malicious, may result in a suit for slander of title by the owner of the real property.[58]

Under Mississippi's lien law, the only property subject to a lien is property upon which improvements were actually made. There are no construction lien rights on any other property held by the owner of the property that has been improved.[59] Such property is, by statute, "liable for the debt contracted and owing,

---

[52] Miss. Code Ann. § 85-7-135 (Supp. 1972).

[53] *Id.* § 85-7-137; Brown v. Gravlee Lumber Co., 341 So. 2d 907, 910 (Miss. 1977).

[54] Miss. Code Ann. § 85-7-131 (1972).

[55] Wenger v. First Nat'l Bank, 174 Miss. 311, 164 So. 229, 231 (1935).

[56] Miss. Code Ann. § 85-7-201 (1972).

[57] Manderson v. Ceco Corp., 587 F. Supp. 445, 446 (N.D. Miss. 1984).

[58] Walley v. Hunt, 212 Miss. 294, 54 So. 2d 393, 396 (1951).

[59] Miss. Code Ann. § 85-7-131 (1979).

for labor done or materials furnished, or architectural engineers' and surveyors' or contractors' service rendered about the erection, construction, alteration or repairs thereof."[60]

For subdivision property, the lien will attach to the entire subdivision when the labor, materials, or services have been provided upon the whole subdivision. In other cases, the lien extends only to the particular part of the subdivision that has been improved by the labor, materials, or service. For city property, the lien extends to the whole lot upon which the improvement is being erected, constructed, altered, or repaired. For rural property, the lien encompasses all of the real property upon which the improvement is located up to a maximum of one acre. The lienholder is entitled to set the boundary of this one acre upon which the lien attaches.[61]

When the property upon which the improvement is made is rented and a tenant authorizes the work, the lien encompasses only that part of the property on which the work was actually performed *and* is limited to the estate of the tenant.[62] This limitation does not apply when the owner has given written consent to the work.[63]

[C] Notice Requirements

Mississippi has strict filing requirements for construction liens. Such a lien will take effect only upon the filing and recording of a notation of the lien in the *Notice of Construction Liens* book in the office of the chancery clerk for the county in which the property is located.[64] The lien will take effect as to subsequent purchasers or encumbrancers for value only from the time of commencing suit to enforce the lien, or from the time of filing the contract (or notice thereof) in the office of the chancery clerk.[65]

A suit to enforce the lien must be filed within 12 months of the date when the indebtedness secured by the lien became due and payable to the lienor.[66] When materials have been delivered to the project in installments and no date for payment is fixed by the contract, the suit must be filed within one year from the date of delivery of the last lot of materials.[67] The one-year limitation, although strictly applied, may be tolled by intervening events, such as the owner's bankruptcy.[68]

For liens based upon a claim for materials used on the job, the lienor need

---

[60] *Id.*

[61] *Id.*

[62] *Id.* § 85-7-137 (1972).

[63] Brown v. Gravlee Lumber Co., 341 So. 2d 907, 910 (Miss. 1977).

[64] MISS. CODE ANN. § 85-7-133 (Supp. 1998).

[65] *Id.* § 85-7-131; Self v. Nelson, 402 So. 2d 822, 825 (Miss. 1981).

[66] MISS. CODE ANN. § 85-7-141 (1972).

[67] Billups v. Becker's Welding & Mach. Co., 186 Miss. 41, 189 So. 526, 528 (1939).

[68] Home Bldg. Mart, Inc. v. Parker, 370 So. 2d 916, 919 (Miss. 1979).

only prove that materials were delivered to the jobsite. Such proof constitutes prima facie evidence of incorporation into the project.[69] Once this proof of delivery is made, the opposing party must persuade the court that the materials were not incorporated into the work.

Mississippi law allows only one suit to be brought to enforce a lien, and all parties who have filed a lien or other claim on the same property may intervene or be joined as parties to protect their interests.[70] Mississippi Code Annotated § 85-7-141 contains several technical requirements that must be carefully followed in bringing suit to enforce a lien.

Lienholders are permitted to file a notice of their lien in the lis pendens record in the chancery clerk's office upon compliance with certain technical requirements. The lienholder must also inform the owner of the property that the notice has been filed, and this must be done in person or be sent by certified mail, return receipt requested.[71]

Filing in the lis pendens record is not the same as filing in the *Notice of Construction Liens* book as provided in § 85-7-133. In order to have maximum protection, the lienholder should file in both places.[72]

If the lienor succeeds in prosecuting its suit to enforce the lien, Mississippi statutes provide special proceedings for enforcing the judgment. The lienholder may obtain a special order for the sale of the property upon which the lien exists or obtain execution for any residue that remains unpaid after the sale of the property.[73] A lienholder may obtain reasonable attorneys' fees incurred in prosecuting and enforcing its lien.[74] This provision may be of particular benefit to holders of small liens, by making the enforcement of liens a more cost-effective remedy than it has been in the past.

[D] Lien Priority

Typically, a priority question arises between a lienholder who has improved the property and a financing institution that has provided financing for the improvement under a construction loan and deed of trust. Construction lenders usually will have filed a deed of trust before the filing of any lien for work on the property. Consequently, the holder of a deed of trust will ordinarily have priority over a subsequently filed lien. However, the Mississippi Supreme Court has created some special rules governing priority for construction lenders.

The rights of lenders with prior recorded claims are superior to subsequently

---

[69] MISS. CODE ANN. § 85-7-131 (1979).

[70] *Id.* § 85-7-143 (1972).

[71] *Id.* § 85-7-197 (1984).

[72] Hicks v. Greenville Lumber Co., 387 So. 2d 94, 97 (Miss. 1980).

[73] MISS. CODE ANN. § 85-7-151 (1972). Sections 85-7-153 through 85-7-157 provide details of the procedures by which a judgment of the lien may be enforced.

[74] *Id.* § 85-7-151 (1972).

filed construction liens only to the extent that funds loaned pursuant to the deed of trust were actually used in the construction, or when the construction lender can show that it used reasonable diligence in disbursing the construction loan.[75] The rules on what constitutes "reasonable diligence" continue to evolve. However, at a minimum, a lender should obtain affidavits from the owner (and those with a direct contractual relationship with the owner) that no money is owed on the property as of the time the funds are disbursed. In addition, the lender should regularly check the records of the chancery clerk to determine whether any construction liens have been filed.[76]

With respect to priority questions when a construction lender is not involved, the lienholder will generally be protected against subsequent purchasers or encumbrancers for value without actual notice, provided the contract for the improvement has been filed or lis pendens notices are filed.[77] In order to be fully protected, a lienholder should always file a lis pendens notice. Such a notice is binding upon the owner and all other interested persons from the date of filing.[78]

§ 25.04 STOP PAYMENT NOTICE

Although subcontractors, materialmen, and laborers who have no contract with the owner have no right to file a construction lien, Mississippi law does provide some alternative protection. By giving the owner of the property a written *stop payment notice,* subcontractors, material suppliers, and laborers who deal directly with the general contractor may bind sums in the hands of the owner that are otherwise due to the prime contractor.[79]

There are certain, well-defined limitations on the right to enforce a stop payment notice. For example, the right is granted only to those with a direct contract with the prime contractor. Those who contract with or provide labor or materials to a subcontractor do not have stop payment rights.[80] Also, a stop payment notice does not have the effect of binding funds in the hands of the prime contractor that are due to a subcontractor.[81] Significantly, if the prime contractor has provided the owner with a contract surety bond, the right to claim protection

---

[75] Wortman & Mann, Inc. v. Frierson Bldg. & Supply Co., 184 So. 2d 857, 860 (Miss. 1966); Guaranty Mortgage Co. v. Seitz, 367 So. 2d 438, 441 (Miss. 1979).

[76] Deposit Guar. Nat'l Bank v. E.Q. Smith Plumbing & Heating, Inc., 392 So. 2d 208, 209, 212 (Miss. 1980).

[77] Miss. Code Ann. § 85-7-131 (1979); Southern Life Ins. Co. v. Pollard Appliance Co., 247 Miss. 211, 150 So. 2d 416, 421 (1963).

[78] Miss. Code Ann. § 85-7-197 (1984).

[79] *Id.* § 85-7-181 (1987).

[80] Monroe Banking & Trust Co. v. Allen, 286 F. Supp. 201, 207 (N.D. Miss. 1968).

[81] Redd v. L&A Contracting Co., 246 Miss. 548, 151 So. 2d 205, 207 (1963).

on the bond, if it exists at all, is the sole remedy available to the claimant.[82] Also, a federal district court has construed the stop payment notice as allowing no protection to claimants who provide rental equipment.[83]

Stop payment notices should be sent promptly to assure maximum protection under the statute. For instance, because the statute operates to bind only those funds that the owner is actually holding on the date it receives the notice, a notice received after the owner has paid the prime contractor fails to result in protection for the claimant.[84]

The statute provides the procedure for claiming the protection of the stop payment notice. The notice must be sent to the owner, and it must be in written form. It must state the amount due and should state that it is for the purpose of claiming the protection of the statute. Although the statute does not specify the particular manner of delivering written notice, a claimant would be wise to send it certified mail, return receipt requested, or to hand deliver it, obtaining a receipt for such delivery. Moreover, a copy should be sent to the contractor who has failed to pay the claimant.

Should the owner, after receiving the stop payment notice, choose to pay the prime contractor in derogation of the notice, the owner does so at its peril and may become liable to those who have given notice, up to the amount paid to the prime contractor. Under any circumstances, the owner's liability to all claimants is limited by the amount of the contract.[85] If the owner is holding less than the amount of all claims, the claimant is then entitled to pro rata protection with respect to any other claims that may be filed.

The stop payment provision is also to be read together with the lis pendens recording statute, Mississippi Code Annotated § 85-7-197. Accordingly, a party who is granted a stop payment right is also entitled to record its claim in the lis pendens record, and the procedure for this recording and the effect of the recording are the same as for a lienor who files a lis pendens notice.

As with suits to enforce a construction lien, only one suit is allowed to adjudicate the rights of all parties when a stop payment notice has been filed. All persons who claim an interest in the fund are to be joined as parties to the lawsuit, and any party not included may intervene.[86] When suit is filed, the owner may elect to pay into the court the sums otherwise due the contractor or to pay into court an amount sufficient to satisfy all of the claims for which notice has been received. If the owner chooses either of these options, the owner may be entitled to dismissal of the suit without risking liability for court costs.[87] If, however, the

[82] Dickson v. USF&G, 150 Miss. 864, 117 So. 245, 248 (1928).

[83] Coatings Mfrs., Inc. v. DPI, Inc., 926 F.2d 474, 478 (5th Cir. 1991).

[84] Corrugated Indus., Inc. v. Chattanooga Glass Co., 317 So. 2d 43, 47 (Miss. 1975).

[85] Miss. Code Ann. § 85-7-181 (1987).

[86] *Id.*

[87] *Id.*

owner denies the indebtedness to the contractor, the case will be tried, and if judgment is rendered against the owner, the judgment becomes a lien on the property dating back to the date of service of the original notice. A recent amendment to the stop payment statute allows for attorneys' fees to be recovered by a party who enforces its stop payment rights, thereby making this remedy more likely to be enforced.[88]

[88] *Id.*

CHAPTER 26

MISSOURI

Keith Witten
Bernard L. Balkin

§ 26.01 TYPES OF CONSTRUCTION BONDS

Construction bonds in Missouri commonly consist of three different types of bond. Bid bonds help to assure that the bidder will execute a satisfactory contract and file proper payment or performance bonds, or both, as required by a construction contract. Performance bonds provide a means of assuring the complete performance of a construction contract. Payment bonds assist in assuring that those who provide labor and materials to be incorporated into a project will receive payment.

§ 26.02 BID BONDS

There is no general statutory requirement in Missouri that bid bonds be provided under either private or public construction contracts. Bid bonds or a deposit in lieu thereof are required for contracts for construction of roads, bridges, or culverts when the engineer's estimate of cost exceeds $500,[1] as a guaranty on the part of the bidder that, if its bid is accepted, the bidder will, within ten days after receipt of notice, enter into a contract and bond to do the work advertised, and, upon default forfeit and pay 10 percent of the engineer's estimate of costs.

§ 26.03 PERFORMANCE BONDS

No general statutory authority requires that performance bonds be obtained by a public body from contractors on public contracts, but numerous regulations promulgated by state, county, and city agencies contain such requirements. Missouri statutes do not require a performance bond to the public entity, except for construction of roads, bridges, and culverts, but state agencies customarily require such bonds, and certain public entities and municipalities often provide for such bonds by ordinance or code.

Another statute relating to contracts for road, bridge, or culvert work, requires a contractor to enter into a bond with an authorized surety, conditioned that the contractor would faithfully discharge its duties under the contract within the time and manner provided and furnish and promptly pay for all labor employed and materials used and equipment rented in the performance of the contract.[2] That statute authorizes the state, county, or political subdivision or any laborer, materialman, or other person injured by breach of such contract to sue on such bond.[3]

---

[1] Mo. Rev. Stat. § 229.050 (1986).

[2] *Id.* § 229.060.

[3] Missouri State Highway Comm'n *ex rel.* Licking State Bank v. Coopers Constr. Serv. Co., 220 Mo. App. 401, 286 S.W. 736 (Mo. 1926).

§ 26.04 PAYMENT BONDS

[A] Common Law Payment Bonds

If a contractor on a private project furnishes a payment bond, the bond would be a common law payment bond as there is no statute requiring the furnishing of a payment bond on a private project. On private construction projects, Missouri law, instead, provides mechanics' lien rights to contractors, subcontractors, materialmen, and laborers who perform labor or furnish material for any building or erection of improvements upon land or for repairing the same. Missouri also does not provide any statutory procedure for bonding around liens of subcontractors or materialmen so as to discharge the real estate from mechanics' liens.

[B] Statutory Payment Bonds

The Missouri statutes requiring a bond for guaranteeing payment of labor and materials on certain public works are Missouri Revised Statutes §§ 107.170 and 229.050 (1986). The second statute deals specifically with construction of roads, bridges, and culverts and also requires a performance bond to the public entity. No lien may be imposed by a contractor upon public projects or publicly owned property. Missouri statutes require officers of the state and certain political subdivisions of the state to obtain bonds from contractors making contracts for public works conditioned upon payment of labor and material as described in the statutes.

§ 26.05 GENERAL PRINCIPLES OF BOND LAW

Missouri recognizes the tripartite nature of suretyship and distinguishes it from insurance in that the surety is secondarily liable and has rights of reimbursement from its principal.[4] A surety may be discharged of liability to the obligee if there is a material alteration of the underlying contract by the principal and obligee without the surety's consent.[5] When, however, the surety is compensated, then the alteration must be material to the risk, and the extent of discharge is measured by the prejudice suffered by the surety.[6]

Absent a provision in a bond requiring notice to a surety of its principal's default, there is no requirement either by case law or statute that notice of default be given to the surety, although a surety may show delay in notice as grounds for a partial release for escalating costs and other damages that may arise in the interim.[7]

---

[4] Ensco Envtl. Servs., Inc. v. United States, 650 F. Supp. 583 (W.D. Mo. 1986).

[5] Continental Bank & Trust Co. v. American Bonding Co., 605 F.2d 1049, 1056 (8th Cir. 1979).

[6] McKinney v. Lynch, 102 S.W.2d 944 (Mo. Ct. App. 1937).

[7] Continental Bank & Trust Co. v. American Bonding Co., 605 F.2d 1049, 1056 (8th Cir. 1979).

Missouri recognizes the common law obligation of a principal to reimburse the surety for payments the surety is obligated to pay by reason of the suretyship relationship.[8] A surety may also proceed against its principal for exoneration as an equitable remedy before paying the obligee.[9] Furthermore, if a surety performs the obligations of its principal, the surety becomes subrogated to the rights of the obligee against the principal and others, and such rights relate back to the date of execution of the bond and take priority over an assignee of the contractor for money due under the underlying contract.[10]

[A] Surety's Right to Demand that Obligee Sue Principal

Missouri provides by statute that any person bound as a surety for another in any bond, bill, or note for the payment of money or delivery of property may, at any time after an action has accrued, require in writing that the person having that right of action commence suit against the principal debtor and the other parties liable, and if suit is not commenced within 30 days after service of notice and pursued with due diligence to judgment and execution that the surety shall be exonerated from liability to the person so notified.[11] This statute is not applicable to fidelity bonds, fiduciary bonds, or public official bonds,[12] but has been recognized as enforceable on other surety obligations.[13]

[B] Liability of Principal as Measure of Liability of Surety

The surety's liability is generally coextensive with the principal,[14] and the surety is not liable if the principal is not liable.[15]

[C] Principles of Contract Construction Apply

Construction and interpretation of the surety contract is generally in accordance with contract principles. Earlier Missouri cases held that the extent of the surety's liability is measured by the strict terms of the surety contract and cannot be extended by construction or implication. However, the rule of strict construction does not apply to compensated sureties, and ambiguities in the insurance contract will generally be construed against the surety as drafter.[16]

---

[8] Krebs v. Bezler, 338 Mo. 365, 89 S.W.2d 935, 936 (Mo. 1936).

[9] Riddle v. Dean Mach. Co., 564 S.W.2d 238 (Mo. Ct. App. 1978).

[10] First State Bank v. Reorganized Sch. Dist. R-3, 495 S.W.2d 471 (Mo. Ct. App. 1973).

[11] Mo. Rev. Stat. §§ 433.010, 433.030 (1986).

[12] *Id.* § 433.040.

[13] United States v. Shafer, 627 F. Supp. 181 (W.D. Mo. 1985).

[14] Estate of Kauppi v. Bridges, 462 S.W.2d 694 (Mo. 1971).

[15] J.R. Watkins Co. v. Lankford, 363 Mo. 1046, 256 S.W.2d 788 (Mo. 1953).

[16] City of St. Louis v. Maryland Cas. Co., 122 S.W.2d 20 (Mo. Ct. App. 1938); City of St.

[D] Choice of Law

The governing law with regard to performance and payment bonds and rules of construction has been held to be the place of contracting.[17] The contract and bond are to be construed according to ordinary rules of contract construction, with the meaning determined from the four corners of the contract for the purpose of determining the intent of the parties.[18]

[E] Statutory Bonds

A bond that purports to be a statutory bond will include all obligations required by the statute, which will be deemed to be written into it.[19] The parties can add other provisions in their bonds beyond the obligations provided by statute, and these provisions will be enforceable as common law bonds.[20]

[F] Statutes of Limitation

An action on either a statutory bond or a private bond may be brought at any time within the period allowed by the general statutes of limitation covering contract claims. Some confusion exists as to whether this is five years under § 516.120, which governs "all actions upon contracts, obligations or liabilities, express or implied, except those mentioned in § 516.110," or under § 516.110, which provides that an action may be brought within 10 years "upon any writing, whether sealed or unsealed, for the payment of money or property."[21]

Missouri by statute prohibits any contract or agreement that either directly or indirectly limits the time in which any suit or action may be instituted.[22] A provision for a 90-day required notice to the surety was recognized and held valid, but such notice requirement does not limit the 10-year statute within which suit may be filed.[23] The time for giving notice of a claim under a bond requiring notice within a specified time will not be extended by the furnishing of small additional items, when the reason for furnishing those items was to circumvent the notice

---

Joseph *ex rel.* Consolidated Stone Co. v. Pfeiffer Stone Co., 224 Mo. App. 895, 26 S.W.2d 1018 (Mo. Ct. App. 1930); La Salle Iron Works, Inc. v. Largen, 410 S.W.2d 87 (Mo. 1966).

[17] Audrain County *ex rel.* First Nat'l Bank of Mex. v. Walker, 236 Mo. App. 627, 155 S.W.2d 251 (Mo. Ct. App. 1941).

[18] *Id.*

[19] Camdenton Consol. Sch. Dist. No. 6 *ex rel.* W.H. Powell Lumber Co. v. New York Cas. Co., 340 Mo. 1070, 104 S.W.2d 319 (Mo. 1937); State *ex rel.* Winebrenner v. Detroit Fidelity & Sur. Co., 326 Mo. 684, 32 S.W.2d 572 (1930).

[20] Audrain County *ex rel.* First Nat'l Bank of Mex. v. Walker, 236 Mo. App. 627, 155 S.W.2d 251 (Mo. Ct. App. 1941).

[21] State *ex rel.* Enterprise Milling Co. v. Brown, 106 S.W. 630 (Mo. 1907); Missouri, K&T Ry. Co. v. American Sur. Co., 291 Mo. 92, 236 S.W. 657 (Mo. 1921); Superintendent of Ins. v. Livestock Mkt. Ins. Agency, Inc., 709 S.W.2d 897, 900 (Mo. Ct. App. 1986).

[22] Mo. Rev. Stat. § 431.030 (1986).

[23] Frank Powell Lumber v. Federal Ins. Co., 817 S.W.2d 648 (Mo. Ct. App. 1991).

provision.[24] However, furnishing labor or material necessary for the proper performance of a contract, done in good faith at the request of the general contractor or owner, does extend the time.[25]

Although one division of the court of appeals has approved city ordinances that have required a bond claimant to give written notice of its claim within 90 days of completion of a contract in order to make a valid bond claim,[26] another division has more recently held that a requirement in a city ordinance for suit to be filed within three months from the completion of the contract and acceptance by the city is void and in violation of the state constitution as being inconsistent with the 10-year statute of limitations for commencement of a suit on a bond.[27]

§ 26.06 LIABILITY OF SURETY

[A] Bid Bonds

A bid bond provides security to the obligee in case the successful bidder fails either to execute a construction contract or furnish an acceptable performance bond.[28] A bid bond is an indemnity bond and, unless it specifically provides for forfeiture of the entire penal sum as liquidated damages, both the principal and surety are liable only for the lesser of the obligee's actual damages or the penal sum of the bond.[29] The surety's issuance of a bid bond does not require it to furnish a payment and performance bond.[30]

As with other bonds, the surety on a bid bond is generally liable only to the same extent as the principal and may assert the same defenses as its principal could.[31] For example, the surety may assert the defense of (1) the failure of the owner to follow the terms of the bid instructions in reletting the job,[32] (2) the owner's reletting of the contract with changed conditions and specifications,[33] and (3) notice to the owner of a serious mathematical error in the bid.[34]

---

[24] School Dist. v. Reliance Ins. Co., 904 S.W.2d 253, 256 (Mo. Ct. App. 1995).

[25] *Id.*

[26] City of St. Louis *ex rel.* Atlas Plumbing Supply Co. v. Aetna Cas. & Sur. Co., 444 S.W.2d 513 (Mo. Ct. App. 1969).

[27] City of Kansas City v. St. Paul Fire & Marine Ins. Co., 639 S.W.2d 903 (Mo. Ct. App. 1982).

[28] Bolivar Reorganized Sch. Dist. v. American Surety Co., 307 S.W.2d 405, 410 (Mo. 1957).

[29] 64 Am. Jur. 2d Public Works and Contracts §§ 61 and 83 (1972).

[30] Den Mar Constr. Co. v. American Ins. Co., 290 N.W.2d 737, 741–42 (Minn. 1979); Travelers Indem. Co. v. Buffalo Motor & Generator, 397 N.Y.S.2d 257, 258 (App. Div. 1977); Green River Gas v. United States Fidelity & Guar. Co., 557 S.W.2d 428, 430 (Ky. Ct. App. 1977).

[31] Bolivar Reorganized Sch. Dist. v. American Surety Co., 307 S.W.2d 405, 410 (Mo. 1957).

[32] Hanover Area Sch. Dist. v. Sarkisian Bros., Inc., 514 F. Supp. 697, 703–04 (M.D. Pa. 1981).

[33] William J. Morris, Inc. v. Lanzilotta & Teramo Constr. Corp., 405 N.Y.S.2d 508, 509 (App. Div. 1978).

[34] H. D. Warren, Annotation, Rights and Remedies of Bidder for Public Contract Who Has Not Entered into a Contract, Where Bid was Based on His Own Mistake of Fact or That of His Employees, 52 A.L.R.2d 792 (1957).

[B] Performance Bonds

A performance bond protects the owner or obligee from the failure of the principal to perform the construction contract according to its terms. Frequently, performance bonds give the surety the option upon the contractor's default of remedying the default, performing the contract, or soliciting bids to obtain performance, although some bonds do not provide options.

Claimants supplying labor and materials may seek to recover against a performance bond if there is no payment bond, if claims against the payment bond exceed its penal sum, or if the claimant can not bring a valid claim under the payment bond because it failed to give a required notice or does not have the required relationship with the principal. Although a performance bond is intended to provide protection for the owner, some cases have allowed materialmen and suppliers to recover if the underlying contract requires payment to all laborers and materialmen, if the bond does not expressly limit recovery to the named obligee.[35] For example, if the bond expressly incorporated the underlying provisions of the contract and did not expressly limit recovery to the named obligee, the materialmen could assert a valid claim against the performance bond.[36]

The penal sum of a performance bond is the limit of the surety's liability, except for prejudgment interest when the obligee's claim exceeds the penal sum and the principal is found to be liable. If the surety litigates the issue of liability, it can be liable for prejudgment interest from the date of the demand.[37] However, the surety cannot be liable for prejudgment interest if the judgment against the principal did not allow interest.[38]

When a performance bond does not exclude liability for consequential damages, the obligee may be able to recover consequential damages such as loss of profits, delay damages, costs of borrowing, and costs of capital incurred by the breach.[39] Missouri law allows recovery of lost profits as consequential damages when the amount is not speculative.[40] The surety's liability for consequential damages will depend, however, on whether the principal's default was a proximate cause of the losses sustained.[41] A surety may be liable for such items as the cost of supervision, overtime wages, furnishing temporary power, operating sanitary facilities, providing drinking water, fixed overhead and staffing.[42]

A surety is generally not liable for its principal's tortious acts, either intentional or negligent.[43] However, a contractor and its surety may expressly undertake

[35] LaSalle Iron Works, Inc. v. Largen, 410 S.W.2d 87, 92 (Mo. 1966).

[36] Ill-Mo Contractors, Inc. v. Aalcan Demolition & Contracting Co., 431 S.W.2d 165 (Mo. 1968).

[37] Howard Constr. Co. v. Teddy Woods Constr. Co., 817 S.W.2d 556 (Mo. Ct. App. 1991).

[38] J.R. Watkins Co. v. Lankford, 256 S.W.2d 788 (Mo. 1953).

[39] Havens Steel Co. v. Randolph Eng'g Co., 813 F.2d 186 (8th Cir. 1987).

[40] Collegiate Enters., Inc. v. Otis Elevator Co., 650 F. Supp. 116 (E.D. Mo. 1986).

[41] State *ex rel.* Nelson v. Hammett, 203 S.W.2d 115 (Mo. Ct. App. 1947).

[42] General Ins. Co. v. Hercules Constr. Co., 385 F.2d 13 (8th Cir. 1967).

[43] J. Louis Crum Corp. v. Alfred Lindgren, Inc., 564 S.W.2d 544 (Mo. Ct. App. 1978).

such obligations.[44] Also, if a statute or ordinance requires a bond, it may provide that the bond will cover negligent or tortious acts.[45]

In the absence of a contrary provision in a takeover agreement, a completing surety will be liable for the full amount of the completion costs, but it is also entitled to a credit for the contract balances to which the contractor would have been entitled had it not defaulted.[46]

A performance bond surety may be discharged if the principal and obligee agree without the surety's consent to a material modification to the bonded contract.[47] Such alterations may include a change in the scope of the contract, extensions of time for the principal to pay or perform.[48] However, a provision in a bond that the surety waives notice of alterations or modifications in the contract may prevent the surety from claiming discharge.

A mere failure of the parties to observe the technical requirements of processing change orders will not discharge the surety and Missouri courts generally require proof that the surety was prejudiced.[49] Indeed, increases in costs alone do not constitute an alteration in the nature of the work or changes in the scope of the contract so as to discharge a performance bond surety.[50] However, an increase of 300 percent in the cost of work over the original estimate was been held to be a substantial modification of a contract.[51]

Nor is lack of notice to the surety of the principal's default normally a defense to liability on a performance bond.[52] However, even without a notice provision in the bond or contract, the obligee may not deliberately delay notifying the surety of the principal's default and attempt to recover escalated costs in completion between the date of default and its demand.[53]

A surety may also argue that the obligee's release, loss, or misapplication of security prejudiced its rights and that it is entitled to be discharged on its performance bond obligations by such activity. Because a surety has a beneficial interest in all collateral provided by the principal to the obligee, an obligee has an affirmative obligation to perform those acts necessary to secure its collateral.[54] If the obligee fails to secure the collateral, the surety will be released of liability to the extent of its prejudice.[55] When a contract does not give the owner authority

---

[44] City of Univ. City *ex rel.* Mackey v. Frank Miceli & Sons Realty & Bldg. Co., 347 S.W.2d 131 (Mo. 1961).

[45] Weinhaus v. Massachusetts Bonding & Ins. Co., 210 S.W.2d 710 (Mo. Ct. App. 1948).

[46] Continental Bank & Trust Co. v. American Bonding Co., 630 F.2d 606 (8th Cir. 1980).

[47] Restatement of the Law of Security, § 128(b) (1941).

[48] Dickherber v. Turnbull, 31 S.W.2d 234 (Mo. Ct. App. 1930).

[49] Massachusetts Bonding & Ins. Co. v. John R. Thompson Co., 88 F.2d 825 (8th Cir. 1937).

[50] Continental Bank & Trust Co. v. American Bonding Co., 605 F.2d 1049 (8th Cir. 1979).

[51] Peter Kiewit Sons' Co. v. Summit Constr. Co., 422 F.2d 242 (8th Cir. 1969).

[52] American Sur. Co. v. United States, 317 F.2d 652 (8th Cir. 1963).

[53] Continental Bank & Trust Co. v. American Bonding Co., 605 F.2d 1049, 1057, n.17 (8th Cir. 1979).

[54] Lewis v. Paul Brown Realty & Inv. Co., 193 S.W.2d 13 (Mo. 1946).

[55] McKinney v. Lynch, 102 S.W.2d 944 (Mo. Ct. App. 1937).

to withhold funds from the principal, the surety cannot complain of prejudice arising from the owner's payment to the contractor upon completion.[56]

The obligee's release of the principal may also discharge the surety. But in order to discharge the surety, the release must release the principal of its obligation on the bonded project. A release between the principal and obligee as to some other matter, even though related to the bonded project, will not discharge the surety. Thus, where the obligee on a construction project released the principal and surety's indemnitors as guarantors on promissory notes, the release did not affect the principal's duty to complete the project and, the surety could not claim a discharge on its performance bond.[57]

[C] Payment Bonds

[1] Generally

All official boards or agents of the state or any county, city, town, township, school, or road district in the state must require every public works contractor to provide a bond guaranteeing payment of labor and material as detailed in the statute.[58] The statute further provides that coverage under such bonds shall be deemed to be coextensive with the statutory requirements. In 1995, the Missouri General Assembly amended the statute by making it the duty of "all public entities" to require a statutory public works payment bond, rather than listing various public bodies to which the duty applied. Similarly, rather than using a laundry list of the various types of supplies and materials covered by the bond, some of which were rather archaic (e.g., "hay, feed, coal"), the new statute simply requires the bond to cover "materials, incorporated, consumed or used in connection with the construction of such work, and all insurance premiums, both for compensation, and for all other kinds of insurance, said work [sic], and for all labor performed in such work whether by subcontractor or otherwise."[59]

The new statute provides, however, that no bond need be provided if the cost of the public work involved is estimated not to exceed $25,000. Furthermore, professional engineers, architects, licensed land surveyors, and those who provide environmental assessment services need not be required to provide a statutory public works payment bond. Finally, the new statute allows public entities to indemnify their officers and employees against claims arising out of an alleged act or omission occurring in the performance of their duties under the statute, except in cases of malfeasance in office or willful or wanton neglect of duty.

No mechanics' lien may be obtained for work performed or material furnished on public works. Some contracts with state entities are held not to be

[56] J.R. Meade & Co. v. Barrett & Co., 453 S.W.2d 632 (Mo. App. E.D. 1970).

[57] Continental Bank & Trust Co. v. American Bonding Co., 605 F.2d 1049 (8th Cir. 1979).

[58] Mo. Rev. Stat. § 107.170.

[59] *Id.*

within the coverage of the statute, such as those with the curators of state universities or the State Highway Commission, but bonds provided may be enforced as private or common law bonds.[60] Property owned by the operator of a natural gas pipeline pursuant to franchise with a city, which was reasonably necessary for public use, and city utility easements on which the natural gas pipeline lay were not subject to a mechanics' lien.[61] The right of action to sue on the bond required under § 107.170 is given by § 522.300, which provides that every person furnishing material or performing labor, either as an individual or as a subcontractor, shall have a right to sue on such bond.

[2] Liability of Public Officials for Failing to Require Payment Bond

Public officials have been held liable to materialmen or laborers for the failure of public officials to obtain the bond required by statute.[62] The decision of whether to accept a particular bond is a discretionary act for which public officials are entitled to official immunity.[63] However, the failure to require any bond is a violation of a ministerial duty rendering the public officials liable.[64] If a subcontractor does not allege that public officials failed to require a contractor to post a bond, the subcontractor may not assert a claim directly against the contractor.[65] In order for a public official to be liable, the claimant must demonstrate that the arrangement on which the public entity allegedly should have required a statutory public works payment bond was an enforceable contract.[66]

[3] Remoteness

Subcontractors and their laborers and materialmen are expressly covered by the statutory provisions of §§ 107.170 and 522.300, but one supplying material

---

[60] Geller, Ward & Hasner Hardware Co. v. Trust Co., 234 S.W. 1019 (Mo. Ct. App. 1921).

[61] River's Bend Red-E-Mix, Inc. v. Parade Park Homes, Inc., 919 S.W.2d 1 (Mo. Ct. App. 1996).

[62] C.A. Burton Mach. Co. v. Ruth, 194 Mo. App. 194, 186 S.W. 737 (Mo. Ct. App. 1916); Austin v. Ransdell, 207 Mo. App. 74, 230 S.W. 334 (Mo. Ct. App. 1921); Rupard Asphalt Co. v. O'Dell, 382 S.W.2d 832 (Mo. Ct. App. 1964); Layne, Inc. v. Moody, 886 S.W.2d 115 (Mo. Ct. App. 1994) (commissioner of the Missouri Office of Administration could be liable for failure to require bond); George Weiss Co. v. Dwyer, 867 S.W.2d 520 (Mo. Ct. App. 1993) (superintendent and members of school board who accepted payment bonds that listed a fictitious issuer were personally liable to subcontractor); National Oil & Supply, Inc. v. Vaughts, Inc., 856 S.W.2d 912 (Mo. Ct. App. 1993) (county commissioners could be liable to material supplier for failing to require contractor to furnish a payment bond, even though contractor had no written contract with county); Energy Masters Corp. v. Fulson, 839 S.W.2d 665 (Mo. Ct. App. 1992) (school district directors personally liable to architectural firm for failing to require contractor to furnish statutory public works payment bond).

[63] George Weis Co. v. Dwyer, 956 S.W.2d 335, 338 (Mo. Ct. App. 1997).

[64] S&W Cabinets, Inc. v. Consolidated Sch. Dist., 901 S.W.2d 266, 268-69 (Mo. Ct. App. 1995).

[65] City of Keytesville v. Kelco Indus., Inc., 773 F. Supp. 1264, 1266 (E.D. Mo. 1991).

[66] Layne, Inc. v. Moody, 956 S.W.2d 325 (Mo. Ct. App. 1997).

to a materialman who, in turn, sells to a subcontractor or contractor has been held not be within the coverage of the statutory bond.[67] Construction lenders as such are not covered by a statutory bond, even though the loan proceeds were used to pay covered labor and material obligations.[68]

[4] Prevailing Wages

The surety on a public works project was held liable under the payment bond for prevailing wages and the doubling penalties, interest, and attorneys' fees, when the bond specifically made the surety liable for prevailing wages.[69] The prevailing wage statutes make a suit brought by a worker to recover the doubling penalties and attorneys' fees allowable by the prevailing wage statutes a suit for wages and give any judgment entered in favor of a worker for those amounts the same force and effect as other judgments for wages.[70]

[5] Attorneys' Fees

Another new statute allows a court or arbitrator to award reasonable attorneys' fees and interest at a rate up to one and one-half percent per month to the prevailing party in litigation involving private construction work.[71] Furthermore, it precludes the use of a contractual provision making payment from a contractor to a subcontractor, trade contractor, specialty contractor, or supplier contingent on receipt of payment from any other private party, including a private owner, as a defense to a petition to enforce a mechanics' lien.[72]

Persons who enter into contracts for private construction work, other than for the building, improvement, repair or remodeling of owner-occupied residential property of four units or less, must make all scheduled payments pursuant to the terms of the contract. Any person who is not paid in accordance with the provisions of such a contract may bring an action in a court of competent jurisdiction against a person who has failed to pay. In such an action, or in an arbitration action, the court or arbitrator may, in addition to any other award of damages, award interest at the rate of up to one and one-half percent per month from the date payment was due under the terms of the contract, and reasonable attorneys' fees, to the prevailing party.[73]

---

[67] City of St. Louis v. Kaplan-McGowan Co., 108 S.W.2d 987 (Mo. Ct. App. 1937).

[68] Audrain County *ex rel.* First Nat'l Bank of Mex. v. Walker, 236 Mo. App. 627, 155 S.W.2d 251 (Mo. Ct. App. 1941).

[69] City of Kansas City v. Integon Indem., 857 S.W.2d 233 (Mo. Ct. App. 1993).

[70] Mo. Rev. Stat. § 290.300 (1993).

[71] *Id.* § 431.180 (Supp. 1997).

[72] *Id.* § 431.183.

[73] *Id.* § 431.180.

[6] Prompt Payment Act

A statute enacted in 1990[74] requires that any "public works contract"[75] must provide for prompt payment by the public owner to the contractor and prompt payment by the contractor to subcontractors and material suppliers.[76] If a contractor, without reasonable cause, fails to make any payment to its subcontractors and material suppliers within 15 days after receipt of payment under the public construction contract, the contractor must pay to its subcontractors and material suppliers, in addition to the payment due them, interest in the amount of one and one-half percent per month calculated from the expiration of the 15-day period until fully paid.[77]

The statute recognizes that there can be valid reasons to withhold payment from a subcontractor, such as unsatisfactory job progress, defective construction work, and so on.[78] However, it requires that when a contractor receives any payment from the owner, it must pay each subcontractor in proportion to the work completed, less retention.[79] It also prohibits a contractor from applying for payment to the owner for an amount which it intends to withhold from the subcontractor.[80] If a contractor determines, after having received payment from the owner, that moneys should be withheld from a subcontractor for any of the reasons mentioned by the statute, the contractor must deduct the moneys withheld from the subcontractor from its next application for payment to the owner.[81] Finally, if a contractor that withholds payment does not do so in good faith for reasonable cause, a court may impose interest at one and one-half percent from the date of the invoice and award reasonable attorneys' fees to the prevailing party.[82]

[7] Extra-contractual Liability

Missouri does not recognize a common law bad-faith claim of an insured against its insurer.[83] A surety has been deemed to come within the definition of an insurer[84] and as such is subject to the provisions of Missouri Revised Statutes § 375.420. The statute has been held to preempt any common law right against the insurer and provides instead a statutory remedy for vexatious refusal to pay

---

[74] *Id.* §§ 34.057 *et seq.*

[75] *Id.* § 34.058.1.

[76] *Id.* § 34.057.1.

[77] *Id.* § 34.057.1(7).

[78] *Id.* § 34.057.5.

[79] *Id.* § 34.057.1(6).

[80] *Id.* § 34.057.2.

[81] *Id.* § 34.057.3.

[82] *Id.* § 34.057.6.

[83] Duncan v. Andrew County Mut. Ins. Co., 665 S.W.2d 13 (Mo. Ct. App. 1983); Halford v. American Preferred Ins., 698 S.W.2d 40 (Mo. Ct. App. 1985).

[84] State *ex rel.* United States Fidelity & Guar. Co. v. Walsh, 540 S.W.2d 137 (Mo. Ct. App. 1976).

claims, which is limited to 20 percent of the first $1,500 of loss and 10 percent of any excess amount, together with reasonable attorneys' fees.[85]

§ 26.07 MECHANICS' LIENS

On private construction projects, Missouri law provides mechanics' lien rights to contractors, subcontractors, materialmen, and laborers who perform labor or furnish material for any building or erection of improvements upon land or for repairing the same. No lien may be imposed by a contractor upon public projects or publicly owned property. Missouri statutes require officers of the state and certain political subdivisions of the state to obtain bonds from contractors making contracts for public works conditioned upon payment of labor and material as described in the statutes.

The purpose and intent of the Missouri mechanics' lien statute is to give those who supply labor or material that has enhanced the value of an owner's property security in the owner's property.[86] The lien statute is remedial in nature and should be construed as favorably to those persons as its terms will permit.[87] However, favorable construction does not relieve the claimant of reasonable and substantial compliance with statutory requirements.[88] Special statutes allow for labor and material liens against railroads.[89]

§ 26.08 ARCHITECTS

Registered architects or corporations registered to practice architecture, registered professional engineers or corporations registered to practice professional engineering, registered landscape architects or corporations registered to practice landscape architecture, and registered land surveyors or corporations registered to practice land surveying who render such service directly connected with the erection or repair of any building or other improvement under a contract with the owner or lessee or the owner or lessee's agent, trustee, contractor or subcontractor, or without a contract if ordered by a city, town, village or county having a charter form of government to abate the conditions that caused a structure on that property to be deemed a dangerous building under the local ordinances may obtain a lien on building or improvement to the extent of one acre.[90]

Furthermore, any design professional or corporation authorized to have such lien rights may have a lien whether or not actual construction has commenced if it contracts with one who is the owner or lessee or the owner or lessee's agent or

---

[85] Housing Auth. *ex rel.* Evans Elec. Constr. Co. v. Baumann, 512 S.W.2d 436 (Mo. Ct. App. 1974); State *ex rel.* United States Fidelity & Guar. Co. v. Walsh, 540 S.W.2d 137 (Mo. Ct. App. 1976).

[86] Vasquez v. Village Ctr., Inc., 362 S.W.2d 588 (Mo. 1962).

[87] R.L. Sweet Lumber Co. v. E.L. Lane, Inc., 513 S.W.2d 365 (Mo. 1974).

[88] Farmington Bldg. v. L.D. Pyatt Constr., 627 S.W.2d 648 (Mo. Ct. App. 1981).

[89] Mo. Rev. Stat. §§ 429.440 *et seq* (1992).

[90] *Id.* § 429.015 (Supp. 1999).

trustee contracted for such professional services directly with the design professional or corporation asserting the lien either at the time the contract is made or the time the lien is filed.[91] Priority between a design professional or corporation lien claimant and any other mechanics' lien claimant shall be determined pursuant to the provisions of Missouri Revised Statutes § 429.260 on a pro rata basis. Finally, in a civil action, the owner or lessee may assert defenses which include the actual construction of the planned work or improvement has not been performed in compliance with the professional services contract, is impracticable, or is economically infeasible.[92]

§ 26.09 ENVIRONMENTAL REMEDIATION

There is no case law in Missouri on whether contractors who perform environmental remediation are entitled to claim a mechanics' lien.

§ 26.10 WAIVER

Missouri has no statutory provision that permits an affirmative waiver of lien rights. However, failure of the contractor or owner to comply with the notice and consent requirements of the lien statutes or the subcontractor's or supplier's failure to assure itself of the owner's consent, may have the effect of a waiver of lien rights. A contractor's service of a notice of intent to file a mechanics' lien, filing of a mechanics' lien, and filing of a suit to enforce the mechanics' lien do not waive the contractor's right to enforce a contractual arbitration provision.[93] Missouri statute specifically provides for a notice that must be given by the prime contractor and makes reference to the owner's right to demand a lien waiver from all persons supplying material or services for the described work. A statute enacted in 1992 provides that an agreement to waive lien rights is not enforceable and against public policy when the agreement is in anticipation of and in consideration for the awarding of a contract or subcontract to perform work or supply materials for an improvement to real property.[94]

Lien waivers signed by contractors, subcontractors, laborers, or materialmen are generally enforceable to the extent of the dollar amount and dates set forth in the lien waiver. A party who executes a lien waiver is estopped from asserting its invalidity as against an owner or mortgagee who has paid out money or otherwise changed its position to its detriment in reliance upon the waiver.[95] However, if there has been no such detrimental change of position, the claimant may assert a defense of invalidity.[96] For example, a postdated check that was later returned for

[91] *Id.* § 429.105 (1992).

[92] Henges Co. v. Doctors' N. Rds. Bldg., Inc., 409 S.W.2d 489 (Mo. Ct. App. 1966).

[93] Silver Dollar City, Inc. v. Kitsmiller Constr. Co., 874 S.W.2d 526, 534-35 (Mo. Ct. App. 1994).

[94] Mo. Rev. Stat. § 429.005 (1992).

[95] Mid-West Eng'g & Constr. Co. v. Campagna, 397 S.W.2d 616 (Mo. 1965).

[96] *See, e.g.,* Tharp v. Keeter/Schaeffer Invests., Ltd., 943 S.W.2d 811, 817-21 (Mo. Ct. App. 1997).

insufficient funds allowed the party executing a lien waiver at the time of receiving the check to assert that the lien waiver was invalid.[97]

§ 26.11 ELEMENTS RECOVERABLE BY A MECHANICS' LIEN CLAIMANT

The Missouri lien statute requires that to establish a lien a person shall "do or perform work or labor upon, or furnish any material."[98] By case law, a claimant is required to prove that such labor or material entered into the improvement and became part of its value.[99] However, evidence of delivery to the site amounts to substantial evidence of incorporation of material into an improvement.[100] Materials need not be incorporated into the improvement if they were "used or consumed" in the improvement, such as heating oil to maintain heat during construction.[101] However, a supplier has the burden of proving that material delivered to the original contractor that does not actually go to the job site actually goes into the making of improvements on the owner's land.[102]

In light of the liberal construction given to the statute, most types of work are covered under the statute, whether for original improvements or for repairs, although a lien for repairs to existing improvements will not have priority over existing encumbrances on the underlying land.[103] Excavation and grading services are lienable when performed as an integral part of a total plan to construct improvements, even though they may not be part of the contract of construction.[104] Material need not be actually incorporated into the improvement to be lienable. It is sufficient if the material is necessarily consumed in the performance of the improvement,[105] such as fuel oil to heat the building.[106] However, material that has been prepared or furnished for an improvement but has not been used in the improvement is not lienable.[107]

Superintendence charges of both the original contractor or a subcontractor are lienable.[108] Installation of personalty may be lienable, but only if the personal

---

[97] St. Louis Flexicore, Inc. v. Lintzenich, 414 S.W.2d 787 (Mo. Ct. App. 1967).

[98] Mo. Rev. Stat. § 429.010 (Supp. 1999).

[99] Farmington Bldg. v. L.D. Pyatt Constr., 627 S.W.2d 648, 651 (Mo. Ct. App. 1981).

[100] Stuart C.&M. Co. v. James H. Stanton Constr. Co., 433 S.W.2d 76, 79 (Mo. Ct. App. 1968); Continental Elec. Co. v. Ebco, Inc., 365 S.W.2d 746, 752 (Mo. Ct. App. 1963), *rev'd on other grounds,* 375 S.W.2d 134 (Mo. 1964).

[101] Oliver L. Taetz, Inc. v. Groff, 363 Mo. 825, 253 S.W.2d 824 (Mo. 1953).

[102] Davidson v. Fisher, 258 S.W.2d 297 (Mo. Ct. App. 1953).

[103] Elliott & Barry Eng'g Co. v. Baker, 134 Mo. App. 95, 114 S.W. 71 (Mo. Ct. App. 1908).

[104] H.B. Deal Constr. Co. v. Labor Discount Ctr., Inc., 418 S.W.2d 940 (Mo. 1967).

[105] Boyer Lumber, Inc. v. Blair, 510 S.W.2d 738 (Mo. Ct. App. 1974).

[106] Oliver L. Taetz, Inc. v. Groff, 363 Mo. 825, 253 S.W.2d 824 (Mo. 1953).

[107] Davidson v. Fisher, 258 S.W.2d 297 (Mo. Ct. App. 1953).

[108] Fagan v. Brock Motor Car Co., 282 S.W. 135 (Mo. Ct. App. 1926); Fuhler v. Gohman & Levine Constr. Co., 346 Mo. 588, 142 S.W.2d 482 (Mo. 1940).

property becomes a fixture attached to realty.[109] Costs of necessary transportation of material are lienable, as well as reasonable delivery and commission charges.

Outdoor irrigation installation is specifically described by statute as lienable work.[110] Purchase of trees, shrubs, bushes, plants, or landscaping goods or services are also lienable, but are enforceable only against the property of the original purchaser of such plants unless the lien is filed against the property before the conveyance of the property to a third person.[111]

A lien is provided for labor and material provided for the construction of any street, curb, sidewalk, sewerline, waterline, or other pipeline in front of, adjacent to, along, or adjoining any lot, tract, or parcel in any town, city, or village.[112]

The lien statement may include overhead and profit in claiming the reasonable value of the improvements, labor, or materials furnished, but claims that are substantially overstated will be denied enforceability.[113]

§ 26.12 ELEMENTS NOT RECOVERABLE BY A MECHANICS' LIEN CLAIMANT

Loans advanced to a contractor or materialman for the purchase of material or the financing of labor costs for improvements to realty are not lienable items.[114] Legal services are not part of lienable items and will not be awarded as part of a mechanics' lien judgment.[115]

§ 26.13 ISSUES RELATING TO THE FORM OF A MECHANICS' LIEN STATEMENT

The required contents of the lien statement are mandatory, and the statement must substantially comply with the statute.[116] The statute does not detail the

---

[109] Drew's Hardware & Appliance Co. v. Willis Hous. Projects, 268 S.W.2d 596 (Mo. Ct. App. 1954).

[110] Mo. Rev. Stat. § 429.010 (Supp. 1999).

[111] *Id.*

[112] *Id.* § 429.020.

[113] Dave Kolb Grading, Inc. v. Lieberman Corp., 837 S.W.2d 924 (Mo. Ct. App. 1992).

[114] Putnam v. Heathman, 367 S.W.2d 823 (Mo. Ct. App. 1963). A mechanics' lien claimant may recover prejudgment interest on any liquidated amount owed, either at the rate of nine percent under Mo. Rev. Stat. § 408.020, when the parties have not agreed to a rate of interest, or at the rate provided for in the contract, if any. Judgments bear interest after entry at nine percent, except that judgments on contracts bearing more than nine percent interest bear interest at the rate provided for in the contract. Bolivar Insulation Co. v. R. Logsdon Builders, Inc., 929 S.W.2d 232 (Mo. Ct. App. 1996).

[115] Allied Pools, Inc. v. Sowash, 735 S.W.2d 421 (Mo. Ct. App. 1987).

[116] Farmington Bldg. v. L.D. Pyatt Constr., 627 S.W.2d 648, 651 (Mo. Ct. App. 1981); L. Waldo & Assocs. v. PVO Foods, Inc., 852 S.W.2d 424 (Mo. Ct. App. 1993) (holding that subcontractor's lump-sum billing did not satisfy requirement of "just and true account of the amount due").

contents of the subcontractor's notice, but case law and practice suggest at least the following:

1. Name of the person or persons to whom notice must be given
2. Name of claimant
3. A description of the improvement
4. Location of the property
5. Name of the person or persons with whom the claimant made the contract
6. Amount of the claim
7. Basis of the claim (labor, material)
8. Date of the notice
9. Signature of the claimant.

[A] Requirement of Verification

A lien statement must contain a verification of the lien statement by the oath of the filer or some credible person for the filer.[117]

[B] Requirement of Itemization

A lien statement must contain a just and true account of the demand due after all just credits have been given.[118] Itemization has been required by case law in cases involving priority over a mortgage claimant or when the claim is based upon quantum meruit.[119]

[C] Description of Real Property

A lien statement must contain a true description of the property, or so near as to identify the same, upon which the lien is intended to apply.[120] The description of the property need not be the legal description if it clearly identifies the property upon which the lien is intended to apply,[121] especially if the rights of third parties

---

However, a concrete subcontractor's mechanics' lien statement was sufficient to meet the statutory requirements even though it did not list the depth of the concrete, because the contractor billed for its concrete flatwork on a square footage basis and the invoices itemized the square footage. Construction Equip. Management, Inc. v. Dunhill Dev. Corp., 892 S.W.2d 639, 642 (Mo. Ct. App. 1995). Similarly, hauling charges listed in the statement were not insufficient because they failed to state the driver's hourly rate and the number of hours it took to deliver the concrete, when the hauling charge was determined by the cubic feet of concrete delivered, not the amount of time it took to deliver it. *Id.*

[117] Mo. Rev. Stat. § 429.080 (1992).

[118] *Id.*

[119] S&R Builders & Suppliers, Inc. v. Marler, 610 S.W.2d 690 (Mo. Ct. App. 1980).

[120] Mo. Rev. Stat. § 429.080 (1992).

[121] Paradise Homes, Inc. v. Helton, 631 S.W.2d 51 (Mo. Ct. App. 1981).

are not involved. One lien statement may be filed when the improvements consist of two or more buildings upon the same or contiguous lots, if erected under one general contract.[122]

A mechanics' lien extends to the building, erection, or improvement and the land upon which it is situated to the extent of three acres, but if the improvement is upon a lot of land within a city, town, or village, or if it is for manufacturing, industrial, or commercial purposes and not within a city, town, or village, the lien extends to the lot, tract, or parcel of land on which the improvement is situated, not limited to three acres.[123]

A lien applies only to the right, title, and interest of the owner of the improvement. A lien may attach to an improvement erected by a claimant at a lessee's order, but by statute is limited to a lien upon the improvements and the leasehold interest,[124] unless the claimant can establish that the lessee had been constituted the agent of the lessor. An example of such agency has been found when the lease required the tenant to erect the improvements or the leased premises required remodeling or repair to meet the specific purpose of the lease.[125] The lienholder on a leasehold interest may not remove improvements that have been constructed or repaired, nor may the claimant remove additions if removal will cause irreparable harm to the original structure.[126]

[D] Description of Owner

A lien statement must contain the name of the owner or contractor, or both, if known to the person filing the lien.[127] In order to be lienable, the labor and material furnished must arise out of a contract between the original contractor and the owner, or with its agent, trustee, contractor, or subcontractor.[128] The contract may be written or oral, express or implied.[129]

The authority of an agent for the owner may be either express or implied from evidentiary facts. A lessee does not have the authority to subject the lessor's property to a lien unless an agency may be implied from the terms of the leasehold, such as the lessee's requirement to make substantial improvements.[130]

A mechanics' lien can be established against property held under a tenancy by the entirety only if both husband and wife join in the contract.[131] The authority

---

[122] Mo. Rev. Stat. § 429.040 (1992).

[123] *Id.* § 429.010 (Supp. 1999).

[124] *Id.* § 429.070.

[125] Branick Constr. Co. v. Taylor, 585 S.W.2d 282 (Mo. Ct. App. 1979); Bates v. McKay, 724 S.W.2d 565 (Mo. Ct. App. 1986).

[126] Orear v. Dierks Lumber Co., 188 Mo. App. 729, 176 S.W. 467 (Mo. Ct. App. 1915).

[127] Mo. Rev. Stat. § 429.080 (1992).

[128] *Id.* § 429.010 (Supp. 1999).

[129] Otte v. McAuliffe, 441 S.W.2d 733 (Mo. Ct. App. 1969).

[130] Messina Bros. Constr. Co. v. Williford, 630 S.W.2d 201 (Mo. Ct. App. 1982); Branick Constr. Co. v. Taylor, 585 S.W.2d 282 (Mo. Ct. App. 1979).

[131] Morgan Wightman Supply Co. v. Smith, 764 S.W.2d 485 (Mo. Ct. App. 1989).

of one spouse to act as agent for the other may be shown by acts evidencing active approval or participation in the improvements, such as execution of a deed of trust for the purpose of financing the improvements.[132] However, mere knowledge of the contract of the spouse and acquiescence without objection is not sufficient to create the required showing a contract or agency.[133]

§ 26.14 AMENDMENT OF A MECHANICS' LIEN STATEMENT

Although there is no express statutory authority for amending a mechanics' lien statement, a few cases have discussed such amendments.[134] An amendment before the time for filing a mechanics' lien statement would probably not be subject to challenge, unless the original statement was filed in bad faith or with an intention to defraud. Amendment after expiration of the time for filing the lien statement is more risky. It is unclear whether amendments that do not increase the amount claimed or make material changes may be allowed after the expiration of the time for filing a lien statement.

§ 25.15 ASSIGNMENT OF A MECHANICS' LIEN STATEMENT

Missouri law allows for the assignment of a mechanics' lien by statute.[135] However, the statute limits assignment to situations where two or more persons have filed mechanics' liens in the clerk's office. If two or more persons have done so, they may assign their liens to each other or to any other person.[136] The assignee may bring suit in his name and enforce any such assigned lien as if it had not been assigned. Because a mechanics' lien cannot be assigned in the absence of statutory authority,[137] it appears that a single lien claimant may not assign a mechanics' lien.

§ 26.16 LIEN FRAUD

Any original contractor, subcontractor or supplier who fails or refuses to pay any subcontractor, materialman, supplier or laborer for any services or materials provided pursuant to any contract for which the original contractor, subcontractor or supplier has been paid, with the intent to defraud, commits the crime of lien

[132] Stockman v. Estate of Shelton, 526 S.W.2d 349 (Mo. Ct. App. 1975); Morgan Wightman Supply Co. v. Smith, 764 S.W.2d 485 (Mo. Ct. App. 1989).

[133] La Crosse Lumber Co. v. Goddard, 151 S.W.2d 455 (Mo. Ct. App. 1941); Wilson v. Fower, 236 Mo. App. 532, 155 S.W.2d 502 (Mo. Ct. App. 1941). Twin Bridges Constr. Co. v. Ferner, 700 S.W.2d 534 (Mo. Ct. App. 1985); Kenny's Tile & Flooring, Inc. v. Curry, 681 S.W.2d 461 (Mo. Ct. App. 1984); Moellering Concrete, Inc. v. Doerr, 784 S.W.2d 864 (Mo. Ct. App. 1990).

[134] *See, e.g.,* Hill Behan Lumber Co. v. Dinan, 786 S.W.2d 904 (Mo. Ct. App.1990); Woodling v. Westport Hotel Operating Co., 63 S.W.2d 207 (Mo. Ct. App. 1933).

[135] Mo. Rev. Stat. § 429.160 (1992).

[136] *Id.*

[137] Williams Lumber & Mfg. Co. v. Ginsburg, 146 SW.2d 604, 606 (Mo. 1940).

fraud, regardless of whether the lien was perfected or filed within the time allowed by law.[138] A property owner or lessee who pays a subcontractor, materialman, supplier or laborer for the services or goods claimed pursuant to a lien, for which the original contractor, subcontractor or supplier has been paid, shall have a claim against the original contractor, subcontractor or supplier who failed or refused to pay the subcontractor, materialman, supplier or laborer.[139] Lien fraud is a class C felony if the amount of the lien filed or the aggregate amount of all liens filed on the subject property as a result of the conduct described above is in excess of five hundred dollars, otherwise lien fraud is a class A misdemeanor. If no liens are filed, lien fraud is a class A misdemeanor.[140]

§ 26.17 PROCEDURAL ISSUES

[A] Notice Requirements

[1] Original Contractor

Missouri has several specific notice requirements that must be strictly complied with when the interests of third parties are affected and that differ, depending upon the nature of the improvement. The "original contractor" who contracts directly with the owner must give a disclosure notice in writing to the owner in the language of the statute,[141] as a condition precedent to the establishment of any mechanics' lien in its favor. This notice must be given before receiving payment in any form, (1) either at the time of execution of the contract, (2) when the material is delivered, (3) when the work is commenced, or (4) delivered with the first invoice. The notice must be given in 10-point bold type and state:

> **NOTICE TO OWNER**
> **FAILURE OF THIS CONTRACTOR TO PAY THOSE PERSONS SUPPLYING MATERIAL OR SERVICES TO COMPLETE THIS CONTRACT CAN RESULT IN THE FILING OF A MECHANICS' LIEN ON THE PROPERTY WHICH IS THE SUBJECT OF THIS CONTRACT PURSUANT TO CHAPTER 429, RSMo. TO AVOID THIS RESULT YOU MAY ASK THIS CONTRACTOR FOR "LIEN WAIVERS" FROM ALL PERSONS SUPPLYING MATERIAL OR SERVICES FOR THE WORK DESCRIBED IN THIS CONTRACT. FAILURE TO SECURE LIEN**

---

[138] Mo. Rev. Stat. § 429.014.1 (1992).

[139] *Id.* § 429.014.2.

[140] *Id.* § 429.014.3.

[141] *Id.* § 429.012. The contractor must provide the statutorily mandated notice even if the owner is a large and sophisticated corporation. Landmark Sys., Inc. v. Delmar Redevelopment Corp., 900 S.W.2d 258, 261 (Mo. Ct. App. 1995). Even substantial compliance with Mo. Rev. Stat. § 429.012 may not be sufficient when the contractor provides no notice in writing to the person with whom the contract is made. Gauzy Excavating & Grading Co. v. Kersten Homes, Inc., 934 S.W.2d 303 (Mo. 1996).

WAIVERS MAY RESULT IN YOUR PAYING FOR LABOR AND MATERIAL TWICE.

This notice requirement does not apply to new residences for which the buyer has been furnished qualified title insurance protecting against mechanics' liens.

[2] Subcontractor, Supplier, Etc.

An additional requirement is made with regard to the repair or remodeling of, or additions to, owner-occupied residential property of four units or less. The owner must sign a "consent of owner," in 10-point bold type, in the following language:

CONSENT OF OWNER
CONSENT IS HEREBY GIVEN FOR FILING OF MECHANICS' LIENS BY ANY PERSON WHO SUPPLIES MATERIALS OR SERVICES FOR THE WORK DESCRIBED IN THIS CONTRACT ON THE PROPERTY ON WHICH IT IS LOCATED IF HE IS NOT PAID.

Such a consent form is a condition precedent to the creation of a lien by anyone other than an original contractor.[142]

In addition to these notice requirements, any person, other than an original contractor, must give a written notice to the owner, owners, or agent, or either of them, at least 10 days before filing a lien statement, stating that he holds a claim against the improvement, setting out the amount and from whom it is due.[143]

The statute is not clear in defining who is the "owner"—whether the owner at the time of the original contract or subcontract, or at the time of delivery of material or completion of the contract or subcontract. It is indicated in case law that it is at least the owner at the time both the principal contract and the subcontract are made.[144] The term "owner" is defined in the section dealing with subcontractors' liens on residential property.[145]

---

[142] Mo. Rev. Stat. § 429.013 (1992). For a discussion of the definition of "original contractor" requiring notice to the owner under § 429.012, *see* McKenney v. Joplin Union Station, Inc., 867 S.W.2d 245 (Mo. Ct. App. 1993). A contractor was an "original contractor" when it contracted directly with a prior owner who still owned record title at the time, even though that owner had contracted to sell the land to the current land owner; the current owner had not ordered any labor or materials or participated in any meaningful way in the formation or performance of the contract. Landmark Sys., Inc. v. Delmar Redevelopment Corp., 900 S.W.2d 258, 262 (Mo. Ct. App. 1995).

[143] Mo. Rev. Stat. § 429.100 (1992).

[144] R.D. Kurtz, Inc. v. Field, 223 Mo. App. 270, 14 S.W.2d 9 (Mo. Ct. App. 1929).

[145] Mo. Rev. Stat. § 429.013 (1992). It is substantially in accord with R.D. Kurtz, Inc. v. Field, 223 Mo. App. 270, 14 S.W.2d 9 (Mo. Ct. App. 1929). *See also* Dave Kolb Grading, Inc. v. Lieberman Corp., 837 S.W.2d 924 (Mo. Ct. App. 1992).

[B] Where to File

The lien statement itself must be filed with the clerk of the circuit court of the county in which the real estate is located against which the lien is claimed. There are special filing requirements for Jackson County (where Kansas City is principally located)[146] and Lewis County.[147] Filing fees are determined by the county and are partially based upon the number of pages.

[C] When to File

The lien statement itself must be filed within six months after the indebtedness has accrued. The phrase "after the indebtedness has accrued" used in the statute to specify when the lien must be filed has been interpreted to mean the last date on which labor was performed or the last date when material was furnished to the improvement by the claimant.[148] The time for filing a mechanics' lien statement is statutory and cannot be extended by waiver or by contract.[149]

§ 26.18 FORECLOSURE OF A MECHANICS' LIEN

Suit to enforce a mechanics' lien must be commenced within six months after the filing of the statement. Service of process must be issued for suit to be deemed filed.[150] A petition to enforce a mechanics' lien need not allege either the first or last day of work so long as it states that the lien was filed within six months after the indebtedness accrued.[151]

All parties to the contract for performance of the work must be made parties to the suit,[152] and the original contractor must be a party in a subcontractor's suit.[153] However, it has been held that a supplier claimant need not join the original contractor with the owner in its suit to enforce a mechanics' lien, but only the party with whom the claimant contracted.[154] To establish priority, both the trustee and the beneficiary under a deed of trust should be joined as parties. No specific time is provided by statute for obtaining a judgment to enforce a mechanics' lien, but "unreasonable delay" may be a defense.[155]

---

[146] Mo. Rev. Stat. § 478.483 (1987).

[147] *Id.* § 478.353.

[148] Harry Cooper Supply Co. v. Gillioz, 107 S.W.2d 798 (Mo. Ct. App. 1937).

[149] George F. Robertson Plastering Co. v. Altman, 430 S.W.2d 169 (Mo. 1968).

[150] Continental Elec. Co. v. Ebco, Inc., 375 S.W.2d 134 (Mo. 1964).

[151] Refrigeration Supplies, Inc. v. J.L. Mason Missouri, Inc., 872 S.W.2d 105, 107–08 (Mo. Ct. App. 1994).

[152] Vasquez v. Village Ctr., Inc., 362 S.W.2d 588 (Mo. 1962).

[153] Kinnear Mfg. Co. v. Meyers, 452 S.W.2d 599 (Mo. Ct. App. 1970).

[154] Tip-Top Plumbing & Heating v. Gregoric, 860 S.W.2d 22 (Mo. Ct. App. 1993).

[155] Hennis v. Tucker, 447 S.W.2d 580 (Mo. Ct. App. 1969).

§ 26.19 PRIORITY ISSUES

Missouri follows the "first spade rule," and all mechanics' liens relate back to the date of commencement of work or first furnishing of material under the general contract, with each lien holder sharing pro rata.[156] With regard to deeds of trust, a purchase money deed of trust has priority as to land over a mechanics' lien on new construction, but not as to subsequent improvements.[157]

A deed of trust given and recorded before commencement of work for the purpose of financing construction is subordinate to mechanics' lien claimants, both as to the subsequent improvements and land.[158] Mechanics' lien claims for repairs to existing improvements have priority over a prior recorded deed of trust as to the improvements but not the land.[159]

§ 26.20 SPECIAL RULES WHEN MORE THAN ONE CLAIM ASSERTED AGAINST PROPERTY

If two or more lien claims are asserted against the property, then an equitable mechanics' lien suit must be brought, joining all persons claiming interests in the property as disclosed by the public records.[160] The equitable action becomes the exclusive remedy, and all other mechanics' lien actions are stayed. All claimants must join in the action to enforce their liens.[161]

§ 26.21 REMEDIES OF OWNERS

The Missouri lien law has no provisions for allowing the owner to bond against mechanics' lien claims but does authorize the owner to demand lien waivers from the contractor, from all persons supplying material or services for the work described in the contract.[162]

§ 26.22 CLAIM AGAINST OWNER BY ONE NOT IN PRIVITY WITH OWNER

Missouri case law is uncertain as to whether the mechanics' lien statute provides the exclusive remedy to a subcontractor or materialman for a claim

---

[156] Mo. Rev. Stat. § 429.260 (1992). H.B. Deal Constr. Co. v. Labor Discount Ctr., Inc., 418 S.W.2d 940 (Mo. 1967).

[157] Union Elec. Co. v. Clayton Ctr., Ltd., 634 S.W.2d 261 (Mo. Ct. App. 1982).

[158] R.L. Sweet Lumber Co. v. E.L. Lane, Inc., 513 S.W.2d 365 (Mo. 1974).

[159] Mo. Rev. Stat. § 429.050 (1992).

[160] *Id.* § 429.280.

[161] *Id.* § 429.300. IMSE-Schilling Sash & Door Co. v. Kellems, 237 Mo. App. 960, 179 S.W.2d 910 (Mo. Ct. App. 1944).

[162] Mo. Rev. Stat. § 429.012 (Supp. 1999).

against the owner. At least one division of the Missouri Court of Appeals has so held.[163] Another division has allowed the subcontractor to claim for unjust enrichment when the owner has not paid the original contractor.[164]

---

[163] Green Quarries, Inc. v. Raasch, 676 S.W.2d 261 (Mo. Ct. App. 1984) (Western District). *See also* Moellering Concrete, Inc. v. Doerr, 784 S.W.2d 864 (Mo. Ct. App. 1990); Barbara v. Stuart, 708 S.W.2d 136 (Mo. Ct. App. 1989); Lee Bros. Contractors v. Christy Park Baptist Church, 706 S.W.2d 608 (Mo. Ct. App. 1986).

[164] International Paper Co. v. Futhey, 788 S.W.2d 303 (Mo. Ct. App. 1990) (Eastern District); Keopke Constr. v. Woodsage Constr., 844 S.W.2d 508 (Mo. Ct. App. 1992); Landmark Sys., Inc. v. Delmar Redevelopment Corp., 900 S.W.2d 258 (Mo. Ct. App. 1995) (current owner was not unjustly enriched when amount that it paid prior owner, which had contracted for removal and replacement of contaminated soil, for property reflected value placed on property free of contamination and there was no evidence showing that property was worth more than amount paid following contractor's cleanup); Moellering Concrete, Inc. v. Doerr, 784 S.W.2d 864 (Mo. Ct. App. 1990) (no unjust enrichment when owner paid contractor in full, even though contractor failed to pay subcontractor); Barbara v. Stuart, 780 S.W.2d 136 (Mo. Ct. App. 1989) (installer who was not subcontractor need not plead nonpayment of contractor by owner to recover in quantum meruit); Lee Bros. Contractors v. Christy Park Baptist Church, 706 S.W.2d 608 (Mo. Ct. App. 1986) (subcontractor must plead and prove nonpayment of contractor by owner to establish cause of action for quantum meruit).

CHAPTER 27

MONTANA

Lisa A. Banick

§ 27.01 CONSTRUCTION LIENS

The law governing mechanics' liens in Montana, now called construction liens, underwent a major overhaul in 1987.[1] One of the concerns of the legislators in revising the lien law was to eliminate the "secret lien."[2] The secret lien put an owner, unaware of all the potential lien claimants on the owner's project, at risk of having to pay twice for the same work, once to the contractor and again to an unpaid supplier, laborer or subcontractor. Therefore, the legislature added certain procedural notice and filing requirements that must be followed for a valid lien to arise.[3] The purpose of these procedural requirements is to impart notice to the owner of real property that a lien may be or has been filed, and to protect all parties dealing with the property, including subsequent purchasers. The procedural requirements must be closely followed, because the Montana Supreme Court has consistently held that the procedural requirements of the lien law will be strictly construed.[4] Once the procedures have been fulfilled, the lien law will be liberally construed to give effect to their remedial purpose.[5]

[A] Who May File a Lien

A person who furnishes services or materials pursuant to a real estate improvement contract may claim a construction lien to secure the payment of the contract price.[6] The contract price means the amount agreed upon by the contracting parties for performing services and furnishing materials covered by the contract, increased or diminished by the price of change orders or extras, any amounts attributable to altered specifications, or a breach of contract, including but not limited to defects in workmanship or materials.[7] If no price is agreed upon by the contracting parties, the contract price means the reasonable value of all services or materials covered by the contract.[8]

The contracting owner means a person who owns an interest in real estate and who, personally or through an agent, enters into an express or implied contract for the improvement of the real estate.[9] For the purpose of determining whether a person is a contracting owner, agency is presumed, in the absence of clear and

---

[1] MONT. CODE. ANN. § 71-3-521–563.

[2] Senate Judiciary Committee Minutes on Senate Bill 20 (Jan. 16, 1987 and Mar. 12, 1987).

[3] MONT. CODE ANN. § 71-3-521.

[4] Swain v. Battershell, 1999 MT 101, ___ P.2d ___ (Mont. 1999); General Elec. Supply Co. v. Bennett, 626 P.2d 844 (Mont. 1981); Cole v. Hunt, 211 P.2d 417 (Mont. 1949).

[5] General Elec. Supply Co. v. Bennett, 626 P.2d 844, 846 (Mont. 1981).

[6] MONT. CODE ANN. § 71-3-523.

[7] *Id.* § 71-3-522(3)(a).

[8] *Id.* § 71-3-522(3)(b).

[9] *Id.* § 71-3-522(4)(a).

convincing evidence to the contrary between an employer and employee, between spouses, between joint tenants, and among tenants in common.[10]

Under the lien law, a real estate improvement contract is an agreement to perform services, including labor, or to furnish materials for the purpose of producing a change in the physical condition of the real estate. A real estate improvement contract does not have to be in writing for a valid lien to exist.[11]

The statute identifies examples of services and materials that are considered a real estate improvement contract including:[12]

(1) alteration of the surface by excavation, fill, change in grade, or change in a shore, bank, or flood plain of a stream, swamp, or body of water;
(2) construction or installation on, above, or below the surface of land;
(3) demolition, repair, remodeling, or removal of a structure previously constructed or installed;
(4) seeding, sodding, or other landscape operation;
(5) surface or subsurface testing, boring, or analysis; and
(6) preparation of plans, surveys, or architectural or engineering plans or drawings for any change in the physical condition of the real estate, regardless of whether they are used to produce a change in the physical condition of the real estate.[13]

A real estate improvement contract does not include a contract for the mining or removal of timber, minerals, gravel, soil, sod, or things growing on the land or a similar contract in which the activity is primarily for the purpose of making the materials available for sale or use, or a contract for the planting, cultivation, or harvesting of crops or for the preparation of the soil for planting of crops.[14]

[B] Limitation of Lien for Materials

A lien for furnishing materials arises only if the materials are supplied with the intent that the materials are used in the course of construction of or incorporated into the improvement in connection with which the lien arises.[15] The intent can be shown by a contract of sale, a delivery order, delivery to the site by the lien claimant, or by other evidence.[16]

---

[10] *Id.* § 71-3-522(4)(b).

[11] M&R Constr. Co. v. Shea, 589 P.2d 138 (Mont. 1979); Smith v. Gunniss, 144 P.2d 186 (Mont. 1943).

[12] Mont. Code Ann. § 71-3-522(5)(a).

[13] This exception specifically overrules the holding in Kenneth D. Collins Agency v. Hagerott, 684 P.2d 487 (Mont. 1984), in which the Montana Supreme Court found that an architect did not have a lien for services to prepare plans and specifications for an improvement that was never built (interpreting Mont. Code Ann. § 71-3-501, now repealed).

[14] Mont. Code Ann. § 71-3-522(5)(b).

[15] *Id.* § 71-3-524(1)(a)(i).

[16] *Id.* § 71-3-524(1)(a)(ii).

The materials must be incorporated into the improvement or consumed as normal wastage in construction operations, specifically fabricated for incorporation into the improvement and not readily resalable in the ordinary course of the fabricator's business, even though the materials are not actually incorporated into the improvement.

A lien claimant can also lien for materials used for the construction or operation of machinery or equipment used in the course of construction and not remaining in the improvement, subject to diminution by the salvage value of those materials.[17]

A lien for the supplying of tools, appliances or machinery is limited to the reasonable rental value for the period of actual use, if the tools, appliances or machinery is rented. If they are purchased, the lien is for the price, but only if the tools, appliances or machinery were purchased for use in the particular improvement and have no substantial value after completion of the particular improvement.[18]

[C] Amount and Extent of Lien

A person who furnishes services or materials pursuant to a real estate improvement contract is entitled to a lien for the unpaid part of his contract price.[19] A person's lien is reduced by the sum of the liens of other persons claiming construction liens through that person.[20]

A construction lien extends to the interest of the contracting owner in the real estate as the interest exists at the commencement of work or is later acquired.[21] Commencement of work means the date of the first visible change in the physical condition of the real estate caused by the first person furnishing services or materials pursuant to a particular real estate improvement contract.[22]

If an improvement is located wholly on one or more platted lots belonging to the contracting owner, the lien applies to the improvement and to the lots on which the improvement is located.[23] If the improvement is not located wholly on one or more platted lots, the lien attaches to the improvement and to the smallest identifiable parcel of land on which the improvement is located.[24]

If the improvement is to leased premises, the lien applies to the improvement and to the leasehold term. The lien does not attach to the lessor's interest unless the lessor contracted for or agreed to the improvement before it was started.[25]

---

[17] *Id.* § 71-3-524(1)(b)(i)-(iii).
[18] *Id.* § 71-3-524(3).
[19] *Id.* § 71-3-526(1).
[20] *Id.* § 71-3-526(2).
[21] *Id.* § 71-3-525(1).
[22] *Id.* § 71-3-522(1).
[23] *Id.* § 71-3-525(2)(a).
[24] *Id.* § 71-3-525(2)(b).
[25] *Id.* § 71-3-525(3).

If the improvement is to premises held by a contracting owner who owns less than a fee simple interest or a lessee and lease is forfeited by the lessee, a construction lien is not impaired to the extent of the value of the work or improvement that is severable from the real estate.[26] If the work or improvement may be removed without harm to the rest of the real estate, the lienholder may have the value determined, the work or improvement sold separately to satisfy the lien.[27] The purchaser must remove the work or improvement within 45 days of the sale.[28]

If a contracting owner contracts for improvements on real estate not owned by him as part of an improvement on his real estate or for the purpose of directly benefitting his real estate, there is a lien against the contracting owner's real estate being improved or directly benefitted in favor of persons furnishing services or materials to the same extent as if the improvement had been on the contracting owner's real estate.[29]

[D] Notice of Right to Claim a Lien

Unless covered by one of the statutory exceptions, in order to claim a lien a person must give notice of the person's right to claim a lien to the contracting owner.[30] The notice must be given no later than 20 days after the date on which the services or materials are first furnished to the contracting owner. If notice is not given within this period, a lien is enforceable only for the services or materials furnished within the 20-day period before the date on which notice is given.[31]

When payment for services or materials is made by or on behalf of the contracting party from funds provided by a bank or other regulated lender and secured by an interest, lien, mortgage, or encumbrance for the purpose of paying the particular real estate improvement being liened, the notice period is extended to no later than 45 days after the date on which services or materials are first furnished to the contracting owner. If notice is not given within this period, a lien is enforceable only for the services or materials furnished within the 45-day period before the date on which notice is given.[32] This longer notice period does not apply to a contract for improvements for an owner-occupied residence.[33]

[1] Contents of Notice of Right to Claim a Lien

The notice of right to claim a lien must be in writing and state that it is a notice of a right to claim a lien against real estate for services or materials

[26] *Id.* § 71-3-525(4)(a).
[27] *Id.* § 71-3-525(4)(b).
[28] *Id.* § 71-3-525(4)(b).
[29] *Id.* § 71-5-525(5).
[30] *Id.* § 71-3-531(2).
[31] *Id.* § 71-3-531(3).
[32] *Id.* § 71-3-531(4).
[33] *Id.* § 71-3-531(4).

furnished in connection with improvement of the real estate.[34] The notice must contain a description sufficient to identify the real estate against which the lien may be claimed.[35] The notice must contain the information as specified in the suggested statutory form, which generally includes the following information: the name of the owner and the owner's address, the date of mailing or service, the name, address, telephone number and signature of the person providing the notice, a description of the services or materials, the property description, and other information about the ways the owner can protect against construction lien claims.[36]

Often a person who is required to provide notice of right to claim a lien does not know the name of the contracting owner or the property description. To assist a subcontractor or material supplier who must provide notice of right to claim a lien, the subcontractor or supplier can request that the contractor provide a property description, and the name and address of the contracting owner. This information must be furnished to the requestor with five business days.[37]

The notice of right to claim a lien must be sent to the contracting owner by certified mail or delivered personally to the contracting owner.[38] Notice by certified mail is effective on the date the notice is mailed. If the notice is delivered, written acknowledgment of receipt must be obtained from the owner. A person may not claim a construction lien unless the lien claimant has complied with the notice requirement.

A copy of the notice of right to claim a lien must be filed with the clerk and recorder of the county where the improved real estate is located.[39] This copy must be filed no later than five business days after the date on which the notice of right to claim a lien is given to the contracting owner. The signature of the person on the notice of right to claim a lien is not required to be acknowledged by a notary public as is required for other documents filed with the clerk and recorder.[40]

The notice filed with the clerk and recorder for the purpose of public notice is effective for one year from the date of filing. The notice lapses upon the expiration of the one-year period unless the person who may claim a lien files with the clerk and recorder a one-year continuation of the notice prior to the date on which the notice lapses.[41] The clerk and recorder may remove the notice from the public record when it lapses. The continuation statement must include the clerk and recorder's file number of the notice, the date on which the notice was

[34] *Id.* § 71-3-532(1).
[35] *Id.* § 71-3-532(2).
[36] *Id.* § 71-3-532(3).
[37] *Id.* § 71-3-531(7).
[38] *Id.* § 71-3-531(5).
[39] *Id.* § 71-3-531(6)(a).
[40] 42 Mont. A.G. Op. 53 (1988).
[41] MONT. CODE ANN. § 71-3-531(6)(c).

originally filed, and the name of the person to whom the original notice was given.[42]

[2] Exceptions to Notice of Right to Claim a Lien

There are certain exceptions to the requirement for providing a notice of right to claim a lien to the contracting owner. The following persons are not required to give a notice of right to claim a lien:

(1) a person who furnishes services or materials directly to the owner at his request;
(2) a wage earner or laborer who performs personal labor services for a person furnishing any service or material pursuant to a real estate improvement contract;
(3) a person who furnishes services or materials pursuant to a real estate improvement contract that relates to a dwelling for 5 or more families;
(4) a person who furnishes services or materials pursuant to a real estate improvement contract that relates to an improvement that is partly or wholly commercial in character.[43]

The scope of these exceptions has not been adjudicated in any reported Montana case.

[E] Attachment of Lien

A person's lien does not attach and may not be enforced unless, after entering into the contract under which the lien arises, the person has filed a lien not later than 90 days after the person's final furnishing of services or materials or the owner files a notice of completion.[44] The timeliness of filing the lien is often a "gray area" of the lien law, and the facts and circumstances of each case are controlling.[45]

A lien will be invalid if it is filed 90 days after the person last provided materials or services for the project. The final work performed must be to enhance the value of the construction project, and not be done solely to extend the time of the lien. The following work has been held sufficient to extend the deadline for filing a lien: repair of a malfunctioning computer card in an elevator[46] and work valued at $500 to relay carpet.[47]

A lien can also be invalid if it is filed too early. A lien that is filed before the person claiming the lien has substantially furnished services or materials

[42] *Id.* § 71-3-531(6)(c).
[43] *Id.* § 71-3-531(1).
[44] *Id.* § 71-3-535(1).
[45] Frank L. Pirtz Constr., Inc. v. Hardin Town Pump, Inc., 692 P.2d 460 (Mont. 1984).
[46] Devoe v. Gust. Lagerquist & Sons, Inc., 796 P.2d 579, 581 (Mont. 1990).
[47] Frank L. Pirtz Constr., Inc. v. Hardin Town Pump, Inc., 692 P.2d 460, 464 (Mont. 1984).

pursuant to a real estate improvement contract is not effective to create a construction lien unless the lien claimant is prevented from fulfilling the obligation because of the fault of another person.[48] In *Durand v. Dowdall,*[49] both Durand and Lien contracted with the lessee of certain property to remodel a service station into a restaurant. Durand worked for about ten weeks after which it became clear the lessee was not going to pay Durand, and Durand walked off the job, as did Lien. Durand and Lien both filed liens, and brought a lien foreclosure action. The Montana Supreme Court affirmed the trial court's decision that the liens of Durand and Lien were invalid. The Supreme Court found that the contractors failed to provide evidence that the lessee's nonpayment prevented them from completing the work, or that prompt payment was of the essence to completion of their work.

In *Western Plumbing of Bozeman v, Garrison,*[50] the homeowners contracted with Western Plumbing to install a plumbing system and fixtures for their home, and contracted with Metcalf to do certain masonry work. There was no specific agreement as to time of payment for the work. Western Plumbing and Metcalf both filed liens before completion of the work. Western Plumbing completed the rough-in plumbing, but did not hook-up the bathtub or two sinks, and none of the fixtures were installed. Metcalf had installed about 11,500 out of 14,560 bricks for the project. The Montana Supreme Court determined that neither contractor had substantially completed the work, and that the liens were invalid. The Court noted that the agreement between the homeowners and the contractors did not provide for periodic progress payments, and until substantial completion no obligation to pay arises. It will depend on the particular facts of each case whether the nonpayment of an progress payment permits the contractor to abandon the project and claim a lien.[51]

A lien attaches at the commencement of work.[52] Commencement of work means the date of the first visible change in the physical condition of the real estate caused by the first person furnishing services or materials pursuant to a particular real improvement contract.[53] A lien attaches when it is filed if the lien is filed for the preparation of plans, surveys, or architectural or engineering plans or drawings for any change in the physical condition of land or structures that

[48] MONT. CODE ANN. § 71-3-535(4).

[49] 757 P.2d 1302 (Mont. 1988).

[50] 556 P.2d 520 (Mont. 1976).

[51] *Compare* Intermountain Elec., Inc. v. Berndt, 518 P.2d 1168, 1170 (Mont. 1974) (subcontractor who voluntarily abandoned work for non-payment by contractor when work was 40% complete was not entitled to lien) *and* Olson v. Westfork Properties, Inc., 557 P.2d 821 (Mont. 1976) (sewer and water contractor had invalid lien where contractor walked off job, and several hundred feet of water line leaked and backfill was not done according to the specifications) *with* Bauer v. Cook, 596 P.2d 200 (Mont. 1979) (contractor had valid lien where contractor presented evidence that he could not continue work without payment and owners' demand for completion of thirty-one items before payment was found to be total breach).

[52] MONT. CODE ANN. § 71-3-535(5).

[53] *Id.* § 71-3-522(1).

are not used incident to producing a change in the physical condition of the real estate.[54]

[F] Notice of Completion

As noted above, the owner can start the clock ticking on the deadline to file a lien by filing a notice of completion. The contracting owner may file a notice of completion at any time after the completion of any work or improvement.[55] The following acts or events constitute completion of any work or improvement for the purpose of filing a notice of completion:

(1) the written acceptance by the contracting owner, his agent, or representative of the building improvement or structure, but the filing of a notice of completion is not considered as an acceptance of the building improvement or other structure;
(2) the cessation from labor for 30 days upon any building, improvement or structure, or the alteration, addition to, or repair.[56]

The notice of completion together with an affidavit of publication must be filed in the office of the county clerk and recorder of the county where the property is located and must set forth the following information:

(1) the date when the work or improvement was completed or the date on which cessation from labor occurred first and the period of its duration;
(2) the contracting owner's name and address and the nature of the title, if any, of the person signing the notice;
(3) a description of the property sufficient for identification;
(4) the name of the contractor, if any.[57]

The notice must be verified by the contracting owner or the contracting owner's agent.[58] A copy of the notice of completion must be published once each week for three consecutive weeks in a newspaper of general circulation in the county where the land on which the work or improvement was performed is situated.[59] The contracting owner must also give a copy of the notice of completion to any person who has given the contracting owner a notice of a right to claim a lien.

[G] Notification to Owner of Lien

The person claiming a lien must serve a copy of the lien upon each owner of record of the property named in the lien. Service must be made by personal

[54] *Id.* § 71-3-535(6).
[55] *Id.* § 71-3-533(1).
[56] *Id.* § 71-3-533(2).
[57] *Id.* § 71-3-533(3).
[58] *Id.* § 71-3-533(4).
[59] *Id.* § 71-3-533(6).

service on each owner or by mailing a copy of the lien by certified or registered mail with return receipt requested to each owner's last known address.[60] When the requirements for service by mail are followed, service is complete. It is irrelevant to such service who actually receives the notice that has been properly mailed.[61]

[H] Contents of Lien Notice

There is a suggested form of a construction lien contained in the statute.[62] Generally, the lien form must include the following information:

(1) the name and address of the person claiming the lien;
(2) a description of the real property sufficient to identify it;
(3) the name of the person who owns the real property and the name of the person who entered into the contract to improve it;
(4) the name and address of the person with whom the lien claimant contracted to furnish services or materials;
(5) a description of the services or materials provided;
(6) the amount remaining unpaid or if no amount was fixed by the contract, a good faith estimate of the amount identified as such;
(7) the date the services or materials were first furnished by the lien claimant;
(8) the date the lien claimant last furnished services or materials, or if the date has not yet occurred, an estimate of the date on which services or materials will be last furnished and identify the date as an estimate;
(9) the date that the lien claimant gave notice of the right to claim a lien and the name of the person such notice was given, or if notice was not required to be given, identify the exception.[63]

A failure to identify correctly the owner or person whose interest in property is sought to be charged on the notice of lien is fatal to the lien.[64] In *Swain v. Battershell,*[65] the contractor, Battershell, hired Swain to do some concrete work at a mall. Battershell told Swain that he was the owner of the property, when in fact, he was not the owner. Swain performed the concrete work, but Battershell refused to pay Swain after a dispute arose about the quality of the work. Swain filed a lien naming Battershell as the contracting owner. The Montana Supreme Court determined that the misidentification of the owner made the lien invalid.

---

[60] *Id.* § 71-3-534(2).

[61] Sheridan Ready Mix, Inc. v. First Congregation Church of Plentywood, 695 P.2d 456, 461 (Mont. 1985).

[62] MONT. CODE ANN. § 71-3-536.

[63] *Id.* § 71-3-535(3).

[64] Swain v. Battershell, 1999 MT 101, ___ P.2d ___ (Mont. 1999); Cascade Elec. Co., Inc. v. Associated Creditors, Inc., 224 P.2d 146 (Mont. 1950); Blose v. Havre Oil & Gas Co., 31 P.2d 738 (Mont. 1934).

[65] 1999 MT 101, ___ P.2d ___ (Mont. 1999).

Even though Battershell told Swain that he was the owner, Swain had constructive notice of the actual owner of the property through the title records of the clerk and recorder.

Whether the court will apply such a strict construction to the property description in the lien depends on the parties involved. The Montana Supreme Court has said that it will construe the adequacy of the property description more strictly against a lien claimant where third parties are involved than where only the owners themselves are involved, and are presumed to know the location of the property.[66] In *General Elec. Supply Co. v. Bennett,*[67] the lien claimant filed a lien and identified the property as the "office building located on Lots 7 and 8 in Block 1 of Valley View Acres Subdivision." The building was actually located on Lot 9. The invoices attached to the filed lien refer to the "Bennett Office Building." One of the owners of the property was Gary Bennett. In the foreclosure action, the trial court found that the lien was invalid because of the incorrect property description. The Montana Supreme Court reversed. The Court first noted that if, by rejecting what is erroneous in the description, enough remains to identify the particular property sought to be charged, the lien will be upheld.[68] The Court ruled that taken together, the reference to the office building, and the correct block and subdivision were sufficient to identify the property, especially since the owners of the property were the only party involved.

[I] Filing of Lien with County Clerk

The lien must be filed with the county clerk and recorder of the county in which the improved real estate is located.[69] The person claiming the lien must certify to the county clerk and recorder that a copy of the lien has been served on the owner of record and must state whether service was made by delivery or by certified or registered mail.[70]

The signature of the person signing the lien and the signature of the person signing the certification of notification of the property owners must be acknowledged by the person executing it, or if executed by a corporation, by its president, vice president, secretary, assistant secretary or other person duly authorized by corporate resolution and the signature notarized.[71]

[J] Priority of Lienholders

There is equal priority between or among construction lien claimants who contribute to the same real estate improvement project, regardless of the date that

[66] General Elec. Supply Co. v. Bennett, 626 P.2d 844, 847 (1981).
[67] 626 P.2d 844 (1981).
[68] *Id.* at 846.
[69] *Id.* § 71-3-535(2)(a).
[70] *Id.* § 71-3-534(2).
[71] *Id.* § 71-21-203.

the lien claimant first contributed services or materials, and regardless of the date on which the person filed the notice of lien.[72] When the proceeds of a foreclosure sale are not sufficient to pay all construction lien claimants, each claimant receives a pro rata share of the proceeds based on the amount of the respective liens.[73] Construction liens attaching at different times have priority in the order of attachment.[74]

[1] Priority of Liens Compared with Other Claims

A construction lien has priority over any other interest, lien, mortgage, or encumbrance that may attach to the building, structure, or improvement or on the real property on which the building, structure, or improvement is located and which is filed after the construction lien attaches.[75] An interest, lien, mortgage or encumbrance that is filed before the construction lien attaches has priority over a construction lien with two exceptions.

A construction lien has priority, to the extent of the value of the work or improvement that is severable, over an interest, lien, mortgage, or encumbrance that is filed before the construction lien attaches. If the work or improvement may be removed without harm to the rest of the real property, the lien holder may have the value determined, the work or improvement sold separately on foreclosure, and the proceeds used to satisfy the construction lien.[76]

A construction lien has priority over any interest, lien, mortgage, or encumbrance that is filed before the construction lien attached if that interest, lien mortgage, or encumbrance was taken to secure advances made for the purpose of paying for the particular real estate improvement being liened.[77] The rationale behind this exception, as explained by the Montana Supreme Court in *Home Interiors, Inc. v. Hendrickson,*[78] is that a party that lends money to a landowner for a real estate improvement is in the best position to protect against non-payment by the landowner by either withholding funds or by requiring the landowner to obtain lien waivers from the potential lien claimants.

[K] Substitution of Bond

Whenever a construction lien has been filed upon real property or any improvements on the property, the contracting owner of any interest in such property, may at any time before the lien claimant has commenced a lien fore-

[72] *Id.* § 71-3-541.
[73] *Id.* § 71-3-541(1).
[74] *Id.* § 71-3-541(2).
[75] *Id.* § 71-3-542(1).
[76] *Id.* § 71-3-542(3).
[77] *Id.* § 71-3-542(4).
[78] 692 P.2d 1229 (Mont. 1984) (applying former MONT. CODE ANN. § 71-3-502(4)); Beck v. Hanson, 589 P.2d 141 (Mont. 1979).

closure action, file a bond with the clerk of district court in the county where the property is located.

In *James Talcott Constr. Inc. v. P&D Land Enterprises,*[79] Talcott Construction brought an action to foreclose on its construction lien on condominiums. Mountain Bank filed an irrevocable letter of credit with the court on behalf of P&D, 10 days after the lien foreclosure action was started, and the court entered an order dissolving the lien. Talcott appealed and argued that the bond must be filed before the action is commenced. The lower court determined that the statute provided that the bond "may" be filed at any time before the action, but it is not mandatory and the bond can be filed after the action is commenced. The Montana Supreme Court recognized that the right to retain a lien until the debt secured by the lien is paid is a substantive property right. The Montana Supreme Court determined that the statute means that a bond does not have to be filed, but that if one is filed, it must be before the action is commenced.[80] For this reason, a lien claimant sometimes believes it is an appropriate strategy to file simultaneously a lien and a lien foreclosure complaint to take away the property owner's ability to substitute a bond.

The bond must be in amount equal to one and one-half times the amount of the lien and must be either in cash or written by a corporate surety company. If written by a corporate surety company, the bond must be approved by a judge of the district court where the bond is filed.[81] The bond has to be conditioned that if the lien claimant is finally adjudged to recover upon the claim upon which the lien is based, the principal or the surety must pay to the claimant the amount of the judgment, together with any interest, costs, attorneys' fees, and other sums which the claimant may be entitled to recover.[82]

If a bond is filed, the lien against the property is discharged and released in full and the bond is substituted for the lien.[83] An action can be maintained against the bond, and must be commenced within the statute of limitations applicable to a lien foreclosure action.[84]

[L] Lien Foreclosure Action

All persons interested in the property with the lien or having liens on the property may be made parties.[85] The owner or person whose interest is sought to be charged is a necessary party to the action.[86] All actions to foreclose on a lien must be brought within two years from the date of filing the lien.[87] A successful

[79] 862 P.2d 395 (Mont. 1993).

[80] James Talcott Constr., Inc. v. P&D Land Enters., 862 P.2d 395 (Mont. 1993).

[81] Mont. Code Ann. § 71-3-551(2).

[82] *Id.* § 71-3-551(3).

[83] *Id.* § 71-3-552.

[84] *Id.* § 71-3-553(2).

[85] *Id.* § 71-3-561.

[86] Cascade Elec. Co. v. Associated Creditors, Inc., 224 P.2d 146 (Mont. 1950).

[87] Mont. Code Ann. § 71-3-562.

lien claimant is entitled to recover the money paid for filing and recording the lien and a reasonable attorneys' fee in the district and supreme courts, and a defendant against whose property a lien is claimed is entitled to recover reasonable attorneys' fee if the lien is not established in the lien foreclosure action.[88]

[M] Satisfaction of Lien

If the debt which is a lien upon any real estate, structure, building, or other improvement is paid and satisfied, it is the duty of the lien claimant to acknowledge satisfaction, and if a lien claimant fails to do so, he is liable to any person injured by such failure.[89] Therefore, if a lien claimant is paid after filing a lien and the debt is satisfied, the lien claimant should provide the owner with a signed and acknowledged satisfaction of lien. The satisfaction of lien is filed with the county clerk and recorder where the property is located.

§ 27.02 BONDS

Generally there are three parties involved with the execution of a bond: the principal, the obligee, and the surety. The principal is the party that obtains the bond, and for a construction project the principal is usually the contractor. The obligee is the beneficiary of the bond, and is usually the owner of the project. The surety is the bonding company who agrees to be responsible for the obligation of the principal.[90] Often there is an additional party to a bond called the indemnitor, who guarantees the obligation of the principal to the surety in the event that the principal defaults. While there is no requirement that bonds be provided for private construction projects, there are statutory bonding requirements for public projects. The discussion below focuses on the bonding requirements for public construction projects.

[A] Bid Bonds

Bid bonds are required on all public projects, including state, county, municipal, and school district projects.[91] A bid bond is evidence of the good faith on the part of a bidder, and secures the obligation of the successful bidder to enter into the contract at the bid price.[92] The public entity must specify the amount of the bid bond in the advertisement for bids, which cannot be less than 10 percent of the bid price.[93]

Acceptable forms of security for the bid bond include a surety bond executed by a surety corporation authorized to do business in Montana, as well as cash and

---

[88] *Id.* § 71-3-124; Kosena v. Eck, 635 P.2d 1287 (Mont. 1981).
[89] MONT. CODE ANN. § 71-3-537.
[90] *See id.* § 28-11-401.
[91] *Id.* § 18-1-201(1).
[92] *Id.* § 18-1-201(2).
[93] *Id.* § 18-1-202(2).

certain other bank instruments.[94] The bid bonds must be returned to the bidders whose bids are not accepted.[95] If a bid is accepted or a contract is awarded and the successful bidder refuses to sign the proposed contract, the bidder forfeits the posted security, whether it is money, bank instruments, or is liable for the amount of the bid bond.[96] The bidder's liability is limited to the bid bond amount specified by the public authority in the advertisement for bids.[97]

[B] Performance Bonds

A performance bond secures the contractor's obligation to perform all of the provisions of the contract. Performance bonds are required on all public projects, including state, county, municipal, city and town projects.[98] The state or other governmental entity may waive the requirement for a performance bond for building and construction projects that cost less than $50,000.[99] A school district may waive the requirement for a performance bond for building and construction projects that cost less than $7,500.[100]

The bond or other security must be in an amount equal to the full contract price agreed to be paid for the work or improvement and must be to the state of Montana.[101] For a city or town, the municipality may by general ordinance fix the amount of the security and the name of the secured party, but the amount of the security cannot be less than 25 percent of the contract price.[102]

[C] Payment Bonds

Labor and material payment bonds are required on public projects, including state, county, municipal, city and town projects.[103] The payment bond secures the obligation of the contractor to pay all laborers, mechanics, subcontractors, and material suppliers, and to pay all persons who supply the contractor or subcontractors with provisions, provender, material, or supplies for performing the work.[104] The statute requiring payment bonds will be liberally construed to effectuate the overall purpose of compensating those who contribute materials and supplies to a public project.[105]

---

[94] *Id.* § 18-1-203.
[95] *Id.* § 18-1-205.
[96] *Id.* § 18-1-204(1).
[97] *Id.* § 18-1-204(2).
[98] *Id.* § 18-2-201(1).
[99] *Id.* § 18-2-201(4).
[100] *Id.* § 18-2-201(5).
[101] *Id.* § 18-2-203.
[102] *Id.*
[103] *Id.* § 18-2-201(1).
[104] *Id.* § 18-2-201(1)(b)-(c).
[105] Luciano v. Northwest Pipe and Casing Co., 870 P.2d 99, 101 (Mont. 1994).

As for performance bonds, the state or other governmental entity may waive the requirement for a payment bond for building and construction projects that cost less than $50,000.[106] A school district may waive the requirement for a payment bond for building and construction projects that cost less than $7,500.[107] Instead of a surety bond, a governmental entity may accept cash or certain bank instruments.[108] If the governmental entity fails to obtain the bond or other security, the governmental entity is liable to the laborers, mechanics, subcontractors, and material suppliers and persons supplying subcontractors with materials and supplies for the full amount of the debt of any subcontractor or contractor.[109]

The bond or other security must be in an amount equal to the full contract price agreed to be paid for the work or improvement and must be to the state of Montana.[110] For a city or town, the municipality may by general ordinance fix the amount of the security and the name of the secured party, but the amount of the security cannot be less than 25 percent of the contract price.[111]

[1] Right of Action on Bond and Notice to Governmental Entity

All laborers, mechanics, subcontractors, and material suppliers, and all persons who supply any entity or person or subcontractor with provisions, provender, materials, or supplies for performing the work can sue in their own name on the bond or other security furnished by the contractor.[112] There is no right to sue unless within 90 days after the completion of the contract with an acceptance of the work by the appropriate representative of the governmental entity, the laborer, mechanic, material supplier, or subcontractor presents to and files with the appropriate representative of the governmental entity a notice in writing of such person's claim against the bond or other security.[113] The notice required within 90 days after completion and acceptance of the work may not be construed to prevent or delay the payment of money due the contractor under the terms of the contract.[114]

The statute contains a suggested form for providing written notice to the governmental entity. The form requires that the notice must identify the name of the person who provided the work or materials, the amount of the claim, the name of the principal and the person providing the bond or other security, a description of the work, and must be signed by the person providing the notice.[115]

---

[106] MONT. CODE ANN. § 18-2-201(4).
[107] *Id.* § 18-2-201(5).
[108] *Id.* § 18-2-201(3).
[109] *Id.* § 18-2-203.
[110] *Id.*
[111] *Id.*
[112] *Id.* § 18-2-205(1).
[113] *Id.* § 18-2-204(1).
[114] *Id.* § 18-2-208(3).
[115] *Id.* § 18-2-204(1).

[2] Notice to Contractor of Right of Action on the Security

A person or entity furnishing provender, provisions, materials, or supplies for a public project must, not later than 30 days after the date of the first delivery to a subcontractor or subcontractor's agent give a written notice of a right of action on the bond or security.[116] The written notice must be delivered personally or sent by certified mail to the contractor.[117] The written notice must state that it is a notice of a right of action on the security, that the person or entity giving the notice has started to deliver provender, provisions, materials or supplies, the name of the subcontractor or agent who placed the order or to whom the items were delivered, and that the contractor and the contractor's security will be held for the unpaid price if the person or entity is not paid.[118] Failure to give the specified written notice will preclude a lawsuit against the contractor or the bond or other security.[119]

The statute specifically provides that any other type of actual or constructive notice is not sufficient.[120] This provision was added to the statute following the decision in *Robintech, Inc. v. White & McNeil Excavating, Inc.*[121] In *Robintech,* White & McNeil was the general contractor for a water main improvement project. White & McNeil contracted with Waterworks Supplies Co. to supply the pipe. Waterworks in turn contracted with Robintech to supply the pipe. White & McNeil knew that Robintech was supplying the pipe, and a representative of White & McNeil signed for the pipe at the job. The packing lists and receipts were on Robintech letterhead. Robintech gave the required written notice to the city of its claim against the bond, and sent a copy of this notice to White & McNeil. However, Robintech did not give White & McNeil separate written notice as required by § 18-2-206. White & McNeil challenged Robintech's claim against the bond for failure to give White & McNeil written notice. The Montana Supreme Court determined that the statutory notice was waived and the notice provisions were satisfied if the contractor had actual knowledge that materials were being furnished by a particular supplier and consented to this. The packing lists and receipts satisfied the notice requirement.

Because the legislature specifically added language that any other type of actual or constructive notice is not sufficient, it appears that a subcontractor or supplier who failed to give the required notice might not be able to rely on the *Robintech* decision. While there is no reported court decision that interprets and applies the new statutory language, the prudent supplier of provender, provisions,

---

[116] *Id.* § 18-2-206(1).
[117] *Id.* § 18-2-206(2)(a).
[118] *Id.* § 18-2-206(2)(b).
[119] *Id.* § 18-2-206(4).
[120] *Id.* § 18-2-206(3).
[121] 709 P.2d 631 (Mont. 1985).

materials or supplies to a subcontractor on a public project should give timely written notice entitled "Notice of Right of Action on the Security" and include the information required by the statute.

[3] Attorneys' Fees

In a lawsuit brought against the surety or other person liable on the security, the prevailing party is entitled to recover reasonable attorneys' fees. Attorneys' fees will not be allowed in action brought before the expiration of 30 days following the date of filing of the notice required to be given to the contractor.[122]

[4] Exceptions

The statute includes an exception that states that the provisions of the statute do not apply to money loaned or advanced to a contractor, subcontractor, or other person in the performance of the work.[123] In *Luciano v. Northwest Pipe and Casing Co.,*[124] the Montana Supreme Court addressed the scope of this exception. Luciano, the general contractor, entered into a contract with Petroleum Pipe to supply pipe and materials for an irrigation district project. Petroleum Pipe then contracted with Northwest Pipe to provide the pipe. Luciano paid Petroleum Pipe for the pipe, but Petroleum never paid Northwest. Petroleum then filed for bankruptcy. Luciano claimed that because he had advanced funds to his subcontractor, Petroleum Pipe, the subcontractor's supplier, Northwest, was precluded from seeking payment against Luciano's bond under the noted exception. The Court commented that the language of the relevant statute is hardly a model of clarity, and because the statute was enacted in 1931 there is no available legislative history.[125] The Court determined that the statutory exception only prevents a subcontractor or other person from making a claim against the contractor's bond if the contractor has loaned or advanced money to that specific subcontractor or other person. Since Luciano had advanced money to Petroleum, not Northwest, Northwest was entitled to recover against Luciano's bond.

[D] Statute of Limitations

The terms and conditions of the particular bond should be reviewed for any deadline on the time to bring a lawsuit. Generally, the bond has a shorter statute of limitations than the applicable statutory statute of limitations for contracts.

[122] *Id.* § 18-2-207.
[123] *Id.* § 18-2-208(1).
[124] 870 P.2d 99 (Mont. 1994).
[125] *Id.* at 101.

Often the performance bond and payment bond require that a lawsuit must be brought within one year after final payment under the contract.

[E] Extent of Surety's Liability on Bond

In Montana, surety bonds are generally regarded as contracts of insurance and are construed most strongly against the surety and in favor of coverage.[126] Generally, a surety cannot be held liable beyond the express terms of its contract.[127] For example, although a surety bond and the underlying contract must be read together, the surety's obligations are not necessarily coextensive with the obligations of the principal in the underlying contract.

In *Treasure State Industries v. Welch,*[128] an unpaid material supplier, Treasure State sued to collect on the subcontractor's performance bond which named the general contractor as the obligee. Treasure State contended that the performance of the subcontract includes payment of material suppliers, and thus the performance bond should extend to protect unpaid material suppliers. The Montana Supreme Court found that the bond was not intended to protect third-party material suppliers, only the general contractor as the named obligee, because the bond did not include any specific condition or promise concerning payment of material suppliers.

Sureties are subject to the provisions of Montana's Unfair Claim Settlement Practices Act, which prohibits certain claims practices.[129] Thus, if a surety fails to act fairly and in good faith in handling claims under a bond and violates the Act, a claimant, in addition to contract remedies, may be compensated under tort law.

---

[126] State v. American Sur. Co., 255 P. 761 (Mont. 1930).

[127] *Id.* § 28-11-411.

[128] 567 P.2d 947 (Mont. 1977); *see also* Pioneer Concrete & Fuel, Inc. v. Apex Constr., Inc., 664 P.2d 938 (1983).

[129] K-W Indus. v. National Sur. Corp., 754 P.2d 502 (Mont. 1988).

CHAPTER 28

NEBRASKA

Victor E. Covalt, III

§ 28.01 INTRODUCTION

On private projects, Nebraska provides for construction lien rights in favor of contractors, subcontractors, and materialmen under the Nebraska Construction Lien Act. (Lien Act).[1] The Lien Act allows posting of payment bonds in substitution for lien rights both before and after filing of a lien.[2]

There are no construction lien rights on public projects in Nebraska.[3] The prime contractor on public jobs must post a payment bond for the total contract price to insure payment for labor, materials, and the rental of equipment for public improvements for state projects costing more than $15,000 for a state project and for any other public project with a price of more than $5,000.[4]

Performance bonds and bid bonds are statutorily required on state contracts over $40,000 for erection and improvement of buildings, but are not otherwise statutorily required on public projects.[5] However, performance bonds and bid bonds are often requested as part of the bid specifications for public and private jobs.

§ 28.02 BOND LAW

[A] General Concepts

[1] Contract Interpretation

In Nebraska, a construction surety bond is treated as a third-party beneficiary contract.[6] The surety is bound by and its liability is measured by the strict terms of its contract.[7] The bond and the underlying construction contract are read together to determine the extent of the surety's liability.[8]

In order to recover on a bond, a claimant must establish the intention of the parties to the bond to protect the claimant from the express language of the bond.[9]

---

[1] Neb. Rev. Stat. §§ 52-125 to -159 (Reissue 1998).

[2] *Id.* §§ 52-141, -142.

[3] *Id.* § 52-132.

[4] *Id.* §§ 52-118 to -118.02.

[5] *Id.* § 72-803(3) (Reissue 1996).

[6] *See, e.g.,* Haakinson & Beaty Co. v. Inland Ins. Co., 216 Neb. 426, 431, 344 N.W.2d 454, 458 (1984).

[7] Farmers Union Coop. Ass'n v. Mid-States Constr. Co., 212 Neb. 146, 153, 322 N.W.2d 373, 377 (1982) (quoting Rawleigh Co. v. Smith, 142 Neb. 529, 531, 9 N.W.2d 286, 284 (1943)). *See* Cagle, Inc. v. Sammons, 198 Neb. 595, 600, 254 N.W.2d 398, 402 (1977).

[8] Dealers Elec. Supply Co. v. United States Fidelity & Guar. Co., 199 Neb. 269, 258 N.W.2d 131 (1977). However, terms in the bond that contradict the terms of the underlying contract do not necessarily modify the underlying contract. *See* American Sur. Co. v. School Dist. No. 64, 117 Neb. 6, 219 N.W. 583 (1928).

[9] Dealers Elec. Supply Co. v. United States Fidelity & Guar. Co., 199 Neb. 269, 258 N.W.2d 131 (1977). *See* Cagle, Inc. v. Sammons, 198 Neb. 595, 254 N.W.2d 398 (1977) (takeover contractor

A claimant, as a third-party beneficiary, is bound by all of the terms and conditions of the bond.[10]

[a] Ambiguities

Ambiguous bond language has been interpreted under a variety of principles, including in accordance with the purposes of any applicable statute, in accordance with the intent of the parties at the time of contracting, against the surety for compensation, and in favor of the objectively reasonable expectations of the obligee.[11]

[b] Statutory Bond

Bonds issued pursuant to a statutory requirement incorporate the requirements of the statute. If the terms of the statute are in conflict with the terms of the bond, the terms of the statute control.[12] The statutes are given a liberal construction to effect the remedial purposes of the legislature.[13]

Failure of the state to formally accept or approve a statutory bond may or may not be a defense to a surety's liability thereon.[14] "Release of sureties, through mere technicalities, is not to be encouraged."[15]

[c] Extra Work

Quantum meruit claims for extra work may form the basis of recovery against the surety on the project.[16]

---

cannot make claim on payment bond; may recover on equitable subrogation); Twin City Plaza, Inc. v. Central Sur. & Ins. Corp., 409 F.2d 1195 (8th Cir. 1969) (owner who directly contracts with subcontractor to reconstruct work cannot recover from general contractor's surety; direct obligation supersedes prior legal relationship).

[10] Haakinson & Beaty Co. v. Inland Ins. Co., 216 Neb. 426, 431, 344 N.W.2d 454, 458 (1984).

[11] *See* Cornett v. White Motor Corp., 190 Neb. 496, 209 N.W.2d 341 (1973); Abel v. Southwest Cas. Co., 182 Neb. 605, 610, 156 N.W.2d 166 (1968); American Sur. Co. v. School Dist. No. 64, 117 Neb. 6, 219 N.W. 583 (1928); C.F. Iddings Co. v. Lincoln Constr. Co., 104 Neb. 124, 175 N.W. 643 (1920).

[12] State v. Easley, 207 Neb. 443, 446-47, 299 N.W.2d 439, 441-42 (1980). *See* C.F. Iddings Co. v. Lincoln Constr. Co., 104 Neb. 124, 127, 175 N.W. 643, 644 (1920).

[13] McElhonse v. Universal Sur. Co., 182 Neb. 847, 858, 158 N.W.2d 228, 235 (1968); Peter Kiewit Sons' Co. v. National Cas. Co., 142 Neb. 835, 849-50, 8 N.W.2d 192, 199 (1943).

[14] *See* NEB. REV. STAT. § 52-118(3) (Reissue 1998) (public construction contract must be bonded); Nye-Schneider-Fowler Co. v. Roweser, 104 Neb. 389, 177 N.W.2d 750 (1920) (failure to obtain second surety as required voids bond as to executing surety). *But see* State v. Easley, 207 Neb. 443, 446, 299 N.W.2d 439, 441 (1981) (bond for child support obligation).

[15] C.F. Iddings Co. v. Lincoln Constr. Co., 104 Neb. 124, 127, 175 N.W. 643, 644 (1920).

[16] Reischick Drilling Co. v. American Cas. Co., 208 Neb. 142, 303 N.W.2d 264 (1981).

[d] Attorneys' Fees

Recovery of attorneys' fees for a successful claimant is mandatory.[17]

[e] Choice of Law

Nebraska will enforce selection of forum clauses in bonds.[18] As to choice-of-law issues, Nebraska will recognize rationally based choice-of-law selection provisions, and in absence thereof will apply the law of the place of performance.[19]

[f] Equitable Subrogation

Nebraska recognizes the doctrine of equitable subrogation wherein the surety who performs upon its bond becomes subrogated to all rights of the persons to whom payment of performance was rendered.[20]

[B] Performance Bonds

In Nebraska, performance bonds are required to secure "faithful performance" of any contract let by the state in excess of $40,000 for the erection, repair, or improvement of public buildings.[21] Otherwise, performance bonds are not required in Nebraska for either public or private projects.[22]

[1] Contract Interpretation

The surety's liability on a performance bond is limited to the express language of its undertaking.[23] The Nebraska Supreme Court has held that a

---

[17] *Id. See* NEB. REV. STAT. § 44-359 (Reissue 1998); *id.* § 52-141(REISSUE 1998).

[18] Haakinson & Beaty Co. v. Inland Ins. Co., 216 Neb. 426, 344 N.W.2d 454 (1984); NEB. REV. STAT. §§ 25-413 to -417 (Reissue 1995) (Model Uniform Choice of Forum Act).

[19] *See* First Mid-Am., Inc. v. MCI Communications Corp., 212 Neb. 57, 59, 321 N.W.2d 424, 425 (1982) (not a surety case); Farm Mortgage & Loan Co. v. Beale, 113 Neb. 293, 202 N.W. 877 (1925) (promissory note). *Cf.* Twin Plaza, Inc. v. Central Sur. & Ins. Corp., 409 F.2d 1195 (8th Cir. 1969) (Nebraska law applied to Iowa project without discussion).

[20] *See, e.g.,* Indemnity Ins. Co. v. Lane Contracting Co., 227 F. Supp. 143 (D. Neb. 1964); Cagle, Inc. v. Sammons, 198 Neb. 595, 254 N.W.2d 398 (1977); *see also* Smith & Covalt, *Should the Surety Stand on Its Equitable Subrogation Rights or File Its Indemnity Agreement under the Uniform Commercial Code,* 69 Neb. L. Rev. 664 (1990).

[21] NEB. REV. STAT. § 72-803 (Reissue 1996); *id.* § 83-134 (Cum. Supp. 1998).

[22] *Cf.* NEB. REV. STAT. §§ 52-118 to -118.03 (Reissue 1998) (payment bond required); *id.* §§ 39-1348 to -1354 (Reissue 1998) (state highway contracts); *id.* §§ 70-637 to -649 (Reissue 1996) (public power district contracts); *id.* §§ 73-101 to-105 (Reissue 1996) (public lettings); *id.* § 73-106 (Reissue 1996) (school district contracts).

[23] Farmers Union Coop. Ass'n v. Mid-States Constr. Co., 212 Neb. 147, 153, 322 N.W.2d 373, 377 (1982).

materialman may recover on a performance bond if the underlying contract requires the payment of claims for materials and labor.[24]

[2] Notice Requirements

Failure to give timely notice of default pursuant to the terms of the bond will bar liability if such failure prejudices the surety.[25] Similarly, when the owner lets a new contract to correct or modify unsatisfactory work without notice to the general contractor or the surety, the surety on the original contract is not liable for the costs of reconstruction.[26]

[3] Statute of Limitations

The surety's liability to the owner on a performance bond has been held to be limited to the duration of the contractor's warranty to repair or replace defective work.[27]

Although the statute of limitations for actions in written contracts in Nebraska is five years, there is a special statute limiting commencement of actions on breach of warranty as to real property improvements to four years after discovery of the breach if discovered thereafter and barring actions entirely after ten years.[28] The statute begins to run on a cause of action on a bond when the surety's obligation to pay accrues and the contractor's conduct without notice to or consent by the surety does not toll the running of the statute.[29]

[C] Bid Bonds

In Nebraska, a bid bond or a certified check in the amount determined necessary by the department or agency of the state seeking bids is required for bids on state contracts to erect or improve public buildings in excess of $40,000.[30] Otherwise, there are no requirements for bid bonds for public or private projects. For state highway projects, a prequalification system is used.[31] For public power

[24] *Id. See* Abel v. Southwest Cas. Ins. Co., 182 Neb. 605, 156 N.W.2d 166 (1968).

[25] R.C. Walters Co. v. DeBower, 191 Neb. 544, 216 N.W.2d 515 (1974).

[26] Twin City Plaza, Inc. v. Central Sur. & Ins. Corp., 409 F.2d 1195 (8th Cir. 1969) (Nebraska law).

[27] Farmers Union Coop. Ass'n v. Mid-States Constr. Co., 212 Neb. 147, 322 N.W.2d 373 (1982).

[28] NEB. REV. STAT. § 25-205 (Reissue 1995); *id.* § 25-223. *See, e.g.,* Witherspoon v. Sides Constr. Co., 219 Neb. 117, 123-25, 362 N.W.2d 35, 39-41 (1985); Grand Island Sch. Dist. No. 2. v. Celotex Corp., 203 Neb. 559, 279 N.W.2d 603 (1979).

[29] Rawleigh Co. v. Smith, 142 Neb. 427, 7 N.W.2d 80 (1942), *on reh'g,* 142 Neb. 529, 9 N.W.2d 286 (1943).

[30] NEB. REV. STAT. § 72-803 (Reissue 1996). *Id.* § 83-134(5) (Cum. Supp. 1998).

[31] *Id.* §§ 39-1348 to -1354 (Reissue 1998).

projects, determination of responsibility, including financial condition, experience, and ability, is a statutory factor in the letting of the bid.[32]

[D] Payment Bonds

[1] Private Projects

On private projects in Nebraska, payment bonds are not required. However, payment bonds may be posted in lieu of construction lien rights, either before or after lien filing.[33]

[2] Public Projects

For public projects, Nebraska statutes require that before the state or any city, village, county, or other public board or officer may award a contract for erection or improvement of a publicly owned facility, the general contractor must post a payment bond issued by a corporate surety in an amount not less than the full contract price.[34] However, a bond is not statutorily required for any state project costing less that $15,000, or for any other public project costing less than $5,000.[35] However, the contracting body may require payment bonds on small projects in the bid specifications.[36] Subcontractors have no lien, equitable or otherwise, on funds remaining in the hands of the owner on a public project.[37]

If the public contracting body fails to require or obtain a bond, the contract may be void.[38] It may be liable to claimants under a theory of negligence under the State Tort Claim Act or the Political Subdivision Tort Claim Act.[39] The claim may also be filed with Office of Risk Management for consideration by the State Claim Board under the State Miscellaneous Claims Act or the State Contract Claims Act.[40] However, because the bonds posted with public authorities are

---

[32] *Id.* § 70-639 (Reissue 1996).

[33] *Id.* §§ 52-141, -142 (Reissue 1998). *See* § **28.03[H].**

[34] *Id.* §§ 52-118, -118.01, -118.02 (Reissue 1998).

[35] *Id.* § 52-118(2).

[36] *Id.*

[37] Fremont Foundry & Mach. Co. v. Saunders County, 136 Neb. 101, 285 N.W. 115 (1939).

[38] *See* NEB. REV. STAT. § 52-118(3) (Reissue 1998).

[39] Chicago Lumber Co. v. School Dist. No. 71, 27 Neb. 355, 417 N.W.2d 757 (1988). *See* NEB. REV. STAT. §§ 81-8,209 to -8,235 (Reissue 1996) (State Tort Claim Act); NEB. REV. STAT. §§ 13-901 to -926 (Reissue 1997 & Supp. 1996).

[40] NEB. REV. STAT. §§ 81-8.294 to -8.306 (Reissue 1996 and Cum. Supp. 1998) (all contract claims against the state must be filed with the State Claims Board, which can adjudicate the claim unless the party withdraws the claim within 90 days of filing, and only then may a suit be filed in the District Court for Lancaster County, Nebraska).

available for public inspection, the claimant's failure to verify the existence and terms of the bond may create a valid affirmative defense to recovery.[41]

[a] Claimants

The Nebraska statutes provide that any person who has furnished labor or materials or rental equipment "actually used or rented" for the public project may bring suit on the bond if the person has not been paid in full within 90 days after the last day the claimant performed labor, furnished materials, or rented equipment for the project.[42]

[b] Subcontractors Must Give Notice

If the claimant has no direct contractual relationship with a subcontractor, then the claimant must also give written notice of the claim to the general contractor by certified or registered mail within "four months" after the last day upon which work was performed for which the claim is made.[43]

[c] Time Limits to File Suit

Any lawsuit on the bond must be brought within one year after "final settlement" of the principal contract.[44] *Final Settlement* means a determination by the proper authority that the contract has been completed, that final payment is due, and of the amount due.[45] Failure to bring suit in the time allowed bars recovery.[46]

[d] Interpretation

The statutes are remedial in nature and are to be given a liberal construction to effect the purpose of protecting laborers and materialmen on projects for which the general construction lien rights are not available.[47] Payment bonds are third-

---

[41] *See* Chicago Lumber Co. v. School Dist. No. 71, 227 Neb. 355, 417 N.E.2d 757 (1988); Paxton & Vierling Iron Works v. Village of Naponee, 107 Neb. 784, 186 N.W. 976 (1922).

[42] NEB. REV. STAT. §§ 52-118, -118.01.

[43] *Id.* § 52-118.01. *See* Reischick Drilling Co. v. American Cas. Co., 208 Neb. 142, 303 N.W.2d 264, 270-71 (1981); McElhose v. Universal Sur. Co., 182 Neb. 847, 158 N.W.2d 228 (1968) (defines subcontractor based upon substantiality and importance of work to project as a whole; question of fact); *see also* Dockendorf v. Orner, 206 Neb. 456, 293 N.W.2d 395 (1980) (notice requirement on Packers and Stockyards Act bond).

[44] NEB. REV. STAT. § 52-118.02 (Reissue 1998).

[45] Zimmerman's Elec., Inc. v. Fidelity & Deposit Co., 194 Neb. 248, 251, 231 N.W.2d 342, 345 (1975); *see* Boyd v. Benkleman Pub. Hous. Auth., 188 Neb. 69, 195 N.W.2d 230 (1972).

[46] Westinghouse Elec. Supply Co. v. Brookley, 176 Neb. 807, 824, 127 N.W.2d 465 (1964).

[47] *See, e.g.,* Dukane Corp. v. Sides Constr. Co., 208 Neb. 227, 230, 302 N.W.2d 721,723 (1981); McElhose v. Universal Sur. Co., 182 Neb. 847, 858, 158 N.W.2d 228, 235 (1968); NEB. REV. STAT. § 52-118 (Reissue 1998).

party beneficiary contracts, and liability thereon is governed by the terms and limitations of the statutes, the terms and conditions of the bond, and the terms of the underlying contract.[48]

[e] Burden of Proof

The claimant has the burden to bring itself within the terms of the statute and within the coverage of the bond.[49]

[f] Materials and Services Covered

The claimant must show that the labor, material, or supplies furnished were "actually used" in completion of the project.[50] Rental of equipment for performance of the contract will sustain a claim on the bond.[51] Fuel and supplies consumed during performance of the contract are also covered by the bond.[52]

[g] Extra Work

Recovery on a payment bond for extra work on the theory of quantum meruit has been allowed for the reasonable value of the work performed.[53]

[h] Recovery of Interest, Costs, and Fees

Prejudgment interest is recoverable on "liquidated claims" from the date of the claim.[54] Otherwise, prejudgment interest is recoverable from the date the plaintiff makes a formal settlement offer to take judgment at an amount less than

---

[48] *See* Cagle, Inc. v. Sammons, 198 Neb. 595, 254 N.W.2d 398 (1977) (general contractor who took over defaulting subcontractor's work may not recover on payment bond); Westinghouse Elec. Supply Co. v. Brookley, 176 Neb. 807, 824, 127 N.W.2d 465, 475 (1964) (claimant must bring itself strictly within limitations established by statute); Peter Kiewit Sons' Co. v. National Cas. Co., 142 Neb. 835, 8 N.W.2d 192 (1943) (claim for rental of equipment and fuel and supplies consumed but not incorporated into improvement are covered by both statute and bond).

[49] Westinghouse Elec. Supply Co. v. Brookley, 176 Neb. 807, 824, 127 N.W.2d 465, 475 (1964); Concrete Steel Co. v. Rowles Co., 100 Neb. 400, 163 N.W. 323 (1917).

[50] Dukane Corp. v. Sides Constr. Co., 208 Neb. 227, 302 N.W.2d 721 (1981); Quality Equip. Co. v. Transamerica Ins. Co., 243 Neb. 786, 502 N.W.2d 488 (1993).

[51] NEB. REV. STAT. § 52-118 (Reissue 1993); *id.* § 52-118.02 (rental under lease with option to purchase is covered unless and until option to purchase is exercised); McElhose v. Universal Sur. Co., 182 Neb. 847, 158 N.W.2d 228 (1968) (rental of caterpillars to supplier of gravel for road project covered).

[52] Peter Kiewit Sons' Co. v. National Cas. Co., 142 Neb. 835, 8 N.W.2d 192 (1943); West v. Detroit Fidelity & Sur. Co., 118 Neb. 544, 225 N.W. 673 (1929); C.F. Iddings Co. v. Lincoln Constr. Co., 104 Neb. 124, 175 N.W. 643 (1920).

[53] Reischick Drilling Co. v. American Cas. Co., 208 Neb. 142, 303 N.W.2d 264, 270-71 (1981); Ritzau v. Wiebe Constr. Co., 191 Neb. 92, 214 N.W.2d 244 (1974).

[54] NEB. REV. STAT. § 45-103.02 (Reissue 1998).

the final judgment rendered and files a receipt therefor signed by the opponent or its attorney in the action.[55] A claimant may also recover costs and attorneys' fees against the surety.[56]

§ 28.03 CONSTRUCTION LIEN LAW

[A] General Concepts

The Nebraska Construction Lien Act (Lien Act) generally provides for liens against real estate in favor of any person who furnishes services for materials under a real estate improvement contract.[57] Except as provided by the Lien Act, there are no non-consensual liens against real estate for improvements.[58]

Under the Lien Act, there are no lien rights as against property owned by government agencies or political subdivisions.[59]

Under the Lien Act, the primary requirements for obtaining a lien are (1) a "real estate improvement contract" with a contracting owner or agent under which (2) claimant has furnished services or materials to change the condition of the land or a structure thereon and (3) timely recording of a lien.[60]

Because the right to a construction lien is statutory and did not exist in common law or in equity, the claimant must, in the first instance, bring itself within the statutes by complying with the procedure for perfecting such a lien.[61]

[1] Real Estate Improvement Contract

A Real Estate Improvement Contract is "an agreement to perform services, including labor, or to furnish materials for the purpose of producing a change in the physical condition of land or of a structure."[62]

---

[55] *Id.* §§ 45-103.02, -103.04; Knox v. Cook, 233 Neb. 387, 393-96, 446 N.W.2d 1, 5-6 (1989).

[56] NEB. REV. STAT. § 44-359 (Reissue 1998); *id.* § 52-141 (private projects); Reischick Drilling Co. v. American Cas. Co., 208 Neb. 142, 303 N.W.2d 264, 271 (1981).

[57] NEB. REV. STAT. §§ 52-125 to -159 (Reissue 1998) (effective Jan. 1, 1982). The Lien Act was modeled after the construction lien portion of the Uniform Simplification of Land Transfers Act, 14 U.L.A. 312-63 (1980). *See* Action Heating & Air Conditioning, Inc. v. Petersen, 229 Neb. 796, 800, 429 N.W.2d 1 (1988).

[58] NEB. REV. STAT. §§ 52-126, -131 (Reissue 1998).

[59] *Id.* § 52-132.

[60] *Id.* § 52-131.

[61] Hulsinky v. Parrott, 232 Neb. 670, 673, 441 N.W.2d 883, 886 (1989) (citing Ideal Basic Indus., Inc. v. Juniata Farmers Coop. Ass'n, 205 Neb. 611, 289 N.W.2d 192 (1980), and Kotter & Sailors v. Pease, 161 Neb. 774, 74 N.W.2d 538 (1956)).

[62] NEB. REV. STAT. § 52-130 (1) (Reissue 1998).

[2] Contracting Owner

The contracting owner must be a person who owns real estate and contracts to improve it.[63] The owner can contract through an agent for improvements.[64] Agency is presumed between spouses, employer and employee, and joint tenants and tenants in common. Otherwise, the claimant has the burden of proving agency by showing (1) consent to another to act on its behalf by the owner; (2) control over the other by the owner; and (3) consent by the other to so act.[65]

[3] Claimants

Prime contractors, subcontractors and materialmen can be claimants.[66] Suppliers to subcontractors may file construction liens, but suppliers to suppliers or to materialmen are not protected by the Lien Act.[67]

[4] Services Covered

Services specifically included under the Lien Act are excavation and grading; construction or installation; demolition, repair, remodeling, or removal of structures; landscaping; surface or subsurface testing or analysis; and preparation of surveys, architectural and engineering plans, or drawings.[68] However, contracts for mining, timber removal, or crop production are expressly excluded.[69] Banks and financiers are excluded from claiming construction liens.[70] Express and implied contracts are recognized.[71]

---

[63] *Id.* § 52-127(3).

[64] *Id.* §§ 52-127(3), -128. Franksen v. Crossroads Joint Venture, 245 Neb. 863, 515 N.W.2d 794 (1994) (tenant is not agent of landlord to subject fee interest to lien; but lien may attach to fee interest upon termination of lease by merger under equitable estoppel theory). *See also* Landmark Enters., Inc. v. M.E. Harrisburg Assocs., 250 Neb. 882, 554 N.W.2d 119 (1996).

[65] Tuttle & Assocs., Inc. v. Gendler, 237 Neb. 825, 467 N.W.2d 881 (1991).

[66] Neb Rev. Stat. §§ 52-127(8), -136 (Reissue 1998); *see* Action Heating & Air Conditioning, Inc. v. Petersen, 229 Neb. 796, 429 N.W.2d 1 (1988); Blue Tee Corp. v. CDI Contractors, Inc., 247 Neb. 397, 529 N.W.2d 16 (1995).

[67] Hulsinky v. Parrott, 232 Neb. 670, 674, 441 N.W.2d 883, 886 (1989) (dicta). *But see* Neb. Rev. Stat. § 52-134 (Reissue 1984). Blue Tee Corp. v. CDI Contractors, Inc. 247 Neb. 397, 529 N.W.2d 16 (1995) (supplier of steel to fabricator had lien rights; fabricator was proven to be a subcontractor).

[68] Neb Rev. Stat. § 52-130(1)(a) to (f) (Reissue 1998).

[69] *Id.* § 52-130(2).

[70] *Id.* § 52-127(9); Hulsinky v. Parrott, 232 Neb. 670, 441 N.W.2d 883 (1989).

[71] Neb. Rev. Stat. § 52-127(3) (Reissue 1998). Mid-America Maintenance, Inc. v. Bill Morris Ford, Inc., 232 Neb. 920, 442 N.W.2d 869 (1989).

[5] Materials Covered

In order to claim a lien for materials, the materials must be shown to be furnished with intent that they be used for or incorporated into the improvement and they (1) are so used or consumed; or (2) are specially fabricated and not readily resalable; or (3) are used for the operation of machinery or equipment during construction.[72] Delivery to the job site creates a presumption of use or incorporation into the improvement.[73] Suppliers of tools, machinery, and appliances rented for use in construction may claim a lien for the reasonable rental value of actual use and standby time, or, if purchased, if they are consumed or exhausted during construction.[74]

[6] Amount of the Lien

The amount of the prime contractor's lien is the unpaid part of its contract price.[75] The contract price may be increased or decreased by change orders, extras, or breaches of contract.[76] In the absence of a contract price, the lien is for the reasonable value of the goods and services furnished.[77] The lien amount of other claimants is the unpaid amount of their contract price except as discussed below in regard to "residential real estate."[78]

[7] Substantial Performance Required

The Nebraska Supreme Court has held that a contractor who is in default cannot assert a construction lien upon property unless the contractor has substantially performed the contract.[79] In a building contract, substantial performance is

---

[72] NEB. REV. STAT. § 52-134 (Reissue 1998). Blue Tee Corp. v. CDI Contractors, Inc., 247 Neb. 397, 529 N.W.2d 16 (1995) (supplier of steel to fabricator had lien rights); Robinson v. Madsen, 246 Neb. 22, 28, 516 N.W.2d 594, 598 (1994) (claimant has burden of proof to show materials furnished by it were actually incorporated into project).

[73] NEB. REV. STAT. § 52-134(2) (Reissue 1998).

[74] *Id.* § 52-134.

[75] *Id.* §§ 52-131(4), -136(1).

[76] *Id.* § 52-127(2). Prejudgment interest is recoverable only if there is no reasonable controversy as to liability and the amount is liquidated. Lange Indus., Inc. v. Hallam Grain Co., 244 Neb. 465, 482, 507 N.W.2d 465, 477 (1993). *Accord* Blue Tee Corp. v. CDI Contractors, Inc. 247 Neb. 397, 403-04, 529 N.W.2d 16 (1995). *But see* Peterson v. Kellner, 245 Neb. 515, 519-20, 512 N.E.2d 517, 520 (1994) (plain error to award prejudgment interest without compliance with offer-of-settlement procedures required by NEB. REV. STAT. § 45-103.02 (Reissue 1998)). Section 45-103.02 was subsequently amended to provide that the settlement offer requirement applies only to unliquidated claims and to specify that interest accrued on liquidated claims from the date the cause of action arose to the date of judgment at 12 percent. NEB. REV STAT. §§ 45-103.02, -104 (Reissue 1998).

[77] NEB. REV. STAT. §§ 52-127(2), -136 (Reissue 1998).

[78] *Id.* § 52-136(2).

[79] Lange Indus., Inc. v. Hallam Grain, 244 Neb. 465, 473-74, 507 N.W.2d 465, 473 (1993).

shown when all essential elements necessary for full accomplishment of the purpose of the contract have been performed, so that the owner receives substantially what is called for by the contract. Any deviations from the contract must be minor and unimportant. A contractor whose contract was terminated without fault on his part has a construction lien notwithstanding failure to substantially perform the contract but only for the reasonable value of goods and services furnished for the project.[80]

[B] Notice and Filing Requirements

Although the Lien Act provides for certain optional notices to be given,[81] there are no mandatory notice requirements that are prerequisites to claiming a lien. However, the Lien Act provides certain affirmative obligations to furnish information upon request for residential projects.[82]

[1] Time Limits for Filing a Lien

A construction lien may be recorded at any time after entering into a contract under which lien rights arise and no later than 120 days after the final furnishing of services or materials.[83] However, lien rights can be cut off earlier as to "residential real estate" by full payment of the prime contractor by a "protected party contracting owner" unless a "notice of lien liability" has been given[84] or by purchase by a buyer who is a "protected party."[85] Effective use of the "notice of commencement" and "notice of termination" systems can also defeat lien rights before expiration of the 120 day period.[86]

[2] Lien Contents

The construction lien must contain:

1. The name and address of the claimant;
2. The name and address of the contracting owner of the record holder of the contracting owner's interest in the real estate at the time of recording;
3. A description of the real estate;
4. The name and address of the person with whom claimant contracted;
5. A general description of the services performed or to be performed or materials furnished or to be furnished;

---

[80] Tilt-Up Concrete, Inc. v. Star City Fed., Inc., 255 Neb. 138, 582 N.W.2d 604 (1998).

[81] NEB. REV. STAT. §§ 52-135, -141, -145, -146 (Reissue 1998).

[82] *Id.* §§ 52-143, -145(6).

[83] *Id.* §§ 52-131, -137(1).

[84] *Id.* §§ 52-129, -135, -136(2), (3), (4), (5). *See* **§ 28.03[H].**

[85] NEB. REV. STAT. § 52-139(5) (Reissue 1998).

[86] *See id.* §§ 52-137, -138, -139, -145, -146. *See also* **§ 28.03[F][1].**

6. The amount unpaid, whether due or not, or if no amount is fixed by contract, then a good-faith estimate of the amount designated as an estimate;
7. The time the last services or materials were furnished, or if that has yet to occur, then an estimate of the time when it will occur.[87]

[3] Execution and Acknowledgment

A construction lien must be executed and acknowledged by the claimant and recorded with the Register of Deeds office for the county where the land is situated.[88]

[4] Amendments to Liens

The lien can be amended by an additional recording at any time within the original filing time. Thereafter, the lien can be amended only to reduce the amount, reduce the real estate against which it is claimed, or to apportion the lien, such as among lots in a platted subdivision.[89]

[5] Assignments

The Lien Act also provides for recording assignments of liens, but the owner may continue to deal with the original claimant until the owner receives notice thereof and a direction against arrangements or payment without the assignee's consent.[90]

[C] Enforcement of Liens

A lien is enforceable for two years after the date of recording.[91] It must be enforced in a civil action for foreclosure.[92] However, anyone with an interest in the real estate may give and record a demand upon the claimant to institute legal proceedings to enforce the lien.[93] In that case, the lien lapses unless the claimant either commences legal action within 30 days after receipt of the written demand or records an affidavit that the total contract price is not yet due.[94]

---

[87] NEB. REV. STAT. § 52-147 (Reissue 1998).

[88] *Id.* §§ 52-127(13), -147; id. §§ 76-211, -216 to -236 (Reissue 1996) (acknowledgment required for recording); *id.* §§ 64-201 to -209 (Reissue 1996) (defines acknowledgment).

[89] *Id.* § 52-148 (Reissue 1998). The amendment must reference the original filing by date and recording number. *Id.*

[90] *Id.* § 52-149.

[91] *Id.* § 52-140(1).

[92] *Id.* § 52-155. *See id.* §§ 25-2137 to -2155 (Reissue 1995) (foreclosure procedure). All lien claimants may be joined in a single action. *Id.* § 52-155(2) (Reissue 1998).

[93] *Id.* § 52-140(2) (Reissue 1998).

[94] *Id.* § 52-140(2).

[D] Remedies for Wrongful Conduct

The Lien Act provides remedies for wrongful conduct that deprives anyone of its benefits, including the power to award damages and restrain further conduct. If a claimant acts in bad faith in recording the lien, in stating the amount thereof, or in refusing to release a lien, then the court can declare the lien void and award actual damages, costs, and attorneys' fees.[95]

[E] Lien Waivers

Lien rights under the Lien Act may be waived by a written waiver signed by the claimant. No consideration is required, and it is valid whether signed before or after the contract is executed or the goods or services are furnished. A written waiver of construction lien rights waives all rights, unless it is specifically limited to a particular portion of the lien rights or a particular portion of the materials or services furnished. Acceptance or a promissory note or other evidence of debt is not a waiver of lien rights unless it expressly so declares. Ambiguities in the waiver are to be construed against the claimant.[96] There is no requirement that the written waivers be either acknowledged or recorded. A lien waiver does not affect your contract rights.

[F] Lien Priorities

The priority of liens depends upon the time of attachment. Liens that attach at the same time have equal priority and share pro rata in the proceeds.[97] Liens attaching at different times have priority in the order of attachment.[98] The lien attaches upon recording thereof and has prioirity generally at the earlier of the time of recording or "visible commencement" of the improvement.[99] In most cases, liens filed after the project has started have equal priority to each other. The liens "relate back" to a time earlier than the time of filing as an exception to the first in time to file rule.[100] However, if a "Notice of Commencement" is filed, attachment dates may be altered.

[1] Notice of Commencement System

Either the owner or a claimant may record a Notice of Commencement.[101] If the owner files it, is must state the name and address of the contracting owner,

---

[95] *Id.* § 52-157. *See also id.* § 52-156 (liability for improper recording of notice of termination).

[96] *Id.* § 52-144.

[97] *Id.* § 52-138(1).

[98] *Id.* § 52-138(2).

[99] *Id.* § 52-137(3); *see id.* § 52-137(4), (5) (visible commencement for new construction occurs when materials are delivered or excavation or site preparation has begun).

[100] This may allow filing of a lien after bankruptcy has been filed by the property's owner under 11 U.S.C. § 363(b)(3) and 11 U.S.C. § 546(b).

[101] NEB. REV. STAT. § 52-145(1), (5) (Reissue 1998).

the name and address of the fee simple titleholder, the real estate being improved, and that liens filed will attach as of the date of the recording of the notice.[102] If the claimant records it, it must state basically the same information plus the name and address of the claimant and of the persons with whom the claimant contracted.[103] If no duration is stated, it is effective for one year, and no duration of less than six months may be stated.[104] The notice lapses either by its term or by completion of the notice of termination process by the owner.[105] The notice of termination must be recorded, sent to all persons who have requested it, and published for three weeks in a legal newspaper. An affidavit of service and of publication must then be recorded to complete the process.[106]

If used, a Notice of Commencement limits the interest in and the identity of real estate to which liens may attach.[107] Further, all liens recorded while the Notice of Commencement is effective relate back to and attach as of the date it was recorded.[108] A lien recorded within 30 days of the lapse of a Notice of Commencement attaches when it is recorded.[109] A lien filed more than 30 days after the lapse relates back and attaches 31 days after the lapse.[110]

If a claimant records a Notice of Commencement, his lien will have equal priority with all other claimants' filings after the notice is recorded. If the claimant who records the notice has previously recorded its own lien, the priority based on recording of the lien is also preserved for the benefit of other claimants.[111]

While a Notice of Commencement is effective, a transfer of the property or a mortgage or other lien recorded will be junior to construction liens that are not yet recorded, but are recorded thereafter.[112] However, upon lapse of the Notice of Commencement or upon completion of the notice of termination process, a window of 30 days is created within which the property can be sold or encumbered free of unrecorded construction liens.[113]

Further, when "residential real estate" is sold to a "protected party," the buyer takes the same free of all unrecorded liens, whether or not a Notice of Commencement is on file.[114]

If an owner terminates a Notice of Commencement before the project is

[102] *Id.* § 52-145(1).
[103] *Id.* § 52-145(5). A claimant must also send a copy thereof to the contracting owner. *Id.*
[104] *Id.* § 52-145(2).
[105] *Id.* §§ 52-137(2), -145(2), -146.
[106] *Id.* § 52-146.
[107] *See id.* § 52-145(3).
[108] *Id.* § 52-137(2).
[109] *Id.* § 52-137(3)(a).
[110] *Id.* § 52-137(3)(b).
[111] *See id.* § 52-138(3).
[112] *Id.* § 52-139(1).
[113] *Id.* §§ 52-138(2), (3), -139(1), (2).
[114] *Id.* § 52-139(5).

completed or abandoned, the owner becomes personally liable to those persons wrongfully deprived of their lien rights.[115]

[2] Priorities as Against Other Liens

A construction lien is subordinate to liens recorded before the attachment of the lien. Thus, a banker who records its "Construction Security Agreement" and then causes the owner to record a Notice of Commencement can protect his lien priority. However, subsequent advances made upon a prior recorded construction security agreement are junior to intervening liens if made with knowledge of the lien attachment.[116] However, subsequent advances made under a "construction security agreement" may have priority (1) if made in payment of the price of the improvements, or (2) if made for reasonable protection of the lien on the real estate, or (3) if applied to pay any lien or encumbrance that has priority over the construction lien.[117] Further, a subsequent security interest taken to pay a lien with priority over the construction lien is also given priority.[118]

[G] Residential Real Estate

The Lien Act provides special protection for buyers and owners of residential real estate for use as a personal residence.

[1] Protected Party

A *protected party* is an individual who owns, agrees to buy, or grants an interest in residential real estate in which that person or a relative intends to live as a resident.[119] A "protected party" buyer takes title free of any unrecorded liens.[120]

[2] Residential Real Estate Defined

For the purposes of the Lien Act, residential real estate is defined as real estate with improvements which contain no more than four units and having no nonresidential uses for which the protected party is lessor. A condominium is residential real estate even if the condominium development does not otherwise qualify.[121]

---

[115] *Id.* § 52-156.
[116] *Id.* § 52-139(1), (2).
[117] *See id.* § 52-138(3).
[118] *See id.* § 52-139(4).
[119] *Id.* § 52-129(1); Payless Bldg. Ctr. Inc. v. Wilmouth, 254 Neb. 958, 581 N.W.2d 420 (Neb. 1998) (co-trustees under revocable trust are not protected parties under Lien Act).
[120] *Id.* § 52-139(5).
[121] *Id.* § 52-129(2).

[3] Amount of the Lien

The protected party contracting owner's lien liability to any claimant is the lesser of the unpaid amount of the claimant's contract or the unpaid amount on the prime contract at the time the owner receives a notice of lien liability.[122] That is, the owner's total lien liability under a prime contract is the contract amount less all payments made in good faith before receipt of a notice of lien liability and all payments make while withholding sufficient funds to satisfy all claimants who have given a notice of lien liability.[123] Because the prime contractor's lien is reduced by the liens of all claimants claiming through it, the protected party contracting owner has valid setoff rights against the prime based on liens asserted by its subcontractors.[124] If liens are asserted in excess of the balance due under the prime contract, the funds are disbursed to the claimants in order of priority and pro rata to those who have equal priority.[125]

[4] Notice of Lien Liability

A Notice of Lien Liability may be given by any claimant to a protected party contracting owner at any time after entering into a contract under which lien rights arise and before or after a lien is recorded. It must state:

1. The name and address of the claimant;
2. The name and address of the person with whom the claimant contracted;
3. The name of the owner against whom a lien may be claimed;
4. A general description of the services or materials provided or that will be provided;
5. A description of the real estate against whom the lien may be claimed;
6. A statement that the claimant has recorded a lien and the date of recording or, if the lien has not become recorded, a statement that the claimant is entitled to record a lien;
7. The amount unpaid for services or materials whether or not due, or a good-faith estimate of the amount designated as an estimate;
8. The following statement: "Warning. If you did not contract with the person giving this Notice, any future payment you make in connection with this project may subject you to double liability."[126]

---

[122] *Id.* § 52-136(2).

[123] *Id.* § 52-136(5).

[124] *Id.* § 52-136(3); Action Heating & Air Conditioning, Inc. v. Petersen, 229 Neb. 796, 429 N.W.2d 1 (1988).

[125] *Id.* § 32-137(4).

[126] *Id.* § 52-135.

[H] Bonds to Prevent or Eliminate Construction Liens

The Lien Act also provides that posting of a payment bond may substitute for or release lien rights.[127] The bond can be recorded before or after a lien is filed.

[1] Recording of a Bond in Advance Prevents Liens from Attaching

If the owner or the prime contractor procures and records notice of a payment bond, no liens may attach to the real estate. Claims must be brought thereon within one year after the claimant completes performance unless a longer period is provided in the bond. Claimants without a direct contractual relationship with the prime contractor must give notice of nonpayment to the prime contractor withing 90 days after completion of performance. The claimant may proceed directly against the surety without joining the prime contractor and without compliance with the notice and recording requirements of the Lien Act. The prevailing party in this type of bond suit may recover reasonable attorneys' fees and costs.[128]

[2] Posting Bonds to Release Filed Liens

After a lien has been recorded, a person with an interest in the real estate may cause the lien to be released by posting a bond of 115 percent of the amount of the lien with the clerk of the district court and then recording the clerk's certificate as to the posting of the bond. Thereafter, the claimant may enforce its lien rights against the bond by legal action.[129]

[I] Other Remedies for the Owner

The Lien Act affords an owner additional protections including (1) the right to cut off or alter lien rights with a notice of commencement and notice of termination;[130] (2) the right to demand institution of legal action within 30 days or the loss of the lien;[131] and (3) the right to seek voiding of the lien, restraining orders, and damages for wrongful conduct.[132]

---

[127] *Id.* § 52-141.

[128] *Id.* § 52-141. The statute also provides standards for the penal amount of the bond, requires furnishing of copies on request, and provides that the surety's liability on the bond "is not affected by any change or modification of the prime contract." *Id.* "To Record" means to file the bond with the Register of Deeds where the real estate is located. *Id.* § 52-127(13).

[129] *Id.* § 52-142. Gomez v. Kenny Deans, Inc., 233 Neb. 506, 446, N.W.2d 209 (1989); Hormandl v. Lecher Constr. Co., 231 Neb. 355, 436 N.W.2d 188 (1989).

[130] Neb. Rev. Stat. §§ 52-133(1), -137(2), (3), -145, -146 (Reissue 1998).

[131] *Id.* §§ 52-140(2), -152.

[132] *Id.* § 52-157.